CONCISE HISTORIES OF AMERICAN POPULAR CULTURE

CONCISE HISTORIES OF AMERICAN POPULAR CULTURE

edited by
M. Thomas Inge

CONTRIBUTIONS TO THE STUDY OF
POPULAR CULTURE, NUMBER 4

Greenwood Press
Westport, Connecticut

Library of Congress Cataloging in Publication Data
Main entry under title:

Concise histories of American popular culture.

(Contributions to the study of popular culture, ISSN 0198-9871; no. 4)
Bibliography: p.
Includes index.
1. United States—Popular culture—Addresses, essays, lectures. I. Inge, M. Thomas. II. Series.
E169.1.C6668 306'.0973 82-6115
ISBN 0-313-23302-0 (lib. bdg.) AACR2

Library of Congress Catalog Card Number: 82-6115
ISBN: 0-313-23302-0
ISSN: 0198-9871

First published in 1982

Greenwood Press
A division of Congressional Information Service, Inc.
88 Post Road West
Westport, Connecticut 06881

Distributed in the United Kingdom and
Europe by Aldwych Press Ltd., London

Printed in the United States of America

10 9 8 7 6 5 4 3 2 1

For Scott

Contents

Preface

The serious study of popular culture is the most recent consequential development in the humanities on college and university campuses in this country. A great many catalogs list introductory courses on the subject, general and specialized studies appear regularly from the university and scholarly presses, more scholars than ever before are moving from traditional disciplinary areas of inquiry to unexplored interdisciplinary problems in the popular arts, and a body of useful reference materials has begun to accumulate. Beginning guides to this material may be found in the essays published in the three volumes of the *Handbook of American Popular Culture* (Greenwood Press, 1978-1981), edited by the present writer.

This volume brings together some of the most useful portions of the *Handbook* into a more convenient format for those beginning a study of popular culture and some of the specific forms it has taken in this century. It contains fifty chapters, each providing a concise history of a major area or aspect of American popular culture and a selected checklist of the most important books and reference works on the subject. All of the historic overviews from the *Handbook* are included here, the majority revised and updated by the original contributors and some completely rewritten. In addition, there are two new essays on dance and fashion by Loretta Carrillo and an original essay by Michael Bell on approaches to the study of popular culture.

The intention is to provide overviews and starting points for students, researchers, and general readers who for professional, academic, or personal reasons are beginning studies in the popular arts and mass culture. The reader may then move to the fuller bibliographic essays in the *Handbook* or consult the listed specialized reference guides beyond the *Handbook*. This volume is a combined history, bibliography, and textbook designed to encourage and further our understanding of the cultural environment in which we live.

M. Thomas Inge

Advertising

Elizabeth Williamson

Advertising has been described as an institution, a business, an industry, a discipline, a profession, a science, an art, and a talent. It has been defined as news, salesmanship in print, and mass communication. Some of the best minds in the business, outside the business, and on the fringes of the business have attempted to define and deal with this elusive subject. Scholars and advertising men themselves have examined the political, economic, social, ethical, historical, and religious aspects of advertising. Each of them has told us what advertising is, how it works, how it should work, and why it does not work; each has told us that advertising either deceives, informs, pleases, or frightens us.

Advertising has been attacked and defended by almost every segment of society. When it is advantageous, someone will admit to having used or even liked advertising. When it is not, the vindictiveness against advertising flies, even from public relations, marketing, and retailing specialists. Some popular culture books deal with advertising, but generally by including disparaging remarks. Examine a typical American history book and you will probably find little or no mention of advertising. Yet, to look at the advertisements of a nation is essentially to view most aspects of its existence. Advertising is the story of a nation's people. And, although advertising certainly did not originate in America, this country has probably done more than any other nation to use and foster advertising. It has been said that some foreign politicians have observed American advertisements as a gauge for measuring and understanding America's tastes and values. Advertising is probably the most pervasive form of popular culture and, surprisingly, has rarely been examined from this perspective.

Although the origins of advertising have been traced back to several very early sources, no one is exactly sure when the trade began. However, several evidences of written advertisements have been discovered and offered as the first recorded efforts in selling. The ones most often suggested are a Babylonian clay tablet announcing the services of an ointment dealer, scribe, and shoemaker, and a piece of papyrus from the ruins of Thebes offering a reward for the return of runaway slaves. The early history of advertising, replete with its accounts of Grecian town criers and Roman shop signs, is a fascinating one, and the reader is advised to consult the definitive histories listed elsewhere in this essay for a more thorough survey of early advertising history. Because of space limitations, we must necessarily begin with colonial America, which was beginning to implement already existing advertising methods, especially the shop sign and posted notices.

Advertising in America, which grew in conjunction with the expanding colonial economy, found its greatest impetus in newspapers, once the press had won its right to exist. As early as 1704 *The Boston Newsletter* carried advertisements for the return of some men's clothing and for the reward and capture of a thief. By the time of the Revolution, there were some thirty newspapers in America, each carrying substantial amounts of advertisements, mostly classified and local.

Although American advertising had reached a considerable sophistication and circulation, it was Benjamin Franklin who has earned—along with his many other credits—the title of father of American advertising, because he made important improvements in advertising methods. As a printer and a newspaperman, Franklin made major changes in the style and format of American advertisements. Most newspaper advertisements, which consisted of three- and four-line notices, were printed in various and uneven typefaces and were difficult to read. Franklin cleaned up the ads by separating individual notices with white spaces and then by adding bolder headings, thus making each ad distinctive from the rest. To make the advertisements even more distinctive, Franklin began using illustrations representative of the individual advertiser. He experimented with different symbols, such as ships, tools, horses, and books, which indicated the general contents of the advertisements. These symbols ranged in size from one and one-quarter inches to half columns and full columns and served as either borders or major graphics for the advertisements.

In addition to showing graphic expertise, Franklin was also the master of the written word. His knowledge of effective persuasive copy is obvious in the notice he wrote advertising his famous Franklin stove. He stressed not only the functional features of his invention but also the pleasures and comforts it would bring to the ladies. Advertising his brothers' super fine crown soap, he created this angle: "It cleanses fine Linens, Muslins, Laces, Chinces, Cambricks, etc. with Ease and Expedition, which often suffer more from the long and hard rubbing of the Washer, through the ill qualities of the soap than the wearing."

Although some men like Franklin led the way in improving advertising, the general state of advertising was a poor one. Most ads were simply notices for goods, services, land out west, slaves, or lost items. Advertisements were also used to attack competition and to announce the newest wonder drugs. Fraudulent medicine men and patent medicines, most often cited for giving advertising a disreputable image, would remain problems for advertisers for a long time.

Most of the advertisements of the shopkeepers of the late eighteenth century were directed toward the upper classes. Long notices informed the wealthy readers of the latest imported goods from England, Holland, and the Far East. Quality fabrics like chintzes and taffetas, and fragrant balms, spices, and perfumes were signs of wealth and prestige in the New World. The words "imported" and "just arrived" in an advertisement spoke of America's taste and the advertiser's audience, both of which changed after the revolutionary war. After the long struggle with England for independence, America felt drastic changes both socially and economically, and advertisements of that period reflected those changes. Once fashionable to own goods "just imported," it was now fashionable and more feasible to purchase "American-made" products, a tag that began to appear regularly in advertisements.

Newspaper growth matched the increasing American population and income, and, by 1820, some five hundred newspapers were serving more than nine million Americans. Although advertisements were still of uneven quality, they were almost certain to be read since advertisements, a little more than legal notices, flooded the newspapers. Newspapers prided themselves on the number, not the quality, of the ads that appeared in their pages. And the American reading public accepted the inundation of advertisements, along with the editorial policies of American newspapers, which remained highly partisan.

Technological advances in the early 1800s created many kinds of changes in the format and production of newspapers, especially in price reduction. The first penny newspaper, *The New York Sun*, was a 9 × 12 tabloid that rapidly reached a circulation of twenty thousand. Benjamin Day, its founder, soon met competition from a very shrewd editor, reporter, and founder of *The New York Herald*—James Gordon Bennett. Bennett charged two pennies for his paper and soon its circulation doubled that of the *Sun*. Both men experimented with advertisements. Day created a section called "Wants" and charged advertisers fifty cents per ad per day. Bennett immediately created the "Personals" column whose contents read much like those of today.

Bennett saw the power and profit in advertising and soon added restrictions to advertisers in his newspaper. At first he limited the time that a single advertisement could run to two weeks, but he later changed the limitation to one day. He also banned the use of illustrations. His idea was to give all advertisements equal importance and impact. Advertisers protested, but the *Herald's* circulation and the need for and effectiveness of advertising forced the advertisers to submit to Bennett's rules.

Bennett was successful in implementing his restrictions for a brief time until Robert Bonner of *The New York Ledger* matched wits with Bennett and won. Bonner, whose pulp magazine itself accepted no advertisements, did advertise for his magazine elsewhere. Deciding to break Bennett's boycott, Bonner bought whole pages in the *Herald* and simply repeated the announcement for his magazine in bold type over and over again. Sometimes he repeated a complete advertisement as many as ninety-three times in a single issue of the *Herald.*

Such competition and chaos demanded some sort of order, which soon arose in the form of a middle man, the advertising agent. Someone had to inform the advertiser about the various newspapers, rates, and options available to him, and someone had to help the newspaperman keep his pages filled with advertisements. The first advertising agent, Volney B. Palmer, who began as a newspaper advertising solicitor, decided to go "independent" and established several offices selling space for a few newspapers and charged a 25 percent commission for each advertisement. His first competitor was his own protégé, S. M. Pettingill, whom Palmer tried to run out of business by waging a slanderous war against him. Palmer was unsuccessful, however. In fact, Palmer ended up going insane, while Pettingill ended up as a very successful advertising agent and copywriter.

The creation of the advertising agent, which worked for a while, soon created its own competition and chaos. By the time of the Civil War, there were some twenty agents operating in ten cities. Although they claimed to follow the rates established by the newspapers, they often dickered to the point of cutting the editors' rates a healthy percentage, thus increasing their own commissions. The shrewd advertising agent became a wealthy man easily enough.

Out of the advertising agent struggle emerged a man who added stability and respectability to a floundering, but possibly good, system. George P. Rowell bought mass space in one hundred papers across the country and contracted to advertisers. Rowell also guaranteed payment to the newspapers for any ads for which he received a commission. He believed in truth in advertising and even wrote in an essay, "Honesty is by all odds the very strongest point which can be crowded in an ad." Rowell, in addition to his devotion to honesty, is known as the founder of *Printer's Ink* and as the publisher of the first American newspaper directory that gave estimates of the nation's newspaper rates and circulation.

Although Rowell stressed the need for honesty in advertising, he and many other agents made a great deal of money during the Civil War by advertising patent medicines. While it is easy for us today to point a finger at such men and such practices, it would be wise for us to reconsider the times. Even religious publications—the predecessors of magazines and the most influential medium in post-Civil War America—contained inordinate amounts of patent medicine advertisements. In fact, patent medicine advertising comprised 75 percent of all advertising in religious publications. Many temperance papers carried advertisements for medicines that were eighty-proof alcohol.

However, once the secret formulas of patent medicine began to be exposed, the public responded by showing disapproval of both the promoters of the products and of the advertising men. One result of the consumers' behavior was that certain advertising men again tried to clean up their unsavory reputation. F. Wayland Ayer, founder of N. W. Ayer and Son, became personally interested in the reputation of advertising after an associate made disparaging remarks about the nature of Ayer's business. Ayer responded by trying further to stabilize Rowell's efforts to establish rates between advertiser, publisher, and agent. Ayer initiated the open contract, which stipulated the amount of money that would be spent on advertising costs plus the agent's commission. The greatest impact of Ayer's system was that it became clear that the agent represented the advertiser. Ayer is also credited with being the man who first studied the market and produced the first marketing survey.

Most efforts to establish a greater rapport between agents and clients focused on newspaper activity since the few magazines that were successful in the mid-century refused to carry advertisements. J. Walter Thompson was the first advertising man to convince magazine publishers to accept advertisements. His success plus several events in the last three decades of the nineteenth century made magazines and magazine advertising the new American craze. Technological advances such as the Hoe high-speed rotary press and the halftone method of reproducing photographs, in addition to a reduction in second-class postal rates, and a 50 percent increase in the literacy rate, all contributed to the mass circulation of magazines. Mass magazines introduced Americans to the nationwide sale of products and to national advertising.

Today's readers, who complain about the number of advertisements in their favorite magazines, might be surprised to learn that *Harper's*, which initially shunned advertisements, by 1899 carried 135 pages of ads and 163 pages of editorials. J. Walter Thompson, who continued to control much of the advertising in existing magazines—mostly women's—was not the only man to recognize the profit in this area. Cyrus Curtis, magazine magnate, created magazines expressly for the purpose of advertising. Among his creations were *Ladies' Home Journal*, *Cosmopolitan*, and *McClure's*.

The twentieth century heralded in the age of American advertising. Outdoor advertising, the oldest form of the profession, received a new face when the first electric sign was erected in New York in 1891. Retailers actively engaged in advertising. Copywriter Claude Hopkins gave Americans a breakfast product "shot from guns," in addition to giving copy a new status in the advertising campaign. Americans were bombarded with advertising. Newspapers, magazines, transit ads, billboards, posters, and window displays echoed America's progress. The age of mass production, mass selling, and mass advertising had arrived. And Americans appeared to love it. Broadway, "The Great White Way," attracted thousands of tourists, as did the Hudson River steamboat excursions to Albany, during which passengers gazed at the lighted billboards that lined the riverbanks.

But many people began to worry about the moral, psychological, and physical effects that such mass production and mass selling would have on the American public. Outsiders (and insiders, too) wrote exposés attacking the new American way and fraudulent advertising; while on the other side, advertisers themselves grouped together to create organizations and clubs to regulate their own profession. Vigilance committees and campaigns to promote truth in advertising sprang up overnight. Agencies such as the Better Business Bureau, the Association of National Advertising Managers, and the American Association of Advertising Agencies developed policies to improve the effectiveness of advertising and to protect the consumer from fraudulent claims. *Printer's Ink*, the leading advertising trade paper, created a model statute for the regulation of advertising; it vowed to "punish untrue, deceptive, or misleading advertising." In 1916 advertising gained some crucial respectability when President Woodrow Wilson addressed the Associated Advertising Clubs of the World in Philadelphia.

The struggle between advertising groups and consumer groups continued, as did American prosperity, through the 1920s. Advertising benefited greatly from the prosperity and, at the same time, congratulated itself for its contributions to America's growth. The December 7, 1929 issue of *The Saturday Evening Post* carried 154 pages of advertising in a 268-page publication that sold for five cents. Another new medium of the 1920s—the radio—brought advertising billings to three and one-half billion dollars by the end of the decade.

In addition to the stockmarket crash of 1929 and the ensuing economic upheavals, advertisers had to struggle against other factors throughout the 1930s. Muckrakers launched new attacks; the Robinson-Patman Act of 1936 protected the little merchant from unfair competition by the big businessman; the Wheeler-Lea Act of 1938 gave the Federal Trade Commission more power over advertising; and the Federal Food, Drug, and

Cosmetic Act of 1938 gave the administration authority over packaging and labeling.

But in spite of controls and criticism, advertising continued to survive and prosper. Radio remained the major advertising medium until the emergence of television, which quickly gave advertising a new source of expression, new challenges, and new problems. How successfully advertising will survive the electronic age, the problems of shortages, and an uncertain American economic future cannot be accurately predicted. But one thing is certain: advertising will face the new challenges just as it faced the ones presented to it throughout its early history in America.

BIBLIOGRAPHY

Barton, Roger, ed. *Handbook of Advertising Management.* New York: McGraw-Hill, 1970.

Bishop, Robert L., comp. *Public Relations: A Comprehensive Bibliography.* Ann Arbor, Mich.: A. G. Leigh-James, 1974.

Blum, Eleanor. *Basic Books in the Mass Media.* Urbana: University of Illinois Press, 1972.

Borden, Neil H. *The Economic Effects of Advertising.* Chicago: R. D. Irwin, 1942. Reprint. New York: Arno Press, 1976.

The Creative Black Book. New York: Friendly Publications, 1970-.

Cutlip, Scott M., comp. *A Public Relations Bibliography.* 2d ed. Madison and Milwaukee: The University of Wisconsin Press, 1965.

Dunn, S. Watson, ed. *International Handbook of Advertising.* New York: McGraw-Hill, 1964.

Ferber, Robert, Alain Cousineau, Millard Crask, and Hugh G. Wales, comps. *A Basic Bibliography on Marketing Research.* 3d ed. New York: American Marketing Association, 1974.

Hodgson, Richard S. *The Dartnell Direct Mail and Mail Order Handbook.* 2d ed. Chicago: Dartnell Press, 1974.

Madison Avenue Handbook. New York: Peter Gleen Publications, 1958-.

Media/Scope. Dictionary of Terms Useful to Buyers of Advertising. Skokie, Ill.: Standard Rate and Date Service, 1966.

Mott, Frank Luther. *American Journalism: A History of Newspapers in the United States Through 260 Years: 1690 to 1950.* Rev. ed. New York: Macmillan, 1950.

———. *A History of American Magazines.* Cambridge: Harvard University Press, 1957.

Padley, Martin, ed. *A Handbook to Television Advertising.* New York: National Retail Merchants Association, 1969.

Presbrey, Frank. *The History and Development of Advertising.* Garden City, N.Y.: Doubleday, Doran, 1929.

Reeves, Rosser. *Reality in Advertising.* New York: Alfred A. Knopf, 1960, 1961, 1973.

Revzan, David A. *A Comprehensive Classified Marketing Bibliography.* Berkeley: University of California Press, 1951.

Richard, John M. *A Guide to Advertising Information Sources.* Scottsdale, Ariz.: MacDougal Publishing House, 1969.

Sampson, Henry. *A History of Advertising from the Earliest Times.* London: Chatto and Windus, Piccadilly, 1874. Reprint. Detroit: Gale Research Company, 1974.

Standard Directory of Advertisers: The Agency Red Book. New York: National Register Publication Company, 1964-.

Stansfield, Richard H. *The Dartnell Advertising Manager's Handbook.* Chicago: Dartnell, 1969.

Stephenson, Howard, ed. *Handbook of Public Relations: The Standard Guide to Public Affairs and Communications.* 2d ed. New York: McGraw-Hill, 1971.

Thompson, J. Walter, Company. *Advertising: An Annotated Bibliography.* New York: National Book League, 1972.

Turner, E. S. *The Shocking History of Advertising!* New York: E. P. Dutton, 1953.

Urdang, Laurence, ed. *Dictionary of Advertising Terms.* Chicago: Tatham, Laird and Kudner, 1977.

Wight, Robin. *The Day the Pigs Refused to Be Driven to Market: Advertising and the Consumer Revolution.* New York: Random House, 1972.

Wood, James Playsted. *The Story of Advertising.* New York: Ronald Press, 1958.

Young, Margaret Labash, et al. *Subject Directory of Special Libraries and Information Centers.* 4th ed. Detroit: Gale Research, 1977.

Almanacs

Robert K. Dodge

Americans today are only vaguely aware of the importance of almanacs during the first two hundred fifty years of American history. Most of us can quote a few of Poor Richard's sayings and associate them with an almanac; most of us probably remember the story of Abraham Lincoln and his use of an almanac to prove the innocence of a client; and many of us may remember reading in our history books that a Bible and an almanac constituted the only reading matter for most of our pioneers.

Anything else we remember about early American almanacs is probably associated with a sense of the quaint, of people who spelled with a final "k" and who attempted to predict the weather a year in advance.

Almanacs were much more than quaint. They were the forerunners of modern magazines and city directories. They served as calendars and road maps. They helped to publicize the U.S. Constitution. They served as vehicles for advertising and for politics and religion, and they spread humor throughout the country. They provide us an important source of information about American life and attitudes in the seventeenth, eighteenth, and nineteenth centuries.

In 1639 Stephen Daye printed America's first almanac in Cambridge, Massachusetts. For the next two and a half centuries and longer, almanacs constituted an important part of American life.

Most seventeenth-century almanacs appear quite modest. Almost all of them are sixteen-page pamphlets. A few extended to twenty-four or even thirty-two pages, beginning the gradual but steady tendency of American almanacs to lengthen. The sixteen-page almanacs devoted a separate page to each month. (Some of today's "factual" almanacs of a thousand or more pages devote fewer pages to the calendar.) Another page was often used to introduce the calendar and to give information concerning the dates of eclipses. Two of the three additional pages consisted of the front and back covers. The remaining page, usually the inside of the back cover, was sometimes used for advertisements, sometimes to provide information on events of the coming year, and sometimes to present an essay on the science of astronomy.

The calendar, considered the heart of the almanac, contained such information as the time of sunrise and sunset, the beginning date of each season (under the old-style calendar more variable than today), the phases of the moon, and usually some astrological information as well. If the intended readership included commercial fishermen or shippers, the calendar would include information on tides. The longer almanacs often allotted two pages to each month, although at least one twenty-four-page almanac included a nine-page explanation of its twelve-page calendar.

In the eighteenth century the almanac industry became more competitive. After all, the printing of an almanac had become a very profitable sideline for many American printers. They had a guaranteed market among farmers, commercial fishermen, and sailors. Naturally each almanac maker wanted to capture as large a share of the market as possible. It was perhaps competition more than any other influence that led to the changes in the eighteenth-century almanac, changes that make them more interesting to the student of American popular culture than are the majority of the almanacs from the seventeenth century.

Early competition concentrated on the accuracy of the calendar. Almanac makers extolled the virtues of their own calendars and often pointed out real or imagined inaccuracies in their competitors'. Sometimes a free errata sheet for the calendar of a major competitor was offered with the purchase of an almanac.

Another form of competition involved piracy. One of the reasons that bibliographies list so many editions of such popular titles as Thomas Greenleaf's and Abraham Weatherwise's almanacs appears to be that some of the editions were piracies. In at least one case the piracy had more involved motives, at least if Nathaniel Ames, publisher of one of America's first best-selling almanacs, was correct in his assessment of the competition. Ames complained that his competitors had banded together to produce a fraudulent and inaccurate almanac under his name in order to discredit him and his calendars.[1]

Ames and James Franklin can be credited with beginning to change the rules of almanac competition. They realized that the accuracy of a calendar as a sales inducement could be pushed only to a certain point, and they began the process of including other material to sell their almanacs. Ames often included short paragraphs on current events and on morality in general. James Franklin invented the character of Poor Robin, who gave his readers the sayings of Poor Robin.

While Ames and James Franklin began the process of changing the rules of competition, it was Benjamin Franklin who carried the process to its completion. Benjamin Franklin's first almanac burst upon the Philadelphia scene with the creation of Poor Richard and the prediction of the death of Titan Leeds, at the time the most popular almanac maker in the city.

Both the sayings of Poor Richard and the prediction, to which Leeds foolishly responded, helped Franklin's almanac to capture the attention of

Philadelphia, and as Franklin saw the popularity of Poor Richard's sayings grow, he increased their number. The idea for the prediction, like the idea for the sayings, was borrowed: the prediction from Jonathan Swift, a well-known British almanac maker who later developed a reputation for satire; the sayings from his brother. But, while Franklin treated the prediction almost exactly as Swift had, he developed the sayings far beyond what his brother had done.

Other almanac makers soon accepted the idea that material other than the calendar could make their almanacs sell. In the decades following the introduction of Poor Richard, almanacs grew longer and longer as publishers competed to include more and more material that the public would buy. It is such material that makes eighteenth- and nineteenth-century almanacs so interesting to the student of American popular culture.

For example, historians of farming in early America will find hundreds of "valuable receipts" for improving soil, increasing crop yields, and curing diseases in livestock. Many of the receipts appear to be based on superstition, and a few appear to be based on even less than that, but many more seem to represent a real interest in the establishment of an empirical science of farming. Two of the better suggestions include the use of lime as a fertilizer (useful only when the soil is acidic) and the addition of green organic material to the soil.

Other receipts offered cures for various human ailments. The gout, bloody flux, toothache, and nosebleed are provided with "sure and certain" cures. The science of medicine appears even less advanced than that of agriculture, but a trial-and-error methodology was beginning here as well.

Some almanacs included recipes for the preparation and preservation of food. Such recipes impress the modern reader with their emphasis on preservation and with the large quantities they were intended to serve. Measurements tended to be imprecise.

Many of the almanacs contained descriptions of American customs. One almanac printed an essay in favor of the New England custom of bundling. According to the essay, bundlers were almost always pure, and that new fangled innovation, the sofa, was far more dangerous to a woman's chastity. A long poem against bundling appeared in one of the Andrew Beers almanacs for 1793. Unlike the essay, the moralistic poem includes much detail about what its author thought took place in the bundling bed. One quatrain describes a man and a woman who had bundled together, each wearing a full set of clothing and wrapped in a separate sheet. The man, however, caught the itch from the woman, and she caught a bastard from him.[2]

Other described customs included bees and peddling. A few publishers, most notably Robert Thomas of *The (Old) Farmer's Almanack*, opposed the custom of social gatherings known as bees as wasteful of time and property. Thomas believed that a family had plenty of time during the long winter to husk its corn as it became necessary without the expense of entertaining all of the neighbors. Most almanac makers, however, considered bees of all kinds to be either harmless entertainment or positive ways for neighbors to help each other.

Peddlers constituted an important method of distribution for the almanac industry. Other media might criticize the peddler and, perhaps, deservedly so, but, as many of today's newspapers romanticize the newsboy, so did almanacs tend to romanticize the peddler.

Judging from what was printed in almanacs, early Americans must have liked to read about the exotic and the horrible. Indian captivity narratives and other stories of Indian cruelty abound, as do stories of Indian stoicism. Stories of cannibalism in America and Africa are common. Some almanacs described exotic animals, such as the giraffe and the elephant. The myth of the elephant's memory was demonstrated. Sentimental stories were popular as well. Some of the sentimental stories appear grotesque, at best, to the modern reader, but they do represent one form of popular story for the time.

By the last half of the eighteenth century, many of the almanacs had begun to provide pure information in the style of the present *World Almanac and Book of Facts* or the other large present-day almanacs familiar to most of us. The information was usually local, but a selection of almanacs would provide such information for most of the United States. What clubs existed in a particular city? What were the roads and their condition? Who were the political officers? What were the churches and who were the clergymen? Most localities had one or more almanacs that attempted to answer such questions. A few even attempted to name every family in the locality.

Other kinds of information dealt with current events, including politics. The first balloon ascension was noted in many almanacs and even inspired the publication of the *Balloon Almanac.* The settlement of the frontier was a popular topic, as was the American Revolution and later the adoption of the Constitution. Laws and tariffs were reprinted. George Washington's "Farewell Address" was widely reprinted, as were many of the writings of Benjamin Franklin.

Another topic that must interest the student of popular culture is humor. Comic almanacs flourished in the nineteenth century. The David Crockett almanacs are probably the best known, but Josh Billings (Henry Wheeler Shaw), Commodore Rollingpin (John Henton Carter), and others produced comic almanacs. *All-My-Nack*, *Allminax*, and *Allmaniac* were among the comic misspellings. In addition, many of the serious almanacs contained comic material, much as *Reader's Digest* and other magazines do today. Such comic material constitutes one of the few sources of early popular humor still available to us. Between 1776 and 1800, for example, more than 1,500 comic items were published in serious American almanacs. Certainly much of the comedy was literary rather than popular, and much of it was not even very comic. In some cases the comic items seem to have been copied directly from British sources. Nevertheless, this body of humor is worthy of study simply because it does constitute almost the only source of written popular humor before the *Spirit of the Times* and its competing journals, and the almanac remained an important source even after that.

The nineteenth century saw the development of advertising almanacs, especially those advertising patent medicines. Milton Drake says that about fifty patent medicine almanacs were published in the century, many of them in continuous publication for several years.[3] Many other groups used almanacs for advertising in the nineteenth century. Drake lists religious groups, uplift groups, political groups, labor and professional groups, fraternal groups, and pressure groups, as well as straightforward sales-related advertisers such as those printing and distributing almanacs in this century. The *Christian Almanac,* one of the religious almanacs, grew to have a circulation of 300,000 in 1850.[4]

The twentieth century has brought about additional changes in U.S. almanacs. The almanac of pure information has certainly become the dominant form. For some publishers, the word *almanac* has come to mean any yearly compilation of information and statistics, whether in a particular field (for example, the *Nurse's Almanac* and the *Standard Educational Almanac*) or more general (the *World Almanac and Book of Facts*). The calendar, if it exists at all, has been relegated to a very minor role. In the case of a few publications, such as *The People's Almanac* by David Wallechinsky and Irving Wallace, even the characteristic of yearly publication has been dropped. A few old-time or family almanacs are still published. Most prominent among them is the *Old Farmer's Almanac,* a direct descendant of Robert B. Thomas' *Farmer's Almanac.* Its appeal to a sense of nostalgia and quaintness had gained it a circulation of 2 million in 1970.

Scholars interested in American ethnic groups will find that U.S. almanacs have been published in at least twenty languages including twelve European languages and six American Indian languages.

NOTES

1. Samuel Briggs, *The Essays, Humor and Poems of Nathaniel Ames, Father and Son, of Dedham, Massachusetts from Their Almanacks, 1726-1775* (Detroit: Singing Tree Press, 1969), p. 372.

2. "A Song Upon Bundling," *Beers's Almanac for 1793* (Hartford, Conn.: Hudson and Goodwin, 1792), pp. 26-27.

3. Milton Drake, *Almanacs of the United States* (New York: Scarecrow Press, 1962) 1; xiii.

4. Drake, p. x.

BIBLIOGRAPHY

Booker, Elsie H. and Curtis. "Patent Medicines Before the Wiley Act of 1906." *North Carolina Folklore, The Essays, Humor and Poems of Nathaniel Ames, Father and Son, of Dedham, Massachusetts from their Almanacks, 1726-1775.* Cleveland: Western Reserve Press, 1891. Reprint. Detroit: Singing Tree Press, 1969.

Brigham, Clarence. "An Account of American Almanacs and Their Value for Historical Study." *Proceedings of the American Antiquarian Society,* n.s. 34 (October 1925), 3-28.

______. "Report of the Librarian." *Proceedings of the American Antiquarian Society,* n.s. 35 (October 1926), 190-218.

Bristol, Roger P. *Supplement to Charles Evans' American Bibliography.* Charlottesville: University Press of Virginia, 1970.

Dodge, Robert. "Didactic Humor in the Almanacs of Early America." *Journal of Popular Culture,* 5 (Winter 1971), 592-605.

Dorson, Richard M. *Davy Crockett: American Comic Legend.* New York: Spiral Editions, 1939.

Drake, Milton. *Almanacs of the United States.* 2 vols. New York: Scarecrow Press, 1962.

Evans, Charles. *American Bibliography.* 14 vols. Worcester, Mass.: American Antiquarian Society, 1903-55. Reprint. New York: Peter Smith, 1941-67.

Kittredge, George Lyman. *The Old Farmer and His Almanack.* Cambridge: Harvard University Press, 1920. Reprint. New York: B. Blom, 1967.

Leypoldt, F., Lynds E. Jones, and R. R. Bowker. *The American Catalogue.* New York: Bowker, 1880-1911. Reprint. New York: Peter Smith, 1941.

Littlefield, George Emery. "Notes on the Calendar and the Almanac." *Proceedings of the American Antiquarian Society,* n.s. 24 (October 1914), 11-64.

McDowell, Marion Barber (now Marion Barber Stowell). "Early American Almanacs: The History of a Neglected Literary Genre." Ph.D. dissertation, Florida State University, 1974.

Page, Alfred B. "The Almanacs of John Tulley: 1687-1702." *Publications of the Colonial Society of Massachusetts,* 13 (July 1912), 207-23.

Paltsits, Victor Hugo. "The Almanacs of Roger Sherman, 1750-1761." *Proceedings of the American Antiquarian Society,* n.s. 18 (April 1907), 213-58.

Sagendorph, Robb. *America and Her Almanacs: Wit, Wisdom and Weather.* Boston: Yankee-Little Brown, 1970.

Shaw, Henry Wheeler. *Old Probability: Perhaps Rain—Perhaps Not.* New York: G. W. Carleton, 1876. Reprint. Upper Saddle River, N.J.: Literature House/ Gregg Press, 1970.

Shaw, Ralph R., and Richard Shoemaker. *American Bibliography: A Preliminary Checklist for 1801-1819.* 20 vols. New York: Scarecrow Press, 1958-64.

Stowell, Marion Barber. *Early American Almanacs: The Colonial Weekday Bible.* New York: Burt Franklin, 1977.

Wenrick, Jon Stanley. "For Education and Entertainment—Almanacs in the Early American Republic, 1783-1815." Ph.D. dissertation, Claremont Graduate School, 1974.

———. "Indians in Almanacs, 1783-1815." *Indian Historian,* 8 (Winter 1977), 36-42.

Woodward, F. G. "An Early Tennessee Almanac and Its Maker: Hill's Almanac 1825-1862." *Tennessee Folklore Society Bulletin,* 18 (March 1952), 9-14.

Animation

Thomas W. Hoffer

Animated motion pictures of the kind shown to mass audiences in the United States from the early 1920s to the 1950s were literally created frame by frame. Of course, all motion pictures are photographed by this method, usually twenty-four frames taken in one second, processed and projected on a screen at the same rate, fused into the appearance of motion in our mind's eye. Many of the films considered in this section, while created frame by frame with a camera, are first drawn by an artist or a group of artists. But there are other animated films which are created by single-frame exposures of objects, models, miniatures or photographs, manipulating the objects, photographs, or the camera itself between each single exposure. Still other forms of animation completely eliminate the camera and create movement by drawing directly on the film. The unusual patterns of line and geometry come to life when the film is projected, sometimes with a soundtrack created in similar fashion. Present-day electronic technology enables animators to create sound and pictures with multiple synthesizers and computers. This brings us to another type of animated film which is made up of computer generated images based on single frames, created from the mathematical equivalents of line, mass, tone and color in a given scene.

These various forms of animation include the cel drawings of Winsor McCay, Raoul Barré and John Bray; the stop-action tricks of Emil Cohl, Georges Méliès, or Edwin S. Porter; the silhouette cutouts of Lotte Reiniger; the object and puppet animation of Willis O'Brien or George Pal; the animated photographs and drawings of Bob Godfrey or Terry Gilliam; or the drawings on film and soundtracks by Len Lye and Norman McLaren; and the computer generated images orchestrated by John Whitney and Lillian Schwartz.

Animation is more than drawing, of course. Definitions of animation that limit the subject to either photography shot a frame at a time or to movements created frame by frame do not have sufficient breadth to accommodate all of the rich, varied forms noted above. Those examples originate in diverse ways but they share one common element: the manipulation imposed between the frames, whether drawn, photographed individually or generated by a machine. Norman McLaren, of the National Film Board of Canada, defined the process in this manner:

> Animation is not the art of *drawings* that move, but the art of *movements* that are drawn. What happens between each frame is more important than what exists on each frame. Animation is therefore the art of manipulating the invisible interstices that lie between frames. The interstices are the bones, flesh and blood of the movie, what is on each frame, merely the clothing.[1]

Cel-animation is one of the two types that first reached mass audiences as the moving picture evolved in the United States after 1895. This type was manifested in the art of Winsor McCay (Gertie, the Dinosaur; Little Nemo), Otto Messmer (Felix, the Cat), Walt Disney (Mickey Mouse), Max and Dave Fleischer (KoKo, the Clown; Betty Boop), Tex Avery (Porky Pig, Bugs Bunny), Bob Clampett (Bugs Bunny), Chuck Jones (The Roadrunner) and hundreds of others who created their films frame by frame by drawing them individually for the camera through the use of celluloid overlays (cels). The works of those animators resulted in more than movement or simple drawings; they created characters, told stories, used and exploited stereotypes, and caricatured life and personalities.

The types of object-animation are also diverse, developing a deeper tradition in Europe but increasingly featured in American theatrical film and television. There are the pinscreen films of Alexandre Alexeieff and Claire Parker; the puppet films of George Pal and Jiri Trnka; clay animated films of Will Vinton; monstrous miniature films of Willis O'Brien and Ray Harryhausen; cutout films of Lotte Reiniger, Sid Marcus, Jan Lenica, Zofia Oraczewska, Larry Jordan; pixilated films of Bernard Longpre and Andre Leduc; kinestasis animation by Dan McLaughlin and Charles Braverman; stills-in-motion films of Al Stahl and many television documentary filmmakers; and the abstractions of Oskar Fischinger, Viking Eggeling, Hans Richter, and Mary Ellen Bute. The drawing-on-film techniques or cameraless animation is another kind of abstraction which defines its own class because these films by Norman McLaren, Robert Swarthe, Len Lye and others eliminated the camera in the production process. The last category of animated film, incorporating computer generated images, is less than one decade old, at least in terms of innovation. In digital television, using character generators and microprocessors, there is a new technological basis for manufacturing abstract forms and titles. Other electronic and photographic technology has animated, through stop-action, the swirl of clouds in television weathercasts, or the rotation of clouds around Jupiter, reflecting a mixture of new and old technologies, now typical of animation forms in the early 1980s.

The animated drawing was a reality decades before the innovation of the motion picture but the animated film did not evolve until the invention of the film camera and projector. In 1825, drawings were animated in parlor toys and other gadgets such as John Aryton's Thaumatrope (1825, Paris) or the Phenakistiscope (1832). But invention of still photography by Louis Daguerre, based on the work of Joseph Nicéphore Niepce, later ushered in a period of animating still pictures, after 1851. In Philadelphia, for example, Coleman Sellers built equipment which enabled him to project several still photographs in rapid succession. Eadweard Muybridge, Ottomar Anschutz and Jules Marey were among several experimenters who sought to photograph objects in motion and project those pictures, recreating the movement. With the invention of roll film by Hannibal Goodwin and the perfection of moving picture cameras and projectors by Thomas Edison, W. Laurie Dickson, William Friese-Greene, Thomas Armat, Louis and Auguste Lumiere, the technical capability for object and cel animation was available to many creative craftsmen by 1900. Georges Méliès photographed staged narratives, incorporating stop-action tricks and pictorial fantasies performing his "substitution trick" in *The Vanishing Lady* in 1896. He stopped the camera and removed the lady and resumed photography. When the film was projected, she merely "popped off" the set, establishing one of the earliest examples of stop-action photography. This technique was used in hundreds of films after 1896 and became the photographic basis for object animation in films as recent as *The Empire Strikes Back.* In 1900, J. Stuart Blackton drew the face of a fat man who smiled off-and-on again with the animation created by stop-action technique in an early Edison film, *The Enchanted Drawing.* Simple pixilation animation was demonstrated by Oscar B. Dupue when he exposed his films while his camera was positioned on the bow of a ship touring Norway. These 1902 films, exposed at a very slow frame rate, had shown the ship racing through the water at high speed when shown at a faster projection speed. In the 1903 Edwin S. Porter version of *The Great Train Robbery,* two matte shots were incorporated in the dramatic action. Porter covered parts of the scene with light-absorbing black velvet and shot the action of the train interior, then rewound the film backward, matting out the train interior and reframed the camera on a passing landscape. The camera was started again, creating the composite image showing the train interior and the passing landscape through a doorway. Out of these crude examples would eventually come optical printers and traveling matte systems which would enable filmmakers to create various composite shots of actors against all kinds of background plates, such as those pursued by monsters in *Jason and the Argonauts* (1963) or rotoscoped mattes in *Star Wars* (1977).

In the same year that Winsor McCay took to the stage to draw cartoons in his "Seven Ages of Man" cartoon act (1906), J. Stuart Blackton and

Albert E. Smith created an animated film called *Humorous Phases of Funny Faces.* Two years later, Emile Cohl finished his cel-animated film *Fantasmagorie,* released by Gaumont. In 1911, Winsor McCay released an animated film based on the Little Nemo comic strip. After this time, a number of animators had expanded animation from stop-action tricks to a cel medium. In McCay's work, however, there is, by far, a clear distinction in style unmatched by his contemporaries or succeeding generations.

But McCay's technique in full animation, where every frame was painstakingly redrawn, was out-of-step with the increasing demands for films on a regular basis. The period 1912-1915 was one of great change in the motion picture business. Audiences for films were expanding into larger theaters; playbills became longer as features or multi-reelers became available, sometimes requiring as much as $2.00 for an admission to a roadshow engagement. In this era of changing programs and star system, the animated film needed a new production procedure if it were to have any chance of regular exposure to the increasingly mass audience. For obvious reasons of efficiency, but more for the presold nature of the content already widely syndicated by newspapers, most of the early series of animated cartoons were derived from their comic strips.

John Bray and Raoul Barré had been working on a systematic method of producing animated cartoons faster without having to redraw everything in each frame, as did McCay. Barré divided up the labor in cartoon production, assigning various tasks to his staff, spending much of his time supervising their work. This model for work was refined and carried forward by Walt Disney in the early 1930s, supplemented with training sessions, pencil tests, storyboards, script conferences, and other devices to produce a single animated style. Barré's "slash system" enhanced his division of labor by eliminating the expensive effort involved in redrawing everything in each frame, including the stationary portions of the action, as done by Winsor McCay. In Barré's system, only the moving portions of an action would be drawn, with the stationary portions put on another cel. Perhaps Barré's New York studio, organized in 1913, had greater significance since it was the training ground for a new generation of animators including Albert Hurter and Richard Huemer, who would later animate at Disney. One year later, John Bray formed an animation studio in New York, and with Earl Hurd, they pooled their patents which enabled mass production of cartoons on a sound economic basis. Bray originated the concept of "inbetweening," with the animator drawing the extreme movement positions and his assistants drawing all the movements between those extremes. A uniform system of peg registration was developed by Bray and Hurd so the holes placed on each drawing would be perfectly registered with successive drawings. Other technical improvements in the animation production process included

Max Fleischer's rotoscope device, in which live-action footage was traced onto cels, and Bill Nolan's moving background system.

In object animation, there were not any similar mass production innovations. Willis O'Brien produced such a stop-motion short, *The Dinosaur and the Missing Link* (1914), taking two months for the photography, one frame at a time. Special effects techniques, which would eventually incorporate animation, improved with Norman Dawn's single-frame photography of matte shots resulting in less time for composing tedious glass shots.

In the period 1916 through 1926, object and cel animation forms expanded their audiences incorporating a greater range of characters. While the fully animated, fluid movements of McCay animations were not the norm for this decade, a number of characters, mostly based on successful comic strips, appeared before film audiences. They moved in limited fashion often with jerks, cycles and lots of holds. Instead of every frame in sixteen animated in each 35mm foot, animation on "2's" was typical, meaning that two exposures were made for each piece of artwork. The result was limited animation but more cheaply and rapidly produced, enabling more cartoons to reach theater screens and perhaps gain an audience. The more widely distributed animations included the work of Otto Messmer, Max and Dave Fleischer, the Hearst International Film Studio (which included Walter Lantz briefly) and Paul Terry's organization. Sid Marcus designed *Animated Hair* cartoons using cutouts and Tony Sarg animated prehistorical animals in silhouette cutouts. The *Paramount Pictographs* consisted of educational subjects in a magazine format and were usually followed with a Bray cartoon. In fact, many newsreels after 1914 included a cartoon, some of which editorialized or interpreted a news event or satirized a personality. Those working in stop-action forms included Segunde de Chómon, Giovanni Pastrone (Italy), Willis O'Brien, and Marcel Delgado.

Animation and special photographic effects had joined together in the decade before 1926 with live-action scenes combined with animated characters. The use of masks or mattes would become a more reliable method for accomplishing this, beginning with the work of F. D. Williams and his traveling matte system which became an industry standard for years.

While new forms of animation were finding audiences, many films failed to attract much interest beyond their initial release. At first a novelty, cartoons based on successful comic strips became pale reflections of the original works. Even the Disney cartoons, and his live-action *Alice* series combined with animated characters, were not standouts either in terms of style or character.

Disney began his animation career in 1920 with a job at the Kansas City Film Ad Company. His training was largely through trial and error, relying upon Eadweard Muybridge's photo studies and other books. He persuaded his brothers and associates to go to California for a fresh start following the failure in Kansas.

In Europe, painters Viking Eggeling, Georges Braque, and Francis Picabia experimented with abstract animation while their commercial counterparts in America such as Pat Sullivan and Bud Fisher created work for the mass marketplace. Others in the art of abstract animation included Hans Richter, Walter Ruttman, Fernand Leger, and Oskar Fischinger.

The so-called golden age of American animation found its beginnings in the exploitation of sound and color, after 1928. From this exploitation grew a large number of producer organizations in search of characters duplicating Disney's success with Mickey Mouse and his full animated personality style. In this period, 1928-1947, Disney would continue to outdistance the competition, at least in terms of audience appeal and full character animation. Even at the Disney organization in the early 1940s, there were differences over matters of style and out of that rebellion came the United Productions of America (UPA) in the mid-1940s. During this time, animation expanded its functions beyond entertainment, and into instruction and propaganda, mostly because of World War II. Experimentation in animation continued among inventors and independent filmmakers with some small influences from and collisions with the theatrical film establishment. Object-animated films using puppets and miniatures reached new audiences but these were never as influential as an animated form until their incorporation into television advertising, programming and theatrical film special effects years later. Technology also helped establish new styles or maintain existing ones, as in the case of live-action combined with animation in color. Influences from abroad were minimal due to the war, but this would change after 1948. The economics of production and other factors, by 1947, forced some producers to cut back or stop animated short-subject production, signaling the beginning of the end for the animated theatrical cartoon, at least for a decade. The most important regulatory development in this period was the 1948 consent decree which began the breakup of the major film producers' hold on distribution and exhibition. The result was the increasing access to American screens by independents and foreign films, and, some still argue, at the expense of the American animated short.

There is no question that the Disney studio, in this twenty year period 1928-1947, was the most important in terms of personality or character animation, organization, technical achievement, merchandising and exploitation of color and sound. Disney innovated the storyboard, allowing his animators to plan entire films more efficiently. He reinvested money and effort in building a cadre of trained personnel who, according to some, were later exploited by him. He insisted on the best quality work and maximized every opportunity to strengthen the organization by maintaining every conceivable control over this product at a time when other producer organizations were struggling against the double feature that tended to push cartoons out of theaters. Following the success of *Flowers and*

Trees (1932), the first three-strip technicolor sound cartoon, and the popular *Three Little Pigs* (1933), Disney resisted the general industry practice of following a winner with a duplicate offering, a practice still followed in today's phonograph, radio, television and film industries. His shrewd deal with Technicolor insured exclusive use of the new process for two years, undoubtedly nourishing new exhibitor and distributor interest in the animated film. His organization also wrung every ounce of profit from merchandising activity and carried it to new heights, later emulated by the Fleischer brothers. While *Snow White and the Seven Dwarfs* (1937) was not the first animated feature, it was the most economically and artistically successful for many years. In that picture and an earlier short subject, *The Old Mill* (1937), Disney innovated the multi-plane techniques that provided a greater sense of depth. His organization developed checkpoints in the animation process to maintain quality and extend animation to new frontiers. These included the conference technique, key drawings, pencil tests, the Leica reel, and stereophonic sound.

World War II eclipsed commercial cartoon animation but in the few years before that conflict, the Fleischer brothers released their product through Paramount and Walter Lantz released through Universal Pictures. The Fleischer Studios animated Betty Boop (1930), Popeye (1933), and Superman (1941). Paul Terry eventually released his cartoons through Twentieth Century Fox, totaling over 1,200 shorts during the life of his studio but never engaging in feature production. Warner Brothers began with Bosko (1930) and followed with Porky Pig (1935), Bugs Bunny and Elmer Fudd (1940), and The Roadrunner and Coyote (1948) among others. Metro-Goldwyn-Mayer characters came later than the others but eventually included Tom and Jerry (1939). Following labor troubles at the Disney Studio in 1941, a number of artists left and set up United Productions of America (UPA). Their more limited animated style was in considerable contrast to Disney's, with flat, two-dimensional characters and far more abstraction in character and background as in Mr. Magoo (1949) and Gerald McBoing Boing (1951). Like the Disney Studio, UPA also spawned another generation of animators and directors such as John Hubley, Peter Burness, Bill Littlejohn, Bill Melendez, and Jules Engel. For television advertising in particular, the more abstract style of UPA would find a cordial welcome as well as adaptation for reasons of economy and clarity.

Object-animation, models, and puppets still appealed to American audiences although not nearly in the same scope as the cel-animated cartoon. Willis O'Brien's *King Kong* (1933) was an improvement over *The Lost World* (1925). By 1940, George Pal had released the first of his *Puppetoons* with a young Ray Harryhausen assisting. Puppet animation would eventually vanish from American screens to reappear in different form on television.

This period, 1928-1947, also involved some experimentation in the new sound medium, which was married to the cartoon at first in a very literal way. The music became the leader for the action, down to the precise beat of each note. It was as if movies returned to the static state of the first decade in the century, when few dared to manipulate camera angle, image size, or editing. Thus, many cartoons, including early Disney, were merely illustrated radio programs or phonograph records. Fortunately, Disney, the Fleischers and others eventually outgrew the restraints of the early sound technology and turned it around, integrating sound with the picture instead of having the sound determine picture. Radio provided one model for the sound film, including animation, because through sound effects, music, and dialogue, well timed to the action, the soundtrack could take over the narrative function or develop another narrative action in the same or different time frame. The best example of this marriage occurred when Orson Welles brought his Mercury Theater ensemble to Hollywood and made *Citizen Kane* (1941). With voice characterizations such as Mel Blanc's (Porky Pig or Bugs Bunny, for example) and the integration of sound effects in point or counterpoint to the visible action (as in some Warner Brothers' cartoons or the character who spoke in sound effects, Gerald McBoing Boing) American animation achieved greater expressiveness with sound.

King Kong (1933), *The Invisible Man* (1933), and the ghostly story of George and Marion Kirby (*Topper,* 1937) were the memorable illusions created by special photographic effects, mattes and stop-action animation in the 1930s. In the early 1940s, Disney demonstrated live-action combined with animation in Technicolor, but Metro-Goldwyn-Mayer's *Anchors Aweigh* (1944) is the best-remembered sequence, featuring Gene Kelly dancing with an animated mouse, Jerry of the Tom and Jerry duo. With the closing of George Pal's puppet-animation business and Columbia's decision to abandon cel-animation in the late 1940s, early signals for discontinuing animated shorts in the United States were apparent. A combination of factors were involved in this demise, including the difficulty producers had in obtaining commitments from Technicolor, the uncertain status of new color processes such as Polacolor and Cinecolor, higher labor costs in producing shorts and the 1948 consent decree which resulted in the producer organizations divesting themselves of their theaters, and certain trade practices which enhanced the vertical integration of the film industry.

In the next period of American animation, 1947-1963, major studios had less and less automatic access to theater screens. The removal of block-booking practices opened the window for more independent films and foreign pictures on United States screens. The broadcasting industry began its transformation to include national television networks, taking away a substantial portion of the nighttime audience of the film business. At first, film studios refused to sell their film libraries to television, but a trickle soon led to a Niagara and by 1960, television was devouring both the mundane and classic animated films stripped in local programs and network shows. The potential of television and increased availability of foreign films were probably the chief influences on animation in this period, along with the indigenous UPA-style. This flat, abstract cartoon motif, embellished with personality through voicing and sound effects brought new economies to the video medium. Unlike Disney's work, there were more individual styles reflected in the UPA character lineup. *The Unicorn in the Garden* (1953), *My Twelve Fathers* from Czechoslovakia (1958), *The Commissar Comes Home* (1959), and *The Romance of Transportation* (1952) from Canada were additional animated styles available to American audiences. In the experimental or avant-garde community, abstract animations expanded to more specialized audiences which included formally organized festivals and exhibitions, and better distribution plans. Bolder manipulations in animated forms were taken in television advertising, first with the "quick-cut" commercial, giving the appearance of stop-action. Magoo became a spokesman for General Electric lightbulbs. Slowly, a trend in limited-animation commercials took hold, including use of the cel medium, but also including collage, "paper sculpture," and still photography. Partly to lessen costs of full, character animation, quick-cutting or flash-cutting was also incorporated. Following the exhaustion of studio animated libraries, many new limited animation series were started. Dimensional or object-animation found new life on theater screens partly because of the audience's renewed interest in science fiction and the film industry's attempt to lure audiences away from television. A young Ray Harryhausen worked with Willis O'Brien on *Mighty Joe Young* (1949) but surprised investors by filming the black-and-white *Beast from 20,000 Fathoms* (1953) for a cheap $200,000, making a profit in competition with three-dimension, wide screen, and other scoped-and-full-color processes. Slowly incubating were other forms of stop-motion photo animation. The Canadian Film Board's *City of Gold* (1957), recreating the days of Dawson City and the Klondike gold rush by using 300 recovered glass plates, was the predecessor to NBC's "Project Twenty" series, which would reach larger audiences with stop-motion recreations. We had all become accustomed to old photographs gathering dust in hallways and on walls, but rarely had we heard them "talk." In "Project Twenty," animation brought these historic pictures to new audiences.

As in the previous periods, newer technologies were exploited in films such as John Fulton's multiple mattes and animation in the remake of *The Ten Commandments* (1956). The John Oxberry animation stands established new standards for a growing TV commercial industry and made the animated form more widely available to television. At Disney, the three-head optical printer was developed and with the improved technology of the sodium-light-traveling matte process made possible the dazzling *Mary*

Poppins (1964). Videotape was invented and innovated by the end of this period along with the capability to perform simple animation on tape.

Disney was still the dominant studio in theatrical animation but the studio was also changing with the times. The move to combine live-action and animation pictures following World War II turned out to be a steady transition to all-live-action features in the early 1950s. Television saved the Disney enterprises by permitting unbridled promotion of Disneyland, a new amusement park in Anaheim, California. The Mickey Mouse Club was launched in 1955, introducing the Disney name and characters to another generation. Mickey Mouse cartoons were curtailed in 1953, but special animated shorts and two-reelers continued. By the mid-1960s, Warner Brothers and MGM had closed their animation units. For a time, Disney was alone in animation feature production, as costs continued to rise. Reflecting the medium's constant appetite to devour new material on a giant scale, prime time television received "The Flintstones" in 1960, a limited-animation series that lasted six years on the network, and still survives in syndication. With limited animation techniques, there was a sharp rise in television animation by the mid-1960s, sometimes accompanied by the scorn of production professionals who had emulated the Disney techniques of full, character work.

In the period 1964 to present, American animation continued to expand into new forms and was largely conditioned by electronics. Television had become the dominant national advertising medium and chief distributor of animated films, both the Saturday morning variety from U.S. television networks, and some experimental works available through public television stations. Network ratings demonstrated that audiences were attracted to Saturday morning color television offerings on the networks, setting the stage for a three-way race among the competing networks by 1967. Puppets shed their animation technologies in television for videotaped live-action forms such as "The Muppets." Kermit the Frog was called the "Mickey Mouse of the 1970s" by *Time* magazine. Animated theatrical shorts were practically moribund except for Metro-Goldwyn-Mayer's *The Dot and the Line* and Warner's *The Pink Panther* series animated by DePatie-Freleng. At Disney, the results of a talent hunt began to replenish the ranks of retired and dead animators. Ward Kimball broke Disney cel traditions with a short, *It's Tough to Be a Bird* (1969) using cutout collage sequences. Norelco's fourteen-year-old Christmas animation, with some updating, seemed to symbolize the stability of full-and-limited animation advertising in the production marketplace by the end of the 1970s. Animation expanded into other areas of persuasion, beginning in 1964 with television editorial cartoons in New Orleans. Years later, Hal Seegar began "Cartoon-A-Torials," distributed by Post-Newsweek. Perpetual Motion Pictures, New York, editorialized through "Mr. Hipp" on the NBC program, "Weekend," but the series was shortlived. Science-fiction television programs continued the thread of theatrical films of the same type as those of the 1950s, with "Voyage to the Bottom of the Sea" (1964) and "Star Trek" (1966-1969) starting a new era of animation techniques in support of special photographic effects. Kubrick's *2001: A Space Odyssey* (1968) used front projection techniques and a flashy "stargate" sequence that had a large influence on television commercials, proliferating slit-scan, starbursts, and other visual embellishments made for corporate logos and product names. There was far more emphasis on form than content as later films such as *Star Wars* (1977), *The Black Hole* (1979) and *Star Trek: The Motion Picture* (1979) demonstrated. Rod Steiger later typed this resurgence of special effects as "humanized cartoons." And, perhaps taking a cue from EXPO '67, the TV and film producers mixed more of their media. EXPO '67 was the watershed for film and multimedia techniques with a world showcase of mixed media, including animation. In animation the "mix" began with the drawing of cels and their storage on videotape, but the expansion through electronics would later require satellites, telemetry digital storage modes, and computers. *Star Wars* (1977) signalled the full media-mix, including computer animation, rotoscoped mattes, stop-action or dimensional animation, computer directed cameras, synthesized sound effects, miniatures and, of course, live-action. Like *2001,* the picture had a profound impact on other media and on television advertising in particular, but it should be noted that the animator and special effects artists who conceived and executed the designs in *Star Wars* were principally from the television commercial business, not the Hollywood special-effects establishment. About the mid-1960s, television began to acquire a more graphic look in station logos, advertising, network signatures, and main titles. News had long been accustomed to using drawings for judicial trials where TV cameras were routinely excluded. Such graphics began appearing over the shoulders of anchor-persons and reporters, usually symbolizing or stylizing the event with some object. There was an enormous emphasis on making even the live portion of the news "interesting." By 1980, character generators, which made possible quick preparation of long written quotations on TV screens, provided a variety of lettering fonts and other graphic elements such as "colorizing" and tabular outlines. Some systems could perform limited animation.

Despite higher equipment costs when compared to film animators, many experimentalists moved into video technology and achieved limited national exposure but only over public television. Object and cutout animation had a better foothold in television than the previous period (1947-1963), although "Land of the Lost" (NBC-TV, 1974-1978) was shortlived, it was a program which combined dimensional animation with live-action. The zany British import, animated by Terry Gilliam, "Monty Python's Flying Circus" never seemed to wear out with some audiences. In theatrical film, Ray Harryhausen's *Jason and the Argonauts* is still seen as his best work, although a number of other films were produced in recent years. Probes into deep space represented another example of media-mix in animation. Voyager provided pictures of Jupiter and Pioneer flew by Saturn. Representations were broken down into their line components and sent back to earth where they were stored digitally and played back in color in time-lapse fashion.

Computer-assisted and the generation of computer-animated images were the most significant technical breakthroughs in this period, 1964 to the present. Scientists at Bell Laboratories made the first computer-animated films in 1963. Many others developed and exploited theory, hardware and software to evolve computer graphics, first used in the automobile and aircraft industries as an aid to design. The theory and applications from numerical control in engineering had direct implications for computer-assisted work in traditional animation. As experimental filmmakers such as Stan Vanderbeek and John Whitney connected with programmers and the computer technology, a number of computer-animated systems became available commercially.

Animation also contributed substantially to the new form of children's instructional television represented by "Sesame Street" (1969-). Along with *2001: A Space Odyssey,* another cel-and-collage animated film had considerable influence on the graphic quality of television and advertising. Al Brodaux, Heinz Edelman, George Dunning and Fred Wolf led the team to create *Yellow Submarine* (1968), an unusually stylized leap from Disney animation to a fantastic, optical and surrealistic world of graphics and animated characters. In other theatrical animation, adult audiences had new forms in the X-rated cartoon by Ralph Bakshi. Sex was explicit in *Fritz the Cat* (1973), which was the only non-Disney film released in this period to show a profit.

Despite the concerns about violence in children's programming, and proposals to curb advertising in such programs (discarded in early 1981), the audiences for animation were still expanding in the 1980s. The biggest potential for these specialized audiences likely to consume instructional, experimental films, photographic abstractions, and entertainment is in the growing videodisc and videocassette markets. The survival and growth of animation in the late 1950s is attributed to the transition to mass television. Conditions have clearly changed, where animation interests still survive in advertising and mass programming, yet new adaptations are being made in instructional, scientific, editorial and entertainment forms, incorporating a mixture of media.

NOTE

1. Quoted in John Halas, ed., *Computer Animation* (New York: Hastings House, 1974), p. 97. (McLaren's italics.)

BIBLIOGRAPHY

Adamson, Joe. *Tex Avery: King of Cartoons.* New York: Popular Press, 1975.

Brosnan, John. *Movie Magic: The Story of Special Effects in the Cinema.* New York: St. Martin's Press, 1976.

Carbarga, Leslie. *The Fleischer Story in the Golden Age of Animation.* New York: Nostalgia Press, 1976.

Canemaker, John. *The Animated Raggedy Ann and Andy.* New York: Bobbs-Merrill, 1977.

Ceram, C. W. (Kurt W. Marek). *Archaeology of the Cinema.* New York: Harcourt, Brace and World, 1965.

Crafton, Donald Clayton. "Emile Cohl and the Origins of the Animated Film." Ph.D. dissertation, Yale University, 1977.

Curtis, David. *Experimental Cinema.* New York: Universe Books, 1971.

Edera, Bruno. *Full Length Animated Features Films.* New York: Visual Communication Books, Hastings House, 1976.

Fielding, Raymond. *The Technique of Special Effects Cinematography.* 3d ed. New York: Focal Press, 1972.

Gartley, Lynn, and Elizabeth Leebron. *Walt Disney: A Guide to References and Resources.* Boston: G. K. Hall, 1979.

Halas, John, ed. *Computer Animation.* New York: Hastings House, 1974.

Hoffer, Thomas W. *Animation: A Reference Guide.* Westport, Conn.: Greenwood Press, 1981.

Holman, L. Bruce. *Puppet Animation in the Cinema: History and Technique.* New York: A. S. Barnes, 1975.

Laybourne, Kit. *The Animation Book.* New York: Crown, 1979.

Le Grice, Malcolm. *Abstract Film and Beyond.* London: Cassell and Collier Macmillan, 1977.

Madsen, Roy. *Animated Film: Concepts, Methods, Uses.* New York: Interland Publishing Co., 1969.

Maltin, Leonard. *Of Mice and Magic: A History of American Animated Cartoons.* New York: McGraw-Hill, 1980.

Peary, Danny, and Gerald Peary, eds. *The American Animated Cartoon: A Critical Anthology.* New York: E. P. Dutton, 1980.

Reiniger, Lotte. *Shadow Puppets, Shadow Theatres and Shadow Films.* 1970. Reprint. Boston: Plays, 1975.

Renan, Sheldon. *An Introduction to the American Underground Film.* New York: E. P. Dutton, 1967.

Russett, Robert, and Cecile Starr. *Experimental Animation: An Illustrated Anthology.* New York: Van Nostrand Reinhold Co., 1976.

Schickel, Richard. *The Disney Version: The Life, Times, Art and Commerce of Walt Disney.* New York: Simon and Schuster, 1968.

Thomas, Bob. *Walt Disney: An American Original.* New York: Simon and Schuster, 1976.

Youngblood, Gene. *Expanded Cinema: The Audio-Visual Extension of Man.* New York: E. P. Dutton, 1970.

Architecture

Richard Guy Wilson

Of all the elements that make up popular culture, architecture is surely the most omnipresent. One can turn off the Rolling Stones, refuse to watch "Charlie's Angels," ignore Harold Robbins, be revolted by Big Macs, and reject the message of Mr. Clean; yet, unless one becomes a hermit and retires to the mythical cave, the man-made environment intrudes. The buildings one lives in, works in, and plays in, reveal personal and cultural values; they are records of growth, progress, decay, and decline and, if properly understood, they can serve as an environmental diary. While to some eyes architecture is only the very rarefied "high art" or the top 5 percent of the built environment, if properly construed, architecture is concerned with all forms of design—from skyscrapers and homes of the wealthy to highways, McDonald's restaurants, suburban ranches, mobile homes, plastic pink flamingos in the yard, and Ethan Allen settees.

The vast array of the mass environment, whether it is called popular architecture or modern vernacular, constitutes at least 95 percent of our surroundings. There is a need to understand this environment in all its aspects, not just the currently popular subjects of fast-food palaces and the strip, but other aspects as well, such as urban sprawl, shopping centers, ranch-styled homes, and the symbolic meanings people ascribe to or invest in their buildings. Since the late eighteenth century and the development of a modern consciousness, most historians have felt that buildings are concrete expressions of a culture and a world view. While this idea is perhaps more easily acceptable in terms of such public or semipublic monuments as the East Wing of the National Gallery of Art in Washington, D.C., or the Chartres Cathedral in France—to take two extremes—recently there have been other views. Richard Oliver and Nancy Ferguson, in writing about fast-food restaurants, diners, gas stations, and historical villages, claim that "by their very familiarity, they can and do act as mirrors of our culture." The profound shifts created by the industrial revolution have affected the built environment in many ways, most of which have been ignored. A radical discrepancy exists between the tastes, needs, and preferences of professionals—historians, critics, architects, urban designers and planners, and the decision makers whose policies they inform—and the people whose lives they influence.

Popular architecture, as does all architecture, generally fulfills two functions: first, it encloses or houses some type of activity, and second, it communicates. The methods of communication through different signs and symbol systems are at the core of the study of popular architecture. The physical elements of coach lanterns and shutters on a house, the twisting nudes in front of Caesar's Palace in Las Vegas, and the blinking lights of "OVER A BILLION SOLD" convey messages of social status, association with the past, and information. To understand popular architecture, we must look at it not simply as an art of building, but as a tangible expression of a way of life.

In the West before the late eighteenth century, nearly all architecture was of two basic types, either folk (or vernacular or traditional) or academic high art. By folk architecture we mean buildings of a preindustrial society—whether houses, shops, or barns—that are based on one or a very few types that admit of only a few individual variations. The architect or designer, as such, does not exist; the building type is carried in the collective consciousness of the culture. Construction is either by the final consumer or a tradesman not far removed from the consumer, and local materials are used. Academic high-art architecture refers to specialized buildings, each one an original or unique creation (though self-consciously in a "style"), and the designer is a professional or an amateur who specializes in or has aspirations to the creation of significant monuments.

Popular architecture emerged with the industrial revolution. With popular architecture, production is changed; building materials and even entire buildings are mass-produced by a team or teams of specialists who are generally far removed from the ultimate consumer. Instead of one building type prevailing, there are many, with innumerable variations within each type. The forms, plans, and images of the buildings are products of fashion and are acquired through popular magazines, trade journals, books, governmental agencies, travel, and the media. The images refer to history, high art, technology, status, patriotism, and individual fantasies. Semiotically, popular architecture is fashion- or style-consciousness, and the symbols are generally chosen for their immediate impact.

Academic high-art architecture has continued, of course, in the modern world. Modern architecture strives for subtle symbols, abstractions of ideas and emotions that are available only to the initiated. High-art architecture lacks the directness and immediacy of most popular architecture.

Who designs popular architecture? The answer is anybody and everybody, although some are more responsible than others. Buildings by academically trained architects are not necessarily examples of high art; in fact, architects have been responsible for the mass-produced Mobil service station, ranch-styled homes, and Miami Beach hotels. There is hardly a building activity of the modern age that architects have not participated in, and they serve on the design staffs of Holiday Inns, Disney World, the Rouse Corporation, and the Winnebago Company. But there are others, such as industrial designers, who have also designed mass-produced commercial buildings. The profession of the industrial designer did not emerge until the 1930s, but he quickly became the hero of the new technological mass-production age. Walter Dorwin Teague, one of the first, designed the enamel-paneled, machinelike Texaco service station. Another source for the designs of popular architecture is the builder or contractor. Building is an old and honored tradition, but its increasing technological nature precludes much design by actual workers today. And, of course, there is finally the consumer, who decides to add a clip-on mansard roof to his storefront or put a French Provincial door on his ranch house and a plastic deer in the front yard.

The relationship between popular architecture and high-art architecture has never been stable; and, in spite of the elitist "trickle down" theory that high art always informs low art or that popular architecture "rips off" high-art architecture, the reverse is often true. Taste, which used to be a sign of class and wealth, is no longer an operable guide; the nouveaux riches have taken care of that. Who actually informs the taste of architecture and the processes by which it trickles down, or up, or sideways needs considerable study. But it is evident that plans, forms, and images constantly shift from one level to another. Recently, there has been a great spurt of interest by academic high-art architects in the archetypal image of the 1930s—the sleek, shiny streamlined diner. Now, as they are passing out of existence to be replaced by colonial- and Mediterranean-styled diners, they are discovered and appropriated. Or one can look at materials such as shingles, which have moved over the years from a vernacular exterior covering-up into the range of high art, back into the hands of the builder and Levittown, and once again back to becoming the chic material.

Communication of the styles and motifs of popular architecture is generally transmitted by one of two methods: experientially, through observation and travel; or secondhand, through books, magazines, and trade journals. The first method, of course, is nebulous and depends on studying specific individuals; the second method—the media—has, however, left a more tangible record. Early in the nineteenth century in the United States books that spread knowledge of stylistic details began to appear, intended for mass circulation. The earliest were builders' guides such as Asher Benjamin's *The American Builder's Companion* and Minard Lafever's *The Modern Builder's Guide*. Their contents were plates illustrating details or ornament and construction, with possibly a few elevations and plans of complete buildings. They helped spread the fashion for styles such as federal, then Greek revival, and finally gothic revival to builders, carpenters, and of course consumers. Their continuation in print, in some cases nearly thirty years after first publication, accounts for the *retardare* appearance of some buildings in more provincial areas.

About mid-century, a new type of publication appeared, the house pattern book, which was filled with plans and designs of complete buildings. The most popular of these were Andrew Jackson Downing's *Cottage Residences* and *The Architecture of Country Houses*, Gervase Wheeler's *Rural Homes*, and Samuel Sloan's *The Model Architect*. While many designs of large pretentious homes were illustrated in these books, there were also "working men's cottages," "laborers' cottages," and other small houses shown, along with details that would allow anyone with either skills or some funds to update their homes. This type of publication continued throughout the nineteenth century in a virtual flood of titles and editions, such as George Woodward's *Woodward's National Architect*, E. C. Gardner's *Homes and how to make them*, and the Palliser Company's *New Cottage Homes and Details*. These books served as dream manuals for the masses. House details could be adapted from them by a local builder or architect, and, in many cases, such as that of the Palliser Company, complete sets of plans could be purchased at a nominal cost. The men responsible for these books were a varied lot: a few had some architectural background, but many were simply glorified carpenters who adopted high-art styles for mass consumption.

Another method of communication was through magazines. Between 1846 and 1892, *Godey's Lady's Book* published four hundred fifty house designs. In the 1860s, several magazines that were directed specifically at the builder and carpenter, such as *The American Builder* and the *Architectural Review and American Builder's Journal*, came into being. The first professional architectural magazine in the United States, *The American Architect and Building News*, was not founded until 1876.

With small modifications, these same patterns have remained into the 1970s. Certainly one of the greatest influences on home design has been the mass-circulation homemaker magazines. Although they advocated different approaches to architectural style, interior furnishings, and gardens, a study of these magazines is essential to any understanding of the popular culture of the home. Some of these advocated strong points of view at different times. In its early years, *The House Beautiful* supported the arts and crafts movement and bungalow design. More famous was the *Ladies' Home Journal*, which, at the turn of the century, sponsored home design by architects such as Frank Lloyd Wright. It was through Wright's designs in the *Journal* that many builders and homeowners learned to imitate his work. Other *Journal* architects were more conservative and advocated styles ranging from colonial to Mediterranean. Other magazines, such as *The American Home*, have been almost single minded in their sponsorship of "early American" as the fit style for Americans. Today, the strong direction in homemaker magazines such as *Better Homes and Gardens* is twofold: first, a natural trend, and second, a rich eclecticism.

Tangential to the homemaker magazines are how-to-do-it magazines such as *Early American Life*, which is filled with nostalgia of the "good old" days. The advertisement states: "Your Dream Home—there's at least one house in every issue of *Early American Life*, complete with floor plans." These can be in any number of styles, but most frequently in the stockade and Cape Cod styles. *Popular Mechanics*, the best known of the how-to-do-it magazines, has always exercised a strong influence on taste in home and furniture design.

Specialized trade journals are probably the major new contribution of the twentieth century. Professional architectural magazines such as *Progressive Architecture* and *The Architectural Record* have affected popular taste minimally, but they are important for tracing ideas. Far more important are magazines such as *House & Home: The Magazine of Housing*, *Qualified Remodeler*, and *Professional Builder*, which are directed at the construction industry. They deal with products and styles in articles such as "Bathroom Design: The Opulant Look" and "How to Facelift Old Buildings Without Losing Their Charm." Then there are specialized trade journals of other industries such as service stations and restaurants. The impact of fast-food can be felt in many of the magazines, for example, *Restaurant Business* and *Nation's Restaurant News*. Many of them feature articles on designs and images of the fast-food industry.

Books or specialized issues of magazines devoted to home design have had a long history in the twentieth century. Most have been on the order of the house pattern books and present images and ideas that can be adapted or copied at will. Collections of designs by architects, such as *The Architectural Record Book of Vacation Houses* or *A Treasury of Contemporary Houses*, are important since a vast range of styles from radical to conservative are shown. *The Building Guide* of *House & Garden* magazine for 1963-1964 offered forty houses and plans ranging from the contemporary to the traditional and included designs entitled "A Combination of Ranch and Colonial" and "The Plantation House in Miniature." Some books convey conventional wisdom. *The Book of Houses* advised in a chapter entitled "What Price Style?" that "Style, of course, is a subjective factor and if a family is emotionally drawn toward a 'Cape Cod' or a 'Georgian,' serious consideration should be given to a home of that type."

Images of other building types are communicated in much the same manner. Books on office design, shopping centers, and factories abound, although they are of course directed at the professional in the field rather than toward the public. But books such as *Motels, Hotels and Restaurants* by Architectural Record have influenced buildings around the world.

While popular architecture began to emerge in the eighteenth century with the Industrial Revolution, it and the associated components in the man-made environment have not been the subject of serious study until very recently. Among architects and historians, the reasons are fairly obvious: popular architecture was not serious and lacked the imprint of *Kultur*. The study of architecture, whether historical or contemporary, has been usually confined to monuments: churches, temples, memorials, theaters, forums, palaces, homes of the elite, and buildings designed by architects who aspire to greatness. A result of Germanic pedantic scholarship and English dilettantism, architecture is usually studied chronologically, and concentration is on a critical and evaluative analysis of the styles, forms, plans, ornament, and details. While the culture and the purpose of a building are sometimes noted, the building is generally seen as existing independently in space and time. From the 1930s onwards, the preoccupation in both the United States and Europe with "modern architecture" led to a further separation from the field of popular architecture. Concerned with totally abstract designing in modern materials and techniques and completely removed from the area of historical recall, nostalgia, or recognizable motifs, modern architecture developed its own language. While the historians of modern architecture have paid some attention to issues of prefabrication and industrial warehouses and factories, they have focused largely on a history of designs by major architects. In these studies, as in the more traditional historical studies, the mention of a Howard Johnson restaurant, a cozy Cape Cod cottage from Mount Vernon estates, or an entryway to Forest Lawn Cemetery in southern California, would be only in the most negative terms.

Variations from the study of certifiable monuments can be seen in the interest in early American and vernacular architecture. Early American architecture is basically preindustrial vernacular, and the study of this type and regular vernacular have been more concerned with the details and recording of buildings than with any investigation into meanings of the buildings and their culture. One exception has been the work of Henry Glassie in his two major books, *Patterns in the Material Folk Culture of the Eastern United States* and *Folk Housing in Middle Virginia*. In the latter book, Glassie applies the structuralism of Claude Lévi-Strauss and Noam Chomsky to vernacular houses; while his results are dense and open to question, he offers some suggestions for studying popular architecture.

Along with the other revolutions of the 1960s, a sense of crisis in the architectural and design world has led, in the 1970s, to a greater recognition of popular architecture and the necessity for understanding the entire man-made environment. One significant change was the sense of failure of modern architecture; the brave new world envisioned in the 1930s, where "total design" could improve man's life, was a hoax. Most consumers disliked, if not downright hated, modern buildings, not only for their sterile quality and uncomfortable feeling, but also because they simply did not work well. Urban renewal, a product of modern architectural city planning, proved to be worse than the illness it was supposed to correct. When it was published in 1961, Jane Jacobs's *The Death and Life of Great American Cities* was viewed as heretical for her celebration of the messy vitality of the street. Today, it is the received orthodoxy. While there are still many architects and critics who profess an admiration for modern architecture, the continual bombardment of questions and alarming failures has opened the doors for some recognition of popular architecture.

The Museum of Modern Art in New York—the citadel of avant-garde modern chic—provided several new directions in the mid-1960s. In 1964, the exhibit *Architecture Without Architects* by Bernard Rudofsky (and his book of the same name) presented the thesis that centuries-old buildings executed by common men without the aid of designers could present eternal themes of architecture. The exhibit showed not only homes and temples of primitive peoples but also granneries and fertilizer bins. Rudofsky has gone on to exploit this unself-conscious theme in *The Prodigious Builders*. In 1966, the Museum of Modern Art published Robert Venturi's *Complexity and Contradiction in Architecture*, the first openly critical look at the theories of modern architecture.

Robert Venturi and Charles Moore have been among the leaders of architects who argue that popular architecture is worthy of study. Venturi's *Complexity and Contradiction* was concerned more with a rather dense design philosophy and, except for the notorious phrase, "Main Street is almost alright," was not really concerned with popular architecture. But, *Learning from Las Vegas* by Venturi, Denise Scott Brown, and Steven Izenour was concerned with popular architecture and argued that architects should look at the strip; for in spirit, if not style, it approached the grandeur of the Roman Forum, or "Las Vegas is to the Strip what Rome is to the Piazza." Charles Moore's writings have been felicitous with significant comments on suburban and motel culture. Another harbinger of the change has been the example of Peter Blake. In 1964, he published *God's Own Junkyard*, a great diatribe against popular architecture. But within ten years, he was writing admiring articles on the virtues of Disney World and the strip. *Progressive Architecture* magazine, the high priest of modern architecture, devoted its June 1978 issue to "Taste in America" and contained articles on McDonald's design evolution and on suburbia.

The other critical shift that began in the 1960s and still continues is the burgeoning historic preservation movement. As a movement, historic preservation can be traced back to the mid-nineteenth century in the United States and abroad. Until the 1960s, it was generally viewed as elitist and concerned with historic houses and recreations of olden times in Williamsburg and other museum villages. But in the 1960s, historic preservation became more populist in outlook and less concerned with the individual high-art building and more concerned with entire neighborhoods. Nods of approval have been given to lesser classes of structures such as service stations, billboards, and even outhouses. Preservation studies have been carried out in working-class neighborhoods such as the Old West Side in Ann Arbor, Michigan, which is a blue-collar, German enclave.

In the last few years, other writers, such as architectural and art historians, sociologists, planners, and anthropologists, have spluttered forth a variety of papers, articles, and books that have contributed to knowledge in the area. However, the field is still virtually wide open, and, while some research progresses on diverse topics such as gas stations, fast-food restaurants, and amusement parks, there is plenty for everybody to do. Basic research needs to be done in every area, and methodological approaches need to be discussed. Several societies dealing with different aspects of popular architecture have been founded recently, but they have delivered little and seem more interested in collecting dues.

BIBLIOGRAPHY

Appleyard, Donald, Kevin Lynch, and John R. Meyer. *The View from the Road.* Cambridge: MIT Press, 1964.

Banham, Reyner. *Los Angeles: The Architecture of Four Ecologies.* New York: Harper & Row, 1971.

Clay, Grady. *Close-up: How to Read the American City.* New York: Praeger, 1973.

Columbia University. *Avery Obituary Index of Architects and Artists.* Boston: G. K. Hall, 1963.

______. *Avery Index to Architectural Periodicals.* 2d ed. Boston: G. K. Hall, 1973. 15 vols. plus supplements.

Fishwick, Marshall, and J. Meredith Neil, eds. *Popular Architecture.* Bowling Green, Ohio: Bowling Green Popular Press, n.d. [1975].

Gebhard, David, and Harriette Von Brenton. *L. A. in the 30's.* Santa Barbara, Calif.: Peregrine Smith, 1975.

Giedion, Sigfried. *Mechanization Takes Command: A Contribution to Anonymous History.* New York: Oxford University Press, 1948.

Glassie, Henry. *Pattern in the Material Folk Culture of the Eastern United States.* Philadelphia: University of Philadelphia Press, 1968.

———. *Folk Housing in Middle Virginia: A Structural Analysis of Historic Artifacts.* Knoxville: University of Tennessee Press, 1975.

Gowans, Alan. *Images of American Living: Four Centuries of Architecture and Furniture as Cultural Expression.* Philadelphia and New York: J. B. Lippincott, 1964.

Gutman, Richard, "Diner Design, Overlooked Sophistication." *Yale Perspecta,* 15 (1975), 41-55.

Hall, Ben M. *The Best Remaining Seats.* New York: C. N. Potter, 1961.

Halprin, Lawrence. *Freeways.* New York: Reinhold, 1966.

Harris, Cyril M., ed. *Dictionary of Architecture and Construction.* New York: McGraw-Hill, 1975.

Kouwenhoven, John. *The Arts in Modern American Civilization.* New York: Norton, 1948.

Kyriazi, Gary. *The Great American Amusement Parks.* Secaucus, N.J.: Citadel Press, 1976.

Renwick Gallery, National Collection of Fine Arts, Smithsonian Institution. *Signs of Life: Symbols in the American City.* New York: Aperture, 1976.

Venturi, Robert, Denise Scott Brown, and Steven Izenour. *Learning from Las Vegas.* Cambridge: MIT Press, 1972. Rev. ed., 1971.

Whiffen, Marcus. *American Architecture Since 1780: A Guide to the Styles.* Cambridge: MIT Press, 1969.

Wolfe, Gary Herbert. "The Gas Station: The Evolution of a Building Type as Illustrated Through a History of the Sun Oil Company Gasoline Station." Unpublished Master's thesis, University of Virginia, 1974.

Automobile

Maurice Duke

Although man had dreamt of a self-propelled vehicle for centuries, it was not until the end of the nineteenth century that a practical road machine capable of sustained distances emerged for general use. Historians disagree on the actual inventor of the first American automobile, but it is widely known that men such as George B. Selden, Charles E. Duryea and J. Frank Duryea, John William Lambert, Gottfried Schloemer, Charles Black, Charles Brady King, and Ransom Eli Olds, among others, were constructing and testing gasoline engine vehicles in the last two decades of the century.

It was not until the first decade of the twentieth century, however, that the automobile emerged as a commercially practical business and industrial venture. Still sought after by collectors, the early Oldsmobile, followed shortly by a host of other American automobiles, was the first successfully produced and marketed motorcar in the United States. From an inauspicious beginning in 1901, the year in which 425 Oldsmobiles were manufactured and sold, the automobile industry grew to become a giant that has influenced our physical, intellectual, and moral lives in a way that is unequalled in modern times. By mid-century, nearly fifty million automobiles were registered in the United States. There are indeed few Americans who can truthfully claim that the motorcar has had no place in their lives.

When the automobile first appeared, it was treated as a curiosity, a plaything for the rich and a tinkering project for the inventors or the hapless blacksmith who might be called upon to aid a motorist who by some mechanical malfunction had suddenly become a pedestrian. The automobile quickly took hold, however, capturing people's minds as well as their imaginations. Born into an America that had virtually no road system, it soon began to shrink the size of the continent of whose vastness and inexhaustibility St. Jean deCrèvecoeur had boasted just over a century before. Although still not completely trustworthy for long distance touring, automobiles became popular for cross-country expeditions— giving rise, incidentally, to a number of early automobile travel narratives and novels—and for exploring places that mere decades before were out of range of the traveller or adventurer who had to rely on the horse, the ship, or the train.

When the automobile emerged from its novelty stage, its influence on American life became markedly greater. The mass production of Henry Ford's Model T, which began in 1908, ushered in a new era of attitudes and convictions about the motorcar. Ford proved that his vehicle—and presumably others as well—could be produced cheaply and could be made to operate efficiently. Both the joys and woes of owning self-propelled wheels had now come to mid-America. Although sudden death might lurk around the next curve and the neighborhood horses might be terrified, not to mention the emerging noise and pollution problems, there was a new sense of freedom across the land. Urban dwellers could escape to the country for a day; isolated rural residents could visit each other and the nearby towns and cities more easily; lovers had a ready-made mobile bedroom; and businessmen could move more quickly in their daily routines.

As the automobile became a way of life in America, so American life had to adjust to accommodate it. While the motorcar was shrinking the size of the continent, it was also altering both its physical and moral landscape as well. Service stations, garages, and parts warehouses popped up around the country at the same time that legislators and judges were pondering complex problems about how the use of the automobile should be governed. Also, both culturally and socially other changes were taking place. Society took a negative attitude to women driving automobiles, for example, steering wheels sometimes carrying a warning sign that read "Men and Boys Only." Clothes styles were altered to be more in keeping with what the motorist would need. Hotels began giving way to the more modern motel, a combination of the words *motor* and *hotel*, and city dwellers found they could live outside urban areas and motor to work, thus creating America's vast and sprawling suburbs.

When America emerged, chauvinistic and sassy, from World War I, the automobile, already firmly planted in American life, was there to help it celebrate its victory. In the decade of the 1920s, important social distinctions began to be made between owners and drivers of the myriad cars available in the country. Ford's Model T had been superseded by the more manageable and sleeker Model A; the rumble seat came into its own; and the owner of expensive cars, such as Cadillacs, Buicks, Chryslers, and Packards, set them aside from those who drove the more plebian Fords and Chevrolets. The female driver also came into her own, with such automobile manufacturers as, for example, Jordan, actually making a sales pitch to women. The liberated woman, so the ads implied, should choose a Jordan; and advertising pictures of this sleek car would often show a woman driving, with a man sitting beside her on their way to the club, tennis, or golf. And the Dusenberg, one of the great prestige cars of the era, is still preserved in an outdated phrase in our language: "It's a Doosy!"

Throughout the 1920s and 1930s, the automobile continued to be the great emancipator of middle America. It was not until the belt-tightening occasioned by World War II that serious thoughts about the longevity of the automobile began to be considered. Entering their first period of gasoline rationing, Americans now had to queue up to receive rationing stickers. "Is this trip necessary?" became the question of radio newscasters and politicians alike. The wheels of the country began to turn more slowly, but the speed was destined to be regained and even vastly accelerated in the next decade.

Emerging victorious from World War II, the American, as Lewis Mumford would later write in *The Highway and the City*, "sacrificed his life as a whole to the motorcar." Freeways and interstates took the place of the prewar highways, which now became relegated to secondary road status. Drive-in movies, dubbed passion pits by their critics, drive-in restaurants, drive-in churches, and even drive-in funeral parlors made their appearance across America. And the cars of yesteryear began reappearing on the nation's roads after having been reworked into custom vehicles, whose youthful creators steadfastly maintained reflected their innermost personalities. Although he applied the term to different cars at a later date, as cultural critic Tom Wolfe said, the 1950s and early 1960s marked the era of "the kandy*kolored, tangerine*flake, streamline baby." America was the car and the car was America.

Then something happened. In the early 1970s Americans began to face the reality that fossilized fuels might indeed be depleted in the foreseeable future. Moreover, the motorcar, long suspected as a serious atmospheric pollutant, came under the study of scientists who proved such to be the case. Adding to the already major problems the one of safety, the automobile thus became a political issue, and Detroit car manufacturers found themselves dictated to more by Washington than by their own boards of directors. Suddenly, the automobile became in many people's minds the great enemy, and ominous rumblings from the federal government were a portent of intentions to break up the American's love affair with his wheels. One can only guess as to where such sentiments will eventually lead. As *Car and Driver* magazine speculated some months ago, America might be waking up with a hangover from the greatest party in human history.

From the beginning of recorded history, man has been a competitive creature. One aspect of this competition has manifested itself in sports, the leisure-time play world of the adult. Sports are surveyed elsewhere in this book; but because the automobile has occupied a unique role in American sports, its place in competition has been reserved for this section.

The automobile had hardly emerged as a functioning mechanical entity from the small factories of America than one of its special uses came to be competition. That competition has grown, and the groups that sponsor it have become so organized, that automobile sports in America is now a multi-million dollar entertainment industry. Whether it is a local businessman racing in amateur weekend events, or A. J. Foyt making his bid for an unprecedented fourth career win at Indianapolis, the automobile has changed the sports pages of America's newspapers and the Monday morning quarterbacking in America's offices in a permanent way.

Historians agree that the first officially recognized American automobile race occurred in November 1895 when the Chicago *Times-Herald* Race, from Chicago to nearby Evanston, Illinois, was run over a distance of just fifty-five miles. Quite naturally, other sanctioned races soon followed in great numbers. During these early days of racing, competitors took to the open public roads to stage their events, but legislators quickly identified and acted against this kind of racing because of the dangers that it imposed upon life and property. Accordingly, sanctioned racing, using specially made cars that were usually modifications of those available to the public, took to horse racing tracks, where they could run in an orderly circle before grandstand-seated spectators.

With the passage of time, however, the automobile manufacturers recognized the need for specialized courses that would accommodate the peculiar needs of automobile racing as distinct from horse racing. This included hard-surface tracks, provisions for spectator safety, and an area where the cars could be worked upon before, or often during, a race. Accordingly, large wooden oval tracks were constructed. Similar in design to the present-day Indianapolis track, they were widely used throughout the 1920s. Later, when better surfacing materials became available, these kinds of tracks gave way to the conventionally paved courses, such as those now widely in use in all parts of the country. The best known of these courses is undoubtedly the Indianapolis Motor Speedway, although the annual race there is only one on the yearly circuit sponsored by the United States Auto Club (USAC). One of the major sponsors in American racing, the USAC also sponsors sprint car, dirt car, midget, stock, and road-racing events.

Until the close of World War II American automobile racing was conducted almost exclusively on the oval tracks of the Indianapolis type. Following the war, however, other forms of racing began to emerge. They now include stock-car racing, road racing, drag racing, and off-road racing. Each form has contributed markedly to the overall sport of motor racing.

Stock-car racing had its beginnings in the South and is an outgrowth of the illegal whiskey industry, which has permeated Southern culture for years. Moonshiners, who of necessity had to produce their wares out of the view of the law enforcement officers, early discovered methods of engine and chassis preparation that would allow them maximum speed and minimum risk. For this operation, they chose inconspicuous American sedans and then set about preparing them for their unique duty. Often the drivers of these cars would run whiskey during the week and then show up at a local track on the weekend to race against each other.

In the early 1950s, stock-car racing, as it came to be called, underwent marked changes. In the first place it was organized on a national level by the National Association of Stock Car Racing (NASCAR). Further, it took on a new respectability and spread nationwide with headquarters in Daytona Beach, Florida. With the proliferation of this popular form of racing came an interest on the part of the Detroit manufacturers. Precisely how much sponsorship is involved between the top NASCAR teams and the companies that make the cars they race is not known. Indeed, the manufacturers constantly and categorically deny involvement in racing, but the influence is surely there. National advertising alone is enough to suggest that such is the case.

At the same time that stock-car racing was moving from the backwoods brush country of the South and into national prominence, another form of racing was introduced to America. This was road racing, which brought to the American racing scene not only a new kind of motorized competition, but also the influence of and interest in international racing, long popular in Europe. It was not long before the names of such great European drivers as Tazio Nuvolari, Rudolf Caracciola, Graham Hill, Mike Hawthorne and the South American Juan Manuel Fangio became, if not household words, common enough to racing across America.

The revival of road racing in America, where it had been virtually unknown since before the days of the wooden race courses of the pre-1920s, came about as the result of the introduction of the now legendary MG-TC sports car following World War II. Upon their return from duty in Europe, many GI's brought with them these small English sports cars, a kind of vehicle that was unknown to Americans of the time. Nimble and swift if operated by a seasoned driver, these machines quickly came to be used in competitive events. Soon the town of Watkins Glen, New York, today internationally known for its support of road racing, became the site of races that were run through the streets of the village. About this time the Sports Car Club of America (SCCA) was formed to promote both amateur and professional competition. In order to be a member of this organization, the applicant had to own a sports car; he was dropped from membership when he divested himself of it.

Over the years the SCCA has grown to the point that it sponsors major professional road races throughout the country on closed courses designed to simulate actual road conditions and, in addition, all the amateur road racing events that are conducted each year from coast to coast. International in flavor, road racing is now one of the major spectator events on the American racing scene.

Drag racing, another popular form of American automobile sport, had its origins at the same time that road racing was being reintroduced to America, although the two groups are quite different.

Automotive writer Brock Yates, the iconoclastic senior editor of *Car and Driver* magazine, has speculated that drag racing had its beginning in California, where city fathers attempted to slow down traffic by installing traffic lights at intersections that normally would not need them. The outcome was, Yates speculated, that youthful hot-rodders would stop beside each other at a red light and then race to the next one, and so on down the street.

No matter what the precise origin of this form of racing, which involves driving a specially prepared car in a straight line to its maximum speed, its early forms doubtless took place on public streets and highways. With the passing of time, however, the drag racers moved to special straight tracks prepared for this kind of sport and became organized under the National Hot Rod Association (NHRA). This form of racing, in which the cars regularly run at speeds in excess of two hundred miles per hour, is often said to be a mechanic's sport rather than a driver's sport, since the preparation of the car rather than driving skill, some maintain, is more crucial.

Off-road racing is a relatively new and highly controversial kind of motorized competition. It involves competing in vehicles specially prepared to negotiate rough terrain, but not on a prepared course, and withstand the mechanical strain for hundreds, often thousands, of miles.

One other kind of racing deserves mention here, before we turn to the myriad material available for the study of the automobile. That is the Grand Prix circuit, one or two of whose races are conducted yearly on American soil.

The Grand Prix, consisting of a series of races run throughout the year in various countries, is considered by many to be the pinnacle of motorcar racing. The world champion driver is decided each year from the ranks of this group, and its drivers regularly receive more international publicity than those on any other circuit. Each year, in October, one of the Grand Prix races is run at Watkins Glen, and recently there has been added a Grand Prix West, which is run through the streets of Long Beach, California. Because the drivers on the Grand Prix circuit have played so crucial a part in the American racing scene, any study of the American automobile that omitted them would be less than complete.

Whether the future of American automobile racing is inextricably intertwined with the future of the American passenger car is impossible to say. There is the likelihood that even if the American family car as we know it disappeared from the landscape, automobile racing would still continue. After all, the spectators at the chariot races of antiquity were not themselves drivers of chariots. At this point it is safe to say that American automobile racing is not suffering the same illnesses as the automobile at large in our society. The hangover from the party of racing is one confined largely to escalating costs, not to a general malaise and disenchantment with the automobile that now permeate a large segment of society.

BIBLIOGRAPHY

The Automotive History Collection of the Detroit Public Library: A Simplified Guide to Its Holdings. 2 vols. Boston: G. K. Hall, 1966.

Bledsoe, Jerry. *The World's Number One, Flat-Out, All-Time Great, Stock Car Racing Book.* Garden City, N.Y.: Doubleday, 1975.

Bochroch, Albert R. *American Automobile Racing.* New York: Viking, 1974.

Dettelbach, Cynthia Golomb. *In the Driver's Seat: The Automobile in American Literature and Popular Culture.* Westport, Conn.: Greenwood Press, 1976.

Duryea, J. Frank. *America's First Automobile.* Springfield, Mass.: Donald M. Macaulay, 1942.

Flink, James J. *America Adopts the Automobile, 1895-1910.* Cambridge, Mass.: MIT Press, 1970.

______. *The Car Culture.* Cambridge, Mass.: MIT Press, 1975.

Georgano, G. N., ed. *The Complete Encyclopaedia of Motor Cars.* London: Ebury Press, 1968.

Glasscock, C. B. *The Gasoline Age: The Story of the Men Who Made It.* Indianapolis: Bobbs-Merrill, 1937.

Hill, Frank Ernest. *The Automobile: How It Came, Grew, and Has Changed Our Lives.* New York: Dodd, Mead, 1967.

Kouwenhoven, John. *Made in America: The Arts in Modern Civilization.* New York: W. W. Norton, 1948.

Lewis, Albert L., and Walter A. Musciano. *Automobiles of the World.* New York: Simon and Schuster, 1977.

Marx, Leo. *The Machine in the Garden: Technology and the Pastoral Ideal in America.* Oxford, Eng.: Oxford University Press, 1964.

Mumford, Lewis. *The Highway and the City.* New York: Harcourt, Brace and World, 1963.

Nader, Ralph. *Unsafe at Any Speed.* New York: Grossman, 1965.

Pirsig, Robert M. *Zen and the Art of Motorcycle Maintenance.* New York: William Morrow, 1974.

Pritchard, Anthony, and Keith Davey. *The Encyclopaedia of Motor Racing.* London: Robert Hale, 1969, 1973.

Rae, John B. *The American Automobile: A Brief History.* Chicago: University of Chicago Press, 1965.

Wolfe, Tom. *The Kandy* Kolored Tangerine* Flake Streamline Baby.* New York: Farrar, Straus, and Giroux, 1965.

Best Sellers

Suzanne Ellery Greene

Before an historic overview of American best sellers can be undertaken, several points must be established. The first is the nature of the best sellers to be considered. Although the Bible, several cookbooks, and a few other reference works have outsold most other books in the United States, these will be excluded from this essay. All other fiction and nonfiction works will be considered. Second, in such a brief account, only the major trends can be noted. The best sellers of a given period are never homogeneous. Within every period, books more typical of an earlier era continue to appear and gain popularity. During this century, the number of popular books has grown so rapidly that broad categorizations are exceedingly difficult to establish. The function of this overview will be to provide a brief account of the major new developments and leading trends in best-selling literature from colonial times to the present.

The first press in America opened in 1638 in Cambridge, Massachusetts, in conjunction with Harvard College. Its early output consisted of almanacs, sermons, catechisms, and *The Whole Booke of Psalmes*, generally known as *The Bay Psalm Book* (1640). Most books were imported from England, and booksellers reported sales of romances, collections of poetry, school books, and religious books. By the 1660s, American presses had begun to publish books in large enough editions and of sufficiently general interest that their products began to gain a wide circulation. Religious books dominated the market, while books about peculiarities of the New World, especially tales of captivity among the Indians, also gained a large readership.

Traditionally, the first American best seller is said to be *The Day of Doom*, a versified account of the final judgment day written by Michael Wigglesworth in 1662 and printed by Samuel Green in Cambridge. Even a century later, some school children were required to memorize the seemingly endless stanzas about people doomed to an eternity in hell and about the lucky few who were chosen by God for heavenly bliss. In 1664, the first of four editions printed over thirty years of Richard Baxter's collection of sermons, *A Call to the Unconverted*, appeared. This was translated by John Eliot for circulation among the local Indian tribes. Books such as *The Pilgrim's Progress* by John Bunyan, reprinted in Cambridge in 1681, *Husbandry Spiritualized* (1709) by John Flavel, an anonymous *The History of the Holy Jesus* (1745), and James Hervey's *Meditations and Contemplations*, published in Philadelphia in 1750, mark a continuation of the wide appeal of religious subjects.

The Captivity and Restoration of Mary Rowlandson (1682) and John Williams's *The Redeemed Captive* (1707) exemplify the popular captivity tales. Adventure stories complete with massacres, survival through various sorts of cleverness, an eventual return home, all punctuated by Christian devotion, made lively reading for colonists who felt threatened by God's order and by the wilderness outside their small towns. These narratives provide a valuable indication of the English settlers' attitudes toward the Indians as well as their heavy reliance on God.

As the colonial period progressed, literary concerns grew wider, and the philosophical points of view of the authors became more varied. During the 1740s, American editions of Samuel Richardson's sentimental and didactic tale *Pamela* (1744) and Alexander Pope's *Essay on Man* (1747) were best sellers. The decade before the Revolution was marked by the appearance of political best sellers representing all points of view. John Dickinson's conservative *Letters from a Farmer in Pennsylvania* (1768), a treatise entitled *Conciliation with America* (1775) written by Edmund Burke, and Thomas Paine's provocative *Common Sense* (1776).

The titles of the best sellers that were published from the 1770s until the end of the eighteenth century sound like a reading list for an English literature course. Many of these works came to be considered classics, and, despite the Revolution, the majority were authored by Englishmen. This list includes such novels as *The Vicar of Wakefield* (1772) by Oliver Goldsmith, *Clarissa* (1786) by Samuel Richardson, *Tristram Shandy* (1774) by Laurence Sterne, and *Charlotte Temple* (1794) by Susanna Rowson. Poetry such as John Milton's *Paradise Lost* (1777), William Cowper's *The Task* (1787), and an edition of Robert Burns's *Poems* (1788) sold well. Thomas Paine's *Age of Reason* (1794) and Benjamin Franklin's *Autobiography* (1794) were both widely read. *The Federalist* (1788), arguing for the adoption of the new constitution, had a large audience. *Paradise Lost* and John Fox's *Book of Martyrs* (1793) indicate that religion had not been forgotten although it was relegated to a less central position than it had held a century earlier. It is quite evident that the readers of best sellers had a wide range of interests, were heavily influenced by British literary culture, but also read many American products.

History and heroism dominated the best sellers of the first three decades of the nineteenth century. Books written in America about American subjects predominated for the first time. Parson Mason Weems's *Life of Washington* (1800), in which the cherry tree story first appeared, was read avidly, even in rural areas where it was carried by itinerant book peddlers. Washington Irving's *History of New York* (1809) and his later *Sketch Book* (1819) enjoyed wide sales. Jane Porter's novels about patriotic heroes, *Thaddeus of Warsaw* (1804) and *Scottish Chiefs* (1810), helped prepare the way for the enormous success of the tales of adventure and nationalism by Sir Walter Scott, including *Guy Mannering* (1815), *Rob Roy* (1818), *Ivanhoe* (1820), and *Kenilworth* (1821). James Fenimore Cooper created a prototype American hero and his adventures as in *The Spy* (1821) and the Leatherstocking stories of *The Pioneers* (1823). *The Last of the Mohicans* (1826) and *The Deerslayer* (1841) were almost as widely read as Scott's novels. The popularity of Scott and Cooper continued through the century.

The 1830s and 1840s are marked by long lists of books that sold extremely well, in part because of the new practice of issuing cheap reprints of recent popular books. First in newspaper format, then in paperbound books, best sellers became available in twenty-five-cent editions. From this time on, cheap editions of popular books were always on sale for readers who could not afford the more expensive originals. Charles Dickens was an enormously popular author whose novels of sentiment and social reform were snatched up on issue. His sickly children, impoverished innocents, and evil rich men reduced thousands of American readers to tears and helped prepare the way for the American-produced, tear-jerking, sentimental novels that followed.

Dickens's works were not the only ones whose sales benefited from the inexpensive reprints. Readers who had not bought the earlier dollar editions of Scott and Cooper could now afford book purchases. Imitators of Scott, Cooper, and Dickens abounded. The best known was Joseph Holt Ingraham, who wrote thrillers such as *The Pirates of the Gulf* (1836), religious novels such as *The Prince of the House of David* (1855), and novels about life in the city such as *Jemmy Daly, or the Little News Vendor* (1843). Historical novels such as *The Last Days of Pompeii* (1834) by Edward Bulwer-Lytton and *The Three Musketeers* (1844) by Alexandre Dumas were popular, as were histories such as Jared Sparks's *Life of Washington* (1839), William Prescott's *Conquest of Mexico* (1843), and Thomas Macauley's *History of England* (1849). Maria Monk's *Awful Disclosures* (1836), an anti-Catholic tract purporting to reveal the scandals of life in a nunnery, added a bit of sensationalism to the best-seller lists.

Mid-nineteenth-century America supported the rise of the sentimental domestic novel, often written by and about women and problems such as poverty, prostitution, drunken and perfidious husbands and lovers—all presented from a woman's point of view. Nathaniel Hawthorne complained that "America is now wholly given over to a damned mob of scribbling women." Some examples of the more famous products of this group include *The Wide, Wide World* (1850) by Susan Warner and *The Lamplighter* (1854) by Maria S. Cummins. T. S. Arthur's *Ten Nights in a Bar-Room* (1854), written in a similar vein, was used as a temperance tract by various prohibition societies. Mrs. E. D. E. N. Southworth, the most prolific of the best-selling women authors, wrote over sixty novels, including *Ishmael* (1864) and *Self-Raised* (1864), which sold over two million copies each.

While the sentimental novels dealt with many of the problems that concerned the nation's reformers, the most divisive issue of all was largely ignored in the best sellers of the day. *Uncle Tom's Cabin*, written in 1852 by Harriet Beecher Stowe, was one of the few that directly attacked the slavery system and wielded an enormous impact in converting many disinterested readers into active opponents of slavery. Stowe's tear-jerking episodes and moralistic base closely resembled those of the other sentimental writers. *Uncle Tom's Cabin* stands as one of the few examples of a novel that clearly had a major impact on popular thought. Swinging many Northern readers to an antislavery position, the book gained acceptability by emphasizing the physical brutality and destruction of families inherent in slavery while omitting the questions of political rights and racial equality which, at that point, seemed an issue only to the most radical abolitionists.

The period of the late nineteenth and early twentieth century is marked primarily by the diversity of the popular forms, with no one innovation predominating. Sentimental and domestic novels, religious books, local color stories, historical fiction and nonfiction, adventures, some rather sensationalist exposés, and a few detective stories all gained wide readership throughout the period. Despite the fact that very few of these are read today, even by students of literary history, the period is important in that it marked out the broad categories of fictional best sellers as they have continued to the present day. Limitations of space permit only brief examples of these types to be given.

While Laura Jean Libbey produced sentimental domestic novels of the prewar sort, a new group of "glad-books" began to appear. Many centered on a child character and became children's classics. These include *Rebecca of Sunnybrook Farm* (1904) by Kate Douglas Wiggin and *Pollyanna* (1913) by Eleanor Porter. Grace Livingston Hill and Gene Stratton-Porter produced other glad-books, called "molasses fiction" by their critics, that remained best-selling types through World War I.

Religious novels like *St. Elmo* (1867) by Augusta J. Evans and *Barriers Burned Away* (1872) by Edward Payson Roe paved the way for some enormously popular writers like Lew Wallace, whose *Ben Hur* (1880) sold over a million copies through the Sears, Roebuck and Company mail-order catalog alone. Charles Sheldon's *In His Steps* (1897), in which he presented accounts of how contemporary people would change their lives if they really followed Christ's teachings, sold even more copies. Harold Bell Wright, in books like *The Shepherd of the Hills* (1907) and *The Eyes of the World* (1914), combined religious morality with the strenuous outdoor life and a love story, thus putting together a very successful formula that combined several of the most popular subjects of fiction. Lloyd Douglas, who later produced novels like *The Magnificent Obsession* (1929) and *The Robe* (1942), followed in this same tradition.

Not all historical novels were religious. Winston Churchill's historical stories such as *Richard Carvel* (1899) and *The Crisis* (1904) made him one of the most popular writers of the turn of the century. Owen Wister's *The Virginian* (1902) put before the American reading public a character who is sometimes described as the first cowboy hero. Westerns and other masculine adventure stories grew in popularity. Zane Grey, whose more than fifty novels were read by millions, remained on the best-seller lists from the appearance of *The Spirit of the Border* in 1906 through 1924 with *The Call of the Canyon*. Writers like H. Rider Haggard and Rudyard Kipling set their adventures in the more exotic settings of Africa and India. Jules Verne's fantasies about outer space and the world beneath the sea moved even further away from the familiar. Mystery stories like those of Arthur Conan Doyle in the late nineteenth century and Mary Roberts Rinehart in the early twentieth century marked the beginning of the rise to predominance of yet another sort of escapist adventure.

Two new kinds of literature caused an enormous sensation in the early twentieth century. The muckrakers' exposés about business, industry, and politics were read avidly. Books like Upton Sinclair's *The Jungle* (1906) about the Chicago meatpacking business shook the public. More sensationally, Elinor Glyn's *Three Weeks* (1907) drew both enthusiastic readers and official banning with its vivid account of a seduction scene and the following affair between an Englishman and a princess.

The questioning and criticism of society's traditional values and behavior patterns grew more pronounced and more popular during the 1920s. Readers turned away from political questions and emphasized a search for meaning in the life of the individual. Even Sinclair Lewis's social criticisms like *Main Street* (1920) and *Babbitt* (1922) showed the effect that forced conformity had on the individuals involved. More typical of the best-selling novels of the decade were *The Sheik* (1921) by Edith M. Hull and *The Private Life of Helen of Troy* (1925) by John Erskine, in which the characters simply took off and did their own thing. Nonfiction lists were dominated by histories, biographies, and fad books such as *Diet and Health* by Lulu Hunt Peters (1924), crossword puzzle books, and sagas of the South Seas.

The 1930s saw a swing back to historical novels. The leading characters almost invariably stood as successful examples of the old American rugged individualism. In books like *Drums Along the Mohawk* (1936) by W. D. Edmonds and *Northwest Passage* (1937) by Kenneth Roberts, the heroes prevailed against overwhelming odds by dint of their own hard work and intelligence. Two epics headed the best-seller lists for two consecutive years: *Anthony Adverse* by Hervey Allen in 1933 and 1934 and *Gone with the Wind* in 1936 and 1937. An obvious search for stable, moral values appeared in novels like Pearl Buck's *The Good Earth* (1931) and Lloyd Douglas's *The Magnificent Obsession* (1929) and *Green Light* (1935). Despite the severity of the Depression and the rising tide of nazism in Germany, neither fiction nor nonfiction best sellers dealt deeply with either problem until the very end of the decade.

Best sellers that appeared during the years from World War II to the present can be treated as one unit, despite some changes that have taken place. The major noticeable feature of all these books, both individual works of fiction and the aggregate yearly lists of both fiction and nonfiction, is the recognition of the complexity of the world. Politics, religion, sex, psychology, health, love, and many other topics are combined in one book and certainly over the lists of books. Social concerns, from poverty to minority rights to ecology, are reflected in the best sellers. Several major trends can be picked out of the enormous variety, which itself is the most outstanding feature of the period.

From the appearance of *Mein Kampf* on the best-seller list of 1939 through the middle 1950s, both fiction and nonfiction lists revealed a very wide interest in World War II and subjects related to it. Other than that, the best sellers reflected few political concerns until after 1955, when books like *On the Beach* (1957) by Neville Shute, *Dr. Zhivago* (1958) by Boris Pasternak, *Exodus* (1959) by Leon Uris, and *The Ugly American* (1959) by William Lederer and Eugene Burdick heralded increasing political awareness that was to continue, albeit unevenly, into the 1970s.

The historical romantic adventure story, a leading type of best seller for so long, declined in favor of novels like those mentioned above that treat contemporary problems and, a new favorite, suspense stories like two that came out in 1969—*Airport* by Arthur Hailey and *The Salzburg Connection* by Helen MacInnes. Many books, like Peter Benchley's sensational *Jaws* (1974), were made into films, which led to still higher book sales.

One other strong trend since World War II is the increasingly explicit descriptions of sex, both in the fictional characters' actions and in nonfiction best sellers like A. C. Kinsey's *Sexual Behavior in the Human Male* (1948) and the William H. Masters and Virginia E. Johnson study, *Human Sexual Response*, published in 1966. Popularized science, psychology, and health books, like Eric Berne's *Games People Play* (1965) and Jean Nidetch's *The Weight Watcher's Cook Book* (1968), received wide readership also.

From even a brief, oversimplified historical survey of American best sellers, it is clear that they do change drastically both in topics and in style, reflecting changes in the attitudes and the values of the readers. These are useful tools for looking at popular concerns in any given period and tracing their changes over a period of time.

BIBLIOGRAPHY

BOOKS

Bowker Annual of Library and Book Trade Information. New York: R. R. Bowker, 1955-.

Greene, Suzanne Ellery. *Books for Pleasure: Popular Fiction 1914-1945.* Bowling Green, Ohio: Bowling Green University Popular Press, 1974.

Hart, James D. *The Popular Book: A History of America's Literary Taste.* New York: Oxford, 1950.

Leavis, Q. D. *Fiction and the Reading Public.* London: Chatto and Windus, 1965.

Lewis, Freeman. *Paper-Bound Books in America.* New York: New York Public Library, 1952.

McQuade, Donald, and Robert Atwan. *Popular Writing in America.* New York: Oxford, 1974.

Mott, Frank Luther. *Golden Multitudes: The Story of Best Sellers in the United States.* New York: Macmillan, 1947.

Nye, Russel B. *The Unembarrassed Muse: The Popular Arts in America.* New York: Dial Press, 1970.

Smith, Roger H. *The American Reading Public: What It Reads.* New York: R. R. Bowker, 1964.

Waples, Douglas. *Research Memorandum on Social Aspects of Reading in the Depression.* New York: Social Science Research Council, 1937.

Wilson, Louis R. *The Geography of Reading.* Chicago: American Library Association and University of Chicago Press, 1938.

INDEXES

Book Review Index. Detroit: Gale Research, 1965-.

International Index to Periodicals. New York: H. W. Wilson, 1907-1965.

National Library Service Cumulative Book Review Index, 1905-1974. Princeton: National Library Service Corporation, 1975.

New York Times Book Review Index. New York: Arno Press, 1973.

Readers' Guide to Periodical Literature. New York: H. W. Wilson, 1904-.

Social Sciences and Humanities Index. New York: H. W. Wilson, 1966-1974.

Social Sciences Index. New York: H. W. Wilson, 1975-.

PERIODICALS

Book Review Digest. New York, 1905-.
Booklist. Chicago, 1905-.
Bookman. New York, 1895-1933.
Library Journal. New York, 1876-.
New York Review of Books. New York, 1963-.
New York Times Book Review. New York, 1896-.
Publishers Weekly. New York, 1872-.
Saturday Review. New York, 1952-.
Saturday Review of Literature. New York, 1924-1951.

Children's Literature

R. Gordon Kelly

The relationship between children's literature and the mainstream of the nation's literary and intellectual life was particularly close in the late nineteenth century, when, for example, three successive editors of the *Atlantic Monthly*, Thomas Bailey Aldrich, Horace Scudder, and William Dean Howells, all, at one time or another, wrote expressly for children. In this century, however, there has been significantly less overlap. Few major twentieth-century American authors have written for children, and in the development of higher education, the study of children's books was relegated to the intellectual periphery of schools of education and library science. Until recently, writing about children's books, as well as the books themselves, issued with a few notable exceptions from a cozy enclave cut off in large measure from modern literary and intellectual trends. As a consequence, "children's literature" all too often designates a narrowly belletristic tradition that excludes much that is of interest in the history of books for children, including works of great popularity. From the ubiquitous primers of the seventeenth and eighteenth century to the phenomenally popular stories of Horatio Alger in the nineteenth and the adventures of Nancy Drew and the Hardy boys in the twentieth, some children's books, however undistinguished in literary quality, have reached very large numbers of readers. Moreover, much of the literature directed to children is "popular" literature in the sense that it is highly conventional and intended to appeal to the largest possible audience. This is as true of the moral tale, the principal form of antebellum fiction for children, as it is of the works of Alger and the numerous series books produced early in this century under the direction of Edward Stratemeyer, to cite only three of the most conspicuous examples of popular children's literature. Thus there is ample justification for including a chapter on children's literature in a history of popular culture.

Although there has been an increasing interest in the history and criticism of children's literature in the last ten years, much of the work that has appeared reflects a conventional and unimaginative belletristic orientation, lacking scope and theoretical sophistication. Fortunately, the most interesting and promising work in the field deals with the cultural significance of popular books for children: the antebellum moral tale, the novels of Alger, and the Oz fantasies of L. Frank Baum. Children's books are especially deserving of a contextualist approach because they give form and specificity in ways considered appropriate for impressionable minds to matters of crucial importance: cultural definitions of what *is*; what is good, true, and beautiful; what things go together. Children's books are an accessible, readily available feature in an elusive enterprise—the creation, maintenance, and modification of meaning in society. We have hardly begun to examine children's books in America from this perspective and to locate them in the cultural contexts in which they were written, read, and selectively preserved and made available to successive generations of American children.

The following summary of the history of books for children in the United States departs in two important ways from the capsule histories to be found, for example, in most textbooks on children's literature. First, it emphasizes changes in the social and intellectual factors shaping the creation of children's books. One does not have to be a philosophical idealist to admit that concepts of the child and his or her needs constitute crucial aspects of an author's intention, nor need one be a Marxist to accept that changes in technology can significantly affect the production of books, including books for children. Second, I have not assumed that the development of literature for children can easily or unambiguously be interpreted as an increasingly faithful delineation of social reality appropriate to the child's needs and interests, for the very concept of these needs and interests has undergone significant change in the last two centuries and is changing even now.

Histories of children's literature have often been written as if fidelity to life and a due regard for the true nature of the child are asymptotic with the present—that as we approach the present, books for children, with numerous exceptions duly noted, are, on balance, both truer to life and truer to what we take to be the essence of childhood than books published decades or centuries ago. The view is understandable though scarcely pardonable. The children's books of colonial America especially lie on the far side of a cultural divide that few would-be historians of children's literature have endeavored to cross, being content to dismiss books written before the first quarter of the nineteenth century as narrowly sectarian, gloomy, and morbid, to name a few of the charges leveled at them by modern commentators. What is being condemned, however, is not the literature so much as the view of human nature, including child nature, that pervades the primers and catechisms, those most popular of children's books produced in the seventeenth and eighteenth centuries. However, literature for children was more diverse than that, for in addition to the religious manuals and conduct books, there was biography, fiction, animal stories, riddles, fables, nursery rhymes, fairy tales, and picture books. A leading historian of early books for children only slightly overstates the situation when he observes: "Speaking broadly, I know of no kinds of children's books published today which were not also published in the seventeenth century."[1] Moreover, it is clear that writers for children sought in a variety of ways to appeal to and to influence the mind of the child reader—as they understood it—since a major aim was to arouse in the child the desire for saving knowledge.

The emergence of modern children's literature is conventionally dated from the middle of the eighteenth century and credited, rather too narrowly, to the entrepreneurial genius of John Newbery, whose first venture in colorfully printed books written to amuse as well as edify children was *Pretty Little Pocket Book* (1742), by which time books for children had been highly vendible for several decades. From the 1750s, Newbery's little books were imported or pirated by American printers and booksellers, most notably Isaiah Thomas in Worcester, Massachusetts.

Americans remained heavily dependent on British books for children until well into the nineteenth century, but in the 1820s, the spirit of literary nationalism began to stir interest in the creation of a truly American literature for children. Much of the literature was religious, though not narrowly sectarian. Interdenominational tract societies, such as the American Sunday School Union, established in 1818, and the American Tract Society, founded the following year, produced vast quantities of books and pamphlets for the religious and moral edification of American youth, most of it presented in the attractive format that derived from Newbery and his American imitators.

The future of American children's literature, however, did not lie in the efforts of the tract societies but in the work of such popular and prolific antebellum moralists as Jacob Abbott and Samuel Griswold Goodrich, better remembered as the genial, avuncular "Peter Parely." Goodrich eventually wrote over one hundred books designed to introduce his young readers to the facts of geography, history, and natural science in an informal and entertaining way—often by employing a travelogue format. Abbott, trained as a Unitarian minister, was even more prolific than Goodrich. In a series of books devoted to the educational and moral development of a good boy, Rollo, Abbott managed to hint at how an individualized child character might be created, and in a later series, the *Franconia* stories, he drew on his childhood memories of Maine in describing a group of children growing up in a rural village.

Until the 1850s, the moral tale, designed primarily to instruct the young in the civic virtues of obedience, piety, self-reliance, and self-discipline, was the principal form of secular fiction addressed to American children, but in the decade before the Civil War, there was a perceptible broadening of children's literature. William Taylor Adams, writing as "Oliver Optic," introduced more adventure into boys' books while still adhering, in an early book like *The Boat Club* (1855), to the moral values of the day. Like the adventure tale, stories of family life, later a staple of girls' fiction, also have their origins in the 1850s in such popular works as *The Wide, Wide World* (1850) of "Elizabeth Wetherell" (Susan Bogart Warner) and Maria Cummins' *The Lamplighter* (1854), both of which illustrate the rewards accruing to faith, fortitude, and patience. Even fantasy, a form generally uncongenial to the New England temperament, can be traced to the 1850s in the work of the minor transcendentalist Christopher Pearse Cranch, *The Last of the Huggermuggers* (1855).

After the Civil War, American children's literature flowered in a manner that surprised even the most hopeful critics of children's books a decade before. Most of the differences that set off early nineteenth-century books for children from their counterparts in the 1870s and 1880s can be traced in large measure to the altered views about the nature and needs of children typically held by children's authors, publishers, and later librarians. By 1850, the concept of infant depravity ceased to be a major factor in shaping books for children and was replaced by a conception of the child as innocent and good.

Childhood came to be acknowledged as a separate stage of life valuable in itself, a time during which the child's capacity for wonder and imagination could be freely and safely indulged. This view of childhood affected virtually every aspect of child nurture from discipline to clothing and diet and had a profound effect on books for children. The extraordinary achievements in children's literature from 1865 to the turn of the century are owed directly and decisively to widespread acceptance of this altered view of the child.

Other factors of a more mundane sort also contributed to the expansion, diversification, and specialization of publishing for children that occurred after the Civil War. Population increases and comparatively high levels both of income and of literacy in the United States contributed to a rapid expansion of audiences for books of all kinds. Developments in printing technology speeded up the process of publication, making possible more attractive books at lower prices. Improvements in transportation, especially the creation of a continental rail system, meant that the market for children's books could be organized on a national basis. The growth of public education and the founding of public libraries also stimulated the demand for children's books.

To these demographic and technological factors, which in isolation merely describe a capacity for growth, must be added factors of belief and value. The development of literature for children after the Civil War was owed not only to the new views of childhood described earlier but also to the profound faith in the social and individual benefits of education—a faith deeply rooted in democratic thought—and to a conception of art, which, in its more exalted formulations, promised a kind of secular salvation through works of imaginative genius.

As a consequence of these views, writers for children, as well as editors and publishers, rejected the overt didacticism that had characterized the antebellum moral tale and sought to shift the emphasis in children's books from instruction to entertainment and pleasure. Nevertheless, this shift in emphasis can be overstated. The rejection of a particular form of moralizing after 1860 did not entail rejecting the moral values espoused by earlier writers, such as Goodrich and Abbott. Self-reliance, courage, and independence, if not religious faith, composed a core of values that underwent little change in the course of the century, although the literary forms in which they were expressed changed markedly. An astute student of the change correctly observes: "The assertion of freedom from moral didacticism, far from being a move toward aesthetic autonomy, was made within a definite and circumscribed moral framework."[2]

Much of the history of children's literature in the last third of the nineteenth century is foreshadowed in books and periodicals that appeared in the five years following the Civil War. The most notable single work is Louisa May Alcott's *Little Women* (1867), which provided a model for much subsequent fiction centered on family life. Earlier practitioners of the boys' adventure story, such as "Oliver Optic," were joined by "Harry Castlemon" (Charles Austin Fosdick) and Horatio Alger, Jr., whose *Ragged Dick* (1868) was the first of more than one hundred novels depicting the rise (or, often, the restoration) to respectability of impoverished, often homeless, boys. A popular sentimental girls' series began in 1867 with the publication of *Elsie Dinsmore* by Martha Farquharson Finley.

The works of "Castlemon," Alger, and Finley defined a gray area of literary and moral respectability—not as objectionable as the dime novels and story papers, a rank undergrowth of cheap, sensational fiction that flourished despite the contempt heaped upon it by custodians of the nation's cultural life—but certainly not as praiseworthy as the work of Harriet Beecher Stowe, John Townsend Trowbridge, Louisa May Alcott, and a host of other, mainly New England, writers who dominated the quality juvenile periodicals of the period: *Our Young Folks, The Riverside Magazine*, *Wide Awake*, *Youth's Companion*, and preeminently *St. Nicholas*. In the thirty years following its establishment in 1873, *St. Nicholas*, under the able editorship of Mary Mapes Dodge, made available to American children the work of the best regarded juvenile authors in Britain and the United States.

With the turn of the century, new types of children's books appeared, but there was little change in the social and intellectual factors underlying the creation of children's literature. Interest in folk and fairy tales, formerly limited almost exclusively to British materials and the work of the Grimm brothers and Hans Christian Andersen, broadened to include the traditional tales of other countries. Animal stories became popular after the turn of the century, with the publication of Jack London's *The Call of the Wild* (1903), Alfred Ollivant's *Bob, Son of Battle* (1898), and the work of Ernest Thompson Seton. An even more popular new form was the school sports story, which reflected the increasing prominence of athletics in the national life in the 1880s and 1890s. The Frank Merriwell stories of "Burt L. Standish" (Gilbert Patten), derived in large measure from the dime-novel tradition, but the work of more ambitious juvenile novelists, such as Ralph Henry Barbour, owed much to Thomas Hughes' widely read story of life at Rugby, *Tom Brown's School Days* (1857).

Such books as Kate Douglas Wiggins' *Rebecca of Sunnybrook Farm* (1903) and Dorothea Canfield Fisher's *Understood Betsy* (1917) were notable contributions in the early twentieth century to the well-established domestic story tradition inaugurated by *Little Women*, while L. Frank Baum enriched the rather thin tradition of American fantasy with *The Wonderful Wizard of Oz* (1900) and more than a dozen sequels. Another staple of juvenile publishing, the series adventure for boys, underwent development at the turn of the century at the hands of Edward Stratemeyer, who followed up his success with the Rover Boys by creating the Motor Boys, the Bobbsey Twins, and Tom Swift, among others. Retaining control of each series' concept, Stratemeyer hired writers willing to work to his formula and published their work under a series pseudonym. Following his death in 1930, Stratemeyer's production-line methods of quality control were successfully continued by his daughter, Harriet Stratemeyer Adams, who created Nancy Drew.

Stratemeyer's rationalization of series book production has an analogue in the world of quality publishing for children. The growth of children's libraries and the professionalization of children's librarianship in the late nineteenth and early twentieth century, together with the establishment of National Book Week in 1919, the appointment in the same year of Louise Seaman Bechtel as children's book editor at Macmillan, and the concentration of children's book reviewing in the hands of librarians and educationists—all influenced the creation of children's literature, especially after 1920, in ways that are not yet well understood. Part of the effect, however, has been to maintain critical standards that appear to have changed little since the 1880s.

The decade of the 1930s saw the publication of some notable examples of the family story and the juvenile historical novel as well as some excellent retellings of traditional folk tales. The picture book, however, is the principal form of children's book in which there has been dramatic improvement, owing largely to new color printing processes. The achievements of writers in the 1930s notwithstanding, the history of American children's literature in the century following the Civil War is marked by a proliferation of types but a singular continuity of underlying cultural values and assumptions.

It is not really until the 1960s that significant changes occur in American children's books, changes that have their origins in a heightened sensitivity to racial, ethnic, and gender discrimination as well as in the emergence of alternative concepts of the child that permitted, indeed demanded, franker and more explicit treatment of social problems: divorce, drug abuse, and mental illness, for example. Although it is possible to point to the kind of apparent qualitative changes that characterize any period—the emergence recently of more sophisticated science fiction and fantasy for young people is an example—major changes in children's books involve a shift in the concept of childhood as occurred in the middle of the nineteenth century and appears to be occurring now in efforts to define the rights of children, including the right of access to children's books of unprecedented frankness.

NOTES

1. William Sloan, *Children's Books in England and America in the Seventeenth Century* (New York: King's Crown Press, 1955), pp. 4-5.
2. E. Geller, "Somewhat Free: Post-Civil War Writing for Children," *Wilson Library Bulletin,* 51 (1976), p. 175.

BIBLIOGRAPHY

Blum, John Morton, ed. *Yesterday's Children: An Anthology Compiled from the Pages of Our Young Folks, 1865-1873.* Boston: Houghton Mifflin, 1959.

Children's Books in Print. New York: Bowker, 1970-.

Children's Catalogue. 13th ed. New York: H. W. Wilson, 1976.

Darling, Richard L. *The Rise of Children's Book Reviewing in America, 1865-1881.* New York: R. R. Bowker, 1968.

Egoff, Sheila, ed. *Only Connect.* Toronto: Oxford University Press, 1970. 2d rev. ed., 1981.

Erisman, Fred. "L. Frank Baum and the Progressive Dilemma." *American Quarterly,* 20 (Fall 1968), 616-23.

Field, Carolyn W., ed. *Subject Collections in Children's Literature.* New York: R. R. Bowker, 1969.

Gottlieb, Gerald. *Early Children's Books and Their Illustration.* Brookline, Mass.: David R. Godine, 1975.

Gruber, Frank. *Horatio Alger, Jr.: A Biography and a Bibliography.* West Los Angeles, Calif.: Grover Jones, 1961.

Haviland, Virginia, ed. *Children's Literature: A Guide to Reference Sources.* Washington, D.C.: Library of Congress, 1966.

Kelly, R. Gordon. *Mother Was a Lady: Self and Society in Selected American Children's Periodicals, 1865-1890.* Westport, Conn.: Greenwood Press, 1974.

Kirkpatrick, Daniel, ed. *Twentieth Century Children's Writers.* London: St. James; New York: St. Martin's, 1980.

Lanes, Selma G. *Down the Rabbit Hole: Adventures and Misadventures in the Realm of Children's Literature.* New York: Atheneum, 1971.

MacLeod, Anne Scott. *A Moral Tale: Children's Fiction and American Culture, 1820-1860.* Hamden, Conn.: Archon, 1975.

Meacham, Mary. *Information Sources in Children's Literature.* Westport, Conn.: Greenwood Press, 1978.

Meigs, Cornelia, et al. *A Critical History of Children's Literature.* Rev. ed. New York: Macmillan, 1969.

Monson, Dianne, and Bette Peltola. *Research in Children's Literature.* Newark, Del.: International Reading Association, 1976.

Pellowski, Anne. *The World of Children's Literature.* New York: R. R. Bowker, 1968.

Rosenbach, A.S.W. *Early American Children's Books.* Portland, Me: Southworth, 1933.

Sale, Roger. *Fairy Tales and After: From Snow White to E. B. White.* Cambridge: Harvard University Press, 1978.

Sloane, William. *Children's Books in England and America in the Seventeenth Century.* New York: King's Crown Press, 1955.

Welch, D'Alté. "A Bibliography of American Children's Books Printed Prior to 1821." *Proceedings of the American Antiquarian Society,* 73 (1963), pt. 1:121-324, pt. 2:465-596; 74 (1964), pt. 2:260-282; 75 (1965), pt. 2:271-476; 77 (1967), pt. 1:44-120, pt. 2:281-535.

Wohl, R. Richard. "The Rags to Riches Story: An Episode in Secular Idealism." In *Class, Status and Power,* edited by Reinhard Bendix and Seymour M. Lipset. Glencoe, Ill.: Free Press, 1953.

PERIODICALS

Children's Literature. New Haven, 1972-.

Children's Literature in Education. London, England, 1970-.

Phaedrus: An International Journal of Children's Literature Research. Boston, 1973-.

Circus and Outdoor Entertainment

Don B. Wilmeth

Of all forms of early American popular entertainment, excluding popular theatre, only the outdoor amusement industry and the circus have managed to survive changing times and tastes, despite noticeable alterations. The traveling tent circus has largely given way to presentation in permanent indoor arenas, and the traditional amusement park, despite the struggling survival of some, has evolved into the "theme" park, such as Disneyland or Six Flags Over Texas. To most observers, the differences between the various forms—be they circus, carnival, fair, or amusement park—are largely irrelevant. The memories evoked from each blur and meld into a single sensory recall. In reality, the various forms are quite different, and myriad examples can be isolated under the general heading of "outdoor entertainment" or, more correctly, "outdoor entertainment and environmental forms." In William F. Mangels's excellent but tentative survey, *The Outdoor Entertainment Business*, a long list of identifiable entertainments are enumerated: circuses, carnivals, amusement parks, carousels, roller coasters, dance halls, shooting galleries, penny arcades, world fairs, menageries, and so on. In this survey chapter, however, I have chosen to deal with only two major categories: (1) the circus and wild west exhibitions, and (2) outdoor amusements (fairs, exhibitions, pleasure gardens, amusement parks, carnivals, seaside resorts, and theme parks). Although the other public amusements indicated by Mangels are legitimate individual forms, the two areas of concern here represent the major forms of American outdoor entertainment past and present, incorporating a number of the other items mentioned by Mangels.

THE CIRCUS

In 1968 Marcello Truzzi, in "The Decline of the American Circus," defined the circus as "a traveling and organized display of animals and skilled performances within one or more circular stages known as 'rings' before an audience encircling these activities." This definition, which provides a workable framework for a study of the circus, includes the traditional circus and the wild west exhibition under the general category of a circus, but it excludes the carnival, which is socially a very distinct organization and depends, as does the amusement park, on its audience's active participation. The circus, on the other hand, demands a high degree of emotional empathy and passive involvement and thus is more closely related to traditional theatre, whereas the carnival and its kin have evolved from the medieval fair tradition. Despite Truzzi's identification of the wild west as a form of circus, its evolution and form are distinctive enough to be dealt with independently.

In its various forms, the circus is one of the oldest forms of popular entertainment. Historians have rather unsuccessfully attempted to trace the individual circus acts to antiquity, but the modern circus's connection with Rome's Circus Maximus or even earlier traditions is tenuous at best. The circus, as we know it today, more likely dates from the equestrian training circle of a much later period. Its clearest progenitor was Philip Astley who, in 1770, opened what amounted to a one-ring circus in London, featuring horsemanship acts and ultimately developing a form of theatre called "hippodrama." The European circuses stayed close to Astley's original form, often in fixed locations, although adding in time clowns, acrobats, jugglers, trapeze artists, trained animals, and other acts. In America the early trend was toward size and movement. In the course of the circus's history, there have been in America, Mexico, and Canada since 1771 over eleven hundred circuses and menageries (an even earlier tradition and one of the definite predecessors of the circus in England and America). The peak period of the American circus was in 1903, with approximately ninety-eight circuses and menageries in existence. The pattern since 1903 has been one of steady decline.

The early American circus, then, was virtually transported from England. Although elements of the circus existed prior to 1793 in the form of individual acts, the man who brought the previously disparate elements together in Philadelphia in 1793 was John Bill Ricketts, a Scotsman who arrived in America in 1792. In his permanent building in Philadelphia, Ricketts presented trick riding, a tightrope walker, and a clown. Ricketts had been a pupil of Charles Hughes, whose Royal Circus at Blackfriar's Bridge in London had been rival to Astley's since 1782. Subsequently, Ricketts's circus made appearances in New York, Boston, and Albany, as well as other cities in the United States and Canada.

The opening of the Erie Canal in 1825 afforded the increasing number of American circuses greater freedom in travel; traveling animal menageries had continued to parallel the increasing number of circuses. By the end of the first quarter of the nineteenth century, efforts were made to merge the menagerie and the circus. The elephant, which was to have a key role in the American circus, was first exhibited in 1796; the second and the most famous early elephant in the new country, Old Bet, was shown by Hackaliah Bailey with great success until 1816. Old Bet has mistakenly been associated by historians with Nathan Howe's circus. Howe and his partner Aaron Turner also have been credited mistakenly with the introduction of the circus tent around 1824. Recent research indicates, however, that the tent was probably not introduced until 1826 by J. Purdy Brown.

During the first half of the nineteenth century, distinctive characteristics of the American circus began to evolve. The first circus parade dates from 1837, when a short-lived circus marched through the streets of Albany; in 1838, the circus first used rail travel as transportation (from Forsythe to Macon, Georgia); the first boat circus (under Gilbert Spalding and Charles Rogers), a forerunner of the show boat, dates from 1852. The 1890s and early years of this century saw many small railroad circuses traveling across the country, although wagon shows continued well into the twentieth century. Nevertheless, in time, motorized transportation and the railroad displaced mule power and horsepower. The circus of Tom Mix made the first transcontinental tour of the United States by a motorized circus in 1936.

Among the major changes in the pattern of the American circus, in addition to mobility, was the introduction of multiple rings, in contrast to the European one-ring format. Around 1873, William Cameron Coup added a second ring to the circus, utilizing the name of P. T. Barnum; in 1881, James A. Bailey negotiated the merger of several great circus operations, including Barnum's circus, and opened with a three-ring show. By 1885, virtually all American circuses had adopted the three rings. The circus now incorporated the menagerie, the concert, the side-show, and the street parade as integral ingredients.

The period between 1830 and 1870 saw the emergence of numerous prominent circuses in the history of the American circus, each with colorful and important histories: the George F. Bailey Circus; circuses utilizing the name of the "Lion King" (Isaac Van Amburgh); the several circuses of Seth B. Howes; the Mabie Brothers Circus; the Yankee (Fayette Ludovic) Robinson Circus; the John Robinson Circus; the Spalding and Rogers Circus; the Dan Castello Circus; the Dan Rice Circus (capitalizing on the name of the early American clown); and the W. W. Cole Circus.

The so-called golden age of the American circus—which lasted until about 1917—began in 1871, when W. C. Coup persuaded P. T. Barnum, the showman and museum entrepreneur, to become a partner in a circus enterprise. Barnum lent his name to other shows in addition to Coup's, which ultimately caused a split with Coup in 1875. In 1880, Barnum joined James A. Bailey and James L. Hutchinson in a new operation. This lucrative partnership lasted until 1885 when Barnum refused to deal further with Bailey, and Bailey sold his interest to James Cooper and W. W. Cole. In 1887, after Barnum had experienced a number of setbacks, including the loss of a Madison Square Garden contract to the rival Adam Forepaugh

Circus, Barnum gave Bailey full control of the circus and added his name to the new "Barnum & Bailey Greatest Show on Earth." During this golden age, a number of the older circuses continued to compete or operate in their own regional circuits; other new prominent circuses came into their own, including the Sells Brothers Circus, the Great Wallace Circus, and the Lemen Brothers Circus.

The Ringlings, the name most frequently associated with the circus today, were late arrivals on the circus scene. None of the five brothers was involved until 1882. After seeing a traveling circus in their hometown of Baraboo, Wisconsin, they began to do a variety show around Wisconsin. In 1895, after adding more circus acts and animals to their menagerie, they made their first tour outside the Midwest and entered Barnum and Bailey's territory in New England. A year after Bailey's death in 1907, the Ringlings bought the Barnum and Bailey Circus; they finally merged as one in 1918, becoming "Ringling Brothers and Barnum & Bailey Combined Shows."

Various competitors tried to shut out the Ringlings, but the circus had become big business, and their efforts were fruitless; after 1910, the circuses had declined in number and in extravagance. The street parade became obsolete; menageries virtually vanished; and even the big top would practically disappear. Mechanization deprived the circus of its uniqueness and flair; individual initiative became dampened as well. Today, only a dozen or so circuses travel in the United States and they are only a faint reminder of the glories of the traveling tent circus of the turn of the century. During the 1940s and 1950s, the larger circuses—the Clyde Beatty, the King Brothers, and the Ringling shows—experienced a series of disasters. In 1957, "The Greatest Show on Earth" was forced to put away its big top and perform only in permanent facilities, thus depriving the major circus in the United States of one of its great attractions. Ironically, despite the near disappearance of the circus, its total audience continues to grow (thanks in part to television and films) and its revenue to swell. As the modern circus adjusts to modern demands, its age-old appeal apparently continues unabated.

THE WILD WEST EXHIBITION

The so-called Wild West show is invariably associated with William Frederick "Buffalo Bill" Cody, who found the association of his enterprise with that of the circus or the use of the word "show" anathema. His billing was invariably "Buffalo Bill's Wild West," without the "show," and, if pressed, his general manager John M. Burke would insist that it was an exhibition. In its most ideal form, then, a Wild West show may be defined as an exhibition illustrating scenes and events characteristic of the American Far West frontier.

The exact origin of the Wild West show is difficult to pinpoint. The rodeo is related in part to the Wild West exhibition, insofar as a traveling rodeo with hired contestants would fit a common definition; yet the rodeo is normally a competitive sport in which the contestants pay an entrance fee and receive no pay except prize money. Thus, the kinship between the rodeo and the Wild West show should not be stressed, although, as mentioned below, they share a common beginning in terms of popularity. The Wild West actually evolved in part from the "specs" (or spectacular pageants) of the circus, the old traveling menageries, early exhibitions of cowboy skills and Indians dating from the 1820s, and the numerous plays, novels, and cheap popular literature of the nineteenth century.

Most historians of the Wild West show credit Cody with the consolidation and popularization of this form of entertainment. After ten seasons of performing in mediocre border melodramas built vaguely around his life and exploits as a scout, a buffalo hunter, and a frontiersman, Cody returned to his home of North Platte, Nebraska, in the summer of 1882. Upon his return, he was cajoled into planning the "Old Glory Blow-Out," a Fourth of July celebration of cowboy skill acts climaxed by a buffalo hunt in which Cody demonstrated with blank ammunition his methods of killing buffalo. This date in 1882, then, marks the upsurge of both the Wild West show and the rodeo, although doubtless not the first examples of either. (The rodeo harks back to the byplay and showoffs of early cattle roundups; an early form of the Wild West show was seen in New York by way of Boston in 1843; other elements of Cody's show existed prior to 1882.) What was new in Cody's Wild West exhibition was the combination that spelled success. In its ultimate form, Cody's Wild West became a dominant form of outdoor amusement, reaching its peak of popularity around 1893.

Cody's Wild West was on the upswing in 1883. Initially, his operation was not very successful although it spawned a host of imitators. With the aid of Nate Salsbury, who joined Cody in 1884, and Dr. William F. Carver, whom he met in 1882-1883 (later, both Carver and Salsbury claimed to be the originator of the Wild West concept), Cody, who was not a consummate showman, began to experience phenomenal success. With the puffed releases of his colorful press agent-manager, "Arizona" or "Major" John M. Burke, Cody's show became the epitome of the romanticized and glamourized American West, particularly in Europe, where Cody made several successful tours. At the beginning of its history, the Wild West appeared to be a representation of the contemporary western scene but, as the old West vanished, it soon transcended the reality and created a legendary West based largely on illusion.

In its first decade, then, the Wild West show had a contemporary interest that began to fade after the turn of the century. The format, which originally had been new and unique, lacked variety, and showmen fell victim to the temptation to combine it with a circus or to add circus acts to its own pageantry. Gordon William Lillie, known as "Major Lillie," "Pawnee

Bill," or "the White Chief of the Pawnees" (an early performer with Cody), thought the solution was to restyle his show as "Pawnee Bill's Historic Wild West and Great Far East." The latter included "every type of male and female inhabitant"—Hindu magicians, Singhalese dancers, Madagascar oxen cavalry, Australian bushmen, and so forth. Other shows featured notoriety. "Cummins's Wild West and Indian Congress" featured Red Cloud, Chief Joseph, Geronimo, and Calamity Jane. Despite the changing nature of the Wild West show after the 1890s, the largest number of such entertainments flourished in the early years of the twentieth century. In the course of its history, according to Don Russell, the foremost historian of this phenomenon, there were over one hundred Wild West shows. With the great proliferation of such organizations at the turn of the century, the shows became quite shabby. Cody's last European tour began in 1902 and by 1909 he had to merge his operation with that of Pawnee Bill. By 1908, the "101 Ranch Wild West Show," which began in 1892, became a permanent institution and major competition for the Cody-Pawnee Bill show. World War I marked the end of the golden era of outdoor show business, including the Wild West show. By 1918, there were no major Wild West shows, their popularity having been eclipsed by the increasing popularity of motion pictures and the growing appeal of the more "believable" portrayal of the movie cowboy.

OUTDOOR ENTERTAINMENT

The American outdoor amusement industry evolved, as did the circus, from European traditions—the medieval fair and carnival and the seventeenth-century pleasure garden. Indeed, it is possible to trace elements of the carnival, fair, and amusement park back to antiquity. Before the American Revolution, pleasure gardens, modeled on London's most famous gardens, Vauxhall and Ranelagh, appeared in major cities on the East Coast. Like Vauxhall, which was the first internationally famous pleasure garden when it opened in 1661, the American version offered visitors food, drink, music, and free variety acts. As in England and France, the simple pleasure of strolling, eating, and drinking became tiresome, and amusements of a more thrilling and exciting nature were sought.

The end of the nineteenth century saw similar places of amusement develop, however, as a result of improved transportation and technology. With the invention of the trolley came the institution of so-called trolley parks. Dozens of such parks were established by street railways at the end of the line all over the country as an economical method of encouraging weekend riders to use the cars. Initially, these parks offered little that could not have been found at the earlier pleasure garden. During the nineteenth century, however, amusements offered at the gardens and at rural picnic groves and shore resorts began to increase in number and in sophistication. Also, by the 1880s, thanks to new technology, mechanical pleasure rides such as the carousel and a device called "the Ferris wheel" developed.

The most obvious stimulus for the outdoor amusement industry first began when the Vienna World's Fair was held at "The Prater" in Vienna in 1873. A new concept in outdoor entertainment was presented with its large array of amusement "machines" or rides, fun houses, games of chance, and other activities, which created a new and exciting kind of park. Although Jones's Woods, a grove of some one hundred fifty acres along the East River, offered New Yorkers in the early nineteenth century a large variety of amusements, it was not until 1893 and the World's Columbian Exposition in Chicago that American showmen sensed the lucrative potential of outdoor amusements.

The true emergence of the American carnival and the exploitation of amusement rides and concessions, then, is usually cited as 1893. Although an area outside the exposition fair proper, called the "Midway Plaisance," began slowly, when the concessionaires hyped its promotion and agreed that the assembled attractions should be moved to various cities, the idea of the street fair or modern carnival had been born. The traveling carnival was fully realized that same year when Frank C. Bostock presented a collection of attractions at Coney Island, the location later of the amusement park's great growth. Bostock's entertainment has been called the first modern carnival in that his efforts mark the first attempt to make portable a group of attractions. Initially these early carnivals were moved by horse-drawn wagons, but by 1914 the "Smith Greater Shows" was moved by truck.

As early as 1883 the more traditional state fairs were invaded by the amusement business and amusement zones were included at all the world fairs after Chicago in 1893. The trolley companies mentioned above followed suit and patterned a number of the trolley parks after such amusement areas. Today, the carnival business is a large industry. One of the largest of the traveling carnivals, the "Royal American Shows," travels on eighty double-length railroad cars loaded with 145 massive pieces of equipment. Their midway features more than fifty rides and attractions and seven under-canvas shows, illustrating vividly the three distinctive features of the carnival—riding devices, shows or exhibits, and concessions.

The modern concept of the amusement park developed at Coney Island, a beach resort in Brooklyn, New York, which contained a series of parks and independent entertainments. There, beginning in 1895, street railway companies and seaside entertainment entrepreneurs had witnessed the evolution of the ultimate model on which to base their operations. Coney Island's fame began when Billy Boynton built Sea Lion Park in 1895, followed by George C. Tilyou's Steeplechase Park in 1897, and then the purchase in 1903 of Boynton's park by Frederic W. Thompson and Elmer (Skip) Dundy. They rebuilt the Boynton park into a lavish version of the

Midway Plaisance—Luna Park—at a cost of nearly $1 million. Luna offered, on a more or less permanent basis, a wildly eclectic environment of attractions, illuminated at night by more than two hundred fifty thousand incandescent lights. Across Surf Avenue from Luna, a real-estate speculator named William Reynolds quickly countered and spent $3.5 million to build Dreamland Park, where everything was on an even more exuberant scale, all lit by one million bulbs.

The great period of the traditional amusement park dates from Coney Island's spectacular growth at the turn of the century to about World War II, although its decline began, as did that of all outdoor entertainments, around World War I. However, while it lasted, the Coney Island model inspired countless other Luna Parks and Dreamlands all over America, until, by the early years of the new century, the amusement park had become a fixture of most large cities. From World War II to the present, the decline of the traditional amusement park has been slow but steady, with the announcement of the closing of major amusement parks a commonplace event. The lack of needed materials during the war, ultimate patrons' boredom with the aging attractions, natural disasters, and vandalism have all contributed to the traditional amusement park's demise.

According to a recent survey, there are, nonetheless, still more than one hundred major amusement parks in the United States. A large number of these parks, however, represent the latest phase of the outdoor amusement industry. As traditional parks declined in popularity, they were replaced by the "theme" parks, dating from the conception of Disneyland in Anaheim, California, which began in 1954. Apparently, the popularity of the amusement park is not waning. During the summer of 1976, over seventy-five million people attended such parks; more patrons rode roller coasters in 1977 than attended professional football and baseball games combined. Possibly, as Brooks McNamara has suggested, we are now approaching a kind of saturation point for this type of entertainment. If so, definite indications of such a development have yet to materialize fully.

BIBLIOGRAPHY

Badger, Reid. *The Great American Fair.* Chicago: Nelson-Hall, 1979.

Braithwaite, David. *Fairground Architecture: The World of Amusement Parks, Carnivals, and Fairs.* New York: Frederick A. Praeger, 1968.

Chindahl, George L. *History of the Circus in America.* Caldwell, Idaho: Caxton Printers, 1959.

Coxe, Antony D. Hippisley. *A Seat at the Circus.* Rev. ed. Hamden, Conn: Archon Books, 1980.

Croft-Cooke, Rupert, and Peter Cotes. *Circus: A World History.* New York: Macmillan, 1976.

Durant, John, and Alice Durant. *Pictorial History of the American Circus.* New York: A. S. Barnes, 1957.

Fried, Frederick A. *Pictorial History of the Carousel.* New York: A. S. Barnes, 1964.

Funnell, Charles F. *By the Beautiful Sea: The Rise and High Times of That Great American Resort, Atlantic City.* New York: Alfred A. Knopf, 1975.

Griffin, Al. *"Step Right Up Folks!"* Chicago: Henry Regnery, 1974.

Kasson, John F. *Amusing the Million: Coney Island at the Turn of the Century.* New York: Hill and Wang, 1978.

Kyriazi, Gary. *The Great American Amusement Parks.* Secaucus, N.J.: Citadel Press, 1976.

May, Earl Chapin. *The Circus from Rome to Ringling.* 1932. Reprint. New York: Dover Publications, 1963.

McCullough, Edo. *World's Fair Midways: An Affectionate Account of American Amusement Areas from the Crystal Palace to the Crystal Ball.* 1966. Reprint. New York: Arno Press, 1976.

McKennon, Joe. *A Pictorial History of the American Carnival.* Sarasota, Fla.: Carnival Publishers, 1972.

McNamara, Brooks. "Come on Over: The Rise and Fall of the American Amusement Park." *Theatre Crafts,* 11 (September 1977), 33, 84-86.

Mangels, William F. *The Outdoor Entertainment Business.* New York: Vantage Press, 1952.

Rennert, Jack. *100 Posters of Buffalo Bill's Wild West.* New York: Darien House, 1976.

Russell, Don. *The Wild West or, A History of the Wild West Show.* Fort Worth: Amon Carter Museum of Western Art, 1970.

Sell, Henry Blackman, and Victor Weybright. *Buffalo Bill and the Wild West.* New York: Oxford University Press, 1955.

Shirley, Glenn. *Pawnee Bill: A Biography of Major Gordon W. Lillie.* Lincoln: University of Nebraska Press, 1958.

Speaight, George. *A History of the Circus.* San Diego and New York: A. S. Barnes, 1980.

Thayer, Stuart. *Annals of the American Circus 1793-1829.* Manchester, Mich.: Printed for the author by Rymack Printing Co., 1976.

Toole-Stott, Raymond. *Circus and Allied Arts, A World Bibliography.* 4 vols. Derby, England: Harpur, 1958-1971.

Towsen, John H. *Clowns.* New York: Hawthorn Books, 1976.

Truzzi, Marcello. "The Decline of the American Circus: The Shrinkage of an Institution." In *Sociology and Everyday Life.* Edited by Marcello Truzzi. Englewood Cliffs, N.J.: Prentice-Hall, 1968.

______, ed. "Circuses, Carnivals and Fairs in America." *Journal of Popular Culture,* 6 (Winter 1972), 531-619.

Ulmer, Jeff. *Amusement Parks of America: A Comprehensive Guide.* New York: The Dial Press, 1980.

Note: See also the bibliography for STAGE ENTERTAINMENTS.

Comic Art

M. Thomas Inge

The daily and Sunday comic strips, and comic books, are part of the reading habits of more than one hundred million people at all educational and social levels in the United States. Any mass medium that plays so heavily on the sensibilities of the populace deserves study purely for sociological reasons, but comic art is important for other reasons as well. While the roots of comic art may be partly European, the comics as we know them today are a distinctively American art form that has contributed heavily to the culture of the world, from Picasso to the pop art movement. They derive from popular patterns, themes, and concepts of world culture—just as Dick Tracy was inspired by Sherlock Holmes (notice the similarity in noses), Flash Gordon and Superman draw on the heroic tradition to which Samson, Beowulf, Davy Crockett, and Paul Bunyan belong. The comics also serve as revealing reflectors of popular attitudes, tastes, and mores, and they speak directly to human desires, needs, and emotions.

While some historians would trace the comic strip to prehistoric cave drawings, the medieval Bayeux tapestry, the eighteenth-century print series of such artists as William Hogarth, the illustrated European broadsheet, the nineteenth-century illustrated novels and children's books, or European and American humorous periodicals, the American comic strip as we know it may have been influenced by all of these antecedents, yet it remains a distinct form of expression unto itself and primarily is an American creation. It may be defined as an open-ended dramatic narrative about a recurring set of characters, told with a balance between narrative text and visual action, often including dialogue in balloons, and published serially in newspapers. The comic strip shares with drama the use of such conventions as dialogue, scene, stage devices, gesture, and compressed time, and it anticipated such film techniques as montage (before Eisenstein), angle shots, panning, close-ups, cutting, and framing. Unlike the play or the film, however, the comic strip is usually the product of one artist (or an artist and a writer) who must be a combined producer-scriptwriter-director-scene designer at once and bring his characters to life on the flat space of a printed page, with respect for the requirements of a daily episode that takes less than a minute's reading time. It is these challenges that make fine comic art difficult to achieve and contribute to its distinct qualities.

Identifying the first comic strip is not easy. Some would suggest James Swinnerston's 1895 feature for the San Francisco *Examiner*, *Little Bears and Tykes*, in which bear cubs, who had been used in spot illustrations for the newspaper since 1893, adopted the human postures of small children. Others more commonly suggest Richard Outcault's *The Yellow Kid*, who first appeared in the May 5, 1895, issue of the New York *World*, a street urchin in the middle of riotous activities set in the low-class immigrant sections of the city and identified by the title "Hogan's Alley." Unlike Swinnerston, Outcault developed a central character in his use of the Kid, always clad in a yellow shift on which his dialogue was printed, and by 1896 had moved from a single panel cartoon to the format of a progressive series of panels with balloon dialogue, which would become the definitive form of the comic strip.

Outcault's use of contemporary urban reality in his backgrounds, which had counterparts in the naturalistic novels of Stephen Crane, Frank Norris, and Theodore Dreiser, would not reappear in the comics for over two decades (and even then in the safe Midwestern environment of Sidney Smith's *The Gumps* of 1917, which emphasized the pathos of lower middle-class life, and Frank King's *Gasoline Alley*, a year later, where the use of chronological time first entered the comics in following the growth of a typical American family). Most of the popular strips that came on the heels of the Kid in the following three decades used humor and fantasy as their major modes, such as Rudolph Dirks' *The Katzenjammer Kids*, now in its eightieth year and the longest running comic strip in existence; Frederick Burr Opper's several wacky creations *Happy Hooligan, Maude the Mule*, and *Alphonse and Gaston*; Richard Outcault's penance for his illiterate outlandish Kid, *Buster Brown*; Winsor McCay's *Little Nemo in Slumberland*, the most technically accomplished and aesthetically beautiful Sunday page ever drawn; Bud Fisher's *Mutt and Jeff*, the first daily comic strip and the first successful comic team in the funnies; George Herriman's classic absurdist fantasy and lyrical love poem *Krazy Kat*; Cliff Sterret's abstractly written and drawn family situation comedy, *Polly and Her Pals*; George McManus's *Bringing Up Father*, whose central characters, Maggie and Jiggs, became a part of American marital folklore; Billy DeBeck's tribute to the sporting life, *Barney Google*; Elzie Segar's *Thimble Theater*, which in 1929, after a ten-year run, introduced Popeye to the world; and Frank Willard's boarding house farce, *Moon Mullins*. These were the years when the terms *comics* and *funnies* became inseparably identified with this new form of creative expression, even though comedy and humor were not to remain its primary content.

Although some adventurous continuity and suspense had been used in

C. W. Kahles' burlesque of melodrama, *Hairbreadth Harry* in 1906, Roy Crane's *Wash Tubbs* of 1924 and George Storm's *Phil Hardy* and *Bobby Thatcher* of 1925-27 established the adventure comic strip, and Harold Gray's *Little Orphan Annie* also of 1924 drew on the picaresque tradition in a successful combination of exotic adventure and homespun right-wing philosophy. The adventure strip would not become a fully developed genre, however, until 1929 and the appearance of the first science fiction strip, *Buck Rogers,* by Richard W. Calkins and Phil Nowlan, and the successful translation of the classic primitive hero from the novels of Edgar Rice Burroughs, *Tarzan* (most beautifully drawn in those years first by Harold Foster and later by Burne Hogarth). The 1930s and 1940s were to be dominated by adventure titles, such as Chester Gould's *Dick Tracy,* Vincent Hamlin's *Alley Oop,* Milton Caniff's *Terry and the Pirates* and his postwar *Steve Canyon,* Alex Raymond's *Flash Gordon,* Lee Falk's *Mandrake the Magician* (drawn by Phil Davis) and *The Phantom* (drawn by Ray Moore), Harold Foster's *Prince Valiant,* Fred Harman's *Red Ryder,* Fran Striker's *The Lone Ranger* (drawn primarily by Charles Flanders), Alfred Andriola's *Charlie Chan* and *Kerry Drake,* Will Eisner's *The Spirit,* and Roy Crane's second contribution to the tradition, *Buzz Sawyer.* Related by the use of the same devices of mystery and suspense and also developed during these years were the soap opera strips, among the best known of which were *Mary Worth,* by Allen Saunders and Dale Connor (a reincarnation of Martha Orr's 1932 antidote for the Depression, *Apple Mary*); writer Nicholas Dallis' *Rex Morgan, M. D.* (drawn by Marvin Bradley and Frank Edgington), followed in 1952 by *Judge Parker* (drawn by Dan Heilman and later by Harold LeDoux), and in 1961 by *Apartment 3-G* (drawn by Alex Kotzky); and Stanley Drake's 1953 collaboration with writer Eliot Caplin on *The Heart of Juliet Jones.*

The 1950s proved to be the era in which satire flourished in the comics. As early as 1930, Chic Young's *Blondie* had gently satirized at first the flappers and playboys of the jazz age and later the institution of marriage, but Al Capp's *Li'l Abner* of 1934 would eventually become a significant forum for illustrating the hypocrisies and absurdities of the larger social and political trends of the nation. Just as Capp used the hillbilly life in Dogpatch as his main vehicle for satire, his successors would use other and often more imaginative vehicles, such as the fantasy world of children in *Barnaby* by David Johnson Leisk and *Peanuts* by Charles Schulz, the ancient form of the animal fable by Walt Kelly in *Pogo,* military life in *Beetle Bailey* by Mort Walker, the world of prehistoric man by Johnny Hart in *B. C.*, and the fanciful world of a medieval kingdom in *The Wizard of Id* by Hart and Brant Parker. The most recent entries in this tradition, however, demonstrate two radical trends for the 1970s, with Russel Myers' *Broomhilda* moving toward a totally abstract world in the tradition of George Herriman's *Krazy Kat* and Garry Trudeau's *Doonesbury* moving into the realistic world of the radical student generation of the last decade.

The earliest comic books were reprint collections of favorite comic strips, such as *The Yellow Kid*, *Mutt and Jeff*, and *Barney Google*, bound in cardboard covers. The comic book as we know it, however, began in 1933 when ten thousand copies of *Funnies on Parade* were printed, with thirty-two pages of Sunday color newspaper reprints within a paper-covered booklet about 7½″ by 10″ in size and intended to be given away as a premium for using the products of Proctor and Gamble. The give-away comics were so successful that in 1934 Dell Publishing Company, at the instigation of Max C. Gaines, sold through chain stores for ten cents a copy thirty-five thousand issues of *Famous Funnies*, which then became the first monthly comic magazine and reached a circulation peak of nearly one million copies during its twenty-year existence. While other publishers would begin successful imitations of this reprint comic book, such as *Popular Comics*, *Tip Top Comics*, and *King Comics*, a major innovation occurred when in 1935 National Periodical Publications issued *More Fun*, the first comic book to publish original material specifically written and drawn for its unique page size and format.

The same publishers began *Detective Comics* in 1937 (thus the firm's better known initials "D. C."), the first title devoted to a single theme, but it was not until they issued in June 1938 the first number of *Action Comics*, which introduced writer Jerry Siegel's and artist Joe Shuster's creation, Superman, that the comic book truly became a commercial success and spawned thousands of subsequent super-heroes during the 1940s, such as Batman, the Human Torch, Sub-Mariner, Captain Marvel, Wonder Woman, Captain America, Plastic Man, Blackhawk, Daredevil, and Airboy, among others. The industry would not again witness such a proliferation of super-heroes until 1961 when Stan Lee created a popular set of characters beset with human problems and neuroses despite their superior strength, such as Spiderman, the Hulk, Thor, and the Fantastic Four. Parallel with the super-hero titles, publishers also introduced humorous and funny animal books, among the most popular of which were *Archie*, as drawn by Bob Montana and first introduced in *Pep Comics* in 1941; *Walt Disney's Comics and Stories*, with Donald Duck and his Uncle Scrooge as delineated by Carl Barks, beginning in 1942; and in 1945, *Little Lulu*, with art by John Stanley.

A trend in realistic crime stories developed when editor Charles Biro and publisher Lev Gleason initiated *Crime Does Not Pay* in 1942. Eight years later, horror, science fiction, and war became prominent when William M. Gaines, the son of Max C. Gaines who had helped create the comic book, began publication of such titles as *Crypt of Terror*, *The Vault of Horror*, *The Haunt of Fear*, *Weird Science*, *Weird Fantasy*, *Crime Suspenstories*, and *Two-Fisted Tales*, under the "EC" (Entertaining Comics) imprint. These series proved to include some of the best written and most imaginatively drawn stories in American comic book history. Just as the EC team was hitting its stride, however, in 1954, a psychiatrist named Dr. Fredric Wertham published his book, *Seduction of the Innocent*, the culmination of a war against comic books by those who felt they contributed to juvenile delinquency. When a United States Senate Subcommittee on Juvenile Delinquency was established to investigate this charge, the major publishers responded by creating their own Comics Code Authority as a self-censoring agency. Unable to work under the code's stringent guidelines, Gaines changed his successful satiric comic book *Mad* into a magazine in 1955 and thereby continued to provide America with some of its finest satiric humor in this century.

American comic art, in both comic strip and comic book form, faces a most uncertain future. The space allotted to comic strips by newspapers has grown increasingly smaller while syndicate and editorial preference weeds out the most creative and therefore possibly unsettling strips, even though such formerly forbidden topics as homosexuality, premarital sex, and abortion have entered the funnies. The comic book seems impossibly shackled by the economic and editorial strictures which prevail in the industry, even though a few bright moments have occurred in the 1970s with the appearance of such titles as *Conan the Barbarian*, *The Swamp Thing*, *The Shadow*, and *Howard the Duck*. The most promising work has been accomplished by artists working for the underground press, many of whose "comix" have made genuine advances in the art form. Yet comic art, a little over eighty-five years old, has not realized its full potential and promises yet to become a powerful form of humanistic expression.

BIBLIOGRAPHY

Bails, Jerry, and Hames Ware, eds. *The Who's Who of American Comic Books.* 4 vols. Detroit: Jerry Bails, 1973-1976.

Becker, Stephen. *Comic Art in America.* New York: Simon and Schuster, 1959.

Berger, Arthur Asa. *The Comic-Stripped American.* New York: Walker and Co., 1973.

Couperie, Pierre, et al. *A History of the Comic Strip.* Translated by Eileen B. Hennessy. New York: Crown, 1968.

Daniels, Les. *Comix: A History of Comic Books in America.* New York: Outerbridge & Dienstfrey, 1971.

Dorfman, Ariel, and Armand Mattelart. *How to Read Donald Duck: Imperialist Ideology in the Disney Comic.* Translated by David Kunzle. New York: International General, 1975.

Estren, Mark James. *A History of Underground Comics.* San Francisco: Straight Arrow Books, 1974.

Fleisher, Michael L. *The Encyclopedia of Comic Book Heroes.* New York: Macmillan, 1976-. Eight volumes projected.

Goulart, Ron. *The Adventurous Decade.* New Rochelle, N.Y.: Arlington House, 1975.

Horn, Maurice, ed. *The World Encyclopedia of Comics.* 1 and 2 vol. editions. New York: Chelsea House, 1976.

Kempkes, Wolfgang. *International Bibliography of Comics Literature.* Detroit: Gale Research Co., 1971. 2d rev. ed. New York: R. R. Bowker/Verlag Dokumentation, 1974.

Kunzle, David. *The Early Comic Strip.* Vol. I: *History of the Comic Strip.* Berkeley: University of California Press, 1973.

Lupoff, Dick, and Don Thompson, eds. *All in Color for a Dime.* New Rochelle, N.Y.: Arlington House, 1970.

O'Sullivan, Judith. *The Art of the Comic Strip.* College Park: University of Maryland, Department of Art, 1971.

Overstreet, Robert M. *The Comic Book Price Guide.* Cleveland, Tenn.: Robert M. Overstreet, 1970-.

Perry, George, and Alan Aldridge. *The Penguin Book of Comics.* New York: Penguin Books, 1969. Rev. ed., 1971.

Reitberger, Reinhold, and Wolfgang Fuchs. *Comics: Anatomy of a Mass Medium.* Translated by Nadia Fowler. Boston: Little, Brown, 1972.

Robinson, Jerry. *The Comics: An Illustrated History of Comic Strip Art.* New York: G.P. Putnam's Sons, 1974.

Sheridan, Martin. *Comics and Their Creators.* Boston: Hale, Cushman & Flint, 1942. Reprinted. Brooklyn, N.Y.: Luna Press, 1971. Reprinted. Arcadia, Calif.: Post-Era Books, 1973.

Thompson, Don, and Dick Lupoff, eds. *The Comic-Book Book.* New Rochelle, N.Y.: Arlington House, 1973.

Walker, Mort. *Backstage at the Strips.* New York: Mason/Charter, 1975.

Waugh, Coulton. *The Comics.* New York: Macmillan, 1947. Reprinted. Brooklyn, N.Y.: Luna Press, 1974.

Wertham, Fredric. *Seduction of the Innocent.* New York: Holt, Rinehart and Winston, 1954. Reprinted. Port Washington, N.Y.: Kennikat Press, 1972.

Dance

Loretta Carrillo

Dance at its most popular level in America has served as a form of social, participational recreation. Country or folk dancing and city or social dancing together describe the major patterns. The history of recreational dance in this country, moreover, parallels the development of dance as a form of popular stage entertainment and testifies to the great influence each form has had upon the other. Nineteenth-century minstrels borrowed jigs and clog dances from white and Black folk dancers who performed at city and plantation festivities as much as the spectacular Broadway musicals of the 1920s and 1930s borrowed from social dance of the time. What the history of dance in America clearly shows is that Americans have not only enjoyed watching dance, but they have also nurtured a rich and varied tradition of dance as a form of popular social recreation.

In early America, as in all lands, dance initially played a purely ceremonial role as part of religious observances. Ritualistic Indian circle dances, replete with complex formations and incantations, constituted the only form of dance European settlers in the New World encountered. The Puritans themselves brought no dance tradition with them and were, in fact, strongly discouraged from engaging in couple dancing. Increase Mather preferred "unmixed" dancing, and his condemnation of "promiscuous" couple dances dates from the 1680s in the pamphlet "An Arrow Against Profane and Promiscuous Dancing Drawn Out of the Quiver of Scriptures." On the other hand, a later more tolerant religious sect living in Albany, New York, the Shakers or "Shaking Quakers" of Revolutionary days, actually incorporated step and round dances into their religious ceremonies. Taking the opposite view as the Puritans, the Shakers believed dancing was an angelic activity which helped rid them of sin and bring them closer to an ecstatic, ideal communion with God.

Other English, French, and Spanish colonists brought rich native traditions of folk dancing which included hornpipes and jigs in addition to stately court dances such as the minuet and gavotte. In England, John Playford's *The English Dancing Master or Plaine and Easie Rules for the Dancing of Country Dances, with the Tune to Each Dance,* published in the 1650s, became a standard country dancing manual for English and European dancing masters. The publication of *The English Dancing Master* began the standardization of country dances which made their way into society circles and challenged for the first time, according to historian Richard Nevell, the popularity of fancy drawing room dances of the wealthy.

Despite the railings of Puritan ecclesiastics such as Mather, good numbers of New England Puritans and other colonists continued to dance. By 1716 Boston claimed two rival dancing masters, one of whom was forced to move to New York when the rivalry for authority and for students became too keen. John Griffith, the most famous of the colonial dancing masters, is said to have travelled along the Eastern seaboard from Rhode Island as far south as Charleston, South Carolina, renting space, advertising in newspapers and giving instructions in the popular dances of the day. By the mid 1700s, Virginians were dancing the court gavotte as well as the country reels outlined in Playford's manual. George Washington was reported to have especially enjoyed dancing the "Sir Roger de Coverly" which later became the "Virginia Reel." In Philadelphia, the first "Assembly" or ball was held in 1748 which established a tradition of a yearly social gathering with dancing as the main activity. By the days of the American Revolution, city people and country folk in all the colonies were performing traditional contra dances as well as new occasional ones with names such as "Jefferson and Liberty" and "The Washington Quickstep." Moreover, the wealthy classes in all regions of the country continued the tradition of court dances.

In the late eighteenth century, French entertainers and dancing masters such as the Alexander Placide family, who came to America to escape the terrors of the French Revolution, greatly influenced the course of theatre as well as social dancing in America. Having the greatest influence in high society circles of Newport, New Hampshire, New York and Philadelphia, the French dancing masters brought sophisticated versions of country dances which they renamed *"les contredanses."* So widespread was the French influence, that the French quadrille, a slowed down version of the minuet, became the forerunner of the American square dance. Also quite important was the effect French and all dancing masters in America had well into the late nineteenth century upon improvising and complicating the country dance steps, and upon standardizing their execution as well as developing dance rules of etiquette.

Anti-British sentiment in America in the late eighteenth and nineteenth centuries fostered general preference for the French quadrille over English contra dances, although rural areas of New England kept alive the English folk dancing tradition. In the Southern Appalachian mountains of Kentucky, West Virginia, North Carolina and Tennessee, the Scottish and Irish settlers and their descendants continued to jig and clog which eventually became the trademark of Southern country dancing. Using native African rhythms and dances such as the "Giouba," which used figures of the court dances with hip movements of the Congo, the Black slaves on Southern plantations during this period incorporated the jig footwork rhythms into their own peculiar dance styles. This early Black dance tradition was later perfected by the nineteenth-century jig and clog dancers or "buckdancers" such as William Henry Lane, known as Master Juba (derived from the "Giouba" dance) who gained wide popularity in America and Europe. Southern regional Black dance in America, in addition, eventually blossomed in the early twentieth century into the tap and jazz forms perfected by Black professional dancers. In another region of the country, Western settlers and cowboy dancers of the period favored the cotillion with the "caller" who shouted out the dance formations. Western square dancers of the day danced *The Wagon Wheel* and *The Texas Star.*

In the city, social dancing became increasingly refined and adapted rules of etiquette under the guidance of the dancing masters. Hundreds of manuals such as *Dick's Quadrille Book* (1878) were published during the 1800s dictating correct placement and deportment. Couple dancing had been popularized in the first half of the nineteenth century by the waltz and the polka—European country dances which were both integrated into the quadrilles of the day. Initially considered scandalous because of the close contact of the couple, the waltz grew so popular that the dancing masters were forced to accept a refined version of it. However, the extent to which social dance in America was breaking away from the control of dancing masters was seen when in 1883, fearful that dance would become vulgar without proper instruction, they formed the American National Association of Masters of Dancing to preserve the genteel way of dancing.

In a further attempt to exert control over social dance of the day, Allen Dodworth, New York's leading dancing master, published a manual in 1885 designed to show the proper, refined way to execute ballroom dancing. The manual, *Dancing and Its Relation to Education and Social Life, with a New Method of Instruction, with 250 Figures,* placed importance on dancing as a form of cultivated behavior and contained a system of teaching with diagrams and musical scores. Also contributing to the effort to keep social dancing refined were regular articles in popular periodicals such as *Godey's Ladies Book* which contained rules on proper dance deportment.

By the early 1900s the waltz, the polka and the schottische were the favorite social dances. Mrs. Cornelius Vanderbilt II was staging balls as the most important social events of the season, and "correct" dancing was fully accepted as a cultivated activity for high society. Social dancing was also established as a fixed feature of American social life at all levels. Around this time, however, the rich musical and dance traditions of Southern Blacks which had been nurtured in New Orleans was being heard more frequently and was to permanently change the face of social dance in America by introducing a new sense of rhythm. New Orleans saloon music known as "ragtime," with its "ragged" or syncopated rhythm, gave rise to the Turkey

Trot, Grizzly Bear, Bunny Hug, and the Kangaroo Dip. So popular did these dances become that they set off a dance craze that lasted well into the late 1920s. Far more daring than the tame waltz had been, these new dances allowed couples to hang on to each other and dance cheek-to-cheek.

Society matrons now thundered that deportment and etiquette had been completely lost in the new dances. Irene and Vernon Castle came to society's rescue, however, when between 1912 and 1919 they did much to popularize a refined way of performing the popular social dances of the period. The Castles performed the Turkey Trot, the Tango and the Hesitation Waltz with equal grace and elegance. Performing at afternoon "*thes dansants*" or "tea dances" held at ballrooms and cabarets, the Castles gave rise to a new emphasis upon refined social dancing. The Castles even created new dances such as the Castle Walk and gained wide popularity touring the United States and Europe giving demonstrations. Other dance demonstrators quickly followed the Castle lead and performed in halls and ball-dining rooms in major cities all across America. Maurice and Walton, Joan Sawyer and Jack Jarret, and Arthur Murray and Irene Hammond were all dance demonstrators during the period 1910-1920.

Given the immense popularity of social dancing during this period, popular music began to concentrate on music to dance by. Irving Berlin's "Alexander's Ragtime Band" was extremely popular as was the "jazz" music of Black musicians which was now a more familiar sound to the white American public. The Black Bottom, the Shimmy and the Varsity Drag, dances adapted from the Black tradition, were all summarily denounced as immoral. Paying no attention to pulpit preachers, however, the enthusiastic dancers of the 1920s continued performing all of the new dances in public halls all over the country. The Charleston, appearing in the 1923 Black performers' review "Running Wild," along with Harry Fox's improvised routine in the Ziegfeld Follies, the Foxtrot, quickly became the dances of the 1920s.

The public dance arena gained wide popularity during the 1920s when hundreds of dance halls sprang up in San Francisco's Barbary Coast, New Orleans' French Quarter, Chicago's South Side and New York's Bowery and Tenderloin District. Several types of halls catering to different clientele and social classes developed. Municipal districts and civic groups such as clubs and lodges sponsored dances at public halls. Another type of public dance arena, the "Taxi-dance" ballrooms, were for men only and offered dance partners for the price of a ticket. More elaborate dance palaces, complete with chandeliers and gilt drapes, could be found in major cities. The Roseland and the Savoy in New York, the Trianon and Aragon in Chicago, the Hollywood Paladium in Los Angeles, and similar arenas in Detroit, Cleveland, Cincinnati and Denver entertained millions of dancers throughout the decades of the 1920s and 1930s.

The decade of the 1930s is perhaps best known as the classic period of the Broadway musical and the Hollywood film, both of which featured dancing. Musicians such as George Gershwin, Irving Berlin, and Cole Porter were composing music for Broadway shows, and Fred Astaire and Ginger Rogers reigned as the dance couple of Hollywood film. James Cagney, Shirley Temple, Bill "Bojangles" Robinson, George Raft, and Buddy Ebsen all performed routines and also contributed toward making dance the center of stage and film entertainment during the decade. In the social dance arena, Arthur Murray's mail order dance instruction business was flourishing and the Lindy Hop, created on the occasion of Charles Lindbergh's 1927 cross-Atlantic flight, became a very popular dance that incorporated the energetic movements of the Charleston and the Black Bottom. Young people were increasingly becoming the biggest followers of dance fads, particularly when the big dance bands and swing music along with jitterbugging became popular during the closing years of the decade.

Benny Goodman, Tommy Dorsey, Duke Ellington, Glenn Miller and swing music became the rage in the 1940s. Jitterbugging quickly became the favorite dance of American servicemen and their dance partners in entertainment centers and Canteens. The jitterbug, however, was unquestionably perfected at Harlem's Savoy Ballroom where dancers incorporated gymnastic feats such as airborne turns and tosses into the dance and the best performers became dance demonstrators in their own right. The second feature of social dance during this period was the rage for Latin music and dances. Cesar Romero and Carmen Miranda performed the samba, rumba, conga, and mambo to music by Xavier Cugat, Tito Puente and Perez Prado for an American dance public who diligently tried to learn the syncopated rhythm and hip movements. Generally, they settled for less complicated versions of Latin dances; however, the interest for the Latin rhythm never died. The resurgence of interest in social dance in the 1970s, in fact, was due to a great extent to the popularity of the Hustle, a New York City Hispanic youth dance which required complex timing and an acute sense of rhythm.

With the decade of the 1950s came Elvis Presley and rock-and-roll music and dancing. In 1956 "American Bandstand," a television program developed in Philadelphia and hosted by Dick Clark, provided an arena for teenagers to dance to the new music. Adults still preferred the fox trot and the cha-cha and vocal hits by Frank Sinatra and Rosemary Clooney. The younger generation, on the other hand, danced the Stroll and listened to music by Jerry Lee Lewis, Bill Haley and The Comets, the Everley Brothers, and the Platters.

Chubby Checker and the Twist, a dance that both adults and teenagers found easy to perform, dominated the rock-and-roll dance scene in the early 1960s. The period also produced such fad dances as the Mashed Potatoes and the Jerk, which like the Twist, separated the dancing couple and stressed the ingenuity of individual styles and movements. The French discotheque became popular in American during this time and developed as the night spot where one could dance amid strobe lights and glittering decor. Black music and dance of the period came to be called the "Motown Sound" (the record label under which much of the music was produced). Such stars as Diana Ross and the Supremes, The Temptations, and Smokey Robinson and the Miracles were "Motown" celebrities. Social dancing in the mid- and late 1960s waned, however, as the Beatles began to revolutionize rock music. The rock concert replaced dancing as the popular social entertainment pastime when young people preferred listening to popular singers Jimi Hendrix, Janis Joplin, and the Jefferson Airplane sing at rock festivals such as Woodstock and the Monterey Pop Festival. By the late 1960s, the drug culture had inspired and produced "acid rock," the ulimate in undanceable music.

In the 1970s, a return to dancing brought back the discos and a new, updated version of "American Bandstand." The 1971 show "Soul Train" featured Black dances such as The Breakdown and the Scooby Doo which incorporated variations of the "lock step" and showed once again Black dance's emphasis upon complicated rhythm and timing. The Hustle, a dance originating in Hispanic *barrios* of New York City, was at the center of the dance craze in the 1970s and is credited with bringing back technique to social dancing. The New York City disco, Studio 54, became the fashionable dancing spot for such celebrities as Liza Minelli and ballet superstar Mikhail Baryshnikov. In addition, the 1977 movie *Saturday Night Fever* gave the dance craze of the 1970s new life. Studios and instructors once again became popular, and television came up with programs such as "Dance Fever" where dancing couples from across the country competed for prize money. The period also witnessed a nostalgic yearning for the good old days of dancing, and afternoon tea dances, held at hotels and clubs, featured programs of music from the 1930s and 1940s while couples glided across dance floors.

In more recent times, the popularity of New Wave and Punk Rock music of the late 1970s and early 1980s attests to a new breed of dancers. Sporting Mohawk hairdos dyed pink, purple or blue, and wearing leather clothing, these newest dancers reject recent stylized movement. Their dancing is often performed in New York City and other urban area street corners and parks and may consist of repetitious, ritualistic-like jumping up and down while shivering and shaking the body. The contemporary cult of both Punk Rock and New Wave music provides the latest evidence that popular music and dancing are so closely connected that one inevitably influences and shapes the direction of the other.

While social dance developed in the late nineteenth and early twentieth centuries as the most popular form of recreational dance in America, country dancing remained popular in isolated regions and changed much less drastically than did social dance, particularly in the twentieth century. City dancing, as has been shown, responded to the innovations in popular music. Country dance, on the other hand, retained the patterns and innovations developed prior to the Civil War. Although such movement innovations as the "swing" and "waltz" steps were integrated, for example, into the square dances of the 1880s and 1890s, country dancing in America remained essentially unchanged through the nineteenth century. Country dancing and folk culture, however, experienced a revival with the 1918 publication of Elizabeth Burchenal's *Twenty-Eight Contra Dances, Largely from the New England States.* Country dances from Maine to Massachusetts were rediscovered, and a sense of their historical value and that of folk lifestyles as well inspired the founding of centers committed to preserving and studying American folk cultures. In addition, Western country dance was kept alive by Dorothy and Lloyd Shaw in Denver, Colorado. Lloyd Shaw's *Cowboy Dances,* published in 1939, renewed interest in Western square dance, as did his troupe of demonstration dancers who toured the United States and Europe.

The last category of dance developed in America as a form of popular culture is defined as "national" or "ethnic" folk dance. While the English, Irish, and Scottish country dance traditions have had the greatest influence upon the development of American country dance, other ethnic groups have kept alive national dances that reflect the mother country's culture. Defined more as demonstration rather than participational dances, ethnic folk dances such as the Israeli *hora* dance, the Mexican *el jarabe* courtship dance, the Scottish Highland Fling, and the Italian *tarantella* have symbolic value in and of themselves. Though they can be and very often are performed by non-trained dancers, their fullest expression is usually given by trained dancers in demonstrations at celebrations, festivities, or especially staged performances. An example can be seen in the Spanish *flamenco* dancers who have not only mastered the intricate footwork but who can also execute the stylized body movements that suggest the sensuality at the heart of *flamenco* dances. Moreover, national or ethnic folk dances usually express a facet of the culture's history or are meant to show themes—love, death, war—common to all ethnic folk dances. Lastly, American ethnic folk dances express this country's heterogeneous, cultural make-up and the influence all folk cultures have had upon shaping a popular American dance tradition.

BIBLIOGRAPHY

Buckman, Peter. *Let's Dance, Social, Ballroom and Folk Dancing.* New York: Penguin Books, 1978.

Burchenal, Elizabeth. "Folk Dances of the United States: Regional Types and Origins." *International Folk Music Journal,* 3 (1951), 500-506.

Calabria, Frank M. "The Dance Marathon Craze."' *Journal of Popular Culture,* 10 (1976), 54-69.

Croce, Arlene. *The Fred Astaire and Ginger Rogers Book.* New York: Galahad Books, 1974.

Dannett, Sylvia G. L., and Frank R. Rachel. *Down Memory Lane, Arthur Murray's Picture Story of Social Dancing.* New York: Greenberg Publishers, 1954.

Emery, Lynne F. *Black Dance in the United States from 1619-1970.* Palo Alto: National Press Books, 1972.

Fernett, Gene. *Swing Out, Great Negro Dance Bands.* Michigan: The Pendell Company, 1970.

Kendall, Elizabeth. *Where She Danced.* New York: Alfred A. Knopf, 1979.

Kraus, Richard. *Folk Dancing, A Guide for Schools, Colleges and Recreation Groups.* New York: The Macmillan Company, 1962.

______. *Square Dances of Today and How to Teach and Call Them.* New York: The Ronald Press Co., 1950.

Lange, Roderyk. *The Nature of Dance, An Anthropological Perspective.* New York: International Publications Service, 1976.

Marks, Joseph E., III. *America Learns to Dance.* New York: Exposition Press, 1957.

Magriel, Paul, ed. *Chronicles of the American Dance from the Shakers to Martha Graham.* New York: DaCapo Press, 1978.

McCarthy, Albert. *The Dance Band Era: The Dancing Decades from Ragtime to Swing, 1910-50.* New York: Chilton Book Company, 1971.

McDonaugh, Don. *Dance Fever.* New York: Random House, 1979.

Nevell, Richard. *A Time to Dance, American Country Dancing from Hornpipes to Hot Hash.* New York: St. Martin's Press, 1977.

Nye, Russel B. "Saturday Night at the Paradise Ballroom: or Dance Halls in the Twenties." *Journal of Popular Culture*, 7 (1974), 14-22.

______. "Minstrels to Musicals." In *The Unembarrassed Muse: The Popular Arts in America.* New York: The Dial Press, 1970, pp. 162-180.

______. "The Big Band Era." In *The Unembarrassed Muse: The Popular Arts in America.* New York: The Dial Press, 1970, pp. 326-340.

Mueller, John. *Dance Film Directory.* Princeton, N.J.: Princeton Book Company, 1979.

Smith, Frank H. *The Appalachian Square Dance.* Berea, Ky.: Berea College, 1955.

Sonnenshein, Richard. "Dance: Its Past and Its Promise on Film." *Journal of Popular Culture,* 12 (1978), 500-506.

Sterns, Marshall and Jean. *Jazz Dance: The Story of American Vernacular Dance.* New York: Schirmer Books, 1968.

Terry, Walter. *The Dance in America.* New York: Harper and Row, 1971.

Wright, Louis B. *The First Gentlemen of Virginia.* Charlottesville: University Press of Virginia, 1964.

Death

Robert A. Armour and
J. Carol Williams

Throughout American history, popular customs have reflected general American attitudes toward death. From the seventeenth-century folk art of tombstone carving, to the more elaborate nineteenth-century monuments, to this century's reproductions of Michelangelo's masterpieces in famous Forest Lawn Cemetery, the art that has adorned our cemeteries has made visible the values we have placed on death. Likewise, the rituals associated with death also represent popular values: hiring an *aanspreecker* in colonial Dutch American communities to visit the homes of friends of the deceased to announce the death; the quick burial in mass graves of the soldiers killed on Civil War battlefields; or the sight of an entire nation in mourning as it watches the riderless horse lead the body of a slain president to its resting place. The goal here is to provide an overview of popular attitudes toward death in America. Because of the many ethnic and religious variations that have existed side by side in this land, it is impossible to make generalizations about the attitudes toward death, which have varied with culture and time, but we can pinpoint some writers and events that were typical of their day.

One of the first books published in the Old World about America was an illustrated version of Thomas Hariot's *A Briefe and true report of the new found land of Virginia* (1590). This book, written by a fine scientist sent over by Sir Walter Raleigh to record the history of the new colony at Roanoke Island, was one of the earliest accounts of the customs of the people native to this land. Among the illustrations by John White is a drawing of an Indian burying ground, which consisted of a platform on high wooden columns inside a thatched hut of considerable size. The skin of a dead chief was stripped from the body, tanned, and then replaced over the skeleton so that the figure of the chief was preserved. Then, according to the caption that accompanies the drawing, the body was placed on the platform where one of the priests in charge of the dead murmured prayers day and night. This, the earliest example of published writing about death in North America, demonstrates that the Indians had concerns for their dead that are similiar to those still held by a large segment of the population: interest in the preservation of the body, reverence for the dead, and acceptance of the role of the clergy.

As the Europeans began to populate the eastern seaboard, they brought with them, along with their political, economic, and artistic attitudes, ideas about death. Those ideas found quick expression. During the first winter in the new land, fifty-two of the original one hundred two settlers at the Plymouth colony died before spring. And in Virginia, of the roughly 1,650 people who had come to the colony by 1625, approximately one thousand had died; over three hundred had been killed in the Indian massacre of 1622. The deaths in Virginia were accepted as expected events; John Smith, in his *History of Virginia* (1624), simply refers to the deaths and rails at the leaders whose stupidity caused them. God is given credit for the good things that happened at Jamestown, but He is not blamed for the suffering. This attitude established a pattern that was carried on in the southern colonies throughout the colonial period. The writings of William Byrd II discuss sicknesses and deaths, but there is only brief mention of the dying process and no doubt of the afterlife. Even deists such as Thomas Jefferson believed without much question in a future state of rewards and punishment, and the words of Philip Vickers Fithian, the tutor for the family of Robert Carter of Virginia just before the Revolution, typify the concern for the afterlife during the Enlightenment. When he thought he might be dying during a serious illness, he resigned "myself body and soul and Employment to god who has the hearts of all in his hand, and who I am persuaded, if he has anything for me to do in Life, will preserve, and in a measure fit me for it, if not, I am in his hand, let him do as seems good in his eyes."

However, the attitude in the colonies controlled by the Puritans was by no means so accepting or passive. These people began early in the education of their children to establish a healthy respect for death. Two of the most popular books of Puritan New England were intended to instill in children their parents' fears. James Janeway, in *A Token for Children* (1676), taught them about the ever nearness of death, and *The New England Primer* used thoughts about death to illustrate some of the letters of the alphabet: "T—*Time* cuts down all/Both Great and Small" and "X—Xerxes the great did die/So must you and I," among others.

Life was viewed by the Puritan as a pilgrimage, a difficult trip whose ultimate goal is heaven. American Puritans were greatly influenced by John Bunyan's *Pilgrim's Progress* (1678), and their expectations for life and death followed closely Christian's pilgrimage through the temptations of life. The goal is the Celestial City, which can be reached only through death. This attitude led to a duality in the Puritan's ideas about death. One side of the Puritan said that death would bring relief from the travails of life and would bring the traveler into the presence of God. This side welcomed death, perhaps even longed for it. The other side of the

Puritan realized that the dying person may not be among those chosen to be saved by God and therefore may well be damned to an eternity without the presence of God. In this manner the Puritan at once both glorified death and feared its consequences.

The words of the Puritan preacher Jonathan Edwards expressed this duality. In his *Personal Narrative* (ca. 1740) he wrote: "The heaven I desired was a heaven of holiness; to be with God, and to spend my eternity in divine love. . . . Heaven appeared exceedingly delightful, as a world of love; and that all happiness consisted in living in pure, humble, heavenly, divine love." Yet in his famous sermon, "Sinners in the Hands of an Angry God" (1741), he describes hell in such terms as to make death a frightening prospect: ". . . it is a great furnace of wrath, a wide and bottomless pit, full of the fire of wrath, that you are held over by in the hand of that God, whose wrath is provoked and incensed as much against you, as against many of the damned in hell. . . ."

The popular image of parsimonious and socially dull Puritans is put to the lie by a description of their funerals. Historical records demonstrate that substantial parts of estates were spent for the funeral of the deceased. In addition to the expected expenses for a coffin, winding sheet, and grave, large amounts of money were spent on gloves and rings for the invited guests at the funeral and for extensive amounts of spices, cider, and rum. The costs of the alcoholic beverages became one of the largest single expenses in a Puritan funeral. The practice, of course, was not restricted to the Puritan colonies, and people in other colonies also began to complain about the high cost of dying, especially the costs of providing gifts and drinks for the guests.

The importation of the romantic movement from Europe as the eighteenth century turned into the nineteenth led to a different attitude toward death in America. The romantics were fascinated with death, and thoughts of death dominated the "graveyard" writers who were central to the movement. Many writers in the early romantic period, such as Philip Freneau and William Cullen Bryant, meditated on the meaning of death; but perhaps the American writer best known for his compulsion about death was Edgar Allan Poe. Many of his poems and stories about death demonstrate a duality of horror and longing, but none illustrates the point better than some verses from "Annabel Lee" (1849), which describes the death of the narrator's girfriend:

And this was the reason that, long ago,
   In this kingdom by the sea,
A wind blew out of a cloud by night
   Chilling my Annabel Lee;
So that her highborn kinsmen came
   And bore her away from me,

To shut her up in a sepulchre
  In this kingdom by the sea.

The angels, not half so happy in Heaven,
  Went envying her and me—
Yes!—that was the reason (as all men know,
  In this kingdom by the sea)
That the wind came out of the cloud chilling
  And killing my Annabel Lee.

Some of the nineteenth-century theologians continued the Puritan concepts even though the Puritan movement itself had died out. John Owen, writing in Philadelphia in 1827, made an impassioned plea for the Calvinistic view of the afterlife. In *The Death of Death in the Death of Christ*, which was endorsed by thirteen other ministers from the city, Owen reinforced and restated the basic tenets of Calvinism: ". . . let these doctrines, of God's eternal *election*, the free grace of *conversion*, *perseverance*, and their *necessary* consequences, be asserted." In other words, salvation depended on God's determination to save a particular soul. This was not an uncommon view of death at the time, but one that was to be given less credence as the nineteenth century passed.

A few years later, another book, *The Tree and its Fruits or, The Last Hours of Infidels & Christians Contracted* (1839), coming out of the same city but written by the American Sunday-School Union, focused on the last hours of the dying. The effort was to show that the good died easily and the evil died with difficulty. "It is a fact," the Union writes, "which appears worthy of being more prominently held up to the view of all whose minds are in any degree interested in the great concerns of eternity, that nearly all those who have been conspicuous in the ranks of infidelity, have left this world in a tempest of horror and dismay, as though the anathema maranatha, pronounced against all who love not the Lord Jesus, had withered them before their time; whilst it is notoriously true, that those who meet death with the greatest composure, and who triumpht over all his terrors, are the men whose lives have adorned the gospel of God their Saviour."

A more moderate and eloquent view of death was presented in the dedication speech for Hollywood Cemetery in Richmond, Virginia, in June of 1849. Oliver Baldwin's view of death was no less traditional than those of Owen or the Union, but his ideas were more tempered with charity: "The Grave, the Grave, how simply but powerfully it speaks through the eye of the soul, and bids it meditate upon itself and its destiny. An ancient writer has said that man was taken from the dust of the earth to prompt him to humility. But a still stronger incentive to humility is the fact which he daily witnesses that to dust he must return." Dust, according to Baldwin, is the fate of all, not just those who are elected by

God for salvation or those who have lived without sin and can expect an easy death. Baldwin went on to discuss at some length the value of a fine cemetery, both to those who expect to reside there shortly and to those who visit old friends and relatives there.

In 1859 Charles Darwin published *The Origin of Species*, which eventually changed the attitudes of many Americans toward death. Darwin, of course, challenged the historical accuracy of the Bible, but, in one way, his method was more of a challenge than his content. He had used science to arrive at conclusions that affected religion, and humankind was forced to decide between science and religion or to find a way to reconcile the two. Among the first to try the latter was William Rounseville Alger in *A Critical History of the Doctrine of Future Life* (1867). Alger was by no means a scientist, but he did view humankind as living in a scientific cycle in which all plants and animals have a place and a role: "The individual man dies . . . for the good of the species, and that he may furnish the conditions for the development of a higher life elsewhere. It is quite obvious that, if individuals did not die, new individuals could not live, because there would not be room. It is also equally evident that, if individuals did not die, they could never have any other life than the present." Alger claimed that this consideration made death a "necessity and benignity," rather than a horror; and he maintained that "the noble purpose of self-sacrifice enables us to smile upon the grave."

By the end of the century, writers were more consciously trying to reconcile Darwin with their own views of death. John Fiske, in *The Destiny of Man* (1892), attempted to show that his own Christian faith was not at odds with the theory of evolution. In his last chapter, he considered the afterlife, which is after all, he suggested, a religious matter not to be considered scientifically but accepted as a point of faith. Fiske put limits on the use of science and maintained that one must go beyond science to discover the truth about death. William James engaged himself in the same debate but used science to arrive at his conclusions in *Human Immortality* (1898). James wanted to show that the scientific assumption that life ends when the brain is dead is too limited. He argued that the brain has several functions: ". . . our soul's life, as we here know it, would none the less in literal strictness be the function of the brain. The brain would be the individual variable, the mind would vary dependently on it. But such dependence on the brain for this natural life would in no wise make immortal life impossible,—it might be quite compatible with supernatural life behind the veil hereafter."

While the intellectuals were trying to decide how to deal with the scientific problems raised during the century, others were finding different expressions of their ideas about death. Well-known writers, such as Henry Wadsworth Longfellow and Oliver Wendell Holmes, wrote poems that sought the solace of death; and writers less well known at the time, such as Walt Whitman and Emily Dickinson, adopted death as a major theme. Among the popular writers, however, death remained uncomplicated by theories of evolution and scientific methods. The elegiac and funeral verses of some sentimental poets received wide circulation and represented an altogether different attitude toward death than did the theories of ministers and psychologists or the poetry of Whitman and Dickinson. Julia A. Moore, the "Sweet Singer of Michigan," was renowned for her crude poetry inspired by the deaths of children:

LITTLE ANDREW

Andrew was a little infant,
And his life was two years old;
He was his parent's eldest boy,
And he was drowned, I was told.
His parents never more can see him
In this world of grief and pain,
And Oh! they will not forget him
While on earth they do remain.

One bright and pleasant morning
His uncle thought it would be nice
To take his dear little nephew
Down to play upon the raft,
Where he was to work upon it,
And this little child would company be—
The raft the water rushed around it,
Yet he the danger did not see.

This little child knew no danger—
Its little soul was free from sin—
He was looking in the water,
When, alas, the child fell in.
Beneath the raft the water took him,
For the current was so strong,
And before they could rescue him
He was drowned and was gone.

Oh! how sad were his kind parents
When they saw their drowned child,
As they brought him from the water,
It almost made their hearts grow wild.
Oh! how mournful was the parting
From that little infant son.
Friends, I pray you, all take warning,
Be careful of your little ones.

In the first decades of the twentieth century, the attitudes toward death did not change radically from those at the end of the previous one. Samuel McChord Crothers ended his *The Endless Life* (1905) with the allegory of Mr. Honest who dies peacefully: "Our doubts and fears vanish when we see Mr. Honest standing by the river's bank talking with happy earnestness with his friend Good-conscience. . . . Those who share that faith recognize, in all humility, their own limitations." And G. Lowes Dickinson in *Is Immortality Desirable?* decides, to no one's surprise, that it is: "To sum up, then, the immortality which I hold to be desirable, and which I suggest to you as desirable, is one in which a continuity of experience analogous to that which we are aware of here is carried on into a life after death, the essence of that life being continuous unfolding no doubt through stress and conflict, of those potentialities of Good of which we are aware here as the most significant part of ourselves."

Such attitudes remained typical through the middle part of the twentieth century; and indeed, it is possible to find some writers even in the seventh decade who claim to hold such traditional views. However, the growing importance of science, including the science of trying to understand the mind, and the diminishing importance of religion have changed attitudes. But some of the most significant changes in the attitudes toward death have resulted from other societal changes. The concept of the family has changed from one in which there were several generations of one family living under the same roof (as with the fictional Walton family on television) to one in which there are normally only two generations within a household—and then only until the children are old enough to move out on their own. This change, coupled with the growth of homes for the elderly and with increased mobility, means that children are less likely to see their grandparents die.

Another factor influencing that phenomenon is the growth of modern hospital facilities and the tendency for the aging to spend their last weeks in a hospital, both benefiting and suffering from life-prolonging treatment. The result is that very few people die at home now, as people did a century ago. If a person does not die accidentally on a highway, the likelihood is that he or she will die in the unfamiliar surroundings of a hospital room. The entire family probably will not be present, and surely the youngest children will be absent. One result of these changes is that children are likely to reach adulthood before they are in the presence of a dying person; the act of death becomes a mystery only to be described by older persons, or perhaps never even discussed at all.

Another change in our society that has influenced our attitudes concerns the growing dependence on the funeral home for its services. Early in this century, the undertaker would come to the home of the deceased and embalm the body there. It would be laid out in the parlor until time for the services and the body would then probably have been taken to a church for the religious service and from there to the grave site for burial. Many changes began to alter this procedure. First, the process of embalming was moved to the facilities of the undertaker, where the family was not bothered with the unpleasantness of it and where the risks of spreading contagious diseases were diminished. Then, many people found that rising building costs were forcing them to forego the luxury of a parlor, which formerly had been little used except for Sunday afternoon visits from the preacher and for funerals. Some houses were built without parlors, and, in others, the television set was moved in and the room became the family room or den, hardly places suitable for the display of a body. To complicate matters more, the size of the front door was reduced for architectural reasons, and the caskets would no longer fit through. The result was that the undertaker began to provide space in his building for the display of the body and for visitation by family and friends. The presence of death was taken from the home and moved to this other place, significantly called a "funeral home," and the room set aside for visitation was called the "parlor." The person who operated such an establishment no longer simply performed the basic services of an undertaker, but became a professional overseeing the entire process of the funeral. He, and even today he is almost always a man, gave himself a new title—"funeral director." He added a chapel to the building so that the body did not have to be taken to a church for services, and ultimately he relieved the family of much of the organizational responsibility for arranging for the disposition of a relative's body.

These changes mean that the presence of death is physically removed from the household and that some of the trauma of dealing with a death is passed from the hands of the family to those of a professional who is paid for his services. Those in the colonial period who complained about the high costs of funerals would be astounded by the bills presented today by hospitals, rest homes, and funeral directors for services rendered during a person's last days and the funeral that follows. But these professionals provide services that have become accepted by the large part of Americans at mid-twentieth century.

For many Americans, death has become an unfamiliar event, made mysterious and frightening by the fact that so few people experience its presence during their formative years. But there have been intellectual challenges to this system that have been influential. In 1963 Jessica Mitford wrote *The American Way of Death*, which was an exposé of the funeral industry. This book, and others like it, became the impetus for a more careful look at the funeral practices that had become so widely accepted. It challenged the necessity for embalming, expensive caskets, and elaborate cemetery plots; and some people began asking if the high expenses of a funeral were justified. The most pointed attack, however, was directed at the funeral directors themselves, who were accused of creating a myth about the value of their services. Mitford's book was sensational, and she used isolated cases, in some instances, to support her points; but the overall message of the book was accurate and led many people to question the methods of the American way of death.

Then, in 1969, Elizabeth Kubler-Ross wrote *On Death and Dying,* which became a major challenge to the way we have been treating our dying patients. Kubler-Ross, herself a medical doctor, demonstrated that often the dying patient is given good medical treatment but poor death counseling by medical professionals whose primary goal is the saving of life. Few physicians are trained to deal with the traumas of death and are not capable of assisting their patients with the problems of dying. Kubler-Ross has interviewed hundreds of dying patients and listened to their tales, and this book is in part a record of what they have told her and in part a plea for a better understanding and for more sensible treatment of the dying patient. It, like Mitford's book, has forced the American public to reconsider its attitude toward death.

These influences have led to mixed attitudes toward death in contemporary America. While the majority of Americans still insist on what they think of as a traditional view of death and funerals, there are signs that Mitford, Kubler-Ross, and others have had their impact. That attitudes have been changed somewhat is reflected in the general acceptance of college courses and church seminars on death, newspaper and magazine articles on the costs of funerals, memorial societies that discuss alternative means of disposing of the body, and television shows that even bring the presence of death into situation comedies. Suggestions for reform, however, meet with widespread resistance, and demonstrate that attitudes toward death are deep seated in our society. It is difficult to say whether the attitudes toward death in today's society lean toward tradition or openness; probably the former, but the tendency toward openness suggests that there may be continuing changes in attitudes.

BIBLIOGRAPHY

Aries, Philippe. *The Hour of Our Death.* New York: Knopf, 1981.

Badham, Paul. *Christian Beliefs About Life After Death.* New York: Barnes and Noble, 1976.

Beauchamp, Tom L., and Seymour Perlin. *Ethical Issues in Death and Dying.* Englewood Cliffs, N.J.: Prentice-Hall, 1978.

Becker, Ernest. *The Denial of Death.* New York: Macmillan, 1973.

Bermann, Eric. *Scapegoat: The Impact of Death-Fear on an American Family.* Ann Arbor: University of Michigan Press, 1973.

Bowman, Leroy. *The American Funeral: A Study in Guilt, Extravagance, and Sublimity.* Westport, Conn.: Greenwood Press, 1959.

Dumont, Richard G., and Dennis C. Foss. *The American View of Death: Acceptance or Denial.* Cambridge, Mass.: Schenkman Publishing, 1972.

Funeral Industry Practices. Washington, D.C.: Bureau of Consumer Protection. Federal Trade Commission, 1978.

Funerals: Consumers Last Right. Mount Vernon, N.Y.: Consumers Union, 1977.

Furman, Erna. *A Child's Parent Dies: Studies in Childhood Bereavement.* New Haven: Yale University Press, 1974.

Habenstein, Robert W., and William Lamers. *The History of American Funeral Directing.* Milwaukee, Wis.: Bulfin Printers, 1962.

Harlow, Rabbi Jules, ed. *The Bond of Life: A Book for Mourners.* New York: The Rabbinical Assembly, 1975.

Harmer, Ruth Mulvey. *The High Cost of Dying.* New York: Collier Books, 1963.

Jackson, Charles O. *Passing: The Vision of Death in America.* Westport, Conn.: Greenwood Press, 1977.

Kubler-Ross, Elizabeth. *Living with Death and Dying.* New York: Macmillan, 1981.

______. *On Death and Dying.* New York: Macmillan, 1969.

Kutscher, Austin H., Jr., and Austin H. Kutscher, eds. *A Bibliography of Books on Death, Bereavement, Loss, and Grief: 1935-1968.* New York: Health Science Publishing, 1969.

Kutscher, Austin H., Jr., and Martin Kutscher. *A Bibliography of Books on Death, Bereavement, Loss, and Grief: Supplement 1, 1968-1972.* New York: Health Science Publishing, 1974.

Mack, Arien, ed. *Death in the American Experience.* New York: Schocken Books, 1974.

Miller, Albert Jay, and Michael James Acri. *Death: A Bibliographic Guide.* Metuchen, N.J.: Scarecrow Press, 1977.

Mitford, Jessica. *The American Way of Death.* New York: Simon and Schuster, 1963.

Moody, Ralph, Jr. *Life After Life.* New York: Bantam Books, 1975.

Russell, O. Ruth. *Freedom to Die: Moral and Legal Aspects of Euthanasia.* New York: Human Sciences Press, 1975.

Stannard, David E., ed. *Death in America.* Philadelphia: University of Pennsylvania Press, 1975.

______. *The Puritan Way of Death: A Study in Religion, Culture, and Social Change.* New York: Oxford University Press, 1977.

Toynbee, Arnold, et al. *Man's Concern with Death.* New York: McGraw-Hill, 1968.

Weir, Robert F., ed. *Ethical Issues in Death and Dying.* New York: Columbia University Press, 1977.

Debate and Public Address

Robert H. Janke

A study of debate and public address as an element of American popular culture could appropriately begin with a frequently quoted statement by William Norwood Brigance from the preface to his celebrated work, *A History and Criticism of American Public Address:* "Most of the mighty movements affecting the destiny of the American nation have gathered strength in obscure places from the talk of nameless men, and gained final momentum from leaders who could state in common words the needs and hopes of common people."[1] This momentum might come from the sophisticated inaugural address of a patrician president or from the outspoken words of an uneducated civil rights worker. Great speakers through the ages have shared the ability to move their listeners to action, whether at a political meeting, a religious assembly, or an outdoor rally, or through broadcasts on radio and television. In the democratic American process, the people, responding either directly or indirectly to these speakers, take action that determines the course of historical events. This essay deals with such speakers and their words.[2]

The history of debate and public address in the United States is, in essence, the religious, political, and social history of the nation. Therefore, a compact treatment of value to the student should include, in chronological order, a selection of the most significant speakers, popular issues, and contemporary events that have contributed to this history.

The most significant speakers of early New England were the preachers, who exerted considerable influence, for they were also leaders and teachers whose sermons adapted the established theology to everyday application. What many consider to be the first notable speech delivered in America is John Winthrop's speech on liberty. Winthrop, who was chosen the first governor of the Massachusetts Bay Colony, opposed broad democracy. In 1635, he argued that man was not free to do simply as he wished but must submit to civil and lawful authority, an authority which encompassed a moral covenant between God and man, an authority which was looked upon as the "ecclesiastical elect."

This theological approach, known as theocracy, was upheld by four generations of the Mather family, who, as America's first dynasty, were predominant in shaping the lives of the colonists during the later seventeenth and early eighteenth centuries. Richard Mather advocated the liberalizing of the means to attain church membership; his son, Increase Mather, assuming the pastorate of Boston's North Church, upheld the Puritan views of church and state. Increase's son, Cotton Mather, became recognized as New England's leading preacher. He spoke out on the vital issues of the time, including support for the inoculation against smallpox, but he is known today largely for his part in the Salem witch trials of 1692. Cotton's son, Samuel Mather, the fourth generation of the dynasty, succeeded his father and grandfather as pastor of North Church but was less influential than his illustrious predecessors.

Changing concepts in religion gradually spread throughout the Colonies. Soloman Stoddard, preacher in Northampton, Massachusetts, espoused a doctrine of predestination. In 1727, he was succeeded in the pulpit by his grandson, Jonathan Edwards. From among Edwards' hundreds of sermons, the best known is "Sinners in the Hands of an Angry God," preached in 1741, which epitomized his theme that all men were sinners facing damnation and could be saved only through God's arbitrary, predestined choice. Traveling evangelist George Whitefield preached more than 18,000 sermons, primarily on New Calvinism, which offered personal salvation through the acceptance of Christ and sanctioned a sense of freedom previously unknown to the Colonists.

During this same period the seeds of freedom were also developing in the political sphere. The concept of the town meeting, which took many forms throughout the Colonies, gave the Colonists the opportunity to air grievances and discuss issues in a democratic manner. Increasingly these issues centered on British rule and the union of the Colonies. As early as 1754, addressing the representatives to the congress at Albany, Benjamin Franklin of Philadelphia advocated a confederation. In Boston, Samuel Adams, a highly effective orator, aroused the citizens to the cause with his fiery speeches, one in particular delivered in Faneuil Hall in 1770 following the massacre of five colonists by British soldiers; at a meeting three years later his heated oratory triggered the dumping of the tea into Boston harbor.

While such men as Samuel Adams and his compatriot James Otis were addressing assemblies for the revolutionary cause in Boston, Patrick Henry was arguing for American independence in Virginia. His speech in that state's House of Burgesses in opposition to King George III's Stamp Act of 1765, delivered to shouts of "Treason!" is recognized as a triumph in American oratory. Henry's statement delivered on March 23, 1775, at St. John's Church in Richmond, is now part of American folklore: "I know not what course others may take; but as for me, give me liberty, or give me death!"[3]

Some of the most intense and significant debates of this period in American history took place in 1787 and 1788 as the various states deliberated the proposed Federal Constitution. In Virginia, the opponents were evenly matched. The Antifederalists, led by Patrick Henry who thought that Virginia should refrain from immediate ratification, lost by a narrow margin to the Federalists, led by James Madison who cogently refuted the points made by Henry. In a similar dispute in New York, Alexander Hamilton's oratory in favor of the Federalist cause defeated the Antifederalists under the leadership of Governor Clinton. Eventually the Constitution was ratified, and the fledgling government was launched as George Washington assumed the presidency in 1789. Washington's statement from his "Farewell Address" of 1797 is frequently quoted in political debate: " 'Tis our true policy to steer clear of permanent alliances with any portion of the foreign world."[4]

The popular issues treated in the debates and public addresses during the first half of the nineteenth century included such matters as tariffs, New England manufacturing, foreign interests, centralization of government, expansion, internal improvements, sectionalism, slavery, nullification, and secession. These issues were debated at thousands of rallies, platforms, and "stumps" across the country, as well as in the famed halls of the nation's capitol.

Three of America's most distinguished orators emerged during this early national period, a period referred to as America's Golden Age of Oratory: Henry Clay from the West, the North's Daniel Webster, and the Southerner John C. Calhoun, known as the Great Triumvirate. Clay's eloquent speech on the New Army Bill delivered before the House in 1813, rallied the forces necessary to bring the War of 1812 to a successful conclusion. In 1824 his speech to the House on the Greek Revolution, supporting the Greeks in their conflict with the Turks, was received abroad with great interest. Clay, popularly called the Great Pacificator during the Missouri controversy in 1820, continued to play this role throughout his long career. Daniel Webster, considered America's foremost public speaker, was known equally for his political, legal, and platform or special occasion speaking. He is best remembered for his debate in the Senate in 1830 with Robert Y. Hayne of South Carolina, who argued for the states' right of nullification, the right to put liberty first and union afterward. Webster's famous reply, concluding with the statement, "Liberty *and* Union, now and forever, one and inseparable!"[5] has ever since been identified with popular American oratory. Calhoun was the most effective orator from the South, a leading spokesman for states' rights and slavery. But in the final speech of his career, on the Clay Compromise Measures of 1850, he could not persuade his fellow senators to support his stand against Clay and Webster in their combined efforts to preserve the Union.

Other prominent public speakers of the early nineteenth century included

John Quincy Adams, known for his compromises on the Treaty of Ghent and arguments for the Monroe Doctrine; Thomas Hart Benton, long-time senator from Missouri whose oratorical skills were directed at western expansion; and Thomas Corwin, political leader from Ohio whose speech, "Against War with Mexico," delivered to the Senate, caused him to be burned in effigy as a traitor in 1847.

Some twenty years earlier had begun an era of what was called platform speaking, reflected in the emergence and development of professional orators who addressed themselves, either voluntarily or for a fee, to specific issues, usually concerned with some demand for social reform, such as abolition, women's rights, or prohibition.

Antislavery spokesmen included William Lloyd Garrison of Massachusetts, who agitated against slavery through the New England Antislavery Society, the American Antislavery Society, and numerous other abolitionist societies which he helped to establish; Wendell Phillips, public orator noted for his speech delivered in 1837 to an overflowing crowd in Boston's Faneuil Hall on the murder of abolitionist Elijah Lovejoy; and Charles Sumner, who is best known for his offensive "Crime against Kansas" speech, delivered to the Senate in 1856 in opposition to the Kansas-Nebraska bill. (This speech resulted in Sumner's being severely assaulted by his opponents and left unconscious on the floor of the Senate.) Edward Everett was a well-known and highly skilled orator who, as circumstances evolved, was the principal speaker at the ceremony dedicating the cemetery on the battlefield at Gettysburg in 1863, an occasion made famous by the brief address of Abraham Lincoln.

Numerous blacks also spoke in public on the slavery question, chief among these being Frederick Douglass, an exslave whose greatest speeches included "The Meaning of July Fourth for the Negro," delivered in Corinthian Hall, Rochester, New York, on July 5, 1852, and the "West India Emancipation" speech delivered at Canandaigua, New York, on August 4, 1857. Other black speakers prominent during this period were Charles Lennox Remond, Henry Highland Garnet, Samuel Ringgold Ward, James McCune Smith, and Robert Purvis. Some decades later, Booker T. Washington, founder of Tuskegee Institute, became the major voice of the Negro. His most celebrated speech, delivered in Atlanta, Georgia, at the Cotton States and International Exposition in 1895, while conceding that progress would be a struggle, sought the "blotting-out of sectional differences and racial animosities and suspicions."[6]

Abraham Lincoln was among the most effective popular orators of the mid-century period. Upon accepting the Republican nomination in Illinois for the U.S. Senate in 1858, he declared: "A house divided against itself cannot stand. I believe this government cannot endure, permanently half *slave* and half *free*."[7] His opponent, Stephen A. Douglas, the Little Giant, refuted Lincoln's statement several weeks later by arguing that the people should have the right to decide for themselves. The stage was thus set for a series of seven debates which attracted audiences numbering into the thousands across the prairies of Illinois. These debates are still the best known in American history. Although Douglas won the Senate seat, the debates provided the path to the presidency for Lincoln only two years later. Lincoln's masterpiece, the "Gettysburg Address," delivered on November 19, 1863, and since memorized by millions of schoolchildren, ranks among the world's great speeches. Also considered a special work of oratorical literature is his "Second Inaugural Address," delivered March 4, 1865, famed for the words: "With malice toward none, with charity for all, with firmness in the right as God gives us to see the right, let us strive on to finish the work we are in."[8]

Following the Civil War the issues facing the nation were new and varied, but no popular debate topic was more crucial than that dealing with the reconstruction of the Southern states. Robert G. Ingersoll was known for his verbal brilliance while defending the cause of the Northern Republicans. Georgia's Henry Grady became known as the spokesman for the New South.

A distinctive feature of this era of platform speaking, a period when the role of women in American society was universally acknowledged as being inferior to that of men, was that women, despite resistance and sometimes ridicule, emerged as public speakers on popular issues. With an address on July 4, 1828, in New Harmony, Indiana, Frances Wright became the first woman orator, appealing for reforms in education. Other women orators followed, such as Angelina Grimké, a Southerner who moved Northern audiences to the antislavery cause, and Abbey Kelley Foster, who spoke out fiercely on the issues of women's rights and temperance, often denouncing her audiences and frequently meeting with public disapproval. The speaking career of Ernestine L. Rose was largely concerned with human rights, particularly the rights of women; and Lucy Stone traveled and spoke extensively for women's rights. Pioneer black women orators, concerned mainly with antislavery and women's rights, were Sojourner Truth, Frances Ellen Watkins Harper, and Sarah P. Remond. In 1848 in Seneca Falls, New York, Elizabeth Cady Stanton addressed the first Women's Rights Convention, which she and Lucretia Mott had promoted. A leading advocate for the cause of prohibition was Frances E. Willard, who crusaded widely for temperance, presiding over the National Women's Christian Temperance Union and eventually broadening her advocacy to include labor reform and women's liberation.

Susan B. Anthony was foremost in the women's movement as a speaker and organizer. She lectured for more than forty-five years, and her influence on popular culture was reflected in 1979 when her likeness was sculptured for the obverse of the one dollar coin.

During the nineteenth century two uniquely American media concerned with public address were the "lyceums" and the "Chautauquas." Thousands of lyceums, organized and staffed by civic-minded volunteers, flourished in cities across the nation at this time, operating mainly in auditoriums during the winter months. Originally intended to provide a platform for series of educational lectures by local specialists, the lyceums soon attracted the nation's leading statesmen and scholars touring as professional lecturers, drawing large crowds, and earning large fees. The long list of traveling speakers included such prominent personalities as Henry Ward Beecher, Ralph Waldo Emerson, Horace Greeley, Oliver Wendell Holmes, James Russell Lowell, Theodore Parker, and Daniel Webster. Wendell Phillips's "The Lost Arts," delivered some two thousand times over a period of forty years, was a major attraction.

The Chautauquas originated and operated in a different manner. At Lake Chautauqua, New York, during the summer of 1874, John H. Vincent offered a program of lecture courses. Based on the success and growth of his project, he acquired a partner, Keith Vawter, and in 1904 organized what became known as "traveling Chautauquas." The Chautauquas, traveling with tents mostly through the rural areas during the summer months, were particularly popular with the masses, and their programs featuring distinguished speakers on appealing topics catered to mass tastes. William Jennings Bryan and Russell H. Conwell were audience favorites. Conwell presented his lecture, "Acres of Diamonds," to over six thousand audiences during a period of more than fifty years and with his huge profits founded Temple University. It is estimated that during a single year Chautauqua programs were offered in some ten thousand communities, with a total audience of four million.

As the various lyceums either disappeared or merged to form literary societies during the period after the Civil War, newly formed lecture bureaus supplied speakers who gave audiences what they wanted to hear, utilizing local facilities for public address and providing eminent speakers for substantial fees. James B. Pond became a major entrepreneur whose contracted speakers included the best that money could attract: Henry Ward Beecher, Chauncey M. Depew, John B. Gough, Robert G. Ingersoll, and Wendell Phillips, to name only a few. Mark Twain was extremely successful on the lecture circuit, earning more money from public address than from publication. With the coming of the economic depression of 1929, the traveling Chautauqua phenomenon waned, but through the 1930s and 1940s lecture bureaus continued to supply large and enthusiastic audiences with such speakers as Richard Halliburton, Eleanor Roosevelt, and Lowell Thomas.

From the early days of Colonial "theocracy" through the expansion into the many different denominations existing today, the clergy wielded considerable persuasive power. Some of these individuals made significant contributions to American popular culture. Theodore Parker's noteworthy sermon, "The Transient and the Permanent in Christianity," delivered in a South Boston church in 1841, established him as an advocate of modernist doctrines and aroused wide criticism. He became known for his sermons against slavery, the most noted being his denunciation of Webster for his speech of March 7, 1850. Henry Ward Beecher, like his father, Lyman

Beecher, was a powerful orator for many causes, including the antislavery movement, and is recognized as the greatest American preacher of the nineteenth century. His "Memorial Sermon on Abraham Lincoln," delivered April 23, 1865, is a sublime example of oratorical tribute.

Skillfully organized revivalism became big business during the latter half of the nineteenth century, and the best-known revivalist was Dwight L. Moody. Not ordained, Moody preached in convention halls, warehouses, and theaters to audiences numbering well into the thousands. Following Moody by a generation and addressing audiences into the early decades of the twentieth century, Billy (William A.) Sunday, a former baseball player with the Chicago White Sox, also not ordained, continued in the tradition of Moody in "saving souls." Sunday was an energetic preacher who put sawdust on the floor so that sinners would not make a noise as they walked down the aisle to the foot of his speaking platform, a ritual known as "hitting the sawdust trail." Archbishop Fulton J. Sheen, a Roman Catholic traditionalist with a commanding presence and a sharp intellect, brought his evangelism to a radio and television audience estimated at thirty million at its peak. His television program, "Life Is Worth Living," won an Emmy Award in 1952. Presently, Billy (William F.) Graham, the foremost Protestant evangelist, attracts large audiences with a quiet yet forceful and sincere manner. A recurrent theme of Graham's sermons calls for humility before God.

As the nineteenth century drew to a close, the Populists were advocating free coinage of silver, agrarian reform, and a graduated federal income tax. Involved in these issues was the most prominent speaker of the period, William Jennings Bryan, a Nebraskan Democrat with Jeffersonian principles. His address to the Democratic convention in Chicago in 1896, "The Cross of Gold," advocating the cause of labor and the farmer, is considered a highpoint in convention oratory. Bryan had a long and popular career as a proponent for humanity, democracy, and religious orthodoxy, which culminated in 1924 in the world-famous Scopes "Monkey Trial" in Dayton, Tennessee, where he argued eloquently for the cause of the divine creation of man. He was resoundingly defeated by Clarence S. Darrow, the lawyer for the defense of the theory of evolution.

The popular hero of the Spanish-American War, Theodore Roosevelt, New York Republican, assuming the presidency in 1901, spoke extensively and successfully to break up the trusts of big business and the railroads and to promote conservation. Roosevelt's well-known speech calling for decency in government, "The Man with the Muck-Rake," delivered in Washington, D.C., in 1906, reflected the tenor of the time. Other progressives noted for public address were also campaigning for reform, including Albert J. Beveridge, Robert M. LaFollette, and William E. Borah.

In the early years of the twentieth century, issues of war and peace, as well as reform, engulfed Democratic President Woodrow Wilson, a crusading, intellectual speaker. Wilson's famous "Peace Without Victory" speech delivered to the Senate on January 21, 1917, intended to convince the warring European powers to resolve their conflict, was to no avail: three months later, on April 2, Wilson had to appear before a joint session of Congress to ask for a declaration of war. This momentous "War Message" was enthusiastically endorsed, and the nation embarked on its first world war. Following the conclusion of this war, against strong opposition from the Senate led by Henry Cabot Lodge, Wilson traveled to Versailles, and on January 25, 1919, appealed to the international delegates for the formation of a League of Nations as a means to render justice and maintain peace. Although the world was not then ready for Wilson's idealistic dream, his concepts would find realistic expression a generation later in the formation of the United Nations.

Faced with the darkest depression known in this country, Democrat Franklin D. Roosevelt assumed the presidency on March 4, 1933, and the era of the New Deal was launched. His inaugural address, transmitted by radio, was heard by more people than any previous public address, and his words brought a renewal of hope and confidence:

> This great Nation will endure as it has endured, will revive and prosper. So, first of all, let me assert my firm belief that the only thing we have to fear is fear itself—nameless, unreasoning, unjustified terror which paralyzes needed efforts to convert retreat into advance.[9]

A week later, on March 12, Roosevelt gave his first radio "fireside chat," in which he personalized the workings of government. The fireside chat's success was immediate. Roosevelt continued to bring the problems and solutions of government directly to the people, who responded by backing him in his programs for recovery and reform. Roosevelt used a fireside chat as a means of addressing the nation on December 9, 1941, after the Japanese had attacked Pearl Harbor: "Together with other free peoples, we are now fighting to maintain our right to live among our world neighbors in freedom and in common decency, without fear of assault. . . . We are going to win the war and we are going to win the peace that follows."[10]

The "peace that followed" ushered in an era known as the Cold War. An "iron curtain," a term employed by Winston Churchill in a speech delivered at Westminster College in Fulton, Missouri, on March 5, 1946, was drawn between the forces of communism and the free peoples of the Western world. Democratic President Harry Truman, faced with a major crisis when the communist army of North Korea invaded South Korea in June 1950, used a radio address to declare a national emergency. Less than a year later, in an historic controversy over military policy, Truman relieved General of the Army Douglas MacArthur of his command of the United Nations Forces in the Far East, and MacArthur was honored with an invitation to address a joint session of Congress. On April 19, 1951, the respected World War II hero, receiving a tremendous ovation, stated his position and bid good-bye:

But I still remember the refrain of one of the most popular barrack ballads of that day which proclaimed most proudly that "Old soldiers never die; they just fade away." And like the old soldier of that ballad, I now close my military career and just fade away—an old soldier who tried to do his duty as God gave him the light to see that duty.[11]

A new type of participatory government, made possible by electronics, was introduced with the debates and public addresses of the two national political conventions and the succeeding presidential campaigns in 1952, when for the first time these proceedings were brought directly to the people coast-to-coast via television. Never before had so many people witnessed history in the making. The Republicans nominated General of the Army Dwight D. Eisenhower; the Democrats nominated the articulate governor of Illinois, Adlai E. Stevenson. Eisenhower was elected by the largest popular vote ever cast for a presidential candidate, and his "Inaugural Address," televised on January 20, 1953, was the first to be seen and heard by millions of people throughout the country.[12]

The power of television as an element in determining the course of political events was dramatically emphasized during the fall of 1960, when the Republican candidate for the presidency, Vice President Richard M. Nixon, faced the Democratic nominee, Senator John F. Kennedy. Although the original impression of the electorate was that the candidates were equally qualified, Kennedy's fluency and charisma, transmitted to millions of viewers through the medium of television, carried the debates and, ultimately, the election. Kennedy's concise, eloquent "Inaugural Address," telecast on January 20, 1961, noted for its epigram, "Ask not what your country can do for you—ask what you can do for your country,"[13] sought to inspire a new beginning, a New Frontier, in attempts to solve problems both at home and abroad.

The major domestic problem facing the nation during this period was civil rights. In the forefront of black protest was Martin Luther King, Jr., who delivered hundreds of speeches and organized marches, boycotts, and sit-ins to achieve his vision of nonviolent integration. King's "I Have a Dream" speech, delivered on August 28, 1963, from the steps of the Lincoln Memorial to a crowd of more than 200,000 blacks and whites who had marched on Washington, is the most renowned public address of the civil rights movement. Advocating an opposing point of view was Malcolm X (Malcolm Little), whose address, "The Ballot or the Bullet," delivered on April 3, 1964, in Cleveland, pressed for black nationalism. Black rhetoric became more militant with Stokely Carmichael, who coined the slogan, "Black Power," and H. Rap Brown, who threatened armed confrontation. The revolutionary public statements of Black Panthers Huey P. Newton, Eldridge Cleaver, and Bobby Seale expressed the ideology of Marx and Lenin. As the struggle continued into the 1970s, the debate and public address of black revolution became less inflammatory.

Concurrent with black agitation as a vital oratorical issue was the complex problem of the war in Vietnam. The question of how to achieve a permanent peace divided the nation. President Kennedy's commencement address at American University, delivered June 10, 1963, calling for peaceful solutions to international problems, led to the Nuclear Test Ban Treaty and detente with the Soviet Union. Outspoken against appeasement with the Soviet Union was conservative Republican Senator Barry M. Goldwater, whose speech delivered at a rally sponsored by the Detroit Economic Club on March 25, 1964, urged for peace through strength. As the Vietnam War continued, prominent vocal advocates of peace included Senators J. William Fulbright, George McGovern, Eugene McCarthy, and Robert F. Kennedy. The administration's Vietnam policy was openly probed on television by the Senate Foreign Relations Committee. Amid great dissension within the leadership of his own party, Democratic President Lyndon B. Johnson in an historic nationally televised address on March 31, 1968, announced both the cessation of bombing in Vietnam and his decision to resign at the end of his term. Unrest in the country was strong. Educators, clergymen, and other groups addressed themselves to the war issue, but young people across the nation became the most potent voice for peace. Hundreds of student demonstrations and protests on college and university campuses, some peaceful, others violent, emphatically expressed opposition to the war. Such public expression undoubtedly contributed greatly to the ceasefire agreement, effective January 28, 1973, with which the Nixon administration brought U.S. involvement in Vietnam to a close.

During this same period, the Space Age became a popular issue of debate and public address. Astronaut John H. Glenn, Jr., following his orbital flight around the earth, an exploit witnessed by an estimated 135 million television viewers, declared before a joint session of Congress on February 26, 1962, that "what we have done so far are but small building blocks in a huge pyramid to come."[14] Seven years later, on July 20, 1969, Neil Armstrong became the first human being to set foot on the moon, the first person to address the planet Earth from a planetary body. Millions of people all over the world watched and listened as Armstrong proclaimed: "That's one small step for a man, one giant leap for mankind."[15]

During the 1970s, one of the popular issues debated endlessly was women's rights, including the passage of the Equal Rights Amendment. This issue was exemplified by the public addresses and activities of Representative Shirley Chisholm, the first black woman elected to Congress, who in 1972 actively sought the Democratic presidential nomination. Other prominent issues of the decade included the energy crisis, culminating in an antinuclear rally in Washington, D.C., in 1979; and homosexual or "gay" rights, whose activists also marched on Washington during that year.

Earlier, the 1976 presidential campaign had been distinguished by three nationally televised debates between Republican President Gerald R. Ford and Democratic candidate Jimmy Carter, marking the first such encounter since the Kennedy-Nixon debates. Four years later, on October 28, 1980, incumbent President Carter faced Republican candidate Ronald Reagan in a single televised debate witnessed by more than one hundred million Americans. Although the impact of these conflicts on the electorate was considered difficult to assess, they afforded maximum mass involvement in debate and public address.

The debate and public address, however, having the greatest impact on popular culture during the past decade focused on two historic events. First, as part of the aftermath of the Watergate incident, the American public witnessed the televised debate by the Committee on the Judiciary of the House of Representatives in 1974, as members considered the possible impeachment of President Nixon. Less than two weeks later, in an address unprecedented in American history, speaking to the nation via television from the White House, Nixon announced his resignation.

The other historic event of major oratorical importance during this period was the celebration of the United States' Bicentennial during 1976. Speech activities across the nation involved many thousands, including students from more than 8,500 high schools, colleges, and universities, who argued pertinent topics as part of the Bicentennial Youth Debate program. At one Bicentennial ceremony, President Ford, in a brief address delivered at the National Archives in Washington, D.C., on July 2, 1976, praised the far-sighted Americans who framed the Bill of Rights, "which protects us day and night in the exercise of our fundamental freedoms—to pray, to publish, to speak as we please."[16]

From the town meeting to the march on Washington, debate and public address, stimulated and magnified in modern times by radio and television, has been an integral part of American popular culture. Through the power of public speaking the American people have reached the crucial decisions that have governed the country as well as the personal choices by which they have lived. Essentially, the debate and public address of America's past not only has served the immediacy of particular occasions but also has provided a rich heritage of permanent and popular literature.

NOTES

1. William Norwood Brigance, ed., *A History and Criticism of American Public Address,* 2 vols. (New York: McGraw-Hill, 1943; reprint ed. New York: Russell & Russell, 1960), 1; vii.

2. Debate and public address in the United States are two distinct but related areas within the academic discipline of speech communication. The study of debate is frequently grouped with argumentation or included as a component of forensics, whereas the study of public address is often coupled with rhetoric. In this essay, however, debate and public address are considered as a single area of inquiry.

3. Patrick Henry, "Liberty or Death," in *American Speeches,* eds. Wayland Maxfield Parrish and Marie Hochmuth (New York: Longmans, Green, 1954), p. 94. Many

of the popular speeches from which brief passages are quoted in this essay, of course, can be found readily in other sources.

4. George Washington, "Farewell Address," in *Famous Speeches in American History,* ed. Glenn R. Capp (Indianapolis: Bobbs-Merrill, 1963), p. 40.

5. Daniel Webster, "Second Speech on Foote's Resolution—Reply to Hayne," in *American Speeches,* eds. Wayland Maxfield Parrish and Marie Hochmuth (New York: Longmans, Green, 1954), p. 229.

6. Booker T. Washington, "Atlanta Exposition Address," in *The Voice of Black America: Major Speeches by Negroes in the United States, 1797-1971,* ed. Philip S. Foner (New York: Simon and Schuster, 1972), p. 582.

7. Abraham Lincoln, "A House Divided," in *American Forum: Speeches on Historic Issues, 1788-1900,* eds. Ernest J. Wrage and Barnet Baskerville (New York: Harper & Brothers, 1960; reprint ed. Seattle: University of Washington Press, 1967), p. 180.

8. Abraham Lincoln, "Second Inaugural Address," in *Famous Speeches in American History,* ed. Glenn R. Capp (Indianapolis: Bobbs-Merrill, 1963), p. 94.

9. Franklin D. Roosevelt, "First Inaugural Address," in *Contemporary Forum: American Speeches in Twentieth-Century Issues,* eds. Ernest J. Wrage and Barnet Baskerville (New York: Harper & Brothers, 1962; reprint ed. Seattle: University of Washington Press, 1969), p. 157.

10. Franklin D. Roosevelt, "America's Answer to Japan's Challenge," in *Selected American Speeches on Basic Issues 1850-1950*), eds. Carl G. Brandt and Edward M. Shafter, Jr. (Boston: Houghton Mifflin Riverside Press, 1960), pp. 413, 420.

11. Douglas MacArthur, "American Policy in the Pacific," in *Representative American Speeches: 1951-1952,* Vol. 24, No. 3 of *The Reference Shelf,* ed. A. Craig Baird (New York: Wilson, 1952), p. 30.

12. There had been a limited television coverage of Harry Truman's inaugural address on January 20, 1949.

13. John F. Kennedy, "Inaugural Address," in *Representative American Speeches: 1960-1961,* Vol. 33, No. 3 of *The Reference Shelf,* ed. Lester Thonssen (New York: Wilson, 1961), p. 39.

14. John H. Glenn, Jr., "Address before the Joint Meeting of Congress," in *Representative American Speeches: 1961-1962,* Vol. 34, No. 4 of *The Reference Shelf,* ed. Lester Thonssen (New York: Wilson, 1962), p. 206.

15. Neil Armstrong, quoted by John Noble Wilford, "Astronauts Land on Plain; Collect Rocks, Plant Flag," *New York Times,* July 21, 1969, p. 1. See also Wernher Von Braun, "The First Men on the Moon," *Encyclopedia Americana,* International Ed., Vol. 25 (New York: Americana Corp., 1976), p. 360.

16. Gerald R. Ford, "Bicentennial of American Independence," in *Representative American Speeches: 1976-1977,* Vol. 49, No. 4 of *The Reference Shelf,* ed. Waldo W. Braden (New York: Wilson, 1977), p. 196.

BIBLIOGRAPHY

Adalian, Paul T., Jr., ed. *Speech Communication Abstracts.* Pleasant Hill, Calif.: Theatre/Drama & Speech Communication Information Center, 1974-.

Barrett, Harold, ed. *Rhetoric of the People: "Is There Any Better or Equal Hope in the World?"* Amsterdam: Rodopi N. V., 1974.

Baskerville, Barnet. *The People's Voice: The Orator in American Society.* Lexington: University Press of Kentucky, 1979.

Boulware, Marcus H. *The Oratory of Negro Leaders: 1900-1968.* Foreword by Alex Haley. Westport, Conn.: Negro Universities Press, 1969.

Braden, Waldo W., ed. *Oratory in the Old South: 1828-1860.* Baton Rouge: Louisiana State University Press, 1970.

Brigance, William Norwood, ed. *A History and Criticism of American Public Address.* 2 vols. New York: McGraw-Hill, 1943. Reprint. New York: Russell & Russell, 1960. See Hochmuth, Marie Kathryn, ed., below.

Brockett, Oscar G., Samuel L. Becker, and Donald C. Bryant. *A Bibliographical Guide to Research in Speech and Dramatic Art.* Glenview, Ill.: Scott, Foresman, 1963.

Browne, Ray B., ed. *Abstracts of Popular Culture: A Quarterly Publication of International Popular Phenomena.* Bowling Green, Ohio: Bowling Green University Popular Press, 1976-.

Cleary, James W., and Frederick W. Haberman, comps. and eds. *Rhetoric and Public Address: A Bibliography, 1947-1961.* Madison: University of Wisconsin Press, 1964.

Enos, Richard Leo, and Jeanne L. McClaran, eds. *A Guide to Doctoral Dissertations in Communication Studies and Theater.* Ann Arbor, Mich.: University Microfilms International, 1978.

Hochmuth, Marie Kathryn, ed. *A History and Criticism of American Public Address.* Vol. 3. New York: Longmans, Green, 1955. Reprint. New York: Russell & Russell, 1965. See Brigance, William Norwood, ed., above.

Holland, DeWitte, ed. *America in Controversy: History of American Public Address.* Dubuque, Iowa: Wm. C. Brown, 1973.

———. *Preaching in American History: Selected Issues in the American Pulpit, 1630-1967.* Nashville, Tenn.: Abingdon Press, 1969.

Jones, Louis Thomas. *Aboriginal American Oratory: The Tradition of Eloquence Among the Indians of the United States.* Los Angeles: Southwest Museum, 1965.

Kruger, Arthur N. *Argumentation and Debate: A Classified Bibliography.* 2d ed. Metuchen, N.J.: Scarecrow Press, 1975.

Matlon, Ronald J., comp. *Index to Journals in Communication Studies Through 1979.* Annandale, Va.: Speech Communication Association, 1980.

Miller, Marion Mills, ed. *Great Debates in American History: From the Debates in the British Parliament on the Colonial Stamp Act (1764-1765) to the Debates in Congress at the Close of the Taft Administration (1912-1913).* 14 vols. New York: Current Literature, 1913. Reprint. (3 vols.) Metuchen, N.J.: Mini-Print, 1970.

Mulgrave, Dorothy I., Clark S. Marlor, and Elmer E. Baker, Jr. *Bibliography of Speech and Allied Areas, 1950-1960.* Philadelphia: Chilton, 1962. Reprint. Westport, Conn.: Greenwood Press, 1972.

Oliver, Robert T. *History of Public Speaking in America.* Boston: Allyn and Bacon, 1965. Reprint. Westport, Conn.: Greenwood Press, 1978.

Speech Communication Directory, [1935-] (formerly *Speech Communication Association Directory*, and *Speech Association of America Directory*). Annandale, Va.: Speech Communication Association, 1935-.

Sutton, Roberta Briggs. *Speech Index: An Index to 259 Collections of World Famous*

Orations and Speeches for Various Occasions. 4th ed. rev. and enl. New York: Scarecrow Press, 1966. See also 4th ed. supp., 1966-1970, and 4th ed. supp., 1971-1975.

Tandberg, Gerilyn. *Research Guide in Speech.* Morristown, N.J.: General Learning Press, 1974.

Thonssen, Lester, and Elizabeth Fatherson, comps. *Bibliography of Speech Education.* New York: Wilson, 1939. See also supp., 1939-1948.

Tucker, Raymond K., Richard L. Weaver, II, and Cynthia Berryman-Fink. *Research in Speech Communication.* Englewood Cliffs, N.J.: Prentice-Hall, 1981.

Vital Speeches of the Day. Southold, N.Y., 1934-.

Wallace, Karl R., ed. *History of Speech Education in America: Background Studies.* New York: Appleton-Century-Crofts, 1954.

Detective and Mystery Fiction

Larry N. Landrum

Mystery and detective fiction have been among the most popular fictional genres to emerge in Western literature. The roots of mystery fiction have been traced into antiquity, and arguments have been made for the universality of many of its characteristics. Puzzles and narrative riddles are found in the folklore of all cultures, and the investigation of wrongdoing and the search for solutions to problems found in detective fiction reaches beyond recorded history. The particular forms that such interests take are not universal; they emerge in particular cultures at particular times, pass into and come to dominate appropriate modes of expression, and reveal tendencies found in their parent cultures. Detective stories demand keen observation, superior reasoning, and the disciplined imagination of their protagonists. The immediacy of physical danger may require a strong arm, fighting skills, or a quick gun. In any case the narrative must provide a suitable challenge with high enough stakes so that the measures taken by the detective seem appropriate.

Mysteries are less specialized than detective stories and often verge on the gothic. There is often some sense in which the mystery threatens to escape rational explanation. Such uncertainty is expressed in other ways: the narrator is vulnerable, caught in a web of intrigue, or susceptible to the frailties of ordinary people. The central figure of a mystery is usually the narrator, and the weight of suspense allows little distance between the narrator and the reader. In the detective story, distance is established by focusing the reader's attention on detection and often by placing the recorder of the experience, the Watson figure, between the reader and the detective. While many structural similarities suggest a common origin for gothic and mystery fiction, mysteries clearly reflect the growing influence of rational explanations of mysterious causes that marked early nineteenth-century popular literature.

The origins of the detective story, it is generally agreed, are found in the work of a single writer, Edgar Allan Poe. Though mystery and detection figure in numerous Poe stories, those that most influenced the detective tradition are "The Murders in the Rue Morgue" (1841), "The Mystery of Marie Rôget" (1842-43), and "The Purloined Letter" (1844). Most historians of the genre agree that nearly all the conventions of the classic detective story achieve their earliest coherent form in these tales, though later variations are important to the development of the genre.

Poe's major contribution was the celebration of independent observation and reason in the investigation of the murkier levels of human affairs. In "The Murders in the Rue Morgue," C. Auguste Dupin concludes a friend's train of thought for him by reconstructing the clues to his associative thoughts. In "The Mystery of Marie Rôget" the author attempts to solve a real crime by using only the evidence available to him in the newspapers; and in "The Purloined Letter," Dupin illustrates that imagination is crucial to the solution of problems conceived by intelligent criminals. Poe himself drew in part on the fanciful reminiscences of Francois Eugene Vidocq, a thief who was hired to catch criminals in Paris and who published his memoirs in 1828-29. Poe considered Vidocq only "a good guesser and a persevering man" who often erred because he failed to see the whole as well as the parts.

Numerous writers in subsequent years failed to mark Poe's caution and created a legion of detectives whose solutions relied heavily on luck. Others created police detectives rather than the inspired amateur or private investigator. In the long run, however, policemen were considered competition for the private detective or too dull or compromised or rule-bound for the serious intellectual business of crime detection, unless some special status gave them the freedom and independence to see the whole picture and the leisure to pursue the unusual and bizarre. Throughout much of the rest of the nineteenth century, the narrative form in which the detective appeared remained relatively open. The detective's investigation tended to merge in most novels with themes from gothic fiction, domestic romance, courtroom exposition, exposés, and picaresque adventure stories.

Developments in Europe often appeared in America almost simultaneously. Dickens' works were eagerly awaited and often pirated within a few days of publication. Only his Inspector Bucket in *Bleak House* (1852-53) and the unfinished novel, *The Mystery of Edwin Drood* (1870), have direct influence, but his descriptions of low life and sharply etched characters influenced popular writers on both sides of the Atlantic. Dickens' son-in-law Wilkie Collins came closer to the genre. The first of his books, *A Woman in White* (1860), finds a young artist called to a remote country house where mysteries began to build around a beautiful heroine and her stigmatized but brilliant sister. In the story told through witnesses' accounts, the young man is disappointed in love, disappears for a time from the narrative, then in book three returns to conduct an investigation that carries him into old court records and a battle of wits with a master criminal-spy. With the 1868 publication of *The Moonstone*, serialized in

America in *Harper's Weekly,* Collins captured many of the conventions and nuances that became formulas in later detective fiction.

However, it was Anna Katherine Green's *The Leavenworth Case* in 1878 that brought the disparate elements together for the classic detective novel. Her portly detective, Ebenezer Gryce, soon became well-known on both sides of the Atlantic. A novel of detection as well as mystery, *The Leavenworth Case* eliminated many of the threads of extraneous genres and created a suspense that kept readers close to the action. In the next decade Green's work was eclipsed by the shadow of Arthur Conan Doyle, whose work was as popular in the United States as it was in England. *A Study in Scarlet* (1886) got off to a slow start, but with the publication of Fergus Hume's *The Mystery of a Hansom Cab* in 1887, British detective fiction achieved a popularity that Doyle led for many years.

The classic story appeared in slick magazines and hardcover novels, making its strongest appeal to the upwardly mobile middle class. By the turn of the century the novel of pure detection and the mystery novel whose central figure was forced into uncertain detection were distinct genres and both were popular. Jacques Futrelle's *The Thinking Machine* (1907) stories featured observation and analysis. His short story, "The Problem of Cell 13," is a classic of its kind. R. Austin Freeman's Dr. Thorndyke, first appearing in *John Thorndyke's Cases* in 1909, was a scientist whose laboratory methods fascinated readers. Thorndyke carried a compact laboratory kit with which he was able to do immediate analysis of physical clues. In *The Singing Bone* (1912), Freeman tells the murderer's story, then allows the reader to follow the detective's investigative procedures, relying on the interest in the method of detection to hold his readers.

The mystery strain developed by Anna Katherine Green is polished to perfection in the mysteries of Mary Roberts Rinehart. Probably best known for her introduction of the "had I but known" element, Rinehart's handling of suspense led to many imitations. *The Circular Staircase* (1908) established her reputation as a mystery writer and subsequent novels made her one of America's highest paid authors. Carolyn Wells' *The Clue* (1909), the first of her Fleming Stone mysteries, led to a formulaic approach that she outlined in *The Technique of the Mystery Story* (1929). Many later mystery and detective writers would attempt to explain the secret of writing the successful mystery novel. The middle-class dream in the classic story is apparent in the novels of Willard Huntington Wright, who wrote under the pen name of S. S. Van Dine. His detective, Philo Vance, first appeared in *The Benson Murder Case* in 1926, a scholarly eccentric who carried out meticulously detailed investigations in a milieu of conspicuous consumption. Rex Stout avoids this tendency, or rather balances his opulent Nero Wolfe with the tough Archie Goodwin, an updated and sophisticated Watson figure. Stout's fiction, beginning with

Fer-de-lance (1934), represents a masterful balance of entertaining tales and detection.

If the tale of pure detection is expressed most faithfully in the seemingly impossible problem, then its most concise form is the locked room mystery, best expressed in America in the novels of John Dickson Carr, who also writes as Carter Dickson. Beginning with *It Walks by Night* (1929), Carr developed a series of fascinating puzzles for alert readers. In *The Hollow Man* (1935), his detective, Dr. Gideon Fell, launches into a lengthy thesis on types of locked room situations.

In this period, often called the "golden age" of detective fiction, Earl Derr Biggers' *The House Without a Key* (1925) began a series of novels that immortalized Charlie Chan, the Honolulu detective who inverted the image of the Oriental mastermind popularized in the Fu Manchu figure created by Sax Rohmer in the first decade of the twentieth century. Another detective that achieved immortality during this period was detective-author Ellery Queen. Created by Frederic Dannay and Manfred B. Lee in *The Roman Hat Mystery* (1929) and appearing in numerous subsequent stories and novels, Ellery Queen narrated his own novels and was drawn into cases to help his police inspector father. Queen has consistently given the reader a fair chance to solve the mystery, the "fair play" rule for writers, and has kept this tradition alive. Though the tight construction of the more or less pure story of detection continues to the present day, a second strain of detective fiction evolved that reached its peak in the 1930s. It is often seen as burgeoning independently out of the heads of a few key writers, but its roots are actually in the nineteenth century. The form that evolved out of the dime-novel tradition and reached its flowering in well fertilized pages of the pulps is the hard-boiled detective story.

The figure of the detective emerged slowly and tentatively in the story papers and dime novels from a vigilante figure of instant justice to a special representative of the government, and from the West to the urban East. The rise of the Eastern detective figure roughly parallels the shift of crime from the West to the East, or as Arthur Schlesinger notes, between the James Brothers' aborted attempt to rob the Northfield, Minnesota, bank on September 7, 1876, and the Jimmy Hope gang's $3,000,000 robbery of the Manhattan Savings Institution in New York on October 27, 1878. The first dime-novel detective is generally agreed to be the Old Sleuth, who first appeared as a serial titled, "Old Sleuth, the detective; or, The Bay Ridge Mystery" in the *New York Fireside Companion* in 1872.

The success of Green's *The Leavenworth Case* may have inspired editors to print translations of Emile Gaboriau's more adventurous French detective stories, and they appeared in quantities in 1879-80 and after. At least eighteen appeared in Munro's *Seaside Library* during these years. By 1883 the *New York Detective Library* and the *Old Cap Collier Library* were both entirely made up of detective stories. In 1885 the *Old Sleuth Library* began by reprinting the 1872 "Bay Ridge Mystery." Early paper libraries featured a variety of detectives of various ages, ethnic origins, occupations, and both sexes. Of these, Old King Brady and Nick Carter became most popular.

Though Old King Brady is now remembered mainly by collectors, over 100 Nick Carter stories have been reprinted recently in paperbacks. *The Nick Carter Weekly* began in 1891 and as late as 1933 there were still 400 paper volumes in print. J. Randolph Cox counted 78 serials and 115 short stories in *Street & Smith's New York Weekly*, 282 issues of the *Nick Carter Detective Library*, 819 issues of the *Nick Carter Weekly*, 160 issues of *Nick Carter Stories*, 127 issues of *Detective Story Magazine* and 40 issues of *Nick Carter Magazine*, as well as scattered stories elsewhere. The detective's exploits were written by various hands and have emerged in radio, film, and television. Nick Carter was a man of breeding, education, and polish who liked an after-dinner cigar and a glass of port, but he was also a tough man of action known for his great strength and courage. In short, he combined the classic attributes of the urban gentleman detective with the Western adventure hero.

Changes in the copyright law, the invention of cheaper wood pulp paper, the rise of yellow journalism and more widespread adult literacy made the pulps possible in the 1890s. Detectives appearing in pulp magazines were at first extensions of those in dime novels, but soon evolved into fully urbanized figures. Dialogue and backgrounds began to be more authentic and Prohibition made the underworld chic. Exposés of city politics and gangster activities, postwar disillusionment, and literary naturalism made conventional adventure heroes seem less believable. Though the relatively genteel puzzle story reached its greatest popularity during the first quarter of the twentieth century, hard-boiled detective fiction began to deal with the feelings and reactions of the lower middle class. Pulp detective stories circumvented the social restrictions of the classic story to reveal the shocking rawness of American materialism. Authenticity seemed to demand a rejection of the social complacency found in the formal story, to require a commitment that went beyond the specific investigation of a case. The metaphorical link that evolved in the 1920s was the contract between an independent detective and a person willing to pay for his services.

It is not surprising that writers should grope for a style to express feelings about the predatory quality of society nor that they should be drawn to follow the lead of writers who successfully captured them. The pattern can be seen in the detective fiction of *Black Mask* (1920-51), a magazine initially financed as a money-making scheme by George Jean Nathan and H. L. Mencken. The stories of Carroll John Daly, who created the detective Race Williams, owed much to the dime novels, but his stories had a grit and cold violence that were rare in earlier fiction. Within a few years the magazine, especially under the editorship of Joseph T. Shaw, had attracted a number of superior writers who refined and fashioned the violence into a style for the 1920s and 1930s. Numerous pulps, such as *Dime Detective, Detective Story, Detective Fiction Weekly,* and others picked up stories in the hard-boiled style. By the late 1940s, however, the pulps were disappearing.

Many of the pulp detective writers were soon forgotten and relatively few saw their work in hardcover editions. Some reached great fame as novelists as well as writers of detective fiction. Dashiell Hammett's work is probably most significant. From his *Red Harvest* (1929), which introduced the Continental Op, through *The Maltese Falcon* (1930) where the Op becomes the private detective Sam Spade, to the mystery, *The Glass Key* (1931), Hammett explored the potentials of the hard-boiled genre. Raymond Chandler wrote numerous stories for *Black Mask* and other pulps and became the spokesman for the hard-boiled school. Beginning with *The Big Sleep* (1939), Chandler's novels capture almost perfectly the balance between the vulnerable mystery narrator in a predatory milieu and the detective who must assert his solution to the crime.

If one of the risks of the classic story is that it becomes too mechanistically concerned with plot, a risk of the hard-boiled story is that the detective becomes an extension of the atmosphere rather than its mediator. Dashiell Hammett's Continental Op in *Red Harvest* feels himself afflicted with the epidemic killing in "Poisonville," and Mickey Spillane's Mike Hammer, in *I, The Jury* (1947) is stricken with the disease. Spillane became identified with the excesses and distortions of McCarthyism, but from 1947 to 1951 his first seven novels were bestsellers and have now sold about forty million copies. Many critics saw this formulaic expression of the hard-boiled world as a dead end, much as earlier critics had seen the puzzle story as the end of the classic detective story. Yet writers continue to produce variations on the puzzle story, and the violence implicit in the hard-boiled form continues to be metaphorically viable.

Erle Stanley Gardner had shown with his first Perry Mason novel, *The Case of the Velvet Claws* (1932), that the hard-boiled world could be softened by adopting some of the conventions of the classic detective story in the form of a courtroom drama. So successful was this approach that together with his other detective fiction Gardner sold more than one hundred million copies. Ross Macdonald (Kenneth Millar) represents another direction. His early novels are close to the Hammett tradition, but his later novels show a turn to greater subtlety in which his detective, Lew Archer, is an extension of the author's moral sensibilities. His *On Crime Writing* (1973) includes an essay on the writing of *The Galton Case* (1959). Chester Himes's detective fiction is similarly complex and hard-boiled, but while Macdonald compresses much of his violence into metaphor, Himes infuses his police detectives Coffin Ed Johnson and Grave Digger Jones with a picaresque comic spirit. Other contemporary writers have explored the potentials of mystery, as the superb work of Margaret Millar attests, or followed the criminal into the psychology of crime and social concepts of justice found in the work of Patricia Highsmith.

No single writer or school of writers presently dominates detective fiction, possibly because no investigative style can very accurately reflect the turbulent social conditions and attitudes of the times. Fictional detectives do not, as even their nineteenth-century detractors were fond of pointing out, correspond very closely to their real life counterparts. Instead they seem to represent a way of reflecting upon the darker social metaphors of life and the problems in the way to their understanding. Throughout the history of detective fiction, literal investigation has been closely followed by a more metaphorical form. Police memoirs and procedurals have been closely followed by fictional detectives who reestablish human proportions. Over time writers of detective and mystery fiction have evolved conventions that allow readers the opportunity to share in setting proportions right.

BIBLIOGRAPHY

Ball, John, ed. *The Mystery Story.* San Diego: University of California, in cooperation with Publishers's Inc., 1976.

Barzun, Jacques, and Wendell Hertig Taylor. *A Catalogue of Crime.* New York: Harper and Row, 1971.

Cawelti, John G. *Adventure, Mystery, and Romance.* Chicago: University of Chicago Press, 1976.

Champigny, Robert. *What Will Have Happened: A Philosophical and Technical Essay on Mystery Stories.* Bloomington: Indiana University Press, 1977.

Charney, Hanna. *The Detective Novel of Manners: Hedonism, Morality and the Life of Reason.* Rutherford, N.J.: Fairleigh Dickinson University Press, 1981.

Eames, Hugh. *Sleuths, Inc.: Studies of Problem Solvers: Doyle, Simenon, Hammett, Ambler, Chandler.* Philadelphia: J. B. Lippincott, 1980.

Hart, James D. *The Popular Book: A History of America's Literary Taste.* New York: Oxford University Press, 1950.

Haycraft, Howard, ed. *The Art of the Mystery Story: A Collection of Critical Essays.* New York: Simon and Schuster, 1946.

———. *Murder for Pleasure: The Life and Times of the Detective Story.* New York: Appleton-Century, 1941.

LaCour, Tabe, and Harold Morgensen. *The Murder Book: An Illustrated History of the Detective Story.* London: Allen and Unwin, 1971.

Landrum, Larry N., Pat Browne, and Ray B. Browne, eds. *Dimensions of Detective Fiction.* Bowling Green, Ohio: Bowling Green University Popular Press, 1976.

Macdonald, Ross. *On Crime Writing.* Santa Barbara, Calif.: Capra Press, 1973.

Mundell, E. H., and G. Ray Rausch, comps. *The Detective Short Story: A Bibliography and Index.* Manhattan: Kansas State University Library, 1974.

Murch, Alma Elizabeth. *The Development of the Detective Novel.* Port Washington, N.Y.: Kennikat Press, 1968.

Nevins, Francis N., ed. *The Mystery Writer's Art.* Bowling Green, Ohio: Bowling Green University Popular Press, 1971.

Reilly, John M., ed. *Twentieth-Century Crime and Mystery Writers.* New York: St. Martin's Press, 1980.

Ruehlmann, William. *Saint with a Gun: The Unlawful American Private Eye.* Washington, D.C.: American University Press, 1974.

Steinbrunner, Chris, and Otto Penzler. *Detectionary: A Biographical Dictionary of Leading Characters in Detective and Mystery Fiction, Including Famous and Little-Known Sleuths, Their Helpers, Rogues Both Heroic and Sinister, and Some of Their Most Memorable Adventures as Recounted in Novels, Short Stories, and Films.* Woodstock, N.Y.: Overlook Press, 1977.

______. *Encyclopedia of Mystery and Detection.* New York: McGraw-Hill, 1976.

Symons, Julian. *Mortal Consequences: A History from the Detective Story to the Crime Novel.* New York: Schocken Books, 1973.

Winks, Robin W. *Detective Fiction: A Collection of Critical Essays.* Englewood Cliffs, N.J.: Prentice-Hall, 1980.

Winn, Dilys. *Murder Ink: The Mystery Reader's Companion.* New York: Workman Publishing, 1977.

______. *Murderess Ink: The Better Half of the Mystery.* New York: Workman, 1979.

Editorial Cartoons

Nancy Pogel and
Paul P. Somers, Jr.

Although editorial cartooning has a long history in the United States, it originated in Europe. The key words—"cartoon" and "caricature"—derive from the Italian *cartone*, "a large sheet of paper," and *caricare*, "to exaggerate, change, or overload." The Englishman William Hogarth, whose moral indignation led him from fine art to satirical engravings denouncing the evils of his society, may be considered the first cartoonist. His successors, Thomas Rowlandson, George Cruikshank, and, especially, James Gillray, inspired emulation. Since that time, other Englishmen such as John Tenniel, David Low, and Ronald Searle, along with the Frenchmen Honoré Daumier and Jean Louis Forain, have influenced American artists. In recent years, the Australian Patrick Oliphant and the Canadian Paul Szep have become quite popular here. For the most part, however, the American editorial cartoonists have reflected the political and social moods of the nation, refining and simplifying their work to insure the maximum impact on a public with little time to ponder the complex drawings and lengthy captions of earlier times.

Herbert Block (Herblock) has defined the editorial cartoonist as "the kid who points out that the Emperor is without his clothes." From Ben Franklin to Jeff MacNelly, America has produced a long line of artists—left, right, and center—idealists and cynics whose work has tried to keep politics honest. Unfortunately, the political or editorial cartoonists who have not also been accepted by "high culture" enthusiasts as painters, printmakers, or major illustrators, have been relegated to secondary or backseat positions, as have so many artists in a variety of popular culture categories.

The editorial cartoon has been around much longer than the comic strip and it was taken seriously at an earlier date. No matter how poorly it was drawn or how tasteless it might have been, a widely distributed cartoon attacking a king or, in the United States, a president, could not be ignored.

American editorial cartooning probably began in 1747 with "Non Votis" or "The Wagoner and Hercules," the designing and/or drawing of which are attributed to Benjamin Franklin. Franklin is also associated with the second oldest extant political cartoon, "Join or Die," the representation of the colonies as a disjointed snake, which appeared in his *Pennsylvania Gazette* for May 9, 1754. The engraver was Paul Revere, whose 1770 engraving "The Boston Massacre" was widely circulated for its propaganda value. Revere had copied a drawing by Henry Pelham, stepbrother of John Singleton Copley.

Shortly before the Revolution, Franklin supposedly designed the cartoon "Magna Britannia: her Colonies Reduced" for distribution in England, hoping the symbolic representation of Britannia fallen from her place of eminence at the top of the globe, her limbs (each bearing the name of a North American colony) severed, would help sway England toward a more lenient colonial policy. Indeed, up to the point at which the French entered the war, mezzotints and engravings in London supported the colonists.

Few cartoons appeared during this period: Frank Weitenkampf has located a mere seventy-eight produced before 1828. An exception to the busy cartoons of the day—and one that seems almost modern in its simplicity—was drawn by Elkanah Tisdale in 1812. Gilbert Stuart has traditionally received the credit, but it was Tisdale who added a few pencil strokes to the map of Governor Elbridge Gerry's ingeniously contrived Essex County senatorial district, thus creating the dragonlike "gerrymander" and adding a word to our language.

Given the bitterness of partisan politics that characterized the early—not to mention the later—years of the Republic, it is surprising that there are so few cartoons of George Washington, who was scurrilously derided by his foes. William Murrell surmises that "too ardent" patriots have destroyed unflattering cartoons of the Father of Our Country. Thomas Jefferson was not so fortunate, and several cartoons survive that mock his Gallic and democratic proclivities. In fact, the first American cartoon designed for newspaper reproduction in the *New York Evening Post* (1814), dealt with Jefferson's highly unpopular Embargo Act.

Although Franklin, Tisdale, and others were well known, Edinburgh-born William Charles was the first to become famous here primarily as a political cartoonist. Charles drew heavily upon the works of English cartoonists Gillray and Rowlandson and left no disciples after his death in 1820, but he deserves to be remembered, nevertheless, for popularizing the political cartoon.

The next phase in the history of American editorial cartoons was initiated by the development of lithography, a process that was much faster than woodcuts and engravings. The first lithographed cartoon appeared in 1829; thereafter, lithographed cartoons flourished. Most of them were produced by the firms of Henry R. Robinson and Currier & Ives. Robinson's company produced many political lithographs between 1831 and

1849, and some were superior to those by Currier & Ives, a name that has become synonymous with lithography. The Currier & Ives firm produced over seven thousand different titles between 1840 and 1890 and sold some ten million copies, only eighty of which titles were political cartoons. They were realistic: faces were copied from photographs; and numerous balloons filled with finely printed dialogue floated over the stiff figures. As the Civil War approached, the firm often marketed cartoons, sometimes drawn to order, on both sides of a controversial issue. It is precisely the drawn-to-order nature of these cartoons that makes them seem so woodenly quaint today.

Although Currier & Ives documented the mid-century discord with their lithographs, especially those dealing with the campaigns of 1856 and 1860, the Civil War, and Abraham Lincoln, there were other media germinating that would soon leave the lithographers in the shade and would begin another phase in American editorial cartooning. Englishman Henry Carter arrived here in 1848, changed his name to Frank Leslie, and, by the mid-1850s, was embarked on a series of magazine ventures, the most successful of which was *Frank Leslie's Illustrated Newspaper* (later *Frank Leslie's Illustrated Weekly*). Other Leslie publications included *The Jolly Joker*, *The Cartoon*, *Chatterbox*, and *Phunny Phellow*. An impressive list of artists was employed by Leslie, as well as by *Vanity Fair*, *Harper's Weekly*, and the scores of other publications that appeared and disappeared abruptly: the Anglo-Irishman Frank Bellew, who was popular before the war and whose elongated caricature of Lincoln is still remembered, and many others, most notably the German Thomas Nast and the Viennese Joseph Keppler.

Born in Landau, Germany, in 1840, Thomas Nast came to New York City at the age of six. He became deeply interested in art, especially in the great English cartoonists Leech, Tenniel, and Gilbert. Nast said that he was indebted to Tenniel for his striking use of animals as symbols. At fifteen, he won a job with *Frank Leslie's Illustrated Weekly*. During the Civil War, his illustrations for *Harper's Weekly* were extremely popular. He soon turned to a more emblematic, less reportorial style, which was sometimes allegorical, nearly always emotionally powerful. So effective a voice for the Union did he become that Lincoln called him "our best recruiting sergeant."

The South had its own German-born artist, Adalbert J. Volck, a Baltimore dentist who produced a few excellent caricatures, most notably twenty-nine "Confederate War Etchings" (1863). He scathingly portrayed Lincoln as a clown, a Negro, a woman, and an oriental dancer. Apparently, he gave up cartooning after the war.

Nast, however, continued to draw, and his style evolved into caricature. Eventually, it was through his battle against the Tweed Ring that he made his mark as one of America's most powerful editorial cartoonists. Incensed by the corruption of Boss Tweed, Nast began to fire his volleys from the pages of *Harper's Weekly*. He took Tammany Hall's own tiger and made it into a fearful symbol of marauding lawlessness, to be used against Tweed in the election of 1871. Tweed lost and went to jail in 1873. He escaped, only to be identified and arrested again in Spain because an official recognized him from one of Nast's cartoons. Unfortunately for Nast, right and wrong were never again so plainly distinguishable. His attacks remained formidable, but he was sometimes at a loss for a target, as his own Republican party proved itself susceptible to corruption. He quit *Harper's* in 1887 and lost much of his effectiveness. His investments failed, and by 1902 he had no choice but to accept the post of U.S. Consul to Guayaquil, Equador, where he died in December of the same year. But he left behind him such long-lasting symbols as the Tammany tiger and the Republican elephant, the less durable rag baby of inflation, and the Democratic donkey, which he did not create but did popularize. By his influence on public opinion, he demonstrated that a popular, forceful editorial cartoonist was someone to be reckoned with.

The passing of Nast did not leave a vacuum, however, for there arose the comic weeklies. Joseph Keppler, who came to St. Louis from Vienna in late 1867 or early 1868, started two German-language comic weeklies, both of which failed. In 1872, he went to New York and worked for Frank Leslie. He founded a German-language weekly, *Puck*, in 1876 and an English version in 1877. The magazine thrived and in less than ten years had a circulation of eighty thousand. An excellent cartoonist himself, Keppler employed many of the best artists of the time.

Puck's heyday partly overlapped Nast's decline. In 1884, Nast was disgruntled by the Republicans' nomination of the tainted James G. Blaine and expressed himself in a cartoon. The Democratic *Puck* joined in and revived an idea Keppler had used against Grant: the tattooed man. Bernard Gillam drew the scandalous series, depicting the husky Blaine in his undershorts, covered with tattoos representing his opponents' allegations of "corruption." The Republicans responded with Frank Beard's cartoon in *Judge*, dramatizing a rumor that Grover Cleveland was the father of an illegitimate child. Perhaps the most telling shot in the cartoon war was "The Royal Feast of Belshazaar Blaine and the Money Kings," drawn by Walt McDougall for the New York *World*. In the drawing, patterned after the *Last Supper*, Blaine, Jay Gould, and other New York financiers feast on such dishes as "patronage." Displayed on billboards around the state, the cartoon contributed to Blaine's defeat in New York and in the national election. According to Charles Press, this marked the real beginning of daily editorial cartooning as a profession.

One of *Puck*'s two great rivals, *Judge*, was founded in 1881 by a dissatisfied *Puck* cartoonist, James A. Wales. Perhaps *Judge*'s most famous symbol was the "Full Dinner Pail," cartoonist Grant Hamilton's embodiment of the prosperity of Republican William McKinley's first administration. As Stephen Becker points out, these "Full Dinner Pail" cartoons drawn by Hamilton and by Victor Gillam represented an advance in cartooning technique because of their greater simplicity and, therefore, immediacy, as compared to the crowded panel cartoons of the late nineteenth century. The third great comic weekly of the period was *Life*, founded in 1883 by *Harvard Lampoon* graduates led by J. A. Mitchell. Much, although not all, of its satire was social rather than political.

The development of newspaper cartooning was gradual; James Gordon Bennett had started the New York *Telegram* in 1867 and had used sensationalism to boost sales. In the first regular use of cartoons in a newspaper, he printed a front-page cartoon every Friday. Joseph Pulitzer, who bought the New York *World* in 1883, made an even bigger impression with editorial cartoons such as the devastating "Feast of Belshazaar." William Randolph Hearst took over the New York *Journal* in 1895 and began the great circulation war. He brought with him from San Francisco Homer Davenport, who is perhaps best remembered for his caricatures of Republican National Chairman Mark Hannah as smug and bloated, his suit decorated with dollar signs. Hearst snatched Frederick Burr Opper from *Puck* in 1899. Although critics have been condescending toward his technique, Opper was a cartoonist of great versatility and popularity, with a successful comic strip, "Happy Hooligan," and several telling series of political cartoons, such as "Alice in Plunderland" and "Willie and His Poppa." His career was unusual because of its variety and length and also because he was one of the few cartoonists able to make the changeover from the comic magazines, with their complicated, multifigured cartoons, to the daily newspapers, whose deadlines necessitated a more direct style and simpler designs.

The war with Spain provided cartoonists with inspiration for a while, but Theodore Roosevelt literally sustained them for years. His teeth, mustache, and glasses made him easy to draw. He was a favorite subject for two of the early twentieth century's best-known cartoonists: John T. McCutcheon and Jay N. (Ding) Darling. Charles Press has put them at the head of a group of cartoonists he labels "bucolic."

John Tinney McCutcheon was one of the most notable of a large group of outstanding midwestern cartoonists active around the turn of the century. He drew editorial cartoons and nostalgic panels, and illustrated books, such as his famous *Boys in Springtime*. Of his political cartoons for the Chicago *Tribune*, perhaps the best known are his 1932 Pulitzer Prize winner, "A Wise Economist Asks a Question," and "The Mysterious Stranger" (1904), which shows Missouri standing in line with states of the Republican column after it deserted the solid South to vote for Roosevelt.

Another durable midwesterner was Jay N. (Ding) Darling of Iowa. His "The Long, Long Trail," a 1919 tribute to Teddy Roosevelt, has often been reproduced. The duration of his career is shown by the dates of his Pulitzer Prizes—1924 and 1943; he received his last award when he was sixty-six. According to Stephen Becker, however, by that time he was "almost a throwback" to the less sophisticated days of the early part of the century.

In approximately the middle of these men's careers came the next major event in American History: World War I. During the three years of war before the American entry, major U.S. newspaper cartoonists, all but one of whom favored intervention on behalf of the French and English, were busy drawing German atrocities. The interventionist artists included W. A. Rogers and Nelson Harding of the Brooklyn *Eagle*. Dutch artist Louis Raemaekers, whose work appeared in the Hearst papers, is generally considered to be better than the Americans who drew for the Allied cause. The lone pen wielded in defense of neutrality belonged to Luther D. Bradley of the Chicago *Daily News*. He died early in 1917, before his antiwar convictions were tested. With the United States in the war, a Bureau of Cartoons, set up under the direction of George J. Hecht, successfully channeled cartoonists' work into the war effort by suggesting topics and otherwise maximizing the propaganda value of cartoons.

Luther Bradley was the only cartoonist for an important newspaper to oppose the war, but the radical cartoonists also opposed it and became prominent in the development of modern political cartooning. Much of their work appeared in *Masses* (1911-1917) and *Liberator* (1918-1924), because their uncompromising political views were unacceptable to the mainstream. They did not put their shoulders to the wheel of the Allied cause, but instead produced cartoons such as Robert Minor's in 1915, which presented the Army medical examiner's idea of the "perfect soldier": a muscular giant with no head.

Three of the radical cartoonists who were most important and most satisfied to be called cartoonists were Boardman Robinson, Art Young, and Robert Minor. Boardman Robinson was the most influential in terms of his effect on subsequent generations of political cartoonists, partly by virtue of his pioneering technique using crayon on grained paper, as Daumier and Forain did before him, and partly because of his position as an instructor at the Art Students League in New York from 1919 to 1930. Among those he influenced may be listed his fellow radical cartoonists Robert Minor and Clive Weed, as well as Oscar Cesare, Rollin Kirby, and Edmund Duffy.

Robert Minor gave up his successful career as a mainstream artist to draw cartoons that reflected his socialist and antiwar beliefs. He simplified his style to increase the impact of the intensely political cartoons he drew for *Masses*.

Art Young probably received the widest distribution of any of the radical cartoonists, partly because he came to socialism relatively late in life, after he had been on the staffs of several major newspapers. With *Masses* editor Max Eastman, Young was also sued unsuccessfully by the Associated Press for libel and was prosecuted in vain by the government under the Espionage Act for obstructing recruitment into the armed forces. In spite of government suppression, *Masses*, in its various forms, provided a forum for some of the best cartoonists of the period. Indeed, art editor John Sloan, along with George Bellows and George Luks, were acclaimed artists of the Ashcan school. It is precisely this exceptional degree of talent, coupled with a technique perfectly suited to the expression of moral outrage, that has made the names and influence of the radical cartoonists last longer than their more moderate contemporaries.

In 1922, the first Pulitzer Prize for editorial cartooning was awarded; it went to Roland Kirby of the New York *World*. If winning prizes is any indication, he was the dominant editorial cartoonist of the 1920s, winning again in 1925 and in 1929 (Nelson Harding won in 1927 and 1928). Kirby is considered to be a transitional figure between the early multifigure cartooning and the modern single-figure panels.

Many of the best comic artists of the 1930s drew social rather than political cartoons for magazines such as *The New Yorker*, *Vanity Fair*, and *Time*. The Depression, however, along with FDR and his NRA eagle, gave editorial cartoonists plenty of inspiration. As it happened, most cartoonists and most publishers were against Roosevelt. Notable exceptions were C. D. Batchelor, D. R. Fitzpatrick, and, at first, John T. McCutcheon.

Edmund Duffy, who has been called Kirby's heir, won three Pulitzer Prizes in the next decade: 1931, 1934, and 1940. Just as Rollin Kirby's famous "Mr. Dry" was not represented in any of his prize-winning cartoons, so Duffy's chinless little Ku Klux Klansman was also overlooked by the judges. Like Kirby, Duffy was influenced by Boardman Robinson and he is credited by Stephen Becker with continuing Kirby's move away from the crowded panels of the nineteenth century and toward the single-figure cartoon of those dominant figures of the mid-twentieth century, Herblock and Bill Mauldin.

The 1930s also gave cartoonists the slant-eyed figure of Japanese militarism and the easily caricatured Mussolini and Hitler. The St. Louis *Post-Dispatch*'s Daniel R. Fitzpatrick, in a style reminiscent of Boardman Robinson, made effective use of the swastika as a symbol of oppression. Fitzpatrick, who had won a Pulitzer Prize in 1926, would win another in 1955.

During World War II, Bill Mauldin's work in *The Stars and Stripes* provided a welcome relief from patriotic propaganda. He was a combat veteran himself, and his characters, Willie and Joe, were survivors, not heroes. The public took to them immediately. In 1945, Mauldin won the Pulitzer Prize. His popularity continued after the war, with some diminution: his style and the savagery behind it were too grating for a public that wanted amusement, not a crusade. When he returned to cartooning in 1958 with the St. Louis *Post-Dispatch*, he had switched to a lighter grease pencil and opened up his cartoons. And, as his Pulitzer Prize in 1959 for an anti-Russian cartoon showed, the targets were fatter. The civil-rights struggles of the 1960s provided him with the southern redneck to ridicule. Overall, Mauldin may be said to have moved in the same general direction as his liberal counterpart, Herbert Block.

Although Herbert L. Block, "Herblock," was an active cartoonist throughout the 1930s and was awarded the Pulitzer Prize in 1942, his preeminence generally begins after the war. He was one of the first cartoonists to oppose the anti-Communist hysteria, and he also assailed Senator Joseph McCarthy courageously. "Mr. Atom," his sinister personification of the bomb, ranks among the most effective cartoon symbols of the mid-twentieth century.

Among the younger men who have begun to challenge the dominance of Herblock and Mauldin is Patrick Oliphant, who came from Australia in 1964 to work for the Denver *Post*. As the story goes, he and his wife studied the past Pulitzer Prize-winning drawings, and he won one in 1966. Influenced by British cartoonist Ronald Searle, Oliphant has in turn influenced other artists with his fine, exuberant line and emphasis on sheer humor. A true satirist, he gets his laughs at the expense of the foolish, no matter what party or profession they belong to. He is presently with the Washington *Star*.

Another comparatively recent addition to the top echelon actually predates Pat Oliphant. An Iowa devotee of Ding Darling, Paul Conrad left the Denver *Post* in 1964 for the Los Angeles *Times*. Lawsuits filed by Mayor Sam Yorty and the Union Oil Company attest to Conrad's effectiveness there. Stephen Hess and Milton Kaplan's inclusion of Conrad in the "big four" with Herblock, Mauldin, and Oliphant is not universally accepted, but he is unarguably one of the very top cartoonists today. He may be accused of lack of subtlety, for he sometimes breaks bones in the process of drawing blood, but the sheer wildness of his concepts and his skill in executing them with fine and intricate lines make him deadly when he is on target. He won Pulitzer Prizes in 1964 and 1971.

The other important cartoonists drawing today are too numerous even to list here. Further, any attempt to classify them is bound to be unsatisfactory, for cartoonists resist being categorized just as adamantly as do writers. Keeping these caveats in mind, it is convenient to begin with the so-called new wave, a term used in the early 1960s to include Hugh Haynie of the Louisville *Courier-Journal*, Bill Sanders of the Milwaukee *Journal*, the resurgent Bill Mauldin, his Chicago contemporary John Fischetti, and other, generally liberal cartoonists such as Tony Auth of the Philadelphia *Enquirer*. Especially hard-hitting and somewhat younger, at least in terms of national prominence, are Tom Darcy of *Newsday*, Bill Shore of the Los Angeles *Herald Examiner*, and Paul Szep of the Boston *Globe*. A liberal, humanitarian cartoonist who often attains this high impact is Draper Hill of the Detroit *News*. Hill is also a leading American authority on the editorial cartoon. A "second beach head" was established by Don Wright of the Miami *News*, who has influenced Mike Peters of the Dayton *Daily News*, Doug Marlette of Charlotte *Observer*, Bob Englehart of the Dayton *Journal Herald*, and Duane Powell of the Raleigh *News Observer*.

Conservative cartoonists include Don Hesse of the St. Louis *Globe Democrat*, Charles Werner of the Indianapolis *Star*, Tom Curtis of the Milwaukee *Sentinel*, Wayne Stayskal of the Chicago *Tribune*, Jim Boardman of the Cincinnati *Enquirer*, and Karl Hubenthal of the Los Angeles *Herald-Examiner*. Jeff MacNelly of the Richmond *News Leader*, winner of two Pulitzer Prizes, comes closer than any of these to the free-swinging hilarity of Oliphant.

There is some disagreement as to whether or not Gary Trudeau and Jules Feiffer's use of the strip medium instead of the single panel disqualifies them as editorial cartoonists, although the awarding of the 1975 Pulitzer Prize to Trudeau is strong evidence on their behalf. At any rate, it is impossible to deny Trudeau's popularity among young people and liberals. Feiffer has been effective since the late 1950s, not only in his merciless forays against the liberals' nemeses, but also in his equally merciless exposure of the self-deception and hypocrisy to which so many liberals fall prey.

Again, it must be emphasized that these groupings are approximate at best, for each cartoonist reacts according to his instincts, not according to some rigid party or liberal-conservative alignment. If there is a trend in editorial cartooning today, it is toward originality and spontaneity of style, with an increasing emphasis on humor for its own sake.

BIBLIOGRAPHY

Becker, Stephen. *Comic Art in America*. Simon and Schuster, 1959.

Blaisdell, Thomas C., Jr., and Peter Selz. *The American Presidency in Political Cartoons: 1776-1976.* Santa Barbara: Peregrine Smith, 1976.

Campbell, Mary, and Gordon Campbell. *The Pen, Not the Sword: A Collection of Great Political Cartoons from 1879 to 1898*. Nashville: Aurora Publishers, 1970.

"Caricature, Cartoon, and Comic Strip." *Encyclopaedia Britannica*. 15th ed., vol. 3, 909-22.

Chase, John, ed. *Today's Cartoon*. New Orleans: Hauser Press, 1962.

Cooper, Frederick Taylor, and Arthur Bartlett Maurice. *The History of the Nineteenth Century in Caricature*. New York: Dodd Mead, 1904. Reissued, Detroit: Tower Books, 1971.

Craven, Thomas, ed. *Cartoon Cavalcade.* New York: Simon and Schuster, 1943.
Fitzgerald, Richard. *Art and Politics.* Westport, Conn.: Greenwood Press, 1973.
Foreign Policy Association. *A Cartoon History of U. S. Foreign Policy Since World War I.* New York: Vintage, 1968.
Geipel, John. *The Cartoon: A Short History of Graphic Comedy and Satire.* London: David & Charles, 1972. New York: A. S. Barnes, 1972.
Hess, Stephen, and Milton Kaplan. *The Ungentlemanly Art.* New York: Macmillan, 1968. Rev. ed., 1975.
The Image of America in Caricature and Cartoon. Fort Worth, Tex.: Amon Carter Museum of Western Art, Swann Collection and Lincoln National Corp. of Fort Wayne, 1976.
Keller, Morton. *The Art and Politics of Thomas Nast.* New York: Oxford University Press, 1968.
Lynch, John Gilbert Bohun. *A History of Caricature.* London: Faber and Gwyer, 1926.
Malcolm, James P. *An Historical Sketch of the Art of Caricaturing.* London: Longman, Hurst, Rees, Orme, and Brown, 1813.
Murrell, William. *A History of American Graphic Humor.* 2 vols. New York: Whitney Museum, 1933, 1938. Reissued, New York: Cooper Square Publishers, 1967.
Nelson, Roy Paul. *Cartooning.* Chicago: Henry Regnery, 1975.
______. *Comic Art and Caricature.* Chicago: Contemporary Books, 1978.
Nevins, Allan, and Frank Weitenkampf. *A Century of Political Cartoons.* New York: Charles Scribner's, 1944. Reprinted, New York: Farrar, Straus & Giroux, 1975.
Parton, James. *Caricature and Other Comic Art.* New York: Harper and Bros., 1878. Reprinted, New York: Harper & Row, 1969.
Shikes, Ralph E. *The Indignant Eye.* Boston: Beacon Press, 1969.
Spencer, Dick, III. *Editorial Cartooning.* Ames: Iowa State College Press, 1949.
______. *Pulitzer Prize Cartoons.* Ames: Iowa State College Press, 1951.
Weitenkampf, Frank. *American Graphic Art.* New York: Holt, 1912. Revised. New York: Macmillan, 1924. Reprinted, New York: Johnson Reprint, 1970.
______. "Keppler and Political Cartooning." *Bulletin of the New York Public Library,* 42 (December 1938), 906-908.

Fashion

Loretta Carrillo

One of the many ways in which the Jamestown settlers of 1607 reflected their status as English colonists was in their style of clothing. Men dressed in standard doublet, trunk hose and boots while women wore wide, cut-away farthingales and stiff, straight bodices. Half a century later in the 1650s the Virginia Cavaliers were still following the London dress fashions. Men wore knickerbockers gathered with ribbons at the knees and women wore the latest fashions of billowing sleeves and gummed, black silk patches of stars or crescent moons on the face. The southern Virginia wilderness settlers, on the other hand, were much less fashionably dressed. Their clothing was in the popular mode, but was of a more simple cut and made of leather and homespun fabrics. North and South Carolina frontier dress followed similar fashions as the rest of the region with the exception of Charleston where fashionable dress was featured when the city became a fashionable cultural center in the late eighteenth century.

The fashions of the New England Pilgrim settlers at Plymouth conformed generally to the current English dress mode but were stripped of ornamentation. The Pilgrim men wore the traditional doublet and hose and the women simple farthingales. Their dress, however, had been influenced to a degree by Dutch fashion, since the Pilgrims had spent many years in exile in the Low Countries. The Puritans of Massachusetts Bay who came later to the New World, having departed directly from the mother country, dressed in the current English mode more faithfully than their Pilgrim counterparts. In time, New England society developed a heterogeneous population consisting of Puritan ecclesiastics, merchants and merchant adventurers, yeomen and tenant farmers, and African slaves, all of whose rank in society was reflected in their dress. The Puritan fathers dressed in the severe Puritan garb of broad-brimmed hat, black doublet, coarse stockings and heavy, square-toed shoes. They attempted to lay down dress codes by sermonizing against extravagance in dress, but had little success in doing so. The merchant class dressed much as did the Virginia colonists while the wealthy classes in both colonies followed London high fashions. The tenant farmer class dressed as simply as did their counterparts in England while the slaves were relegated to hand-me-downs and crudely constructed clothing of coarse fibers.

During this period and continuing for the better part of America's fashion history, wearing fashionable clothing was directly related to a person's social standing in the community, since only wealthy persons could afford imported clothing and fine silks and satins. Upper-class women in the seventeenth century Virginia and New England colonies were dressed in silks, fur-lined hoods, lace, and ribbons. Less wealthy persons relied on coarse fibers and crude construction which attempted, more often unsuccessfully, to follow fashionable styles.

In other developing regions, the same class distinctions could be seen in fashions. The Quaker settlers of Pennsylvania were of the peasant class and wore sober, plain dress in the style of the period. Philadelphia, on the other hand, grew into a bustling trade center by the late eighteenth century where imported dresses and fabrics made the wealthy class as well attired as their counterparts in New England and Virginia.

Later, the American Revolution and the resulting stress on equalitarianism popularized more simple, less ornamented dress. In more practical terms, the growing emphasis on simplicity was a result of the cut-off of commerce between the colonies and Europe, due to the British blockade. Hatred of the British allowed a greater French influence on American fashions after the 1783 peace treaty; nevertheless, the mother country's dress continued to predominate over American fashion styles.

By the late 1700s, powdered wigs and frilled shirts were no longer fashionable for men, and male dress settled into a variation of the recognizable form known today as jacket and trousers. Influenced by post-revolutionary French fashions, women's dress in America underwent a "Classical Revival" that featured short-bodiced gowns, high waistlines and low necklines.

During this time period, but on another front, Westward expansion in America gave rise to a more rugged lifestyle reflected in the functional, simple clothing of the frontier settlers. From Canada to Spanish Florida, Texas, and the Southwest, the hunting smock, loose tunic, moccasins, and leggings were standard men's dress. Much use was made of animal hides and furs for jackets and caps. Women's dress was hardly fashionable but was sturdy, useful, and made of crude homespuns. Unlike the leisured classes of the colonies and their descendants, the frontier families had greater use for functional as opposed to purely fashionable, ornamented dress. Spanish colonization of the United States Southwest introduced the prevailing Spanish and Mexican mode of dress to the region. In addition, the functional *vaquero* or Mexican cowboy attire greatly influenced the dress of the American cowboy and frontiersman.

The increasing industrialization of America in the early 1800s created a thriving American textile industry which accounted for enormous increases in cotton production over the period 1815-1830. The single invention that democratized fashion in America as well as in England was the sewing machine, invented in 1830 by the French tailor Barthelemy Thimmonier but patented in the United States in 1851 by Issac Singer as a more elaborate instrument with eye-point needle and under-thread shuttle. The sewing machine allowed fashion as an industry to form quickly, and exporters, importers, wholesalers, and department and retail stores quickly developed to participate in the burgeoning trade. As the American clothing industry continued to grow, the large labor force required to run the industry inevitably exerted an important influence from 1900 onward when the International Ladies Garment Workers Union organized to demand reform of appalling working conditions in the factories.

Further allowing the middle-class women in America access to stylish clothing was the development of the paper pattern industry. In the 1850s, women could obtain basic paper dress patterns in women's magazines, either diagrammed or printed as tissue supplements. Enterprising women and men such as Madame Ellen Louise Demorest and William Jennings Demorest along with Ebenezer Butterick and James McCall recognized the current and potential market for patterns and developed the industry so that by the 1860s a thriving market for patterns copied from English and Parisian designers in several sizes with explicit sewing instructions were available in department stores, retail outlets and mail order houses to middle and lower class women.

The American paper pattern industry not only brought fashionable dress to the average woman, but it also created a fashion press. In 1860, the Demorests introduced *Madame Demorest's Quarterly Mirror of Fashions* devoted exclusively to fashion news, and they later inserted a fashion section in the weekly *New York Illustrated News.* Butterick's dress pattern business was so successful that by 1867 he issued the *Ladies Report of New York Fashions,* and in the 1870s he had established wholesale depots in Chicago and Montreal for Butterick patterns.

Other more established women's periodicals such as *Godey's Ladies Book, Peterson's Magazine, Leslie's,* and *Harper's Bazaar* which carried diagrams and tissue supplements found competition in the newer fashion journals. So established was the paper pattern industry by the late 1800s that the 1876 Centennial Exhibition at Philadelphia displayed two pavilions of women's paper dress patterns, one by the Demorests and the other by Ebenezer Butterick.

An important feature of women's fashions during the mid-nineteenth century which focused attention on women's health rather than on the aesthetics of fashion was the Dress Reform Movement of the 1850s. This small but vocal group in America protested against the dangerous, constricting features of tight bodices that threatened women's health and anatomical development. The cumbersome bustles and dragging trains that collected street filth were also presented as dangerous features of popular women's fashions of the period. In protest, Amelia Bloomer introduced the knee-length skirt worn over baggy trousers known as "Bloomers," but the outfit was never generally accepted. Only at the century's end was it used and then simply as a cycling outfit. Similar dress reform groups in England and Germany also did not fare well with either popular or mass fashions.

Haute couture had formally emerged in Paris and London when in the late 1850s "couturiers" such as Charles Frederick Worth designed garments for European nobility and the upper classes and displayed and sold specially designed and manufactured garments in elite salons. During the early twentieth century in America, New York City, Boston, and Chicago emerged as the country's fashion capitals, all of which took their cues from Paris. The heart of the clothing industry in America, however, was the mass production of clothes, including copies of designers' styles which provided the average woman her level of haute couture.

By 1914, World War I brought the fashion business to a halt in Europe, and America was subsequently cut off from European designers. Edna Woolman Chase, editor of *Vogue,* responded by putting on a fashion show with live models to show original American designs. After the war, Hollywood and its stars and American culture itself began to have a greater share of influence upon American fashion. The Jazz Age produced Hollywood stars such as Pola Negri, Gloria Swanson, and Greta Garbo all of whom popularized bobbed hair, cloche hats, heavy eye-makeup and the "vamp" look. Also originating during this decade was the cocktail dress, shortened calf-length dresses, lowered waistlines and strap shoes for women while for men the grey-flannel trousers or "Oxford Bags" became popular. The high fashion designer, Coco Chanel, greatly influenced the fashions of the decade when she introduced a simple, natural look in the boxy suit which resembled the convent uniform she had worn as a girl. The Chanel look made women appear young and boyish in contrast to the popular Oriental designs of one of Chanel's counterparts in Paris, Paul Poiret. Chanel also facilitated mass manufacture of couture designs by using simple fabrics such as jersey and cotton which made copying easier. Lastly, the period was known for such fashion items as the "Eton Crop" hairdo, long strings of pearls and "slave" bracelets.

In reaction against the boyish look generated by the Chanel suit and hip-length waist dresses of the 1920s, the fashions of the early 1930s were influenced by Italian-born designer Schiaparelli and stressed normal waistlines, rounded bust, longer hair and lowered, mid-calf dress and skirt lengths. The Depression and its hardships inevitably influenced fashions of the latter part of the decade. A more masculine trend appeared in ladies' suits which emphasized wider shoulders and shoulder pads; however, the short, full-skirted, ballet-length, dinner dress became very popular in America during the period and contrasted sharply with the severe day suit. Despite catastrophic financial setbacks of the decade, the 1930s was also the period when designers and manufacturers stressed the importance of accessories and presented coordinated collections of handbags, shoes, and gloves.

Inevitably, World War II influenced fashions of the 1940s, for the better part of the decade featured the "Austerity Look." Fashion historians point out that this decade marks the first time fashion was dictated by the masses and not by elite designers. Skirt lengths were short, jackets were long and square-shouldered, and hair was set in rolls at the nape of the neck and tied with scarves knotted at the top of the head. This "no-frills" look appeared to suit the world's anxious, wartime mood. Claire McCardell further pioneered an "American Look" that was essentially casual when she revealed a taste for simple fabrics such as seersucker, cotton, and voile. In many ways, McCardell may have set the precedent for the casual look Americans have since preferred in their clothing, epitomized in the American love for denim which blossomed in the 1960s.

On the high fashion scene, Christian Dior soon tired of the austerity look and introduced "The New Look" in 1947 which reigned for the entire decade of the 1950s. Round shoulders, corseted waists, long, billowing skirts, dinner gloves and stiletto high-heeled shoes signaled a return to femininity and prosperity. An interesting and important feature of wartime austerity which Dior incorporated into high fashion and popularized was the use of synthetic fibers such as Rayon and Lurex. Though previously despised, the artificial fibers which later included Banlon and Orlon proved durable, easy to care for and an attractive alternative to natural fibers.

The decade of the 1950s is critical to American fashion history because it marks America's complete dominance in the ready-to-wear trade. Ready-to-wear clothing had been an infant industry in the post Civil War period and had blossomed in the last decade of the century. By the decade of the 1950s, the American ready-to-wear production and merchandizing experts had so perfected their trade that millions of profit dollars were being made on copies of European haute couture designer clothing. In time, European designer houses as a group saw the light and eventually set up boutiques in America to sell their own copies. But by the early 1960s, they had rivals in American designers such as Bill Blass, Geoffrey Beene and Calvin Klein who were all making huge profits from off-the-rack copies of clothing designed specifically for the ready-to-wear market. These fashions stressed the casual, suburban lifestyle that came to dominate the American scene. By 1966, individual American ready-to-wear designer houses could boast of profits in the $200 million range.

The 1960s was indisputably the decade of ready-to-wear, denim and blue jeans, pop fashions, including mini skirts, vinyl dresses, unisex clothing and the breakdown of all classic fashion rules in America and in Europe as well. Fashion was now ruled over by the middle and working classes, by youth and, to a great extent, not by dictates at all but by personal taste. British ready-to-wear designer Mary Quant popularized denim and above-the-knee hemlines and model Twiggy, with her long, lean, boyish figure, popularized the mini skirt. The Hippie culture in the late 1960s influenced mass fashion by popularizing peasant garments and mixing clashing patterns and textures of clothing. Fashion personalities such as Jacqueline Kennedy were created by the now neatly organized New York fashion press. As an avid consumer of fashion, Jackie Kennedy exerted enormous influence over popular fashion trends for the entire decade, making everything from low-heeled buckle shoes to Spanish *mantillas* popular. The 1960s were important, too, because the decade marked the period when men's fashions were given more attention by high-fashion designers Pierre Cardin and John Weitz.

The Hippie craze for ethnic and peasant dress was carried over into the early 1970s and assimilated by high fashion. The mood in dress, however, was still anti-haute couture, with jeans, work clothes, and casual sportswear predominating. The pantsuit for both casual and evening wear was most popular with women in the early 1970s while hemlines came to below-the-knee in mid-decade, several years after the public completely rejected the midi-length hemline. In the late 1970s, London's punk rock look, complete with leather jackets, dyed purple and pink hair and safety pin earrings, influenced American fashion, particularly the youth in urban centers.

A sizable reaction against the tough, punk look in the early 1980s, however, has been the "classic" look which stresses a simple, neat and tailored appearance. The fashion extravagances of the 1960s have given way in the 1980s to a casual though refined appearance that is essentially conservative and traditional. This trend has influenced women's fashions, particularly the way in which women dress in the business world. The recent flurry of "Dressing for Success" books and manuals attempt to show women executives, administrators, office managers and other businesswomen how to dress in order to be accepted into management and business circles. The stress is usually on conservative, tailored fashions that purportedly show women appropriately dressed for the serious, no-frills world of work.

On the more popular level, contemporary popular fashion, interestingly, again puts emphasis upon the couture designers who had been told in the 1960s to take their cues from popular fashion. The craze now appears to be for the designer label—Bill Blass, Dior, Givenchy, Calvin Klein—on everything from jeans to scarves, perfume, and luggage. After two decades of stress upon individuality and personal taste in fashion, the American public of the early 1980s now values the designer label, apparently for its declaration of status and wealth. More importantly, perhaps, the American fashion consumer craves designer labels on everything from sunglasses to brassieres in order to affirm its own ability to buy items that previously were reserved only for the wealthy, elite class.

BIBLIOGRAPHY

Bell, Quentin. *On Human Finery.* New York: Schocken Books, 1978.
Bender, Marilyn. *The Beautiful People.* New York: Coward-McCann, Inc., 1967.
Bigelow, Marybell S. *Fashion in History, Apparel in the Western World.* Minne-

apolis, Minn.: Burgess Publishing Co., 1970.

Black, J. Anderson, and Madge Garland. *A History of Fashion.* New York: William Morrow and Co., Inc., 1980.

Carnes, Valerie. "Icons of Popular Fashion." In *Icons of America.* Eds. Ray B. Brown and Marshall Fishwick, Bowling Green, Ohio: Bowling Green University Press, 1978, pp. 228-40.

Carter, Ernestine. *The Changing World of Fashion, 1900 to the Present.* New York: G. P. Putnam's Sons, 1977.

Daves, Jessica. *Ready-Made Miracle: The Story of Fashion for the Millions.* New York: Putnam, 1967.

Dorner, Jane. *Fashion in the Twenties and Thirties.* New Rochelle, N.Y.: Arlington House Publishers, 1973.

———. *Fashion: The Changing Shape of Fashion Through the Years.* London: Octopus Books, 1974.

Gordon, Eleanor, and Jean Nerenberg. "Everywoman's Jewelry: Early Plastics and Equality in Fashion." *Journal of Popular Culture,* Vol. 13, No. 4 (Spring 1980), 629-44.

Jarnow, Jeannette A., ed. *Inside the Fashion Business.* New York: John Wiley and Sons, Inc., 1965.

Kidwell, Claudia B., and Margaret C. Christman. *Suiting Everyone: The Democratization of Clothing in America.* Washington, D.C.: Smithsonian Press, 1974.

Lauer, Jeanette C., and Robert H. Lauer. "The Battle of the Sexes: Fashion in 19th Century America." *Journal of Popular Culture,* Vol. 13, No. 4 (Spring 1980), 581-89.

———. "The Language of Dress: A Sociohistorical Study of the Meaning of Clothing in America." *The Canadian Review of American Studies,* Vol. 10, No. 3 (Winter 1979), 305-23.

Levin, Phyllis. *The Wheels of Fashion.* New York: Doubleday, 1965.

Ley, Sandra. *Fashion for Everyone: The Story of Ready-to-Wear, 1870-1970.* New York: Charles Scribner's Sons, 1975.

McClellan, Elisabeth. *Historic Dress in America, 1607-1870.* 1904. Reprint. New York: Benjamin Blom, Inc., 1969.

Newton, Stella Mary. *Health, Art and Reason, Dress Reformers of the 19th Century.* London: John Murray Publishers, Ltd., 1974.

Riegel, Robert E. "Women's Clothes and Women's Rights." *American Quarterly,* Vol. 15, No. 3 (Fall 1963), 390-401.

Roach, Mary Ellen and Joanne Bubolz Eicher, eds. *Dress, Adornment, and the Social Order.* New York: John Wiley & Sons, Inc. 1965.

Sichel, Marion. *Costume Reference.* 7 vols. Boston: Plays, Inc., 1978.

Walsh, Margaret. "The Democratization of Fashion: The Emergence of the Women's Dress Pattern Industry." *The Journal of American History*, Vol. 66, No. 2, (September 1979), pp. 299-313.

Warwick, Edward, Henry C. Pitz, and Alexander Wyckoff. *Early American Dress.* New York: Benjamin Blom, Inc., 1965.

Weibel, Kathryn. "Images of the Fashionable Woman." In *Mirror, Mirror: Images of Women Reflected in Popular Culture.* New York: Doubleday, 1977, pp. 175-226.

Wilcox, Ruth Turner. *The Mode in Costume.* New York: Charles Scribner's Sons, 1958.

Film

Robert A. Armour

The date was December 28, 1895. The place was the basement of a cafe in Paris. The audience was the first public one to pay its way to watch movies, paying to be fascinated by moving images of a baby eating his meal, workers leaving a factory, and a train rushing into a station. The scenes were taken from ordinary life, but the experience was far from ordinary. This event was produced by the Lumière brothers, but the technology that led to this moment had been the result of the imagination and persistence of many inventors, both in Europe and America.

Eadweard Muybridge in 1877 had discovered that sequential still photographs of a horse running could be placed in a series and "projected" in such a manner as to make the photographic image of the horse appear to be running. In New Jersey in the late 1880s Thomas Edison and his crew led by William Dickson developed the idea of putting photographs on a single piece of continuous film, and George Eastman supplied the film. For projection Edison decided on the Kinetoscope, a peephole machine through which the film could be shown to one person at a time. Several creative inventors worked on the idea of a projector, but it was finally the Lumière brothers who were able to adapt Edison's ideas and develop the first practical means of allowing many people to view a movie simultaneously. The history of this new art form was then to be written in light.

Once the photographic technology had been developed, the next stage was to decide what to do with it. Obviously audiences could not long be enthralled by shots of a baby eating and would demand more. Both the Lumières and Edison attempted to expand the cinematic subject matter; but it was another Frenchman, George Méliès, who first achieved major success at telling a story with film. He was a magician who used the medium as part of his act, but in the process he began to depict plot as well as action. His most famous film was *A Trip to the Moon* (1902) which described a fanciful space voyage.

In order to develop a narrative process for film, the filmmaker had to learn to manipulate both space and time, to change them, and to move characters and action within them much as a novelist does. What Méliès had begun, others, especially Edison and his new director of production, continued. Edwin S. Porter learned how to use dissolves and cuts between shots to indicate changes in time or space, or both; the result was *The Great Train Robbery* (1903). This Western, shot in the wilds of New Jersey, told the complete story of a train robbery, the chase of the bandits, and their eventual defeat in a gunfight with the posse. Cross-cutting allowed Porter to show in sequence activities of both the posse and the bandits that were supposed to take place at the same time.

Businessmen began to realize the financial potential for movies. While movies were first shown as part of other forms of entertainment, they soon became the featured attraction themselves. By 1905 the first nickelodeon had opened in Pittsburgh, where customers each paid a nickel to see a full program of a half dozen short films. The opening of theaters completed the elements necessary for an industry: product, technology, producer, purchaser, and distributor.

In 1907, a would-be playwright came to Edison with a filmscript for sale. Edison did not like the script, but he hired its author, David Wark Griffith, as an actor. Griffith refused to use his real name, but he needed money and accepted the job. Thus began the career of the man who would turn this entertainment into an art. He began making films himself shortly. His tastes in plots were melodramatic, but his interests in technique were both innovative and scientific. Guided by his cameraman, Billy Bitzer, he began to experiment with editing and shots, finding many ideas for cinematic technique in the sentimental novels and poems of nineteenth-century literature. Gradually he persuaded both audiences and company bosses to accept the idea of a more complicated plot told in a lengthy movie. The result was the first major, long film. In 1915, after unheard-of amounts of time in production, Griffith released *The Birth of a Nation*, a story of the South during the Civil War and Reconstruction. The racial overtones of the film caused considerable controversy, but the power of the images and the timing of the editing created a work of art whose aesthetic excellence is not questioned. In response to the criticism of his racial views, the next year Griffith directed *Intolerance*, which interwove four stories of intolerance into a single film. Griffith was to continue as one of America's leading directors until audiences began to lose their taste for melodrama, and other directors had learned his methods. He had been responsible for launching the careers of several directors, such as Raoul Walsh, and Frank Powell, and numerous actors, such as Lillian and Dorothy Gish, Mary Pickford, and H. B. Walthall.

While Griffith was learning how to get the most from screen actors, Thomas Ince was polishing the art of telling a story efficiently. In the early 1900s, he directed a few films (*Civilization*, 1916, is the best known), but he quickly turned his attention to production, leaving the details of directing to others under his close supervision. His talent was for organization, and today he is credited with perfecting the studio system. Film is actually a collaborative art, and Ince learned how to bring the talents of many different people into a system that produced polished films, without the individualizing touches found in those films of Griffith or others who work outside the strict studio system.

One man who learned his trade from Griffith was Mack Sennett. Sennett worked for Griffith for a few years as a director and writer, but his interests were more in comedy than in melodrama. In 1912 he broke away and began to work for an independent company, Keystone. Here he learned to merge the methods of stage slapstick comedy with the techniques of film; the results were the Keystone Cops, Ben Turpin, and Charlie Chaplin. Sennett's films used only the barest plot outline as a frame for comic gags that were improvised and shot quickly. From the Sennett method, Charlie Chaplin developed his own technique and character. He began making shorts under the direction of Sennett, but in 1915 he left and joined with Essenay which agreed to let him write and direct his own films at an unprecedented salary. Here he fleshed out his tramp character; one of his first films for Essenay was *The Tramp* (1915). He continued making films that combined his own comic sense and acrobatic movements with social commentary and along with Mary Pickford became one of the first "stars." Later he made features, such as *The Gold Rush* (1925) and *Modern Times* (1936). Sennett and Chaplin began a period of great film comedy. Buster Keaton combined a deadpan look with remarkable physical ability and timing. He too began making shorts, but soon was directing and starring in features, such as *The General* (1926). Harold Lloyd (*The Freshman*, 1925) and Harry Langdon (*The Strong Man*, 1926) also created comic characters that demonstrated their individuality and imagination.

From these ingredients came the studio system and the star system. The demands of the moviegoing audiences created a need for a great number of films, and small companies were unable to meet the demands. Adolph Zukor at Paramount and Marcus Loew, Louis B. Mayer, and Irvin Thalberg at Metro-Goldwyn-Mayer quickly learned the means of applying American business methods to this new industry. They bought out their competition and eventually controlled film production, distribution, and exhibition. Even the actors and directors got into the act as Chaplin, Griffith, Pickford, and Douglas Fairbanks joined together to create United Artists, intended at first to distribute the various productions of its founders. Later it too became a studio force, along with Columbia, Fox, Warners, and others.

With the studios came the stars. The public hungered for new heroes and new sex objects, and the studios were quick to give the public what it wanted. Along with the stars who had been established in the early

1900s came the new generation of the 1920s: Rudolph Valentino, Gloria Swanson, Clara Bow. The stars soon became the nucleus of American myth, and the public followed the stars' affairs, marriages, and extravagant lives with keen interest. This was the stuff Hollywood was made of. Fortunately there were behind these stars creative directors, such as Cecil B. DeMille, Eric Von Stroheim, and Henry King, who were able to mold the talents of the stars into movies.

During the 1920s American films dominated the worldwide industry, but they were greatly influenced and enhanced by developments and personalities from Europe. The Russians Sergei Eisenstein (*Potemkin,* 1925) and V. I. Pudovkin (*Mother,* 1926) were especially influential in their understanding of montage (the relationship of the images to each other and the meaning that results). American interest in fantasy was influenced both directly and indirectly by *The Cabinet of Dr. Caligari* (1919) directed by the German Robert Wiene and *Destiny* (1921) directed by an Austrian working in Germany, Fritz Lang.

Some Europeans came to America to make films: Ernst Lubitsch, Victor Seastrom, and F. W. Murnau, for examples. The influence on American film of these films and filmmakers was profound; they left their strong impression on what came to be known as the Hollywood movie.

The story surrounding the coming of sound to movies is a complex and complicated one. The idea of connecting sound to the visuals was an old one; Edison had in fact entered the movie business because he was searching for visuals to go with the phonograph he was already marketing. To convert the movie technology to sound was expensive. Despite development of the necessary technology (most notably in this country by Lee de Forest), the industry was reluctant to invest in the change. In the mid-1920s Western Electric developed a method for putting the sound on a disk that could be roughly synchronized with the film. None of the big studios could be convinced to try it, but Warners Brothers was about to be forced out of business by the other, larger companies. It had little to lose and decided to take the risk. For a year Warners distributed a program with short sound films of slight interest, but on October 6, 1927, it premiered *The Jazz Singer* with Al Jolson. Sound was used to help tell the story, and the public loved it. Quickly, Warners established its financial base, and other studios rushed to emulate them; but problems developed. Studios had to reequip themselves. The camera, which had been struggling to free itself and discover new methods of expression, found itself confined to a large box and immobile. Actors had to learn to speak to their audiences, and exhibitors had to invest in sound projectors and speakers. Once the problems were overcome, however, the marriage of sound to the visuals became a natural extension of the art.

The period between the coming of sound and World War II was dominated by the studios. They controlled the production—including story, the role of the directors, and the selection of actors—distribution, and exhibition (they owned their own theaters). In the 1930s America went to the movies; by the end of the decade some eighty million people saw a movie every week. The studios provided them with the means to live out their fantasies, find heroes, and escape from the Depression.

One factor directly affecting the films of the 1930s was censorship. Hollywood movies in the late 1920s and early 1930s had become rather open in their use of sex, and the scandals in the private lives of the stars shocked the public even as it hungered for vicarious living. Fear of government intervention and of the Depression forced the studios to censor themselves. They established the Hays Office under the directorship of Will Hays, former postmaster-general, and this office published a strict moral code for on-screen activities and language. The results stifled creativity, but the new moral tastes of the public were satisfied.

The stars captured the public's imagination as in no other time in American popular culture: Fred Astaire and Ginger Rogers, Jean Harlow, Clark Gable and Vivian Leigh, Edward G. Robinson, and Marlene Dietrich. The comics maintained the traditions of the silent comedians: Charlie Chaplin continued to make movies and was joined by the Marx brothers, Mae West, and W. C. Fields.

At the same time, the directors had to find a path through the maze created by the studios, the Hays Office, and the stars. They had to bring all these divergent elements together and make movies. Men such as John Ford and Howard Hawks created their own visions of America and discovered methods of capturing the American myth on film. Many of the directors of the period were immigrants: Josef von Sternberg, Alfred Hitchcock, Fritz Lang, Otto Preminger, and Frank Capra. Each discovered for himself the essence of this country and its people. Perhaps that essence was most fittingly expressed in a film that came at the end of the prewar period, *Citizen Kane* (1941), the first film Orson Welles directed.

The war changed the industry. Many residents of Hollywood took time off to participate in the war effort. Some like John Ford and Frank Capra made films for the government. Others like Fritz Lang continued to make commercial films, but they were propaganda-oriented and helped build morale. The stars went to the battle areas to entertain the troops. Even studio space was commandeered to produce war documentaries, and war films became a dominant fictional genre.

After the war the rate of change accelerated. Anti-trust suits broke up the large companies and forced them to sell their theaters. And television began to keep the public at home. The movie industry responded with attempts at expanding the medium to attract new interests: 3-D, CinemaScope, Technicolor; and it continues to experiment: quadraphonic sound, sensurround, holographic images, and giant leaps in special effects have been tried.

However, in responding to competition from television, the use and type of subject matter has taken precedence over the development of technology. The movie makers have thought it necessary to give the public something that cannot be beamed into private living rooms. The results have been increased depiction of explicitness in sex and violence. Both sex and violence have been staples of the movies since the beginning, but the contemporary cinema has found new methods of enticing the public with them.

As the major Hollywood studios began to lose their domination of the American movie industry and turn their attention to television production, the leadership was taken up by independent producers and directors, making their own films and then distributing them through the networks originally established by the Hollywood companies. Stanley Kubrick, Robert Altman, Arthur Penn, Peter Bogdanovich, and Francis Ford Coppola have provided America with a new group of filmmakers, men who have demonstrated a certain independence of subject and method. Part of the void left by the diminishing importance of Hollywood has been filled by foreign filmmakers whose films have been greeted with enthusiasm by American audiences. Ingmar Bergman, François Truffaut, and Federico Fellini have dominated, but for the first time countries outside of Europe have begun to leave their mark. Japan has been especially productive.

Perhaps, however, the most important change in movies in recent years has been in the audience. By no means the number of people who went to the movies in the late 1930s still do, but those who do go are younger and more knowledgeable about film. They read the books, subscribe to film journals, watch filmed interviews with movie people on television, and read daily reviews. Many in today's audience are college-educated and have taken film courses while in school; they can talk intelligently about montage, jump cuts, and fade outs. It is for this audience that *Scenes from a Marriage* is imported from Europe and *Star Wars* is made.

BIBLIOGRAPHY

The American Film Institute Guide to College Courses in Film and Television. Princeton, N.J.: Peterson's Guides, 1978.

Andrew, J. Dudley. *The Major Film Theories.* New York: Oxford University Press, 1976.

Armour, Robert A. *Film: A Reference Guide.* Westport, Conn.: Greenwood, 1980.

Balio, Tino, ed. *The American Film Industry.* Madison: University of Wisconsin Press, 1976.

Barnouw, Erik. *Documentary: A History of the Non-fiction Film.* New York: Oxford University Press, 1974.

Bawden, Liz-Anne. *The Oxford Companion to Film.* New York: Oxford University Press, 1976.

Bluestone, George. *Novels into Film.* Berkeley: University of California Press, 1957.
Braudy, Leo, and Morris Dickstein, eds. *Great Film Directors: A Critical Anthology.* New York: Oxford University Press, 1978.
Brownlow, Kevin. *The Parade's Gone By.* New York: Ballantine, 1968.
Bukalski, Peter J. *Film Research: A Critical Bibliography.* Boston: G. K. Hall, 1972.
Clarens, Carlos. *An Illustrated History of the Horror Film.* New York: Capricorn Books, 1967.
Cripps, Thomas. *Slow Fade to Black.* New York: Oxford University Press, 1977.
Eisenstein, Sergel. *Film Essays and a Lecture.* New York: Praeger, 1970.
Fenin, George N., and William K. Everson. *The Western.* New York: Orion, 1962.
Giannetti, Louis D. *Understanding Movies.* Englewood Cliffs, N.J.: Prentice-Hall, 1976.
Grant, Barry K. *Film Genre: Theory and Criticism.* Metuchen, N.J.: Scarecrow, 1977.
Haskell, Molly. *From Reverence to Rape.* New York: Holt, Rinehart and Winston, 1973, 1974.
Hurt, James, ed. *Focus on Film and Theatre.* Englewood Cliffs, N.J.: Prentice-Hall, 1974.
Jacobs, Lewis. *The Rise of the American Film.* New York: Teachers College Press, 1939, 1968.
Kaminsky, Stuart M. *American Film Genres: Approaches to a Critical Theory of Popular Film.* New York: Dell, 1977.
Limbacher, James. *Feature Films on 8mm and 16mm.* New York: R. R. Bowker, 1977.
MacCann, Richard Dyer, ed. *Film: A Montage of Theories.* New York: E. P. Dutton, 1966.
______, and Edward S. Perry. *The New Film Index.* New York: E. P. Dutton, 1975.
Mast, Gerald. *The Comic Mind.* Indianapolis: Bobbs-Merrill, 1973.
______. *A Short History of the Movies.* Indianapolis: Bobbs-Merrill, 1981.
Renan, Sheldon. *An Introduction to the American Underground Film.* New York: E. P. Dutton, 1967.
Richardson, Robert. *Literature and Film.* Bloomington: Indiana University Press, 1969.
Rosen, Marjorie. *Popcorn Venus.* New York: Coward, McCann, and Geoghegan, 1973.
Sarris, Andrew. *Interviews with Film Directors.* New York: Avon, 1967.
Youngblood, Gene. *Expanded Cinema.* New York: E. P. Dutton, 1970.

Foodways

Charles Camp

Few subjects occupy a larger place in the American consciousness than food. In both a literal and a figurative sense, food serves to define individual and group identities; culturally acquired and nurtured matters of taste demark ethnic, regional, racial, and spiritual differences between Americans that otherwise might lack concrete expression. Indeed, within the maze of identities that characterizes contemporary American society, food offers one of the oldest and most evocative systems of cultural identification. While many characteristics of American ethnic groups, for example, have been obscured in our postindustrial society, we sense and know the difference between Italian and Greek pastries and between a Polish sausage and the common hotdog. We may lack very scientific procedures for describing the differences between these foods, but we regularly employ such distinctions as a way of defining (and celebrating) ethnic cultural diversity.

The past five years have seen an explosion of interest in food that apparently draws its energy from a variety of sources. The back-to-nature and whole-earth movements of the 1960s have contributed an increased public sensitivity to matters of diet and to the economic system that supplies most Americans with their daily bread. Interest in old-time ways of life, which led to something of a boom for American folklife studies, also sparked a more general curiosity about home cooking and other aspects of American domestic life. In the early 1970s, American industry began to catch up with European competitors in the manufacture of home cooking equipment that would permit the average American cook to produce virtually any dish desired. With the elevation of the Cuisinart food processor to the status of a mid-1970s icon, food became a general grid for plotting status and social position. *Time* and *Newsweek* covers heralded the "Cooking Boom," and, overnight, dozens of magazines, cookbooks, courses, and television programs sprang up to meet an ever-growing appetite for information.

The groundwork for the present food boom lies of course in the long-standing love affair that well-to-do Americans have had with French and other continental cuisine. As part of the social heritage that defined the elite, gourmet cooking (as it has been traditionally termed) places food within a European symbolic system that most Americans have found difficult to understand much less imitate. The food boom brought together grass-roots interest in American foodstuffs and domestic traditions and a system of defining social achievement and status that was previously restricted to the wealthier classes. The result is a curious mixture of Americana and gourmet styles, but also a refreshingly open consideration of the variety of American cookery.

The history of American food mirrors the history of American society, with its periodic fluctuations between a longing admiration of European ways of life and an intense pride in things distinctively American. With the exception of native American contributions to American foodways, the development of a distinctively American food pattern has consisted of adapting a much larger range of native foodstuffs to immigrant cookery styles (and vice versa). Unlike European cookery, during the eighteenth and nineteenth century American food was noted for the quality of foodstuff (meat, fruits, and vegetables chiefly) and not for the quality of preparation. The domination of the food industry in nineteenth-century America by descendants of prominent English families did not advance the concept of a truly American way of eating, although, by mid-century, American oysters, shrimp, beef, and whiskey had begun to distinguish themselves.

Although European travelers in America often describe the crudity of American inns and other eateries, the simplicity of American foods and the bountiful supply of beef, seafood, and wild fowl impressed many visitors. What average Americans ate during that time is more difficult to determine; but it is clear that in the style of the log cabin, in which native materials are combined as simply as possible, the everyday diet of early Americans was based chiefly on local crops and meat and game supplies. This dependence on local foodstuffs defined the regional character of American cookery—a feature that is perhaps the most obvious distinction of American foodways.

The development of industrialized food technology and the use of railroads for shipping livestock and foodstuffs allowed for a wider choice of materials for the late nineteenth-century American cook. However, at the end of the century, most Americans had established a balance between the ethnic traditions in which their culture (and approach to food) was based and the regional food supplies. The result—a Texas German food style distinctively different from a mid-Atlantic German style, for example, —has not changed markedly in this century, despite the growing diversity of foodstuffs available to the average cook.

The goal of American agriculture and food technologists to supply the average cook with food supplies that defy season and locale was reached with the development of mechanized food preservation and transportation industries. With summer produce available year round, both frozen and fresh, the last physical limitation on American cookery was removed and the last regional boundaries were struck down. Restaurant systems that made use of standardized food technology quickly developed, and it was soon possible to follow a chain of franchised fast-food restaurants across the country in a string of virtually identical meals.

While critics at the time lamented the passing of cookery traditions that were grounded in time and space, it has become plain that Americans have developed a pluralistic approach to food much like the double vision with which they perceive popular entertainment, music, and other aspects of daily life. Frozen vegetables and syndicated fast-food have found their place in American life, but Americans still eat ten times as many tomatoes in the summer as in the winter, and the consumption of sausage, soups, and barbecue still varies widely from region to region.

BIBLIOGRAPHY

Barer-Stein, Thelma. *You Eat What You Are: A Study of Ethnic Food Traditions.* Toronto: McClelland and Stewart Limited, 1979.

Bennett, John. "An Interpretation of the Scope and Implications of Social Scientific Research in Human Subsistence." *American Anthropologist,* 48 (October 1946), 553-73.

Brown, Dale. *American Cooking.* New York: Time, Inc., 1968.

Collin, Richard. *New Orleans Underground Gourmet.* New York: Simon and Schuster, 1973.

Committee on Food Habits, National Research Council. *Manual for the Study of Food Habits.* Bulletin of the National Research Council Number 111, January 1945. Washington, D.C.: National Research Council, 1945.

Cummings, Richard Osborn. *The American and His Food: A History of Food Habits in the United States.* Chicago: University of Chicago Press, 1940.

Cussler, Margaret, and Mary Louise de Give. *Twixt the Cup and the Lip: Psychological and Socio-Cultural Factors Affecting Food Habits.* New York: Twayne Publishers, 1952.

Dickson, Paul. *Chow: A Cook's Tour of Military Food.* New York: New American Library, 1978.

Douglas, Mary. "Deciphering a Meal." In Clifford Geertz, ed., *Myth, Symbol and Culture.* New York: W. W. Norton, 1971, pp. 61-81.

Hillman, Howard. *The Book of World Cuisines.* New York: Penguin Books, 1979.

Journal of American Culture. Vol. 2, No. 3 (Fall 1979). Special Issue: Focus on American Food and Foodways. Issue Editors: Kay Mussell and Linda Keller Brown.

Lincoln, Waldo. *American Cookery Books, 1742-1860.* Worcester, Mass.: American Antiquarian Society, 1954.

Pyke, Magnus. *Food and Society.* London: John Murray, 1968.

Root, Waverly, and Richard de Rochemont. *Eating in America: A History.* New York: William Morrow, 1976.

Schweid, Richard. *Hot Peppers: Cajuns and Capsicum in New Iberia, Louisiana.* Seattle: Madrona Publishers, 1980.

Sokolov, Raymond. *Fading Feast.* New York: Farrar, Straus, and Giroux, 1981 (A collection of the articles Sokolov wrote for *Natural History* on regional foodways.)

Trillin, Calvin. *American Fried.* New York: Penguin Books, 1975.

Western Folklore. Vol. 11, No. 1 (January 1981). Special Issue: Foodways and Eating Habits: Directions for Research. Issue Editors: Michael Owen Jones, Bruce Giuliano, and Roberta Krell.

Wilson, Christine S. "Food Habits: A Selected Annotated Bibliography." *Journal of Nutrition Education,* 5 (January-March 1973), supp. 1, 39-72.

Yoder, Don. "Folk Cookery." In Richard M. Dorson, ed., *Folklore and Folklife: An Introduction.* Chicago: University of Chicago Press, 1972, pp. 325-50.

Games and Toys

Bernard Mergen

Games and toys, as part of the larger topic of play, have been studied by anthropologists, folklorists, psychologists, and historians for a century, and there is general agreement that both are significant in shaping individual personality and cultures. While the use of games and toys is not limited to childhood, it is obvious that in our society these terms are usually reserved for children's activities, with the prefix "adult" attached to games and toys that are not primarily meant for minors. On the other hand, as Jac Remise has pointed out, most toys are made by adults to appeal and sell to other adults.[1] When is a painted replica of a soldier a toy, and when is it a miniature? When is throwing a ball a game, and when is it a sport? Purpose and context can help make some useful distinctions, but the study of games and toys quickly leads to related subjects such as leisure, child development, education, sport, and recreation. Indeed, it is difficult to abstract games and toys from the whole study of work and play.

Games must be subdivided into at least three categories: physical skill, strategy, and chance. Most games involve some combination of the three, and, more often than not, some kind of competition is involved between teams, players, or an individual with himself. Competition may be the key element in distinguishing between games and play since most recent definitions of play emphasize process rather than any specific activity. As Stephen Miller has written: "There are goals in play, but these are of less importance in themselves than as embodiments of the process involved in obtaining them. Process in play is not streamlined toward dealing with goals in the shortest possible way, but is voluntarily elaborated, complicated, in various patterned ways."[2] All games are played, but not all play is a game. Similarly, all toys are played with, but not all play involves toys. Toys may be thought of as props in activities that may involve competition, chance, learning, fantasy, entertainment, or even "doing nothing." Games and toys, especially those of children, provide us with material for understanding the development of the mind—of imagination and communication, of ritual and innovation.

The games and toys of colonial children were those of their British, French, Dutch, and German ancestors. Paintings and engravings by Pieter Breughel, Jacob Cats, and other Dutch artists show children playing tag, blindman's bluff, jump rope, and leapfrog. They also depict a variety of stilts, hoops, tops, dolls, kites, and musical instruments. The sixteenth- and seventeenth-century child had a rich assortment of playthings, and there is no reason to suppose that the colonial child did not share in this abundance. Neither the rigors of frontier life nor the strictness of New England Puritanism could eliminate games and toys. Peter Wagner has recently noted that as early as 1649, Thomas Shepard castigated his congregation for spending the Sabbath "in rioting and wantonness, in sports and foolishness."[3]

Prosperity and changing values brought even greater variety to the toy market in the eighteenth century. Benjamin Franklin recalled buying imported toys in Boston in 1713, and English, German, and American potters made miniature dishes and tea sets in increasing quantities. The earliest surviving dolls' house, now in the collection of the Van Cortlandt Museum in New York City, is believed to date from 1774. If we extend the definition of toys, as Katharine McClinton does, to include "antiques of American childhood,"[4] we find interesting examples of silver whistles with coral and bells that were given as christening presents. These small noisemakers are often shown in eighteenth-century portraits of children, either held in a hand or worn on a silver chain around the child's neck. Silversmiths also made nursing bottles, porringers, and vessels with long spouts called "papboats" for the children of wealthy Americans. Pottery cradles made in England also found their way to the colonies, where they were sold for christening and birthday presents.

Older children and adults played with ivory or hardwood "cup and ball" toys, in which the object was to catch the ball in the cup or on the point of the handle that fitted into a small hole in the ball. Battledore and shuttlecock were popular outdoor games, as were marbles and ball games. Each game had its season; marbles came first, in the early spring, followed by kites, tops, and hoops. In New York, the sequence was slightly different, according to the adage: "Top-time's gone, kite-time's come, and April Fool's day will soon be here." Ball games—rudimentary forms of soccer and baseball—were played on holidays. According to William Wells Newell, "in Boston, *Fast-day* (the first Thursday of April) was particularly devoted to this sport. In England, the playing of ball at Easter-tide seems to have been a custom of the festival, inherited probably from pre-Christian ages. Foot-ball was a regular amusement on the afternoon of a New England Thanksgiving."[5] Bowling, hand ball, and hockey were other forms of ball games in seventeenth- and eighteenth-century America.

Indoor games of the same period included backgammon, chess, billiards, and various card games. As early as 1775, the *Pennsylvania Packet* advertised a card game to teach geography; but the heyday of educational card and board games was in the nineteenth century. The appearance of animals in many eighteenth-century family portraits suggests that pets were important elements in children's play. Dogs, cats, birds, squirrels, lambs, and even deer were part of the domestic scene. The legacy of Puritanism clouded the enjoyment of some of this kind of play, however, since the 1773 edition of *The New England Primer* illustrated the letter C with the rhyme: "The Cat doth play, And after slay." Samuel Goodrich described another indoor pastime of late eighteenth-century boys: "During my youthful days I found the penknife a source of great amusement, even instruction. Many a long winter evening, many a dull, drizzly day . . . have I spent in great ecstasy making candlerods or some other simple article of household goods, for my mother, or in perfecting toys for myself and my young friends. . . ."[6]

A generation later, Edward Everett Hale grew up with "an infinite variety of amusements—almost everything we wanted for purposes of manufacture or invention. Whalebone, spiral springs, pulleys and catgut, for perpetual motion or locomotive carriages, rollers and planks for floats . . . good blocks for building, carpenter's tools, a work-bench, and printing materials. . . . When we became chemists we might have sulphuric acid, nitric acid, litmus paper, or whatever we desired, so our allowance would stand it. I was not more than seven years old when I burned off my eyebrows by igniting gun-powder with my burning glass."[7] The 1830s and 1840s witnessed the birth of the American toy and game industry. William S. Tower, a carpenter in South Hingham, Massachusetts, organized a guild of toymakers in the late 1830s, and Franklin Peale exhibited a small steam locomotive made by Matthias Baldwin at the Peale family's Philadelphia museum. For the next forty years, wooden and metal toys were usually produced as a sideline by craftsmen engaged in cabinetmaking or tool manufacturing.

Paper toys and games were developed by stationers and lithographers. The titles of some board and card games echo the concerns of the period. In 1843, W. & B. Ives of Salem, Massachusetts, issued a highly moralistic board game, "The Mansion of Happiness," intended to teach young Americans to practice the virtues of industry, honesty, and sobriety. The following year introduced "The Game of Pope or Pagan or the Missionary Campaign or the Siege of the Stronghold of Satan by the Christian Army." By the 1860s, moralism began to be replaced by current events and an emphasis on material success. Milton Bradley's tremendously popular "The Checkered Game of Life," which appeared in 1860, alternated squares printed with "wealth," "happiness," "industry," and "ambition," with others labeled "gambling," "poverty," "jail," and "suicide."

"In 1868," according to McClinton, "four games of war and patriotism were packaged together under the title 'The Union Games.' "[8] Anagrams, puzzles, Zoetropes (a slotted revolving drum that gives the viewer the sense of moving pictures), and conversation cards gained in popularity through the 1860s. Conversation cards, which printed questions such as "Have you ever been in love?" and "What is your favorite food?," were intended to enliven the "cold and ceremonious" social gatherings that European travelers often found in the United States. The McLoughlin Brothers' catalog of 1867 lists seven kinds of conversation cards, including "Loves and Likes," "Comical Conversation Cards," "Conversations on Marriage," and "Quizzical Questions and Quaint Replies." Another type of game involving dialogue is illustrated by "Japhet Jenkins and Sally Jones visit to Boston," copyrighted in 1867. In this game, cards with brief sentences are shuffled and dealt to the players who take turns reading them and filling in blanks in a book that tells the adventures of a pair of country bumpkins visiting the city.

In 1883, sixteen-year-old George S. Parker invented his first game, the "Game of Banking." Subsequent games also reflected the concerns of the Gilded Age. "The Game of Moneta: or Money Makes Money" appeared in the Montgomery Ward catalog of 1889, and a "Game of Business" came out in 1895. One of the most popular games of the period was marketed by the Crandalls in 1889 under the name "Pigs in Clover." This puzzle required the player to maneuver four marbles through a maze into a cardboard enclosure. Hundreds of thousands were sold, and the game seems to have been especially popular in Washington, D.C., where the symbolism of the spoils system was obvious. Political election games appeared regularly in the late nineteenth century, and an interesting study could be done by comparing the "Centennial Presidential Game" of 1876 with the "Presidential Election" game of 1892, "Politics" of the 1950s, and "Bigwig" in 1973.

Games and toys were inspired by every conceivable event. The Chicago Columbian Exposition of 1893 was commemorated in games, puzzles, and building blocks. "Sherlock Holmes" and "The Amusing Game of Innocence Abroad" profited from the popularity of the books that preceded them. "White Squadron Picture Puzzles" helped to make the names of the war ships *Baltimore*, *Chicago*, and *Monterey* familiar to American children. The 1886 catalog of sporting goods and games sold by the Peck & Snyder Company lists chess, checkers, lotto, dominoes, Parcheesi, cards, bagatelle, cribbage, tetotums or spinning dice, and dice, as well as a board game called "The Monopolist." "On the board," the catalog reads, "the great struggle between Capital and Labor can be fought out to the satisfaction of all parties, and, if the players are successful, they can break the Monopolist, and become Monopolists themselves." Again, it would be instructive to compare this game with the well-known Parker Brothers game, "Monopoly," introduced in 1935. Robert H. Canary's essay on "Monopoly" and the 1950s "Game of Life" and James M. Hughes's comparison of "Monopoly" and "The Cities Game" are suggestive beginnings. The "Class Struggle" game, marketed in 1978 by political science professor Bertell Ollman, offers still another point of comparison.

The plethora of games in the twentieth century reveals much about American culture. Since most of these games involve elements of chance as well as strategy, they may reflect a growing uncertainty about the future and the desire to prepare individuals "to endure bad times in the hope of brighter futures." This is the hypothesis advanced by J. M. Roberts and Brian Sutton-Smith in their work on "Child Training and Game Involvement" in non-Western societies. Luck has always played a significant, if neglected, role in American thought, and a study of gambling games, especially among children, would be rewarding. The problem, of course, is that like other illegal activities, few records exist that describe gambling games. One of the few comes from Stewart Culin, an anthropologist and museum curator, who described "Street Games of Boys in Brooklyn, New York" in 1891. Culin found a game that the boys called "Pictures," which was played by shooting the cards found in cigarette packages toward a wall, the winner being the boy whose card landed nearest the wall. The winner then threw all the cards into the air and kept the ones that fell face up. Culin's ten-year-old informant claimed to be ignorant of the related game—penny pitching. "It was regarded among his associates as a vulgar game, and only practiced by bootblacks and boys of the lowest class, such as compose the 'gangs' that are a well-known feature of street life among the boys of our cities."[9]

There are many other kinds of toys that parallel adult activities. Toy models of steam engines, trains, telegraphs, telephones, washing machines, automobiles, and airplanes appeared soon after their introduction in the adult world. In some cases, an inventor seems to have no clear purpose and tries out his invention in toy form. Edison put one of his early phonograph cylinders in a "Talking Doll" in 1890. Dolls' houses and doll house furniture are obvious examples of toys that follow the fashion and changes in technology. Building materials are another example. In 1901, a British inventor, Frank Hornby, patented a set of construction materials made of thin strips of metal with perforations for nuts and bolts. His "Mechanics Made Easy," or "Meccano," was soon copied in the United States as "Erector" sets, allowing American children to build skyscraper skeletons to mirror those outside their bedroom windows. Charles Pajeau's 1914 patent for "Tinkertoys" followed the same general idea of building in outline, but his colorful rods, knobs, and pulleys seem closer to the abstract forms of the Armory Show than to the cantilever of the Queensboro Bridge. Pajeau may also have borrowed his idea from Friedrich Froebel, whose rods, strings, and balls inspired the young Frank Lloyd Wright in 1876.

Occasionally, however, the power of toys to mold the habits and talents of children fails. During World War I, Edward Hurley, chairman of the United States Shipping Board, decided that Americans should learn the value of the merchant marine and persuaded the Ives Toy Manufacturing Company to make a copy of the standard merchant ship being constructed by the Emergency Fleet Corporation. In his letter to the company, Hurley wrote: "It is none too early to begin waking Americans to the importance of ships, putting ships and the sea into their daily thought and work, and making ships appeal to the imagination of everybody in the country. We want to reach the children as well as the grown-ups, and, in this connection knowing how closely toys follow popular interest and what an educative value they have, it has been in my mind to have this great new national interest before the men who invent and design your goods."[10] When the Ives catalog for 1919 appeared, the advertising copy echoed Hurley's patrotic note: A boy "can get thoroughly interested in the great game of commerce and the big Merchant marine of his country. He can talk it, play it and interest his chums in it. . . .Who knows but what it may lead them into the big business of transportation by sea that is going to play such a wonderful part in the future world trade of the United States?" The ironic end to this effort to build support for an American merchant marine was the bankruptcy of the Ives Company in 1929, a collapse that Ives's accountants attributed in part to poor sales of the toy merchant fleet.

Turning from toys to games played without equipment, the historical record is strongest for the years since 1883, when folklorists, psychologists, and anthropologists first began to study children's play systematically. In that year, William Wells Newell, linguist, poet, and folklorist, published *Games and Songs of American Children.* This collection of almost two hundred folksongs and counting-out rhymes, clapping and ring games, tag and guessing games gives us a sense of the complexity and formality of games in the 1870s. Few adults or children today would be willing to memorize the long poem, "Knights of Spain," that accompanied a popular kissing game. Some songs, such as the familiar "Barbara Allen," were used to circumvent the religious ban on dancing. As the ballad was sung, couples kept time with slow movements without changing place. Newell's research showed that most American games and songs had British and European origins. He was impressed by the conservatism of children in preserving these games, but he was also afraid that increased immigration, urbanization, and industrialization were destroying traditional games.

There is some evidence that cities made play difficult. In 1892, Washington, D.C., passed an ordinance that declared it unlawful "for any person or persons to play the game of football, or any other game with a ball, in any of the streets, avenues, or alleys in the cities of Washington and Georgetown; nor shall it be lawful for any person or persons to play the game of bandy, shindy, or any other game by which a ball, stone, or other substance is struck or propelled by any stick, cane, or other substance in any street, avenue, or alley. . . ."[11] In the same year, Helen and Robert Lynd tell us, Muncie, Indiana, made it illegal to pitch quoits or coins, to play cricket, bandy, cat, townball, or any other game of public amusement, or to discharge a gun, pistol, or firearm on Sunday. Both laws tell us a great deal about the play life of small cities and towns and about the kinds of games and where they were played. Whether the motive was a reformist hope that play could be regulated in school yards and playgrounds, or a conservative desire to maintain fundamental religious values, the 1890s and early twentieth century saw numerous efforts to redefine games and play.

Observers unanimously agreed that most children were "doing nothing" and wasting their time when they were not working. A survey in Milwaukee, Wisconsin, in 1911, put the percentages at 19 percent working, 31 percent playing, and 50 percent doing nothing on a typical November day.[12] A similar survey in Cleveland, Ohio, on June 23, 1913, found 10 percent working, 50 percent playing, and 40 percent of the city's children doing nothing.[13] Of those who were playing, 43 percent were described as "just fooling." Doing nothing and just fooling were categories that included: breaking windows, chalking suggestive words on buildings, standing around on corners, fighting, looking at pictures of women in tights on billboards, stealing, and gambling with dice, cards, buttons, marbles, and beer bottle tags. Joseph Lee, Luther Gulick, Henry Curtis, and others sought to improve opportunities for urban recreation under the supervision of professional playground directors. The founding of the Playground Association in 1906 and the publication the following year of the first issue of *The Playground* (now *Parks and Recreation*) mark the beginnings of highly organized children's games and play in the United States.

Typical of the way in which traditional games were appropriated by the recreation movement is a list published in the *Seventh Annual Report of the Department of Playgrounds* of Washington, D.C., in 1918. Games were divided into "Low Organized Games," "High Organized Games," "Quiet Games," "Races," "Relay," and "Memory and Sense Games." An example of each included: "Prisoners Base," "Basketball," "Boiler Burst," "Wheelbarrow," "All up Indian Club," and "Ghosts." Early surveys of games and play suggest that there have been important changes in game preferences among American children. For example, T. R. Croswell, who studied about two thousand schoolchildren in Worcester, Massachusetts, in 1896, found only four of one thousand boys playing cowboys and Indians and only two who mentioned playing with toy soldiers. Girls' game preferences seem to have changed more than boys' in the past century, with many more girls playing games that were played exclusively by boys in the past, such as leapfrog and red rover. Boys and girls now play few singing and dialogue games such as those recorded by Newell, and many of the rhymes that were recited with those games are now used in jump rope.

Brian Sutton-Smith argues that children's play has become more sophisticated and that fantasy play and games involving the manipulation of symbols have been encouraged by middle-class parents.[14] Playground planners in the United States are trying to introduce "Adventure Playgrounds," in which children are encouraged to organize and develop their own games and to build their own play structures. A new vocabulary has entered the playground movement: "loose parts," "ambiguity," "flexibility," "diversity," "change," and "open-endedness." The contemporary student of games is faced with a bewildering variety of theories and an equally confusing body of raw data. Games, toys, and play serve many functions, not the least of which is to help cope with a chaotic, violent, and even dangerous world. We should not be surprised to find much that is shocking in play, but we must try to understand what is actually going on, rather than imposed preconceived definitions of what is play and what it is not. We must try to discover what games and toys mean to the players.

NOTES

1. Jac Remise, *The Golden Age of Toys* (Greenwich, Conn.: New York Graphic Society, 1967), p. 11.
2. Stephen Miller, "Ends, Means, and Galumphing: Some Leitmotifs of Play," *American Anthropologist*, 75 (February 1973), 97.
3. Peter Wagner, "Literary Evidence of Sport in Colonial New England: The American Puritan Jeremiad," *Stadion*, 2 (1976), 235.
4. Katharine McClinton, *Antiques of American Childhood* (New York: Bramhall House, 1970).
5. William Wells Newell, *Games and Songs of American Children* (New York: Harper & Brothers, 1883), p. 176.
6. Elizabeth George Speare, *Child Life in New England 1790-1840* (Sturbridge, Mass.: Old Sturbridge Booklet Series, 1961), p. 18.
7. Speare, p. 19
8. McClinton, p. 227.
9. Stewart Culin, "Street Games of Boys in Brooklyn, New York," *Journal of American Folklore*, 4 (July-September 1891), 234-35.
10. *Emergency Fleet News*, January 1, 1919, p. 9.
11. U.S. Department of Labor, Children's Bureau, *Facilities for Children's Play in the District of Columbia* (Washington, D.C.: Government Printing Office, 1917), p. 68.
12. *The Playground*, 6 (May 1912), 51.
13. George Johnson, *Education Through Recreation* (Cleveland: The Survey

Committee of the Cleveland Foundation, 1916), p. 49.

14. Brian Sutton-Smith, "The Two Cultures of Games," in *The Folkgames of Children* (Austin, Tex.: Published for the American Folklore Society by the University of Texas, 1972), pp. 295-311.

BIBLIOGRAPHY

Avedon, Elliott M., and Brian Sutton-Smith, eds. *The Study of Games.* New York: John Wiley, 1971.

Brewster, Paul G. *Children's Games and Rhymes.* Durham, N.C.: Duke University Press, 1952.

———. *American Nonsinging Games.* Norman: University of Oklahoma Press, 1953.

Champlin, John D., and Arthur E. Bostwick. *The Young Folks' Cyclopaedia of Games and Sports.* New York: H. Holt, 1890.

Herron, R. E., and Brian Sutton-Smith, eds. *Child's Play.* New York: John Wiley, 1971.

Howard, Dorothy. *Dorothy's World: Childhood in Sabine Bottom, 1902-1910.* New York: Prentice-Hall, 1977.

Huizinga, Johan. *Homo Ludens: A Study of the Play Element in Culture.* Boston: Beacon, 1960.

Kirshenblatt-Gimblett, Barbara, ed. *Speech Play.* Philadelphia: University of Pennsylvania Press, 1976.

Knapp, Mary, and Herbert Knapp. *One Potato, Two Potato . . . The Secret Education of American Children.* New York: Norton, 1976.

McClintock, Inez, and Marshall McClintock. *Toys in America.* Washington, D.C.: Public Affairs Press, 1961.

Mergen, Bernard. "The Discovery of Children's Play." *American Quarterly,* 27 (October 1975), 399-420.

———. *Play and Playthings of American Children: A History and Reference Guide.* Westport, Conn.: Greenwood Press, 1982.

Newell, William Wells. *Games and Songs of American Children.* New York: Harper & Brothers, 1883. Reprinted. New York: Dover Books, 1963.

Opie, Iona, and Peter Opie. *The Lore and Language of School Children.* Oxford: Clarendon Press, 1960.

———. *Children's Games in Street and Playground.* Oxford: Clarendon Press, 1969.

Plumb, J. H. "The New World of Children in Eighteenth-Century England." *Past and Present,* 67 (May 1975), 64-93.

Roberts, J. M., M. J. Arth, and R. R. Bush. "Games in Culture." *American Anthropologist,* 61 (1959), 597-605.

Rosenberg, B. G., and Brian Sutton-Smith. "Sixty-Years of Historical Change in the Game Preferences of American Children." *Journal of American Folklore,* 74 (January-March 1961), 17-46.

Schwartzman, Helen B. *Transformations: The Anthropology of Children's Play.* New York: Plenum, 1978.

Sutton-Smith, Brian. *The Folkstories of Children.* Philadelphia: University of Pennsylvania Press, 1981.

———. *The Folkgames of Children.* Austin: University of Texas Press, 1972.

______. "The Play of Girls." In *Becoming Female: Perspectives on Development.* Edited by Claire B. Knapp and Martha Kirkpatrick. New York: Plenum, 1979, pp. 229-57.

Ward, Colin. *The Child in the City.* New York: Pantheon, 1978.

PERIODICALS

The Playground. New York, 1907-1915; Cooperstown, N.Y., 1916-1923; Greenwich, Conn., 1923-1924; New York, 1924-1929; *Playground and Recreation,* New York, 1929-1930; *Recreation,* New York, 1931-1965; *Parks and Recreation,* Arlington, Va., 1966-.

Playthings. New York, 1903-.

Gothic Novels

Kay J. Mussell

The gothic novel had its greatest general popularity in a relatively brief period of literary history, the end of the eighteenth and the beginning of the nineteenth centuries. It was originally an English literary form, although authors and readers in other countries quickly adopted gothic fiction and its conventions for their own. The influence of the gothic in fiction, however, has been much more significant than its relatively short period of great popularity would indicate. In addition to its contributions to the detective novel, science fiction, horror stories, the popular melodrama, and the works of such writers as Poe, Hawthorne, Irving, James, and Faulkner, the gothic novel also continued as a form in itself, although much less well defined and less pervasive than it had been in its heyday. The audience for the gothic novel, from the works of Ann Radcliffe in eighteenth-century England to those of Phyllis Whitney in twentieth-century America, is primarily female. Women are attracted to gothic novels by the combination of romance and terror, a blend that has remained relatively constant over the past two hundred years.

Like all popular formulas, the gothic novel is fiction with a characteristic world view supported by a particular set of conventions. It consists of a story set in a remote place or a remote time in which a usually improbable and terrifying mystery is completely intertwined with a successful love story. Unlike the detective story, gothic novels do not provide a logical solution to the mystery; to the contrary, the mystery and the love story are so coincidentally interconnected that it is virtually impossible to separate them. The solution of the mystery removes the impediments to the coming together of the lovers. Women are victimized by finding themselves in a situation (castle, monastery, crumbling mansion) where a gothic villain can threaten them. The novels depend upon a setting in which the social structure is hierarchical; the conventions of gothic fiction, such as mysterious inheritances, hidden identities, lost wills, family secrets, inherited curses, incest and illegitimacy, require a world in which social mobility takes place through family identity and marriage rather than individual worth. The novels also depend upon the audience's belief that the successful courtship and marriage of the characters is the most satisfactory conclusion of the plot, elevating the place of family formation through love to a supreme position.

Although the gothic novel as a form is capable of containing and exploring sensitive and sophisticated questions in fiction, as shown by the work of such writers as Poe and Hawthorne, in its popular version it has been both formulaic and predictable. The world view of the gothic novel offers vicarious danger and romantic fantasy of a type that is particularly appealing to female readers. The heroine is cast as a victim in a man's world, but through the demonstration of feminine virtues, she proves herself worthy of the love of the hero, who becomes her deliverer from the terrors to which she is vulnerable. The gothic villain, on the other hand, manipulates terrifying props and produces fear and danger before he or she is defeated by the power of true love. The gothic novel over two centuries reaffirms the romantic belief in love as the cure for and defense against evil.

Scholarly consideration of the gothic novel in America is long overdue, but the study has been hampered by a variety of legitimate difficulties beyond the traditional resistance to the study of popular art forms. The term *gothic* does not lend itself to easy definition and has not been consistently applied. In its earliest British form, as written by Horace Walpole, the gothic novel was synonymous with supernatural horror; but within a few years, in the works of Ann Radcliffe and Clara M. Reeve, among others, the gothic took on more sentimental and romantic characteristics, almost as though the work of Samuel Richardson had been overlaid with gothic props. In Ann Radcliffe's works, the "supernatural" is explained as the manipulations of the gothic villain who threatens the lovers. Clara Reeve's gothic novels were historical romances that used the exotic trappings of medieval chivalry to provide excitement. It was these latter types of the gothic that were most appealing and influential in America.

After the early nineteenth century, the word *gothic* was not consistently applied to formula novels until recently, even though the form flourished between those dates. In 1960, Gerald Gross, an editor at Ace Books, titled a paperback series of romantic mysteries designed for women *gothics.* The term caught on immediately as it characterized so aptly one of the most active and lucrative areas of publishing from 1960 through the mid-1970s. The gothic boom of this period was not entirely dependent upon new material; some of the most popular titles were published long ago, and either were never out of print or were returned to print to satisfy readers. The gothic novel may have been submerged or out of vogue during some periods, but it was never entirely absent from the literary scene.

Beyond the problem of definition, another impediment to the serious study of gothic fiction is that the audience for the form has been primarily female, relatively inarticulate, and lacking in access to the outlets for critical expression. The forms influenced by the gothic, on the other hand, have been much more thoroughly documented and studied. When the original gothic novels lost their vitality for readers, the tradition splintered in a number of directions. Gothics influenced detective fiction, science fiction, and the Western, especially in the works of James Fenimore Cooper. In Europe, although not in America, they were influential in the development of horror stories, such as *Frankenstein* and *Dracula.* Their influence on serious American writers has been well documented.

For the late eighteenth and early nineteenth centuries, as well as for the mid-twentieth century, there is relatively firm agreement upon what a gothic novel is. However, the definitions from the two periods are not entirely congruent, and for the century and a half between there is no such agreement. The first gothic novels, those of Horace Walpole, Ann Radcliffe, Clara M. Reeve, "Monk" Lewis, and others, were read in America and influenced American fiction. The rise of the novel in America coincided with the peak popularity of gothic fiction in Britain, and since American fiction was very derivative of British models, much early American fiction was strongly influenced by the gothic. Critics of gothic novels traditionally have divided them into several categories: sentimental-gothic, terror-gothic, historical-gothic, and some subcategories of lesser significance. Sentimental-gothic novels emphasize the love story and use supernatural terrors with rational explanations. The primary writer of this type in Britain was Radcliffe, and her work was most influential upon American fiction. Terror-gothic novels, like those of Walpole and Lewis, emphasize the supernatural, often using depraved monks or nuns as villains. Their influence was most marked upon serious writers in America, but the terror-gothic tradition never developed fully in this country. Historical-gothic novels were much more influential in America. Such works romanticized the past, usually with anachronistic elements, exploiting the exoticism of a remote time to heighten the atmosphere of terror.

Although the gothic was influential in America, there are several reasons why it never developed fully here. The most important was that the American society and landscape did not provide the necessary moldering castles, sinister monasteries, and hierarchical social structure so necessary to the novels. A second was the American antipathy to fiction as "not true" and "not instructive." A third was that, in the absence of international copyright laws, it was simpler and cheaper for American printers to pirate the works of British popular authors than to pay American writers for original material. For more than a century, American fiction writers were hampered by the cheaper competition of British authors, who, in turn, complained loudly about the lack of payment for their work. Even today, the most popular gothic writers are British, and American authors are not only derivative but also rely heavily upon British settings. In American fiction, then, the sentimental-gothic and historical-gothic modes flourished, especially in their more sensational elements. The supernatural developed only in the works of serious authors. The popular audience was much more interested in terrors with rational explanations than in explorations of the irrational or the psychological. Alexander Cowie suggests that the gothic novel in America used gothic conventions in a frame of sentimental romance.

Charles Brockden Brown was the first major American writer to use the gothic in his fiction. He was particularly influenced by the terror-gothic mode, although he often supplied rationalistic or quasi-scientific explanations for apparently supernatural effects, using the potential of terrorizing material to explore psychological states and experiments. His novels, including *Wieland* (1798), *Ormond* (1799), and *Edgar Huntly* (1799), have American settings. A lesser contemporary of Brown was Isaac Mitchell, the author of one of the most popular novels of the period, *The Asylum, or Alonzo and Melissa* (1804), a gothic romance hinging upon the opposition of a father to his daughter's proposed marriage. To heighten the gothic atmosphere in an American setting, Mitchell set his book in a medieval castle on the shore of Long Island Sound. Another novel that resembles British models, *Julia, or the Illuminated Baron* (1800), by Sally Wood, is set in eighteenth-century France. The plot depends upon the hidden identities of Julia and her suitor, who endure many dangers before being united. In the end, both are revealed as aristocrats, but in deference to American democratic sentiments, they renounce their titles. Wood used traditional gothic elements including a dangerous chateau, visits to tombs, kidnappings, and an attempted rape. Other novels by Wood, similar in type, are *Dorval, or the Speculator* (1801), *Amelia; or the Influence of Virtue: an Old Man's Story* (1802?), and *Ferdinand and Elmira: a Russian Story* (1804).

Other novelists of the early period, some anonymous, who wrote gothic fiction include Ann Eliza Bleecker, and the women who used the pseudonyms "A Lady of Massachusetts," and "A Lady of Philadelphia." *Laura* (1809), by "A Lady of Philadelphia," is about a nun who comes to America and endures many terrors in a yellow fever epidemic. Chapbooks and magazines were also filled with gothic fiction. George Lippard's *The Quaker City, or The Monks of Monks' Hall* (1844) used many gothic conventions.

After the heyday of the gothic novel in Britain and America, the tradition splintered in a number of directions. Poe was influenced by the gothic in both his stories of detection and his stories of horror. Science fiction was also indebted to the gothic for its premise of the seemingly supernatural (or strange) explained by rational means. The stage melodrama often resembled gothic novels in world view as well as conventions. Some critics have even suggested that the Western was influenced by the gothic, especially in its use of Indians and the dangers of the wilderness as a form of American gothic terror. However, all of these uses of the gothic go beyond the imaginative world posited by the original gothic novelists.

Because the American democratic and practical mind was never quite comfortable with the gothic of terror, the heirs of the early gothic novels can be found in the women's novels of the nineteenth and twentieth centuries. Many writers of sentimental romances wrote novels that today would be called *gothics*, novels that are dependent upon the models of Radcliffe or the Brontes for their plot and their world view. Even at their most tame, the domestic and sentimental novelists often relied upon gothic conventions for suspense. Probably the most important of these writers was E.D.E.N. Southworth, whose novels were written over many years of the nineteenth century. In books like *The Hidden Hand* (1859) and *The Curse of Clifton* (1852), she used gothic conventions (lost heirs, evil villains, virtuous maidens, nobles, and castles) within novels that reflected the world view of the gothic. That fictional world by the mid-nineteenth century was one in which life itself was precarious, but especially for young women. There was always someone—a villain, a jealous woman, a rival for an inheritance—who could jeopardize the romantic happiness of a young heroine by the manipulation of gothic threats. Another important writer of the period was "Bertha M. Clay," the pseudonym for a group of writers, beginning with Charlotte M. Breame, who wrote women's novels in the gothic mode for Street and Smith's dime-novel series. The popularity of the gothic is further demonstrated in this period by one of the major dime-novel publishers, Norman Munro, who once published Walpole's *Castle of Otranto* in a story paper without acknowledging the source by either author or title. Gothic novels of this period, however, were rarely novels of the supernatural, although they were indebted to the gothic for conventions and techniques. Most were very long, written in a highly romantic style, and full of coincidences in plot and anachronisms in setting. They were often written very quickly in order to satisfy the voracious appetite of their large audience.

The turn of the century saw an increase in reader interest in historical romances, many of which relied upon gothic conventions and world view. Some followed the tradition of Clara M. Reeve and others in Britain, mining past ages of Europe for romantic and exotic material. But, by the end of the nineteenth century, most historical gothics were no longer set in the Middle Ages. Colonial America and the Revolutionary period, as well as the Civil War, became more appropriate settings. Mary Johnston, the Virginia author, wrote several novels in this form. Her *To Have and To Hold* (1900), one of the most popular historical romances in American publishing history, is the tale of a young aristocratic woman who flees Britain and comes to Jamestown in a shipment of potential brides in order to escape a villainous suitor. In America she is purchased by a settler who, after surviving a number of dangers with her, saves her from her pursuer and falls in love with her. Johnston adapted gothic conventions to the American landscape better than many other authors.

Authors of the early twentieth century who used gothic material in romances include Mary Roberts Rinehart, Mignon G. Eberhart (both better known as detective and mystery writers), Kathleen Norris, Emilie Loring, and Kathleen Winsor. These authors and others have never been studied with consistency, but their popularity is demonstrated by the number of their books written long ago that are still in print in paperback. The demand for Rinehart and Loring is especially insatiable.

Gothic novels again attracted the attention of publishers early in the 1960s; however, the origins of the 1960s gothic boom were evident at least as early as the 1930s, with the publication and immense popularity of Daphne duMaurier's *Rebecca* (1938) in England. Among the major gothic novelists of recent years are two Americans, Phyllis A. Whitney and Anya Seton, who first published novels in the 1940s and are still writing today. It is impossible in this period, however, to ignore the influence of British writers on the American formula.

In 1960, the first novel by Victoria Holt (a pseudonym of Eleanor Burford Hibbert) was published in America. *Mistress of Mellyn,* a novel derivative of both Charlotte Bronte's *Jane Eyre* and duMaurier's *Rebecca,* sparked the interest in gothic fiction in America in two ways: by creating a larger market for the writings of popular British writers (Mary Stewart, Barbara Cartland, Dorothy Eden, and Hibbert herself under her various pseudonyms) and by inspiring publishers to promote such established American novelists as Phyllis Whitney, Anya Seton, and Daoma Winston as well as to seek out new writers such as Dorothy Daniels (Norman Daniels), Marilyn Ross (Dan Ross), and Edwina Noone (Michael Avallone). These contemporary gothic novels can also be divided into categories. Some are gothics with contemporary settings in which the strange and terrifying events come from the exotic nature of the environment; an example is Phyllis Whitney's *Black Amber* (1964), which takes place in Turkey. Others are classic gothic stories set in the past in which a young woman (governess, new bride) endures the terrors of an old house with ancient legends, superstitions, and family secrets; an example is Anya Seton's *Dragonwyck* (1944).

Recently, a new type of fiction related to the gothic has been gaining popularity, overshadowing and outselling the work of Whitney and Seton. Novels by such new authors as Rosemary Rogers, Kathleen Woodiwiss, Claire Lorrimer, and Lolah Burford are historical gothics, published as paperback originals and much longer than gothics issued a few years ago. Rogers's *Wicked, Loving Lies* (1976) is set in the eighteenth and nineteenth centuries in Spain, England, France, Tripoli, Louisiana, and Texas. The heroine is raped innumerable times, almost always by the same man (who is, of course, the hero). She is, for a time, Napoleon's mistress, a prisoner in a harem, a British noblewoman, a quadroon slave in the American South, and an heiress. These books are much more sexually explicit than many of the earlier gothics, but their world view remains the same, indicating that the twentieth-century audience is becoming more tolerant of sexual deviation and adventuring but still wishes some of its vicarious romance in gothic form.

Contemporary gothics rarely reach the bestseller lists; however, their sales figures and continuing availability demonstrate their popularity among their primarily female audience. Although there has been some change, the value system of gothic novels has remained relatively stable over the years. The stories still occur in a world in which marriage is seen as the best of all possible states for women and in a world that, because women have very little control over their lives, is especially precarious for them. Despite the irrationality of gothic dangers in a twentieth-century context, these books are still replete with old houses, corrupt aristocrats, disguised identities, lost heirs, supernatural effects rationally explained, and melodramatic reconciliations.

It is clear that there is much more research and study to be done on gothic novels, for their continued popularity over the last two centuries shows that they are significant cultural indicators of the interests, tastes, tensions, and values of their primarily female audience. All of the other inheritors of the original gothics (mysteries, science fiction, melodrama, and Westerns) have gone on to become the subjects of full-scale scholarly studies. Only the gothic novel for women has been neglected, and it is clearly deserving of the same analytic treatment in its own right.

BIBLIOGRAPHY

Birkhead, Edith. *The Tale of Terror.* New York: E. P. Dutton, 1921; New York: Russell and Russell, 1963.

Boyle, Regis Louise. *Mrs. E. D. E. N. Southworth, Novelist.* Washington, D.C.: Catholic University Press, 1939.

Brown, Herbert Ross. *The Sentimental Novel in America 1789-1860.* Durham, N.C.: Duke University Press, 1940; New York: Octagon Books, 1975.

Cawelti, John G. *Adventure, Mystery, and Romance: Formula Stories as Art and Popular Culture.* Chicago: University of Chicago Press, 1976.

Clark, Kenneth. *The Gothic Revival: An Essay in the History of Taste.* London: Constable, 1928; New York: Holt, Rinehart and Winston, 1962.

Coad, Oral Sumner. "The Gothic Element in American Literature Before 1835." *Journal of English and Germanic Philology,* 24 (January 1925), 72-93.

Cowie, Alexander. *The Rise of the American Novel.* New York: American Book Co., 1948, 1951.

Duffy, Martha. "On the Road to Manderley." *Time,* 97 (April 12, 1971), 95-96.

Fiedler, Leslie A. *Love and Death in the American Novel.* New York: Criterion, 1960; Dell, 1966.

Grimsted, David. *Melodrama Unveiled.* Chicago: University of Chicago Press, 1968.

Hart, James D. *The Popular Book: A History of America's Literary Taste.* New York: Oxford University Press, 1950; Westport, Conn.: Greenwood Press, 1976.

McNutt, Dan J. *The Eighteenth-Century Gothic Novel: An Annotated Bibliography of Criticism and Selected Texts.* New York: Garland Publishing Co., 1975.

Mussell, Kay J. "Beautiful and Damned: The Sexual Woman in Modern Gothic Fiction." *Journal of Popular Culture,* 9 (Summer 1975), 84-89.

______. *Women's Gothic and Romantic Fiction: A Reference Guide.* Westport, Conn.: Greenwood Press, 1981.

Nye, Russel B. *The Unembarrassed Muse.* New York: Dial Press, 1970.

Peterson, Clell T. "Spotting the Gothic Novel." *Graduate Student of English,* 1 (1957), 14-15.

Petter, Henri. *The Early American Novel.* Columbus: Ohio State University Press, 1971.

Railo, Eino. *The Haunted Castle.* London: George Routledge, 1927; New York: Gordon Press, 1974.

Redden, Sister Mary Mauritia. *The Gothic Fiction in the American Magazines (1765-1800).* Washington, D.C.: Catholic University Press, 1939.

Thompson, G. Richard. "Introduction: Gothic Fiction in the Romantic Age: Context and Mode." In *Romantic Gothic Tales 1790-1840.* New York: Harper and Row, Perennial Library, 1979, pp. 1-54.

Varma, Devendra P. *The Gothic Flame.* New York: Russell and Russell, 1957, 1966.

West, Katharine. *Chapter of Governesses: A Study of the Governess in English Fiction 1800-1949.* London: Cohen and West, 1949.

Whitney, Phyllis A. "Writing the Gothic Novel." *The Writer,* 80 (February 1967), 9-13, 42-43.

Wright, Lyle H. *American Fiction 1774-1850.* San Marino, Calif.: Huntingdon Library, 1939.

______. *American Fiction 1774-1900.* Louisville, Ky.: Lost Cause Press, 1970.

Historical Fiction

R. Gordon Kelly

Any consideration of historical fiction begins with the troublesome matter of definition. What is an historical novel? Sir Walter Scott, whose Waverly novels effectively established a model adhered to by writers for nearly a century afterward, was less dogmatic on the subject than some of his successors. In giving to *Waverly* the subtitle "It Is Sixty Years Past," he implied a setting at least two generations in the past; while in his preface to *Ivanhoe*, he offered few prescriptions, concentrating rather on defending his practice against the anticipated charge of "polluting the well of history with modern inventions." Ernest Leisy, author of the principal study of American historical fiction, adopted the broadest of definitions—"A historical novel is a novel the action of which is laid in an earlier time"—and reduced Scott's half century in the past to a generation, "so rapid are changes [in the United States]." And Avrom Fleishman, with Georg Lukács, the most theoretically oriented commentator on the historical novel, accepts essentially the same definition, adding only the specification that "real" historical persons be present in the story: "When life is seen in the context of history, we have a novel; when the novel's characters live in the same world with historical persons, we have a historical novel."[1] For the purposes of this essay, however, the broader definition is preferable in order to avoid excluding those costume historical romances that might not qualify under Fleishman's slightly more restrictive definition. Because it is with the *popular* historical novel that we shall be concerned in this essay, little attention is given to those classic works of American fiction—*The Scarlet Letter* or *The Red Badge of Courage*, for example—which a broad definition of historical fiction would otherwise warrant including.

The historical novel has been a staple of American publishing since the first quarter of the nineteenth century, when, following the War of 1812, the call for a national literature and an American Scott was as explicit as Rufus Choate's oration "The Importance of Illustrating New England History by a Series of Romances like the Waverly Novels" (1810). The form was especially popular with readers in the 1820s and 1830s, again at the turn of the century, and in the 1930s and 1940s. With *The Spy* (1821), James Fenimore Cooper successfully demonstrated that Scott's methods could be applied to American materials. Dramatizing the fratricidal nature of the Revolution in his depiction of the Warren family's divided loyalties, Cooper laid the foundations for an international reputation and encouraged a host of imitators. So well-received were *The Spy* and *The Pilot* (1823) that Cooper projected a series of thirteen historical novels, one for each of the Revolutionary colonies, although he completed only one, *Lionel Lincoln* (1825). His subsequent historical fiction included *The Wept of Wishton-wish* (1829), set during King Philip's War; *Wyandotte* (1843), set in western New York State during the Revolution; and *The Oak Openings* (1848), set in frontier Michigan during the War of 1812. He also wrote three novels with European settings in which he deliberately set out to show the differences between his and Scott's perceptions of the same things: eighteenth-century Venice (*The Bravo*, 1831); Germany on the eve of the Reformation (*The Heidenmauer*, 1832); and Switzerland in the early eighteenth century (*The Headsman*, 1883). Cooper's Leatherstocking novels are too well known to require description.

By the mid-1820s, "with Waverly galloping over hill and dale; the 'Spy' lurking in every closet; the mind everywhere supplied with 'Pioneers' on the land and soon to be with 'Pilots' on the deep," American writers were rushing to imitate Cooper.[2] Faced with the number of historical novels coming to market as early as 1824, a critic for *The North American Review* began a review of *The Wilderness, or Braddock's Time* on a note of asperity: "It has been a question seriously agitated among our cisatlantic literati, even at so late a period as since the publication of this journal [begun in 1815] whether America did or did not afford sufficient materials for a new and peculiar historical romance; yet now, so prolific are we in this species of production that the reader who keeps pace with the outpourings of the press . . . must have some industry and a great deal of patriotism."[3] Among the most successful with the reading public were southern romancers like William H. Caruthers in *The Cavaliers of Virginia* (1834) and John Pendleton Kennedy, who found in the Virginia planter an American analogue to Scott's English noble or Scottish laird in *Swallow Barn* (1832) and *Horse Shoe Robinson* (1835). The most prolific of southern historical novelists was William Gilmore Simms, who drew judiciously on Scott and Cooper for structural elements and on his own early experience, as well as on research, for convincing detail in describing early colonial South Carolina in *The Yemassee* (1835), for example, a novel of Indian warfare that still repays reading for its treatment of the Yemassee Indians and their allies. In Simms's wake, John Esten Cooke continued to romanticize southern life until well past mid-century, by which time the historical romance, increasingly out of fashion because of the rise of literary realism, became ever more hackneyed and conventionalized.

The three most popular historical novels published before the Civil War are instructive of the principal ways in which American writers made use of the past. Two of the novels exploited the nation's constitutive conflicts—warfare with the Indian and separation from the British. Robert Montgomery Bird dramatized the former in his bloody, widely read account of frontier revenge, *Nick of the Woods* (1837), while Judge Daniel P. Thompson's *The Green Mountain Boys* (1839) celebrated his forebears' struggle to defend their homes, first against land jobbers and then against Burgoyne and his soldiers. The third best-selling historical romance of the antebellum period, Joseph Holt Ingraham's *The Prince of the House of David* (1855), depicted the chief episodes in the life of Jesus as seen by a young Jewess and demonstrated the profits to be made from tapping the populace's religious idealism, as romances of the Revolution had already amply demonstrated with regard to nationalism and patriotism.

The mid-1850s to the mid-1880s was a period of lessened popularity for historical fiction as a genre. The historical romance continued to attract readers, but the decades were without conspicuous best-selling historical novels. A number of works from the 1870s and 1880s were informed by realism and the increasing preoccupation with local color: for example, Edward Eggleston's *The Circuit Rider* (1874); Mary Hartwell Catherwood's novels of France's New World colonies such as *The Romance of Dollard* (1888); George Washington Cable's *Old Creole Days* (1879) and *The Grandissimes* (1880); and Harold Frederic's *In the Valley* (1890), a tale of the Mohawk Valley in the French and Indian War. By the mid-1890s, however, the historical romance was once more the reigning form of popular fiction. Frank Luther Mott, the principal historian of best sellers, claims that fully half of the best-selling fiction of the period 1894-1902 consisted of historical romances. The revival of the genre's popularity began quietly enough in 1880 with the publication of a religious novel set in Rome at the time of Christ, which was dismissed initially by reviewers as anachronistic. By 1896, however, a nationwide survey revealed that *Ben-Hur: A Tale of the Christ,* by the Civil War general Lew Wallace, was circulated more than any other book in eight out of ten libraries. Widely imitated (for example, Marie Corelli's *Barrabbas,* 1894; and Florence Kingsley's *Titus, A Comrade of the Cross,* 1894), *Ben-Hur* eventually appeared in editions that were authorized by the Holy See as well as retailed by Sears Roebuck—an achievement probably without precedent in American publishing. Combining the historical values of Scott and the moral values of the genteel tradition, it has been credited with battering down the last vestiges of prejudice against fiction.[4] With this last resistance overcome, with Stevenson and Kipling reviving the romance in England, and with patriotism in this country aroused by our adventuring in Cuba and the Philippines, the historical romance flourished and dominated popular fiction until the 1920s.

The stream of historical fiction flowed in several channels at the turn of the century. The commercial success of Anthony Hope Hawkins's *The Prisoner of Zenda* (1894), set in the mythical Balkan kingdom of Ruritania, established a vogue for costume romance that lasted a decade and encouraged a number of American imitators, among the more successful of whom were Richard Harding Davis in *The Princess Aline* (1899) and Harold MacGrath in *Arms and the Woman* (1899) and *The Puppet Crown* (1901). However, the Ruritanian formula was most successfully exploited by George Barr McCutcheon, an obscure Indiana journalist, in *Graustark* (1901), a tale that combined love and adventure with the unabashed celebration of the American virtues of its clean-cut hero. The inordinate popularity of the pseudohistorical romance waned as sales of *Graustark* tailed off—McCutcheon's sequel *Beverly of Graustark* (1904) failed to surpass *Graustark*'s sales. The publication in 1907 of George Ade's parody of the Ruritanian romance, *The Slim Princess*, put an end to the popularity of that formula. In the same year, however, the publication of Elinor Glyn's *Three Weeks* presaged the form's survival in the "bosom and bravado" historical novels of the 1930s, by adding sex—three weeks of lovemaking in a Graustarkian setting—to the Hope-McCutcheon formula.

Romances with historical European settings, as opposed to the misty midregions of Ruritania, were also popular with American readers at the turn of the century. F. Marion Crawford wrote more than forty novels with European settings, for example, *Via Crucis* (1898) and *In the Palace of the King* (1900); S. Weir Mitchell's *The Adventures of Francois* (1898) was set during the French Revolution; Robert Chambers's *Ashes of Empire* (1898) was based on the Franco-Prussian War; and Charles Major's *When Knighthood Was in Flower* (1898) told in archaic language of Mary Tudor's love for a man who was her social inferior. All were best sellers and were more credible historical fiction than the Ruritanian romances.

American settings predominated, however, and among the writers who both rode the crest of the historical romance's popularity and distinguished themselves somewhat from the mass of journeymen writers on the basis of their narrative skill and historical knowledge were S. Weir Mitchell, Paul Leicester Ford, Winston Churchill, Mary Johnston, and Maurice Thompson, author of the very popular tale of the Revolution in the Old Northwest, *Alice of Old Vincennes* (1900). Mitchell's revolutionary war tale of a free or fighting Quaker, *Hugh Wynne* (1898), was not only a commercial success, but also an influential model for writers seeking psychological realism. Paul Leicester Ford brought the knowledge and research skills of a trained historian to his writing of *Janice Meridith* (1899), a tale of the Revolution set in New Jersey.

Winston Churchill won acclaim for three novels especially: *Richard Carvel* (1899), a story of the Revolution, in which the Annapolis-trained Churchill presented a virtuoso description of the battle between John Paul Jones's *Bonhomme Richard* and the British man-of-war *Serapis*; *The Crisis* (1901), in which Churchill portrayed the bitter division of feeling in Missouri, particularly in St. Louis, before and during the Civil War; and *The Crossing* (1904), a story of George Rogers Clark's campaign in the Northwest Territory during the Revolution.

Mary Johnston, the daughter of a Confederate officer, wrote more than twenty historical novels, mostly set in the South during the Revolution or the Civil War. Beginning her career with *The Prisoners of Hope* (1898), she hit her stride in *To Have and to Hold*, a best seller in 1900. In *The Long Roll* (1911) and in *Cease Firing* (1912), she traced the course of the Civil War with meticulously researched detail and evident Southern sympathies.

So great was the popularity of historical fiction that a number of writers, whose earlier works were in a different vein, temporarily joined the ranks of historical novelists. Mary E. Wilkins Freeman's *The Heart's Highway* appeared in 1900, the year that saw the publication, too, of Edward Bellamy's *The Duke of Stockbridge*, a story of Shays's Rebellion that had appeared as a magazine serial in 1879. The following year saw the publication of Sarah Orne Jewett's *The Tory Lover*. Frank Stockton's *Kate Bonnet* was published in 1902.

By 1905, the extraordinary popular appeal of the historical novel was waning and did not really revive until the 1930s, when enthusiasm for Hervey Allen's sprawling tale of the Napoleonic era, *Anthony Adverse* (1933), proved to be a prelude to the unprecedented popularity of Margaret Mitchell's *Gone with the Wind* (1936). Nevertheless, interest in the historical novel had increased in the wake of World War I, and the 1920s saw the publication of a number of notable historical novels: James Boyd's *Drums* (1925) and *Marching On* (1928), which dealt with the Revolution and Civil War respectively and were informed by a soldier's knowledge of military tactics; Walter D. Edmond's *Rome Haul* (1929), a painstakingly accurate portrayal of life along the Erie Canal in its heyday; and Edna Ferber's *Cimarron* (1930). The Revolution and the Civil War, pioneer life, and the opening of the West would continue to furnish historical novelists with their staple subjects.

A new note in the historical fiction of the 1930s was the blend of scrupulous historical research and unconventional interpretation of men and events, exemplified in the work of Kenneth Roberts, who produced a half-dozen well-crafted, exciting novels during the decade. In *Arundel* (1930),

Roberts's hero is none other than tradition's archtraitor Benedict Arnold; and in *Oliver Wiswell* (1940), Roberts presented the Revolution from the loyalist point of view. Even more revisionist in orientation was the work of Howard Fast, whose *The Last Frontier* (1941) was an indictment of the Indian Wars of the 1870s, and whose *The American* presented a defense of John Peter Altgeld, the Illinois governor maligned for his pardon of the convicted Haymarket anarchists. Fast's special interest, however, was the Revolution, which he explored in five novels: *Two Valleys* (1933), *Conceived in Liberty* (1939), *The Unvanquished* (1942), *Citizen Tom Paine* (1943), and *The Proud and the Free* (1950).

Fiction of the flashing rapier and heaving bosom school also enjoyed a considerable measure of popularity during the 1940s, paced by such commercial successes as Kathleen Winsor's *Forever Amber* (1944), a lineal descendant of Elinor Glyn's pioneering *Three Weeks*; by Thomas Costain's costume pieces such as *The Black Rose* (1945) and *The Silver Chalice* (1952); and by the indefatigable Frank Yerby, whose *The Foxes of Harrow* (1946) was followed by twenty-two more novels, which have sold some twenty million copies to date.

Although the popularity of *Gone with the Wind* has not been matched by any subsequent historical novel, that fact should not obscure the considerable popularity of the form down to the present day. According to Russel B. Nye, at least one historical novel has reached the best-seller lists every year since 1931, and he estimates that 10 percent of all books published in paperback today may be considered historical fiction.[5] The extraordinary popularity of John Jakes's multivolume saga of an American family, beginning with *The Bastard* (1976), offers convincing proof that *mutatis mutandis* the spirit of nationalism that Cooper and his contemporaries so successfully exploited is alive and well.

NOTES

1. Avrom Fleishman, *The English Historical Novel* (Baltimore: Johns Hopkins University Press, 1971), p. 4.
2. Lydia M. Child, *Hobomok, a Tale of Early Times*, quoted in Ernest Leisy, *The American Historical Novel* (Norman: University of Oklahoma Press, 1950).
3. *North American Review*, 19 (July 1824), 209.
4. James D. Hart, *The Popular Book* (New York: Oxford University Press, 1950), p. 164.
5. *The Unembarrassed Muse* (New York: Dial Press, 1970), p. 46.

BIBLIOGRAPHY

Aaron, Daniel. *The Unwritten War: American Writers and the Civil War*. New York: Alfred A. Knopf, 1973.

Beard, James F. "Cooper and the Revolutionary Mythos." *Early American Literature,* 11 (Spring 1976), 84-104.

Bell, M. D. "History and Romance Convention in Catherine Sedgwick's *Hope Leslie.*" *American Quarterly,* 22 (Summer 1970), 213-21.

Bernbaum, Ernest. "The Views of the Great Critics on the Historical Novel." *PMLA,* 41 (June 1926), 424-41.

Butterfield, Herbert. *The Historical Novel: An Essay.* Cambridge: Cambridge University Press, 1924.

Clarke, John H., ed. *William Styron's Nat Turner: Ten Black Writers Respond.* Boston: Beacon, 1968.

Dahl, Curtis. "New England Unitarianism in Fictional Antiquity: The Romances of William Ware." *New England Quarterly,* 48 (March 1975), 104-15.

Dickinson, A. T., Jr. *American Historical Fiction.* 3d ed. Metuchen, N.J.: Scarecrow Press, 1971.

Feuchtwanger, Lion. *The House of Desdemona, or the Laurels and Limitations of Historical Fiction.* Trans. Harold A. Bisilius. Detroit: Wayne State University Press, 1971.

Garrett, G. P. "Dreaming with Adam: Notes on Imaginary History." In *New Directions in Literary History.* Edited by Ralph Cohen. Baltimore: Johns Hopkins University Press, 1974.

Henderson, Harry B. *Versions of the Past: The Historical Imagination in American Fiction.* New York: Oxford University Press, 1974.

Hofstadter, Richard, and Beatrice Hofstadter. "Winston Churchill: A Study in the Popular Novel." *American Quarterly,* 2 (Spring 1950), 12-28.

Holman, C. Hugh. "William Gilmore Simms's Picture of the Revolution as a Civil Conflict." *Journal of Southern History,* 15 (November 1949), 441-62.

Kammen, Michael. *A Season of Youth: The American Revolution and the Historical Imagination.* New York: Alfred A. Knopf, 1978.

Leisy, Ernest E. *The American Historical Novel.* Norman: University of Oklahoma Press, 1950, 1952.

Levin, David. *In Defense of Historical Literature.* New York: Hill and Wang, 1967.

Lively, Robert A. *Fiction Fights the Civil War.* Chapel Hill: University of North Carolina Press, 1957.

Lukacs, Georg. *The Historical Novel.* Trans. Hannah and Stanley Mitchell. Boston: Beacon, 1963.

Mott, Frank Luther. *Golden Multitudes.* New York: Macmillan, 1947.

Nye, Russel. *The Unembarrassed Muse.* New York: Dial Press, 1970.

Osborne, William S. "John Pendleton Kennedy's Horse Shoe Robinson: A Novel with 'the Utmost Historical Accuracy'." *Maryland Historical Magazine,* 59 (September 1964), 286-96.

Peck, H. D. "Repossession of America: The Revolution in Cooper's Trilogy of Nautical Romances." *Studies in Romanticism,* 15 (Fall 1976), 589-605.

Ringe, Donald A. "The American Revolution in American Romance." *American Literature,* 49 (November 1977), 352-65.

Van Auken, S. "Southern Historical Fiction in the Early Twentieth Century." *Journal of Southern History,* 14 (May 1949), 157-91.

Williams, Jay. "History and Historical Novels." *American Scholar,* 26 (Winter 1956-1957), 67-74.

Illustration

James J. Best

The history of popular illustration in the United States dates from the eighteenth century, but illustrations were not widely used until the Civil War, when technological developments and popular demand resulted in an enormous growth in their use. As with many American cultural phenomena, the roots of popular illustration can be traced to England, where illustrations by Thomas Rowlandson, William Blake, and Thomas Bewick were popular and were soon "copied" (frequently without attribution) by colonial engravers. Alexander Anderson was the first American to achieve stature as a "native" American illustrator, but F. O. C. Darley was the first illustrator of importance whose work was widely used and recognized. During the period 1840-1860 Darley dominated the field of American illustration, illustrating works by Washington Irving, *The Sketch Book of Geoffrey Crayon, Esq.* (1848), *A History of New York* (1850), *The Alhambra* (1851), and *The Life of George Washington* (1855-1859); Francis Parkman, *The California and Oregon Trail* (1849); James Fenimore Cooper, (thirty-two volumes published between 1859 and 1861); as well as a number of volumes of *The Library of Humorous American Works* (1846-1869). His illustrations were distinctly "American," unpretentious, frontier-oriented, and humorous in an earthy way; they appealed to readers who recognized themselves and their fellow men in the pictures Darley created, pictures which were both familiar and "real."

The Civil War and an increasingly literate public created a demand for comprehensive coverage of Civil War battle action, both in words and pictures. *Harper's Weekly* and *Leslie's Illustrated Weekly* dispatched reporters and artists to cover major battles, and readers saw pictures of battles within weeks of their occurrence. Battlefield illustrators did rough sketches, which were dispatched to New York where engravers, frequently using their imaginations to fill in the voids, translated the rough sketches into front page visual images. So successful was *Harper's Weekly* that its press run at the peak of the Civil War reached 250,000 copies, and its Civil War issues represent a vivid history of the period. The best of the war illustrations can be seen in commemorative volumes published by the two weeklies, *Harper's Illustrated History of the Civil War* (1895) and *Leslie's Illustrated History of the Civil War* (1895), which feature illustration by the leading war illustrators William and Alfred Waud, Thomas Nast, and Winslow Homer.

The success of *Harper's Weekly* led the House of Harper to expand its use of illustrations in its monthly magazine, *Harper's Monthly Magazine,* its children's magazine, *Harper's Young People,* and in its books. Under the direction of art editor Charles Parsons *Harper's Monthly* recruited a staff of illustrators—most notably Edwin Abbey, A. B. Frost, Alfred Kemble, and Howard Pyle—who became leading figures in the Golden Age of American illustration. As the circulation of *Harper's* increased, two other monthlies—*Century* and *Scribner's*—entered the field of quality illustrated magazines. These three magazines dominated the field of magazine illustration during the period 1890-1915, the Golden Age of illustration, and an illustrator who had his work published in any of these three was a "recognized" illustrator.

Although magazine illustration provided the most fruitful field for illustrators, book illustration was also attractive. Book illustration paid more, meant more work on a particular topic, and allowed greater artistic freedom. Not all of the leading magazine illustrators were also successful as book illustrators; only a handful achieved recognition in both fields. Most notable among this select group were Howard Pyle, N. C. Wyeth, Howard Chandler Christy, Charles Dana Gibson, Elizabeth Shippen Green, Jessie Wilcox Smith, and Maxfield Parrish.

Preeminent among this group of illustrators was Howard Pyle. Pyle received recognition for his early book illustrations in *Robin Hood* (1883), *Pepper and Salt* (1886), *The Wonder Clock* (1888) and *Otto of the Silver Hand* (1888), as well as his black and white line drawings, half-tones, and color illustrations for *Harper's Monthly.* More important, Pyle established the first school for the training of illustrators, and his success as a teacher was reflected in the work of his students. N. C. Wyeth, Frank Schoonover, Maxfield Parrish, Elizabeth Shippen Green, and Thornton Oakley were among his students at Chadds Ford, Pennsylvania, and in Wilmington, Delaware, and their artwork appeared in all the major illustrated magazines of the day. Pyle's emphasis on capturing the essence of the action in a story, on involving the reader in the illustration, and on historical accuracy in his student's artwork resulted in illustrations which were stylistically and substantively different from those of their contemporaries. One has only to contrast the women portrayed by Elizabeth Shippen Green and Jessie Wilcox Smith with the Gibson and Christy "American beauties."

At the same time a tradition of western or "cowboy" illustration was developing, led by Frederic Remington and Charles Russell, a tradition continued by Will James in the 1920s and 1930s. Quite frequently it was part of an illustrator's training that he "go West" to get a feel for the land and its people. N. C. Wyeth's first illustrations were based on a trip to the West that he had taken in 1904 and that trip supplied him with a continuing supply of commissions for western illustrations.

The Golden Age of American illustration was far more reflective of American society than it was of European illustration. Pyle and his students, with their emphasis on romantic realism, and Christy, Gibson, and James Montgomery Flagg, with their idealization of the American woman, are quite different from the leading English illustrators of the period, who were illustrating fantasy worlds of faeries and elves (Arthur Rackham, Edmund Dulac, and W. Heath Robinson) or introducing Art Noveau to the world (Aubrey Beardsley and Kay Nielsen). Rackham's illustrations for *Alice's Adventures in Wonderland (1907), Poe's Tales of Mystery and Imagination* (1935), and *Peter Pan in Kensington Garden* (1906); Dulac's illustrations for *Tanglewood Tales* (1918) and *Stories from the Arabian Nights* (1907); W. Heath Robinson's illustrations for *Bill the Minder* (1912) and *Shakespeare's Comedy of a Midsummer's Night's Dream* (1914); Beardsley's drawings for *The Rape of the Lock* (1896); and Kay Nielsen's color work for *East of the Sun and West of the Moon* (1922) are decidedly different from those of their American contemporaries. The most popular American illustrators at the turn of the century were romantic realists, primarily concerned with accurately depicting the historical past, which their readers had never seen, or idealizing the present, to which their readers could aspire. Even the fantasy illustrations of W. W. Denslow in the most popular children's book of the period, *The Wonderful Wizard of Oz* (1900), placed a very real girl from Kansas in the company of a scarecrow, a lion, and a tin woodman. And Dorothy is certainly different from the children who decorate the page of Kate Greenaway's *Under the Willows* (1879) and *The Pied Piper of Hamlin* (1888), the most popular English children's books of the time.

In one area of popular illustration—poster art—American illustrators copied the styles and techniques of their European counterparts. The modern poster dates to France in the 1870s and 1880s, where Chèret and Toulouse-Lautrec created a new form of popular illustration. British poster art developed differently from the French, influenced heavily by Japanese block prints which made extensive use of large masses of solid colors and shapes. As a result Chèret's posters are quite different from those of John Hassall, Dudley Harley, and the Beggarstaffs. It was these men, and Aubrey Beardsley, who were instrumental in introducing the Art Nouveau period, and American posters for books, newspapers, and various magazines reflect that influence. The most prominent American poster artists prior to World War I were Will Bradley, Edward Penfield, and Maxfield Parrish. Penfield and Parrish moved easily between magazine and book illustration and poster art; Penfield's posters for *Harper's* are strikingly similar to his magazine illustrations while Parrish used the same asexual adolescent in his prize-winning *Century* poster and his frontispiece for *Poems of Childhood* (1904). Will Bradley, on the other hand, worked mainly in poster art and on some magazine covers, particularly for *The Inland Printer* and *The Saturday Evening Post.* It is in Bradley's work that one can see most clearly the impact of the Art Nouveau illustrators.

World War I had a major impact on American illustration. A number of illustrators, under the auspices of the Society of Illustrators (founded in 1901), devoted their very considerable energies to creating posters for the government. Howard Chandler Christy, C. B. Falls, James Montgomery Flagg, J. C. Leyendecker, Joseph Pennell, Coles Phillips, and Harrison Fisher (to name but a few) lent their talents to promoting war bond drives, raising money for the Red Cross, recruiting volunteers for the armed services, and publicizing German atrocities. James Montgomery Flagg's poster of himself in a top hat and cutaway jacket in red, white, and blue saying, "Uncle Sam Wants You," created an image which persists to the present.

But World War I marked the end of the Golden Age of American illustration, signalling a change in the demand for and use of illustrations. Posters were never again popular as an advertising medium, as billboards began to dot the roadsides. The nature of magazine illustration also changed. Whereas the first decade of the century saw *Century, Harper's,* and *Scribner's* as the leading illustrated magazines, by the 1930s these three had been replaced by *The Saturday Evening Post, Collier's, Cosmopolitan, Woman's Home Companion, Redbook, Ladies Home Journal,* and *American,* general mass market or women's magazines, which published the greatest number of illustrations. And color illustrations appeared only as covers, so that doing a cover for *The Saturday Evening Post* was a sure sign of recognition. Because of the shift in the market for illustration, very few magazine illustrators who were popular before World War I retained their popularity into the 1930s. Charles Dana Gibson's "Gibson Girl" looked out of place on the pages of *Life* in the early 1930s. The two most prominent illustrators who made the transition were Norman Rockwell, whose covers for *The Saturday Evening Post* over forty years display an amazing ability to change content and style to keep pace with a changing society, and J. S. Leyendecker, whose idealized men were the 1930s equivalents of the Gibson Girls, which made them outmoded by the 1940s. During their careers Leyendecker and Rockwell each completed more than three hundred *Post* covers.

With the decline in the number and quality of illustrated magazines, many illustrators shifted their energies to a new market—the "pulps." In the twenty years following World War I cheap specialized magazines proliferated, offering war stories, romances, detective thrillers, and escapist reading at low cost. This market created an increasing demand for illustrators who could work quickly and whose covers would attract newsstand readers. Although this work was not as prestigious as doing covers for the *Post,* it nonetheless provided a livelihood for many illustrators.

The nature of book illustration also changed after World War I. The economics of publishing dictated that book illustrations be done in black and white and, ideally, on the same paper stock as the text. As a result line drawings and black and white illustrations returned and full-page color plates printed on slick paper virtually disappeared. Several new illustrators handled this genre well, notably Rockwell Kent and Lynd Ward. Kent's *Salamina* (1934) and *N by E* (1930) as well as Ward's *Mad Man's Drums* (1930) and *Song Without Words* (1936) are striking in their use of black and white figures against stark contrasting backgrounds. Lynd Ward's work represents a major breakthrough in book illustration; borrowing from the Belgian, Frans Masereel, Ward created "books without words," where illustrations carried the entire burden of conveying the author's message to the reader.

With the changing market for illustrations during the 1920s and 1930s, many illustrators moved into other areas of illustration—such as advertising and children's books. A number of illustrators who had achieved success prior to World War I found themselves doing more advertising work afterward. Frank Schoonover adapted some of his western illustrations for Colt Firearms; Maxfield Parrish did advertisements for Jello, using many of the same characters and layouts he used in magazine and book illustrations; N. C. Wyeth did calendar art for Mazda-Edison; and Cole Phillips used his "fadeaway" illustrations to sell silverware and lingerie. Perhaps the most successful advertising illustrator was J. C. Leyendecker, whose Arrow Shirt advertisements were instantly recognizable.

Children's books became a major market for illustrations, particularly with the decline in demand for mass market book illustrations. And a new generation of illustrators emerged, in which no one figure or "school" dominated as Howard Pyle and his students did at the beginning of the century. They were replaced by Johny Gruelle and his Raggedy Ann and Andy books, Jean DeBrunhoff's Babar the Elephant series, Ernest Shepard and his illustrations for the Winnie-the-Pooh series, the Dr. Seuss books, and illustrated books based on Disney movies and cartoons, as well as books illustrated by Ludwig Bemelmans, Wanda Gag, Willy Pogany, Helen Sewell, and Boris Artzybasheff.

During World War II poster art reemerged as a major form of illustration, although it never achieved the importance and status, nor the artistic impact, of its earlier counterparts. During World War II the government had other, more efficient, media for mobilizing the citizenry, namely motion pictures and radio. As a consequence the number of posters printed was comparatively low and the quality of poster artwork was not particularly high.

The period since World War II has seen some fundamental changes in American illustration. While the quality and use of illustration stagnated during the interwar period, the post-World War II period has seen a renaissance in American popular illustration. Children's books have retained their importance as sources for illustrations, and much of the most creative illustration is to be found there, with illustrations of subtlety, sophistication, and beauty. There has even been an increase in the use of magazine illustrations. Although the mass market magazines like the *Saturday Evening Post* are no longer in print, they have been replaced by an astounding number of specialty magazines, catering to sports fans, car owners, stereo addicts, and the like. *Sports Illustrated,* for example, has become a major publisher of quality illustrations. Of the traditional illustration media, only book illustration has not flourished (surprising, considering the popularity of art and "coffee table" books).

The renaissance in American illustration has been the result of a number of factors. Television has served to make American society more visually oriented, and this phenomenon has created a larger market for illustrations. The development of the airbrush has made illustration easier and greatly improved the quality of the product. Most important, illustrations are now appearing in places unthought of twenty-five years ago—paperback book covers, record jackets, and even the records themselves, for example—and, as a result, the market for illustration artwork has boomed.

The nature of illustration as a professional endeavor has changed as well. There are very few illustrators today whose artwork dominates the field as that of illustrators at the turn of the century. The death of Norman Rockwell marked the end of an era. Now and in the future they will most likely work together in studios, using increasingly sophisticated techniques like computer graphics to produce visual images for a sophisticated audience.

BIBLIOGRAPHY

Allen, Douglas, and Douglas Allen, Jr. *N. C. Wyeth.* New York: Bonanza Books, 1972.

Atwar, Robert, Donald McQuade, and John W. Wright. *Edsels, Luckies, and Frigidaires.* New York: Delacourt Press, 1979.

Bland, David. *The Illustration of Books.* London: Faber and Faber, n.d.

Broder, Patricia James. *Dean Cornwell, Dean of Illustrators.* New York: Watson-Guptill, 1978.

Buechner, Thomas. *Norman Rockwell, Artist and Illustrator.* New York: Henry Abrams, 1970.

Downey, Fairfax. *Portrait of an Era as Drawn by C. D. Gibson.* New York: Scribner's, 1936.

Dykes, Jeff. *Fifty Great Western Illustrators: A Bibliographical Checklist.* Flagstaff, Ariz.: Northland Press, 1975.

Hahler, Christine Anne, ed. *...illustrated by Darley.* Wilmington: Delaware Art Museum, 1978.

Hornung, Clarence. *Will Bradley: His Graphic Art.* New York: Dover, 1974.

Klemin, Diana. *The Illustrated Book.* New York: Charles Potter, 1970.

Lewis, John. *The Twentieth Century Book.* London: Studio Vista, 1967.

McCracken, Harold. *Frederic Remington: Artist of the Old West.* New York: Lippincott, 1947.
Mahoney, Bertha E., Louise Payson, and Beulah Folmsbee. *Illustrators of Children's Books, 1744-1945.* Boston: Horn Books, 1947.
Metzl, Ervine. *The Poster: Its History and Art.* New York: Watson-Guptill, 1963.
Meyers, Susan. *America's Great Illustrators.* New York: Henry Abram, 1978.
______. *James Montgomery Flagg.* New York: Watson-Guptill, 1974.
Pitz, Henry C. *Howard Pyle.* New York: Clarkson and Potter, 1975.
______. *200 Years of American Illustration.* New York: Random House, 1977.
Reed, Walter, ed. *The Illustrator in America: 1900-1960.* New York: Reinhold Publishing, 1966.
Schau, Michael. *All-American Girls: The Art of Coles Phillips.* New York: Watson-Guptill, 1975.
Schmidt, Dorie, ed. *The American Magazine: 1890-1940.* Wilmington: Delaware Art Museum, 1979.
Schnessel, S. Michael. *Jessie Wilcox Smith.* New York: Thomas Y. Crowell, 1977.
Schoonover, Cortland. *Frank Schoonover, Illustrator of the North American Frontier.* New York: Watson-Guptill, 1976.
Wyeth, Betsy James, ed. *The Wyeths.* Boston: Gambit Press, 1971.
Yanker, Gary. *Prop Art.* New York: Darien House, 1972.

Jazz

William C. Bennett

The jazz tradition springs from the American cultural experiment; it is the precise musical analogy to the melting pot. Jazz was spawned in an evolutionary stream whose headwaters mark the point where African culture became Afro-American. True enough, jazz is "black music," but, more importantly, jazz is a music of black Americans. In the absence of either its African or American components, one can only suppose that jazz would not exist.

The most influential—and, not coincidentally, most African—root strain in jazz is the blues. Speaking strictly musically, the blues is a culturally rich and homogeneous musical genre, formally and harmonically quite unlike any other musical development in this world. Its antecedents, which are primarily melodic, are certainly African, but there is similar certainty that the formalization and harmonization of that melodic seed have taken place in the American South. The simple I-IV-V harmonic essence of the blues and the settling of the song form into an even twelve measures are as momentous a development in terms of world music as one could seek in the music of America.

Form and harmony aside, to this day the most striking aspect of the blues remains the so-called blue notes, the celebrated deviations from the tempered scale that shade the emotional spectrum of these powerful, compact songs. The ambiguity, in terms of Western harmony, of these notes, which take the third and seventh degrees of the scale from major to minor and back again, reflects the ambiguous circumstances that the blues have come to symbolize: in a narrow sense, the place of the black man in a white society; in a larger sense, the plight of humanity in a random universe. The blues, which idiomatically trigger the perception and sensation of sadness, are at the same time a celebration, the means of naming the bogey men of modern life and thus making them less fearful. As such, the blues invite the exorcism of individual troubles; and this aspect, along with the basic simplicity of the form, seems to invite improvisation.

The next important melding of African and European elements into an American music came with the advent of ragtime, which developed as a sort of danceable parlor music with the piano at center stage. The syncopations that characterize ragtime are as African as can be, while the melody, harmony, and basic 4/4 meter harken to Europe, specifically to the march and polka. The classic rag might consist of three sixteen-bar strains, which might be arranged A-A-B-A-C-B-C, or very nearly a rondo. Scott Joplin, the best-known of the ragtime composers, eventually went so far as to attempt a ragtime opera, *Treemonisha,* but there were many other musicians at work in the field, including James Scott, James Reese Europe, Luckey Roberts, Joseph Lamb, and Eubie Blake, whose compositions still prove rewarding to student and listener alike.

A third important strain in the development of jazz is the brass band, in all likelihood the legacy of the American martial tradition. Such bands were the cornerstone of the nation's entertainment in the nineteenth century, and nowhere more so than in New Orleans, where French, African, Caribbean, and English cultures met at the mouth of the Mississippi. There is reason, as well as romantic inclination, to believe that the funeral traditions of the New Orleans black community were instrumental in the gestation of jazz. As ragtime rhythms grew popular, it makes sense to imagine the vibrant and possibly blues-tinged marches played on the way back from the cemetery taking on at the urging of some visionary cornetist—perhaps the legendary Buddy Bolden—a sudden wildness, a rhythmic freedom that demanded attention. This, we may believe, was the birth of swing.

Swing is a different, and larger, rhythmic concept than syncopation. Ragtime syncopation is a device, albeit essential to the ragtime style, which generally takes the form of an offbeat anticipation to sustain interest and inspire a sense of melodic momentum. Swing is a more complete homage to the Afro-American's cultural ancestry, allowing variation all around the beat according to the dictates of constantly implied polyrhythmic foundations, the integrity of the phrase, or sheer instinctual bravado.

The swing factor developed gradually from an aberration among the established brass bands of New Orleans into the guiding principle of a number of smaller ensembles playing a rough-hewn, energetic music that came to be called "jass." The word itself apparently derives from a euphemism for sexual activity. In addition to their rhythmic proclivities, these bands relied on improvisation to realize their ensemble playing; what emerged was a kind of spontaneous counterpoint, a collective improvisation unique in musical history. The lead voice belonged to a trumpet or, more often, a cornet; the clarinet took the treble obbligato role, and a trombone filled the baritone void. A banjo established the chord patterns of the chosen melody, while a tuba—later a bass fiddle—followed the oom-pah contours of the march-time polka. The drummer played a fairly limited role in the early ensemble, occasionally dropping into stop-time to highlight the intertwining lines of his compeers.

If we do accept New Orleans as the "birthplace" of jazz, we can at least debunk the role of prostitution as "mother" to the music. New Orleans's fabled red-light district, Storyville, unquestionably afforded many musicians work in the early years of this century, and many of these players were undoubtedly jazz musicians. However, as Duke Ellington has so bluntly put it, "They didn't learn it there."

The finest of the early bands, at least insofar as recorded evidence is concerned, was that of Joe "King" Oliver. His Creole Jazz Band made its recorded debut in 1923, featuring, in support of Oliver's then-nonpareil horn, a young second cornetist named Louis Armstrong.

Armstrong, who would become a worldwide symbol of American talent and opportunity, was far more than just a mugging entertainer: he emerged from under Oliver's stylistic wing to become the first great, and in many ways quintessential, jazz soloist. That Armstrong was building on an established tradition—the contributions of Buddy Bolden, Mutt Carey, Freddie Keppard, and others—cannot be questioned. At the same time, however, there can be little doubt as to the magnitude of Armstrong's contribution. As is so often the case in jazz, there is little point in trying to separate Armstrong's stylistic innovations from his sheer instrumental virtuosity; they are too closely bound to permit such academic dissections. Still, we can point to aspects of the Armstrong sound and document their influence in the larger plane of world music. We know, for instance, that the soulful vibrato with which Armstrong could worry a single note was absent from the vocabulary of nineteenth-century brassmen and that, today, any well-trained trumpet player includes this device among his expressive techniques. But all of Armstrong's trade tricks, even his seamless glissandos and unheard of high notes, cannot account for the compelling personality of his playing. For it was Louis Armstrong who at last brought the swing factor into focus, who refined Afro-American polyrhythmic urges into an improvisational medium that played freely around the established dictates of melody, harmony, and meter. Armstrong at his best is a fine blend of restraint and expansive gesture, ranging from the subtlest rhythmic reinterpretations of a melodic line, through simple embellishments, to full-fledged improvisation.

Armstrong was not alone in blazing this trail into solo territory. Soprano saxophonist Sidney Bechet, with whom Armstrong recorded as early as 1924, brought his instrument out of its traditional obbligato role with his startlingly effective, arpeggio-based style. And cornetist Bix Beiderbecke's delicately crystalline solo structures were, in their way, just as daring as Armstrong's strokes of genius.

From the early, collectively improvised polyphony of jazz to the advent of the soloist was a major step. Sure to follow were ensemble arrangements that drew on the developing jazz tradition in order to frame those solos structurally. Ferdinand "Jelly Roll" Morton's claim to the invention of jazz is suspect, though he probably should be credited with having done the groundwork for the jazz orchestra. Morton's ensemble arrangements (hear his Red Hot Peppers recordings), essentially an extension of his ragtime-derived piano style, reflect a consciousness of form and texture that would blossom in the work of other bandleaders, notably Fletcher Henderson.

Henderson, working initially with saxophonist-arranger Don Redman, began the expansion of the five-to-ten piece jazz band into the thirteen to seventeen pieces characteristic of the "big band" sound.

While Henderson was honing his arranging skills, which would later make such a contribution to the success of Benny Goodman's band in New York, similar trails were being cleared in other parts of the country. Kansas City was the center of one such area of activity, the essence of which came to be represented by the Count Basie Orchestra of the 1930s and 1940s. Basie's band brought together the classic rhythm section (the continuo of jazz) with a number of excellent soloists, including the great tenor saxophonist Lester Young. The sophistication they brought to the riff tune, with its bluesy exuberance and potent call-and-response patterns, helped launch the so-called Swing Era.

Meanwhile, in the New York of the 1920s, Edward Kennedy "Duke" Ellington was beginning the long career that would establish him as one of America's great composers. With Ellington, individualistic if not always virtuosic players were essential to the complex and innovative arrangements that would necessarily change with the band's personnel. While it is generally agreed that the Ellington band reached its peak in the early 1940s, the whole of his fifty years as composer and bandleader will repay intensive study, bringing to light Ellington's brilliant employment of such musical forces as altoist Johnny Hodges, tenor man Ben Webster, bassist Jimmy Blanton, trombonist Joe "Tricky Sam" Nanton, and so many others.

With the establishment of the solo-ensemble format, which may be considered a sophisticated extension of the call-and-response legacy of African music, and the development of the jazz orchestra, the stage was set for the popular success and excesses of the Swing Era. The mainstream standards of jazz had been formed and were soon to be challenged by a new generation of jazz musicians coming of age in the war-torn 1940s. Leaping off from the harmonic achievements of Coleman Hawkins and Art Tatum, young men such as Charlie Parker, Dizzy Gillespie, and Thelonious Monk were responsible for the musical revolution that carried the onomatopoeic monicker be-bop. Armstrong's basic melodic unit, the swung quarter note, suddenly became an eighth note; the range of harmonic extensions available to the improviser similarly opened up. Smaller (four or five piece) soloistic bands were the medium for this complex new music, in which the balance between composition and improvisation shifted once more toward the spontaneous edge.

The harmonic frontiers probed by be-bop prompted some rather more restrained forays in the early 1950s. Led by Miles Davis, a former Charlie Parker sideman, and arranger Gil Evans, this "Cool School" added occasional new voices to the jazz band—the French horn, for instance—and moved at a more introspective pace than had bop; like bop, however, cool jazz was effectively a listener's music, to be danced to at one's own risk. Conversely, the music was played at the musician's own risk, for financial success (read "popularity") visited dance-oriented jazzmen more often than their esoteric counterparts. What is important is that, like so much jazz, dance-oriented or not, the music that came out of the be-bop revolution (including cool, a vertically oriented reduction of be-bop) demands consideration as art music.

Be-bop also produced a linear reduction of itself, which came to be known as "funky" jazz, or hard bop. Hard bop used the small band format of its forebear to carry arrangements blending the harmonic progress of bop with rhythm-and-blues-flavored structures. The bands of Art Blakey and Horace Silver are archtypical hard bop units, though the movement also nurtured more individualistic talents, such as Wayne Shorter, who would reach prominence with later Miles Davis bands, and Sonny Rollins, who in many ways remains to this day the quintessential tenor saxophonist.

An often interesting, just as often pretentious offshoot of cool jazz came to be known as third stream jazz, a conscious effort to meld the jazz tradition with European concert music. Its major proponents included composer Gunther Schuller and pianist John Lewis, who, as music director of the Modern Jazz Quartet, would create a refined and often Baroque-tinged chamber jazz.

The 1950s also spawned a number of great compositions, many of them from the prolific pens of Charles Mingus and Thelonious Monk. Monk, like Jelly Roll Morton a composer whose themes sprang directly from his instrumental style, enjoyed a popular vogue in the 1960s more attributable to the simultaneous "weirdness" and simplicity of his melodies than to the sophistication of their harmonies, both stated and implied. Mingus enriched the mainstream conception of the jazz ensemble with shades of the collectively improvised polyphony of the music's earliest manifestations; in so doing, he presaged and paved the way for the free jazz movement.

Along with the work of Mingus, Monk, the Modern Jazz Quartet, and Sonny Rollins, the contributions of Miles Davis's groups were among the most significant of the 1950s. The forced near-virtuosity of his be-bop days had given way to a more relaxed, more musical approach in his cool phase; his trumpet musings had become an unmistakable voice by the middle of the decade, owing more perhaps to Louis Armstrong than anyone since. Late in the decade, the Davis band, which included John Coltrane, recorded the first, or at least most influential, exploration of modal jazz to date. Coltrane, in his vertically oriented style, would later take these ideas to the extremes of virtuosity, as in "Impressions," and sheer soulful expression, as in "Spiritual."

Meanwhile, innovation blossomed on the West Coast: the quartet of Ornette Coleman and the concept of free jazz. Coleman's scheme depended on relatively simple thematic material fleshed out through collective improvisation and harmonized by implication, often by microtonal degrees. Coltrane would pick up the free spirit, as would Miles Davis, whose mid-1960s quintet remains one of the most successful examples of a collectively improvising band. The avant garde of jazz continues in relatively good health into the

1980s, where the benefits of perspective have introduced often startling allusions to the past glories of jazz.

A footnote that becomes the thesis: The preceding has been a thumbnail tracing of the roots and milestones of jazz, its history considered only in terms of the tradition. The fact remains that the greater significance of jazz may well be defined by future music historians as the scope of its influences on the popular music of the world. The blues is far and away America's most significant formal contribution to world music; similarly, "jazz" is our most important stylistic contribution. Given the musical influences of jazz on America—from Paul Whiteman, through George Gershwin, Cole Porter, Harold Arlen, and other great writers in the American popular song form, to rock bands like Little Feat—we can yet detail much broader cultural influences through which we can better understand the place of jazz in American culture.

Prime examples of such influences would have to include *The Jazz Singer*, which has to rank as one of the world's foremost cinematic malapropisms (recently re-miscast with Neil Diamond in the role "created" by Al Jolson). Indeed, film has contributed greatly to the propagation of jazz *and* its misperception by the public, helping for instance, Louis Armstrong to be christened an Uncle Tom by a later, media-reared generation of black Americans. Films are, after all, a mass entertainment medium, which a purist's jazz has never been; consequently, we are given *The Benny Goodman Story* and *The Gene Krupa Story* rather than film biographies of Duke Ellington or Big Sid Catlett. Beyond this, however, we find Hollywood's cruelty to the music from which it has borrowed so much extending to the propagation of sinister sterotypes, which for all their collective grains of truth have served to maintain jazz's bad name. If a film romanticizes the moody atmosphere of the jazz club, it is sustaining the jazz club, not jazz; the music is left standing at the box office of the concert stage.

The point is that drug addiction, alcoholism, and venereal disease are tragic sociological side issues to the history of jazz. True, Charlie Parker was a heroin addict; but, more importantly, he was a brilliant musician, an improvising artist of the highest order. What jazz musicians have accomplished they have accomplished in spite of the tremendous socioeconomic obstacles in their path. At the same time, however, we must recognize the role of these obstacles in shaping the feelings that, in their turn, have helped to shape the jazz tradition.

BIBLIOGRAPHY

REFERENCE WORKS

Chilton, John. *Who's Who of Jazz: Storyville to Swing Street*. London: Bloomsbury Book Shop, 1970.

Dixon, R.M.W., and J. Godrich. *Blues and Gospel Records, 1902-1942*. 2d ed. London: Storyville, 1969.

Feather, Leonard. *The Encyclopedia of Jazz in the Sixties.* New York: Horizon Press, 1967.

———. *The New Edition of the Encyclopedia of Jazz.* New York: Horizon Press, 1960.

———, and Ira Gitler. *The Encyclopedia of Jazz in the Seventies.* New York: Horizon Press, 1977.

Harris, Sheldon. *Blues Who's Who: A Biographical Dictionary of Blues Singers.* New Rochelle, N.Y.: Arlington House, 1979.

Jepsen, Jorgen Grunnett. *Jazz Records: A Discography, 1942-1965.* Holte, Denmark: Knudsen, 1963-1965.

Keepnews, Orrin, and Bill Grauer, Jr. *A Pictorial History of Jazz.* 2d rev. ed. New York: Crown, 1966.

Kennington, Donald. *The Literature of Jazz: A Critical Guide.* Chicago: American Library Association, 1971.

Kinkle, Roger D. *The Complete Encyclopedia of Popular Music and Jazz, 1900-1950.* New Rochelle, N.Y.: Arlington House, 1974.

Rust, Brian. *Jazz Records, 1897-1942.* London: Storyville, 1970.

HISTORY AND CRITICISM

Collier, James Lincoln. *The Making of Jazz: A Comprehensive History.* Boston: Houghton Mifflin, 1978.

Gitler, Ira. *Jazz Masters of the Forties.* New York: Macmillan, 1966.

Hodeir, Andre. *Jazz: Its Evolution and Essence.* New York: Grove Press, 1956.

Jost, Ekkehard. *Free Jazz.* Graz: Universal Edition, 1974.

Murray, Albert. *Stomping the Blues.* New York: McGraw-Hill, 1976.

Oliver, Paul. *The Story of the Blues.* New York: Chilton Book, 1969.

Schafer, William J., and Johannes Reidel. *The Art of Ragtime.* Baton Rouge: Louisiana State University Press, 1973.

Schuller, Gunther. *Early Jazz: Its Roots and Musical Development.* New York: Oxford University Press, 1968.

Stearns, Marshall W. *The Story of Jazz.* New York: Oxford University Press, 1956.

Titon, Jeff Todd. *Early Downhome Blues: A Musical and Cultural Analysis.* Urbana: University of Illinois Press, 1977.

Ulanov, Barry. *Duke Ellington.* New York: Creative Age Press, 1946.

Williams, Martin. *Jazz Masters of New Orleans.* New York: Macmillan, 1967.

———. *The Jazz Tradition.* New York: Oxford University Press, 1970.

———, ed. *The Art of Jazz.* New York: Oxford University Press, 1959; reprint ed. New York: Da Capo Press, 1979.

Leisure Vehicles, Pleasure Boats, and Aircraft

Bernard Mergen

The subject of recreational travel is large and complex; it is also a matter of considerable economic and social importance.[1] Despite the high rate of inflation and gasoline shortages, the manufacture and sales of pickup trucks, motor homes, vans, off-road vehicles, snowmobiles, trail bikes, motorcycles, motorboats, and airplanes have increased enormously. Bicycles, sailboats, canoes, gliders, and balloons have also proliferated. Statistics showing the number of participants in cycling, boating, flying, vanning, and "truckin'," while impressive, tell only part of the story. For the student of American popular culture, the study of recreational travel, pleasure boating, and flying offers ways of combining some of the major issues of our time in research that has public policy as well as academic usefulness.

The issue of leisure, what it is and what it means in our society, is the most obvious area of investigation. How do people conceive of and use their nonwork time? What are the relationships between such variables as class, race, age, sex, and region and the use of recreational vehicles, pleasure boats, and aircraft? What are the appeals of speed, fantasy, and competition in the kind of play associated with the use of these artifacts of modern technology? A second issue, commercialism, raises the question: to what extent is our leisure time manipulated by businessmen interested in selling machines without regard to safety or environmental damage? The leisure vehicle industry—manufacturing, marketing, and servicing—is inextricably linked to both national and international economics. What role should the government play in the regulation of these industries? What control is necessary of individual owners of planes, boats, and vehicles? The third major issue, that of conservation of natural resources, raises the question of the future. How will those subcultures which support each of the recreational vehicle, boat, and aircraft types respond to shortages of fuel and restrictions on land and water use? As recently as 1974, a group of recreation and natural resource experts developed a set of future leisure environments for the U.S. Forest Service that included restriction of off-road vehicles in public recreation areas and the banning of private aircraft from metropolitan airports by 1980. At the same time, they predicted air strips and helicopter ports at most popular recreation areas and small private submarines as common as snowmobiles today by the year 2000. By 2050, their report concluded, only foot travel would be allowed in major public parks, but hover craft would be widely used, as would jet-powered back packs and one-man low-speed helicopters.[2]

Recreational vehicles are a product of our economy, technology, and value system. They must be studied in the context of many related activities, especially when we see that a person's choice of a leisure activity is often closely related to his work, social class, educational level, age, and family status. The use of a camper, van, boat, or plane is obviously related to such ancillary activities as hunting, fishing, scuba diving, photography, amateur radio operating, and camping. As the history of boating, flying, cycling, and recreational driving reveals, each activity has unique origins. Unlike less mechanized and less expensive pastimes, their present is a product of past decisions made deliberately and consciously by individuals who had much to gain and often much to lose.

Of the forms of transportation considered in this essay, boating was clearly the earliest. The pleasure yacht was introduced into England in the seventeenth century by the Dutch, and by 1713 American shipbuilders had developed the schooner, a small, fast ship which could be used for fishing and coastal freight. Impromptu races between fishermen inspired wealthier colonists to invest in "well-fitted pleasure boats" through the eighteenth century. In Ireland and England the aristocracy organized yachting clubs to regulate the growth of pleasure boating and to supervise races among members. Many historians point to George Crowninshield's brigantine, *Cleopatra's Barge,* built in 1816, as the first American yacht, but Thomas Doubleday was sailing his twenty-foot sloop in Cape Cod Bay in the same year. The two basic types of pleasure boating, the day sailor and the ocean cruiser, seem to have appeared simultaneously.

By the 1830s, the first generation of American yachtsmen were testing their ships in competition and making technical improvements based on their experience. Robert L. Stevens, Edwin A. Stevens, and John C. Stevens, sons of the great inventor, turned their talents to sailing and their boat, *Gimcrack,* designed by George Steers, became the first ship of the fleet of the New York Yacht Club when it was organized in 1844. Seven years later, Steers's yacht, *America,* astounded the British by winning the Queen's Cup at Cowes.

The end of the Civil War signaled the beginning of ostentatious yachting by American millionaires. The transatlantic race among *Vesta,* owned by Pierre Lorillard, Jr., *Fleetwing,* owned by George and Franklin Osgood, and *Henrietta,* which belonged to James Gordon Bennett, Jr., drew national attention in 1866. The 1870s witnessed the diffusion of yachting across the nation and the founding of clubs on both coasts, the Gulf of Mexico, and the Great Lakes. One of the first journals devoted to water sports, *Aquatic Monthly and Nautical Review,* appeared in 1872, with news of rowing contests and yacht club regattas. By 1884, when the National Watercraft Collection of ship models was begun, yachting was firmly in the hands of professional marine architects such as Edward Burgess and Nathaniel Greene Herreshoff and devoted amateur sailors such as George I. Tyson and Malcolm Forbes. Burgess's *Puritan,* which successfully defended the America's Cup in 1885, broke with the tradition of broad beam, shallow draft sloops by adding a lead keel and reducing the waterline length. Five years later, Herreshoff continued this trend toward narrow, deeper-hulled craft in his *Gloriana.* Like most changes in yacht design, these were made solely to increase speed and to circumvent the rules regarding size, weight, and sail area.

The 1880s were also a decade of steam yachts and naphtha-powered motor launches, heralding the age of motorboating in the twentieth century. In the 1890s, journals such as *American Yachtsman* and *Rudder* helped to popularize small boat racing as well as cruising. Joshua Slocum's solo voyage around the world in 1895-1898, the poetry of John Masefield, and the popular spy novel, *The Riddle of the Sands* (1903) by Erskine Childers all helped to create a romantic image of the sea and encouraged thousands of young men and women to take up sailing. Professional marine photographers such as N. L. Stebbins and Henry Greenwood Peabody published their work in books and magazines for thousands more who would never walk a deck or hoist a sail but who participated vicariously in every America's Cup challenge and Bermuda Race. Although the automobile caused a brief decline in yachting, the work of L. Herreshoff, William Gardner, who developed the "Star" class sailboat in 1911, and John Alden, whose designs led to the construction of more than five thousand boats, contributed to the democratization of yachting. Sailing dinghies led the revival of yachting in the 1920s and 1930s. Collegiate racing, junior racing, and ladies racing all became an accepted part of yacht club activities. The gasoline engine brought new kinds of boating activity, as exemplified by Gar Wood's *Miss America* speed boats, which were approaching 100 miles per hour by 1928. Flying and yachting were pursued by many both in the United States and abroad as the journals *Flugzeug und Yacht* and *Aviation and Yachting* suggest.

Although the Depression and World War II disrupted yachting, the postwar years were a bonanza for the boating industry. New technology produced safer, less expensive boats of all types. In the late 1970s almost 50 million Americans participated in some kind of boating. *Boating* has a circulation over 200,000, and *Sail* about 170,000. *Canoe,* the publication of the American Canoe Association which celebrates its centennial in 1980, has 30,000 subscribers. Although the variety of boating activities makes it difficult to generalize about the people who own and operate the "Snipes," "Sunfish," "Lightnings," "Tempests," and various motorboats, it is clear that the old masculine world of yachting is being replaced by a familial one. The past decade has seen the publication of innumerable books with titles like *Family Under Sail: A Handbook for First Mates* by Jane Kirstein, *The Woman's Guide to Boating and Cooking* by Lael Morgan, and *How to Be a First-Rate Mate: A Sailing Guide for Women* by Gloria Sloane. This trend affects the other forms of recreational travel as well.

Cycling also began as a male activity but eventually became a vehicle (literally) of women's liberation. Today bicycling is generally considered a family activity, and even motorcycling is promoted as a way to meet "the nicest people." Cycling, like ballooning, was French in origin, and the two remained linked until late in the nineteenth century. Neither developed very rapidly. In 1817, Baron Karl von Drais de Sauerbrun developed a bicycle with a fork over the front wheel to allow steering by handlebars; still later, in 1839, Kirkpatrick Macmillan, a Scottish blacksmith, added cranks attached to a system of rods and levers.

Almost a generation later, in the 1860s, Pierre Lallement and Pierre Michoux placed the cranks and pedals on the front wheel to create the highly successful velocipede. The next cycle, the ordinary or penny-farthing, with its large front wheel, required skill and practice to operate. Acrobats were quick to incorporate it into their acts, and French cycling instructors helped to give bicycling a continental, high-status image. Bicycles were promoted at the Philadelphia Centennial Exhibition, and in 1877 Colonel Albert A. Pope began his campaign for the bicycle and better roads. Two years later, *Bicycling World* began publishing news and technical information, becoming the official journal of the League of American Wheelmen (LAW) in 1880.

The perfection of the safety bicycle in 1884 led to the cycling boom of the 1890s. The LAW had over 100,000 members by the end of the century, many of them women whom reformers encouraged to discard their corsets and confining garments and take up cycling as healthful exercise. Almost as suddenly as it had begun, the cycling mania ceased, as bicyclists left their wheels to younger brothers and sisters and took up motoring. It was not until 1972 that bicycles again outsold automobiles. Almost the same fate was suffered by the motorcycle. Although inventors had tried to attach steam engines to bicycles and tricycles since the late 1860s, it was not until 1885 that Gottlieb Daimler successfully attached a gasoline engine to a frame similar to a velocipede. Further improvements made cheap, reliable motorcycles widely available by 1906, when *Motorcycle Illustrated* began publication.

From the beginning, motorcycles were associated with a violent, libidinous, antisocial male subculture. As Sam Kent Brooks points out in his excellent study of the motorcycle in American culture, the association of the motorcyclist with the lone horseman of Western mythology was strong, despite the fact that motorcyclists tended from the beginning to form clubs and ride in groups. By 1912, Andrew Carey Lincoln and Lieutenant Howard Payson had created a fictional world of "motorcycle chums" for boys to read and emulate. Perhaps, as Brooks suggests, the appeal of the motorcycle was even deeper than the image of the cowboy. "To the practiced and regular rider," Brooks quotes the authors of an 1898 book on cycling, "the motorcycle becomes so far like the lower part of the centaur that steering is almost unconscious and the balancing a matter of instinctive bodily sway."[3]

Curiously, motorcycling made a comeback in the 1960s under the stimulus of economic prosperity and an aggressive advertising campaign by Japanese manufacturers. Today the image of the motorcyclist is paradoxically split between the outlaw "Hell's Angels" and "Easy Rider" type and the weekend touring cyclist. The problems posed by the current popularity of cycling is neatly summarized in a recent publication of the Bureau of Outdoor Recreation (now the Heritage Conservation and Recreation Service). Noting that different users consume trails "psychologically" in different ways, the report argues that bicyclists, like hunters, are goal-oriented, needing point-to-point trails in which the trail is more important than the scenery. Motorcyclists and snowmobilers are more concerned with the stimulus from their machines, so their trails should emphasize difficulty of terrain.[4]

Snowmobiles are second only to minibikes in popularity among off-road or all-terrain recreational vehicles. The A. C. Nielsen Company calls it the third fastest growing sport in the United States, just behind tennis and skiing, with more than 7 million participants driving almost a million machines. Yet snowmobiles are only a small part of the leisure vehicle industry. Since the perfection of the Model A, the automobile industry has encouraged the development of pleasure driving. In 1914, the *Ford Times* claimed "campers received motor-morphic medicine because of the laws of motion. Babies were put in cradles, children rode rocking horses, savages swayed to sinuous dances, and grandmother rocked ceaselessly in a rocking chair."[5] As auto camping caught on, car owners began to modify and customize their machines. Trailers were made by cutting an old car in half and hitching the rear seat and wheels to another automobile. Home-built vans were made to look like Pullman cars, clapboard cottages, and prairie schooners. By 1930, the Covered Wagon Company of Mt. Clemens, Michigan, was mass producing trailers, and a new industry was born.

Although trailer owners had organized as early as 1919, as the Tin Can Tourists, the 1930s was the decade of rapid expansion and public awareness. *Trailer Travel Magazine* began publication in 1936, and popular periodicals such as *Fortune*, *Harper's*, *Nation*, and *Time*, discovered "The Trailer Epidemic." Wally Byam's Airstream trailer made its appearance in 1935, a product of new technology and styles. Until the 1950s, recreational vehicles were limited to trailers and converted automobiles and trucks. Developments of the past thirty years have redefined the term. Today the recreational vehicle (RV) may be defined as "a permanent compartment carried by a motorist to cook and/or sleep in."[6] This includes pickup campers, motor homes, camping trailers, travel trailers, and fifth-wheel trailers. It excludes the off-road and all-terrain vehicles such as jeeps, dune buggies, snowmobiles, and trail bikes. Vans, too, should be considered another category.

The reasons for these distinctions are partly technical and partly sociological. RV owners tend to be older, married with children, and in the middle-income group. The image the RV industry seeks to project is solidly "middle American." "In their own small way," writes a spokesman in 1979, "RVs have strongly contributed to the rejuvenation of family life. Children find out how much fun parents can really be and that regular TV is not a necessity. At the same time RVs are an aid in bringing families together in a wholesome outdoor setting. Children are also learning the fundamentals of conservation and ecology."[7]

Off-road vehicle owners, on the other hand, tend to be younger, less affluent, and a good deal noisier. They seek action, adventure, and speed. Although the Jeep appeared in 1940, the greatest diffusion of four-wheel drive vehicles has been in the past ten years. *Off Road* magazine, which claims a circulation of 125,000, began publishing in 1969 and was quickly followed by *4 w d,* published by *Road and Track;* and *Pickup, Van & 4-Wheel Drive.* The impact of off-road vehicles tends to be localized and seasonal, but in some parts of the country the organizations and subcultures associated with them are highly visible and politically powerful. Perhaps most visible on city streets are the vanners in their customized, elaborately painted and decorated vehicles. According to one observer, vanners are often former hot rodders who have turned to vanning after getting married and having children and because the results of their customizing are more satisfying. The pleasure of customizing a van is "glancing over your shoulder and seeing you're surrounded by an environment of your own making. . . . Whether for families or for single people, the van is a playground for personality, a space to shape fantasy."[8]

Of all the fantasies man has indulged in, perhaps the greatest is flight. Flying for pleasure may date from Icarus and Daedalus or the twelfth-century Chinese, but for Americans the connection is again French. Following Jacque and Joseph Montgolfier's balloon ascent in 1783, French balloonists gave frequent demonstrations in the United States. The first American balloonist is said to have been thirteen-year-old Edward Warren, who volunteered to ride in a balloon constructed by Peter Carnes. His ascent, made at Bladensburg, Maryland, on June 24, 1784, preceded Josiah Meggs's in New Haven, Connecticut, by a year. For the next forty-seven years only Frenchmen attempted flights in the United States. In 1835, however, John Wise began to generate interest in ballooning by selling rides in his hot air balloon, *The Meteor.* Within a few years Wise had a rival in the person of Thaddeus Sabieski Constantine Lowe, known as Professor Carlincourt, whose balloon, *Enterprise,* became the model for several that Lowe built for the Union Army. After the Civil War, Wise continued his career as showman and scientific experimenter until his disappearance in a balloon over Lake Michigan in 1879.

Experiments in gliding and parachuting were also being conducted by

Americans and Europeans. In the 1890s Octave Chanute made over 7,000 glider flights in Dune Park, Indiana, and in 1894, Charles Proteus Steinmetz of General Electric organized the first club, the Mohawk Aerial Navigation and Exploration Company. Although Germans and Russians were far ahead of Americans in developing the technology of gliders, the fact that the Wright Brothers succeeded in attaching a motor to one of their gliders overshadows the other achievements. Most of the energy of American inventors and engineers went into perfecting the airplane, yet gliders continued to play a role in the general development of aviation. In 1928, Charles Lindbergh lent his enormous prestige to Hawley Bowlus, who designed sailplanes that were competitive with European models. Anne Morrow Lindbergh was the first American woman to obtain a glider pilot license, while Richard Du Pont used his family connections to bring the best German ideas on soaring to the attention of Americans. When World War II broke out, however, there were only 165 glider pilots in the United States, compared to 186.000 in Germany. In the past twenty years, soaring as a pastime and for competition has become increasingly popular, and American pilots have set altitude and distance records. *Soaring and Motorgliding* magazine claims a circulation of 16,000. Moreover, the development of flexible-wing kite-like gliders by Francis M. Rogallo and others in the late 1940s has led to the boom in hang gliding, a less expensive and more accessible recreation than monoplane gliding.

Like soaring, parachuting is not yet a mass sport, but it has two popular journals, *Parachutist* and *Sky Diver Magazine,* the former with a circulation of 16,000. Experiments with parachutes began with ballooning, but parachute jumps remained a novelty until the development of powered aircraft. Although a barnstormer named Tiny Broadwick is said to have made the first intentional free fall from a plane in 1914, it was not until after World War II that American parachutists began to develop the skills that have led to maneuvers involving as many as fifty skydivers in elaborate patterns. The passing of objects between men and women falling at several hundred miles an hour through thousands of feet of space has become seemingly routine in television commercials, but it is a development of the past twenty-five years. Technological improvements in the parachutes themselves have made jumps of great accuracy possible and have attracted thousands of new participants. Even though only one-quarter of those who try jumping repeat the experience, sky diving is a growing recreational activity.

Flying private airplanes for pleasure, however, remains the most popular of all forms of airborne recreational travel. From 1911, when John and Alfred Moisant opened the first flying school in the United States, to the present, millions of Americans have received pilot's licenses. Today it is estimated that there are 750,000 weekend flyers in the United States flying 150,000 planes. Although owning a plane is expensive—a new two-seater costs at least $20,000—a number of manufacturers have provided small planes suitable for pleasure flying since 1907, when Alberto Santos Dumont, the Brazilian flyer and aeronautical engineer, introduced his *Demoiselle*. In 1937, Piper Aircraft Corporation, which absorbed the Taylor Aircraft Company, began to manufacture the small planes which have become synonymous with private flying. Cessna, Beechcraft, Grumman, and, in the 1950s, Lear Jet, joined Piper in providing a wide range of models for business and pleasure flying.

This brief survey of leisure transportation underscores the need for research and writing that will place leisure activities in the context of history. While we know that the use of recreational vehicles, pleasure boats, and aircraft is correlated with income and, to a degree, with region and social status, we need to know more about the men and women who make and use these objects. Studies of companies, clubs, and individuals should be undertaken by scholars who can evaluate the place of leisure travel in American culture. Because recreational travel occurs in every place in the country, it should be relatively easy to begin compiling information. Students should be encouraged to read and analyze trade journals and club newsletters for clues to cultural beliefs and values. Oral histories can be gathered and archives begun. Only then can we answer the question posed recently on a church billboard: "Will recreation wreck creation?"

NOTES

1. I would like to thank the following individuals for their help in preparing this essay: Julia Herron, Administrator, Member Communications and Publications, Recreational Vehicle Industry Association; Judy Hinds, Editor, Recreational Vehicle Dealers Association; John Haifley, Tempest sailor; Robert Humphrey, Department of Anthropology, George Washington University; Dom Pisano, Reference Librarian, National Air and Space Museum; Tom Narbeth, Assistant Reference Librarian, George Washington University; Donald Berkebile, Curator, American Division of Transportation, Museum of American History; and Andrew Mergen, expert.

2. Elwood L. Shafer, George H. Moeller, and Russell E. Getty, "Future Leisure Environments," U.S. Department of Agriculture, Forest Service Research Paper, NE-301, Upper Darby, Penn., 1974, p. 7.

3. Sammy Kent Brooks, "The Motorcycle in American Culture: From Conception to 1935" (Ph.D. diss. George Washington University, 1975), p. 38.

4. Bureau of Outdoor Recreation, "America's Trails," *Outdoor Recreation Action*, 42 (Winter 1976), 39.

5. Reynold M. Wik, *Henry Ford and Grass Roots America* (Ann Arbor: University of Michigan Press, 1972), p. 27.

6. Al Griffin, *Recreational Vehicles* (Chicago: Regnery, 1973), p. 7.

7. James B. Summers, "The RV Industry and Its Future," *RVDA News*, 12 (June 1979), 4.

8. Arnold Wolfe, *Vans and Vanners* (Matteson, Ill.: Greatlakes Living Press, 1976), pp. 2, 4.

BIBLIOGRAPHY

Brooks, Sammy Kent. "The Motorcycle in American Culture: From Conception to 1935." Ph.D. dissertation, George Washington University, 1975.

Chapelle, Howard I. *The History of American Sailing Ships.* New York: Norton, 1935.

Clark, Arthur Hamilton. *The History of Yachting, 1600-1815.* New York: Putnam's, 1904.

Dwiggins, Don. *On Silent Wings.* New York: Grosset & Dunlop, 1970.

Duthie, James H., and Michael A. Salter. "Parachuting to Skydiving: Process Shifts in a Risk Sport," in *Play as Context.* Edited by Alyce Taylor Cheska. West Point, N.Y.: Leisure Press, 1981, pp. 167-81.

Edwards, Carlton. *Homes for Travel and Living.* East Lansing, Mich.: Carl Edwards, 1977.

Francis, Devon. *Mr. Piper and His Cubs.* Ames: Iowa State University Press, 1973.

Griffin, Al. *Recreational Vehicles.* Chicago: Regnery, 1973.

Lindbergh, Charles. *We.* New York: G. P. Putnam's Sons, 1927.

Milbank, Jeremiah. *First Century of Flight in America.* Princeton, N.J.: Princeton University Press, 1943.

Pelto, Pertti J. *The Snowmobile Revolution: Technology and Social Change in the Arctic.* Menlo Park, Calif.: Cummings, 1973.

Phillips-Birt, Douglas H. C. *The History of Yachting.* London: Elm Tree Books, 1974.

Robinson, Bill. *The Great American Yacht Designers.* New York: Knopf, 1974.

Rockland, Michael Aaron. *Homes on Wheels.* New Brunswick, N.J.: Rutgers University Press, 1980.

Smith, Robert A. *A Social History of the Bicycle: Its Early Life and Times in America.* New York: American Heritage Press, 1972.

Wolfe, Arnold. *Vans and Vanners.* Matteson, Ill.: Greatlakes Living Press, 1976.

PERIODICALS

Boating. Chicago, 1956-.

Flying. New York, 1927-.

Journal of Leisure Research. Arlington, Va., 1969-.

Off Road. Los Angeles, 1969-.

Outing. New York, 1882-1923.

Popular Mechanics. New York, 1902-.

Rudder (combined with *Sea*). New York, 1890-.

Sail. Boston, 1970-.

Trailer Travel Magazine. Chicago, 1936-. (Continued as *Woodall's Trailer Travel.* Highland Park, Ill., 1976-.)

Magazines

Dorothy Schmidt

More than any other medium, magazines represent America. Other nations produce periodicals, but nowhere else is there the multi-colored, multi-voiced flood of print that inundates Americans weekly, monthly, and quarterly. With a readership of more than eighty percent of the population, American magazines are not only dazzling in their design and diversity, but complex in content and purpose. As consumer products, magazines accurately predict and satisfy the tastes of contemporary Americans; as primary advertising tools of business and industry, magazines help provide the market which supplies the demand for products; and as instruments of entertainment and enlightenment, magazines both create and respond to current social values and the panorama of American culture.

The idea of such a periodical apparently arose almost concurrently in France, England, Germany and other European countries, but the term "magazine" was first used in English in the early eighteenth century. The *New English Dictionary* cites the *Gentlemen's Magazine,* founded in 1731, as its first example of the word used to describe a collection of articles, fiction, poetry and "miscellany" gathered into one place, as in a storehouse, or treasure chest. The descriptive term caught on so well that by midcentury several publications included "magazine" either in their titles or subtitles. And two and a half centuries later, magazine is still the preferred and most commonly used designation for thousands of miscellaneous collections for the general public. Other terms, such as bulletins, journals, quarterlies, or reviews are used for more specialized publications including business, professional, trade, and scholarly periodicals, but even many of these are actually consumer or mass magazines.

In addition to content, form and frequency of publication have been used as criteria for differentiating between magazines and other periodicals, especially newspapers. While no entirely satisfactory or mutually exclusive categories of periodicals have been established, magazines are usually produced in pamphlet form, with a stitched, stapled, or glued cover, rather than as broadsheets or tabloids. As for frequency of publication, magazines have traditionally been monthly publications, but again, exceptions can be noted, especially in the modern weekly newsmagazines which offer analysis and commentary on current events to augment the news coverage of radio, television, and newspapers.

A recent expansion of the use of the "magazine" label based largely on content occurred with the initiation of TV magazine programs, for example, *Sixty Minutes* and *20/20*, which provide viewers with a variety of features, including human interest stories, personality profiles, news analysis, and interpretations of various aspects of American life in a cross-media adaptation of the usual contents of the printed periodical.

Difficult to define as they may be, magazines yet hold a unique place in American print media. In form, content, and periodicity, magazines are more durable than newsprint, less formidable than hardbound books, less precipitate than newspapers, yet more timely than books. Furthermore, magazines must be designed to attract and hold reader allegiance to ensure either repeated purchases or continuing subscriptions.

While no single magazine has ever claimed the allegiance of the total American reading public, over 180 million persons read magazines regularly, and most read five or six different publications. The perennial world circulation leader has been the *Reader's Digest,* but currently the most widely distributed magazine in America is *TV Guide,* with a circulation approaching the 50 million mark. *TV Guide* contains not only television programming schedules and criticism, but lucid articles on current personalities and events as well, and its popularity is an ironic refutation of the predicted doom of print media with the advent of electronic media. Instead, not only have magazines survived, but they have thrived, and many have achieved record circulations, in the tens of millions. Other publishers have successfully and profitably identified a more limited market and produced periodicals specifically for that segment of the mass market. Thus magazines on the American scene have changed, and are changing, but there seems to be no stemming of the flood. Each calendar year brings some new magazine addressed to a topic or market not yet tapped.

Today thousands of titles, ranging from *Analog* to *Sesame Street Magazine,* from *Scientific American* to *Rolling Stone,* from the *New Yorker* to *Handyman* tempt readers to exercise private interests and hobbies, while general magazines such as *Reader's Digest, Ladies Home Journal, Atlantic,* and *Time* have broad circulations. Increasingly, historians, sociologists, and cultural anthropologists have begun to acknowledge the importance of magazines as material artifacts and historical sources far more revealing of the culture of their times than any other single source, thus recognizing, in truth, magazines' initial and continuing function as a very "storehouse" of information and diversion.

Obviously, the development of magazines had to await the invention of printing in 1450. Most examples of the new process were either single flat sheets, appropriately called broadsides, or bound volumes such as Bibles and other treatises. A subsequent development was the printing of several flat sheets folded together without binding as tabloids, but finally someone decided to put a stitch through the fold to keep the pages from sliding around, and the magazine began its distinctive existence. In large degree, however, form followed content in magazine development so that the early English magazines were single sheet issues, looking almost exactly like their contemporary newspapers, but containing comment rather than news.

Content of magazines was varied almost from the beginning. Daniel Defoe, credited with starting one of the first magazines in England, in 1710 used *The Review* as a kind of privileged communication among members of his immediate society. A little later Joseph Addison and Richard Steele, in first the *Tatler* and then the *Spectator,* commented on a wide variety of issues then current in London. Essays and short stories originated in the pages of early magazines.

Although printing presses were among the first cargoes to the American colonies, it was not until 1741 that an American magazine somewhat imitative of its English cousins was printed and identified as such.

If asked, most Americans would probably name the *Saturday Evening Post,* founded by Benjamin Franklin, as the oldest American magazine—a misconception on both counts fostered by the cover claims of that widely known publication. Although purporting to have been established in 1728, the magazine was actually begun in 1821, using the offices and press of the defunct *Pennsylvania Gazette,* which, though owned by Franklin, had been founded by someone else and was actually a newspaper, not a magazine. Franklin *almost* printed the first magazine in the colonies, but his *General Magazine, and Historical Chronicle for all the British Plantations in America* lost that premier position to the *American Magazine, or A Monthly View of the Political State of the British Colonies* issued three days earlier by rival publisher Andrew Bradford. Such are the near-misses in historical firsts.

Although neither magazine survived even a full year of publication, other magazines were soon launched. Rogers and Fowle's *American Magazine and Historical Chronicle,* founded in Boston in 1743, lasted three years, thus earning the laurel of magazine historian Frank Luther Mott as the "first really important American magazine."

Several other magazines, including another *American Magazine and Monthly Chronicle* by Bradford, the *New American Magazine,* the *Royal American Magazine,* and other variations on the same theme enjoyed brief lives, but the political foment of the colonies during the next quarter century did not offer a favorable environment for sustained publication. According to Mott, only two American magazines, the *Pennsylvania Magazine,* which employed Thomas Paine, and the *United States Magazine,* were printed during the course of the Revolution.

The post-Revolutionary period was characterized by a number of other firsts: the first acknowledgement of women's interest in magazines, with the *Gentleman's and Lady's Town and Country Magazine;* the first children's periodical; the first magazine for music lovers which contained music scores; and the first sectarian magazine, briefly edited by Methodist Bishops Coke and Asbury.

Magazine content included political news, essays on various aspects of society, short fiction and sketches, poems, and not infrequently, polemics. Little advertising, beyond a few classifieds, was sold, and revenue consisted mainly of subscription fees from a limited circulation. Even the distribution of the periodicals was somewhat haphazard and sporadic by modern standards. With early postal regulations seldom being clear about the status of periodicals, some earnest postmasters making their own interpretations barred magazines from the mails entirely. But even in adverse environments, American magazines flourished because Americans wanted to read them.

The emergence of periodicals dominated by strong editorial figures was one characteristic of the early nineteenth century. James Playsted Wood, in *Magazines in the United States* (1956), writes, "A strong editor, even a strongly wrong-headed editor, has usually meant a strong and influential magazine; whereas intelligent editors of moderate means and no firm opinions have often produced colorless and comparatively ineffective magazines." One early example of a strong editor was Joseph Dennie, whose magazine *Port Folio* (1807-1821) served as a model for subsequent literate and urbane publications. Dennie's strength is indicated by the survival of his periodical even while it espoused the unpopular Tory cause. Another editor and publication worthy of note was Charles Brockden Brown and his *Monthly Magazine and American Review,* called by Mott, "second only to *Port Folio* in importance." Under various titles, Brockden Brown edited the *Literary Magazine* for almost a decade.

The proliferation of magazines during this period included an expansion of magazine content and purpose beyond literature and public opinion. New magazines were directed toward religious groups, the medical profession, women, farmers, and other groups, thus beginning the trend toward specialization which was somewhat deflected by the mushrooming of the great mass magazines in the first half of the twentieth century, but which now has become the mainstream of magazine publishing: the specialized magazine for the special interest group.

One of the most influential women's periodicals of the nineteenth century, indeed, of all time, was *Godey's Lady's Book.* Under the leadership of Sara Josepha Hale, *Godey's* achieved wide circulation during its 68 years of publication. Gowns and other apparel were assiduously copied and sewn from the color fashion plates by dressmakers both amateur and professional. *Godey's,* however, was not merely a fashion book; its contents provided enlightenment for the female mind, and Hale crusaded within its pages for women's right to education in an age which predated women's suffrage in the United States. Within its pages, Edgar Allan Poe described "The Literati of New York," sometimes astutely, and sometimes with rather saccharine sanctimony, and writers like Bryant, Whitman, and Hawthorne were contributors to this popular magazine.

And there were others. Caroline Kirkland spent six years trying to inject a little frontier freshness and literary quality into the *Union* magazine, which publisher John Sartain saw as primarily a showcase for his own outstanding engraving talents. The 1820-1850 time spread contained the births of the *Saturday Evening Post, Graham's Magazine, Peterson's,* the *Scientific American, North American Review, Yale Review, Ohio Farmer, New York Mirror,* and Horace Greeley's *New-Yorker.* In addition, huge quantities of print were unfortunately summarily dismissed as "trash," both by Mott and by contemporaneous editors. These "Penny" magazines and "Family Libraries" abounded, but were often poorly printed, poorly edited collections of pirated or fourth-rate material; however, their very existence testifies to the omnivorous demands of Americans of all levels of sophistication for periodical reading materials. And this was the age in which these demands were answered. Call it the age of expansion, call it America's awakening, or call it the "golden age of periodicals" as Mott did, this country did not again see such a burgeoning of print until after 1900.

The pre-Civil War decade saw the establishment of other familiar names: *Harper's Monthly* (1850), *Country Gentleman* (1853), various regional *Christian Advocates* (1850-), *Atlantic Monthly* (1857), and a spate of short-lived university publications. By this time magazines had progressed in form and appearance far beyond their earlier resemblance to newspapers and had blossomed into handcolored and embellished, highly illustrated offerings whose engravings were often scissored to grace parlor walls. Although more advertising was being accepted, it was carefully segregated from the editorial and textual materials, and small wonder, for much of it ballyhooed the virtues of everything from laxatives and trusses to cures for baldness, cancer, and impotency (all in the same bottle). The lack of regulation of advertising, either by the magazines themselves or by any publishers or advertisers associations, resulted in ads with little or no regard for truth or good taste.

The Civil War interrupted this expansion of magazines, but during the last forty years of the century, magazine offerings increased in scope and variety. Popular and enduring titles, such as *The Nation, Harper's Bazaar, Scribner's,* and *The American Magazine,* began in the 1860s and 1870s. And the breadth of magazine coverage is only hinted at in these titles: *U.S. Law Review, Instructor, Locomotive, American Brewer, Coal Trade Journal, Popular Science,* and *American Naturalist.* The brief life of *Keepapichinin* (1870-1871) indicates its subscribers didn't, but the popular humor of *Puck* and *Judge* kept Americans laughing right up to and through the turn of the century. And the print media's own magazine, *Publisher's Weekly*, began its observations of this dynamic industry.

Only technological barriers prevented magazines from becoming the mass circulation giants of the twentieth century. Throughout most of the nineteenth century, magazines were printed on flat bed presses, from handset type on single pieces of paper which were hand fed into the presses. Rarely could a magazine print more than 100,000 impressions, not only because of the time and labor consumed by the process, but because type and engravings wore down after repeated prints. Development in the 1890s of rotary presses which were capable of printing 10,000 copies an hour on a continuous "web" roll of paper, the development of cheap wood pulp paper strong enough for this type of printing press, and the use of speedy typesetting machinery removed the barriers to mass production and opened the way for circulations to reach the "magic million."

Not surprisingly, access to such numbers of potential customers drew the attention of industry, and advertising content and revenue grew. The influx of advertising dollars soon matched, then passed, sales input. Beginning with almost equal advertising and circulation income in the 1890s, according to U.S. Bureau of the Census manufacturing data, by the late 1920s advertising revenue was three times greater than subscription and sales income.

The shift of emphasis from magazines as the individual voices of single editors or publishers to their use as the major national advertising medium carried both positive and negative results. Magazines became colorful showcases of American technology and progress, with expensive color advertisements brightening their pages and thickening their issues. Through the first three-quarters of the twentieth century, advertising has become almost as interesting to magazine readers as the editorial contents of a periodical. And rightfully so, for it is through such advertising that most Americans become informed about new products, instructed in their uses, and encouraged to purchase everything from toothpaste to Toronados in an economy increasingly dependent on consumerism.

Despite this bounty, a realistic appraisal of magazine content suggests that with economic dependence came loss of editorial freedom, and that some of the free-swinging, fresh-air aggressiveness of earlier editors has been compromised by the magazines' presence at the table of business and industry. This attitude was angrily espoused by Upton Sinclair in *The Brass Check: A Study of American Journalism* (self-published in Pasadena, 1920) in which he called the Curtis publications a "colossal advertisement-distributing machine" using reading material only to fill the empty spaces between the ads. And more recently, Herbert Schiller in *The Mind Managers* (1973) suggests that one influence of the advertising dollar is to make magazine editors more conservative, less likely to broach topics that are controversial enough to offend either readers or advertisers.

Fortunately magazines have not been muzzled entirely, and their investigative reporting has led to exposes and crusades against giant industries such as drug manufacturers, food processors, auto makers and others including big labor, big government, big business, and even big medicine. But as more and more magazines, in fact the majority of them, are not independent businesses, but owned by corporations or conglomerates with widespread holdings and interests, the range of modern magazines' lances must inevitably be shortened.

Thus magazines in the last quarter of the twentieth century are consumer products which must be sold to two groups: the magazine readers who purchase the magazine and the businesses who buy the advertising space. And because the latter are the more economically powerful, the editor who fails to meet their needs will witness the death of even a magazine with rising subscriptions and circulation. But the editorial genius who finds a formula for a magazine and is able to adapt it to the rapidly changing American society or to an unchanging segment of the society, will have a successful, surviving magazine. Examples of this type of editing and management include the *Reader's Digest, Ladies Home Journal, Atlantic, Harper's, McCall's, Time, National Geographic, Scientific American,* or *Playboy.* But the editor whose publication gets out of step with change, or changes too fast, or never develops a distinct identity, must preside over its funeral—sometimes twice. Notable examples include *Coronet, Flair, Look, Collier's, Woman's Home Companion, Life, Saturday Evening Post,* and *Women Sports.*

It is this delicate interrelationship of the reader, the word, and the world of economic and political reality which validates the function of magazines as accurate imprints of American culture and necessitates their special study apart from other print media.

BIBLIOGRAPHY

Anderson, Elliott, and Mary Kinze, eds. *The Little Magazine in America: A Modern Documentary History.* Yonkers, N.Y.: Pushcart, 1979.

Beer, William. *Checklist of American Magazines 1741-1800.* Worchester, 1923 rpt. from *Proceedings,* American Antiquarian Society, October 1922.

Coakley, Mary L. *Sex, Sisterhood and Self-Delusion: What Happened to Women's Magazines.* New Rochelle, N.Y.: Arlington House, 1980.

Ford, James L. C. *Magazines for Millions.* Carbondale: Southern Illinois University Press, 1969.

Fulton, Len, and Ellen Ferber, eds. *International Directory of Little Magazines and Small Presses.* Annual. Paradise, Calif.: Dustbooks, 1970-.

Katz, Bill, and Berry G. Richards. *Magazines for Libraries.* 3d ed. New York: R. R. Bowker, 1978.

Magazine Editorial Reports: Analysis of the Editorial Content of General, News, Women's, Home, and Fashion Magazines. Annual. New York: Lloyd B. Hall, Inc., 1960-.

MIMP, Magazine Industry Market Place. Annual. New York: R. R. Bowker, 1980-.
Mott, Frank Luther. *American Journalism: A History,* 3d ed. New York: Macmillan, 1962.
______. *A History of American Magazines, 1741-1930.* 5 vols. Cambridge: Harvard Belknap Press, 1957-1968.
National Research Bureau. *Working Press of the Nation,* vol. II, *Magazine Directory.* Annual. Chicago: NRB, 1979.
Peterson, Theodore. *Magazines in the Twentieth Century.* Urbana: University of Illinois Press, 1964.
Price, Warren C., and Calder M. Pickett. *An Annotated Journalism Bibliography, 1958-1968.* Minneapolis: University of Minnesota Press, 1970.
Richardson, Lyon N. *A History of Early American Magazines: 1741-1798.* New York: Nelson, 1931; rpt. Octagon, 1967.
Tassin, Algernon. *The Magazine in America.* New York: Dodd, Mead, 1916.
Tebbel, John W. *The American Magazine: A Compact History.* New York: Hawthorn Books, 1969.
______. *A History of Book Publishing in the United States.* 3 vols. New York: R. R. Bowker, 1975-1978.
Wolseley, Roland E. *The Changing Magazine.* New York: Hastings House, 1973.
______. *Journalist's Bookshelf.* 7th ed. Philadelphia: Chilton, 1961.
______. *The Magazine World.* New York: Prentice-Hall, 1951.
______. *Understanding Magazines.* 2d ed. Ames: Iowa State University Press, 1969.
Wood, James Playsted. *The Curtis Magazines.* New York: Ronald Press, 1971.
______. *Magazines in the United States.* 3d ed. New York: Ronald, 1956.
______. *Of Lasting Interest: The Story of the Reader's Digest.* Westport, Conn.: Greenwood Press, 1975, rpt. of 1958 Doubleday ed.
Young, Margaret L., *et al.,* eds. *Directory of Special Libraries and Information Centers.* 4th ed. Detroit: Gale Research, 1976.
van Zuilen, A. J. *The Life Cycle of Magazines: A Historical Study of the Decline and Fall of the General Interest Mass Audience Magazine in the United States during the Period 1946-1972.* Uithoorn, Netherlands: Graduate Press, 1977.

Magic and Magicians

Earle J. Coleman

As the nineteenth-century French prestidigitator Robert-Houdin observed, the theatrical magician can be defined as an actor who is playing the role of a conjurer, that is, a being whose supernatural powers enable him to accomplish what is naturally impossible.[1] Magic, like the closely related performing art of pantomime, is basically grounded upon the production of illusions. In fact, every feat of magic depends upon presenting the spectator with a forgery or counterfeit of some object, action, or state of affairs. While the pantomimist presents an intelligible illusion, the magician exhibits an unintelligible illusion; in the case of the former, one understands how it is effected (through skillful body control developed from a host of ballet-like exercises); in the latter, attributing skill to the performer hardly qualifies as an explanation of how the effect is produced.

Magic and magicians are as at home in American popular culture as the long-running comic strip *Mandrake the Magician* by Lee Falk. Indeed, magic or magical themes have figured prominently in American versions of such diverse forms of entertainment as the impromptu street performance, stage show, circus, dime museum, carnival, nightclub, novel, drama, short story, film, radio, and television. Occasionally, a term used by magicians has found its way into wider circulation in American society. The word *gimmick*, for instance, by which magicians describe a concealed device needed as the means for some magical effect, was eventually adopted by the advertising industry to designate anything that attracts attention by injecting an element of novelty. By definition, popular arts are widely enjoyed, but magic is more than popular; it is actually universal in its appeal. A native of China and a citizen of Italy may have real difficulty in grasping, much less appreciating, the dance, music, literature, painting, or architecture of each other's culture, but both individuals are readily entertained by the magician, for in causing a coin to vanish or levitating a woman the conjurer violates the laws of nature under which all human beings live and with which their experience vividly familiarizes them.

That sleight of hand was practiced in ancient Egypt is shown by a wall painting from a Beni Hasan tomb (ca. 2500 B.C.) depicting a performer presenting the classic "cups and balls mystery." Moving from magic in antiquity to the beginnings of American magic and magicians, one discovers that the Colonial climate was decidedly inhospitable to conjurers, actors, and other entertainers; in fact, all such performers were banned from Jamestown, Virginia, in 1612. Perhaps frivolous entertainment was simply deemed incompatible with the sternness that the struggle for survival demanded of the early colonists. While Virginia still outlawed public magic performances in 1740, a member of the state council, William Byrd II, is reported to have enjoyed a private magic show in June of that year; and, by June of 1769, Virginia no longer forbade magicians, for George Washington wrote in his diary entry of September 19, 1769: "went to see slight (sic) of hand performed"; this presentation took place in Alexandria, Virginia. Washington was also present when Peter Gardiner, a magician-puppeteer, presented his act on November 17, 1772, in Williamsburg, Virginia. In the same year, Jacob Meyer, the first American magician to appear in Europe, was entertaining Catherine II in Focsani, Romania. Meyer favored the stage name "Philadelphia," which he borrowed from his native city and found had a sufficiently exotic ring to European ears. Just over a decade later, in 1783, the famous Philadelphian Benjamin Franklin was solidly defeated in a chess game by a chess-playing automaton, which was the brainchild of a Baron Wolfgang von Kempelen. The match took place in Versailles while Franklin was serving as the U.S. ambassador to France. As we shall see, it remained for another celebrated American to argue that the automaton was actually a magic stunt operated by a concealed, chess-playing assistant in the body of the mannequin figure. The year 1783 is also significant because it marks the birth of Richard Potter in Boston (date of death unknown), the first American to succeed as a magician in his own country. Featuring effects such as the standard "cups and balls," Potter attracted appreciative crowds in Canada as well as the United States. As the dark-skinned son of a British tax collector and his black slave, he has the dubious distinction of being the first American magician to experience racial prejudice during a twelve-day engagement in Mobile, Alabama.

On seeing the automaton chess player in Richmond, Virginia, the still largely unknown American writer and poet, Edgar Allan Poe, offered his theory of the phenomenon in the *Southern Literary Messenger* of April 1836. Later history revealed that Poe had been partially correct in his analysis of the talented machine. As he suspected there actually was a concealed chess player, but this person was not located in the body of the automaton itself as Poe believed; rather, the unseen player was hidden in the desk upon which the mannequin rested. A quarter of a century later, John Henry Anderson, a European who advertised himself as "The Great Wizard of the North," was vividly confronted with the fermenting slavery issue in the United States. Irate citizens of Richmond, Virginia, destroyed the advance publicity posters of this charlatan from the North who dared to trespass upon Southern soil! Explaining that Anderson was from northern Scotland was to no avail.

In 1861, the outstanding German conjurer, Carl Hermann, brought his magic to the White House where he performed for President Lincoln. A contemporary, but native American magician, John Wyman, went further by performing for Presidents Van Buren and Fillmore, as well as entertaining Lincoln four times. It was Wyman who pioneered in the exposing of fraudulent spirit mediums who bilked the public, a crusade which obsessed Harry Houdini in his final years. But it was undoubtedly Senior Blitz of London who performed the most memorable magic for Lincoln. In July of 1863, at an outdoor gathering, Blitz produced a pigeon from Lincoln's hat. Attached to the bird's wing was a slip of paper with the message, "Victory, General Grant." The reference, of course, was to the intense battle then being waged at Gettysburg.

By 1884 Harry Kellar, the first native American magician to achieve international fame, had begun his longest run, 267 performances at the Egyptian Hall in Philadelphia. During this engagement, members of the audience included two of his friends, the noted actor Edwin Booth and the equally prominent writer Mark Twain. Born in Erie, Pennsylvania, on July 11, 1849, Kellar performed on five continents before being recognized as a monarch of American magic. His stylishly mounted levitation of a woman illusion was justifiably the centerpiece of his full-evening show.

Although an often neglected topic, American Indian conjuring is the subject of an entire chapter in Melbourne Christopher's excellent *The Illustrated History of Magic.* Perhaps it should not be surprising that Indian magicians favored producing snakes from bags over extracting rabbits from hats. At the Louisiana Exposition of 1904, Shungopavi, an Indian who billed himself as a medicine man, employed an eagle feather for flourishes in place of the traditional magic wand.

Harry Kellar passed his mantle to Howard Thurston, an American born in Columbus, Ohio, on July 20, 1869. Thurston, who specialized in large-scale illusions, presented his own version of the famous Indian rope trick in which a rope tossed upward remains in mid-air, a boy climbs the rope, and he eventually vanishes. It is worth mentioning parenthetically that the original Indian version of the effect, in which the mystery was presented outside in broad daylight, appears to be purely mythical. Thurston and other magicians offered substantial sums of money to buy a single performance of the trick, and in 1934 the *Times* of India offered 10,000 rupees for one performance; there were no takers. During the same year, Thurston brought an elaborate magic show to the White House of President Roosevelt. One year later, while on what he planned as his farewell tour, Thurston died in Charleston, West Virginia. Having held his title as the United States' leading illusionist for nearly three decades, he had surpassed even the expectations of his predecessor, Kellar.

At about the time that Thurston took over the Kellar show, Thomas Nelson Downs was establishing himself as the greatest coin manipulator in the history of magic. Born in Montour, Iowa, on March 26, 1867, Downs's masterful production of an apparently inexhaustible supply of coins from thin air ensured bookings at first-rate theaters in the United States and on the Continent. One of the most tragic episodes in the history of American magic took place in 1918, when a contemporary of Downs, William E. Robinson, was accidentally shot to death during the performance of his sensational bullet-catching effect. Robinson, who used the stage name Chung Ling Soo, through make-up and costuming convinced his audiences that he actually was an Oriental. A somewhat later figure, Theodore Bamberg (1875-1963), also masqueraded as an Oriental and actually managed to fool even his Oriental audiences.

If the first quarter of this century belonged uniquely to any magician, it belonged to the master escape artist Harry Houdini (1874-1926). Born in Budapest, the son of a rabbi, Houdini, whose real name was Ehrich Weiss, insisted in later years that he was American born. He undoubtedly felt like an American, given that he was brought to the United States while still a child. Several of the biographies on Houdini give credence to the cliche that truth can be stranger and more exciting than fiction. Among his effects were: walking through a brick wall, causing an elephant to vanish on the stage of the New York Hippodrome theatre, and escaping from an endless series of restraining devices—including handcuffs from Scotland Yard. Eventually, Houdini's exploits won him a motion picture contract, his first of several films, *The Grim Game*, being shot in 1919. At the height of his success he received $3,700 a week, the largest salary ever paid to a single performer at the Palladium in London. On each anniversary of Houdini's death, members of the Society of American Magicians demonstrate their regard for him by making a pilgrimage to his Long Island tomb.

During the first three decades of this century, American theater was truly enriched by the phenomenon that came to be known as the full-evening magic show. These productions were extravanganzas which sometimes actually lived up to the superlatives in their advertisements. Elephants, lions, tigers, bears, horses, doves, rabbits, ducks, eagles, or camels, dozens of assistants, elaborate backdrops and scenes which changed frequently, and the use of over a hundred costumes for one performance were the kind of ingredients that contributed to these pageants. But the Depression that hit in 1929 delivered a death blow to most of these elaborately framed presentations. In such an economic climate, the production costs of full-evening shows were prohibitive. The advent of "talkies" in motion pictures and the great popularity of radio also increased the economic risks of large-scale magic shows. Therefore, a majority of American magicians shifted to performing smaller nightclub acts. One magical genius of this era was Cardini (1899-1939). Born Richard Valentine Pitchford, in Wales, Cardini achieved international acclaim for his suave nightclub act which featured unexcelled playing card and cigarette manipulations. For many aspiring American magicians, Cardini's routines became the paradigm of perfection. A few figures such as Harry Blackstone, who was born Henri Bouton in Chicago, and Dante, whose real name was Harry Jansen, carried the full-evening show into the 1940s. Fortunately for contemporary lovers of magic, Harry Blackstone, Jr., is now performing some of his father's magical masterpieces in the baroque environment of Las Vegas hotels. Any chronicle of contemporary American magicians would surely include Joseph Dunninger, whose mental magic gained him popularity from the 1930s through to the 1960s. Dunninger's predictions and demonstrations of telepathy made him extremely successful on stage, radio, and television. In fact, he is one of very few performers who has ever had a series on all three television networks.

Magic today is happily enjoying a rebirth as magicians adapt their art of unreality to the realities of the final quarter of this century. Witness, for example, the popular Broadway play, *The Magic Show,* which fuses the color, flash, and mystery of the old full-evening show with rock music. One of the oldest forms of magic, street conjuring, has been revitalized by artists like Jeff Sheridan, who performs in New York's Central Park. The intimacy of the television camera has enormously increased the audience for close-up magic, which would normally be visible to only one or two dozen spectators. A million-dollar contract with a major Las Vegas hotel has recently been signed by the magic team of Sigfried and Roy, making them the most handsomely paid magicians in history. Causing tigers and other big cats to appear, vanish, or become transformed into human beings, Sigfried Fischbacker and Roy Horn have also appeared in their own program on network television. Senior magicians who lecture to magic societies are finding a growing number of members in these organizations. Bars and restaurants that feature magicians are proliferating throughout the country. In numerous schools from the elementary level to the university a number of magicians specialize in entertaining students. A further expanding market for magic acts has been created by the phenomenon of the theme park. Many of these amusement parks feature half-hour, condensed versions of the full-evening show. In fact, there is now a magic franchise; Mark Wilson, once the star of his own television series, trains and choreographs performers for magic shows at the Busch Gardens theme parks. Even the Houdini escape act has been resurrected by magicians such as the great Randi. Kreskin, drawing perhaps too heavily from the mentalist, Dunninger, has made his mental magic pay through numerous television appearances. It is sobering to realize that the magician who makes one network television presentation has a greater audience than Houdini had in a lifetime. Shimada, the Japanese magician, has reintroduced the exquisite beauty of Oriental magic and is in demand at magic conventions throughout the world. A number of contemporary magicians are being lucratively rewarded for their "commercial magic," that is, magic that is employed to sell a product or service at trade shows and conventions. In our post-Watergate era, the magician can be seen as refreshingly honest; he is the one person who openly announces that he will deceive you and then lives up to his word.

BIBLIOGRAPHY

BOOKS

Bamberg, Theodore, with Robert Parrish. *Okito on Magic.* 2d ed. Chicago: Magic, Inc., 1968.

Blackstone, Harry. *Blackstone's Secrets of Magic.* New York: Garden City Publishers, 1958.

Bobo, J. B. *The New Modern Coin Magic.* 2d ed. Chicago: Magic, Inc., 1966.

Christopher, Melbourne. *Houdini: The Untold Story.* New York: Cassell, 1969.

______. *The Illustrated History of Magic.* New York: Thomas Y. Crowell Co., 1973.

Claflin, Edward, with Jeff Sheridan. *Street Magic.* New York: Doubleday, 1977.

Doerflinger, William. *The Magic Catalogue.* New York: E. P. Dutton, 1977.

Fitzkee, Dariel. *The Trick Brain.* California: St. Raphael House, 1944.

Ganson, Lewis. *Dai Vernon's Ultimate Card Secrets.* London: Unique, 1967.

______. *The Magic of Slydini.* London: Unique, 1960.

______. *Routined Manipulation.* Part I, 1950. Part II, 1952. Part III, 1954. London: Unique.

Gibson, Walter Brown. *The Complete Illustrated Book of Card Magic.* New York: Kaye and Ward, 1969.

Hay, Henry. *The Amateur Magician's Handbook.* New York: Cromwell, 1950.

Hilliard, John Northern. *Greater Magic.* Minneapolis: Carl Waring Jones, 1938.

Hoffmann, Professor. *Modern Magic.* New York and London: Routledge, 1876.

LePaul, Paul. *The Card Magic of LePaul.* New York: Louis Tannen, Inc., 1959.

Marlo, Edward. *The Cardician.* Chicago: Magic, Inc., 1953.

Nelson, Robert Alan. *The Encyclopedia of Mentalism and Allied Arts.* Calgary: Hades, 1971.

Rice, Harold R. *Encyclopedia of Silk Magic.* Vol. I, 1948. Vol. II, 1953. Vol. III, 1962. Cincinnati: Silk King Studios.

Scarne, John. *Scarne's Magic Tricks.* New York: Crown, 1951.

Tarbell, Harlan. *The Tarbell Encyclopedic Course in Magic.* 7 vols. New York: Louis Tannen, 1941-1972.

ANTHOLOGIES AND REPRINTS

Erdnase, S. W. *The Expert at the Card Table.* Nevada: Gamblers Book Club, 1967.

Maskleyne, Nevil, and David Devant. *Our Magic.* England: Routledge, 1911.

Scot, Reginald. *The Discovery of Witchcraft.* Reprint of 1930 edition which was based on 1584 publication. New York: Dover, 1972.

Medicine and the Physician

Anne Hudson Jones

LITERATURE

In Western culture, medicine and the physcian have been subjects of literature since ancient times. Early Greek and Roman dramatists, epigrammatists, and satirists frequently aimed barbs at physicians. The first works of prose fiction were popular romances and Milesian tales, which included physicians as minor characters.[1] In later European literature the physician became a stock character, ridiculed or portrayed as a quack. Chaucer's *The Canterbury Tales,* Boccaccio's *Decameron,* and the *commedia dell'arte* provide early examples; the famous physicians in Molière's plays follow.[2] The physician as a character taken seriously and portrayed sympathetically, however, did not begin to emerge until the nineteenth century, in the novels of Balzac's *Human Comedy*[3] and in Zola's *Doctor Pascal.* This changed presentation of physicians in fiction seems to have resulted from the advances in scientific knowledge, which gave physicians greater professional stature.[4] European literature is rich in its use of the physician and medical themes and has supplied the material for several book-length studies.[5]

It is easier to trace the history of presentations of medicine and the physician in American literature than it is to decide which of those presentations constitute popular rather than high culture. In nineteenth-century American literature, for example, Nathaniel Hawthorne presents physician-scientists in many of his stories and novels, and Herman Melville satirizes surgeons in several of his works. Later in the century, the physician was portrayed sympathetically in novels of two physician-writers, Oliver Wendell Holmes and S. Weir Mitchell. Fictional women physicians appeared as major characters for the first time in the 1880s, in novels by William Dean Howells, Sarah Orne Jewett, and Elizabeth Stuart Phelps Ward. Certainly the best-known physician-scientist of American literature is Sinclair Lewis's Martin Arrowsmith, who appeared in *Arrowsmith* in 1925. Throughout American literature, physician characters appear frequently and in works of such varied writers as Henry James, Ellen Glasgow, James Gould Cozzens, Robert Penn Warren, John Steinbeck, Katherine Anne Porter, Carson McCullers,

William Carlos Williams, William Faulkner, Joyce Carol Oates, and Walker Percy.

Among works of American popular literature dealing with medicine and the physician, none has had more long lasting effects than the seven Dr. Kildare novels, written between 1940 and 1943 by Frederick Faust, under the pseudonym Max Brand. Several movies, a weekly radio program, and two television series have been based on these books. Also important are Lloyd C. Douglas's novels, especially *Doctor Hudson's Secret Journal* (1939), which inspired a television series in the mid-1950s. Frank Slaughter's novels, many about physicians and medicine, began appearing in the 1940s; they now number more than fifty and have sold more than fifty million copies worldwide. His *Women in White* was the basis for a four-part television drama in 1979. Important in the 1950s were Morton Thompson's *Not As a Stranger* and Gerald Green's *The Last Angry Man;* both were made into popular films. Richard Hooker's series of *M*A*S*H* novels came out in the 1960s, and Robin Cook's *The Year of the Intern* and *Coma* were published in the 1970s. A recent smash hit, billed as a medical *Catch-22,* is Samuel Shem's *The House of God,* published in 1978.

Two popular genres, detective fiction and science fiction, use physicians in fairly predictable ways. Physicians' training in observation and diagnosis makes them naturals for detective work. Television's *Quincy* is just the latest version of the physician-detective whose line began with Sir Arthur Conan Doyle's Sherlock Holmes, modeled on the surgeon Dr. Joseph Bell, and Dr. Watson.[6] In science fiction, the role of the physician has usually been combined with that of the research scientist, producing almost a stock character, familiar from the time of Mary Shelley's *Frankenstein* in 1816.[7]

With the development of psychiatry and the spread of its influence in American culture, the psychiatrist has become a favorite character in literature and appears with increasing frequency beginning in the 1930s, in works by "standard" authors such as F. Scott Fitzgerald, Eugene O'Neill, Tennessee Williams, and Arthur Miller[8] as well as works by "popular" authors such as Mary Jane Ward, Theodore Isaac Rubin, and Elliott Baker. At least one recognizable subgenre of popular fiction has resulted, derived from a combination of the novel, autobiography, and psychological case history. The outstanding example of this subgenre is Joanne Greenberg's *I Never Promised You a Rose Garden,* published under the pseudonym Hannah Green in 1964. Hospital settings, especially mental asylums, and metaphors of madness abound in modern popular literature. The institutional environment serves as a microcosm of society as a whole, and the insane are often depicted as being more sane than their medical keepers. Ken Kesey's *One Flew Over the Cuckoo's Nest,* published in 1962, is one of the best-known examples.

Recent plays on Broadway reflect a new popular concern with prolonged illness and death and dying. In one year, 1979, Brian Clark's *Whose Life Is It Anyway?,* Bernard Pomerance's *The Elephant Man,* Arthur Kopit's

Wings, and Steve Carter's *Nevis Mountain Dew* were all playing on Broadway, and Michael Cristofer's *The Shadow Box* was touring the country. Like Sam Shepard's *Inacoma,* based on the Karen Quinlan case, all these plays are responses to possibilities created by sophisticated medical technology.

CARICATURE AND COMICS

European medical caricature dates back to the Renaissance, but medical caricature did not develop in the United States until the Civil War period. The first medical cartoon published in this country has been identified as "The Quarantine Question," which appeared in *Harper's Weekly* in 1858. Medical cartoons were published in the 1880s in early American magazines such as *Puck* and *Life,* and gradually they began to appear routinely in most major American newspapers and magazines. The best-known newspaper comic strip featuring a physician as its main character is *Rex Morgan, M.D.* Written by a psychiatrist, Dr. Nicholas Dallis under the pseudonym Dal Curtis, and drawn by Marvin Bradley and Frank Edgington, *Rex Morgan, M.D.* has run continuously since its first appearance, on May 2, 1948, until the present. Comic books have featured few practicing physicians as heroes, although some use scientist-physicians such as Dr. Andrew Bryant, Dr. Hugo Strange, and Dr. X.

MEDICINE SHOWS

Medicine shows, which originated as a form of entertainment designed to help quacks and streethawkers sell their patent medicine wares, also have a long European heritage, dating back to medieval times. They flourished in this country from the eighteenth century until they were virtually closed down by legislation in the twentieth century. The real heyday of medical show impresarios such as William Avery Rockefeller, "Nevada Ned" Oliver, John E. Healy, "Texas Charley" Bigelow, and John Austen Hamlin was the nineteenth century, but some, such as Dudley J. LeBlanc, the promoter of Hadacol and the Hadacol Caravans, were well known even as late as the 1950s.

FILM

Literally hundreds of physician characters have appeared in American films during this century. The earliest presentation of doctors on the screen was around the turn of the century in peep shows such as *The Doctor's Favorite Patient* and *The Downward Path.* Country doctors were featured in many early films, and three different films bore the title *The Country Doctor*—D. W. Griffith's in 1909, Rupert Julian's in 1927, and Henry King's in 1936. Better known films about the country doctor are those in the Dr.

Christian series, appearing from 1939 to 1941. Of major importance is the series of nine Dr. Kildare films, which appeared in the 1930s and 1940s. The first was *Internes Can't Take Money* in 1937, followed in 1938 by *Young Dr. Kildare*, which introduced the famous Lew Ayres (Dr. Kildare) and Lionel Barrymore (Dr. Gillespie) team. Soon a radio show was based on the films, and two television series followed in the 1960s and 1970s. The movie *M*A*S*H* had equally great success in 1970, inspiring a television series that has lasted longer than any other medical series in the history of television.

Physician characters have appeared in many comedies, domestic dramas, westerns, and detective thrillers, but serious films about physicians are relatively few. Of special interest for their critique of the medical profession are *Arrowsmith* in 1931, *Men in White* in 1934, *A Doctor's Diary* in 1937, *The Citadel* in 1938, and *Not As a Stranger* in 1955. More recent serious films about medicine include *Promises in the Dark* in 1979 and *Elephant Man* in 1980.

The most important physician characters in American films and by far the most often studied are the psychiatrists, who began appearing in minor roles as early as 1906 in the comedy *Dr. Dippy's Sanitarium*. However, only a few films from the early decades of this century depict psychiatric treatment seriously; they include D. W. Griffith's *The Restoration* in 1909; *The Cabinet of Dr. Caligari*, made in Germany in 1919 and distributed in the United States in 1921; and *Private Worlds* in 1935. By the 1940s, there was boom in psychological films. *King's Row* appeared in 1941, *Lady in the Dark* in 1944, *Spellbound* in 1945, *The Dark Mirror* in 1946, *Nightmare Alley* in 1947, and *The Snake Pit* in 1948. Notable psychological films of the 1950s and 1960s include *Harvey* in 1950, *The Cobweb* in 1955, *The Three Faces of Eve* in 1957, both *David and Lisa* and *Freud* in 1962, and *A Fine Madness* in 1966. The indisputable hit of the 1970s crop of psychological films was *One Flew Over the Cuckoo's Nest*, whose anti-psychiatric story found a most receptive audience in 1975. *I Never Promised You a Rose Garden*, released in 1978, did not have the popular success of *Cuckoo's Nest*.

Films that feature male physicians often include women as patients, nurses, lovers, wives, or, occasionally, even as physicians. But films that feature a female physician as the major character are unusual. The first was the 1921 comedy *Kitty Kelly, M.D.* Other, more serious films about women doctors include *Dr. Monica* in 1934, *Private Worlds* in 1935, *Woman Doctor* in 1939, *Spellbound* in 1945, *Girl in White* in 1952, *Strange Lady in Town* in 1955, *I Never Promised You a Rose Garden* in 1978, and *Promises in the Dark* in 1979. Films featuring nurses as main characters (more important than doctors) are not as rare as films featuring female physicians. As early as 1908 the nurse was featured in *The Romance of a War Nurse*. Other films followed, most notably *The White Angel* in 1936, about Florence Nightingale in the Crimea; *War Nurse* in 1930 and *The*

Mad Parade in 1931, both about World War I nurses; *So Proudly We Hail* and *Cry Havoc,* both in 1943 and both about the nurses on Bataan; *Vigil in the Night* in 1940; and *One Flew Over the Cuckoo's Nest* in 1975.

RADIO

Radio serials began in the 1920s. Many used physicians as characters, and by the 1930s several were featuring physicians as the main characters of their own series. One of the earliest daytime network serials to do so was "Peggy's Doctor," which began in 1934 and was discontinued in 1935. "Dr. Christian" ran from 1937 until 1953; "Doc Barclay's Daughters" from 1939 to 1940; "The Doctor's Wife" from 1952 through 1956; and "The Affairs of Dr. Gentry" from 1957 through 1959. The longest running of the daytime serials was "Young Dr. Malone," which began in 1939 and continued through 1960. A spin-off from the earlier Dr. Kildare films and novels was the weekly radio program "Young Dr. Kildare," which began in 1939 and continued through the 1950s.

At least two of radio's daytime network serials featured women physicians: "Joyce Jordan, Girl Interne" (later "Joyce Jordan, M.D."), which ran from 1938 through 1948 on CBS and was then revived by ABC for the 1951-52 season; and "The Life and Loves of Dr. Susan," which ran only one year, 1939. Others featured nurses: "Woman in White," from 1938 through 1940; "Kate Hopkins, Angel of Mercy," from 1940 through 1942; and "Junior Nurse Corps," about Clara Barton. As intriguing as these radio programs sound to students of popular culture, very few of them have been preserved in either tape or script form.

TELEVISION

The most important medium in American popular culture for the presentation of physicians and medical themes is television. Beginning in the early 1960s, television's daytime network serials picked up where radio left off. Both "General Hospital" and "The Doctors" began on the same day in 1963, and "Days of Our Lives" began in 1965. All three programs are still continuing. Shorter-lived daytime television serials presenting physicians and medical themes have included "Dr. Hudson's Secret Journal," from 1956 to 1957; "Young Dr. Malone," from 1958 to 1963; and "The Nurses," from 1965 to 1967.

Far more impressive than the daytime medical serials have been the prime-time medical shows. From 1952 through 1980 there have been well over thirty of these using physicians as main characters and medical themes as the main subject material. Among the first were "City Hospital," from 1952 to 1953; "Doc Corkle," a comedy about a dentist, in 1952; "The Doctor," from 1952 to 1953; and "Medic," from 1954 to 1956. The most successful of the early shows were "Ben Casey" and "Dr. Kildare," both beginning in 1961 and running through 1966. They are the classics of the first-generation doctor shows, and their successful format, an old mentor and a young man, was imitated by many other shows attempting to cash in on their success.

By far the most successful of the second-generation medical series was "Marcus Welby, M.D.," which ran from 1969 through 1976 and ranked among the top ten shows in the Nielsen ratings for the first three of those seasons. "Medical Center," which also began in 1969 and ended in 1976, was not far behind "Welby" in the Nielsen ratings for three of its first four seasons. Another successful medical series that began in 1969 was "The Doctors," one of four segments making up the dramatic series "The Bold Ones"; "The Doctors" was the only one of the four to last until 1973.

Ushering in the third generation of doctor shows was "M*A*S*H," the still continuing hit which premiered in 1972. In six of its first seven seasons, "M*A*S*H" was in the top twelve shows in the Nielsen ratings. By now, it is the longest-lived of any prime-time medical series to date. "Emergency!" began the same year as "M*A*S*H" and lasted for six seasons. Among the many less successful medical shows that began (and ended) in the 1970s were "Young Dr. Kildare," in 1972; "Doc Elliot," from 1973 to 1974; "Medical Story," "Doctors Hospital," and "Doc," all from 1975 to 1976; "The Practice," from 1976 to 1977; and "Westside Medical" and "Rafferty," both in 1977. Medical shows that continue into the 1980s include—along with "M*A*S*H"—"Quincy," which began in 1976, and "Trapper John, M.D." and "House Calls," which both began in 1979.

Unlike the movies, which have featured so many psychiatrists, television has favored physicians who are general practitioners or surgeons. The four series featuring psychiatrists have lasted only a season or two: "The Eleventh Hour," from 1962 to 1964; "Breaking Point," from 1963 to 1964; "Matt Lincoln," from 1970 to 1971; and "The Psychiatrist," in 1971. However, a comedy series about a psychologist, "The Bob Newhart Show," lasted six seasons, from 1972 to 1978. Series featuring women have fared even less well than those about psychiatrists. The only television series to feature a woman physician, "Having Babies" (changed to "Julie Farr, M.D."), lasted all of five weeks in 1978. Shows featuring nurses have been more successful. The first, "Janet Dean, Registered Nurse," aired in 1954. "The Nurses" ran for two seasons, from 1962 to 1964, before being changed to "The Doctors and the Nurses" for one more season. (The daytime serial "The Nurses," which ran from 1965 to 1967, was based on the earlier prime-time series.) "Julia," unusual because it featured a black nurse, was the most successful and ran from 1968 to 1971. In 1981 a new series, "Nurse," based on Peggy Anderson's book *Nurse,* began.

Factual medical shows providing information about medicine to the general public have not met with great success. Among the best of the attempts have been "Medix," "Today's Health," and "Feelin' Good." Another kind of show, factual but with dramatic intent, was "Lifeline," based on activities of real-life physicians involved in life-and-death situations. It premiered in 1978 but did not last a complete season despite the astronomical sums spent filming each episode.

NOTES

1. Darrell W. Amundsen, "Romanticizing the Ancient Medical Profession: The Characterization of the Physician in the Graeco-Roman Novel," *Bulletin of the History of Medicine,* 48 (Fall 1974), 320-37; and Darrell W. Amundsen, "Images of Physicians in Classical Times," *Journal of Popular Culture,* 11 (Winter 1977), 642-55.

2. John H. Dirckx, "The Quack in Literature," *Pharos,* 31 (January 1976), 2-7; and Christine E. Petersen, *The Doctor in French Drama 1770-1775* (New York: AMS Press, 1966).

3. F.N.L. Poynter, "Doctors in *The Human Comedy,*" *Journal of the American Medical Association,* 204 (April 1, 1968), 105-8.

4. "Literature and Medicine," *MD Medical Newsmagazine,* 6 (August 1962), 117-18.

5. Examples are Herbert Silvette, *The Doctor on the Stage: Medicine and Medical Men in Seventeenth-Century England* (Knoxville: University of Tennessee Press, 1967); Saul Nathaniel Brody, *The Disease of the Soul: Leprosy in Medieval Literature* (Ithaca, N.Y.: Cornell University Press, 1974); Gian-Paolo Biasin, *Literary Diseases: Theme and Metaphor in the Italian Novel* (Austin: University of Texas Press, 1975); Susan Sontag, *Illness as Metaphor* (New York: Farrar, Straus & Giroux, 1977); and E. R. Peschel, ed., *Medicine and Literature* (New York: Neale Watson Academic, 1980), which also includes a few essays about American literature.

6. E. P. Scarlett, "Doctor Out of Zebulon: The Doctor in Detective Fiction With an Expanded Note on Dr. John Thorndyke," *Archives of Internal Medicine,* 118 (August 1966), 180-86; and Nancy Y. Hoffman, "The Doctor and the Detective Story," *Journal of the American Medical Association,* 224 (April 2, 1973), 74-77.

7. Thomas D. Clareson, "The Scientist as Hero in American Science-Fiction 1880-1920," *Extrapolation,* 7 (1965), 18-28.

8. See, for example, David W. Sievers, *Freud on Broadway: A History of Psychoanalysis and the American Drama* (New York: Hermitage House, 1955).

BIBLIOGRAPHY

Dunning, John. *Tune in Yesterday: The Ultimate Encyclopedia of Old-Time Radio 1925-76.* Englewood Cliffs, N.J.: Prentice-Hall, 1976.

Gehman, Richard. "Caseyitis." In *TV Guide: The First 25 Years.* Edited by Jay S. Harris. New York: Simon & Schuster, 1978, pp. 63-65.

Gussow, Mel. "The Time of the Wounded Hero." *New York Times,* April 15, 1979, sec. 2, pp. 1, 30.

Halberstam, Michael J. "An M.D. Reviews Dr. Welby of TV." *New York Times Magazine* (January 16, 1972), pp. 12-13, 30, 32, 34-35, 37.

Head, Murdock. "Rx for TV Doctors." *Television Quarterly,* 4 (Spring 1965), 28-33.

Hopkins, Anthony. "Physical Models and Spiritual States: Institutional Environments In Modern Fiction." *Journal of Popular Culture*, 6 (Fall 1972), 383-92.

Kalisch, Beatrice J., Philip A. Kalisch, and Mary McHugh. "Content Analysis of Film Stereotypes of Nurses." *International Journal of Women's Studies,* 3 (November-December 1980), 531-58.

Leake, Chauncey D. "Medical Caricature in the United States." *Bulletin of the Society of Medical History of Chicago,* 4 (April 1928), 1-29.

McNamara, Brooks. *Step Right Up: An Illustrated History of the American Medicine Show.* Garden City, N.Y.: Doubleday, 1976.

McNeil, Alex. *Total Television: A Comprehensive Guide to Programming from 1948 to 1980.* New York: Penguin Books, 1980.

Newcomb, Horace. "Doctors and Lawyers: Counselors and Confessors." In *TV: The Most Popular Art.* Garden City, N.Y.: Anchor/Doubleday, 1974, pp. 110-34.

Rabkin, Leslie Y. "The Celluloid Couch: Psychiatrists in American Films." *Psycho-cultural Review,* 3 (Spring 1979), 73-89.

Real, Michael R. "Marcus Welby and the Medical Genre." In *Mass-Mediated Culture.* Englewood Cliffs, N.J.: Prentice-Hall, 1977, pp. 118-39.

Redlich, Frederick C. "The Psychiatrist in Caricature: An Analysis of Unconscious Attitudes Toward Psychiatry." *American Journal of Orthopsychiatry,* 20 (July 1950), 560-71.

Roffman, Peter, and Jim Purdy. "The Doctors," and "More Neuroses—Alcoholism and Insanity." In *The Hollywood Social Problem Film: Madness, Despair, and Politics from the Depression to the Fifties.* Bloomington: Indiana University Press, 1981, pp. 155-58, 257-61.

Schneider, Irving. "Images of the Mind: Psychiatry in the Commercial Film." *American Journal of Psychiatry,* 134 (June 1977), 613-20.

Schorr, Thelma. "Nursing's TV Image." *American Journal of Nursing,* 63 (October 1963), 119-21.

Sklar, Robert. "Prime-Time Psychology." *American Film,* 4 (March 1979), 59-63.

Spears, Jack. "The Doctor on the Screen." In *Hollywood: The Golden Era.* New York: Barnes, 1971, pp. 314-22.

"Through the Years with Dr. Kildare." *TV Guide,* 21 (January 20, 1973), 15-18.

Wagner, Melinda. "Psychiatrist at the Drawing Board." *Today's Health,* 41 (August 1963), 14-17, 58-60, 63.

Walsh, Mary Roth. "Images of Women Doctors in Popular Fiction: Comparison of the 19th and 20th Centuries." *Journal of American Culture,* 1 (Summer 1978), 276-84.

Wilmer, Harry A. "Psychiatrist on Broadway." *American Imago,* 12 (Summer 1955), 157-78.

Winick, Charles. "The Psychiatrist in Fiction." *Journal of Nervous and Mental Disease,* 136 (1963), 43-57.

Wolfe, Kary K., and Gary K. Wolfe. "Metaphors of Madness: Popular Psychological Narratives." *Journal of Popular Culture,* 9 (Spring 1976), 895-907.

Minorities

Faye Nell Vowell

Although for years it has been accepted that the United States is a nation of immigrants whose individual backgrounds have contributed to shaping the nation's culture, the relationship of minorities to popular culture has been of only minor interest to scholars. This neglect may be due, partly, to the fact that popular culture is at once so amorphous and all pervasive. There are, however, among the many works in the general field of minority or ethnic studies, a sizable number that can introduce the beginning student to the subject of minorities in popular culture.

The influence of minorities on popular culture has, indeed, been great, and a comparatively short essay such as this could not hope to treat that topic adequately in all its complexity and scope. I have, therefore, chosen to focus on the contributions made by three ethnic minority groups: the Indians, the Chicanos, and the blacks. Not only are these three groups the most visible and politically vocal of all ethnic groups, but scholarship dealing with these groups is also more available currently. They are also more likely to interest a student of popular culture.

I should take the opportunity at the outset to discuss my definition of crucial terms and categories. If popular culture is defined as the culture of the mainstream or mass of Americans, then the impact of minorities on this culture may be seen in a number of ways. First, that mainstream culture will possess some vision, or perhaps stereotype, of those minorities based on its contact with them (or its ignorance of or lack of contact with them). Those minorities will possess a corresponding vision of the dominant culture, and the resultant attitudes of both will become manifest in their respective cultures. In addition to this kind of interaction is the inter-cultural "borrowing" between groups. When performed by the ethnic group, this borrowing is called acculturation or assimilation. But the mainstream culture does much the same thing when it popularizes the music or dances of an ethnic group or when, for example, white entrepreneurs sell ethnic foods in fast food chains. Other less obvious evidences of interaction include popular literature by and about minorities, movies, television, politics, folklore, and superstition.

Indians have inhabited the land which is now the United States much longer than any other people. Archeologists hypothesize that they migrated across the Bering Strait and followed the game southward to the warmer climates of Central and South America, eventually founding such great civilizations as the Mayan and the Aztec. As early as four to five thousand years ago the Indian was growing corn in what is now New Mexico.

The first known Indian contact with Europeans was with Spanish conquistadors in the sixteenth century. Between the years of 1521 and 1528 Florida was explored by Ponce de León, Vásquez de Ayllon, and Panfilo de Naváez. Francisco Vásquez de Coronado's expedition pushed north from Mexico through southeast Arizona to New Mexico looking for the Seven Cities of Cibola. In a search for the kingdom of Quivira the Spaniard penetrated as far north as Oklahoma and Kansas. Not until 1598 was there a Spanish attempt at colonization.

Contact between Indians and Europeans on the east coast of the United States quickly assumed a typical pattern of initial friendship on the part of the Indian and exploitation and destruction on the part of the Europeans as they sought to push the Indian toward the interior. By June 1637 the New England Puritans had annihilated the Pequots. In 1675 the independent power of New England Indians was broken by their defeat in King Philip's War. The colonists' side of the story is recounted in such captivity narratives as that of Mrs. Mary Rowlandson. What is usually left out of the story is the savagery of the colonists who would not even allow Philip to be buried after he had been killed and his body mutilated: his head was exhibited on a pole, and his hand was cut off and sent to Boston where it was placed on public display.

A similar pattern of European-Indian relationships may be seen in the South. By 1680 the Westo tribe of South Carolina had been destroyed. In the early 1700s the Yamasee had been forced from their home in South Carolina south to Florida. When in 1817 Spain ceded Florida to the United States, the government was ready to turn its attention to totally removing the Indian threat in the South. Andrew Jackson's administration passed the Indian Removal Act in 1830. In 1838-39 the mass movement of the Cherokees, Chickasaws, Choctaws, Creeks, and Seminoles to lands in Oklahoma began. On this Trail of Tears, one-fourth of the Cherokee nation died.

The subjugation of the Indians of the Southwest began in earnest with the 1848 Treaty of Guadalupe Hidalgo ending the Mexican War. Although troops had to be withdrawn during the Civil War, allowing Apaches led by Cochise and Mangas Coloradas temporarily to regain control of areas of Arizona and New Mexico, the Indians were eventually subdued through the efforts of such men as Generals James H. Carleton and George Crook. After much violence, the Northwest was secured with the surrender of Chief Joseph of the Nez Perce.

The Indians of the northern Great Plains held out against white encroachment the longest. Adapting their culture to fit the horse and the rifle introduced by the Europeans, they used the mobility and firepower gained to retain their freedom for over twenty-five years of continuous warfare. The war years 1866-91 saw such watershed battles as the Sand Creek Massacre by the government of over three hundred Cheyenne and Arapahoe, the defeat of General George A. Custer and nearly three hundred men of the Seventh Cavalry at the Battle of the Little Big Horn, and the slaughter of approximately two hundred men, women, and children by remnants of the Seventh Cavalry at Wounded Knee. The struggle for the continent ended with the defeat of the Sioux at Wounded Knee on December 28, 1890.

For the next fifty years the fortunes of the Indian went steadily downward—confined to reservations, viewed as a ward of the government, controlled by the Bureau of Indian Affairs. However, World War II brought an increased involvement in the affairs of the mainstream. This involvement accelerated with the civil rights movement of the 1960s and 1970s. The National Youth Council was formed in 1960, followed by the more militant American Indian Movement in 1969. The various tribes began to see that red power or Indian power was a possibility and that strength lay in a pan-Indian movement. Evidence of the new militancy followed with the takeover of the island of Alcatraz from November 20, 1969 to June 11, 1971, the "Trail of Broken Treaties" demonstrations just before the 1972 elections, and the occupation of Wounded Knee in 1973.

A generation of articulate Indians such as Vine Deloria, Jr., has arisen to fight the white man again—this time with words and legal maneuvers as well as force. They are battling the old stereotypes: the Puritan's vision of the cruel savage, the beautiful Indian maiden Pocahontas protecting Captain John Smith, the noble savage, and even Jay Silverheels saving the Lone Ranger. Deloria sees a close relationship among the plights of the Indian, the black, and the Chicano. In *We Talk, You Listen: New Tribes, New Turf* he also attacks "traditional stereotypes [which] pictured the black as a happy watermelon-eating darky whose sole contribution to American society was his indiscriminate substitution of the 'd' sound for 'th'." He further notes that "Mexicans were generally portrayed as shiftless and padded out for siesta, without any redeeming qualities whatsoever." Neither stereotype approaches the reality of the situation.

Mexican-Americans view their claim to land in the Southwest as pre-dating that of colonists from Europe. Their heritage began with the Indian tribes who settled *Aztlan* (the southwest United States) before journeying on south and whose blood became mixed with that of the Spaniards when Hernando Cortés landed near present-day Vera Cruz in 1519. Descendants of those original settlers of mixed Indian-Spanish blood still live in such areas of the Southwest as Tierra Amarillo in New Mexico. Although they have inhabited the area for a much longer time, the history of the Mexican American technically begins with the Treaty of Guadalupe Hidalgo which ended the Mexican-American War on February 2, 1848.

By the terms of this treaty, the United States paid Mexico $15 million as an indemnity and acquired over a million miles of territory—an area encompassed by the states of Arizona, California, Nevada, New Mexico, part of Colorado, and Texas. If Mexican citizens elected to stay on their land, they were to be granted citizenship and their property rights were guaranteed. Actual treatment of those Mexicans who elected to remain fell far short of the ideal. They were soon faced with an onslaught of Anglos speaking a different language and living by a different code of laws. In actual practice, most Mexican Americans lost their land. Anglos had gained dominance in California by the 1870s. In New Mexico, the Mexican Americans retained control longer because of the alliance of the *ricos* (upper-class Mexican Americans) and wealthy Anglos. However this alliance did not benefit the small farmer or sheep herder who steadily lost ground. The situation of the Mexican American was probably the worst in Texas. There he faced racial and religious prejudice from Anglo settlers who had come primarily from the fundamentalist-Protestant South and despised the Mexican Americans for their dark skins and their Catholicism. The original Mexican Americans thus came to find themselves in a situation analogous to that of the Indian: they were a conquered people possessing a culture which they had to struggle to retain.

Although the border between the two countries presented no barrier, immigration from Mexico to the United States was minimal until the Mexican Revolution of 1910. Between 1910 and 1920 civil disruption caused some one million Mexicans to flee their homes. Most did not plan to stay in the United States and did not become citizens. They found work in the newly irrigated fields of Arizona, Texas, and California as well as with the railroads and steel companies. During this time they replaced cheap labor from Asia and Europe cut off by the exclusion acts and the Immigration Act of 1924.

But this time of relative prosperity ceased with the Depression of 1929. To reduce welfare rolls, the government began a massive repatriation program. Often there was no discrimination between the Mexican and the Mexican American as they were loaded onto the train that left Los Angeles for Mexico once a month from 1931 to 1933. Mexican Americans met further discrimination during World War II. Two famous incidents are the Zoot Suit Riots, when sailors cruised the streets of Los Angeles assaulting *pachucos,* and the Sleepy Lagoon murder case. In spite of this prejudice, Mexican Americans served the United States well during World War II.

After the war, many took advantage of G.I. benefits to better their education. They also began to demand more equal treatment forming such organizations as the G.I. Forum and the Mexican American Political Organization to assert their civil rights. Their situation was complicated by the continual influx of immigrants from Mexico. *Mojados* (wetbacks), *braceros* (temporary workers brought over under contract), and later "blue carders" and "green carders" continued to come to the United States for economic reasons, thus depressing working conditions. In 1954, the U.S. government initiated "Operation Wetback" to alleviate the labor situation, but indiscriminate deportation of "Mexicans" only resulted in more alienation and mistrust.

Thus in the 1960s Mexican Americans were ready to join the Indians and blacks in a more militant effort to gain their civil rights. The Chicano movement was especially influential among young students who formed such organizations as Mexican American Youth Organization (MAYO) and Movimiento Estudiantil Chicano de Aztlan (MECHA). This movement exalted the Indian side of the Mexican-American heritage and glorified such concepts as *Aztlan* and *La Raza*.

The movement gained support from other areas also. Four charismatic leaders have come to the forefront. In New Mexico, Reies Lopez Tijerina formed the Alianza Federal de Pueblos Libres in 1963. Its purpose was to regain original land grants. The Alianza made headlines in 1967, when members raided the courthouse at Tierra Amarilla, New Mexico. In Texas in 1970, José Angel Gutierrez led La Raza Unida party to political victory in the twenty south Texas counties where Chicanos constitute a majority of the population. The party has since won school board and city council elections in Crystal City, Texas, and city council elections in Carrizo Springs and Cotulla.

In Denver in 1965, Rudolfo "Corky" Gonzalez founded a civil rights organizaton, the Crusade for Justice. The organization sponsored the Chicano Youth Liberation Conference, where *El Plan Espiritual de Aztlan* was articulated in 1969. Gonzalez is also the author of an influential epic poem, "I Am Joaquin" (1967). From California has come the best-known Chicano leader, Cesar Chavez, founder of the United Farm Workers Organizing Committee (UFWOC). In 1965 Chavez initiated a five-year strike, *la huelga*, against California grape growers. Chavez's policy of nonviolence has earned him widespread respect, and he remains a unifying force among Chicanos. *La huelga* was influential in shaping a sense of identity among Mexican-Americans.

A revolutionary peoples' theater developed out of the strike. *Actos* such as *Los Vendidos* by Luis Valdez use the stereotypes Anglos have created of the Chicano and eventually turn them against their creator. Today's Chicano is politically aware and rapidly outpacing the stereotypes of Speedy Gonzales or the Mexican peon taking his siesta under a cactus.

Blacks, the largest ethnic minority in the United States, have also come a long way in destroying the traditional stereotypes possessed by mainstream culture. They share a sense of identity and commonality of problems with the Indians and Chicanos. The epic story of the black man in America also begins with the earliest explorers. Blacks came to America with Hernando de Alarćon and Franciso Vásquez de Coronado, Panfilo de Naváez and Cabeza de Vaca. A black named Esteban himself led the expedition from

Mexico into Arizona and New Mexico in 1538. As settlers they came not long after. In 1619 twenty blacks landed at Jamestown, Virginia—the first of a long line of Africans to be brought to America against their will. These first Africans were treated as indentured servants, but by 1661 Virginia had made statutory recognition of slavery, preceded only by Massachusetts in 1641 and Connecticut in 1650. Maryland followed in 1663, New York and New Jersey in 1664, South Carolina in 1682, Rhode Island and Pennsylvania in 1700, North Carolina in 1715, and Georgia in 1750.

From the beginning, blacks resisted. As early as 1658, a group of blacks and Indians rebelled in Hartford, Connecticut; in 1712 blacks revolted in New York, burning a building and shooting nine white men before the uprising was put down and twenty-one of the blacks executed; in the same city in 1741 fears of a slave uprising led to the execution of thirty-one more—eighteen hanged and thirteen burned alive. For both humanitarian and economic reasons slavery diminished in the North. In the South it flourished as plantation owners looked for cheap labor to grow their money crop: cotton. By 1830 there were more than two million slaves.

Life for black Americans within the system of slavery was based on the premise that they were not people but property. They had no legal rights. They could not engage in commerce. They could not socialize with whites or freed blacks. They could not assemble unless supervised by a white person. They could not defend themselves against whites. They could not leave the plantation without the owner's approval. They could not possess firearms. In short, they had no rights at all—except the right to work in a system in which they accrued no money and made no gains.

Just as they had during Colonial times, blacks resisted. In 1822 Denmark Vesey organized a revolt in and around Charleston, South Carolina, that included thousands of blacks. Perhaps the most famous resistance movement of this time took place in 1831, when Nat Turner and his followers killed more than sixty whites in Southampton County, Virginia, before being defeated by state and federal troops.

Despite such acts of rebellion, black Americans stood little chance in their armed confrontations with whites; inevitably, they were simply outgunned. But if active, armed battles were doomed to failure, other measures were open to them—notably, escape through the Underground Railroad. Fostered by the Abolitionist Movement, which grew steadily after 1815, a network of sympathetic "operators" sprang up to aid those blacks who fled organized slavery. Levi Coffin and John Fairfield stand out among the white "conductors"; Jane Lewis, Elijah Anderson, John Mason, and Harriet Tubman among the blacks. It is conjectured that Tubman, perhaps the most famous of all, accounted for approximately three hundred escapes. Although accurate counts are difficult to come by, it has been estimated that more than 100,000 slaves migrated north along the clandestine route of the Underground Railroad during the years between 1810 and 1850.

The decade of the 1850s, filled with increasing tension between North and South and with patchwork attempts at compromise, ended with two events that indicated the inevitability of war: John Brown's raid in 1859 and the election of Abraham Lincoln in 1860. When it came the war left the South devastated both physically and culturally. In the aftermath of the devastation, another war was fought—the war for political and economic control of the area.

Blacks lost ground rapidly in the South after the war. As early as 1866 groups of Southern whites harassed both blacks and Northern whites by forming vigilante groups. In the late 1860s and 1870s they were joined by groups such as the Knights of the White Camellia, the White Brotherhood, the White League of Louisiana, and the Knights of the Ku Klux Klan.

In 1890 a Mississippi convention passed a suffrage amendment that effectively disenfranchised blacks in that state; in 1895 South Carolina accomplished the same; and in 1898 Louisiana introduced the "grandfather clause." Shortly thereafter, all other Southern states would follow in the pattern; and, by 1910, for all intents and purposes, the blacks had lost the right to vote throughout the South. In 1875 the first "Jim Crow" law appeared in Tennessee; soon, the statutes were laden with such laws. When the Supreme Court outlawed the 1875 Civil Rights Act in 1883, blacks in the South found themselves legally separated from whites in almost all areas of their lives, and whites enforced such segregation in the courts by law and in the streets and countryside by violence and terror. In the first two years of the twentieth century there were over two hundred lynchings in the South; by the beginning of World War I over eleven hundred had occurred.

In the face of such organized prejudice and such brutal tactics, black Americans looked for options. Booker T. Washington offered advice that now seems naively tailor-made to the era of the rise of the industrial giants. He urged his fellow blacks to learn agricultural and industrial skills and to emulate the Puritan habits of thrift, good moral behavior, and perseverance; in his view, blacks had to develop a base of skilled craftsmen in a complicated agrarian and industrial nation before they could aspire to more lucrative goals, and he dedicated the Tuskegee Institute to that end. During the years 1895 to 1915, Washington became the most powerful and influential black in the United States, and, when he spoke, both Northern and Southern whites felt that he spoke for all black Americans.

But the lure of the city, particularly in terms of the freedom and economic opportunities to be sought in the Northern city, drew blacks away from farmlands in increasing numbers. In both the North and South, awareness increased among blacks that they needed to organize in order to battle for their rights. In 1909 the nucleus of the Niagara Movement begun by W. E. B. Du Bois and William Monroe Trotter joined with other blacks and whites in the formation of the National Association for the Advancement of Colored People, an organization which has remained important to the black community to the present time.

The NAACP, frequently criticized by militant blacks in the 1960s as too conservative, hardly seemed so at the time of its founding. With Du Bois as its director of publicity and research, the organization quickly launched a campaign against lynching and brutality, called for protection within the law for Southern blacks, and sought to broaden economic opportunities for blacks across the country. As the means to communicate its message, the NAACP launched a magazine, *The Crisis,* edited by Du Bois, which became the first important national publication to provide a voice for black Americans. In addition, in 1911, the National Urban League was formed, its primary mission being to help blacks in their adjustment to life in the nation's cities.

During World War I, black soldiers performed well, many of them experiencing freedoms in Europe that they had never previously enjoyed. They returned to a United States that to most of them must have seemed symbolized by the resurgence of the Ku Klux Klan, which, within a year of the war's end, had grown from a relatively sparse movement to a membership of over 100,000 hooded white men. In the South they persecuted blacks; in the West, the Japanese.

During the decade following World War I, increasing numbers of blacks migrated to Northern industrial centers where they frequently found jobs in the growing automobile industry, paper and bag companies, the food and clothing industries, and transportation and communication. The American Negro Labor Conference, meeting in Chicago in 1925, sought to organize the efforts of black farmers and industrial workers in the hope of bringing more and more blacks into organized labor. During the same year, A. Philip Randolph organized the Brotherhood of Sleeping Car Porters and Maids; although the industry's full recognition of Randolph's union was delayed until 1937, it marked the beginning of significant black unionizing. The Great Depression of the 1930s eliminated many of the gains for which blacks had worked.

When World War II loomed on the horizon, blacks again played a large and meaningful role in the war effort. However, it was not until after the war in 1948 that President Harry S. Truman, in Executive Order 9981, ordered the desegregation of the armed forces.

In the 1950s the civil rights movement gained momentum. Its most important year was 1955. In that year the Supreme Court ordered school desegregation to move "with all deliberate speed" and banned segregation in public recreational facilities; the Interstate Commerce Commission ordered an end to segregation in buses, waiting rooms, and coaches involved in interstate travel; advances in organized labor were symbolized by the elections of two blacks, A. Philip Randolph and Willard Townsend, as vice presidents in the combined AFL and CIO; and, in Montgomery, Alabama,

Martin Luther King, Jr., initiated the famous bus boycott on December 5—an action that has come to symbolize the concentrated effort to bring meaningful change in American social structure through organized passive resistance.

From that time to the present, meaningful actions have occurred every year on the march to black equality. In 1957 the Southern Christian Leadership Conference was organized. Sit-ins, marches, freedom rides, and other means of resistance were used to make educational, political, and economic gains.

Violence, unprecedented in its continuing intensity, was directed toward the movement as black Americans took the initiative across a broad front to gain equality. Black churches were burned; black leaders were attacked and murdered; white civil rights activists, often young people working summers in the South, were harassed, beaten, and sometimes killed; working-class whites in Northern cities resorted to mob violence in their efforts to keep blacks from moving into their neighborhoods.

In the South, state public officials of the highest ranks led a battle against the inevitable workings of the law. In the North the more subtle forms of segregation in employment, education, and housing were more difficult to confront, although the NAACP, the Urban League, and newer and more militant organizations like the Congress of Racial Equality (CORE) and the Student Nonviolent Coordinating Committee (SNCC) fought for improvements in these areas. Perhaps it was the very subtlety of Northern racism that led to the frustration that fostered the explosions of race riots in black ghettos during the summer of 1964 and for several years thereafter. In 1964 the black areas of New York City, particularly Harlem and Bedford-Stuyvesant, exploded, and the conflagration spread to Rochester, Jersey City, Paterson, Elizabeth, Chicago, and Philadelphia. In 1965 a black area of Los Angeles, Watts, became the scene of insurrection as blacks battled white police and National Guardsmen. In the following three years major riots occurred in Chicago, Lansing, Waukegan, Atlanta, Nashville, Tampa, Cincinnati, Buffalo, Durham, Minneapolis, Birmingham, Detroit, Memphis, Milwaukee, Cleveland, Gary, and Miami.

On April 4, 1968, Martin Luther King, Jr., was assassinated in Memphis. His death symbolized an end to one era of the black American struggle for equality. Since 1955, the year in which the bus boycott began in Montgomery, some relatively rapid changes had taken place on the surface of black-white relations in the United States. The issues of public accommodations, educational opportunities, the issue of equal housing, and others had been resolved. What remained to be done involved the gnawing difficulties of removing the subtle obstacles so familiar as to become almost unconscious factors in the mores and the manners of the culture.

Some of the black militants of the late 1960s and the beginning of the 1970s, particularly groups like the Black Panthers, stated loudly that events had swept over Martin Luther King, Jr., his beliefs, and his methods. It is important to remember, however, that at the time of his assassination he was not in Memphis to organize a bus boycott or a voter registration drive or a department store sit-in. Those tasks belonged to an earlier time. He was in Memphis to help organize a movement for higher pay for striking sanitation workers—more specifically an economic rather than a racial commitment. Clearly, at the end of his life, King was shifting his sights to the economic imbalances in the United States, imbalances which adversely affect working-class people both white and black. He knew that the way to equality in the United States was in the way to wealth, that economic power and the distribution of wealth were the issues of the future. One of the followers of Dr. King and a long-time activist in the Southern Christian Leadership Conference, Jesse Jackson, now leads a movement called "Operation Push." Its objectives are economic in nature, and, while based in the black community, Operation Push seeks a more broadly based constituency. Its cry of "green power" may represent the wave of the future.

Blacks have also made inroads politically, electing black mayors such as Maynard Jackson of Atlanta and congressional representatives such as Julian Bond, Barbara Jordan, and Yvonne Braithwaite Burke. Andrew Young's appointment as ambassador to the United Nations further symbolized the success of the black in American society. But such recent developments as the May 1980 riots in Miami signal that a large group of blacks are still dissatisfied with their position in the United States.

BIBLIOGRAPHY

INDIANS

Armstrong, Virginia Irving, and Frederick W. Turner, III. *I Have Spoken: American History Through the Voices of the Indians.* Chicago: Sage, 1971. Reprint, New York: Pocket Books, 1972.

Bierhorst, John. *The Red Swan: Myths and Tales of the American Indians.* New York: Farrar, Straus & Giroux, 1976.

Brown, Dee. *Bury My Heart at Wounded Knee: An Indian History of the American West.* New York: Holt, Rinehart and Winston, 1970.

Deloria, Vine, Jr. *Custer Died for Your Sins: An Indian Manifesto.* New York: Macmillan, 1969.

Densmore, Frances. *American Indians and Their Music.* New York: Woman's Press, 1926. Reprint. New York: Johnson, 1970.

Fisher, Dexter, ed. *The Third Woman: Minority Women Writers of the United States.* Boston: Houghton Mifflin, 1980.

Haywood, Charles. *Bibliography of North American Folklore and Folksong.* New York: Dover, 1961.

Keiser, Albert. *The Indian in American Literature.* New York: Oxford University Press, 1933. Reprint. New York: Octagon, 1970.

Miller, Wayne Charles, et al. *A Comprehensive Bibliography for the Study of American Minorities.* 2 vols. New York: New York University Press, 1976.

Rothenberg, Jerome. *Shaking the Pumpkin: Traditional Poetry of the Indian North Americas.* Garden City, N.Y.: Doubleday, 1972.

CHICANOS

Boatright, Mody C. *Mexican Border Ballads and Other Lore.* Dallas: Southern Methodist University Press, 1967.

Campa, Arthur L. *Treasure of the Sangre de Cristos: Tales and Traditions of the Spanish Southwest.* Norman: University of Oklahoma Press, 1963.

Gonzalez, Rudolfo. *I Am Joaquin: An Epic Poem.* New York: Bantam Books, 1973.

Martinez, Julio A. *Chicano Scholars and Writers: A Bio-Bibliographical Directory.* Metuchen, N.J.: Scarecrow Press, 1979.

Nabokov, Peter. *Tijerina and the Courthouse Raid.* Albuquerque: University of New Mexico Press, 1969.

Paredes, Américo. *"With His Pistol in His Hand"—A Border Ballad and Its Hero.* Austin: University of Texas Press, 1958.

Robinson, Cecil. *Mexico and the Hispanic Southwest in American Literature.* University of Arizona Press, 1977.

Simmen, Edward. *The Chicano: From Caricature to Self-Portrait.* New York: New American Library, 1971.

Trejo, Arnulfo D. *Bibliografia Chicana: A Guide to Information Sources,* Detroit: Gale Research, 1975.

BLACKS

Bogle, Donald. *Toms, Coons, Mulattoes, Mammies and Bucks.* New York: Bantam, 1974.

Carmichael, Stokely, and Charles V. Hamilton. *Black Power: The Politics of Liberation in America.* New York: Random House, 1967.

Cleaver, Eldridge. *Soul on Ice.* New York: McGraw-Hill, 1968.

Dance, Daryl Cumber. *Shuckin' and Jivin': Folklore from Contemporary Black Americans.* Bloomington: Indiana University Press, 1978.

Franklin, John Hope. *From Slavery to Freedom: A History of Negro Americans.* New York: Knopf, 1967.

Gross, Seymour L., and John Edward Hardy. *Images of the Negro in American Literature.* Chicago: University of Chicago Press, 1966.

Liebow, Elliott. *Tally's Corner: A Study of Negro Streetcorner Men.* Boston: Little Brown, 1967.

Little, Malcolm. *Malcolm X Speaks: Selected Speeches and Statements.* New York: Grove Press, 1966.

Page, James A. *Selected Black American Authors: An Illustrated Bio-Bibliography.* Boston: G. K. Hall, 1970.

Ploski, Harry A., and Warren Marr. *The Negro Almanac: A Reference Work on the Afro American.* New York: Bellwether, 1976.

Shockley, Ann Allen, and Sue P. Chandler. *Living Black American Authors.* New York: Cowles, 1973.

Music

Mark W. Booth

While thoughtful attention to popular music is relatively new, the music itself has been vigorously alive in this country for a long time. Some of the music brought to the New World by the colonists was serious academic music; some was what we now call *folk music*, belonging to the community by tradition and freely. Some, however, was popular music, printed and sold in broadsides and song books or performed by professional entertainers to paying audiences. The source of this popular music was the mother countries of the new Americans, chiefly England. The same ballads sold in the streets of London were sold in the colonial American cities and towns; the same ballad operas and other musical entertainments were heard in English and American theaters.

During the eighteenth century an increasing amount of this popular music was written in the colonies for colonists. During the years of the Revolution, the sentiments of Americans were expressed in anti-British broadsides that could hardly have been imported, but a significant number of these broadsides were specific parodies of British songs. They set anti-British words to British music. As such they remained, however rebellious, colonial popular music. The forms of the lyrics as well as of the music were indebted to the model brought over from England.

To decide, then, where we can mark the beginning of American popular music, it is necessary to find the stage in the developing history of music that has been enjoyed by Americans where not only the actual writing, printing, and selling of the music take place on American ground, but where the product itself has an American quality—some flavor that is not borrowed or inherited.

English music remained in the American marketplace throughout the nineteenth century, but it gradually became mixed with, then edged by, popular music that is distinctly native. Where this genuine American popular music really began cannot be said for certain. A sign of the beginning can be located in 1827. Among the few scattered relics of the music sold or professionally performed a century and a half ago that we know were hits of the day, two songs suggest in retrospect that that year marks a turning point. In *Variety Music Cavalcade 1620-1969*, Julius Mattfeld, the editor, lists four prominent songs for 1827 and of the four, two, "My Long-Tail Blue" and "The Coal-Black Rose," were popularized by the minstrel singer George Washington Dixon. Dixon, whom Mattfeld calls "a Negro minstrel," was a white man performing in blackface. He was neither the first nor the most successful performer in that masquerade tradition, which was still alive more than a century later, but he can be taken to represent with these two hits an emblem, or a portent, of the course of American popular music. The native American note we are looking for was struck in the meeting of Afro-American and Euro-American styles.

Most popular songs in the years after 1827 continued to be the work of English writers or indistinguishable from English work; tunes continued to be borrowed, as the tunes of "Yankee Doodle" and "The Star-Spangled Banner" had been borrowed, from English songs, but a new way had been opened. The music that slaves brought with them from west Africa evolved into an Afro-American folk music and then evolved into a variety of styles of professional performance for black audiences. In themselves these styles are an American popular music. Throughout their history, in all their forms, they have also exerted an influence on the shaping of the rest of American popular music.

Alec Wilder argues that the first truly native American popular songs are those a generation after George Washington Dixon, at the next stage of interaction between black and white music, the songs of Stephen Foster. Foster was influenced not only by the minstrel mimicry of slave music but also by Negro church music. After Foster's death in 1864, Wilder contends, the disruption of the Civil War and Reconstruction in the lives and culture of black men and women kept black music away from the ears of white Americans, and popular music entered a recession that ended in the 1890s when the sounds of ragtime played by young black pianists began to be heard by a white public. The distinctively American feeling that derived from ragtime rhythm enters the mainstream of those major songwriters of the twentieth century whose work Wilder traces. Often very remote from ragtime—or from the successors of ragtime, blues and jazz—American music continued to show the rhythmic and harmonic signs of inspiration from the black tradition, from Tin Pan Alley to swing bands to rock, with a contribution by the way to country and western.

Popular music is a marketplace art. American popular music was the commercial extension of the eighteenth-century publishing and theater business as it had evolved in London and been imitated in New York. This publishing and theater system, in nineteenth-century American cities and towns, met with an American buying public and gradually learned to offer that public music flavored by American folk music styles, most distinctively black music. The evolution came slowly, and when something clearly American predominated at the end of the nineteenth century, it was the product both of American musicians and of the American genius for commercial promotion. (An entertaining account of this evolution is given in the first chapter of Ian Whitcomb's *After the Ball.*) A massive market was sought out, or built, by promoters and salesmen for shows, for sheet music, and for pianos to play the music. Some of the sold entertainment still had, at the turn of the century, the prestige of being European, but the booming American music business drew on a growing body of native writers and performers and sold to a public gaining in cultural self-confidence in spite of itself.

Thomas Edison built the first phonograph in 1877, but for half a century phonograph records would be only a smaller or larger minority of popular music sales. Joseph Murrells, in his *Book of Golden Discs*, supplies the lore of successful recordings: the first to sell a million in 1902 and a couple of dozen of them by the 1920s for home phonographs and juke boxes.

At the opening of the twentieth century the decisive influence of the ragtime pianists fell on white audiences tiring of the minstrel show and willing to pay to hear black performers. At the same time the American band was being heard everywhere, promoted by John Philip Sousa, the most successful musician of his time, and testifying among other things to pugnacious nationalism. Both phenomena would modulate into dance bands playing vigorous dance music. Burgeoning displays of sheet music in neighborhood stores, often music calling itself *rag*, attracted a diverse public, much of which never heard the concerts of the creators of ragtime. Modest as well as prosperous homes had a keyboard, either a piano or the less expensive reed organ: the industry built 107,000 harmoniums a year in 1900, and 177,000 pianos. By 1909, the figure was 364,000 pianos. Piano music was available beyond the proportion of the population that could play: by 1925, more than half the pianos produced were automatics, using player rolls for current hits (see Cyril Ehrlich, *The Piano: a History*). Such instruments, giving out more and better sound than the evolving phonograph had yet mastered, tuned the audience more closely than ever before to the latest fad in music.

A boom in social dancing began during the second decade of the twentieth century, along with the first recognition of music called *jazz.* Nat Shapiro quotes *Variety* as estimating that in the mid-1920s there were 60,000 dance bands playing on the dance floors of jazz age America. Beginning in 1920, radio broadcasting brought recorded and live music into homes, posing an economic challenge to pianos and combining with the Depression in 1929 to decimate record and phonograph sales. The music that America absorbed through these media came mostly from New York, from Tin Pan Alley publishing houses and from the flourishing Broadway stage, reproduced also in vaudeville houses across the country. When in the middle of the 1920s recording engineers developed microphones to replace recording horns, a new softer "crooning" performance became possible and stylish on records and over the radio.

Al Jolson's songs on screen in 1927 opened another medium. When the Depression crippled the New York musical theater, Hollywood studios became the patrons of much of professional songwriting, for the movies that were the country's largest entertainment indulgence during the 1930s. The record industry struggled back late in the decade, dominated by the big swing bands and their vocalists. As the war overtook the United States, a significant economic struggle surfaced in musical entertainment. The American Society of Composers, Authors, and Publishers (ASCAP) had been formed in 1914 to collect performance royalties for the owners of song copyrights. By 1939 it held monopoly power over popular music performance, and a contract dispute with radio broadcasters led to the formation of Broadcast Music Incorporated (BMI) as a rival guild. Following a ten-month interval in 1941 during which no ASCAP music could be played on the radio, causing a boom in classical, folk, and public domain music generally, ASCAP entered into a new broadcast contract, but BMI continued and grew. BMI, growing out of the dispute where its rival stood for established interests, came to represent popular music from outside the New York-Hollywood establishment, and local markets compared with the network emphasis of ASCAP. An institution had appeared to reflect the regional, rural, and minority interests in the music world that would gain great audience support after the war.

When the war ended, the entertainment industry responded to the ready money of a new public, more urbanized, but less in touch with Broadway sophistication, and with expanding young families preparing to be the next generation of popular music consumers—raised with unprecedented pocket money and leisure time and with an unsuspected susceptibility to the energies of rock and roll they would first hear in 1954. Carl Belz describes the recording industry in the years after the war as dividing its market in the interest of stability and consequently producing for the general market dull, or at least highly controlled and predictable, music. Small independent record companies sold to the country and Western and rhythm and blues markets, while the major companies guided the music of the largest pop market down a narrow channel, with a slow succession of new songs and much repetitive recording by competing stars.

Rock and roll, which the industry learned to ride to a staggering new sales volume, also jarred that industry into new patterns: new companies, new small-group recording economics, new audience definitions, and new relationships to radio broadcasting. Some of the story can be told in terms of technical innovations. Television as the surging home entertainment medium turned radio stations toward the disc jockey format of record programming. New sizes, speeds, and materials for the records themselves may have had wide implications. Belz makes an interesting analysis of the cultural meaning of the shift from 78 to 45 rpm records, as streamlining the experience of recorded music toward casualness, especially for young audiences, while their parents bought the more substantial 33 long-playing records that emerged at the same time in the early 1950s. The later movement of rock and its audience into long-playing records reflects the triumphing cultural and economic power of the same young generation, along with a growing seriousness and self-confidence of the makers of rock music.

The relationship of popular culture to ideology in the 1960s and into the 1970s has become of interest to academic sociology, although the alarmed interest of politicians has given way to accommodation. The relationship of the entertainment favored by highly visible classes of teenagers and young adults to the behavior of that audience, and especially its use of drugs, is probably now still too current an issue for full perspective and confident judgment. The history of popular music suggests that it is very unlikely that musical entertainment can induce new behavior, or even introduce new ideas to the audience it must court in order to sell itself. Though popular music has been blamed in the past for undermining community standards or otherwise damaging society, it is a new phenomenon for popular music to have the pervasive presence that prosperity and the portable radio and tape deck have given it lately, and for such conspicuous economic power to be vested in a youth audience. The history of popular music that is now happening cannot be fully schematized and managed by the patterns of earlier popular music. Its development has always been contingent, surprising, and even discontinuous except when we rationalize it with hindsight, and it is continuing that unpredictable development now.

As rock has evolved in the last quarter of a century and brought, among other things, self-conscious seriousness to popular music, it has prompted an immense volume of reportage and analysis, much of it empty but some perceptive and judicious. The attention that rock has demanded has occasioned the first widespread, serious critical attention to the popular arts in general. Nostalgia, publicity promotion, and the university environment of a part of the proprietary audience of rock have contributed to the growing critical and scholarly interest in popular music of the past as well as the present. We are in the process of discovering a heritage; it is certain to contribute to the understanding of our own culture.

BIBLIOGRAPHY

Blesh, Rudi, and Harriet Janis. *They All Played Ragtime*. New York: Knopf, 1950; 4th edition, New York: Oak Publications, 1971.

Bordman, Gerald. *The American Musical Theatre: a Chronicle.* New York: Oxford University Press, 1978.

Chapple, Steve, and Reebee Garofalo. *Rock 'n' Roll Is Here to Pay: The History and Politics of the Music Industry.* Chicago: Nelson-Hall, 1977.

Chase, Gilbert. *America's Music: From the Pilgrims to the Present.* Revised 2d edition. New York: McGraw-Hill, 1966.

Dellar, Fred, and Roy Thompson. *The Illustrated Encyclopedia of Country Music.* New York: Harmony Books, 1977.

Feather, Leonard. *The Encyclopedia of Jazz in the Sixties.* New York: Horizon Press, 1966.

———. *The New Edition of the Encyclopedia of Jazz* New York: Horizon Press, 1960.

———, and Ira Gitler. *The Encyclopedia of Jazz in the Seventies.* New York: Horizon Press, 1976.

Gillett, Charlie. *The Sound of the City: The Rise of Rock and Roll.* New York: Outerbridge & Dienstfrey, 1970.

Hamm, Charles. *Yesterdays: Popular Song in America.* New York: W. W. Norton, 1979.

Harris, Sheldon. *Blues Who's Who: A Biographical Dictionary of Blues Singers.* New Rochelle, N.Y.: Arlington House, 1979.

Horn, David. *The Literature of American Music in Books and Folk Music Collections: A Fully Annotated Bibliography.* Metuchen, N.J.: Scarecrow Press, 1977.

Kinkle, Roger D. *The Complete Encyclopedia of Popular Music and Jazz, 1900-1950.* 4 vols. New Rochelle, N.Y.: Arlington House, 1974.

Malone, Bill C. *Country Music USA: A Fifty-Year History.* Austin: American Folklore Society/University of Texas Press, 1968.

Marsh, Dave, and John Swenson. *The Rolling Stone Record Guide: Reviews and Ratings of Almost 10,000 Currently Available Rock, Pop, Soul, Country, Blues, Jazz, and Gospel Albums.* New York: Random House/Rolling Stone Press, 1979.

Miller, Jim, ed. *The Rolling Stone Illustrated History of Rock & Roll.* 2d edition. New York: Random House, 1980.

Oliver, Paul. *Blues Fell This Morning: The Meaning of the Blues.* New York: Horizon Press, 1960.

Pleasants, Henry. *The Great American Popular Singers.* New York: Simon and Schuster, 1974.

Simon, George T. *The Big Bands.* Revised edition. New York: Macmillan Publishers, 1974.

Southern, Eileen. *The Music of Black Americans: A History.* New York: W. W. Norton, 1971.

Tawa, Nicholas E. *Sweet Songs for Gentle Americans: The Parlor Song in America, 1790-1860.* Bowling Green, Ohio: Bowling Green University Popular Press, 1980.

Tirro, Frank. *Jazz: A History.* New York: W. W. Norton, 1977.

Toll, Robert C. *Blacking Up: The Minstrel Show in Nineteenth-Century America.* New York: Oxford University Press, 1974.

Wilder, Alec. *American Popular Song: The Great Innovators, 1900-1950.* New York: Oxford University Press, 1972.

Newspapers

Richard A. Schwarzlose

As in all significant Colonial matters, the development of the American newspaper closely followed the English prototype in form and content. The printing press had been introduced in England in about 1476 by William Caxton, having made its Continental debut roughly two decades earlier. Although the English monarchs encouraged the early growth of the printing trade, printers and their products needed prior royal approval to escape possible prosecution.

Amsterdam printers, therefore, turned out for British importation English-language pamphlets and books that could not be safely printed in England. Thus, the first English-language news sheet, called a coranto or collection of foreign news items, was published in Amsterdam in December 1620. Seven months later, however, corantos of foreign news were issuing from London printing houses with impunity. It took two more decades and the abolition of the Star Chamber, however, for British printers to attempt domestic news reporting. The first diurnal—the domestic version of coranto—appeared in November 1641, carrying parliamentary proceedings. It was shortly followed by a flood of competing diurnals when it became evident that the authorities would not retaliate. The single-sheet coranto of 1621 gave way within a year to news books of from eight to forty pages, a format utilized by corantos and diurnals until England's first full-fledged newspaper in familiar newspaper format, the Oxford/London *Gazette*, appeared as a semi-weekly in 1665. The term *newspaper* was in common use in 1670. By 1682, with Parliament repeatedly ignoring opportunities to regulate printing, twenty newspapers had appeared. England's first daily newspaper, the London *Daily Courant,* made its appearance on March 11, 1702.

The American Colonies' schedule of newspaper development, while emulating England's, ran between forty years and nearly a century behind the mother country's. The first Colonial press arrived in Cambridge, Massachusetts, in 1638, and after 1654 was associated with Harvard College. The next press appeared in Philadelphia in 1685.

The ill-fated *Publick Occurrences Both Foreign and Domestick* was the Colonies' first newspaper, published in Boston on September 25, 1690, by

Benjamin Harris, who had fled England after serving a prison term for printing a seditious pamphlet. Slightly smaller than a piece of notebook paper, the three-page *Publick Occurrences* (the fourth page was blank) was suppressed by the colonial governor after one issue.

The first paper of continuous publication was the weekly Boston *News-Letter*, begun in 1704 by Boston's postmaster, John Campbell. Looking much like the London *Gazette*, the *News-Letter* carried the line "Published by Authority" in its nameplate, signifying that the colonial governor had approved its contents. This arrangement, in turn, meant that Campbell enjoyed privileged access to the colonial government and received lucrative governmental printing contracts. Many early British and Colonial American newspapers proudly displayed this label.

James Franklin, with brother Benjamin as an apprentice printer, introduced the weekly *New England Courant* in Boston on August 7, 1721, the first paper to survive without governmental ties. Indeed, the *Courant* somehow survived for six, at times stormy years, despite its occasional attacks upon the religious and political powers of Massachusetts.

In the small community setting of Colonial America the newspaper's news function was overshadowed by other, more effective, communication systems, such as pamphlets, broadsides, gossip, tavern conversation, and church and town meetings. A newspaper's significant contribution, then, was weeks' or even months' old foreign news, a smattering of news from other Colonial communities, and the editor's own essay contributions to the community's political and religious discussions. The casual, almost random, Colonial newspaper format—inconspicuous label headlines, only a few crude illustrations, very small type faces, indiscriminate mixing of stories, essays, poems, and advertisements—reflects an editorial priority based on assembling a record of available intelligence rather than on generating a lively, attractive, aggressive news report. Not a lucrative undertaking for most Colonial printers, newspapers were in most communities a financial stepsister to the much more profitable job printing trade.

Until the Revolutionary War had set the political and economic course of the new nation, no more than forty newspapers—mostly weeklies, none more frequent than triweekly—operated in the Colonies, and their growth barely kept pace with population growth. During the eighteenth century most Colonial presses, type, and even paper were imported from England. Two hundred impressions per hour (printing on one side at a time) was considered good press work, and circulations, although difficult to verify, appear to have averaged about five hundered in the largest communities, with a few papers at times claiming more than one thousand copies.

Leading examples of pre-Revolutionary American newspapers and their founding years are: Boston *News-Letter*, 1704; Boston *Gazette*, 1719; *American Weekly Mercury*, (Philadelphia), 1719; *New England Courant*, (Boston), 1721; New York *Gazette*, 1725; *New England Weekly Journal*, (Boston), 1727; Benjamin Franklin's *Pennsylvania Gazette*, (Philadelphia), 1728;

John Peter Zenger's New York *Journal,* 1733; Boston *Evening Post,* 1735; and Williamsburg *Virginia Gazette,* 1736.

Colonial newspapers are regarded as having profoundly affected and sharpened the issues confronting the Colonies and as having hastened the Revolutionary War. The growing political crisis of the late 1760s and early 1770s transformed the leisurely essaying of isolated editors into camps, in places well organized, of hot-penned propagandists. Tory papers included *Rivington's New York Gazetteer,* Boston *Chronicle,* Boston *News-Letter,* Boston *Post-Boy,* and Philadelphia *Pennsylvania Ledger.* Representative of the middle of the road, or Whigs, were the Philadelphia *Pennsylvania Chronicle,* Philadelphia *Pennsylvania Evening Post,* and Boston *Evening Post.* The Radical cause, assisted by the Committees of Correspondence (which have been called America's first wire service), found expression in Benjamin Edes's and John Gill's Boston *Gazette or Country Journal,* Isaiah Thomas's *Massachusetts Spy* (printed in Boston 1770-75 and in Worcester after 1775), John Holt's New York *Journal,* Hugh Gaine's New York *Gazette and Weekly Mercury,* and John Dunlap's Philadelphia *Pennsylvania Packet.*

The end of the Revolutionary War acted as a starter's pistol for American newspaper publishing. Two years after Yorktown, on May 30, 1783, Benjamin Towne converted his Philadelphia *Pennsylvania Evening Post* to daily publication, the first daily in the country. The *Post* was challenged by conversion to a daily of the Philadelphia *Pennsylvania Packet* on September 21, 1784, and the *Post* succumbed within a month. Meanwhile, newspapers of all frequencies of publication were appearing and surviving throughout the young nation at a rate faster than population growth, a trend which continued throughout the nineteenth century. Between 1780 and 1790 total newspapers jumped from 39 to 92, the latter figure including eight dailies. In 1800 there were 235 newspapers, 24 of which were dailies; in 1850 total newspapers was 2,302, 254 of which were dailies; and in 1900 total newspapers was 18,487, 2,190 of which were dailies.

But while the Revolution's outcome provided a stable institutional setting for newspaper growth, the long-standing war of words between the English Whigs and French democrats over the nation's future course persisted and hardened into party labels. In response, the entire generation of post-Revolutionary newspapers became known for its own division into political camps.

This party press movement emerged with Washington's first administration; dominated newspapering until the 1830s or 1840s, and remained in evidence until the end of the Civil War. Although frowned upon today as violating a perceived adversarial relationship between press and government, newspaper's ties with government during the party press period then seemed perfectly appropriate, indeed vital to the interests of both fledgling institutions. Throughout the republic stretched a network of newspapers committed to the cause of the Federalists, Whigs, and Republicans, and a counter-network dedicated to the Anti-Federalists, Democratic-Republicans, and Democrats.

In addition to editorializing and slanting news in favor of the affiliate party, newspapers participated with government in three distinct activities. First, the editor whose man was mayor, governor, or president was that official's mouthpiece, serving in most cases as the public's only avenue to the thinking and policies of that administration. Second, the editor whose party controlled the city council, state legislature, or Congress was likely to be the preferred reporter of legislative proceedings, at times (in the case of Congress, for example) generating through his newspaper's columns the official record of proceedings. Third, select newspapers throughout the nation regularly published laws, orders, and resolutions of Congress. Totaling between forty and eighty, these papers were selected by the State Department, and their selection generally depended on their allegiance to the presidential administration.

John Fenno's *Gazette of the United States* was the first of a series of presidential organs that continued until Abraham Lincoln in 1861 declined to anoint a newspaper editor as his mouthpiece, preferring instead to rely on the Associated Press—which had no apparent political leaning. Administrations and their official organs were as follows: Washington and John Adams, *Gazette of the United States* (which began in New York City and followed the government to Philadelphia in 1790); Jefferson, Madison, and Monroe, *National Intelligencer* (Washington, D.C.); John Quincy Adams, *National Journal* (Washington, D.C.); Jackson, *United States Telegraph* (Washington, D.C.); 1829-31, and Washington, D.C. *Globe*, 1831-37; Van Buren, Washington, D.C. *Globe;* Harrison, *National Intelligencer* (Washington, D.C.); Tyler, *Madisonian* (Washington, D.C.); Polk, Washington, D.C. *Union;* Taylor, Washington, D.C. *Republic;* Fillmore, *National Intelligencer* (Washington, D.C.); Pierce and Buchanan, Washington, D.C. *Union* (which changed its name to *Constitution* on April 13, 1859).

Exuberant and vitriolic, the party press warred ceaselessly with every type of literary artillery against anyone who opposed the home party, the favored policy, or the fair-haired politician. Early examples of the Federalist-Whig brand of newspapers and their founding years are Fenno's *Gazette of the United States* (New York and Philadelphia), 1789; Benjamin Russell's Boston *Massachusetts* (later *Columbian) Centinel,* 1784; Noah Webster's *American Minerva* (New York), 1793; William Cobbett's *Porcupine's Gazette* (Philadelphia), 1797; and the New York *Evening Post* 1801, founded with the assistance of Alexander Hamilton. Those of the Jeffersonian persuasion are Philip Freneau's *National Gazette* (Philadelphia), 1791; Thomas and Abijah Adams' Boston *Independent Chronicle* (a converted pre-Revolutionary paper); Benjamin Franklin Bache's and William Duane's Philadelphia *General Advertiser* (also called the *Aurora),* 1790; and Samuel Harrison Smith's *National Intelligencer* (Washington, D.C.), 1801. A later Whig paper is James Watson

Webb's New York *Courier* and *Enquirer*, merged by Webb in 1829, and a later Democratic paper is Francis Blair's Washington, D.C. *Globe* founded in 1830.

Another type of ideological newspaper appearing during the party press period focused on the Southern slavery question and the plight of Northern blacks. The leading abolitionist voice was William Lloyd Garrison's *Liberator* (Boston), published from 1831 to 1865. Significant among the early black-owned or operated papers, and their periods of existence, are John B. Russwurm's and Samuel Cornish's *Freedom's Journal* (New York), the first black paper, 1827-29; *The Colored American* (New York), 1837-41; *The Ram's Horn* (New York), 1847-48; and Frederick Douglass's *The North Star* (Rochester, N.Y.), renamed *Frederick Douglass' Paper* in 1851, 1847-60.

A much smaller group of papers publishing concurrently with the party or ideological press was the mercantile press, found primarily in large cities and dedicated to factual reporting of business, financial, and shipping news of importance to the business community. The New York *Journal of Commerce,* founded in 1827 by Arthur Tappan but made successful by Gerard Hallock and David Hale, is a prime example of the mercantile press.

Until the 1830s and 1840s newspapers were read almost exclusively by the political or economic elites in America. In the absence of public education, a large middle class, and the technology to produce large quantities of newspapers, editors were content to offer a ponderous political or meticulous mercantile newspaper to the upper classes at about six cents per copy, usually sold by long-term subscription.

In contrast, the penny press editor took advantage of steam-driven, type-revolving presses, which dramatically increased daily production of newspapers, and relied on modest increases in public education and the middle class to offer papers of somewhat wider appeal. Benjamin Day's New York *Sun,* founded in 1833, is considered the first successful penny paper and was followed in this genre by James Gordon Bennett's New York *Herald,* 1835; Horace Greeley's New York *Tribune,* 1841; and Henry J. Raymond's New York *Times,* 1851. Sold for one or two cents by street vendors, the penny press featured street and police news, sometimes embellished with sensationalism, and a variety of political, mercantile, feature, and even sporting news. They were an attempt to bridge the gap between their contemporaries' political-mercantile audience and those one step below on the social ladder. Other early penny papers were the Philadelphia *Public Ledger,* 1836, and the Baltimore *Sun,* 1837.

By the Civil War the penny paper had surpassed the party press's influence in party and governmental affairs and had outreached the mercantile press in gathering and factually presenting news. Their coverage of the Civil War was aggressive and vivid.

The middle third of the nineteenth century saw newspapers attain what is probably their most diverse, interesting, and personal news report. In contrast to newspapering's earlier leadership of propagandists, party workers, and made-over printers, some true writers and thinkers and a few sharp-witted newspaper managers began to populate the news room after the 1830s, giving the news report an esprit, a genuine curiosity about ideas and men, a firmness of opinion without dogmatism, and a new zeal to pursue the news. Newspapers were adopting the more common language of the street and home within story structures that closely resembled the natural flow of events. A sense of reality as experienced daily by people in the streets crept into the news columns.

Type faces remained small, and headlines were still likely to be short labels, except when the news was smashing. Pictures were still few, and advertising still occupied much less than half of a newspaper's column space and amounted to brief business cards or announcements.

Early daily newspapers had hit the streets late in the day, but the coming of telegraphic news dispatches in the late 1840s, coupled with keen competition among newspapers, pushed publication times earlier in the day, until by the Civil War most dailies, whether penny, party or mercantile, were on the street when people went to work, using a midday or late afternoon make-over edition for late local and telegraphic news that materialized during the morning.

Before 1860 Sunday publication was commonly frowned upon as violating the sanctity of the Sabbath, but the urgency of Civil War news forced editors into the Sunday field and thus opened a publishing opportunity which in the twentieth century would become increasingly important to papers' balance sheets.

Between 1865 and 1885 newspapers slowly assumed the structure, news report, and financial support familiar to twentieth-century readers. It was a period when the leaders of the old party, mercantile, and penny press movements left the scene. Some of these papers survived either through progressive management or last-ditch salvage efforts. Notable survivers are: the Baltimore *Sun*, Chicago *Tribune*, Cleveland *Plain Dealer*, Des Moines *Register*, Detroit *Free Press*, New York *Herald*, New York *Tribune*, New York *Times*, Philadelphia *Bulletin*, and Washington, D.C. *Star*. But a tidal wave of new newspapers rolled over the industry, establishing many of our twentieth-century newspaper leaders. Significant members of this new generation and their founding years are the San Francisco *Chronicle*, 1865; Minneapolis *Tribune*, 1867; Atlanta *Constitution*, 1868; Louisville *Courier-Journal*, merged in 1869; Boston *Globe*, 1872; Detroit *Evening News*, 1873; St. Louis *Globe-Democrat*, merged in 1875; Chicago *Daily News* and Dallas *Times-Herald*, 1876; Washington *Post*, 1877; Cleveland *Press* and Minneapolis *Star*, 1878; St. Louis *Post-Dispatch*, merged in 1878; Kansas City *Star*, 1880; Los Angeles *Times*, 1881; and Milwaukee *Journal*, 1882.

Another wave of new leaders, some of them reflecting a return to elitist journalism, appeared around the turn of the century: *Wall Street Journal*, (New York), 1889; Denver *Post*, 1895; Houston *Chronicle*, 1901; *Christian Science Monitor*, (Boston), 1908; and Miami *Herald*, 1910. Only a few papers that have attained national prominence have appeared in recent decades, notably the New York *Daily News,* 1919; Long Island *Newsday,* 1940; Chicago *Sun-Times,* merged in 1948, and vestiges here and there of the old Scripps-Howard and Hearst newspaper chains, the former emerging in the 1880s and the later taking shape after 1900.

Post-Civil War newspapers gradually became big business, fell in with the chamber of commerce crowd, routinized news gathering, formularized news writing, relied more heavily on advertising revenue, and accommodated greater advertising space on news pages. The period also saw the return to dominance of the evening newspaper, marked increases in circulation totals, and realization of machine typesetting and high-speed rotary presses capable of cutting and folding newspapers and printing in four colors on both sides of a continuous sheet of newsprint.

Much of the innovation in newspapering at this time is labeled by the literature as "new journalism" and attributed to Joseph Pulitzer, his St. Louis *Post-Dispatch* after 1878, and his New York *World* after 1883. In sum, "new journalism" included developing a news staff organization and formal news-gathering procedures, adopting promotional and civic improvement projects, enticing greatly expanded advertising patronage onto newspaper pages, keeping the price per paper to two or three cents, depersonalizing editorial columns and objectifying news columns, becoming preoccupied with large circulations, championing the cause of laboring classes, and making greater use of eye-catching illustrations and headlines.

This was also the period when newspaper chains first appeared and when regional and national news-gathering consortiums developed and began to influence newspapers' views of what was "acceptable" news writing. Generally a writing style developed that summarized the news event's most important features in the first few paragraphs and arranged remaining details in descending order of importance, that is the inverted pyramid story structure.

Departmentalization of the news staff, creation of beats for reporters to cover, and introduction of the telephone and typewriter in news operations began to give the news room an organized, if not assembly line, atmosphere. The news report that most newspapers sported by the turn of the century was "objective," superficially comprehensive, and impersonal—informative, yet inoffensive to readers and advertisers alike.

The industry has permitted modest occasional flexibility in that writing formula during this century, especially in some departments, but the bulk of the news report remains much the same as it was by World War I. Indeed, newspapering fought hard to ignore another "new journalism" movement in the 1960s and 1970s. This movement, led by such feature writers and authors as Tom Wolfe, Gay Talese, Norman Mailer, Joan Didion, Hunter S. Thompson, and Truman Capote, was seen by commercial newspaper people as too subjective or fictionalized to warrant newspaper play. In the same two decades, however, newspapers increasingly engaged in "interpretative" journalism, meant to explain or provide background for straight news events, and "investigative" journalism, aimed at exposing corruption and criminal behavior in high places.

Within the first decade of the twentieth century daily and total newspapers reached their full growth at about 2,600 and 18,500, respectively. Average daily circulation per newspaper in 1914 was 11,784, and total daily circulation was about 32 percent of total U.S. population. (In 1974 average daily circulation per newspaper was 34,880, and total daily circulation was 29 percent of total U.S. population.) Between 1915 and 1955 newspaper totals (in all publishing frequency categories) declined, reaching in the latter year a plateau where they have since stayed, with dailies holding at about 1,760 and total newspapers at about 11,200.

The forty-year decline was caused by newspaper oversaturation at the turn of the century which led to numerous suspensions and mergers, a stagnant typesetting and printing technology that became increasingly expensive to operate and maintain, two world wars with attendant manpower and materials shortages which brought the demise of marginal papers, and the growth of other media of mass communication that detracted from newspapers' news product and diverted some advertising revenue to the other media.

Several other newspaper trends and episodes in the past century are worthy of brief note to round out this historical outline.

Some metropolitan newspapers engaged in brief stints of extreme sensationalism. The first, so-called yellow journalism during the decade following 1896, was prompted by William Randolph Hearst's New York *Journal's* challenge to Pulitzer's New York *World.* There were some signs of yellow journalism elsewhere in the country, but New York City bore the brunt of this escapade. The second outbreak of sensationalism, the so-called jazz journalism of the 1920s and especially of the tabloids, was led by Joseph Patterson's New York *Daily News,* 1919; Hearst's New York *Mirror,* 1924; and Bernarr Macfadden's New York *Daily Graphic,* 1924.

Foreign-language newspapers had been sparsely interwoven in America's journalism fabric since Benjamin Franklin's Philadelphia *Zeitung* appeared in 1732, but the upsurge of immigrants after 1880 led to a peak of about 1,200 foreign-language newspapers (about 160 of them dailies) at the start of World War 1. Comparable foreign-language figures in 1980 are about half those totals.

Black newspapers have continued to lead marginal existences in the United States, owing apparently to insufficient advertising revenue and black readers' unwillingness to abandon white-controlled newspapers in their cities. It is estimated that in 1920 there were 492 black newspapers in the United States (none of them dailies), and that in 1970 that number had declined to 325 (two or three being dailies).

Moreover, there has been a constant din of special interest, political, lifestyle, and sensational newspapers in the market. Leftist and pacifist weeklies were much in evidence before each world war. Sensational weeklies, such as the *National Enquirer* and Rupert Murdoch's *Star,* seem to have scored with the grocery store crowd. And during the 1960s and early 1970s, at the height of student unrest over Vietnam and amid counter cultural pursuits, underground or alternative newspapers briefly thrived, only a few surviving as commercial or give-away ventures.

At this writing newspaper totals, despite recent well-publicized newspaper deaths, remain at stable, twenty five-year levels. Absolute circulation figures hold steady while advertising linage and revenue climb slowly in the absence of newspaper competition. While happily settling for a one-newspaper-per-community saturation and the security that rapidly expanding newspaper chains bring, the industry has lately been distressed that its circulation totals have not kept pace with population growth. This concern may breed some interesting tinkerings with the news product in the years ahead.

Meanwhile, the 1970s saw newspapers, among other news media, becoming increasingly aggressive by exposing corruption in high places, publishing classified government documents, using computers to anticipate election returns and to generate public opinion polls, and probing social issues and evils, at times with the help of unnamed confidential sources. Although intended to assist the democratic process and uphold the "public's right to know" at a time of highly charged domestic and international turmoil, such activities have at times backfired as segments of the public, business, and government have objected to perceived and actual negativism, unpatriotism, racism, sexism, and falsehoods in news coverage.

Their credibility thus called into question, newspapers have mounted public relations campaigns, re-examined their news reports, introduced op-ed pages, employed ombudsmen, established press councils, and begun reassessing their codes of ethics. This new public awareness of newspapers as social forces has also been reflected in the past few years in the beginnings of serious academic study of newspaper reporting and writing practices as they affect news events, the governing process, and the public's perceptions of reality.

BIBLIOGRAPHY

Dennis, Everette E., and William L. Rivers. *Other Voices: The New Journalism in America.* San Francisco: Canfield Press, 1974.

Emery, Edwin, and Michael Emery. *The Press and America.* 4th ed. Englewood Cliffs, N.J.: Prentice-Hall, 1978.

Emery, Michael C., R. Smith Schuneman, and Edwin Emery, eds. *America's Front Page News, 1690-1970.* New York: Doubleday, 1970.

Glessing, Robert J. *The Underground Press in America.* Bloomington: Indiana University Press, 1970.

Journalism History. Northridge: California State University Northridge Foundation, 1974-. Quarterly.

Journalism Quarterly. Minneapolis: Association for Education in Journalism, 1924-. Quarterly. (Founded as *Journalism Bulletin.*)

Lee, Alfred McClung. *The Daily Newspaper in America, The Evolution of a Social Instrument.* New York: Macmillan, 1937.

Levy, Leonard W., ed. *Freedom of the Press from Zenger to Jefferson.* Indianapolis: Bobbs-Merrill, 1966.

Lippmann, Walter. *Public Opinion.* New York: Harcourt, Brace, 1922.

McCoy, Ralph E., ed. *Freedom of the Press: An Annotated Bibliography.* Carbondale: Southern Illinois University Press, 1968.

Marbut, F. B. *News from the Capital, The Story of Washington Reporting.* Carbondale: Southern Illinois University Press, 1971.

Marzolf, Marion. *Up from the Footnote: A History of Women Journalists.* New York: Hastings House, 1977.

Mott, Frank Luther. *American Journalism, A History: 1690-1960.* 3d ed. New York: Macmillan, 1962.

Nelson, Harold L., ed. *Freedom of the Press from Hamilton to the Warren Court.* Indianapolis: Bobbs-Merrill, 1967.

Nevins, Allan, ed. *American Press Opinion, Washington to Coolidge.* New York: D. C. Heath, 1928.

Park, Robert E. *The Immigrant Press and Its Control.* New York: Harper & Brothers, 1922.

Pickett, Calder M., ed. *Voices of the Past, Key Documents in the History of American Journalism.* Columbus, Ohio: Grid, Inc., 1977.

Price, Warren C. *The Literature of Journalism.* Minneapolis: University of Minnesota Press, 1959.

———, and Calder M. Pickett. *An Annotated Journalism Bibliography, 1958-1968.* Minneapolis: University of Minnesota Press, 1970.

Schudson, Michael. *Discovering the News, A Social History of American Newspapers.* New York: Basic Books, 1978.

Smith, Anthony. *Goodbye Gutenberg, The Newspaper Revolution of the 1980's.* New York: Oxford University Press, 1980.

Smith, Culver H. *The Press, Politics, and Patronage. The American Government's Use of Newspapers, 1789-1875.* Athens: University of Georgia Press, 1977.

Snyder, Louis L., and Richard B. Morris, eds. *A Treasury of Great Reporting: "Literature under Pressure" from the Sixteenth Century to Our Own Times.* 2d ed. New York: Simon & Schuster, 1962.

Stevens, John D., and Hazel Dicken Garcia. *Communication History.* Beverly Hills, Calif.: SAGE Publications, 1980.

Wolseley, Roland E. *The Black Press: U.S.A.* Ames: Iowa State University Press, 1971.

The Occult

Robert Galbreath

Throughout American history, often during periods of social tension and rapid change associated with secularization, the occult has been conspicuous in popular culture. This has been true of late seventeenth-century New England, the Second Great Awakening and social ferment of the early nineteenth century, industrialization during the Gilded Age, the interwar years of the twentieth century, and the recent countercultural rejection of technocratic society. But popular occultism is by no means confined to periods of social crisis or to a search for alternative values, nor is it adequately defined as rejected knowledge and superstition. For the seventeenth and much of the eighteenth centuries, the occult was part of the dominant value structure of society. In more recent times, the occult has been displaced from the mental universe of the educated elite, although it tends still to be manifested strongly in radical movements in the arts and social thought. At the popular level, the occult seems to have persisted, perhaps without interruption, from the seventeenth and eighteenth centuries to the present.

Popular occultism ranges from traditional folk beliefs and practices to contemporary commercial exploitation, from the persecution of witches to the search for transcendence, from the desire for health and wealth to the reassurance and consolation afforded by belief in postmortem existence. The manifestations of popular occultism speak to many kinds of needs which must be differentiated, not conflated—as in so much impressionistic writing about the occult—into simplistic explanations in terms of cultural decadence or countercultural rebelliousness. Popular occultism has partaken of and contributed to the American preoccupation with optimism, self-development, community, and reform. The study of American popular occultism may thus contribute to the understanding of the persistence and displacement of beliefs, of cultural stratification, and of the processes of social change.

As a concept, "the occult" is unwieldly. By extension from its Latin root, *occulere* (to cover over, hide, conceal), "occult" now signifies anything hidden or secret in the sense of being mysterious to ordinary understanding and scientific reason. "Hidden," however, does not imply "unknowable." Certain phenomena and experiences are believed to be occult in only a superficial, extrinsic sense. Mysterious now, they may eventually be confirmed or disproven by science. In other cases, the occult is said to be an intrinsic quality, inherently unknowable by science, but still accessible, in this view, to certain nonnormative modes of cognition which are themselves occult.

In contemporary popular usage, "occult" and similar terms ("psychic," "esoteric," "paranormal," "mystical," "magical," "supernatural," "metaphysical") encompass at least six broad categories of beliefs, phenomena, experiences, and practices. (1) *Mysteries of human and natural history:* disputed phenomena and theories, such as UFOs, the Loch Ness Monster, the Bermuda Triangle, lost continents, and ancient astronauts, which do not fit into or contradict prevailing scientific and historical knowledge. (2) *Psi phenomena:* the field studied by experimental parapsychology, comprising extrasensory perception (ESP), psychokinesis (PK), and so-called survival phenomena (presumed evidence for postmortem existence), which are all thought to be extrasensorimotor in nature, i.e., outside the person's normal sensory and muscular processes. (3) *Transpersonal experiences:* experiences in which the ordinary personality is transcended, erased, or replaced, as in trance mediumship, spirit or demonic possession, inspiration or enthusiasm, revelation, meditation, and mysticism (oneness with the ultimate). (4) *Occult sciences, arts, or technologies:* disciplines based on the deliberate cultivation of natural or acquired psychic abilities to satisfy specific needs, as in magic (control of natural or occult forces), prediction and divination (including astrology, Tarot cards, the I Ching), characterology (character analysis by means of astrology, phrenology, numerology, etc.), and health and healing (including faith healing, mind cure, psychic surgery, acupuncture). (5) *Occult religions:* organized practices for the primary purpose of worshipping, celebrating, or serving natural forces and pagan or mythological deities, as in both traditional and modern witchcraft, Voodoo, Satanism, and neopaganism. (6) *Metaphysical occultism:* systems of teachings and practices which lead the individual, by means of occult modes of cognition, to personal empirical knowledge of metaphysical truths and principles, as in Theosophy, Anthroposophy, Rosicrucianism, and Gnosticism. Needless to say, these categories overlap. Numerous occult organizations and teachings combine elements from two or more categories. Nor are all six categories equally significant for American popular culture. It is also difficult always to differentiate clearly between the occult and such closely related areas as religious cults and sects, Asian religions in America, positive thinking and self-help, psychotherapy, psychedelics, millennialism, and youth culture.

The history of the occult in America from the first European settlers to the present is far from being fully documented. The available evidence suggests that it involves a complex of Native American and African beliefs, European folklore and customs, medieval and early modern intellectual traditions of geocentrism, correspondence theory, and the efficacy of magic, astrology, and witchcraft, later importations of European and Asian systems of occultism and self-realization, and movements either indigenous to America or distinctively shaped by their experiences here. The occult in seventeenth-century America, with the notable exception of Salem witchcraft in 1692, is still largely unexplored. The English settlers of Massachusetts, Virginia, and Pennsylvania were familiar with magic, astrology, divination, witchcraft, healing, and alchemy, although the extent and significance of that familiarity is by no means clear. Library inventories indicate that occult books were readily available to the literate. Popular almanacs were widely consulted even by the semiliterate for advice on health and future happenings. Court records and religious writings indicate concern that too much reliance was being placed by some colonists on astrology, amulets and good luck charms, and consulting occult practitioners to find lost objects and to cure various afflictions.

Belief in the reality of witchcraft—the practice of evil magic (*maleficium*) in league with the Devil—was commonplace. The greatest wave of witch persecutions in Western Europe was drawing to a close in 1650, the time when witch trials first began in the American colonies. Perhaps sixty to a hundred trials took place (estimates vary) in the second half of the seventeenth century, but it is the events of 1692 in Salem Village (now Danvers), Massachusetts, and the resulting trials in nearby Salem Town which are by far the best known. Although minor by European standards, Salem witchcraft has never ceased to fascinate and appall the popular imagination, perhaps because it is regarded as a microcosm of how a community can be torn apart by suspicion and fear. Approximately 165 persons were accused of witchcraft, thirty-one of them were actually tried and convicted, and of these twenty were executed. Earlier explanations which contended that the accusers were liars and that witchcraft was a fabrication of theologians and clergy are no longer tenable. The reality of witchcraft was mostly taken for granted at the time, and Chadwick Hansen has argued, on the basis of the trial records, that three of the accused probably were guilty of the practice of malefic magic. Hansen has also shown striking parallels between the symptoms of the accusers (victims) and of hysterics described in psychiatric literature. But the process by which a general belief in malefic magic is converted into actual medical hysteria, accusations, trials, and executions in one community and not in another is still not fully understood, although a number of historians have analyzed the social tensions, neighborhood antagonisms, and generational conflicts in Salem Village in an effort to shed light on the origins of the accusations and how they were handled by magistrates.

The decline in trials for witchcraft after Salem is directly related to the decline in belief in malefic magic among judges and magistrates. This decline is part of a general tendency in Western Europe toward the displacement of the occult (sometimes referred to, using Max Weber's phrase, as "the disenchantment of the world") from the public values of the educated elite. Whether this process also marks a general decline in popular belief in the occult is sharply debated by scholars. For eighteenth-century America, Herbert Leventhal has documented the continuity in popular culture of astrology (although, from the evidence of almanacs, in decline), witch beliefs (but not executions), alchemy, geocentrism, the doctrines of qualities, spirits, and humors, and the curious indigenous belief in the supernatural power of rattlesnakes.

By the 1780s, with both revolution and romanticism in the air, European occultism experienced a rebirth. There is no contemporary American parallel to the French enthusiasm over Mesmerism (animal magnetism), the otherworldly visions of Swedenborg, and secret societies. In the late 1820s and 1830s, however, Americans were captivated by the newly imported systems of Mesmerism and phrenology. Their appeal was to the American interest in any purportedly scientific system which claimed to promote health, happiness, and personal improvement on a democratic scale. Phrenology, a form of character divination based on the development of the organs of the brain as revealed by the contours and shape of the skull, had considerable impact on education, penology, medicine, and writers, including Emerson, Melville, Whitman, Poe, and Twain. Mesmerism sought to effect cures by re-establishing the unimpeded flow of animal (or vital) magnetism through the body. It subsequently influenced the development of hypnotism, Spiritualism, and mind cure.

A kaleidoscopic swirl of occultisms, revelations, new religions, and reform movements swept across the United States in the late 1830s and 1840s. There is a complex interweaving of occult ideas and practices with those of millennialists and adventists, utopianists, health reformers, Transcendentalists, Shakers, Mormons, and advocates of social justice. Out of this ferment there arose in 1848 the most influential American contribution to world occultism, Spiritualism.

Spiritualism rested upon two basic beliefs, that the human personality survives bodily death in some form and that it is possible to communicate with the surviving personality or spirit, usually through human mediums. It appealed to those who sought consolation over the loss of loved ones and those who sought scientific, empirical evidence of life after death. The Spiritualist teachings concerning spiritual progress after death derived from Universalism, Transcendentalism, Swedenborg, and especially the Swedenborg-like works of the "Poughkeepsie seer," Andrew Jackson Davis. The Spiritualist phenomena themselves had significant antecedents in Mesmerism, Swedenborgianism, the spirit manifestations among the Shakers, and North American Indian shamanism. But it is the famous spirit-rappings experienced by the Fox sisters in 1848 near Rochester, New York, from which the beginnings of modern Spiritualism are dated. Within the next few years,

Spiritualism swept the country. Mediums held seances in every major city and town at which spirits communicated through raps, table-tipping, written messages, and direct voice utterances. Following the Civil War, Spiritualism took on renewed vitality. New phenomena were manifested and new procedures for communicating were introduced, among them the planchette, spirit photography, trumpet mediums, slate writing, and materializations. Many of these practices were quickly exposed as fraudulent, and public interest began to wane by 1875, although Spiritualism was still to figure prominently in popular romances and in works by Howells, Twain, and James. In response to the exposés and loss of public interest, Spiritualists began to organize themselves into churches and associations for the purpose of training, certifying, and protecting honest mediums.

Spiritualism's emphasis upon empirical phenomena demonstrating the immortality of the soul and life after death not only directly attacked reliance upon ecclesiastical and scriptural authority, it also was seen as the basis for reconciling the competing claims of religious faith and scientific materialism. The often bizarre phenomena and the claims made on behalf of mediums prompted various scholars, scientists, and laypersons to organize psychical research societies in England and America in the 1880s in order to investigate and assess the Spiritualistic evidence. The anecdotal data collected by the psychical research societies is itself an important source on popular attitudes. The philosopher and psychologist, William James, who was also a prominent psychical researcher, offered an illuminating insight into the persistence of popular occult beliefs in modern society in his essay, "What Psychical Research Has Accomplished" (1897). The dominant view of life outside scientific circles, James stated, is "personal" and "romantic." Personal experience lies at the foundation of this worldview—experiences of premonitions, apparitions, omens, visions, dreams, answers to prayers, miracles, and much else that is taken to signify that "events may happen for the sake of their personal significance." James noted that "thousands of sensitive organizations in the United States today live as steadily in the light of these experiences, and are as indifferent to modern science, as if they lived in Bohemia in the twelfth century. They are indifferent to science, because science is so callously indifferent to their experiences." Psychical research, James believed, had attempted to bridge the gulf between impersonal science and personal reality.

As Spiritualism began to decline in public esteem, the Theosophical Society was established in New York City in 1875 by Mme. H. P. Blavatsky, Colonel Henry Steel Olcott, and others. If Spiritualism was the most influential occult movement of the midcentury, Theosophy assumed that role for the late nineteenth and early twentieth centuries, and virtually no subsequent occult organization of importance was left untouched by it. Drawing from American Spiritualism, Oriental religions (especially Hinduism and Buddhism), and the Western occult tradition of Neoplatonism, Hermeticism, and the Kabbalah, Theosophy offered a complex set of teachings covering cosmic and human evolution, human destiny and suffering, karma and reincarnation, and after-death states. Theosophy established the cliché of Tibet as the land of esoteric wisdom and popularized the ideas of karma, reincarnation, and secret masters. Theosophy helped promote the comparative study of religion and encouraged the view that the essential teachings of the major religions are one. The society subsequently had a decisive influence on the revival of Buddhism in Ceylon (Sri Lanka) and to a lesser extent of Hinduism in India; it was also noted for its advocacy of Indian Home Rule. Although the society's headquarters were soon shifted from New York to India, America continued to be a center of Theosophical activity along with England and India. The controversial activities and magnetic personalities of its most prominent leaders over the years—Mme. H. P. Blavatsky, Annie Besant, Charles Leadbeater—assured the society of continuing publicity, culminating in 1929 with the public defection of the young teacher and Theosophical protégé, Krishnamurti. The heady mixture of evolutionary philosophy, ancient wisdom, Oriental religion, modern science, secret masters, and personal initiation appealed to many who rejected both religious dogmatism and scientific materialism without relinquishing either religious concerns or scientific knowledge.

In addition to Spiritualism and Theosophy, mind cure (mental healing) emerged as a third major form of nineteenth-century American occultism. J. Stillson Judah has interpreted all three as examples of "metaphysical" movements, using the term "metaphysics" in a sense originated by New Thought, one of the principal types of mind cure. Emerging from Swedenborgianism, Mesmerism and Transcendentalism, "metaphysics" viewed itself as a practical philosophy, both religious and scientific, concerned with the application to daily life of the absolute truths and deeper realities which are said to exist beyond the dimensions of daily sense-experience. Highly pragmatic, experiential, and optimistic, metaphysics rejected both creedal orthodoxies and blind faith in the name of self-realization through identification with the divine principle within every individual. The metaphysical viewpoint is less apparent in Spiritualism and Theosophy, however, than in the mind cure movements (New Thought, Christian Science, Divine Science, Religious Science, Unity). These movements regarded evil as illusory and illness as the product of unhealthy attitudes. Health, as well as prosperity and pleasure, were the fruits of positive thinking "in tune with the infinite."

During the nineteenth century, America was hospitable to an extraordinary range of occult movements devoted to character analysis, health, metaphysical self-development, communal experiments, and efforts to heal the rift between science and religion. American-style Spiritualism had international impact, as did New Thought. America also became one of the pioneers in psychical research, it was in New York that Theosophy was officially launched, and the World Parliament of Religions at the 1893 Chicago World's Fair introduced Indian Vedanta and Zen Buddhism to the West. But the United States did not participate to any noteworthy extent in the European revival of ritual magic associated with the names of Éliphas Lévi in France and the Hermetic Order of the Golden Dawn in England.

The First World War and the cultural and economic dislocations of the 1920s and 1930s maintained strong popular interest in the occult. An increase in the number of publications on Spiritualism and psychical research occurred during the war and the immediate postwar period. European and Asian occult teachers and spiritual masters became fashionable, among them Count Hermann Keyserling, Rudolf Steiner, G. I. Gurdjieff, P. D. Ouspensky, Krishnamurti, and Paramhansa Yogananda, as did the American psychic diagnostician and prophet, Edgar Cayce. While the major Spiritualist, Theosophical, and New Thought organizations continued, many new eclectic groups appeared, including Psychiana, the I Am Movement, and Mankind United. Popular astrology is also characteristic of the period. Evangeline Adams, who had already achieved some fame as an astrologer before the war and had published successful astrological books in the 1920s, established the first astrological radio show in 1930, the same year that daily horoscopes were introduced by English newspapers. In 1933 *American Astrology*, a pulp, began publication. It is credited with originating the now familiar format of brief, highly general predictions which are supposedly applicable to anyone born under the same zodiacal sign.

After World War II, popular occultism grew steadily, with flurries of public enthusiasm over flying saucers, hypnotic regression to past lives (Bridey Murphy), and Zen Buddhism, until 1966-1968 when the occult captured, or was captured by, youth culture and the mass media. During these years, a number of media events, entertainments, and cultural phenomena coincided and brought home the occult to a vast audience: psychedelics, the flower children, the popularity of Hermann Hesse's novels, *Rosemary's Baby* (book and film), bestsellers on astrology (Linda Goodman's *Sun Signs*) and Edgar Cayce (Jess Stearn's *The Sleeping Prophet*), and news items about Transcendental Meditation, the Church of Satan, and attempts to levitate the Pentagon. It has been argued that this "occult explosion" is historically unique in its convergence with advanced technology, not least of all in media hype and commercial exploitation, and that it constitutes a pop religion which exhibits playful contempt for the supernatural. But it is equally clear from consulting Thomas C. Clarie's *Occult Bibliography*, which annotates 1,856 original and reprint English-language books published in just five years, 1971-75, that there has also been an audience for serious occult ideas and techniques of personal transformation.

Contemporary interest in the occult has concentrated on three broad categories. The first concerns the psychical and spiritual development of the individual and the understanding of others. Meditation, biofeedback, altered states of consciousness, character analysis (e.g., astrology, Tarot cards), spiritual disciplines, and holistic health are some of the primary forms of activity in this area rather than extrasensory perception or psychokinesis (although persons claiming to possess extraordinary psychical abilities have been heavily publicized by the media). The approaches can vary from individual study and experimentation to discipleship under a guru or master (often Oriental, as in Zen Buddhism, Tibetan Buddhism, Sufism, and Yoga, although the tradition can also be Native American, as in the allegedly factual books of Carlos Castaneda). The totalistic cults of Scientology, the Unification Church, and Krishna Consciousness, which are often accused of brainwashing, also emphasize the attainment of particular psychological states.

A second major focus of contemporary occultism is the cosmic, ranging from astrology, UFOs, and ancient astronauts to alleged congruences between modern physics and Eastern mysticism to forms of health, community, and ritual which integrate the person with cosmic harmonies. In this connection, one of the most striking aspects of contemporary occultism has been the appearance and rapid growth of neopagan and witchcraft groups dedicated to the worship or celebration of various natural powers and deities. The ritual practices of modern witchcraft (Wicca) have nothing to do with the malefic magic and devil-worship traditionally associated with witches during persecutions in the past. Modern witch groups mostly claim to be descended, either historically or in spirit, from prehistoric fertility religions or goddess-worship which were subsequently persecuted by Christianity and driven underground. The most thorough investigator of contemporary witchcraft, Margot Adler, has found that its practitioners are not attempting to gain power over others and are not anti-science; rather they have been attracted to witchcraft by the religious freedom, reverence for nature, opportunity for personal growth, feminism, and emphasis on imagination and beauty which they find in it.

By contrast, the third area of contemporary occult activity has been the horrific and diabolic. The most obvious manifestations are found in the popularity of occult horror fiction, most recently exemplified by the novels of Stephen King and Peter Straub, and the flood of horror films, from *Rosemary's Baby* (1968) and *The Exorcist* (1974) to their gruesome imitators. The "horror" in these works is that of possession, of the individual transformed into someone or something utterly alien. The possession need not be done by a demon, vampire, or Satan. Some have argued that the same horror is achieved in real life through the brainwashing techniques ascribed to Scientology, the Unification Church, and Charles Manson's "family."

These manifestations of popular occultism indicate both a strong thirst for personal experience—of occult wisdom, psychic abilities, spiritual reality, human potential, even the demonic—and a wish to revise history, the cosmos, and human nature, to open them to new possibilities—of spiritual evolution, the re-enchantment of the world, and cosmic connections. These tendencies can result in a healthy experimental attitude or an overly credulous and anti-scientific dogmatism; they can be practical and optimistic or escapist and narcissistic. No wonder, then, that popular responses to the occult can be varied and extreme. To the upholders of scientific rationalism, the occult spells irrationalism and the threat of a new Dark Age; to Christian fundamentalists, the occult appears diabolic and portends the Age of the Antichrist; to its enthusiastic advocates, the occult denotes New Age consciousness, the Age of Aquarius. From the varied forms popular occultism has assumed in American history, it is unlikely that any one interpretation can ever be definitive.

BIBLIOGRAPHY

Adler, Margot. *Drawing Down the Moon: Witches, Druids, Goddess-Worshippers, and Other Pagans in America Today.* New York: Viking Press, 1979.

Boyer, Paul, and Stephen Nissenbaum. *Salem Possessed: The Social Origins of Witchcraft.* Cambridge, Mass.: Harvard University Press, 1974.

Braden, Charles S. *These Also Believe: A Study of Modern American Cults & Minority Religious Movements.* New York: Macmillan, 1949.

Bridges, Hal. *American Mysticism: From William James to Zen.* New York: Harper & Row, 1970.

Butler, Jon. "Magic, Astrology, and the Early American Religious Heritage, 1600-1760." *American Historical Review,* 84 (April 1979), 317-46.

Campbell, Bruce F. *Ancient Wisdom Revived: A History of the Theosophical Movement.* Berkeley and Los Angeles: University of California Press, 1980.

Cavendish, Richard, ed. *Man, Myth & Magic: An Illustrated Encyclopedia of the Supernatural.* 24 vols. New York: Marshall Cavendish, 1970.

Clarie, Thomas C. *Occult Bibliography: An Annotated List of Books Published in English, 1971 through 1975.* Metuchen, N.J.: Scarecrow Press, 1978.

Davies, John D. *Phrenology: Fad and Science: A 19th-Century American Crusade.* New Haven: Yale University Press, 1955.

Eliade, Mircea. "The Occult and the Modern World." In his *Occultism, Witchcraft, and Cultural Fashions: Essays in Comparative Religions.* Chicago: University of Chicago Press, 1976, pp. 47-68.

Ellwood, Robert S., Jr. *Alternative Altars: Unconventional and Eastern Spirituality in America.* Chicago: University of Chicago Press, 1979.

______. *Religious and Spiritual Groups in Modern America.* Englewood Cliffs, N.J.: Prentice-Hall, 1973.

Galbreath, Robert. "The History of Modern Occultism: A Bibliographical Survey." *Journal of Popular Culture,* 5 (Winter 1971), 726-54. Reprinted in *The Occult: Studies and Evaluations.* Edited by Robert Galbreath. Bowling Green, Ohio: Bowling Green University Popular Press, 1972.

Hansen, Chadwick. *Witchcraft at Salem.* New York: Braziller, 1969.

James, William. "What Psychical Research Has Accomplished" (1897). In *William James on Psychical Research.* Edited by Gardner Murphy and Robert O. Ballou. New York: Viking Press, 1960, pp. 25-47.

Judah, J. Stillson. *The History and Philosophy of the Metaphysical Movements in America.* Philadelphia: Westminster Press, 1967.

Kerr, Howard. *Mediums and Spirit-Rappers and Roaring Radicals: Spiritualism in American Literature, 1850-1900.* Urbana: University of Illinois Press, 1972.

———, and Charles Crow, eds. *The Occult in America: New Historical Perspectives.* Urbana: University of Illinois Press, 1983.

Leventhal, Herbert. *In the Shadow of the Enlightenment: Occultism and Renaissance Science in Eighteenth-Century America.* New York: New York University Press, 1976.

Melton, J. Gordon. *The Encyclopedia of American Religions.* 2 vols. Wilmington, N.C.: Consortium Books/McGrath Publishing Co., 1978.

———, with James V. Geisendorfer. *A Dictionary of Religious Bodies in the United States.* New York: Garland, 1977.

Moore, R. Laurence. *In Search of White Crows: Spiritualism, Parapsychology, and American Culture.* New York: Oxford University Press, 1977.

Podmore, Frank. *From Mesmer to Christian Science: A Short History of Mental Healing.* New Hyde Park, N.Y.: University Books, 1963. Reprint of *Mesmerism and Christian Science* (1909).

Williams, Peter W. *Popular Religion in America: Symbolic Change and the Modernization Process in Historical Perspective.* Englewood Cliffs, N.J.: Prentice-Hall, 1980.

Zaretsky, Irving I., and Mark P. Leone, eds. *Religious Movements in Contemporary America.* Princeton: Princeton University Press, 1974.

Photography

Richard N. Masteller

Photography has enjoyed popularity in America since 1839, when news of its first widely successful form, the daguerreotype, reached American shores from France. Since these early days, a multitude of photographic formats have entered and passed from the scene, recording it for posterity, shrinking the world while expanding its horizons, and feeding contradictory human desires for scientific information, romantic escapism, and comfortable home truths. Contemporary considerations of the photographic image stress its status as a surrogate reality; the image, could we but learn to read it, might reveal the social construction of reality inherent in the mind of its maker, in the minds of its depicted subjects, perhaps even in the minds of its viewers.

To be considered in the province of popular culture, photography must at least involve a large number of people. It may be useful to divide popular photography into three categories: photography of the people, by the people, and for the people. In its earliest years, the making of photographs by large numbers of people was impossible. Most were without the necessary technical knowledge and financial resources, and the medium itself was experimental and unpredictable. Yet beginning with the daguerreotype and continuing in subsequent forms such as the tintype and the *carte-de-visite*, the photograph drew thousands of people to portrait studios, whether elaborate establishments on Fifth Avenue in New York City in the 1850s or temporary quarters set up by itinerant photographers in hotel rooms across America. The legacy is still alive today—in the portable landscapes and floodlights of the nearby K-Mart. One category of popular photography is, therefore, practiced by commercial photographers: it is photography of the people.

The second category—photography by the people—designates those who take their own photographs but who are relatively untrained photographers. These are the snapshooters, the holiday or vacation practitioners, those who are interested primarily in recording an event or perhaps in capturing a "pretty" picture. Although the outer limits of this group include more serious amateur photographers who join camera clubs and perhaps develop their own films and photographs, the largest number of people in this category are likely to have somebody else (or the camera itself in contemporary "instant" photography) complete the photograph they have taken. In essence, photography by the people designates the work of largely untutored recordmakers.

Photography for the people is the third category of popular photography. It designates the realm of photomechanically reproduced imagery for advertising and information transmission of all kinds, whether in books, magazines, and newspapers, on handbills, bubble gum cards, or political campaign literature. This is clearly an enormous area for research, but it is one that must concern us least here, in part because it borders on areas explored by other analysts of popular culture, and in part because large numbers of people, although exposed to it, do not have the same direct involvement in the production of the imagery as they do in the other two categories of popular photography.

Photography as an artifact of popular culture, then, is most directly photography of the people or by the people: large numbers are exposed to it or engage in it. But unlike photography for the people, such as that taken by photojournalists, photography of or by the people is not translated into another visual medium; and unlike creative photography (photography despite the people?), popular photographers have less artistic and technical training and less desire to produce images for isolated aesthetic contemplation.

Although the world's first photograph, which was the result of an eight-hour exposure, has been dated to 1826, the first technique to receive worldwide acclaim was named by and for its inventor, Louis J. M. Daguerre. As early as 1837, Daguerre produced a permanent image on a daguerreotype, a thin, copper plate which he silvered, sensitized to light, exposed in a *camera obscura*, and developed in mercury vapor. The technical details of his process were made public at a joint meeting of the French Academy of Sciences and the Academy of Fine Arts on August 19, 1839; within five months, over thirty editions of Daguerre's manual had spread the details throughout Europe, to Russia, and to the United States.

Memoirs, letters, newspaper accounts, and cartoons reveal that the public at large was enamored of the "mirror with a memory," especially as refinements in the early 1840s shortened the exposure time and improved the image quality. Although landscapes and cityscapes were common subjects, portraiture was the most prevalent subject matter of daugerreotypes. In 1849, *Godey's Lady's Book* suggested that daguerreotypists were "limning faces at a rate that promises soon to make every man's house a Daguerreian Gallery." Such galleries, often quite elaborate, were opened in major American cities, while itinerant daguerreotypists found eager sitters in smaller towns and villages. To protect the delicate images from tarnish and abrasion, daguerreotypes were most often covered with a brass mat and glass and inserted in elaborately tooled leather cases, padded with silk or velvet. But they were also placed in brooches, medallions, and watch cases. Depending on size and competition, daguerreotype portraits ranged from twenty-five cents to fifty dollars; the average price usually fluctuated from two dollars to seven or eight dollars. In 1853, the *New York Herald Tribune* estimated that approximately three million American daguerreotypes were being produced annually.

Photography of the people soon benefited from additional inventions. Every daguerreotype was unique; although daguerreotype copies of daguerreotypes were made, the mass production of photographic images had to await not only a negative-positive system of picture making, but also a sufficiently detailed image to rival the precision of the daguerreotype. In France in 1850, L. D. Blanquart-Evrard announced his process of printing photographs on a thin paper coated with albumen. In England in 1851, Frederick Scott Archer made negatives composed of light-sensitive collodion on glass, obtaining a more precise image more quickly than had previous negative processes. Ambrotypes on glass, dating from about 1854, and melainotypes or ferrotypes (later called tintypes), dating from 1856, were based on Archer's collodion process. Until near the end of the century, however, the albumen paper print made from a collodion negative was the dominant process in photography.

Predicated on the replicability and mass production inherent in the negative-positive process, the *carte-de-visite* rose in popularity as the daguerreotype waned. *Cartes-de-visite*, patented in France by Disdéri in 1854, were small albumen portraits about 4 by 2½ inches, pasted on cards about 1/16 inch thick. They were made with a camera fitted with multiple lenses which enabled eight exposures to be made on the same negative. At the beginning of the 1860s, "cardomania" skyrocketed. In England, seventy thousand portraits of the Prince Consort were sold during the week following his death. In America during January 1861, the E. and H. T. Anthony Company, the largest photographic company in the nineteenth century, made one thousand portraits a day of Major Robert Anderson, who was a central figure in the attack on Fort Sumter. Images of other soldiers, and of poets, musicians, and entertainers were supplied to meet an insatiable demand. After Lincoln's assassination, photomontage *cartes* appeared of George Washington welcoming Lincoln into Heaven. One's ordinary, earthly neighbors also appeared in *cartes*. An advertisement in *Leslie's* on January 7, 1860, offered "Your Photograph On a Visiting Card: 25 Copies for One Dollar." Although they may not often have been left as calling cards, they were traded with friends and mailed to distant relatives, especially during the Civil War. Although Disdéri died a pauper, he became a millionaire on the strength of his patent. School children today continue the same ritual he first popularized.

The birth of the family album can be dated to 1860, when the photographic industry began to produce albums with specially cut-out pages for the insertion of *cartes*. At first they were only slightly larger than the *cartes*, but albums became more elaborate as picture formats changed. By 1870, the E. and H. T. Anthony Company listed nearly five hundred album styles. Some were simple, but many were lavish: they were several inches thick, leather-bound, gilt-edged, sometimes inlaid with mother-of-pearl, and usually fitted with heavy, engraved metal clasps. Such designs reflect the preciousness attached to photographs of the people.

The albumen print made at a photographer's studio remained the dominant form of photography of the people throughout the last four decades of the nineteenth century, but a variety of merchandising tactics gave the appearance of innovation. Although artificial, painted backdrops were used in England prior to 1851, they were relatively scarce in America during the 1840s and 1850s. Throughout the 1860s they became more common. In the comfort of the studio one could sit in front of a Greek temple or stand before a sylvan scene. Elaborate accessories proliferated—artificial rocks, rustic fences, plaster Grecian urns. In 1870, the studio of José Mora, one of the more flamboyant and successful New York City photographers, was equipped with fifty painted backgrounds—soon to grow to one hundred fifty. His clientele of socialites and celebrities could choose among "plains and mountains, tropic luxuriance and polar wastes," Egypt or Siberia. Matching the proliferation of backgrounds was a proliferation of image sizes. The "cabinet" size, about 4 by 6 inches, became popular in America about 1867. It brought new considerations about retouching negatives and posing sitters because poor technique and less "photogenic" subjects were more apparent in its larger size. "Boudoir" prints, "promenade" prints, and "imperial" prints followed in the 1870s—all were enterprising tactics to foster photography of the people.

Photography by the people can be dated, with some plausibility, to the rise of amateur exchange clubs in the 1850s in England and America. These small groups of people had sufficient funds and sufficient technical training to make their own images of their friends and surroundings. But the flowering of photography as practiced by the masses of people is more logically dated to 1888, when George Eastman announced his Kodak camera with the slogan, "You Push the Button, We Do the Rest." The Kodak was easily portable; it could be held in the hand and weighed only 1½ pounds. It was bought already loaded with a roll of film that would take one hundred circular photographs 2½ inches in diameter. When the roll was fully exposed, the camera was returned to the factory where it was unloaded, reloaded with fresh film, and returned to the owner along with the prints that had been developed from the first film. As Eastman wrote in the owner's manual, "Photography is thus brought within the reach of every human being who desires to preserve a record of what he sees. Such a photographic note book. . .enables the fortunate possessor to go back by the light of his own fireside to scenes which would otherwise fade from the memory and be lost."

The cost of the Kodak camera, together with its first roll of film, was twenty-five dollars; processing the exposed film and loading new film cost another ten dollars. By October 1889, the company was receiving sixty to seventy-five Kodaks and processing six to seven thousand negatives a day. By early 1900, thirty-five different Kodak cameras had been marketed. One of them, the "Brownie," was introduced especially for use by children; it cost one dollar and took six pictures on a roll of film that cost fifty cents to buy and develop. Over one hundred thousand were sold within a year in England and America. Numerous variations of its basic design kept it the most popular roll-film box camera, and it survived in one form or another essentially until the advent of the Instamatic camera in 1963.

In the twentieth century, photography of the people has continued despite the enormous increase in photography by the people, and despite the attack by fine-art photographers on studio portraiture at the turn of the century. The Photo-Secession Exhibition in 1902 and the opening of the Little Galleries of the Photo-Secession in 1905 were the culmination of a decade of increasing antagonism between those who desired to establish photography as an art form, those who practiced photography less seriously as a hobby in the Kodak manner, and those whose commercial aims were paramount. There is not sufficient space here to detail their various battles. But the assumptions behind commercial photography early in the century continued unchanged. Although softly focused imagery replaced the more excessive artificial backdrops of the late 1800s, studio portraiture continued to aim for revelation of "character," and studios continued to produce the formal family portrait, which reasserted solidarity and continuity in the face of social change. At the same time, studios cultivated their role in recording rites of passage: birthdays of children, graduations, weddings, and anniversaries. While the creative photographers whom Alfred Stieglitz chose to welcome to the Photo-Secession evolved into a small circle of confidantes, photographers of the people continued to hold to commercially successful conventions of portraiture. Meanwhile, hobbyists continued to look to burgeoning periodicals of amateur photography, such as *American Photography*, *Photo Era*, and *Photo-Beacon*, for advice on taking pictures. As snapshooters, they continued to indulge in an entertaining, relatively untaxing hobby.

The diverse innovations of twentieth-century photographic technology have attempted to cater to these contradictory aims. We shall note only the most important of these innovations.

The Leica camera was first marketed in 1925 and fully refined by 1932. Offered as a camera for professional photojournalists and serious amateurs, its innovative, compact design provided freedom of movement, while its thirty-five millimeter negative and excellent lens produced detailed images. As a relatively expensive camera, it created a market somewhere between the largest number of casual snapshooters and the professional photographers. While the inexpensive box camera evolved over the years into the Instamatic, the efficient design of the Leica spurred other manufacturers to produce the Contax, the Exakta, the Nikon, and other thirty-five millimeter cameras, and photography by the people spread further across the spectrum of economic and social classes.

Color photography had its first widely celebrated success in 1907, when the Lumière brothers (Auguste Marie, Louis Nicolas, and Louis Jean) marketed their Autochrome process, which produced a unique positive transparency, as did the Kodachrome film first marketed in 1935. In 1941, Kodacolor film was introduced; this negative film allowed any number of positives to be made. Today, the large majority of amateur photographs are in color, in either transparency or positive print form.

The industry's desire to increase photography by the people has not only spurred the invention of various color processes, but it has also led to increasingly simplified, automatic cameras. Photoelectric exposure meters were marketed in the early 1930s and incorporated into some cameras in 1938. Today, a wide range of fully automatic cameras has given new significance to the original Kodak slogan, "You Push the Button, We Do the Rest."

One of the most startling innovations in popular photography occurred despite Kodak's dominance in the marketplace. In 1947, Dr. Edwin Land announced the invention of his instant-picture process, and a year later the first Polaroid-Land camera went on sale. In 1956, the one millionth Polaroid camera was sold. Polaroid's series of innovations, such as shorter development times, more sensitive black-and-white film, instant color film (1963), and development outside the camera (1972), have all helped to make photography by the people easier and, some would say, as dramatic as the original daguerreotype process.

Photography of and by the people will continue to occupy a central position in American popular culture. The average number of photographs taken per household annually has increased from fifty-two in 1965, to seventy-five in 1970, to ninety-four in 1975. Almost thirty-four hundred drive-in photofinishing kiosks were operating in 1976; their yearly growth rate averages 20 percent. Magazines that cater to amateur photographers are thriving. Both *Modern Photography* and *Popular Photography*, begun in 1937, have current circulations of over five hundred thousand, and each month they treat their readers to an endless variety of product news, equipment testing, and picture-making tips. Studio photography—photography of the people—remains largely formal, but it has learned to adopt the candid styles and informal poses that some of these innovations have fostered. Photography by the people today reflects the same fascination with technical innovations and the same desire for effortless records and revelations that accompanied the rise of popular photography in the nineteenth century.*

BIBLIOGRAPHY

Benjamin, Walter. "The Work of Art in the Age of Mechanical Reproduction." In *Illuminations.* New York: Harcourt, Brace, and World, 1968, pp. 219-53.

Braive, Michel F. *The Era of the Photograph: A Social History.* Translated by David Britt. London: Thames and Hudson, 1966.

Darrah, William Culp. *Stereo Views: A History of Stereographs in America and Their Collection.* Gettysburg, Pa.: Times and New Publishing, 1964.

______. *The World of Stereographs.* Gettysburg, Pa.: William C. Darrah, 1977.

Gernsheim, Helmut, and Alison Gernsheim. *The History of Photography from the Camera Obscura to the Beginning of the Modern Era.* 2d ed. New York: McGraw-Hill, 1969.

Halpern, Steven. "Souvenirs of Experience: The Victorian Studio Portrait and the Twentieth-Century Snapshot." In *The Snapshot.* Edited by Jonathan Green. Millerton, N.Y.: Aperture, 1974, pp. 64-67.

Jenkins, Reese. *Images and Enterprise: Technology and the American Photographic Industry, 1839-1925.* Baltimore: Johns Hopkins University Press, 1976.

Jussim, Estelle. *Visual Communication and the Graphic Arts: Photographic Technologies in the Nineteenth Century.* New York: R. R. Bowker, 1974.

Kotkin, Amy. "The Family Photo Album as a Form of Folkore." *Exposure,* 16 (March 1978), 4-8.

Kozloff, Max. *Photography and Fascination.* Danbury, N.H.: Addison House, 1978.

Lesy, Michael. *Wisconsin Death Trip.* New York: Pantheon-Random House, 1973.

______. *Time Frames: The Meaning of Family Pictures.* New York: Pantheon-Random House, 1980.

Lyons, Nathan, and Edward Earle, eds. *Points of View: The Stereograph in America: A Cultural History.* Rochester, N.Y.: Visual Studies Workshop Press, 1979.

Newhall, Beaumont. *The History of Photography from 1839 to the Present Day.* Rev. and enl. ed. New York: Museum of Modern Art, 1964.

______. *The Daguerreotype in America.* 3d rev. ed. New York: Dover, 1976.

______, comp. "Photography." In *Arts in America: A Bibliography.* Edited by Bernard Karpel. Washington, D.C.: Smithsonian Institution Press, 1979.

______, ed. *Photography: Essays and Images.* New York: Museum of Modern Art, 1980.

Ohrn, Karin Becker. "Making Belief: Contexts for Family Photography." Unpublished paper presented at the Biennial Convention, American Studies Association, Boston, October 1977.

*Many of the details in this brief outline have been derived from Beaumont Newhall's *The History of Photography from 1839 to the Present Day,* and from Robert Taft's *Photography and the American Scene: A Social History, 1839-1889.*

Peters, Marsha, and Bernard Mergen. "'Doing the Rest': The Uses of Photographs in American Studies." *American Quarterly,* 29 (1977), 280-303.

Rudisill, Richard. *Mirror Image: The Influence of the Daguerreotype on American Society.* Albuquerque: University of New Mexico Press, 1971.

Sontag, Susan. *On Photography.* New York: Farrar, Strauss and Giroux, 1977.

Stott, William *Documentary Expression and Thirties America.* New York: Oxford University Press, 1973.

Taft, Robert. *Photography and the American Scene: A Social History, 1839-1889.* 1938. Reprint. New York: Dover, 1964.

Thomas, Alan. *Time in a Frame: Photography and the Nineteenth-Century Mind.* New York: Schocken, 1977.

Trachtenberg, Alan. "Introduction: Photographs as Symbolic History." In *The American Image: Photographs from the National Archives, 1860-1960.* National Archives and Record Service. New York: Pantheon Books, 1979, pp. ix-xxxii.

Welling, William *Photography in America: The Formative Years 1839-1900.* New York: Thomas Y. Crowell, 1978.

Physical Fitness

Claudius W. Griffin

America has been concerned about physical fitness (the older term was physical culture) from the country's beginnings. Benjamin Franklin, himself an avid swimmer, advocated lifting weights, sleeping in cold rooms, and drinking great quantities of water to obtain fitness and health. In a letter to Thomas M. Randolph, Jr., in 1787, Thomas Jefferson said, "The time necessary to secure [health] by active exercises, should be devoted to it in preference to every other pursuit."[1] And Noah Webster, in his *Address to Young Gentlemen* in 1790, said that it should be "the business of young persons to assist nature and strengthen the growing frame by athletic exercises."[2] Also in 1790, Secretary of the Department of War Henry Knox proposed to Congress a plan to use the schools as training areas to improve the physical fitness of youth eighteen to twenty years old.

During the nineteenth century, there were three major periods of interest in physical fitness in the United States: the 1830s, the 1860s, and the 1880s. During the 1830s, four different fitness systems became popular. The first stressed the drill and discipline of military academy. Both Pierre Thomas, a Frenchman who was appointed physical educator at West Point in 1814, and Captain Alden Partridge, who opened his first military school at Norwich, Vermont, in 1819, stressed this form of exercise for their students.

About ten years later, Dr. Charles Beck and Charles Follen, two German reformers who had fled repression in Germany, brought the Jahn system of gymnastics to the United States. For Friedrich Jahn, founder of this system of gymnastics, the purpose of exercise was to help German youth grow and develop so that they could free his country from the domination of the French and unite Germany as a democracy. Thus Jahn's system, which was later to influence the United States more heavily through the Turner movement, grew out of and always stressed democracy and social reform. Follen introduced the system at Harvard in 1826, and established the first outdoor gymnasium, consisting of exercise apparatus such as bars, ladders, and ropes. Beck introduced the same system at the Round Hill School in Northampton,

Massachusetts. Following the lead of Follen at Harvard, a few universities, such as Yale, Brown, Amherst, Williams, Charleston, and Bowdoin, organized outdoor gymnasiums and encouraged gymnastic exercises.

A third fitness system, much more natively American, was based on the idea of getting fitness through manual labor. In 1831, leaders of this movement met in New York and organized the Society for Promoting Manual Labor in Literary Institutions. Basing their ideas on the Biblical evidence that God had ordained manual labor, followers of this system advocated the idea that manual labor was the best form of exercise.

A fourth system, also natively American, was the system of calisthenics for girls and women introduced by Catherine E. Beecher in female seminaries in Hartford and Cincinnati. Through simple movements accompanied by music, she aimed to produce grace, good carriage, and sound health.

A second period of emphasis on fitness came in the 1860s, with the introduction of Dr. Dio Lewis's new gymnastics for men, women, and children. Lewis, who attacked the popular notion that great strength was the mark of well-being and that gymnastics was primarily for gymnasts, directed his system to the "fat men, the feeble men, young boys and females of all ages—the classes most needing physical training."[3] His exercises, usually a series of movements performed with handheld implements, were designed to build not strength but flexibility, agility, and general health. Lewis introduced his system in the vicinity of Boston in 1860; it soon became so popular that it was taught in evening classes throughout the area. His book, *The New Gymnastics for Men, Women and Children,* was published in 1862. Feeling that the presence of a teacher was important to fitness development, he began his Normal Institute of Physical Education in Boston in 1861 to train teachers of physical education.

The 1850s and 1860s also saw a resurgence of gym building. In 1853, the University of Virginia constructed a wooden gym; it was followed shortly by the building of brick and stone gyms at Harvard, Yale, and Amherst and later at Princeton and Miami University of Ohio. Thomas Wentworth Higginson, in an article published in the *Atlantic Monthly* for 1861, described public gyms admiringly:

> It is one good evidence of the increasing interest in these exercises, that the American gymnasiums built during the past year or two have surpassed all their predecessors in size and completeness, and have probably no superiors in the world. The Seventh Regiment Gymnasium in New York, just opened by Mr. Abner S. Brady, is one hundred and eighty feet by fifty-two, in its main hall, and thirty-five feet in height, with nearly one thousand pupils. The beautiful hall of the Metropolitan Gymnasium, in Chicago, measures one hundred and eight feet by eighty, and is twenty feet high at the sides, with a dome in the centre, forty feet high, and the same in diameter. Next to these probably rank the new gymnasiums at Cincinnati, the Tremont Gymnasium at Boston, and the Bunker Hill Gymnasium at Charleston, all recently opened.[4]

In 1879, the beginning of the third period of interest in fitness, Mr. Augustus Hemenway gave $110,000 for a new gym to be built at Harvard. Dr. Dudley Allen Sargent, a physician and director of a private gym in New York City, was appointed assistant professor of physical training and director of the Hemenway Gymnasium. Sargent's contribution to the development of fitness was to focus on the individual. Because he believed students were different in physical makeup and physical needs, he developed elaborate measurements of the strength of various parts of the body as well as ways to examine the heart and lungs. This data was then compared to a standard for a given age, and an individual set of exercises was prescribed.

The 1880s saw the second great era of gym building. Colleges such as Smith, Lehigh, Cornell, Tufts, and Johns Hopkins all built gyms. By 1909, 114 colleges had gymnasiums. Physical education departments also began at this time. By 1909, 111 colleges had some sort of physical education department that gave regular instruction in gymnastics.

During the 1890s, a number of movements and people stimulated the growth of fitness. Probably the major influence was the Turner movement, which had begun in the 1840s, diminished in the 1860s, and surged again in the late 1880s and 1890s. In 1848, revolutionary movements had swept over Europe; the German government in particular suppressed demands for a liberal government. As a result of this suppression, thousands of liberal Germans migrated to the United States. Soon these immigrants formed German gymnastic societies, called Turnvereins. The two oldest Turnvereins were organized in Cincinnati and New York in 1848. By 1852 twenty-two such societies had been organized throughout the North.

Emmett A. Rice, in *A Brief History of Physical Education,* describes the Turnvereins in this way:

> The aims of the Turnvereine were to promote physical education, intellectual enlightenment and sociability among members. The Turnvereine building was always provided with a gymnasium where classes in the German system of exercises were conducted for men, women, and children. The teachers in the early period were men who had had experience in Germany. Outdoor games and gymnastic meets and exhibitions were frequent. Education and enlightenment on social problems, political issues and American life in general was accomplished through the library, through lectures, debates and the schools. An atmosphere of brotherhood and friendship pervaded all the activities of the society.[5]

While interest in the movement had fallen off in the 1860s, it picked up again by the 1880s and 1890s. During the 1880s, the number of Turnvereins increased from 186 to 277, and total membership increased from 13,387 to 35,912. The primary influence of the Turners was on physical education in the schools. When leading cities began to introduce systematic exercise and games into school programs, the Turners contributed their long experience and well-trained leaders. Between 1885 and 1890, Kansas City, Chicago, Davenport, Cleveland, St. Louis, and Sandusky accepted physical education as part of regular school activity. All these programs were led by prominent Turners, graduates of the Turner normal college.

But other movements and systems also influenced the development of physical fitness during this period. The Swedish Movement Cure, a system of medical gymnastics from Sweden, thought to be the remedy for certain afflictions, became popular in the 1880s. In the early 1890s, the Delsarte System of Physical Culture also became popular. The creator of this system, Francois Delsarte, a French vocal and dramatic teacher, had developed certain physical exercises to train his students. Adding their own ideas, American teachers of education developed a system of exercises that claimed to produce poise, grace, beauty of face and figure, and health. The system came to be thought of as psycho-physical culture, unifying the body and the mind.

The YMCA, an organization formed in the 1840s to improve the spiritual condition of young men engaged in the trades, had been influenced by the interest in gymnastics that had swept the country in the 1850s. By 1860 the national convention favored the establishment of gymnasiums as "a safeguard against the allurement of objectionable places of resort, which have proved the ruin of thousands of the youth of our country."[6] Robert J. Roberts, the first important physical director of the YMCA, steered its approach to fitness between the two extremes of an emphasis on strength and endurance through difficult feats and the Dio Lewis system of working with very light apparatus. In 1887 the YMCA added a physical department to its newly opened International Training School in Springfield, Massachusetts, to train physical directors for the organization. Dr. Luther Gulick, made head of the department after Roberts resigned, helped increase the number of physical directors from 50 in 1887 to 244 in 1900. For Dr. Gulick, physical training was a vital part of the association program; it worked not only for the body but for the physical and spiritual development of the whole man.

The playground movement, which began in Boston in 1885, also contributed to the development of physical fitness. The first playgrounds were little more than sand gardens for young children, supervised by kindergarten teachers. But soon schoolyards were being designated as playgrounds. In 1889, Boston established a recreation center at Charles Bank, with outdoor gymnasiums and buildings equipped for men, women, and children. New York began to establish playgrounds in 1888, and Chicago followed in 1896 with an outdoor gymnasium and two swimming pools for Douglass Park. By 1900 Philadelphia, Pittsburgh, Baltimore, Hartford, New Haven, San Francisco, and Albany had begun playgrounds.

To the popular mind, one of the most entertaining chapters in the history of physical fitness was created by the strong men of Europe and America and their favorite activity, weight lifting. Weight lifting began in Germany and other Central European countries in the middle of the nineteenth century. Famous European strong men were such giants as Josef Steinbach, Karl Swoboda, and Herman Goerner; others were Arthur Saxon and George Hackenschmidt. Weight lifting began in athletic clubs and in the back rooms of taverns; the strong men performed prodigious feats of strength for crowds in taverns, gymnasiums, and circuses. They were usually heavy, with enormous girths, which came from drinking quantities of beer and eating starchy food.

In the late nineteenth and early twentieth centuries, European strong men toured the United States, entertaining audiences with their feats. The most famous was Eugene Sandow, a trim, well-proportioned showman managed by Florenz Ziegfeld. Other strong men, like the gigantic Canadian Louis Cyr and Warren Lincoln Davis of the United States, became famous. They stimulated a wave of strength seeking in America. In 1903, Alan Calvert began the mail order strength business by establishing the Milo Barbell company. Later he published his book *Super Strength* and a small magazine *Strength.* Much later, in 1938, Bob Hoffman began publishing his magazine *Strength and Health,* which is still being published today, and in 1936 he established the York Barbell company. His York Barbell Club won U.S. weight lifting championships, and in 1940 his Olympic club team won nearly every class.

Part of the history of weight lifting are the "Mr." contests. The Mr. America contest began in 1939 and was followed by the Mr. World and Mr. Universe contests. After World War II, these contests sprang up everywhere. Every small town or section had its "Mr. Greenville" or "Mr. South Bronx" contest. These contests probably did as much harm to strength building as good, for participants did not focus on total fitness but on developing ("pumping up" it was called) certain muscles.

At the end of the nineteenth century, physical fitness had become a major concern in the United States. It was being developed in the schools, in organizations such as the YMCA and the Boy Scouts, on public playgrounds, in gymnasiums, and even in circuses and on the stage. What stands out in the first twenty years of the twentieth century are not any new movements but one organization and two men. The organization was the American Association for the Advancement of Physical Education, created in 1885 and later called the American Physical Education Association. It appointed a committee to develop a set of body and strength measurements that would describe the ideal man and then to create a program of physical education to achieve this ideal. But realizing that such measurements did not measure the efficiency of the body in motion, Dr. Dudley Sargent, mentioned earlier in connection with the Hemenway Gymnasium at Harvard, tried to identify the basic abilities common to many forms of gymnastics and athletics. In 1902, he published his "Universal Test for Strength, Speed, and Endurance." This change, from a static to a dynamic concept of fitness, shifted the emphasis from gymnastics to athletics as the way to develop fitness. Ever since, U.S. physical education has emphasized sports, dance, and other "natural" activities.

Two individuals stand out in the history of fitness during this period. The first, Bernarr Macfadden, was the principal advocate of physical culture in the United States. Macfadden emphasized not only the development of muscular strength but the "strengthening of the entire assimilative and vital system."[7] Even better known are the contributions of President Theodore Roosevelt to the development of fitness. Everyone knows the story of how, with his father's inspiration, Roosevelt exercised in a gym regularly as a child, overcoming his asthma. In *The Strenuous Life,* he said: "In the last analysis a healthy state can exist only when the men and women who make it up lead clean, vigorous, healthy lives; when the children are so trained that they shall endeavor, not to shirk difficulties, but to overcome them; not to seek ease, but to know how to wrest triumph for toil and risk."[8]

Roosevelt was true to his word. During his second administration he discovered that the officers of the U.S. military were not in good shape. On December 2, 1907, he directed the secretary of war to begin a program of annual physical qualification in the U.S. Army, suggesting it be three consecutive days of forced cavalry marches. During the next year he asked that both the Navy and Marines institute similar programs. On January 13, 1909, to shame the Army for complaining against his order to keep fit, Roosevelt himself rode one hundred miles from Washington, D.C., to Warrenton, Virginia, over rough roads.

The story of fitness during the first half of the twentieth century is predominately an up-down history of a nation becoming intensely concerned about the state of its fitness during wartime and apathetic during peace time. During World War I, so many men were rejected from the armed services (during 1915-16, almost 82 percent) that the nation aroused itself. A number of states passed legislation making physical education mandatory in the schools. Soon fitness was much improved. At the end of the war, George E. Fisher said the men who served in the military were "in better condition than any similar number of men have ever been at one time in the United States."[9]

Unfortunately, with the prosperity of the 1920s, America forgot fitness. During the Depression which followed, rural youth migrated in masses to the cities. But even though recreation facilities for them grew, interest in physical fitness waned. At the beginning of World War II, once again the nation became concerned about its level of fitness and preparedness for war. In 1940, the physical endurance of a number of draftees was tested by the classic Harvard Step Test, and, with the exception of farm boys and ex-athletes, the men performed no better than the women. Once again, the number of draftees failing their physical examination because they were unfit was thought to be inordinately high.

The nation mobilized itself. National meetings were held, presidential orders were issued, national committees on fitness were formed, and even councils combining committees with organizations such as the American Medical Association were formed. Again, the government focused on fitness in the schools. A series of pamphlets, brochures, news articles, and fitness manuals were published.

New tests for fitness were developed, and new programs were tried in all branches of the military. Even industry became concerned. The recreation department of the C.I.O., for example, developed a physical fitness program. In spite of all these efforts, one-third of the nation's draftees were still considered unfit for duty. A Senate subcommittee investigated the problem. At the conclusion of its hearings, Senator Claude Pepper, the chairman, stated: "We have learned a profound lesson about the effects of sickness and physical and mental defects. This lesson has been driven home to us by the alarming fact that more than four million young men have been found ineligible for military service.[10]

Unfortunately, the nation had not seemed to learn its lesson, for interest in fitness waned almost as soon as the war was over. During the Korean War, General Hershey, director of Selective Service, reported that the rejection rate of inductees was 50 percent. Even this figure did not stir the public.

But the public did wake up in 1953 when Dr. Hans Kraus and Dr. Sonja Weber reported the results of years of research. Their minimum muscular fitness tests, which were simple strength and flexibility tests, were given to 4,264 American children and 2,870 children in Austria, Italy, and Switzerland. A shocking 57.9 percent of the American children failed, compared with 8.7 percent of the European children. President Eisenhower had Vice President Nixon convene a Conference on the Fitness of American Youth to deal with the problem. On advice from the conference, the president established the President's Council on Youth Fitness and the President's Citizens Advisory Committee on the Fitness of American Youth on July 16, 1956. Groups such as the American Association of Health, Physical Education, and Recreation, the YMCA, and the NCAA also called national conferences.

The result was a national focus on fitness. More national conferences were called by the president, forums on fitness were held, fitness tests were developed, and research studies of the relationship between exercise and fitness, heart disease and exercise, and fitness and age were begun. Knowledge about fitness and its relation to health expanded dramatically.

Interest in fitness remained high during the first years of the Kennedy administration. While he was still campaigning, Kennedy was asked by *Sports Illustrated* to write an article about the importance of sports and physical fitness in American life. In his article, Kennedy called the state of fitness in the United States "a national problem" that "requires national action."[11] He took such action just a month after coming to office by calling a Conference on Youth Fitness, at which he personally addressed the delegates. In July 1961, the President's Council on Youth Fitness released its *Youth Physical Fitness* booklet, which outlined a program for achieving fitness in the schools.

In the middle and late 1960s, books outlining systematic, step-by-step ways to achieve fitness began to appear. One of the first was the *Royal*

Canadian Air Force Exercise Plans for Physical Fitness published in 1962; in 1968 Major Kenneth Cooper published his *Aerobics,* a system that allowed for a variety of ways to achieve and maintain cardiovascular fitness.

Probably it was Cooper's work that stimulated the current interest in running, jogging, and racing, for he felt that jogging was one of the most efficient ways to become fit. Whatever the case, the decade of the 1970s became the decade of the runner. The bookstores are full of new books on running, and there are over fifty magazines and newsletters on the subject.

At last Americans seem to have become aware of the need for fitness. It is not fashionable anymore to have a paunch or to smoke. Suddenly the streets are full of runners, and fitness centers are booming. Perhaps physical fitness has finally come of age in America.

NOTES

1. Julian P. Boyd, ed., *The Papers of Thomas Jefferson,* 18 vols. (Princeton: Princeton University Press, 1955), 11 (January 1 to August 6, 1787), 558.

2. Noah Webster, *Address to Young Gentlemen* (1790), as quoted in Emmett A. Rice, *A Brief History of Physical Education* (New York: Barnes, 1936), pp. 159-60.

3. As quoted in Rice, p. 176.

4. Thomas Wentworth Higginson, "Gymnastics," *Atlantic Monthly,* 7 (March 1861), 283-302, reprinted in *Chronicle of American Physical Education, 1855-1930,* ed. Aileene S. Lockhard and Betty Spears (Dubuque, Iowa: Wm. C. Brown, 1972), pp. 32-33.

5. Rice, p. 162.

6. C. Howard Hopkins, *History of the Y.M.C.A. in North America* (New York: Associated Press, 1951), pp. 33-34.

7. Bernarr Macfadden, *Macfadden's System of Physical Training* (New York: Hulbert, 1895), p. 6, as quoted in Cyril F. Dean, "A Historical Study of Physical Fitness in the United States, 1790 through 1961" (Ph. D. dissertation, George Peabody College for Teachers, 1964), p. 35.

8. Theodore Roosevelt, *The Strenuous Life: Essays and Addresses* (New York: Century, 1899), p. 3.

9. George E. Fisher, "Points of Emphasis in a Post-War Program of Physical Training," *American Physical Education Review,* 24 (1919), 126, as quoted in Dean, p. 35.

10. *New York Times,* July 10, 1944, as quoted in Dean, p. 93.

11. John F. Kennedy, "The Soft American," *Sports Illustrated,* 13 (December 1960), 17.

BIBLIOGRAPHY

Barney, Robert Knight. "Physical Education and Sport in North America." In *History of Physical Education and Sport.* Edited by Earle F. Zeigler. Englewood Cliffs, N.J.: Prentice-Hall, 1979, pp. 171-227.

Carolan, Patrick. "The History, Development, and Evaluation of a Federal Emphasis on Physical Fitness in Civilian Defense, 1940-1945." Ph.D. dissertation, Columbia University, 1952.

Cooper, Kenneth H. *Aerobics.* New York: Evans, 1968.

Dean, Cyril F. "A Historical Study of Physical Fitness in the United States, 1790 through 1961." Ph.D. dissertation, George Peabody College for Teachers, 1964.

Dictionary Catalog of the Applied Life Sciences Library (Formerly Physical Education Library), University of Illinois at Urbana-Champaign, Vols. 1-4. Boston: Hall, 1977.

Drew, Gwendolyn A. "A Historical Study of the Concern of the Federal Government for the Physical Fitness of Non-Age Youth with Reference to the Schools, 1790-1941." Ph.D. dissertation, University of Pittsburgh, 1944.

Eddy, Sherwood. *A Century with Youth: A History of the Y.M.C.A. from 1844 to 1944.* New York: Associated Press, 1944.

Fixx, James F. *The Complete Book of Running.* New York: Random House, 1977.

Hackensmith, C. W. *History of Physical Education.* New York: Harper & Row, 1966.

Higginson, Thomas Wentworth. "Gymnastics." *Atlantic Monthly,* 7 (March 1861), 283-302.

Hopkins, C. Howard. *History of the Y.M.C.A. in North America.* New York: Associated Press, 1951.

Larson, Leonard E., ed. *Fitness, Health, and Work Capacity: International Standards for Assessment.* New York: Macmillan, 1974.

______, and Herbert Michelman. *International Guide to Fitness and Health.* New York: Crown, 1973.

Leonard, Fred Eugene. "German-American Gymnastic Societies and the North American Turnerbund." *American Physical Education Review,* 15 (December 1910), 617-28.

______. *Pioneers of Modern Physical Training.* New York: Associated Press, 1915.

______. "A Select Bibliography of the History of Physical Training." *American Physical Education Review,* 7 (March 1902), 39-48.

______, and George B. Afflect. A *Guide to the History of Physical Education.* 3d ed. Philadelphia: Lea & Febiger, 1947.

Lewis, Dio. "New Gymnastics." *American Journal of Education,* 11 (1862), 531-56; 12 (1863), 665-700.

______. *The New Gymnastics for Men, Women, and Children.* 8th ed. Boston: Ticknor and Fields, 1864.

Lockhard, Aileene S., and Betty Spears, eds. *Chronicle of American Physical Education, Selected Readings, 1855-1930.* Dubuque, Iowa: Wm. C. Brown, 1972.

Metzner, Henry. *A Brief History of the American Turnerbund.* Translated by Theodore Stempfel. Rev. ed. Pittsburgh: National Executive Committee of the American Turnerbund, 1924.

Michener, James A. *Sports in America.* New York: Random House, 1976.

Rice, Emmett A. *A Brief History of Physical Education.* New York: Barnes, 1936.

Staley, Seward C., et al. *Exercise and Fitness: A Collection of Papers Presented at the Colloquium on Exercise and Fitness.* Monticello: University of Illinois College of Physical Education and The Athletic Institute, 1959.

Zeigler, Earle F. *History of Physical Education and Sport.* Englewood Cliffs, N.J.: Prentice-Hall, 1979.

Pornography

Paul P. Somers, Jr.,
and Nancy Pogel

The student seeking out the beginnings of American pornography will hardly be surprised to learn that, along with introducing to America the volunteer fire department, the lending library, and the editorial cartoon, Benjamin Franklin was the first American to own a copy of John Clelland's *Fanny Hill; Or Memoirs of a Woman of Pleasure* (1747). Further, his "Advice to a Young Man on Choosing a Mistress" (1745) was the first indigenous work circulated as pornography. His burlesque, "A Letter to the Royal Academy at Brussels," purporting to have discovered a scientific way to deodorize farts, was written sometime between 1772 and 1782 and circulated in manuscript, and the "Speech of Polly Baker" was published in London's *Gentleman's Magazine* in 1747.

In 1810, Isaiah Thomas of Worcester, Massachusetts, put out the first American edition of *Fanny Hill,* a limited edition under the faked imprint "G. Fenton, 1747." (Understandably, the faked imprint is a protective artifice employed by writers and sellers of erotica, depending on the legality of the enterprise in their particular time and locale.) Pressure from authorities forced him to destroy the unbound editions in 1814.

In 1846 the Irishman William Haynes began to publish erotic books in New York, and the 1850s saw the rise to prominence of George Thompson. Under pseudonyms, the most famous of which was "Greenhorn," he wrote hundreds of pornographic novels such as *The G'hals of Boston* (1850) and *The Delights of Love; Or, The Lady Liberated* (ca. 1850). *Fanny Greely; Or, The Confessions of a Free-Love Sister Written by Herself* (ca. 1850) exploited the story of John Humphrey Noyes's scandalous Perfectionist sect at Oneida, New York, which had been driven out by its outraged neighbors. Also in the 1850s, a series of erotic pocket volumes was published in New Orleans.

The Civil War proved a predictable impetus to pornographers. *Cupid's Own Library* offered to soldiers erotic volumes costing twenty-five cents, fifty cents, and one dollar. *The Rakish Rhymer* (date unknown), an erotic songbook, was widely circulated. Graphic pornography will be discussed later, but obscene prints and photographs circulated among Civil War soldiers and officers.

Among print pornography is Samuel Clemens's scatological satire, *1601: A Conversation as It Was at the Social Fireside in the Time of the Tudors.* Clemens wrote it around 1879 and dedicated it to his friend, the Reverend Joseph Twichell. It was first printed in a limited edition of one hundred copies at the U.S. Military Academy at West Point. H. Montgomery Hyde states that over forty U.S. editions had appeared by 1964. Clemens's *Some Thoughts on the Science of Onanism* (1879), from a speech given by Clemens in 1879 before the Stomach Club, while considered stylistically inferior, has also enjoyed considerable notoriety.

Otherwise, late nineteenth-century fanciers of pornography could always turn to *National Police Gazette,* a barbershop favorite featuring lurid stories of sex and seduction. Pornographic daguerrotypes were increasing in vogue when the first motion picture films were made in 1894. As far as is known, the first pornographic films appeared shortly after, in 1896. So significant was this development to the history of American pornography that its chronicling will require a separate section.

Like Samuel Clemens, many other popular authors wrote pornographic works, primarily for circulation in manuscript among their friends. One of these covert classics was Eugene Field's *Only a Boy* (1896), which was distributed clandestinely but enjoyed a notoriety much wider and greater than its author had originally intended. His homoerotic verse "When Willie Wet the Bed" was printed in some medical journals in the 1880s.

A turn-of-the-century work that is often mentioned in surveys of American pornography is the sado-masochistic *The Memoirs of Dolly Morton; the Story of a Woman's Part in the Struggle to Free the Slaves* (1904). According to Hyde, the book was published in Paris by Charles Carrington, the infamous seller and publisher of pornographic books.[1] It was popular in America and Europe and is said to deal more frankly with the psychology of slavery than does *Uncle Tom's Cabin,* which was "also a favourite with devotees of the whip in spite of its high moral tone."

Some idea of the strictness of American censorship during the Victorian period and after may be gained from a look at the legal difficulties of Theodore Dreiser. In 1900 *Sister Carrie* was withdrawn from the bookstores after a public outcry over its "immorality," even though it contained no explicit descriptions of erotic activity. Merely depicting an "immoral" way of life without condemning or punishing its practitioners was enough to get an author in trouble. In 1916 Dreiser's *The Genius* was banned in Cincinnati, and his publisher withdrew the book when threatened with prosecution.

In 1917 Charles Carrington reissued *The Rakish Rhymer* from the Civil War period as *Some Yarns.* The only extant copy is in the Kinsey collection at the Institute for Sex Research. *My Lives and Loves* (1925-29), the erotic autobiography of Frank Harris, has some claim to inclusion in a survey of American pornography, since its first volume was written in America, although it was published in Germany. Volumes 2 through 4 were written and printed in France. U.S. customs officials were ever alert to keep works such as *My Lives and Loves* out of the country. There was considerable pressure to import such works, for erotic literature flourished in France between the years 1926 and 1956. Olympia Press, for example, published numerous titles.

In 1927 the first volume of *Anecdota Americana* appeared with the false imprint "Joseph Fliesler, ed., Boston." According to Legman in *The Horn Book,* it was probably published in New York by Humphrey Adams.[2] The second volume came out in 1934. The 1930s were also marked by several anonymous American supplements to *My Secret Life,* such as *Marital Frolics* (1934), and by the flourishing of the "eight-pagers."

The eight-pagers were a form of pornography that was quite close to folk art. Originating perhaps in the 1920s, they were small, anonymously drawn comic books (their alternate name, "Tijuana Bibles," gives a clue to one source) which depicted popular cartoon characters such as Popeye, Henry, and so forth, engaged in explicitly erotic activity. They were disseminated variously by distributors of erotic films and naughty novelties and by traveling salesmen, truck drivers, carnival people, and other mobile individuals. Their customers were primarily blue collar and lower-level white collar workers, who had neither the money for "dirty movies" (eight-pagers reached their peak during the Depression) nor the education for more literary erotica. Their popularity waned during World War II and revived briefly in the late 1940s. They disappeared in the 1950s.

The 1930s were a decade of legal battles, such as the famous *Ulysses* decision of 1933. Judge John Woolsey of the U.S. District Court for the Southern District of New York ruled that James Joyce's *Ulysses* was not obscene, and the New York Circuit Court of Appeals upheld his decision. In 1950 folklorist Vance Randolph produced his "unprintable" collection, *Pissing in the Snow and Other Ozark Folktales,* which was long available only in the Library of Congress and at the Institute for Sex Research. At the end of the decade, in 1959, Grove Press published the unexpurgated edition of D. H. Lawrence's *Lady Chatterly's Lover.* In between these years, the decade was characterized by soft-core eroticism. In addition to the obligatory sex scenes in works by major authors such as Erskine Caldwell and Norman Mailer, titillating fiction was provided consistently by Pyramid, Beacon, and other paperback publishers.[3] Orrie Hitt and Jack Woodford were two of the writers who supplied this material. Soft-core continued into the 1960s, although the publication of *Fanny Hill* by G. P. Putnam in 1963 extended somewhat the boundaries of what was permissible.

Events in France had had a strong influence on American publishing of erotic materials with at least some pretense to literary merit, for the French government had begun prosecuting Olympia Press in 1956. According to Michael Perkins in *The Secret Record: Modern Erotic Literature,* "by the early sixties Girodias was confronted with an eighty-year ban on his publishing activities, a six-year prison sentence and a sizable fine; every book he published—including *Lolita*—was banned as soon as it appeared."[4] The French crackdown, plus the relaxing of U.S. censorship, led Girodias to move Olympia Press to New York in 1967. He reissued Olympia's classics and also moved to develop a stable of native erotic authors which eventually included writers of erotic satire such as Ed Martin, Jett Sage, and George Kimball; erotic biographers such as Diane di Prima; surrealists such as Lola Seftali, Renee Auden, Barry Malzberg, and Doreen Peckinpah; and employers of a naturalistic narrative form: Marco Vassi, Angelo d'Arcangelo, and Clarence Major.

In the same year (1967) Milton Luros of Parliament News in North Hollywood undertook an erotic publishing venture reportedly as artistically ambitious as Olympia's. Under the editorship of Brian Kirby, the resultant lines, Brandon House (1967) and, especially, Essex House (1968), Parliament News became the West Coast equivalent of Olympia Press, both for the reprinting of erotic classics and the introduction of new authors. What raised the writers of Essex House above the level of ordinary pornographic writers was not only their superior talent (Kirby forbade the use of pseudonyms) and, in many instances, their willingness to experiment with the form of the novel but also, according to Michael Perkins, their incorporation into their novels of the goals of the youth revolution of the 1960s, which they shared with the somewhat more sophisticated writers of the Olympia Press. Notable Essex House writers include poets Charles Bukowski, *Notes of a Dirty Old Man* (1969), David Meltzer, *How Many Blocks in the Pile?* (1968), Hank Stine, *Thrill City* (1969), Charles McNaughton, Jr., *Mindblower* (1969), Richard E. Geis, *Raw-Meat* (1969), Alice Ramirez, *The Geek* (1969), Paul V. Dallas, *Binding with Briars* (1968), P. N. Dedeaux, *Tender Buns* (1969), Barry Luck, *Gropie* (1969), and well-known science fiction writer, Philip José Farmer, *The Image of the Beast* (1968), *Blown* (1969), and *A Feast Unknown* (1969). Concerned as he is with the literary potential of erotic writing, Perkins concludes that, in spite of possible immaturity, the Essex House novels "considered as a body of work...are the fresh, energetic beginnings of a new erotic literature."[5]

If some of the best erotic novels grew out of the political and social rebelliousness of the late 1960s, so did some of the most vigorous American art. Inspired by the eight-pagers of earlier years, Robert Crumb and S. Clay Wilson began in 1968 to draw adult comic books with titles like *Snatch* and *Jiz*. Underground comics such as these reflected the rebellion of that generation by depicting graphically, sometimes realistically and sometimes grotesquely, sex organs and acts. Crumb was probably the most prominent of the underground cartoonists, although, according to Mike Barrier, "Wilson's work has far more to do with real pornography than does Crumb's since it reflects the fear and disgust felt by pornography readers."[6] Such sex hatred and fear is expressed typically by a cartoon from *Death Rattle* No. 1 (1972), which shows a man making love to a vampirish woman who in the final panel chews off his penis.

Women artists among the underground cartoonists reacted against the sexism of their male counterparts. Some of them were Shary Flenniken (presently an editor of *National Lampoon* and creator of "Trots and Bonnie"), Trina Robbins *(It Ain't Me Babe Comix* and *Tales of Sex and Death),* Willy Mendes, and Meredith Kurtzman. As Mark Estren writes, "Underground cartoonists are preoccupied with sex (as is everyone in our culture), and there is sexism—both kinds. Their irreverence will be their biggest contribution, sexually speaking."[7]

The alacrity with which artists adapt each new art form to the purpose of pornography testifies to its eternal vitality: the Institute for Sex Research has pornographic daguerrotypes dating back to 1839. As mentioned above, the artistic medium of film was used to treat sexual themes and subjects almost from its inception in 1894. Sketchy records exist of some early French erotic films, *Le Bain* (1896) and *Le Voyeur* (1907). In the United States, May Irwin and John Rice delighted audiences and dismayed moral guardians in the essentially innocent *The Kiss* (1896). Edison's camera recorded Fatima, the sensation of the 1893 Columbia Exposition, performing the dance that had made her famous. Censors permitted copies to be shown only after obscuring bars had been placed across forbidden portions of the dancer's anatomy on each frame of every film that was circulated. Early nickelodeon fare, such as *The Bridal Chamber,* was often racier than films shown in theaters. The first municipal boards of censorship were established in 1907.

One of the earliest American stag films was *A Free Ride,* alternately titled *A Grass Sandwich.* Made in 1915, the film is on file at the Institute for Sex Research. Copies also exist of *Strictly Union* (1917) and *On the Beach* (1925). A more modern classic, the 1930s *Mexican Dog,* was distributed as late as the mid-1960s under the title *Sportie.* Some mainstream films of the early twentieth century featured nudity: *Daughter of the Gods* (1916), *A Man's World* (1916), *Ben-Hur* (1925), and *The Sign of the Cross* (1933).

A film which has been regarded as pornographic is *Extase* (1933), in which Hedy Lamarr made her debut at age sixteen. The film won a Golden Lion award at the 1934 Venice Film Festival but was widely banned in the United States.

The Hollywood film industry had its own censor, Will Hayes. In 1934 he cooperated with Catholic decency groups to develop the Motion Picture Production Code, which spelled out in great detail what could *not* be shown on the screen. The Legion of Decency began publishing its list of "condemned" movies in the same year. U.S. Customs also continued to censor incoming films as well as books.

In the gray area of the sexploitation film, Italian immigrant Louis Sonney had founded Sonney Amusements in 1921. Beginning with a "crime doesn't pay" carnival film show, he realized in the 1930s that people were more interested in sex than justice. He therefore turned to the production and exhibition of psuedo-moralistic films such as *Gambling with Souls* and *Forbidden Oats.* In the 1930s and 1940s, distribution of sexploitation films was largely dominated by a group of road show men known as the "Forty Thieves."

Their 1940s successor was Kroger Babb, who produced and marketed "clap operas" such as *Birth of a Baby* (1944). A typical package would include a film, a lecture, and a "nurse" to sell supposedly instructional books. In their excellent book, *Sinema,* Kenneth Turan and Stephen F. Zito interview modern millionaire sexploiter David F. Friedman, who bought out Babb in 1956. Friedman claims Babb as his entrepreneurial idol and says that Babb's *Mom and Dad* grossed $40 million.[8]

From the mid-1950s to the mid-1960s, an increasing number of theaters ventured to show an increasing amount of sex, and later sex and violence, in the form of nudies and roughies to an ever widening audience. The 1955 nudist film *Garden of Eden* was the subject of the Desmond decision, the New York State Court of Appeals' ruling that nudity as such was not indecent. This decision led to a decade of nudie exploitation films like *My Bare Lady* (1962). In 1959 Russ Meyer began his spectacular string of movie successes with *The Immoral Mr. Teas,* a low-budget gag film about a meek man suddenly blessed with x-ray vision. *Mr. Teas* grossed over a million dollars, and Meyer was to make ten more voyeuristic comedies in the next decade. Others followed suit: John McCarthy *(The Ruined Bruin)* and Barry Mahon *(Nude Scrapbook),* to name two.

In 1963 David F. Friedman and Herschell G. Lewis released *Blood Feast,* the first roughie. They also produced such edifying epics as *Color Me Blood Red* (1965). Never one to miss the dollar signs written on the wall, Russ Meyer turned to roughies with *Mud Honey* (1969) and *Faster, Pussycat! Kill! Kill! Kill!* (1966). (Arthur Knight and Hollis Alpert have a classification, called "kinkies," but their boundaries are unclear.)

In 1967 the Supreme Court declined to censor *The Raw Ones'* depiction of frontal nudity. By the mid-1960s, according to Don Druker, some 750 films exploiting sex and violence had been released. Some surpassed the above-mentioned in their violence: George Weiss's and Joseph A. Mawra's *Olga's Girls* (1964) and *White Slaves of Chinatown* (1964). By and large, the censors let the roughies alone.

There were other trends in American erotic films of the 1960s. In the same vein as *Birth of a Baby* and *Mom and Dad,* films like Barry Mahon's *White Slavery* preached against various sex-related evils while depicting them in a most sensational fashion. Toward the end of the decade, even more explicit "educational" films like *Man and Wife* (1969) were being shown.

Also in the 1960s, gay erotic films were made by serious film makers, among them Kenneth Anger *(Scorpio Rising,* 1964), Andy Warhol *(Blow Job,* 1964), and Jack Smith (*Flaming Creatures,* 1963). Los Angeles's Pat Rocco pioneered the gay exploitation film with *Marco of Rio* (1969), *Sex and the Single Gay* (1970), and others.

Foreign films with erotic content hit the United States in two waves: in the late 1950s and early 1960s *La Dolce Vita* (1959), *Monika* (1953), and *Hiroshima, Mon Amour* (1958) were distributed through the exploitation market. Ingenious importers "doctored" some of the films by intercutting sex scenes. A doctored version of *Illicit Interlude* (1952), into which Larry Moyer had introduced a spurious nude bathing scene, was shown and even praised by critics for years. In the late 1960s, even more explicit foreign films such as *I, a Woman* (1965), which grossed $4 million, and *I Am Curious (Yellow)* (1967) were shown in this country.

The year 1967 was a milestone in the history of mass-distributed American erotic films, for that year saw the birth of the "beaver" film in San Francisco. The first gay hard-core loops were made in San Francisco in 1969. More devious efforts were soon necessary when censors forced producers to prove "redeeming social value." According to Kenneth Turan and Stephen F. Zito, the first, best, and most popular of these pseudo-histories was Alex de Renzy's *A History of the Blue Movie* (1970). Bill Osco made *Hollywood Blue Movie* (1971) and *Making the Blue Movie* (1971). *Personals,* directed by Armand Weston and Howard Winters, featured interviews with members of the erotic "scene" intercut with film of their activities.

An oddity of 1970 stands out: Alf Stillman, Jr's. 3-D success, *The Stewardesses.* Although the film showed no explicit sex, the novelty of 3-D and the potency of the stewardess's sexual stereotype made the film a $24 million grosser.

Also in 1970 appeared what was, according to Turan and Zito, the first sixty-minute hard-core 16 mm. film, or at least "the first to be known by name and promoted nationwide." *Mona, the Virgin Nymph* was technically competent and had credible plot and character development.

It was in 1972 that the most spectacularly successful hard-core feature appeared. Made in six days at a cost of $24,000, director Gerard Damiano's *Deep Throat* had grossed some $5 million by mid-1973. That same year, Mitchell Brothers, a San Francisco film group, showed America some hitherto unsuspected attributes of Marilyn Chambers, the Ivory Snow girl, in *Behind the Green Door* (1972). Wakefield Poole's gay hard-core film, *Boys in the Sand* (1971), returned a $400,000 gross on an $8,000 cost.

Although these and other large productions, lavish by the standards of stag films, seemed to signal a new day in slick, even aesthetically pleasing pornographic movies for mass audiences, a 1973 Supreme Court decision put a quick end to such dreams (or nightmares) by making big-budget, X-rated movies impractical due to the legal risks involved.

NOTES

1. Harford Montgomery Hyde, *A History of Pornography* (New York: Farrar, Straus & Giroux, 1965), p. 132.
2. Legman, *The Horn Book: Studies in Erotic Folklore and Bibliography* (New Hyde Park, N.Y.: University Books, 1964), p. 485.
3. Perkins, *The Secret Record: Modern Erotic Literature* (New York: Morrow, 1976), p. 91.
4. Perkins, p. 89.
5. Perkins, p. 125.
6. Cited in *A History of Underground Comics,* by Mark James Estren (San Francisco: Straight Arrow, 1974), pp. 117, 119.
7. Estren, pp. 138-39.
8. Don Druker, "Sex in Two Dimensions: Erotic Movies," in *Our National Passion: 200 Years of Sex in America*, ed. Sally Banes, Sheldon Frank, and Tem Horowitz (Chicago: Follett, 1976), p. 139.

BIBLIOGRAPHY

Aratow, Paul. *100 Years of Erotica: A Photographic Portfolio of Mainstream American Subculture from 1845-1940.* San Francisco: Straight Arrow, 1973.

Ashbee, Henry Spencer. *Catena Librorum Tacendorum: Being Notes Bio-Biblio-Iconographical and Critical on Curious and Uncommon Books.* London: Privately printed, 1885.

______. *A Complete Guide to Forbidden Books.* North Hollywood, Calif.: Brandon House, 1966.

Brewer, Joan Scherer, and Rod W. Wright. *Sex Research: Bibliographies from the Institute for Sex Research.* Phoenix, Ariz: Oryx Press, 1979.

Deakin, Terence J. *Catalogi Librorum Eroticorum: A Critical Bibliography of Erotic Bibliographies and Book Catalogues.* London: Cecil & Amelia Woolf, 1964.

Di Lauro, Al, and Gerald Rabkin. *Dirty Movies: An Illustrated History of the Stag Film, 1915-1970.* New York: Chelsea House, 1976.

Dixon, Rebecca. "Bibliographical Control of Erotica." In *An Intellectual Freedom Primer.* Edited by Charles H. Busha. Littleton, Colo.: Libraries Unlimited, 1977.

Ernst, Morris Leopold, and William Sleagle. *To the Pure.* New York: Viking Press, 1928.

Ginzburg, Ralph. *An Unhurried View of Erotica.* New York: Helmsman Press, 1958.

Haight, Anne Lyon. *Banned Books.* New York: Bowker, 1935. Rev. ed. New York: Bowker, 1955.

Hoddeson, Bob. *The Porn People.* Watertown, Mass.: American, 1974.

Hoffman, Frank A. *An Analytical Survey of Anglo-American Traditional Erotica.* Bowling Green, Ohio: Bowling Green University Popular Press, 1975.

Hughes, Douglas A., ed. *Perspectives on Pornography.* New York: St. Martin's Press, 1970.

Hurwood, Bernhardt J. *The Golden Age of Erotica.* Los Angeles: Sherbourne Press, 1965.

Hyde, Harford Montgomery. *A History of Pornography.* New York: Farrar, Straus & Giroux, 1965.

Knight, Arthur. *Playboy's Sex in Cinema.* 7 vols. Chicago: Playboy Press, 1971-1977. (Vols. 1-3 with Hollis Alpert. Reprints the annual articles published in *Playboy* from 1969 to 1977.)

Kronhausen, Phyllis, and Eberhard Kronhausen. *Erotic Art: A Survey of Erotic Fact and Fancy in the Fine Arts.* 2 vols. New York: Grove Press, 1969-1970.

———. *Pornography and the Law.* 2d ed. New York: Ballantine, 1964.

———. *The Sex People: Erotic Performers and Their Bold New Worlds.* Chicago: Playboy Press, 1975.

Legman, Gershon. *The Horn Book: Studies in Erotic Folklore and Bibliography.* New Hyde Park, N.Y.: University Books, 1964.

———. *Love & Death: A Study in Censorship.* New York: Breaking Point, 1949.

Loth, David. *The Erotic in Literature.* New York: Julian Messner, 1961.

Michelson, Peter. *The Aesthetics of Pornography.* New York: Herder & Herder, 1971.

Nobile, Philip A. *The New Eroticism.* New York: Random House, 1970.

Otto, Herbert A. "The Pornographic Fringeland of the American Newsstand." *Journal of Human Relations,* 12 (1964), 375-90.

Peckham, Morse. *Art and Pornography: An Experiment in Explanation.* Institute for Sex Research Studies in Sex and Society, no. 2. New York: Basic Books, 1969.

Perkins, Michael. *The Secret Record: Modern Erotic Literature.* New York: Morrow, 1976.

The Report of the Commission on Obscenity and Pornography. Washington, D.C.: U.S. GPO, September 1970. (Available from Superintendent of Documents, Washington, D.C. 20402 Stock #052-056-00001-2.) (Paperback ed. New York: Bantam, 1970.)

Rose, Alfred. (Pseud. Rolf S. Reade.) *Register of Erotic Books (Registrum Librorum Eroticorum).* 2 vols. London: Rolf S. Reade, 1936. Reprint ed. New York: Jack Russell, 1965.

See, Carolyn. *Blue Money, Pornography and the Pornographers.* New York: McKay, 1974.

"Sex, Porn and Male Rage." *Mother Jones,* 5 (April 1980), special issue.

Technical Report of the Commission on Obscenity and Pornography. 9 vols. Washington, D.C.: Government Printing Office, 1971-1972. (Available from the Superintendent of Documents, Government Printing Office, Washington, D.C. 20402. Stock #5256-0002 through #5256-0010.)

Turan, Kenneth, and Stephen F. Zito. *Sinema: American Pornographic Films and the People Who Make Them.* New York: Praeger, 1974.

Vassi, Marco. *Metasex, Mirth & Madness.* New York: Penthouse Press, 1975.

Propaganda

Richard A. Nelson

The growth of propaganda in modern life has resulted largely from certain inventive developments in the late nineteenth and early twentieth centuries—(high speed print, telegraphy, films, radio, and more recently television)—which provided governments and private interests with an unprecedented media arsenal useful in times of both war and peace. Despite the continuing role played by commercial advertising and political propaganda in defining our national culture and institutions, Americans by and large bear a traditional antipathy toward the idea (if not the practice) of propaganda. The sobering thought that arises in preparing a topical review such as this is that, notwithstanding an overwhelmingly negative literature condemning propaganda as inimical to freedom (an argument which is itself open to question, but which nevertheless represents a consensus of published opinion), very little has been done to control its spread. That the term continues to hold a strongly pejorative—even sinister—connotation is somewhat surprising since it was Americans who pioneered the implementation of attitudinal methodologies, mass marketing strategies, and media technologies now considered essential to widespread persuasive communication.

Each one of us has been indoctrinated from childhood, and daily we continue to be bombarded with intrusive messages attempting to inform, manipulate, motivate, redirect, and even placate us. An objective observer is forced to conclude that we live at a time when propaganda, far from abating, is becoming an increasingly pervasive force in democratic as well as totalitarian states. Indeed, given the pluralistic nature of contemporary society, some forms of propagandistic social engineering may be necessary if we hope to reach consensus on the vital (but perhaps controversial) issues facing us.

What then constitutes propaganda? Unfortunately, there is no easy answer. Although we have progressed beyond the insular "us versus them" belief that propaganda is something only our enemies engage in (facetiously described as the other side's case put so convincingly as to be annoying!), a definition remains largely a matter of perspective. Writers on the topic regularly devote entire chapters to this one problem due to the imprecision of the term, which has been interpreted variously to include such functions as advertising, public relations, publicity, political communication, special interest lobbying, radical agitation, psychological warfare, and even education. There is, however, general agreement that propaganda is a form of manipulative communication designed to elicit some predetermined response. Not all propaganda is equally embracive, pervasive, or effective in what the persuader asks us to think or do; nevertheless, propaganda is purposive. We can conveniently separate propaganda into those messages which encourage us to buy a commercial product and those which seek to direct our belief structure and personality in a more fundamental way. In many cases, the job of today's propagandist involves not so much changing minds as finding the right audience in order to reinforce and extend existing attitudes. For purposes of this essay, propaganda is defined as the systematic attempt to influence the emotions, attitudes, opinions, and actions of specified target audiences for ideological or political purposes through the controlled transmission of one-sided messages via mass media channels.

One can trace the origins of propaganda to remote antiquity. Aristotle's *Rhetoric*, for example, remains a valuable guide to propaganda techniques despite the passage of more than two millenia. By the Middle Ages, the introduction of the printing press in Europe and the spread of literacy were encouraging greater use of books and tracts designed to sway opinion. Much of this literature was religious, and the term *propaganda* was first used widely by the Catholic Church in 1622, with the founding of the Congregatio de propaganda fide (Congregation for the Propagation of Faith) during the Counter-Reformation.

Drawing on this European heritage, religionists coming to America during the pre-Revolutionary period became active publishers not only of biblical texts but also of literature extolling the virtues of the new land. In this endeavor they were joined by wealthy Colonial trading companies, which issued a number of misleading promotional advertisements designed to encourage settlement of their commercial plantations. The political foundations for modern propaganda emerged late in the eighteenth century, when the idea of inalienable rights advanced during the Enlightenment found flower in the Colonial republics. The Declaration of Independence penned by Thomas Jefferson was widely distributed and proved itself a masterful propaganda document not only by expressing the philosophy of the Revolution in language that all Colonialists could understand but also by justifying the American cause overseas and presaging the rise in importance of public opinion.

One should remember, however, that the American Revolution was not a spontaneous popular uprising. Contrary to myth, it was in reality the work of a small group of dedicated persuaders who created our first national propaganda and agitation campaign in order to overthrow a monarchical government. Even today the work of James Otis, Samuel Adams, Patrick Henry,

Benjamin Franklin, and Thomas Paine (whose circulation of *Common Sense* in 1776 and *The American Crisis* in 1776-83 helped cement opposition to the Crown) continues to be studied by propaganda researchers. Among the techniques these radical pamphleteers inaugurated that are still utilized in contemporary ideological communication are: (1) the realization that propaganda to be effective requires organization (the Sons of Liberty and Committees of Correspondence acted as conduits for revolutionary propaganda throughout the Colonies); (2) the creation of identifiable emotive symbols (the Liberty Tree) and slogans ("Don't tread on me" and "Taxation without representation is tyranny"), which simplify issues and arouse emotions; (3) the utilization of publicity and staged events (such as the Boston Tea Party) to attract media attention and enlist support of key cooperators (religious leaders whose sermons were widely published and distributed); (4) the exploitation of differences rather than emphasizing similarities in order to create discontent leading to change; and (5) the saturation of specified groups as well as mass audiences with monolithic reportage on a sustained and unrelenting basis through control of key organs of opinion (press, pamphlets, broadsides, even songs). The "patriots" proved expert at publicizing their story first so as to establish the agenda for debate, while simultaneously discrediting their loyalist opponents.

During the period of controversy surrounding adoption of the Federal Constitution after the war, a series of newspaper articles now known collectively as *The Federalist Papers* (1787-88) were anonymously prepared by Alexander Hamilton, James Madison, and John Jay to sell Americans on the new government. These proved an effective instrument of propaganda among opinion leaders as well as a thoughtful political treatise of more lasting interest. The freedoms secured by the Constitution led to the development early in the nineteenth century of clearly defined political parties and special interest organizations which readily adopted propaganda technologies for their own purposes. Leading American propagandists of the early 1800s include Theodore Dwight, an effective spokesman for the Federalist cause, and Amos Kendall, who served as Andrew Jackson's chief advisor and later earned the title of "first presidential public relations man."

Fears of undue foreign influence in the new republic led to a series of "anti" campaigns (anti-Illuminati, anti-Mason, anti-Catholic, anti-Irish, anti-Jewish, and so on), which even today flourish sporadically. Early propaganda books, typified by *Six Months in a Convent* which appeared in the early 1830s, helped to focus hatred and were underwritten by interests anxious to control immigrant blocks politically and keep their wages artificially low. The outstanding propaganda novel of the century was Harriet Beecher Stowe's powerful indictment of slavery, *Uncle Tom's Cabin* (1851), which sold an unprecedented 300,000 copies during its first year of publication and contributed significantly to the abolitionist movement. Pro-slavery forces were also active in the period up through the Civil War, issuing tracts and lobbying for support in Congress. In this they were secretly aided by "manifest destiny" expansionists in the North, who flooded the country with literature designed to raise patriotic fervor for war with Mexico. In a real sense, words as much as bullets helped to "Win the West."

As sectional differences became more pronounced and a war between the states inevitable, both the North and South recognized the importance of propaganda to the struggle. Particularly in the North where the war remained unpopular (there were draft riots in New York in 1863 and the so-called Copperhead movement fielded peace candidates as late as 1864), propaganda was utilized to mobilize public opinion both at home and abroad. Many of the trappings of contemporary journalism such as the press conference and the press pass were instituted by military leaders in order to censor battle reportage unfavorable to the Union, and Lincoln personally dispatched up to one hundred special agents to Britain along with a boatload of foodstuffs for unemployed English cotton textile workers so as to counter propaganda gains made by the Confederacy. In the North, too, the art of pamphleteering was advanced by the unceasing efforts of private organizations such as the Loyal Publication Society and the Union League Board of Publications.

The full impact of industrialism and the importance of public opinion began to be felt by the end of the war. Public opinion, which was at first narrowly defined to include only educated white male landowners, gradually came to be extended to the middle and working classes (and later in the twentieth century to women and minorities, changes themselves brought about in part by propaganda). Growing urbanism was accompanied by sweeping improvements in communication which extended the power of the press as a corridor into the minds of millions. In the era of yellow journalism (1890-1914) much of the news was, as it is today, artificial; that is, created and promoted by the newspapers who reported the stories as bona fide events. Although the impact of the press as a propaganda organ dates back before the Revolution, by this period the chains of publications controlled by press barons such as William Randolph Hearst had unrivaled influence on American thought. His *New York Journal* is largely credited with exciting the United States to challenge Spain over Cuba in 1898. Besides quadrupling Hearst's circulation, the events leading up to the war also marked the first time motion pictures were utilized meaningfully for propagandistic purposes. Highly patriotic short films such as *Tearing Down the Spanish Flag!* (1898) electrified U.S. audiences when the hated emblem was replaced by "Old Glory." The tremendous popular success of this picture (although it was actually shot on a roof in New York) spawned a host of imitators once actual hostilities broke out. Since cameramen were often prohibited from gaining access to authentic battleground footage, much of the "reportage," such as the series released under the title *The Campaign in Cuba* (1898), was surreptitiously filmed in the wilds of New Jersey. Screen propaganda already had shown flagrant disregard for truth, but this proved secondary to audiences who clamored for the lifelike images on the screen. This power of "actuality" and "documentation" freed propagandists for the first time from near complete reliance on the written word.

As the United States emerged to become a more important twentieth-century international political factor, European nations competing for continental leadership soon realized that the United States could play a pivotal role in the next war. As early as 1910, Germany began an active propaganda campaign to counteract pro-British biases in the leading organs of U.S. opinion. With the outbreak of hostilities in Europe, both Irish-American and German-American propagandists such as George Sylvester Viereck sought to combat the much more pervasive pro-intervention views spread by English agents working through a well-organized network of native sympathizers, press contacts, cultural exchanges, and business and banking ties. Overcoming isolationist impulses thanks to American gullibility, the British view prevailed and the country was successfully maneuvered into collective hatred of all things German through widespread dissemination of maliciously false (but effective) "anti-Hun" atrocity stories.

Even though we were the last major power to enter the war, the United States ironically was the first belligerent to establish an open, fully coordinated propaganda unit known as the Committee on Public Information (CPI). Headed by advertising executive George Creel, the CPI was given the commission to "sell the war to America." To do this, the CPI organized a national speakers bureau of "four-minute men," who galvanized audiences with carefully timed short propaganda messages supporting Liberty Bond sales drives. Recognizing the power of the screen, the Creel committee also arranged for cooperation between the private film industry (including the newsreel companies) and the military. The poster also emerged at this time as an effective mass war medium, and individual governments literally flooded their nations with millions of propaganda posters designed to muster public support for total victory. Among the American artists who lent themselves to the war effort were Charles Gibson, creator of the "Gibson Girl," and Norman Rockwell. Under CPI auspices alone, more than 100 million enthusiastically patriotic posters and other publications were distributed.

Although in the end much of the propaganda effort by Creel and his Allied counterparts proved (like Wilson's famous Fourteen Points as the basis for a just peace) more hyperbole than fact, World War I is important historically because it commemorates the inaugural deployment of contemporary mass propaganda. While the history of propaganda is indelibly linked to war, the seemingly interminable stalemate that marked most of the years of fighting propelled propaganda to the forefront as an important tool of government for sustaining homeland morale and maintaining ties of alliance. With the end of the war, however, Americans' desire to return to "normalcy" led to the quick disbanding of the CPI and a limiting of government propaganda efforts. On the other hand, during the 1920s and 1930s privately originated propaganda increased as numerous pressure groups formed in attempts to influence individual thought and actions as well as affect government policies by harnessing mass opinion. When the social upheavals wrought by the Great Depression led to installation of a Democratic administration promising a "New Deal," official U.S. propaganda took off once more. The introduction of new social security, public works, labor, housing, agricultural, and other policies required unparalleled peacetime publicity, and the government mobilized all its powers to build a shared consensus. Motion picture advertising (which had already been used for partisan political purposes) was extended, and the Roosevelt leadership further commissioned the filming of a number of documentary films with strong social messages. *The Plow that Broke the Plains* (1936) and *The River* (1937), for example, both pointed to the need for government intervention in conserving natural resources, and their success helped establish a federally controlled U.S. Film Service. Perhaps the most controversial of the early New Deal propaganda campaigns involved the National Recovery Administration (NRA). The totalitarian methods favored by NRA administrators, including enforced display of the blue NRA eagle emblem by "cooperating" businesses, were seen by many as a threat to American democratic principles. Partially on the basis of the propagandistic excesses of its supporters, the NRA was declared unconstitutional and nullified by the Supreme Court.

World propaganda had already entered a new phase with the successes of the Communists in Russia and the National Socialists in Germany. Attention to propaganda issues was further exacerbated by the uncertain economic climate of the period and the increases in the West of ideological movements that used propaganda unhesitatingly for both internal and external distribution. As early as 1919-20, the United States had been engulfed in a "Red scare," but despite this temporary setback Marxist propaganda continued to circulate with growing effectiveness among disenchanted American intellectuals and workers. The sheer amount of propaganda issued by the totalitarian states forced the leading democracies (notably Britain and the United States) to respond with a series of investigations and by upgrading their own propaganda apparatuses. Much of this was once again interventionist in nature, particularly after 1939 and the outbreak of World War II in Europe. Until Pearl Harbor, U.S. antiwar sentiment (epitomized by the America First Committee and the radio sermons of firebrand preacher Father Charles Edward Coughlin) openly competed against the line promoted by Anglophile organizations such as the Fight for Freedom Committee. Even as early as 1938, the United States was moving to shore up its position in Latin America by forming a Division of Cultural Relations in the Department of State, which rigorously issued propaganda designed to portray the United States as an altruistic benefactor in a common struggle against possible foreign aggression.

With the coming of World War II, official U.S. propaganda efforts were mostly directed by the Office of War Information (OWI) which was responsible for internal and external information. The Office of Strategic Services (OSS) conducted clandestine anti-Axis psychological warfare or so-called black propaganda. Coordinating the European operations of the OWI and OSS for military needs was the Psychological Warfare Division at Allied Supreme Headquarters. There were marked differences between U.S. propaganda and that of the Axis powers. Much of the enemy effort relied heavily on radio, and the sarcastic broadcasts of "Lord Haw Haw" (William Joyce) and "Axis Sally" from Germany, "Tokyo Rose" from Japan, and American expatriate poet Ezra Pound from Italy were listened to widely. Apart from broadcasting, the Allies utilized other methods, notably air-dropped leaflets. How effective these were in undermining enemy morale is still debated, but there is no doubt that internally the overall U.S. propaganda effort was successful. On the home front, the major media willingly cooperated in the war effort. The Hollywood studios actively collaborated with federal authorities in grinding out hundreds of racist anti-Japanese and anti-German war epics. Numerous government agencies, including the Treasury Department, took to the airwaves with highly propagandistic radio programs such as *Treasury Star Parade* (1943-44) to sell war bonds and maintain enthusiasm for continuing the fight. Newspapers and newsreels, too, carried regular government-inspired reports and voluntarily censored potentially demoralizing news. Gigantic posters dominated factories and military shipyards to spur production, and even comic books and pulp literature were enlisted to put the country on a war footing unenvisioned even in the darkest days of World War I.

With the defeat of Germany and Japan, U.S. propaganda took on a new direction. Largely because of the struggle with the Soviet Union for postwar dominance, much of the official propaganda issued by the United States since the 1940s has been directed at Eastern Europe and the emerging Third World states. The Voice of America, which transmits news, entertainment, and propaganda worldwide in dozens of languages, now is a division of the new International Communication Agency (USICA), which in 1978 incorporated the former U.S. Information Agency (USIA). The USICA continues to maintain information offices and libraries in sixty countries as well as operate an extensive press and broadcast assistance service. Secret operations are the function of the Central Intelligence Agency (CIA), which for years helped to support the ostensibly private anticommunist Radio Free Europe and Radio Liberty broadcasts. Today the federal government, rather than any Madison Avenue firm or corporate entity, constitutes the single greatest "propaganda machine" in this country. Specialists in forty-seven different federal agencies currently spend over $2.5 billion each year attempting to influence the way Americans think. The government, for example, is the nation's leading publisher and film producer, releasing thousands of magazines and books, hundreds of motion pictures, and countless press releases annually.

For private groups operating nationally, the battle of propaganda is as much as anything else a fight for access to the channels of mass dissemination. Political Action Committees, trade and educational groups, foundations, and other organizations that must compete and lobby for support are often forced to rely on the techniques of propaganda if they are successfully to reach their own institutional goals. Increased use of direct mail and technological breakthroughs may open new doors and opportunities for ideational propagandists as well as those more interested in purely commercial advertising and public relations marketing efforts.

Intervention by the Federal Trade Commission and the Federal Communications Commission in the broadcast advertising marketplace has also helped spur the development of so-called public service announcements (PSAs) that ask us to support approved causes ranging from the United Nations to anti-drug legislation. At the same time, the questionable impact of the FCC-authored "fairness" and "personal attack" doctrines has been to restrict discussions of major issues and limit the content of serious radio and television advertising (advertorials). Other attempts to regulate propaganda have been largely ineffective. The naive assumption voiced by some critics that somehow "rational education" would neutralize "irrational propaganda" has not been borne out by experience.

BIBLIOGRAPHY

Choukas, Michael. *Propaganda Comes of Age.* Washington, D.C.: Public Affairs Press, 1965.

Colby, Benjamin. *'Twas a Famous Victory: Deception and Propaganda in the War with Germany.* New Rochelle, N.Y.: Arlington House, 1974.

Culbert, David, Lawrence Suid, and William Murphy, eds. *Film and Propaganda in America: A Documentary History.* 5 vols. Text and microfiche. Westport, Conn.: Greenwood Press, forthcoming.

Davidson, Philip. *Propaganda and the American Revolution, 1763-1783.* Chapel Hill: University of North Carolina Press, 1941. Republished as *Propaganda in the American Revolution.* New York: Norton, 1973.

Ellul, Jacques. *Propaganda: The Formation of Men's Attitudes.* New York: Knopf, 1965.

Ford, Nick Aaron. *Language in Uniform: A Reader on Propaganda.* New York: Odyssey Press, 1967.

Furhammer, Leif, and Folke Isaksson. *Politics and Film.* New York: Praeger, 1971.

Hamilton, Alexander, James Madison, and John Jay. *The Federalist Papers.* Introduction by Clinton Rossiter. New York: New American Library/Mentor Books, 1961.

Hirst, David. "German Propaganda in the United States, 1914-1917." Ph.D. dissertation, Northwestern University, 1962.

International Propaganda/Communications: Selections from the Public Opinion Quarterly. New York: Arno Press, 1972.

Johnson, Niel M. *George Sylvester Viereck: German American Propagandist.* Urbana: University of Illinois Press, 1972.

Knightley, Phillip. *The First Casualty—From the Crimea to Vietnam: The War*

Correspondent as Hero, Propagandist, and Myth Maker. New York: Harcourt Brace Jovanovich, 1975.

Lasswell, Harold D. *Propaganda Technique in the World War.* London: Kegan Paul, Trench, Trubner, 1927. Reprinted as *Propaganda Technique in World War I.* Cambridge, Mass.: MIT Press, 1971.

______, Ralph D. Casey, and Bruce L. Smith. *Propaganda and Promotional Activities: An Annotated Bibliography.* Minneapolis: University of Minnesota Press, 1935. Reprinted. Chicago: University of Chicago Press, 1969.

______, Daniel Lerner, and Hans Speier, eds. *Propaganda and Communication in World History, Volume 1: The Symbolic Instrument in Early Times.* Honolulu: University Press of Hawaii, 1979.

______. *Propaganda and Communication in World History, Volume II: The Emergence of Public Opinion in the West.* Honolulu: University Press of Hawaii, 1979.

______. *Propaganda and Communication in World History, Volume III: A Pluralizing World in Formation.* Honolulu: University Press of Hawaii, 1980.

Lavine, Harold, and James Wechsler. *War Propaganda and the United States.* New Haven: Yale University Press for the Institute for Propaganda Analysis, 1940. Reprint. New York: Arno Press, 1972.

Lee, Alfred McClung. *How to Understand Propaganda.* New York: Holt, Rinehart, 1952.

______, and Elizabeth Briant Lee. *The Fine Art of Propaganda: A Study of Father Coughlin's Speeches.* New York: Harcourt, Brace, 1939. Reprint. New York: Octagon, 1972; and San Francisco: International Society for General Semantics, 1979.

Linebarger, Paul. *Psychological Warfare.* 2d ed. Washington, D.C.: Combat Forces Press, 1954. Reprint. New York: Arno Press, 1972.

Marks, Barry. "The Idea of Propaganda in America." Ph.D. dissertation, University of Minnesota, 1957.

Mock, James R., and Cedric Larson. *Words That Won the War: The Story of the Committee on Public Information, 1917-1919.* Princeton University Press, 1939. Reprint. New York: Russell & Russell, 1968.

Qualter, Terence H. *Propaganda and Psychological Warfare.* New York: Random House, 1962.

Rhodes, Anthony. *Propaganda—The Art of Persuasion: World War II.* New York: Chelsea House, 1976.

Riegel, Oscar W. *Mobilizing for Chaos: The Story of the New Propaganda.* New Haven: Yale University Press, 1934. Reprint. New York: Arno Press, 1972.

Sethi, S. Prakash. *Advocacy Advertising and Large Corporations: Social Conflict, Big Business Image, the News Media, and Public Policy.* Lexington, Mass.: Lexington Books/Heath, 1977.

Smith, Bruce L., Harold D. Lasswell, and Ralph D. Casey. *Propaganda, Communication, and Public Opinion: A Comprehensive Reference Guide.* Princeton: Princeton University Press, 1946.

Thomson, Oliver. *Mass Persuasion in History: An Historical Analysis of the Development of Propaganda Techniques.* Edinburgh: Paul Harris, 1977.

The Washington Lobby. 3d ed. Washington, D.C.: Congressional Quarterly, 1979.

Wilkerson, Marcus M. *Public Opinion and the Spanish-American War: A Study in War Propaganda.* Baton Rouge: Louisiana State University Press, 1932.

Winkler, Allan M. *The Politics of Propaganda: The Office of War Information, 1942-1945.* New Haven: Yale University Press, 1978.

Pulps

Bill Blackbeard

Until about twenty years ago, the terms *pulp*, *pulp magazine*, and *pulp fiction* were writers' and publishers' trade terms, little known to or used by the general public. Readers who bought such magazines as *Dime Detective*, *Argosy*, *Blue Book*, and *Weird Tales* in the 1930s and 1940s did not think of these popular titles as pulps, but just as fiction magazines, or more generically, according to subject matter, as detective story magazines, adventure story magazines, fantasy magazines, etc. Infrequent and casual articles in such magazines as *Esquire* and *Vanity Fair* dealing with the phenomenon of the popular fiction magazines did, of course, use the term *pulp*, but it did not gain broad usage. From the point of view of the general reader, who once absorbed reams of pulp fiction as he does hours of television today, the paper on which his reading matter was printed was simply irrelevant. A Western novel serialized in the slick paper magazine *Saturday Evening Post* could, in his eyes, be quite as entertaining as another printed in pulp paper *Wild West Weekly*. He read the latter magazine largely because the more eclectic *Post* did not publish enough Western fiction to satisfy his specialized cravings over a given period of time.

To the magazine publisher and his potential advertisers, however, the quality of paper used was a vital concern. So-called slick paper, made of rag content stock, afforded a highly desirable surface for the reproduction of advertisements, particularly those involving a lavish use of color. Unfortunately, slick paper was a costly item and was economically feasible only for very large circulation magazines, such as the *Saturday Evening Post*, *Collier's*, or *Life*, of low newsstand cost supported in large part by their advertising revenue or for more highly priced "quality" magazines, such as *Esquire*, *The New Yorker*, or *Vanity Fair*, with an "elite" appeal, again substantially supported by their advertisements. Pulp paper, on the other hand, prepared from a wood-fiber base and also called *newsprint*, largely in newspaper publishing circles, was much cheaper than slick or coated paper, and its use made it possible for publishers so inclined to reach a mass reading market at low prices without any substantial financial aid from its advertisers. (For this reason, "radical" political journals, that tended to alienate advertisers *per se*, almost always appeared on the cheapest kind of pulp paper stock, generally called *butcher paper* by its left-wing users of the time.)

Many different kinds of magazines with low advertising content utilized pulp paper: the early color comic strip magazines (or comic books); political and cultural journals of all sorts (some of which, like *Harper's* and *The Atlantic*, used a high grade of wood-based paper, called *book paper* in the publishing field); newspaper book review and entertainment supplements; scholastic, library, and book trade publications, etc. However, only the popular fiction or all-fiction magazine acquired the name pulp from its writers and editors in the decades following the turn of the present century, and it is, of course, with this widely circulated, enormously varied body of publications that we are concerned here.

In referring to the pulp fiction magazine in these pages, we are speaking of a specific, readily defined kind of periodical, found only in six sizes and forms, all of which share in common wood-pulp paper and a two-column text. The most frequently encountered form of pulp magazine is a sheaf of several octavo signatures, stapled together at two equidistant points near the spine, enclosed with a slick paper cover attached with glue over the flat area of the spine, and usually featuring interior illustrations, as well as color printing on the outside of the cover. This basic form of pulp magazine is found in three sizes: the large "flat" of about 8½″ × 11″, usually about ¼ to 1 inch thick with trimmed page edges, and composed of three to four signatures (or, very occasionally, perfectly bound, with or without staples); the median, standard size (representing the vast majority of all pulps) of 10″ × 7″ untrimmed, or about 9″ × 6½″ trimmed, averaging ⅓ to ½ inch in thickness (some exceptional pulps of this size can go to two inches or more of thickness), made up of six to twelve signatures (or again, in rare instances, dozens of signatures); and the "digest" size, of about 7½″ × 5″, ¼ to ½ inch thick (with some rare titles reaching an inch or more), almost always trimmed, and involving six to eight signatures (or perfectly bound, with or without staples). A much less frequent form of pulp magazine is the saddle-stitched, single signature variety. The standard form for the nickel thriller and the comic book, it is most often encountered in pulps with the under-the-counter sex story magazines of the 1920s and 1930s. It can also range in size from the flat to the digest form, although the latter is extremely rare in this form, and the median of 9″ × 6½″ is standard.

The all-fiction magazine, by its nature, emphasized a basic broad appeal in its writing and narrative content. Here and there, especially in its later, closing years, the pulp magazine might chance a "difficult," experimental piece of fiction, because of real editorial enthusiasm and a feeling that one such item in a given issue would not alienate finicky readers provided with a half dozen other standard pieces of fiction. Even in such work some kind of straightforward narrative progress had to be in evidence, so that while as bizarre a writer as H. P. Lovecraft or Joel Townsley Rogers could (and did) appear regularly in pulps, a post-*Dubliners* James Joyce or a contemporary equivalent of John Barth probably would not. Basically, the all-fiction magazines provided a market for genre fiction that, often because of peculiar editorial biases as much as any real lack of intrinsic merit, failed to sell to the very limited but higher-paying slick paper magazine markets. While much of the pulp magazine content was, understandably, a mass-produced, stereotyped product seized upon by editors desperate to fill the endless pages of twenty or more titles a month in publishing house after publishing house, virtually all of the fine fiction written in America between the turn of the century and the close of the 1940s found print in these magazines if it could not find it in the slicks or literary journals. Much worthwhile material is still being uncovered today and reprinted to critical applause; indeed, in the case of some long-neglected writers, separate publishing houses with a largely academic clientele have been founded essentially to republish the works of such authors complete in successive, highly priced volumes.

The popular, all-fiction magazine and pulp paper were not, of course, always linked. The American and English predecessors of the American pulp magazine, appearing early in the nineteenth century, generally were printed on the then much cheaper rag content paper. The American "story papers" of the 1850s and later tabloid size nickel weekly journals were crammed inky cheek to jowl with six to eight pages of sensational fiction by such worthies as Nick Carter, Horatio Alger, and Ned Buntline. Their enormous cover illustrations, replete with blood and thunder, were matched by those of the English "penny dreadfuls" of the same period, which carried endless grisly narratives. These were illustrated penny serial parts, 8 pages long, 7 inches x 10 inches, carrying the title of the continued story each featured until slumping sales or author fatigue finally forced a pause before the launching of a new group of continuing narratives, usually penned by the same small group of ferociously productive authors, the most notorious of whom were the prolific G. W. M. Reynolds and Thomas Pecket Prest. Pulp paper first entered the scene with the development of the American weekly novel series of the 1870s in an 8 inches by 11 inches format of sixteen to twenty-four pages, which became as classic during the next few decades as the infamous dime novel. (In fact, the original and definitive dime novels were paperbacked, pocket-sized publications manufactured by Beadle and Adams primarily for Civil War troop use in the 1860s while the later and larger pulp paper thrillers of turn-of-the-century notoriety generally sold for five cents.) These nickel thrillers, an endless series of short novels about such juvenile favorites as Nick Carter, Diamond Dick, Buffalo Bill, Old Sleuth, King Brady, and Old Cap Collier, were the effective forerunners of the publications the next generation of writers called *pulps*. With their lurid, full-color covers (which did not fully supplant the earlier black and white covers until the 1890s), double columns of narrative text, wholehearted focus on sensational fiction, recurrent characters in series novels, pulp paper pages, and regularity of newsstand appearance, these dime novels of the 1870s-1910s lacked only the general dimensions of the definitive pulp magazines of the succeeding period: the popular 7 inches by 10 inches quarto, one hundred page or more in length in which virtually all pulps appeared until the introduction of the pocket-sized or digest-sized pulps of the 1940s.

In moving from the nickel thrillers of the nineteenth century to the pulps of the twentieth, we are, of course, passing from fiction of minimal literacy aimed almost entirely at juvenile readers, or the most naïve of uneducated adults, to a narrative prose intended for a mature mass readership not satisfied by the relatviely small amount of genre fiction available in quality or general content magazines, or in inexpensive paperback book reprints. Interestingly, the first periodical to establish the profitable existence of such a mature mass readership (initially in England rather than America) was not printed on pulp paper at all, nor was it an all-fiction publication. This was the widely famed, slick paper magazine of George Newnes, *The Strand*, in which such fictional figures as Sherlock Holmes and Bulldog Drummond appeared in series after series of novelettes and novels, together with sensational adventure and mystery fiction of all kinds, all profusely illustrated, often with color plates in holiday issues. Sandwiched in was a respectable (though peripheral) stock of nonfiction pieces on prominent personalities, exotic places, pets, and patriotism, so that despite its bounty of popular fiction, parlors that had previously accepted only such dull slick paper periodicals as *Blackwood's*, *Good Words*, and *The Leisure Hour* now received *The Strand*.

Ambitious imitators of *The Strand* appeared almost at once in England, all bounteously illustrated (at the rate of about one cut for every two pages) and replete with thrilling action or detective fiction written by such masters as H. Rider Haggard, R. Austin Freeman, Guy Boothby, E. Phillips Oppenheim, and many others; among these new and sensationally popular magazines were *The Windsor Magazine*, *Pearson's*, *Cassell's*, *Harmworth's* (later *The London Magazine*), and *The Idler*. Many of these published American editions to protect their copyrights in the United States, and their popular impact was much the same here as in England, although direct American imitations were not at all immediately evident (the earliest, possibly, being the *The Cosmopolitan* after 1905, when it was purchased by William Randolph Hearst and immediately took an engaging turn toward broadly popular fiction in great and well-illustrated quantity). American publishers of general magazines, dominated by the images of the more serious *Harper's* and *Scribner's* magazines at the close of the century, seemed to eschew the kind of fun-and-games fiction featured in the new group of British publications, and certainly they avoided any broad body of it in their pages at all times. Even the popularly oriented weekly slick paper magazines of wide dimensions, such as *Collier's* and *Saturday Evening Post* of the 1890s and 1900s, in which the Sherlock Holmes and Raffles stories were reprinted for American consumption, ran only one or two pieces of fiction per issue, with but one or two illustrations apiece, and placed their heavier editorial emphasis on journalistic nonfiction and illustrations of various kinds.

The would-be American consumer of quantitatively published popular action fiction was thus frustrated on two fronts: the imported British magazines, such as *The Strand* and *Pearson's*, were too highly priced for the mass reading public's budget even in American reprint form, while the cheaper popular American magazines, such as *Collier's* and *Saturday Evening Post*, ran about a single evening's worth of engaging fiction per week between them. The stage was thus set in the United States for the emergence of what was to be the single most successful medium for the merchandising of cheap fiction to a mass audience in the history of publishing: the pulps. It was an idea whose time had come, and if one publisher had not developed the concept, another would have in short order. At it happened, however, the man who published the first definitive pulp fiction magazine in 1896, *The Argosy*, did so only as one more step to save a foundering magazine, not as a calculated move in opening a new publishing frontier. Frank Andrew Munsey, who first converted his feebly conceived children's weekly of 1882, *The Golden Argosy*, into a boy's adventure story paper called simply *The Argosy* in 1888, then into a general illustrated monthly magazine of the same name in 1894, finally tried making it a monthly all-fiction adult adventure story magazine companion to his previously successful, general, illustrated *Munsey's Magazine* of 1891. By printing his new 1896 version of *The Argosy* on pulp paper and omitting all illustrative art, Munsey found he could provide a fat bundle of reading matter for a dime, well below the quarter charged at the time by slick paper magazines of similar bulk, such as *Harper's* or *The Century*. Moreover, a great deal of the normal editorial content of such general magazines was pictorial, while in their fastidious prose, nonfiction usually had a marked edge in pages over fiction. On the average, it would be safe to say that a single monthly issue of *The Argosy* of 1896 held more fiction than any six of the leading general monthlies of the time—and it was virtually *all* sensational adventure and mystery fiction of reasonably mature quality.

That this kind of magazine was exactly what the mass adult reading public of the 1890s wanted was at once evidenced by the steep increase in *The Argosy's* circulation. From a rock-bottom low of nine thousand in 1894, the new *Argosy's* sales figures quickly soared to eighty thousand, gradually ascending to a peak of half a million by 1907, a mere decade from its start. *The Argosy* was not long alone in its pulp paper splendor, but it was some time before its burgeoning imitators equalled or surpassed it in overall story quality. The inspired early editorial work in the post-1895 *Argosy* was not that of Munsey, who was much more involved in *Munsey's Magazine* and other projects by that time, but that of Matthew White, Jr., who had joined the Munsey staff in 1886 (and who was later closely aided by Robert "Bob" Davis, a Munsey editor hired in 1904). That White's judgment was sound is indicated by the impressive roster of writers whose early work was printed in *The Argosy* between 1896 and 1910: James Branch Cabell, Upton Sinclair, Mary Roberts Rinehart, Sidney Porter (later "O. Henry"), Susan Glaspell, George Allen England, Albert Payson Terhune, Joseph Louis Vance, Frank L. Packard, William MacLeod Raine, and Ellis Parker Butler, many of whom became regular contributors to the prestigious *Saturday Evening Post* of the upcoming century.

Among the earliest of *The Argosy*'s technical rivals were two other Munsey adventure fiction pulps, *The All-Story* of 1905 (later *All-Story Weekly*) and *The Cavalier* of 1908. Both monthlies and both essentially duplicate *Argosies* with interchangeable authors and cover artists, these two new publications in effect put an over 220-page, all-fiction Munsey magazine on the newsstands three times a month; and when *All-Story* combined with *Cavalier* and went weekly in 1913, there were *five* Munsey adventure pulps for sale every month—and they all sold, voluminously. There seemed to be plenty of people able to devour twelve hundred closely printed pages of Munsey fiction per month—and more, if the sales of other publishers' action fiction pulps are added to those of the Munsey magazines. It must be kept in mind that ten cents in the 1900s would buy about what a dollar will buy today, at a time when most actual incomes were smaller in real purchasing power. It can accordingly be assumed that most buyers of the early pulps rarely bought on impulse or just to read one or two stories by favorite authors; they read their money's worth out of every magazine purchased. A persistent point made in letters to the editors at this time and later is that the readers read every story in every issue; many even rated them in terms of enjoyment derived. Contemporary authors can only weep for that once vast reading public, a public that sustained the pulps for fifty years.

Among the early and most substantial imitators of *The Argosy* were such other 7 inch by 10 inch quarto pulp magazines containing roughly 150 to 200 pages of adventure and action fiction as Street & Smith's *Popular Magazine* of 1904, which reached a quarter million in circulation by 1905; *Gunter's Magazine*, also of 1904, another Street & Smith response to *The Argosy* (with a leavening of romantic fiction in an attempt to appeal to some female readers), which became *The New Magazine* under another publisher in 1910, then returned to Street & Smith as *New Story Magazine* in 1912; *People's Magazine*, a third Street & Smith undertaking of 1906 with an early emphasis on detective fiction rather than straight adventure; *The Top-Notch* of 1910, a final Street & Smith effort in the general action story field issued in an initial dime-novel format, with a bias toward the sports fiction story; *The Blue Book* of 1907 (originally titled *The Monthly Story* Magazine in its 1905 inauguration), a companion magazine to the women-oriented *Red Book* and the later, theater-slanted *Green Book* of the same period; *Short Stories* of 1910, previously an all-fiction reprint magazine of high price and slick paper; and *Adventure* of 1910, the first issue of which actually appeared on slick paper, apparently for promotional reasons. Some of these newcomers carried a fifteen-cent price, justifying it by a modicum of interior illustrations, while the early *Top-Notch*, the smallest in length of the lot, tried for a nickel, but none ever surpassed the enormous circulation lead attained by *The Argosy* or attempted to emulate the weekly publication of *All-Story* (later merged with *The Argosy* into a single Munsey pulp adventure fiction weekly in 1920, after *The Argosy* itself had been a weekly since 1917), although *Popular, Short Stories, Adventure*, and *Top-Notch* eventually went to twice a month publication for varying periods of time.

It soon became evident to some of these pulp fiction entrepreneurs that the needs of their newly tapped reading public might not be wholly met by action fiction in bulk, and that many readers, as indicated by a growing demand in libraries and bookstores, wanted to read rather narrowly along one line of popular fiction, most notably in the 1910s that of detective and mystery narrative, although a spreading interest in Western fiction was not far behind. Street & Smith, of course, had earlier noted this phenomenon in their nineteenth-century nickel library series, where tens of thousands of copies of the weekly *Nick Carter* detective and *Buffalo Bill* Western thrillers vanished off the newsstands every seven days. Munsey, however, was the first to investigate specialized fiction interests when he launched *The Rail-road Man's Magazine* in 1906. A monthly pulp, this publication featured much more nonfiction than the other men's adventure magazines and was actually more of a fraternal journal for railroad employees and locomotive buffs than anythng else; it lasted until 1919 and was revived by Munsey in 1929. More typical of the specialized fiction pulp was a second Munsey effort in this direction, *The Ocean* of 1907. Here, although there was considerable nonfiction, sea stories predominated, with as many as four serials running every month. Munsey's estimate of the public's interest in salt water narratives was misguided, however (in fact, there was never to be a really successful sea story pulp at any time), and he was forced to fold the venture after only a year.

Street & Smith, experimenting a little later in the game, had much better luck. In 1915, they decided to convert the old *Nick Carter* nickel thriller into a new ten-cent semi-monthly pulp magazine of detective fiction, called *Detective Story Magazine*. Nick Carter stories, often serialized, were still featured, but the bulk of the new magazine's contents were purchased from the same freelance authors then supplying the other pulps. Initially only a slim 128 pages, *Detective Story Magazine* quickly fattened to 160 pages, then switched to a weekly schedule at 144 pages with a steadily mounting circulation through the 1920s. Encouraged by their initial success, Street & Smith proceeded in 1919 to alter their successful *Buffalo Bill* weekly nickel thriller into another specialized pulp, this one called *Western Story Magazine.* Like *Detective Story Magazine, Western Story Magazine* was launched as a semi-monthly ten-cent publication of 128 pages. By 1920, however, circulation had swelled to such an extent that *Western Story Magazine,* like its predecessor, became a 144-page dime weekly. Then at 300,000 circulation, it later reached a half million in sales in the mid-1920s when the extraordinarily popular fiction of the hyper-prolific Max Brand (Frederick Faust) began to run in its pages at the rate of two or three serials at a time. A third Street & Smith attempt at a specialized fiction magazine, the fabled *Thrill Book* of 1919, failed because of a lack of courageous editorial direction. Clearly meant to be a magazine emphasizing the weird, bizarre, and fantastic in popular fiction (material which had already proven its wide popularity through its repeated appearance in *Argosy,* where writers famed for fantastic narratives, such as Edgar Rice Burroughs, Abraham Merritt, George Allen England, J. U. Geisy, Francis Stevens, and many others, were acclaimed headliners), *Thrill Book* lacked the nerve to limit its contents to science fiction and fantasy and, by actually taking on the amorphous shape of just another general action pulp, failed to attract the steadfast band of followers who were later to adhere faithfully to such undiluted exponents of fantastic fiction as the *Weird Tales* of 1923 and *Amazing Stories* of 1926. The *Thrill Book* did run some unusual and memorable fantasy—notably Francis Stevens' "The Heads of Cerebus"—but not enough to catch the notice of the multitude of readers who were regularly buying *Argosy* and *All-Story* for the same thing.

Street & Smith continued with their pioneering creation of specialized genre fiction pulps in the 1920s and introduced the long-lived and vastly popular *Love Story Magazine* in 1921 as a 144-page, fifteen-cent weekly—and as a cheaper companion to two older Street & Smith romantic fiction monthlies, *Smith's Magazine* and *Ainslee's Magazine,* once aspiring slicks, but now down-at-the-heel twenty-cent pulps. The following year, Street & Smith made their own attempt at a salt spray magazine with *Sea Stories* (which had to be abandoned by 1930 and converted to a mystery-adventure pulp called *Excitement*); they also introduced the nation's first magazine of collegiate fiction in *College Stories,* anticipating the later peak success in that field of *College Humor. Sport Story* was first published in 1923, as a companion to the sports-oriented *Top-Notch,* while by 1927 another long-established nickel-thriller weekly (actually then selling at seven cents), Harry E. Wolff's *Wild West Weekly*, with its feature novels about Young Wild West, was taken over by Street & Smith as a straight Western fiction weekly with the same name.

In the meantime, other publishers had been busy, particularly in the detective and Western fiction fields. H. L. Mencken and George Jean Nathan, engaged in developing their famed *Smart Set Magazine*, merrily launched three deliberate potboiler magazines in the 1910s to bring in supportive funds for *Smart Set*. The first two of these "louse" magazines, as Mencken and Nathan called them, were routine spicy story pulps of the innocent sort prefigured by Street & Smith's *Live Stories* of 1913 or their earlier *Yellow Book* of 1897, the kind of magazine which sold well in wartime; and Mencken and Nathan's *Parisienne* of 1915 and *Saucy Stories* of 1916 were specifically created with the young, war-excited American in mind. Both were immediate hits, with the second giving the leading naughty story magazine of the time, *Snappy Stories*, strong competition for its position. (It might be mentioned at this point that some variety of risqué pulp fiction was always on sale under dozens of different titles from the turn of the century through the 1950s, many published and distributed in legally *sub rosa* operations. Notable titles in the 1920s and 1930s were *La Paree Stories, Bedtime Stories, 10-Story Book, Saucy Movie Stories, Vice Squad Detective*, *Spicy Mystery Stories*, and *Hollywood Detective*. There were dozens of other titles, and none ever failed financially; every last one was, in fact, ultimately suppressed only by the authorities.) Mencken and Nathan's third "louse" magazine, however, proved to be quite a different matter from the first two; in fact, its reputation eventually overshadowed that of *Smart Set* itself.

Created several years later in 1920, this new monthly action pulp was titled *Black Mask*, and its initial orientation was toward stories of crime, horror, and the quasi-supernatural. Deliberately sensational in title and content, the feisty magazine was intended to attract readers who wanted more fearsome fare than they could find in the relatively sedate *Detective Story Magazine* and *Mystery Magazine* (the latter being a Frank Tousey venture of 1919, a thirty-two-page, 8 inches by 11 inches dime publication featuring cheaply acquired fiction by minor writers). A pitch was made for women readers by the early subtitle wording, "A Magazine of Mystery, Romance, and Adventure," but there was little of the boy-girl romancing that packed the pages of *Ainslee's* or *Love Story Magazine* of the following year; indeed, the cover of the October 1920 issue depicted a young woman cowering from a hot branding iron that has *already* branded her cheek with a livid, smoking image. Although there were a number of generally straightforward detective problem stories in the early issues, these probably reflected the kind of rejects from *Detective Story Magazine* the editors were initially forced to buy, and the obviously desired theme was powerfully rendered in blood and thunder. There was, needless to say, little hint of the restrained, coldly realistic, well-paced fiction that *Black Mask* was later to personify in the writing of Dashiell Hammett, Raymond Chandler, Paul Cain, Raoul Whitfield, and others. Indeed, *Black Mask*, for all of its fame as a pioneering hard-boiled detective story magazine in the 1920s, was in fact a long time in finding its real focus. For most of the 1920s, *Black Mask* was described in its cover subtitle variously as a magazine of air, Western, adventure, and he-man fiction, as well as of detective fiction, and its contents reflected that description. Such later noted writers of tough crime fiction as Whitfield and Horace McCoy initially wrote little but air and Western stories for *Black Mask*. It was not, in fact, until the public impact and circulation rise of the very late 1920s that accompanied the major Hammett serials, such as *Red Harvest* and *The Maltese Falcon*, that *Black Mask* became wholly a magazine of tough detective fiction. In the meantime, there was little influence exerted on other pulp magazines, and the first out-and-out *Black Mask* imitator, *Black Aces*, did not appear until 1931, while such strong and lasting parallel crime fiction magazines as *Dime Detective* and *Detective Tales* did not reach their peaks of quality until the middle 1930s.

In the 1920s, following the advent of *Black Mask* and the minor curiosity called *Mystery Magazine*, the only notable introductions in detective story magazines were Munsey's first move into the field in 1924 with the weekly *Flynn's* (later *Flynn's Weekly Detective Fiction* and finally *Flynn's Detective Fiction Weekly*), starting out with two hundred pages for a dime; Edwin Baird's somewhat earlier *Detective Tales* of 1923, an oddly old-fashioned magazine which quickly jumped to an 8½ inches by 11¼ inches format (the size of the "true" detective and "confession" slicks of the period), but retained its pulp paper as its title changed to a twenty-five cent *Real Detective Tales & Mystery Stories* in 1924; the Priscilla Company's *Mystery Stories* of 1925, a quality twenty-five cent magazine of 160 pages, emphasizing true crime accounts and crime action fiction; W. M. Clayton's *Clues: A Magazine of Detective Stories* of 1926, which directly paralleled *Detective Story Magazine* and ran twice a month for a while in the late 1920s at fifteen cents; Dell's short-lived *Crime Mysteries* of 1927, a fifteen-cent, 120-page monthly which featured much of the interest in the horrific and grisly which characterized the early *Black Mask*; and Harold Hersey's *Dragnet Magazine* of 1928, a twenty-cent, 128-page monthly which was later (in 1931) to become the famed *Ten Detective Aces*, in which such top pulp writers as Lester Dent and Norvell Page wrote monthly novelettes about continuing feature characters in deliberately fantastic and gruesome adventures. The great bulk of the pulps jamming the newsstands of the 1920s were adventures and Westerns, with detectives a slim third, and a random spotting of other early genre pulps, such as *Ghost Stories*, *Weird Tales*, *Amazing Stories*, *Secret Service Stories*, *Sky Birds*, and the like. The earlier adventure pulps had been augmented by such 1920s titles as *The Danger Trail, Complete Stories, Five-Novels Monthly, Tropical Adventures, Thrills, Romance, Ace-High Magazine*, etc., while the Western fiction deluge inaugurated by *Western Story Magazine* counted among its 1920s arrivals *The Frontier, Lariat, Cowboy Stories, West, Rangeland Stories, Western Trails*, and many others.

It was at the close of the 1920s, however, that the real torrent of new pulps (and fresh varieties of pulps) took place. Suddenly, by 1929, all sorts of new kinds of pulp magazines were appearing—World War I action fiction, in such titles as *War Stories* (actually dating from 1926), *Submarine Stories, Navy Stories, Triple-X Magazine, War Novels, Over the Top*, and a sub-genre which quickly outgrew its parent: air war fiction, featuring *Airplane Stories, Wings, Sky Birds, Aces, Air Stories, Eagles of the Air, Sky Riders, Zeppelin Stories*; gangster fiction, typified by such new titles as *Racketeer Stories, Gun Molls, Speakeasy Stories, Gang World, Gangster Stories, Gangland Stories, The Underworld*; and science fiction, reflected by *Amazing Stories, Science Wonder Stories, Air Wonder Stories, Scientific Detective Monthly*, and (just around the corner in 1930) *Astounding Stories of Super-Science*. The quality of pulp fiction had become speedier and breezier, too, with a general dumping of the kind of prolix description and circumlocution which had filled many of those earlier, endless pages in *The Argosy* and *Detective Story Magazine*, and reflected the general tenor of turn of the century fiction. Those writers who had anticipated the looser, swifter style, such as Edgar Rice Burroughs, Max Brand, Dashiell Hammett, Robert E. Howard, Erle Stanley Gardner, continued to flourish in the decade ahead, while many others stodgily prominent in the 1910s and 1920s, vanished completely from the fast-action pulps of the 1930s, much as certain silent film idols, such as John Gilbert and Ramon Navarro, had essentially slipped from view with their own passing medium.

The rising tide of new pulp variations surged into the 1930s, seeing the birth of such minor one-pulp genres as *Prison Stories, New York Stories, Courtroom Stories, Fire Fighters, Jungle Stories, Northwest Stories, Front Page Stories*, and similar titles as well as the introduction of many F. B. I. pulps, such as *Federal Agent, Public Enemy, G-Men, G-Men Detective, Ace G-Man Stories, The Feds*; the formal mixing of genre themes and risqué fiction in such mid-1930s magazines as *Spicy Mystery Stories, Spicy Detective Stories, Spicy Adventure Stories, Spicy Western Stories, Saucy Detective, Saucy Movie Tales, Scarlet Adventures, Hollywood Detective;* the unleashing of a number of sadistic horror fiction magazines, such as *Dime Mystery Magazine, Horror Stories, Terror Tales, Uncanny Tales, Eerie Stories, Thrilling Mystery, Ace Mystery Magazine*; plus even more new detective pulp titles—*Popular Detective, Thrilling Detective, Dime Detective, Detective Tales, New Detective, Crime Busters, Private Detective Stories, Black Book Detective, Double Detective, Strange Detective*

Mysteries; Westerns—*Western Aces, Mavericks, 10-Story Western, Popular Western, Dime Western Magazine, All Western Magazine, Nickel Western, Thrilling Western, Thrilling Ranch Stories*; adventures—*Action Stories, Thrilling Adventures, All-American Fiction, Dynamic Adventures, Excitement, Northwest Stories, Golden Fleece, Oriental Stories, Magic Carpet*; air war—*Air War, Dare-Devil Aces, Sky Aces, Battle Birds, War Birds, Sky Fighters, Sky Devils, George Bruce's Contact, George Bruce's Squadron*; and science fiction—*Miracle Science and Fantasy Stories, Thrilling Wonder Stories, Startling Stories, Marvel Science Stories, Dynamic Stories, Planet Stories.*

Many of the multitude of new magazines were the product of freshly formed pulp chain publishers who carried as many as thirty or more pulp titles apiece; others were the releases of older publishers attracted to the market by the sizable and rising profits in an economic recession (for a nation out of work had little choice but to drink or read, and with bootleg whisky at a quarter a shot, many chose to read cheap fiction much of the time). Among the major publishers who flooded the newsstands with pulps in the wake of Munsey and Street & Smith were Dell Publishing Co., Fiction House, the Hersey Magazines, Clayton Magazines, Popular Publications, Thrilling Publications, Culture Publications, Standard Publications (later Better Publications), the A. A. Wynn magazines, and others, including spinoffs or front publishers set up by established houses to bring out yet more strings of pulps, such as Fictioneers, Inc., backed by Popular Publications, or Trojan Publishing Co., established by Culture Publications, Inc. At the helms of many of the pulps fielded by these publishers, sometimes editing as many as a dozen or more at once, were a number of talented and canny men, such as the much acclaimed Joseph T. "Cap" Shaw of the later *Black Mask*; Harold Brainerd Hersey of *Thrill Book, Ace-High Magazine, The Danger Trail, Clues-Detective*, and *Dragnet*; John W. Campbell, Jr. of *Astounding Science Fiction* and *Unknown Worlds*; John L. Nanovic of numerous Street & Smith titles; Ken White of *Dime Detective*; Farnsworth Wright of *Weird Tales* and *Oriental Stories*; Leo Margulies of the Thrilling chain, who shone in his handling of *Thrilling Wonder Stories* and *Startling Stories*; Henry Steeger of Popular, who supervised almost three dozen titles from *Horror Stories* to *Glamorous Love Stories*; Rogers Terrill, direct editor of all Popular titles under Steeger; Hugo Gernsback of *Amazing Stories* and *Wonder Stories*; Daisy Bacon of *Love Story Magazine*; F. Orlin Tremaine of *Top-Notch* and *Astounding Stories*; A. A. Wynn of *Ten Detective Aces*; Donald Kennicott of *Blue Book*; and others of equal capacity and accomplishment.

Probably the most notable and memorable achievement of the large pulp chain publishers and their editors in the 1930s was the fostering of the rebirth of the hero novel, once so central to the prosperity of the nickel thriller magazines of the 1890s. The first of these new monthly pulps was Gilbert Patten's little known *Swift Story Magazine* of November 1930, which, aside from its twenty-cent price and digest pulp size, itself unusual and innovative for the time, anticipated the content and format of the other hero pulps that followed in every detail: 128-page length, a recurrent hero in a monthly feature novel dominating the magazine—Derek Dane, Sky Sleuth in this case—several illustrations in the lead novel, a group of short stories in the closing pages, a department for the readers, and a lurid cover featuring the hero. Next, five months later, was Street & Smith's *Shadow Magazine* of April 1931, which introduced the dual identity outlaw crime fighter to the hero pulps; then came Standard Publications' *Phantom Detective* of February 1933, a *Shadow* imitation; Street & Smith's *Doc Savage* and *Nick Carter* of March 1933, covering the themes of exotic, fantastic adventure and the private detective respectively; Standard's *Lone Eagle* of September 1933, featuring a World War I air ace; Popular's *Spider* and *G-8 and His Battle Aces* of October 1933, presenting yet another masked crime fighter (the best of the lot) and a second World War I air ace *cum* spy respectively; Street & Smith's *Pete Rice* of November 1933, showcasing the first cowpoke sheriff in the hero pulps; Rose Wyn's *Secret Agent "X"* of February 1934, carrying the fourth hidden identity avenger of crime; Street & Smith's *Bill Barnes,* also of February 1934, a pulp with a contemporary aviation hero like Derek Dane; Popular's *Operator #5* of April 1934, introducing an American master spy facing contemporary enemy operations and foreign invasions; Popular's *Dusty Ayres and His Battle Birds* of July 1934, the first science fiction hero pulp, featuring a future interplanetary war; Popular's *Secret Six* of October 1934, multiplying the dual identity crime fighter by six; Ranger Publications' *Masked Rider* Western of December 1934, starring an imitation of the Lone Ranger of radio; Dell's *Doctor Death* of February 1935, introducing the first criminal lead character, *à la* Fu Manchu, in a hero pulp; and Fawcett Publications' *Terence X, O'Leary's War Birds* of March 1935, a second science fiction air war hero pulp.

The astonishing average was one new hero pulp every two months between January 1933 and April 1935, most of which kept going for the remainder of the decade. Nor did the pace slacken; these seventeen stalwart openers of the heroic way were followed by as many more over the next few years: *Wu Fang, Dr. Yen Sin, G-Men, Public Enemy* (later *Federal Agent*), *The Whisperer, The Skipper, Captain Satan, Captain Hazzard, Captain Combat, Captain Danger, Mavericks, Jungle Stories, Ka-Zar, The Lone Ranger, The Masked Detective, The Ghost* (later *The Green Ghost Detective*), *The Octopus, The Scorpion, The Wizard,* and others, including three short-lived newspaper comic strip adaptations: *Flash Gordon, Dan Dunn,* and *Tailspin Tommy.* Only the paper shortages of

World War II reduced the tide, but even after the war, in the increasing ebb that ultimately foundered almost all the pulps, a few more hero pulps were expectantly launched, such as *Hopalong Cassiday, Captain Zero,* and *Sheena, Queen of the Jungle,* a comic book adaption. The last hero pulp to succumb was the third to be created, *The Phantom Detective* of 1933, which expired with its 170th, quarterly issue in the summer of 1953. In number of issues, however, it was surpassed by *Doc Savage,* with 181 numbers to the summer of 1949, and the twice-a-month *Shadow,* with 325 issues to the same date. The magazine that pioneered the pulp hero concept and format, *Swift Story Magazine* of 1930, curiously, lasted just one issue.

Illustrating the hero pulps, as well as the pulp chain titles in general, was nearly as important for sales by the 1930s as the lurid covers of nickel thrillers had been for their prosperity at the turn of the century. While the earliest pulps (the Munsey titles, *The Popular, Short Stories,* etc.) were chary of interior illustrations when they carried them at all and generally garbed themselves in thematic covers featuring adventurous or sporting males in static poses with little or no relation to specific stories within, the number and quality of interior drawings increased sharply through competition in the 1920s, while direct story delineation on covers—initiated by the Munsey magazines in the 1910s—gradually became the norm. While a very few well budgeted pulps ran virtually an illustration to a page by the mid-1920s and 1930s (notably the stunning *Blue Book Magazine,* which also ran many illustrations in colored ink, *Real Detective Tales,* and the Spicy chain) and a number of others tried to continue with a minimal number of illustrations or none at all (*Best Detective, Great Detective Stories, Scotland Yard, Dragnet,* and *War Stories* were typical), the vast majority carried at least one lead illustration for every story (very short stories were usually excepted) and between two to four for novelettes and novels, plus continuing department heads. Supplying this considerable quantity of artwork was the task of a few dozen well worked professional ink, watercolor, and oil artists, who varied in quality and reputation from the dreariest kind of scrawlers and daubers who worked for Desperation Row (as the skin-of-their-teeth pulp houses were called) to a number of fine artists of international fame who did occasional or regular pulp magazine illustration for bread-and-butter money. Most, of course, were journeymen artists of reasonable competence and occasional flairs of real genius. Among the renowned artists who did a notable amount of pulp cover or interior work were N. C. Wyeth, Rockwell Kent, John Newton Howitt, J. Allen St. John, Gordon Grant, John R. Neill, Jonn Clymer, Austin Briggs, Nick Eggenhoffer, J. C. Leydendecker, and Herbert Morton Stoops; while the most outstanding and popular of the journeymen numbered such memorable talents as Hubert Rogers, Walter M.

Baumhofer, Jerome Rozen, Virgil Finlay, Paul Orban, John Fleming Gould, Frederick Blakeslee, Hannes Bok, Elliot Dold, Edd Cartier, Joseph Doolin, Frank R. Paul, H. W. Wesso, R. G. Harris, Norman Saunders, H. W. Scott, Rudolph Belarski, William Parkhurst, Frank Tinsley, Harold S. DeLay, and Margaret Brundage. Some indifferent comic strip art was introduced experimentally into a few pulps in the 1930s and later, but never with a notable effect on sales or lingering impact, with the possible exception of the classically silly *Sally the Sleuth* in *Spicy Detective Stories*.

The writers, of course—the kids just in from the prairies with their heavy office typewriters in cardboard boxes unloaded on wooden tables in shabby Manhattan furnished rooms, the wealthy top-wordage pulp kings writing from their estates around the world, the five-thousand-words-a-day steady producers in their suburban homes on Long Island or in southern California—these were the mainstay of the whole pulp operation. Following on the early group of pioneer pulp writers in the old Munsey magazines already mentioned, and writing in the 1940s or before, were such gifted and entertaining fictioneers as Edgar Rice Burroughs, whose highly contagious visions of Tarzan and Mars first overwhelmed the mass reading public in Munsey's *All-Story* between January and November 1912; Zane Grey, many of whose best known novels ran in *The Popular, Argosy,* and *All-Story*; Max Brand, who galloped to fame in virtually every early pulp, from *Argosy* and *Blue Book* through *Black Mask* and *Ace High* to *Western Story* and *The Railroad Man's Magazine*; Frank L. Packard, who introduced the dual identity outlaw crime fighter to detective fiction in his Jimmie Dale series for *People's Magazine* and later *Detective Fiction Weekly;* Abraham Merritt, who gripped two generations of readers with his splendid fantasy adventures, such as *The Moon Pool* and *The Ship of Ishtar,* in the Munsey titles; Joel Townsley Rogers, one of the most bizarre writers of suspense prose in American fiction, who wrote both aviation and crime fiction for such disparate magazines as *Wings, Adventure,* and *New Detective;* George Bruce, the finest author of air war fiction in the pulps, who was the first writer to have a pulp named for his work—and not just one pulp, but three (*George Bruce's Aces,* 1930; *George Bruce's Squadron,* 1933; and *George Bruce's Contact,* 1933); Howard Phillips Lovecraft, the finest American writer of macabre fiction since Poe, whose stories had enormous reader impact in *Weird Tales* and *Astounding Stories* and now constitute the base of a small publishing industry; Lester Dent, who wrote most of the *Doc Savage* hero pulps, of which over one hundred have been reprinted in top-selling paperback editions in the 1970s; Dashiell Hammett, who introduced his Continental Op, Sam Spade, and other characters in fresh, hard-bitten prose through the pages of *Black Mask, Brief Stories,* and *Argosy-All-Story*; Carroll John Daly, who created the lone private eye concept in *Black Mask* and augmented it through *Dime Detective, Detective Story, Detective Fiction Weekly,* and a dozen other pulps; Robert E. Howard, the freshest writer of adventure prose since Jack London, who wrote for an endless number of pulps from *Weird Tales* to *Argosy,* and whose work is being avidly reprinted here and abroad in over a hundred hardcover and paperback books; Norvell Page, creator of the *Spider* hero pulp, most powerful and memorable of the hero pulp writers and a regular contributor to many other pulps from *Unknown* to *Dime Mystery Magazine;* Raymond Chandler, who added his own bittersweet cachet to crime fiction in *Black Mask* and *Dime Detective* and even experimented with fantasy in *Unknown;* Ray Bradbury, one of the most noted contemporary American authors, who wrote much of his best fiction for *Weird Tales, Startling Stories, Detective Tales,* and other pulps; Walter B. Gibson, creator of *The Shadow* hero pulp and the indefatigable author of over three hundred novels about his cloaked hero, now in active reprint, as well as of other pulp hero series for such magazines as *Crime Busters* and *Mystery Magazine*; and a host of others of almost equal worth and importance: Robert A. Heinlein, Clark Ashton Smith, Steve Fisher, Frank Gruber, John D. MacDonald, Frederick C. Davis, Raoul Whitfield, Paul Cain, Henry S. Whitehead, Clifford D. Simak, Fritz Leiber, Robert Bloch, Luke Short, H. Bedford Jones, Victor Rousseau, Malcolm Jameson, C. L. Moore, Henry Kuttner, Ted Copp, Vincent Starrett, Erle Stanley Gardner, Frederick Nebel, William J. Makin, Cornell Woolrich, Norbert Davis, Donald Wandrei, Howard Wandrei, Harry Sinclair Drago, Fred MacIsaac, Theodore Tinsley, Theodore Sturgeon, John W. Campbell, Jr., Emile C. Tepperman, Cyril Kornbluth, Eric Temple Bell, David H. Keller, Robert J. Hogan, Paul Ernst, J. J. des Ormeaux, Clarence E. Mulford, Walt Coburn, Paul Chadwick, Huge B. Cave, Jack Kofoed, E. E. Smith, Rex Stout, A. E. Van Vogt, Isaac Asimov —a heady roster of famous names (and some no longer so famous), but one that literally cuts away only some of the cream of the pulps' exciting literary fraternity. There are at least fifty more names as well-known or representing as competent a body a work as any on the preceding list. Some—particularly the writers in the science fiction field and the *Black Mask* school—will be mentioned in other essays in this volume; others will have to wait for a longer study to be properly cited.

As can be seen from the authors noted, almost every area of popular American literature was blanketed by the pulps, and nearly always the involvement was both intimate and massive, leaving a major and permanent impression behind. There never was a time before or since that more good, engaging prose fiction (with, admittedly, a sizable, perhaps essential admixture of rubbish) has been available as cheaply to so many people. It lasted more than half a century, but when it entered its decline, the end came quickly. Many pulp readers of the time could see it coming, although the bulk of the editors and publishers in those later years did not seem so prescient. Since it was, by and large, their new policies and approaches to the fiction they were packaging that hastened the ruin of the pulps, this is perhaps not too surprising.

What happened is that the war years of the 1940s not only led to a reduction in the size of the pulps, their frequency of publication, their abundance of titles, and their very sturdiness (many issues had to be published with only one staple to conserve metal), but to the dismemberment of much of the established editorial staffs as well, with many going into the armed forces or war work. In most cases, these veterans of the great pulp boom of the 1930s, often with little formal schooling and sharing many of the tastes and needs of their readers, were replaced by young, draft-exempt people direct from college with liberal arts degrees in hand, who had rarely had the time or inclination to open a pulp for four or more years previously. Instead of feeling that they were the new, fortunate custodians of a marvelously varied treasure house of ongoing accomplishments and exciting possibilities, most seemed to believe that they had been put in charge of horrendously lowbrow products in antiquated packaging, badly in need of immediate improvement. The improvement they felt necessary, unfortunately, was the discarding of the lurid, raffish veneer, which attracted the bulk of their readership, and supplanting it with a neat, trimmed, proper, respectable, "distinguished" look which would permit the pulp editors to hold their heads up along Publishers Row in the future. The most extreme steps along this line were taken at what had become the economic mainstay of the shortage-racked pulp chains, Street & Smith, and when the prosperous flagship threw the Jolly Roger and the cutlasses overboard and broke out the doilies and teacups, it was really all over for the pulps. Through the 1940s, they were improved to death; in the 1950s, the corpses were interred.

The tragedy was compounded by the fact that, while the Street & Smith pulp packages were being upgraded to invisibility so far as the public was concerned, and their contents made increasingly unpalatable (the editorship of the classic *Detective Story Magazine* was taken over in the 1940s by Daisy Bacon, whose whole previous experience and orientation had been derived from her decades with *Love Story Magazine*), the general level of pulp writing elsewhere was improving enormously. A fresh generation of fine young pulp writers, who had cut their creative eyeteeth on the pulps as kids, was entering the field: Frederic Brown, John D. MacDonald, David Goodis, John McPartland, David Karp, Jack Vance, Philip K. Dick, Harlan Ellison, Evan Hunter, James Causey, Robert Turner, Day Keene, Richard S. Prather, Louis L'Amour, and a great many others. Their beautifully written, highly imaginative and innovative stories filled many of the surviving pulps, notably those of the hardily conservative

Popular chain, as well as most of the burgeoning science fiction pulps. It was to no avail; as the sales of the top-selling Street & Smith chain tumbled in the wake of the deadly new garb of neat propriety imposed on its pulps, national magazine distributors grew more nervous and reluctant about carrying any pulps at all. Individual dealers gave over more newsstand space to the proliferating comic books and cut back on that afforded the slower-selling pulps, often stacking them in odd corners rather than giving them cover display. What people did not see, or did not see well, they were less inclined to look for and buy. (It must be kept in mind, too, that the hard-core, devoted purchasers of particular pulp titles were always in a minority among the largely impulsive pulp public. If *Argosy*, say, was prominently displayed, it sold to some extent through familiarity with the title and the look of the cover; hidden from immediate sight, it was not sought out enough to sustain anything like the previous level of sales.) Basically, the public simply wanted light entertainment. If comic books and the exploding new field of paperback fiction (which demanded less space from dealers than pulps) were more visible than the pulps, the public's money was largely spent in these areas. When one of the two major national distributors of magazines refused to carry pulps any more in the early 1950s, it was all over for the chain publishers. A colorful handful of pulps survived, largely because of strong specialized markets (such as *Ranch Romances*' healthy newsstand pull in the Midwest and Northwest, and the tendency of devoted science fiction fans to buy all of the titles in their field as if they were one publication), but almost all had to adopt the digest pulp size to get even a hope of display at the newsstands. One or two, such as *Argosy* and *Blue Book*, gave up their pulp format and contents altogether and began fresh careers as general slick magazines with male appeal.

Although the bulk of their outlets were gone by the mid-1950s, the new writers remained. Those turning out science fiction had no real problem, for most of their old markets kept publishing, often as the only pulp titles left in the reorganized chains, but other writers had to find fresh sources of income. One of two new digest-size pulps were created with some success to carry some of this material in the crime, detective, and Western fiction fields, notably in Flying Eagle's *Manhunt, Murder! Alfred Hitchcock's Mystery Magazine,* and *Gunsmoke,* but by and large the more adaptable writers turned to the brand new markets for original paperback book fiction, such as Fawcett's Gold Medal Books, Atlas News's Lion Books, and similar title lines at Signet and Dell. These markets were almost exclusively for book-length novels, but paid very well in contrast to the penny-a-word rate still prevailing with most pulps at their demise. A few old-line pulp writers tried these new outlets, as well as the field of hardcover publishing to which most went. Lester Dent of *Doc Savage* tried both, for example, but generally speaking, it was the postwar group of newcomers, such as Day Keene, John D. MacDonald, and David Goodis, who flourished handsomely in the original paperback field.

Still, the pulps as they had been known in their heyday had irrevocably passed from the land. The sight, feel, and smell of them is no more, apart from the shelves of collectors, rare book dealers, and institutions. Only the living heart of their contents beats healthily in the myriad of briskly selling reprints that continue to be unearthed in great quantity from their yellowing pages both here and abroad where—notably in France and Japan—a youthful cabal of interest has sprung up in recent years. The pulps are dead, but at no time has literary and critical awareness of them been livelier than today.

BIBLIOGRAPHY

Bacon, Daisy. *Love Story Writer.* New York: Hermitage House, 1954.

Bedford-Jones, Henry. *This Fiction Business.* New York: Covici-Freide, 1929.

Britt, George. *Forty Years, Forty Millions: The Career of Frank A. Munsey.* New York: n.p., 1935.

Cawelti, John G. *The Six-Gun Mystique.* Bowling Green, Ohio: Bowling Green University Popular Press, 1970.

Cook, William Wallace (John Milton Edwards). *The Fiction Factory.* Ridgewood, N.J.: The Editor Co., 1912.

Day, Donald B. *Index to the Science Fiction Magazines: 1926-1950.* Portland, Oreg.: Perri Press, 1952.

De Camp, L(yon) Sprague. *Science Fiction Handbook.* New York: Hermitage House, 1953. Reprint. Rev. ed. Philadelphia: Owlswick Press, 1975.

Goodstone, Tony, ed. *The Pulps.* New York: Chelsea House, 1970.

Goulart, Ron. *Cheap Thrills: An Informal History of the Pulp Magazines.* New Rochelle, N.Y.: Arlington House, 1972.

Gruber, Frank. *The Pulp Jungle.* Los Angeles: Sherbourne Press, 1967.

Hersey, Harold. *Pulpwood Editor.* New York: Frederick A. Stokes, 1937.

Johanssen, Albert. *The House of Beadle and Adams and Its Dime and Nickel Novels.* Norman: University of Oklahoma Press, 1950. Supplement, 1962.

Jones, H. Bedford. *The Fiction Business.* New York: Covici-Fried, 1929.

Jones, Robert Kenneth. *The Shudder Pulps: A History of the Weird Menace Magazines of the 1930s.* West Linn, Oreg.: Fax Collector's Editions, 1975.

McKinstrey, Lohr, and Robert Weinberg. *The Hero Pulp Index.* Evergreen, Colo.: Opar Press, 1971.

Madden, David, ed. *Tough Guy Writers of the Thirties.* Carbondale: Southern Illinois University Press, 1968.

Mott, Frank Luther. *A History of American Magazines, Volume IV.* Cambridge, Mass.: Harvard University Press, 1957.

Pearson, Edmund. *Dime Novels.* Boston: Little Brown, 1929.

Reynolds, Quenton. *The Fiction Factory, or, From Pulp Row to Quality Street.* New York: Random House, 1955.

Smith, Henry Nash. *Virgin Land.* Cambridge, Mass.: Harvard University Press, 1950.

Radio

Nicholas A. Sharp

It is not easy to summarize the history of radio. In its early days, the medium grew so rapidly and in such diverse ways that time still has not fully clarified what things were important and what were merely interesting. One thing, however, is obvious. Radio in America has gone through three developmental stages—the "pioneer" period from the 1890s through the mid-1920s, the "golden age" of network programs in the 1930s and 1940s, and the "television age" which began in the late 1940s and is still in progress. From the viewpoint of the "old-time radio" fans, this pattern is almost tragic, representing periods of adventurous youth, glorious maturity, and senile decay. From a less partisan position, however, the pattern looks better. It shows a medium that went through a period of early technological and commercial development, then through a boom period of unstable and rapid growth, and finally achieved a stable place in the structure of American business and culture.

The pioneer years can be traced to Heinrich Hertz and the other pre-Marconi investigators of the nineteenth century. For our purposes, however, radio really began in 1895 when the young Italian inventor, Guglielmo Marconi, took his wireless telegraph to England. Customs inspectors smashed his prototype (they thought it was a bomb), but he rebuilt it, obtained British patents, and soon had commercial backers. Before the turn of the century, he had used Morse code to broadcast the results of the America's Cup yacht race, and virtually all of the major Western powers were investigating wireless for military and naval communication.

During the next decade, Reginald Fessenden, Lee de Forest, and scores of other inventors and enthusiasts developed technical improvements—the microphone, the vacuum tube, various crystal receivers—which made radio both inexpensive and exciting.

During World War I, the United States Navy took over almost exclusive control of American radio. It severely limited the use of the medium but made rapid technological progress. Then, in 1919, radio stations again became independent, and the mass production of commercial radio equipment became profitable. General Electric formed the Radio Corporation of America, which took over Marconi's original American company with the idea that the big profits would lie in the production of radio parts. They were not really thinking of broadcasting as anything but a marketing device to help sell radio receivers. The other big electrical companies like Westinghouse and American Telephone and Telegraph had similar ideas. Each of them set up broadcasting stations in order to put interesting things on the air, believing (rightly) that they could sell more receivers that way.

Many other people, however, were also interested in broadcasting. Amateurs broadcast from their garages and basements for the pure joy of contacting people in distant places. Newspapers set up stations to broadcast election results, sporting events, and other notable occurences because they hoped to sell more newspapers by whetting the public's interest. By the early 1920s, dance bands and Broadway plays were being broadcast live from the cramped, ill-equipped studios of pioneer stations, such as WJZ and KDKA, and many stations were beginning to broadcast on regular schedules. Meanwhile, performers were beginning to agitate for payment when they performed on radio.

By 1925, the American Society of Composers, Authors, and Publishers (ASCAP) was insisting on pay scales for radio performances. The National Association of Broadcasters had been formed to protect the interests of station owners, and local stations were using telephone lines to achieve multi-station broadcasts of major events. In Chicago, Detroit, Pittsburgh, and other areas, not to mention New York, stations had established their own regular programs of drama, comedy, and vaudeville, many of them with commercial sponsors. Broadcasting had become a business of its own.

In 1926, the Radio Corporation of American formed the National Broadcasting Company. The network system was born. Within a year, the Columbia Broadcasting System was also operating. NBC contracted to supply each local station with a certain number of programs, most of which originated in New York. Local stations still had considerable time at their own disposal, but they had to carry the programs which NBC sent them. NBC, in turn, sold air time to sponsors. The sponsors were to supply the programs; the network simply used its facilities to broadcast whatever program the sponsors wanted. Sponsors, in turn, wanted to use air time to sell products, and they turned to advertising agencies to produce shows that would sell their wares. The result was that certain advertising agencies became the major employers of actors, singers, directors, writers, and all the other show business professions. Only Hollywood and Broadway could compete as a talent market. Vaudeville died, but radio grew and grew.

A major reason for this rapid development during the 1920s was Herbert Hoover. As Secretary of Commerce, Hoover was able to outmaneuver the Navy, the Department of the Interior, and the Postal Service in claiming regulatory control over radio. His approach to broadcasting aggressively favored corporate free-enterprise; government's role was to eliminate chaos on the airwaves and to insure efficient use of the radio spectrum, nothing else. To do its job, therefore, government had to work closely with the large electronics firms (RCA, Westinghouse, etc.) that had both the capital and the desire to develop radio's economic potential. Hoover called the major corporate heads to a series of conferences during the mid-1920s. At these meetings, he achieved enough coordination among the federal bureaucracy and the various business interests to formulate policies which clearly defined broadcasting as a business enterprise rather than a governmental service. These regulations favored technologically advanced (and, thus, heavily capitalized) firms rather than smaller, less technically sophisticated interests. He worked with both the Congress and the corporate lobbyists to establish the legal base for the Federal Radio Commission (forerunner of today's Federal Communication Commission), and under the FRC's regulation, both radio manufacturing and broadcasting were able to flourish.

Among radio's entrepreneurs, two names stand out—Sarnoff and Paley. At RCA, David Sarnoff directed the development of America's two most significant radio organizations. As head of RCA, he controlled the most important single firm in the manufacturing and marketing of radio receivers. And because NBC, the first and largest of the broadcasting networks, was a subsidiary of RCA, Sarnoff also had a substantial influence on the development of commercial broadcasting, especially on the idea that broadcasters should turn responsibility for program content over to sponsors rather than developing programs for themselves. In contrast, William Paley led the development of broadcasting's most exciting institution, the Columbia Broadcasting System. From the outset, Paley understood programming to be the heart of the broadcasting business, and he was directly responsible for the development of programs, performers, and concepts which still dominate Americans' thinking about the electronic media.

Programming patterns on the networks developed rapidly. At first, comedy-variety shows dominated, and sponsored programs were heard largely at night. In 1929, when Freeman Gosden and Charles Correll took their local Chicago program to New York, "Amos 'n Andy" became radio's first nationwide phenomenon. Soon, other shows with a continued story line and consistent characters became standard nightime fare, though the variety show performers like Eddie Cantor, Ed Wynn, and Al Jolson continued to be the biggest crowd pleasers.

In a relatively short time, the "Amos 'n Andy" concept was metamorphosed into a form designed for daytime listeners, mainly housewives. The daily, fifteen-minute soap opera was born, and within a few years it became almost the only thing that the networks could carry during the day. There were always sponsors for a soap opera.

During the middle and late 1930s, the networks began to discover that they had programming capabilities of their own. They did not have to rely on advertising firms for programs. All of the networks had certain time periods which no sponsor was using, and the networks had to sustain their programming with fillers. So they began using that time for programs, such as the "Columbia Workshop," which were showcases for experimentation. Archibald MacLeish's verse-drama, "The Fall of the City," for instance, was written for and performed as a part of sustaining-time programming. Programs stressing new, dynamic approaches to history, current events, and the arts were developed, and in some cases they became hits. In turn, they stimulated sponsors, such as *Time* magazine, to develop programs, such as "The March of Time," which recreated current events through dramatization.

During the later 1930s two more networks were formed. The American Broadcasting Company was formed when anti-trust actions forced RCA to give up NBC, and NBC was forced to become one network rather than two; ABC had formerly been the NBC "blue" network which supplemented the larger, more popular "red" network. Also, the Mutual Broadcasting System was formed as a more-or-less cooperative venture among stations which wanted more independence than they would be allowed as part of NBC or CBS and yet needed the greater range of programming and services which only a network could provide.

By 1940, the basic programming patterns were set, and they continued through World War II with very little major change. But in the late 1940s, commercial television became a reality. By 1950, television was cutting heavily into radio's market. Network radio tried to respond with some new, creative concepts, such as "Monitor," a weekend program of interviews, satire, and news features. Basically, the entertainment role that network radio programs had filled for two decades was being thoroughly assumed by television. Radio programming, except for news, reverted primarily to the owners of individual stations. Pioneer stations became "Top-40" stations just to survive.

Today, radio programming is still basically a local station phenomenon, though more and more stations find they must turn to prepackaged models ("beautiful music," "adult rock," etc.) to compete for advertising dollars. The networks sponsor a few shows (CBS's "Mystery Theater" is one example), but radio is again a local medium.

Radio is no longer the big business that it was in 1940. It is, however, still a vital, important factor in our society. Like its budgets, radio's pretentions and ambitions have become smaller. Yet it continues to be a medium of essential communication, especially at the local level. Its broadcasts of community events, its occasionally fiery talk shows featuring local luminaries, and its constant barrage of local advertisements make it an integral part of most people's lives. Radio fills a crucial need in our society, and as long as it does, it will continue to be a major part of America's popular culture.

BIBLIOGRAPHY

Archer, Gleason L. *Big Business and Radio.* New York: American Historical Society, 1939.

Barnouw, Erik. *History of Broadcasting in the United States.* 3 vols. New York: Oxford University Press, 1966-70.

Bergreen, Laurence. *Look Now, Pay Later: The Rise of Network Broadcasting.* Garden City, N.Y.: Doubleday, 1980.

Buxton, Frank, and Bill Owen. *The Big Broadcast 1920-1950.* New York: Viking, 1972.

Culbert, David H. *News for Everyman: Radio and Foreign Affairs in Thirties America.* Westport, Conn.: Greenwood Press, 1976.

Dunning, John. *Tune in Yesterday: The Ultimate Encyclopedia of Old Time Radio 1925-1976.* Englewood Cliffs, N.J.: Prentice-Hall, 1976.

Edmondson, Madeline, and David Rounds. *From Mary Noble to Mary Hartmen: The Complete Soap Opera Book.* New York: Stein and Day, 1976.

Fornatale, Peter, and Joshua E. Mills. *Radio in the Television Age.* Woodstock, N.Y.: Overlook Press, 1980.

Harmon, Jim. *The Great Radio Comedians.* Garden City, N.Y.: Doubleday, 1970.

______. *The Great Radio Heroes.* Garden City, N.Y.: Doubleday, 1967.

Head, Sydney. *Broadcasting in America: A Survey of Radio and Television.* 2d ed. Boston: Houghton Mifflin, 1971.

Lyons, Eugene. *David Sarnoff: A Biography.* New York: Harper and Row, 1966.

MacDonald, J. Fred. *Don't Touch That Dial: Radio Programming in American Life 1920-1960.* Chicago: Nelson-Hall, 1979.

Metz, Robert. *CBS: Reflections in a Bloodshot Eye.* New York: Playboy Press, 1975.

Paley, William Samuel. *As It Happened: A Memoir.* Garden City, N.Y.: Doubleday, 1979.

Pitts, Michael R. *Radio Soundtracks: A Reference Guide.* Metuchen, N.J.: Scarecrow Press, 1976.

Poteet, G. Howard. *Published Radio, Television, and Film Scripts.* Troy, N.Y.: Whitston, 1975.

Rosen, Philip T. *The Modern Stentors: Radio Broadcasters and the Federal Government 1920-1934.* Westport, Conn.: Greenwood Press, 1980.

Slate, Sam J., and Joe Cook. *It Sounds Impossible.* New York: Macmillan, 1963.

Sterling, Christopher H., and John M. Kittross. *Stay Tuned: A Concise History of American Broadcasting.* Belmont, Calif.: Wadsworth Publishing Co., 1978.

Summers, Harrison B. *A Thirty Year History of Programs Carried on National Networks in the United States 1926-1956.* Columbus: Ohio State University Press, 1958.

Wertheim, Arthur Frank. *Radio Comedy.* New York: Oxford University Press, 1979.

PERIODICALS

Broadcasting. Washington, D.C., 1931-.

Journal of Broadcasting. Athens, Ga., 1956-.

Records and the Recording Industry

James Von Schilling

"I was never taken so aback in my life," was Thomas Alva Edison's reaction to the initial sounds coming from the machine he had hastily designed to repeat the spoken word, its first words being Edison's own rendition of "Mary Had a Little Lamb." Amazing as that premiere performance of the first phonograph must have been in 1876, even to its inventor, perhaps much more amazing has been its performance in the hundred-plus years since. The phonograph has survived patent struggles and labor disputes, two world wars and a Great Depression, the break-up of monopolies and the breakdown of distribution systems, the advent of motion pictures, radio, and television, along with the rise and fall of musical tastes, styles, and superstars. At times the industry's sales may have dipped, and there were even moments when the phonograph seemed on its last leg and tipping over, but the general trend for over a century has been continuous growth in product, audience, and profits.

Some have argued that the recent emergence of home videocassettes and videodiscs poses a serious threat to the record industry. After all, why pay to hear a performance you can both see and hear—in the privacy of your own home, at your own convenience? But this argument ignores two of the basic principles that have governed the complex history of recorded music. First, the industry has survived and prospered partly by taking advantage of any new medium that appeared to be its rival, or even conquerer. When radio boomed in the 1920s, for example, it seemed to mark the demise of the record industry. Aided by the onset of the Depression, radio was making the notion of *paying* to hear music at home obsolete, or at least foolish. Within a few years, though, radio had introduced America to "swing" music, a style so popular it triggered as a side-effect a whole new boom in record buying. Similarly, the later notion that television might doom the record industry was disproved in the aftermath of the 1964 appearances of the Beatles on the "Ed Sullivan Show," if not the appearances of Elvis Presley on the same show a decade earlier.

The second principle behind the remarkable growth and survival of the record industry reaches all the way back to Edison's reaction to his "child's" first words. At the very heart of recorded music's relationship to American culture has been its power to take each of us aback, as Edison was, throughout our personal lives. Historians of the phonograph have noted that each new development in recording technology was heralded as introducing the ultimate in life-like sound, only to be rendered hopelessly "tinny" by newer technologies, sometimes just a few years later. This suggests we take such claims (for example, the current publicity about digital recording) with a certain skepticism, but it also illustrates an important point. Despite how inferior the recording techniques and results of the past may seem to us now, they created powerful emotional experiences for the audiences of their time. The essential bond has always been between the listener and the recorded sound, and everything else— the technology, the marketing, the profits— has resulted from that bond and its basic power.

In other words, recorded sound does something of great significance to people, and so it has for over one hundred years of American culture. The variety of styles and performers that have been recorded, as well as the variety of audiences that have been affected by these recordings, makes it difficult to determine exactly what this significance is and where its real power resides. "It's got a good beat and you can dance to it," goes the classic explanation for what makes a rock-and-roll record a memorable experience to its audience, but that hardly works with recordings of other genres: jazz, country, Broadway, opera, and so forth. Regardless of genre, however, all recordings do one thing in common: they capture in time a unique combination of music, performance, and artistry and then enable us to make this "timepiece" part of our personal experience.

When we purchase a record, we generally have little knowledge of the history, technology, or economics behind it. But all that may be incidental; the essence of recorded music may simply be the personal actions of bringing that record home, slitting the cellophane "shrink jacket," placing the disc on the turntable, starting the electricity and machinery, and then experiencing internally the timepiece of music, performance, and artistry awaiting us in the grooves. A nursery rhyme in his own voice took Edison aback; today it may require a multi-tracked, million-dollar electronic production, but the results are the same. We are taken hold, and a truly memorable recording will transcend all the history, technology, and business and not let us back into that other world—at least until the music ends.

Thomas Edison invented the phonograph the way Columbus discovered America—accidentally, while looking for something else entirely. Edison was actually seeking to improve the newly emerging telephone system by making it more accessible to the middle and lower classes in America. Home telephone equipment was expensive back in 1876; Edison hoped to design a machine for recording messages, with the results capable of being replayed and transmitted at a centrally located telephone. Precisely why anybody would need to record the message beforehand rather than simply speak into the centrally located phone (for instance, today's public telephones) has never been completely established, not that it really mattered. Edison's idea, which was rendered into a working mechanism by an assistant, John Kruesi, in November 1876, quickly took on new applications when introduced to the public the following year. Edison himself soon envisioned a list of ten general uses for his invention, of which only the tenth dealt with telephones. The others included "letter writing and all kinds of dictation," "reproduction of music" (fourth on his list), and "clocks that announce in accurate speech the time for going home, going to meals, etc."[1]

At first the phonograph generated great publicity as Edison's assistants conducted public demonstrations around the country. But by 1880 Edison had rechanneled his energies and redirected his laboratory toward a new idea, the electric lightbulb, and the phonograph slipped into a state of suspended animation for most of the decade. In October 1887, however, Edison switched gears again, "confessing" to America that, despite his apparent fixation on what he called "the electric business.... Nevertheless, the phonograph has been more or less constantly in my mind."[2] Edison's apparent fickleness was, in reality, a shrewd businessman's response to a rapidly changing commercial climate, as his short-lived monopoly over the machine, the industry, and its future was about to end.

Edison's invention was facing a stiff, serious competitor in 1887, the Alexander Graham Bell-sponsored Graphophone; the following year yet a third rival emerged, Emile Berliner's gramophone. The stage was set for the next thirty years of the fledgling industry's history and a series of complex, exhaustive struggles between the pioneering individuals and companies that emerged from these first three rivals. From a technological perspective, the machine that eventually dominated the market after this "Thirty Years War" was a far cry from Edison's mechanism. Instead, it more closely resembled Emile Berliner's gramophone, recording on discs rather than Edison's cylinder products.

From a business viewpoint, two major companies survived out of the dozen or so that played key roles during these early years; although the ranks of "majors" have changed throughout the decades, these two have always made the list. The first company, Victor Talking Machine, came to life in 1901, when Eldridge R. Johnson, who had been Berliner's equipment supplier, staked his own claim in the industry. Twenty-five years later Johnson sold his controlling interest in Victor for $28 million to a firm that soon merged with the Radio Corporation of America (RCA). Columbia Phonograph, the other permanent leg of the record industry, had its origins way back in 1878, as a subsidiary distributor for Bell's Graphophone. Columbia suffered through periods of hard times and one clear case of bankruptcy. Propped up in 1923 by new owners, it survived the Depression and eventually found a safe haven in the early 1930s under the corporate umbrella of RCA's arch-rival, the Columbia Broadcasting System (CBS).

From a musical standpoint, no single style dominated these early years of the record industry as rock music has since the 1950s. Rather, the catalogs of the pioneer companies featured everything from the arias of Enrico Caruso to the popular ditties of George W. Johnson, "The Whistling Coon." Popular music in general, though, clearly dominated the market, no doubt partly because many early phonographs were coin-operated and served as amusements in public locations. But classical performers, particularly opera stars (orchestras fared poorly under the early recording techniques), became crucial weapons in the fierce publicity battles fought between the pioneer companies. Signing a top European tenor or soprano could help establish a company as an industry leader, even though the bulk of that company's sales were likely to fall in the popular market.

Linked so closely to America's popular culture, though, the record industry was subject to the fluctuations of public taste. The medium experienced its first real boom during the Dance Mania of the mid-1910s. Victor scored a coup by signing the period's ballroom royalty, Vernon and Irene Castle, to "supervise" the recording of dance music, while Columbia trumpeted its own expert, G. Hepburn Wilson, who "dances while the band makes the record." Sales of newly designed phonograph consoles, with prices ranging up to $2,000, soared in the United States and Europe and continued strong through the early 1920s, aided by a popular, shocking, and liberating style of music and dance: hot jazz.

But the focus of popular culture shifted unexpectedly in the mid-1920s to a new medium for speech and music—the radio—with one clear technical advantage over the phonograph. The radio was electric: the amplification processes involved in radio transmission produced sounds far superior in quality to the mechanical diaphragm and stylus system that the early phonograph employed. That technological edge gave radio a jump-start and forced the record industry to adapt by adding radio sets to its consoles and developing electrical recording and playback processes itself. But these changes weren't enough to carry the record industry through a second upheaval later that decade, as the Great Depression placed phonograph records on its list of obviously expendable purchases.

Record sales by 1932 had dropped incredibly—to just 6 percent of the 1927 rate—and sales of phonographs sank to similar depths. The industry did climb back, of course, but doing so took the rest of the decade and involved a number of factors, not the least of which was the New Deal's gradual restoration of consumer confidence in general. Within the industry itself, though, several key developments aided the recovery, most notably the sudden leap to sales prominence of Decca Records, founded by an American, Jack Kapp, and financed by a London stockbroker. With the current industry "majors"—Victor, Columbia, and Brunswick—all selling their discs for seventy-five cents apiece, Decca managed to corral some top performers and peddle their records for only thirty-five cents. "Decca Scoops Music World," headlined their ads, and they did indeed scoop up such pop stars as Bing Crosby, the Mills Brothers, and the Dorseys for their roster. RCA-Victor also contributed significantly to the recovery by marketing a popular, budget-priced phonograph called the Duo, Jr., designed to use the home radio for amplification.

Perhaps the biggest boost to the record industry, though, came from America's popular culture, as the "hot jazz" craze of the 1920s settled into a more mainstream, socially acceptable style of entertainment. America thus entered the "Swing" or "Big Band" era, when purchasing the latest tunes by Benny Goodman, Glenn Miller, Harry James, and others became a basic part of life for a whole generation of young Americans. Radio may have popularized the music in the first place, and jukeboxes whetted the public's appetite, but actually owning an "In the Mood" 78 rpm to play in the parlor was the next best thing to jitter-bugging in front of the bandstand. Sales of records picked up slowly at first and then dramatically, reaching a peak of 127 million in 1941—and then the bubble burst again.

At first the problem this time was World War II and the restrictions imposed on the record industry: all manufacturers of electrical equipment were redirected to the war effort, and 70 percent of the nation's shellac resources (from which records were being produced) were devoted to strictly military purposes. But a heavier bomb fell on the homefront in the summer of 1942, when the American Federation of Musicians voted to strike the record industry on the grounds that recorded music was putting the professional musician out of business, or at least severely curtailing the need for live performances. With its sales concentrated solely in the popular market, Decca suffered the most by not being able to record the latest styles and hits (which could still be heard in live performances on the radio) and was forced to capitulate the following year. The terms of the Decca agreement involved the payment of royalties to the AFM, for the support of unemployed musicians, for every record sold. Columbia and RCA held out for a second year but eventually "surrendered" on the same day Germany signed its peace pact with the Allies.

With conflicts both national and international finally settling down, the record industry may have anticipated a relatively calm postwar period. Instead, the following decade featured an upheaval in technology, a disruption of the industry's economic structure, and a shift in American popular culture of earthquake proportions. The revolution in technology surfaced to the public as the "Battle of the Speeds," with the new 33 1/3 rpm album from CBS in one corner and the new 45 rpm "single" from RCA in the other. Actually, a great deal more than different turnable speeds was involved since Peter Goldmark, the CBS engineer who developed the long-playing 33 1/3 album, had virtually reinvented the entire recording and production process along the way. Nothing would ever be the same after Goldmark's album caught on with the public: not the recording studio, with its dramatically improved microphone system; not the records themselves, with their contents expanded up to ten times the two- or three-minute span of the old 78; not even the industry's long-established hierarchy, with Columbia now the leader and RCA playing "catch up." Countering with its own 45, RCA weakly described the little disc's virtues as the ideal form for the popular single. They were in luck, though, as a figure emerged in America's popular culture (conveniently signed to an RCA contract) who would link the 45, with its oversized hole and its undersized playing time, to millions of young people from that point on: the "Hillbilly Cat" from Tupelo, Mississippi—Elvis Presley.

RCA may have reaped the most benefits from the rise of Elvis Presley from "Hillbilly Cat" to superstardom, but the fact is that neither Elvis, Chuck Berry, Little Richard, the Coasters, nor any of the pioneers of rock and roll would have affected our popular culture had it not been for a new force that developed in the postwar record industry: the independent record company, or "indie." These businesses ranked far below the "majors" in total sales, production and promotional budgets, as well as access to distribution (the "majors" at that time being RCA, Columbia, Decca, Capital, Mercury, and MGM). Yet, for several key reasons, such relatively small-scale operations as Chess, Savoy, and Atlantic Records came to assume a position of great importance and, in fact, permanently changed the direction of popular music and the entire record industry. First and perhaps foremost, these independent companies recorded black music performed by black artists in a style that was known as "rhythm and blues" ("R&B") out of which developed rock and roll. With but a few exceptions (for example, Louis Jordan on Decca), the majors either disavowed black music entirely, shunted it onto less-supported subsidiary labels, or recorded black artists like Nat King Cole who were closer to the white mainstream.

In neglecting to record rhythm-and-blues performers, the majors were simply following a pattern that had been established and reestablished throughout the century, in which black artists influenced—and often determined—the course of America's popular music but white artists profited commercially once the new music reached the public. From the industry's viewpoint, the history of recorded music up to that point had clearly shown that any new music emerging from the black subculture could be directed into the mainstream by the majors, with the ensuing profits diverted from the original sources. Such had been the case with hot jazz and swing music; thus, there was every reason to believe that the system would prevail with rhythm and blues, despite the presence of the independent companies. After all, the majors in the early 1950s were holding a tight grip over all possible distribution routes—jukeboxes, radio airplay, record stores, sheet music—or so they thought. At it turned out, the majors failed to assess two additional factors, one sociological, the other commercial, that nearly toppled the whole system.

In sociological terms, the majors failed to adjust to the new realities of America's racial structure, for World War II had brought blacks and whites in much greater proximity. This was clearly the case in America's Northern cities, where thousands of Southern blacks had relocated during the war to seek jobs and had remained afterwards. Segregation and discrimination were still in force, but the music of a people can sometimes penetrate where the people themselves cannot, especially if an ideal commercial means for that penetration exists. In this case, the music—rhythm and blues—found the perfect means in a handful of young and daring radio disc jockeys, such as Alan Freed, Hal Jackson, and Bill Randle, who felt its power and promoted it to anyone who would listen, black or white. Thus, radio undermined the ability of the majors to orchestrate this new popular music, for the one thing RCA, Columbia, and the others couldn't control was the tuning of the American teenager's bedroom or car radio.

Yet, considering all that the majors *could* control, it's a testimony to the power of rhythm and blues that performers such as Chuck Berry, Fats Domino, Ray Charles, the Coasters, Little Richard, Frankie Lymon, and Bo Diddley—all recording for indies—ever managed to gain a white audience. The majors had direct influence, and often outright control, over the entire production, promotion, and distribution stages in the life of most popular tunes up through the 1950s, and they used all their power to fight for the continued success of their performers, many of whom were holdovers from the Big Band era. Their most infamous tactic was the "cover" record: a white version of a black hit, quickly recorded, released, and promoted in the mainstream white markets and on leading white radio stations (for example, Perry Como's cover of "Kokomo," originally recorded by Gene and Eunice). One especially heavy-handed tactic involved public denunciation of the new music by established mainstream figures; Frank Sinatra, for example, used the words "brutal, ugly, desperate, vicious" to describe rock and roll at a 1958 congressional hearing. With less publicity, but perhaps more effectiveness, the industry developed a third key tactic: revamping their commercial operations and strengthening their promotion departments, especially involving radio airplay. The majors now recognized the importance of releasing pop singles quickly, to capitalize on popular trends, and of marketing their releases thoroughly from coast to coast.

In the short run, the majors lost the struggle with the indies. The number of hit singles produced by independent companies at the close of the 1950s was twice that of the majors, a remarkable shift from the immediate postwar years, when only five out of 162 million-sellers belonged to indies. In the long run, though, the majors won the fight, as few of the independent companies survived the 1960s and the industry retrenchment that decade brought. Once again, the forces behind the new shift were numerous and complex. A well-publicized factor was the 1960 congressional investigation into record industry "payola," or the bribing of radio disc jockeys by record personnel to spur airplay for new releases. The big losers in the scandal weren't the major record companies but the free-wheeling rock-and-roll disc jockeys who had played such key roles in the rise of the new music, especially Alan Freed, whose career and personal life crumbled after the hearings. The indies themselves suffered, too, losing whatever respectability they might have gained during the 1950s. Also, any curtailment of payola activities would hurt the indies more than the majors, who could still rely on their own extensive distribution systems and, in the case of RCA and Columbia, their own nationwide home record clubs.

In addition, the style of popular music had by then progressed from the early years of rock and roll and in a direction that benefited the mainstream industry. With a surprising number of rock pioneers removed from the scene for various reasons (Elvis Presley drafted, Chuck Berry jailed), the sound was decidedly less black "R&B" and more white "pop." Top hits, for example, were recorded by numerous television situation-comedy stars, ranging from Shelley Fabares to Walter Brennan. Another portion of the market belonged to the young performers who recorded for the Philadelphia-centered labels associated with Dick Clark's "American Bandstand" television show. Few members of either group remained successful through the mid-1960s, however their brief tenure at the top clearly presaged two trends that have characterized the record industry ever since. First, the record industry had developed economically to the point where cross-ownership and conglomeration were influencing the musical results, that is, television's non-singers owed their recording careers to the tangled webs being weaved during the 1960s among the various entertainment industries. Second, the record industry was now profiting heavily from the "cult of personality" approach to producing and marketing performers. Whether it was the pompadoured teenage idol or the cashmere-sweatered girl-next-door, the *image* of the performing artist was selling records, perhaps more than the music or performance itself.

Neither trend was exactly new to the record industry. After all, RCA and CBS had been media conglomerates for decades, and numerous recording stars had developed careers in other entertainment fields or had public images that boosted their sales. But it was during the 1960s that the record industry's corporate structure and its promotional apparatus became as important, if not more so, than the recording technology or the music itself. Under such conditions, the companies that did the best weren't necessarily the most inventive or even the most talented, but rather the ones with the strongest economic bases and skills of promotion.

A company whose rise to major status typified the changes in the industry was Warner Records, an independent purchased in the 1960s by Kinney Services, a New York-based conglomerate. With a stock of reasonably talented young performers (based largely in southern California), but with lots of promotional campaigning and enough capital to support its own operations and also acquire Atlantic and Elektra Records, Warner spent the 1960s climbing toward the top of the industry in sales. Warner is often cited as the company best illustrating how the "baby boom" generation and their fixation on popular music brought enormous growth and success to the record industry during the 1960s. Although this sociological approach has obvious validity, it misses the equally obvious point that neither Warner nor the other 1960s majors could have capitalized on the boom and the fixation without their corporate structures and promotional efforts.

Even the Beatles, when viewed in retrospect, were not as spontaneously welcomed by American youth as our popular myths would have us believe. In 1963, the year before "Beatlemania" struck our shores, several Beatles singles were released in the United States on independent labels and caused little reaction. It wasn't until a major company, Capital, bought the distribution rights and launched one of the most extensive promotional campaigns in the history of recorded music that the Beatles attracted their massive following. In other words, "Beatlemania"—along with the other waves of popular music intensity during the last two decades—developed from a combination of factors all present in contemporary America: an unusually large population of young people; the close links that have existed between popular music and the social and emotional lives of young Americans, at least since the mid-1950s and the advent of rock music, although probably extending back through the "swing" and "hot jazz" years; and the existence of well-financed, promotion-oriented record companies to feed huge amounts of product to the vast young audience.

With a large collection of albums and an expensive stereo now important status symbols among American youth, with records now sold everywhere from local supermarkets to coast-to-coast chain stores, and with top performers now rating "cover story" prominence in our national news magazines, it's no surprise that the record industry has climbed past both the radio and the motion picture industry in total annual income. Whether the products on which that climb has been based—the recorded music of the 1960s and 1970s—truly deserve so much promotion, sales, and recognition is subject to debate. Some would draw an imaginary line in the early 1970s to separate, chronologically, the "good" (1960s rock) from the "bad" (1970s disco). Some would draw the line a few years earlier or later, and others would make a distinction throughout both decades between "genuine" popular music expression and "hyped" record industry product.

Still others would argue that all such lines and distinctions are more a reflection of social- and peer-group attitudes than of the relative quality of any of the music. According to this line of thinking, most recorded music since 1960, when the majors began operating on a grander economic scale, has been fashioned with the same basic principles in mind. The ever-present goal has been to maximize profits, as the media conglomerates to which all leading record companies now belong attempt to support current and future acquisitions with all the money generated by all the music. Thus, every trend—even the hint of a trend—is picked up by the industry, worked into salable products, heavily promoted, and eventually dropped by the wayside when a new trend emerges. In the 1970s trends that followed this pattern included country-rock, punk rock, and disco—with "new wave" music perhaps being the first trend to test the pattern's endurance into the 1980s.

The medium of recorded music today is in many ways vastly different from even just one generation past. It now encompasses such new territory as the auto accessory industry, with the advent of cassette and cartridge systems, as well as the fields of demographics and behavior research, with the testing methods now practiced by some companies in their quest for hit records. Today's top albums earn "gold" and "platinum" status not after weeks of high sales but often right at the point of release; some albums cost over $1 million to produce, sell over 10 million units, and bring in over $100 million in gross profits. Today's top recording stars influence fashions, hair styles, sexual mores, drug usage, even social and political decision making. And today's industry scandals are less likely to involve small sums of money paid to free-wheeling disc jockeys than millions of dollars raked in by well-organized "pirates" of illegally copied records and tapes.

In other ways, though, the more things have changed, the more they've remained the same. It took Thomas Edison only months to begin speculating how his new invention, originally a telephone accessory, might expand into new fields and directions: the expansion continues. The industry's early years featured intensely fought struggles between competing companies: the struggles continue with all their intensity. Those first recordings were a mixed lot, mostly based on popular tastes and often disdained by cultural critics: the mixture continues, along with the popular emphasis and critical disdain. And from "Mary Had a Little Lamb" up through "Y.M.C.A.," the sounds of music and voice on record have continued to hold a power all their own, transcending changes in technology and styles of performance. For the future, we can expect both technology and styles to continue changing, with the power remaining strong. It's been over a century now since America played its first record; right now, despite all that's happened to the culture and the industry during those hundred years, there's no sign that the music is about to end.

BIBLIOGRAPHY

Billboard. *Music/Records/200.* New York: Billard, 1976.

Chapple, Steve, and Reebee Garofalo. *Rock 'n' Roll Is Here To Pay.* Chicago: Nelson-Hall, 1978.

Davis, Clive. *Clive: Inside the Record Business.* New York: William Morrow, 1975.

Denisoff, R. Serge. *Solid Gold.* New Brunswick, N.J.: Transaction Books, 1975.

Escott, Colin, and Martin Hawkins. *Catalyst.* London: Aquarius Books, 1975.

Fong-Torres, Ben, ed. *What's That Sound?* New York: Anchor Press, 1976.

Gillett, Charlie. *Making Tracks: Atlantic Records and the Growth of a Multi-Billion Dollar Industry.* New York: Dutton and Co., 1974.

———. *The Sound of the City.* New York: Outerbridge and Dientsfrey, 1972.

Greene, Bob. *Billion Dollar Baby.* New York: Signet, 1975.

Lydon, Michael. *Boogie Lightning.* New York: Dial, 1974.

———. *Rock Folk: Portraits from the Rock 'n' Roll Pantheon.* New York: Dial Press, 1971.

Malone, Bill. *Country Music USA.* Austin: University of Texas Press, 1974.

Marcus, Greil, ed. *Stranded: Rock and Roll for a Desert Island.* New York: Alfred A. Knopf, 1979.

McCabe, Peter, and D. R. Schonfeld. *Apple to the Core.* New York: Pocket Books, 1972.

Miller, Jim, ed. *The Rolling Stone Illustrated History of Rock 'n' Roll.* New York: Random House, 1976.

Morse, David. *Motown and the Arrival of Black Music.* New York: Macmillan, 1971.

Read, Oliver, and Walter L. Welch. *From Tin Foil to Stereo.* New York: Bobbs Merrill Co., 1959.

Roberts, John Storm. *The Latin Tinge: The Impact of Latin-American Music on the United States.* New York: Oxford University Press, 1979.

Shaw, Arnold. *The Rockin' Fifties:* New York: Macmillan, 1974.

———. *The World of Soul: Black America's Contribution to the Pop Music Scene.* New York: Cowles Book Co., 1970.

Spitz, Robert Stephen. *The Making of Superstars: Artists and Executives of the Rock Music Business.* Garden City, N.Y.: Anchor Press, 1978.

Stokes, Geoffrey. *Starmaking Machinery.* New York: Vintage Books, 1977.

Williams, Richard. *Out of His Head: The Sound of Phil Spector.* New York: Outerbridge and Lazard, 1972.

Regionalism

Anne Rowe

Although an awareness of regions or sections has existed in America from the Colonial period to the present, regionalism in literature and the arts generally refers to two periods: the local color period of the late-nineteenth century and regionalism of the 1930s and after.

The beginning of the local color movement is usually cited as 1868, when Bret Harte began publishing stories of California mining camps in the *Overland Monthly.* Many provincial sketches and stories appeared in large-circulation magazines during the 1870s, and the local color vogue reached its height during the 1880s and 1890s, tapering off near the end of the century.

Only after the end of the Civil War, when it became clear that the battle for nationalism had been won, was there a dramatic growth of interest in the many sectional differences of the United States. Local color writing, which emphasized the unique setting of a particular region and reproduced the dialect, customs, provincial types, and other qualities of that region, seemed to satisfy the desire of the American people to take a nostalgic look at the good old days of the preindustrialized, prewar period. Thus, much local color writing was rural-based but intended for city consumption. Local color writing grew out of every region, and representative local colorists included Mary E. Wilkins Freeman and Sarah Orne Jewett of New England, Bret Harte of the West, and George Washington Cable and Thomas Nelson Page of the South. After the fall of the Confederacy there was much national interest in and curiosity about the South, and Southern local colorists were heavily represented in nationally circulated magazines.

Local color writing usually appeared as short stories. Plots were highly contrived and characterization was generally superficial, characters usually not transcending the stereotype. Because of these limitations, local color writing of this period is looked upon today as having been more a popular than an artistic success.

In contrast to the term *local color, regionalism* refers to an intellectual movement of the 1930s which posited that each of the regions of the United States is a geographical, cultural, and economic entity. This new concept of regionalism, which was as much sociological as literary, was apparent particularly in the South. The publication of *I'll Take My Stand: The South and the Agrarian Tradition* by Twelve Southerners in 1930 expressed the desire of its authors to resist standardization and to preserve, as far as possible, an agrarian-based culture. Although the Agrarians, as they were called, including John Crowe Ransom, Robert Penn Warren, Donald Davidson, Allen Tate, and others, did not believe that the South could remain an entirely agricultural society, they argued for a set of values that supported a human rather than machine-dominated society.

During the 1930s a number of works appeared which explored the relationship of the regions to the literary and social culture of America. Carey McWilliams, *The New Regionalism in American Literature,* was an early attempt at defining regionalism. *The Attack on Leviathan: Regionalism and Nationalism in the United States* by Donald Davidson posited an agrarian point of view. *American Regionalism: A Cultural-Historical Approach to National Integration* by Howard W. Odum and Harry Estill Moore argued for an integration of cultural, geographical, and historical factors.

One of the most important literary movements related to regionalism in the 1930s was the Southern Renaissance, out of which came the work of William Faulkner, Thomas Wolfe, Robert Penn Warren, and others. In novels, short stories, poetry, and essays, the literary productivity of the South loomed great. Other major writers of the 1930s, Willa Cather and John Steinbeck, for example, also employed a regional base for their works. The important distinction to be made, then, between local color and regionalism is that the latter brought much more breadth and depth to the depiction of a cultural region.

Regionalism as a cultural force has continued to receive attention since the 1930s. For some artists and critics regionalism has a pejorative connotation; it implies limitation. Regionalism, it is argued, must necessarily limit the universal message of the work of art. Proponents of regionalism argue, perhaps more convincingly, that all art must come out of a particular region or culture. That it does so in no way limits its universal statement. For example, although most of Faulkner's work is set in Mississippi, its meaning extends far beyond the boundaries of that state.

Most recently regionalism has aroused the interests of students of popular culture. Although the development of a formal theory concerning regionalism in popular culture is only in the beginning stages, a number of explorations of the relationship between a region and its culture have been undertaken. A challenging aspect of this study is the fact that with the increasing standardization of the media—television shows that are broadcast nationally, top ten radio programming, films that are released simultaneously in all parts of the country—the question of how many regional distinctions will continue to exist during the remaining decades of this century becomes especially important.

BIBLIOGRAPHY

Bargainnier, Earl F. "The Falconhurst Series: A New Popular Image of the Old South." *Journal of Popular Culture,* 10 (Fall 1976), 298-314.

Bigsby, C.W.E., ed. *Approaches to Popular Culture.* Bowling Green, Ohio: Bowling Green University Popular Press, 1976.

Browne, Ray B., Richard H. Crowder, Virgil L. Lokke, and William T. Stafford, eds. *Frontiers of American Culture.* Lafayette, Ind.: Purdue Research Foundation, 1968.

______, Larry N. Landrum, and William K. Bottorff. *Challenges in American Culture.* Bowling Green, Ohio: Bowling Green University Popular Press, 1970.

Carlson, Alvar W. "Cultural Geography and Popular Culture." *Journal of Popular Culture,* 9 (Fall 1975), 482/130-483/131.

______, ed. "In-Depth: Cultural Geography and Popular Culture." *Journal of Popular Culture,* 11 (Spring 1978), 829-997 [12 articles].

Core, George, ed. *Regionalism and Beyond: Essays of Randal Stewart.* Nashville: Vanderbilt University Press, 1968.

Davidson, Donald. *The Attack on Leviathan: Regionalism and Nationalism in the United States.* Chapel Hill: University of North Carolina Press, 1938.

Gastil, Raymond D. *Cultural Regions of the United States.* Seattle: University of Washington Press, 1975.

Hodge, Clarence Lewis. *The Tennessee Valley Authority: A National Experiment in Regionalism.* New York: American University Press, 1938. Reissued. New York: Russell and Russell, 1968.

Jensen, Merrill, ed. *Regionalism in America.* Madison: University of Wisconsin Press, 1951.

Kirby, Jack Temple. *Media-Made Dixie: The South in the American Imagination.* Baton Rouge: Louisiana State University Press, 1978.

Leary, Lewis. *Articles on American Literature: 1900-1950.* Durham, N.C.: Duke University Press, 1954.

______. *Articles on American Literature: 1950-1967.* Durham, N.C.: Duke University Press, 1970.

Lowenthal, Leo. *Literature, Popular Culture, and Society.* Englewood Cliffs, N.J.: Prentice-Hall, 1961.

Marsden, Michael T., ed. "National Finding List of Popular Culture Holdings Special Collections." *Popular Culture Association Newsletter,* 6 (March 1977).

McWilliams, Carey. *The New Regionalism in American Literature.* Seattle: University of Washington Book Store, 1930. Reprint. Folcroft, Pa.: Folcroft Library Editions, 1974.

Odum, Howard W., and Harry Estill Moore. *American Regionalism: A Cultural-Historical Approach to National Integration.* New York: Henry Holt and Co., 1938.

Rosenberg, Bernard, and David Manning White, eds. *Mass Culture: Popular Arts in America.* Glencoe, Ill.: The Free Press, 1957.

Schrank, Jeffrey. *Snap, Crackle, and Popular Taste: The Illusion of Free Choice in America.* New York: Bell, 1977.

Simpson, Claude M., ed. *The Local Colorists: American Short Stories, 1857-1900.* New York: Harper and Row, 1960.

Spiller, Robert E., Willard Thorp, Thomas H. Johnson, Henry Seidel Canby, and Richard M. Ludwig, eds. *Literary History of the United States.* 2 vols. 3d ed., revised. New York: Macmillan, 1963.

Wolfe, Margaret Ripley. "The Southern Lady: Long Suffering Counterpart of the Good Ole' Boy." *Journal of Popular Culture,* 11 (Summer 1977), 18-27.

Young, Margaret Labash, Harold Chester Young, and Anthony T. Kruzas, eds. *Subject Directory of Special Libraries and Information Centers.* Detroit: Gale Research Co., 1975.

Religion and Self-Help

Roy M. Anker

The notion of self-help has a long, energetic, and prolific life in American culture. Put plainly, past and present self-help ideologies have no common seminal idea or generative figure but vary in emphasis in different historical periods. As this essay title suggests, the numerous mutations of the self-help theme in the flux of American experience stem from diverse and often contradictory strains of popular and elite, religious and secular, and esoteric and conventional influence. As such, the development and the persistence of the self-help ethos are not easy phenomena to delineate. In this tangled knot of influence and expression are found such contrasting spirits as Benjamin Franklin and Ralph Waldo Trine, Andrew Carnegie and Mary Baker Eddy, and William James and Norman Vincent Peale. For better or worse, the self-help heritage perhaps offers one of those unifying modes of thought and feeling that knits together the religious, social, and ethnic pluralism of a change-ridden national history.

The aspiration toward self-betterment does not, of course, arrive new and full-blown in America with the landing of the Pilgrims or the popularity of Horatio Alger's Ragged Dick juvenile novels. As is the case with any human propensity that attains prominence for a while in a given culture, the seeming universality of human nature dictates that other societies in other times and places exhibit, to a lesser degree, similar traits and longings. In all communities, from antiquity to the present, can be found histories and tales of celebrated individuals who, by their own efforts or with divine aid, counter adverse circumstance to better their material and psychic well-being.

By definition, all literature, whether oral or written, has implicit didactic or inspirational elements that bid the listener-reader to emulate the superior qualities of the hero. Those modern books that proclaim their how-to intentions only make this didactic function in literary history fully explicit. The Mesopotamian *Epic of Gilgamesh* (2000 B.C.), for example, heralds the strength, courage, and fortitude of its hero in overcoming vindictive passion to slay monsters and to build city walls that insured the safety of his native people. So, too, the adulation of the wit and guile of Odysseus played a formative role in creating respect for rational control in what came to be classical culture, with its Platonic and Aristotelian confidence that truth and inner tranquility might be attained through the exercise of reason. This central Greek emphasis later formed the basis for a vigorous minority tradition in Christianity. As early as the fourth century A.D.—a theological watershed for historic Christendom—Pelagius, a classically learned English scholar, stressed the potential of each individual to arrive at truth through rational discernment and to achieve salvation through good works, thereby disputing Augustine's insistence on faith and righteousness as the exclusive and irresistible gifts of divine grace. Similarly, the Reformation has Calvinists, heirs of Augustine, confronting heretic Jacob Arminius, who was another proponent of the individual's rational and ethical resolution as sufficient paths to God and Heaven.

Whatever lively currency and effect the notion of self-help has had in American culture, it is clear that this ideal of individual effort and improvement does not first originate in America. The Puritan culture that was to dominate the first century of American life had its roots in England and before that in the European Reformation. Its visions of religion and culture had imbibed the Calvinistic spiritual dialectic between man's radical fallenness and God's gift of grace and salvation. The result was an acute consciousness of the moral insufficiency of natural man. This sense of unworthiness led to a rigoristic ethic in pursuit of sanctification—the acquisition of godliness, which was the long process of righting the self in fulfilling the promise and reality of grace, of making oneself Christlike or fit for God. This religious disposition no doubt found its fruition in John Bunyan's *A Pilgrim's Progress* (1678), an immensely popular tale of worldly temptation, spiritual struggle, and redemption—a fictional how-to rendering of the earthly sojourner's path to salvation. The same impulse for offering practical help and inspiration appeared in Englishman Lewis Bayly's *The Practice of Piety* (1612), which, in its twenty editions, offered advice on the route to godliness, and in Englishman Joseph Alleine's *The Sure Guide to Heaven* (1672), which sold fifty thousand copies in the colonies.

The most influential American expression of the tension between worldly activity and the piety of salvation came in Puritan divine Cotton Mather's *The Christian at His Calling* (1701), in which the author stressed a two-faceted vocation for the believer. The first, or general, calling entailed conversion and allegiance to Jesus Christ. The second stressed worldly vocation, wherein the Christian engaged in practical employment for the benefit of society. Whatever task the Christian undertook was not primarily for personal gain but for the good of his fellows. The importance of Mather's formulation was that it not only emphasized the obligation of gainful activity but it served also as a justification for secular pursuits. The duty of an energetic vocation in the business of supplying others and oneself with necessities and goods repudiated any lingering traditions of quietism or monastic withdrawal. For the Christian, work was founded in gratitude and looked to stewardship.

Some erosion of the Puritan's concept of the meanings and uses of wealth and work came with the Enlightenment and with self-help's most famous poularizer, Benjamin Franklin. For this entrepreneur-inventor-philosopher, who was himself a poor boy made good, wealth itself was a sign of virtues that were the fruit of willed and stalwart action—industry, frugality, and perseverance. In the widely popular collection of Poor Richard's sayings, *The Way to Wealth* (1758), Franklin provided ready advice on the practical values and attitudes necessary to get ahead. Largely missing from this work or from the *Autobiography* (1788), in which Franklin becomes his own hero, is any kind of religious sanction for economic activity. Rather than seeing the accumulation of wealth as beneficial to God or fellow man, it exists largely for the individual and is the product of individual effort. Whereas wealth results from concerted personal initiative and is independent of luck, it reflects on the achiever's character. In the manner of Enlightenment's optimistic rationalism, the requisite traits and virtues are apparent to all and do not flow from and are not directed toward any special notion of Grace. Besides the status enjoyed from amassing wealth, its particular fruit lies in the improved and disciplined character that the individual must forge for himself in order to obtain the wealth.

While Franklin gave his blessing to economic acquisition, other assorted figures in eighteenth-century and early nineteenth-century America wished to sound a note of caution. For one, a less prominent Enlightenment influence from America's patrician sector hoped for a different understanding of the nature of opportunity in an expanding nation. A part of Thomas Jefferson's democratic ideal rested on a broad faith in the potential of small sociopolitical bodies to inspire and to improve their membership. Self-help was here fostered to encourage the development of the whole person, intellectual and moral, and not just his money- or status-making skills. It is safe to say that Jefferson, while insisting on the formal separation of church and state, nonetheless wished to invest the state with functions of inculcating virtue in a manner comparable to a surrogate church. The expanded and learned notion of self-help Jefferson wished to instill effected no constraint on the populace as it and its self-help advocates rushed headlong to embrace the seemingly limitless range of economic possibility.

From a lingering Puritan ambivalence toward wealth through the first half of the nineteenth century came a far greater dissent from a host of popular culture expressions. The famous "ecclectic readers" (1836-1857) of William Holmes McGuffey brought the self-help ethos to more than one hundred million juvenile readers, urging at once the values of assertiveness and diligence and the charity of Christian love. In *Lectures to Young Men* (1844), the famous pulpiteer Henry Ward Beecher counseled that the honest effort leading to wealth was a gift and glory of God that was too easily subverted by greed and uncharitableness. Popular novelist and essayist T. S. Arthur advised in numerous books that the way to success was through hard work that always carries service to others as a primary goal. And far from the image of Horatio Alger as a sponsor of an up-by-the-bootstraps mythos, Alger's many heroes are most always lost orphans with good blood, a lot of luck, modest ambitions, and kindly intentions. In approximately one hundred Alger novels, the greedy, exploitative, and selfishly wealthy or ambitious persons often come upon bad fortune for their unkindness.

During the latter part of the century, which was the height of the Industrial Revolution, the prominent churchman Lyman Abbott, in *How to Succeed* (1882), echoed the attitudes of most Protestant clergy in urging economic success within a proper view of the obligations of stewardship and warnings about greed. It was good to get ahead and use one's full potential, but avarice threatened always to obliterate the import of whatever virtues were exercised in the process of wealth-getting. Success was for an end beyond itself.

The late nineteenth-century caution expressed by Alger, Abbott, and others was partly countered, however, in the enormously successful lecture-pamphlet "Acres of Diamonds" by Baptist minister Russell Conwell, the founder of Temple University. Conwell argued that it was the Christian's duty to acquire wealth, for its accumulation developed character and its possession brought the power to do good. The printed version of the lecture had wide circulation, in addition to the fact that Conwell delivered it some six thousand times throughout his meteoric career.

The self-help tradition initiated in America by Mather and repeated in substance by Beecher, Abbott, and others until the beginning of the twentieth century stressed the primacy of certain virtues of hard work and responsibility as the way toward the improvement of one's character and the acquisition of success. The resources for achievement lay in the makeup of every man, and the attainment of prestige or wealth, seen as a Christian duty in glorifying God and helping neighbor, depended on the individual's fortitude and resolution. Such an ethic is understandable and perhaps appropriate in the open mercantile society of early nationhood on a rich and undeveloped continent.

While the average man, church member or not, was encouraged by manifold religious and secular sources in his culture to pursue economically and socially gainful purposes, he was almost as often cautioned against the invidious and subtle temptation of greed wherein the vision of God and social concern was displaced at enormous cost to the individual and society.

Thus, there exists an almost constant attitude of ambivalence toward the improvement of the individual's material circumstance, and seldom did any self-made man justify his wealth in terms of selfish economic gain or the fair spoils of the victor in a competitive marketplace. Andrew Carnegie's famous Social Darwinist essay, "Gospel of Wealth," in the *North American Review* (1889) stands out as an atypical expression of the business and self-help mentality up to and including Carnegie's own time. Because of greatly changing social and economic conditions, Carnegie's tract sounds the death knell in America for an energetic individualism based on the aspirant's potential for diligence, prudence, and perseverance.

The history of self-help and religion assumes a different character and perhaps even a more significant role in American history from several sources: the life of an innovative and inquisitive New England clockmaker named Phineas P. Quimby, the fathering genius of the New Thought movement; its numerous latter-day offshoots that variously partake of its spirit; and possibly, depending upon the way one reads a shadowy historical record, Mary Baker Eddy's Christian Science. Quimby published only a few articles during his life that in no way account for the seminal and decisive role he plays in the history of American religious life. Rather, his import is felt through the writing and institutional development done by those he treated in his many years of healing practice, notably Mary Baker Eddy. Without Quimby—this modest and comparatively obscure physician of the mind from Maine—the texture of much popular modern self-understanding would be notably different. His influence is readily and daily observable in a myriad of present-day, quasi-Christian, intention-shaping and attitude-inspiring books and assorted electronic media spots. In a thoroughly secular realm, his influence is no less prominent in preparing a receptive ground for the theories and methods of modern psychotherapeutic practice.

An adequate appreciation of Quimby and his curious and mostly unrecognized influence is necessary to understand fully most modern self-help philosophies. Quimby's career and thought began with an accidental self-cure. Apparently doomed by tuberculosis in his early thirties, Quimby attempted to repeat the experience of a friend for whom horseback riding had been curative. Unable to ride because of his weak state, Quimby opted instead for carriage trips. On one such excursion, Quimby's horse balked, and the invalid was forced to run it up a long hill. Soon invigorated by this effort, he drove the beast furiously homeward, arriving there in possession of his old health. The incident planted an intellectual seed in Quimby that was to begin blossoming some years later when he attended a lecture and demonstration by a traveling mesmerist (hordes of whom were then roaming the countryside cashing in on the national curiosity about hypnosis, which was first introduced to America in 1836). Quimby read all he could on the topic and started testing its capability with volunteers. One willing subject, Lucius Burkmar, exhibited unusual clairvoyant powers in the diagnosis of disease and the prescription of remedies.

Eventually, Quimby put together the import of the carriage ride years before and the apparent healing successes obtained through the use of Burkmar. While he still accepted the trance-induced clairvoyant diagnosis of Burkmar, Quimby soon realized that many of Burkmar's patently ridiculous prescriptions could have no causal connection with the cures produced. They were, in effect, placebos in which the patients nonetheless had trusted. Healing was accomplished by the patient's faith in the medicine, not by the medicine itself. From this recognition, it was but a step to the conclusion that the operative and efficacious principles herein were the suggestion of healing at a subconscious level and the confidence of the patient in the remedy prescribed. The disease, then, could be judged to be purely mental or psychological—the product of the patient's mistaken perception of self and reality. Supposing this to be the case, the route to cure was simply a matter of changing the disturbed mental condition or wrong beliefs of the patient, of reshaping the attitudes and the faith of the ill.

Those ideas would always form the base of Quimby's healing theory and practice, although he came to redirect two of its important elements. First, after some years of practice, Quimby became sufficiently knowledgeable and confident about the psychological bases underlying his treatment procedure to discard his previous use of hypnotism as a diagnostic and therapeutic tool. The same diagnostic and therapeutic fruit could be gained, he concluded, through the conscious mind's clairvoyant receptivity to the patient's mood and malady and by explanation and mental suggestion through conversation; these are principles which, in diluted form, constitute important elements in modern psychotherapy.

A second alteration in Quimby's thinking would have great consequence for the history of New Thought and Christian Science as well as for American religious life. Quimby's early experiments with hypnosis and healing arose from a wholly practical and personal incentive—specifically, the matter of getting well. As in the reigning medical practice of the day, Quimby was justly concerned with mundane matters of cause and effect. To an uncertain extent and for obscure reasons—mysteries that plague historians to this day—Quimby gradually moved to spiritualize his previously purely mundane mental cure. He came to believe that he had discovered the healing principle in the miracles of Jesus in the New Testament. This insight involved a re-envisioning of the makeup of the human person, especially in recognizing the existence in each individual of an unconscious, which was deemed by Quimby to be a divine element partaking of the very substance of God. It was this agent or portion of the self—the repository of divine wisdom that was much cultivated by Quimby

—that allowed Quimby to penetrate other minds to treat and diagnose wrong belief that denies the primacy of spirit in the attainment of health. That this radically new method treating bodily ills was effective there was little doubt in either Quimby's mind or the minds of many of his contemporaries. It has been estimated that from his Portland office Quimby treated twelve thousand patients in seven years. Two of his most devoted followers were the daughters of the respected United States Supreme Court Justice Ashur Ware.

Surely the most controversial, if not also the most famous, of all self-help figures who have kinship with Phineas P. Quimby was Mary Baker Eddy, the founder and still-ruling spirit of the Church of Christ, Scientist (or as it is better known, Christian Science), which joins Mormonism as one of the two purely indigenous American religions. Of the multitude of new sects and cults that flourished in the Gilded Age, only Christian Science went on to become a formal churchly body possessed of a governing ecclesiastical structure, a well-defined doctrinal core, and a devotional system of weekly services and evangelical outreach. The Church prohibits publication of membership figures, but recent scholars have estimated that its worldwide membership, mostly located in the United States, has grown since its beginnings in 1879 to one-third of a million members in over three thousand local congregations.

As in the case of its Christian parent religion, of which it is a heretical offshoot, Christian Science can also be said to have started with a fall. On February 1, 1866, the occasional semi-invalid, would-be poetess, and dabbler in occult healing, the then Mrs. Mary Baker Patterson was injured when she slipped and fell on the ice in Lynn, Massachusetts. In her later recollections, she declared that she was miraculously healed from paralysis and probable death while reading the Bible three days after the accident. The notes of her attending physician mention neither the supposed seriousness of the injury nor an immediate restoration of health. Furthermore, in a letter in mid-February to Julius Dresser, later a founder of New Thought, Mrs. Patterson makes no reference to a sudden cure and acknowledges the persistence of her back affliction and asks for physical healing from the man who was a likely successor to Quimby. Without new historical evidence, the controversy over Mrs. Eddy's illness and healing is not likely to dissipate.

Unfortunately, this same historical ambiguity surrounds Mrs. Eddy's personality and several crucial events in her life, including the origin and partial authorship of some of her seminal ideas and writings. On the question of literary origins, debate has raged for decades over whether Eddy stole from Quimby or Quimby from Eddy, and again no resolution of the dispute seems likely on the basis of present evidence. Mrs. Eddy first had contact with Quimby, then well known as a mesmeric healer, in 1862, four years before her famous fall, when she sought his aid for a chronic spinal disorder and nervous exhaustion. She experienced immediate relief and subsequently became a friend of Quimby and his advocate in the press, although she was later to discount his influence on the fully developed system of Christian Science. During her friendship with Quimby, she did have access to numerous unpublished writings of Quimby, now known as the "Quimby Manuscripts." Since the present copies are imprecisely dated, in various handwritings, and possibly the work of some of Quimby's patients, it is difficult to tell when and from whom the sometimes contradictory and fragmentary thoughts actually originated.

Apart from the seemingly irresolvable questions of intellectual indebtedness, it is important to note what Quimby did do for Mrs. Mary Baker Eddy. For some years before encountering Quimby, the frequently bedridden Mrs. Eddy had pursued relief and dabbled in Spiritualism, mesmerism, and various healing theories. During the Gilded Age, these theories were part of a national craze and offered frequent and lively topics of conversation in both taverns and drawing rooms. Her experience with Quimby convinced Mrs. Eddy of the reality of mental healing, and forever after she devoted herself to the genesis and strategies of healing. Quimby also gave Mrs. Eddy an initial step-by-step method by which to go about treating patients, although she was later to discard and indict certain of Quimby's methods, such as the use of manipulation of the head, which is reminiscent of the laying-on of hands.

Defenders of Christian Science have contended that the founder's teachings, which are to this day the exclusive theological core and rule for the Scientist, go far beyond Quimby's thought. Christian Science bears no resemblance to New Thought and was the happy result of the healing method and reality encountered by Mrs. Eddy in the aftermath of her fall in Lynn in 1866. Christian Science's supposed dependence on Quimby, it is argued, results from subsequent interpreters of Quimby, largely Warren Felt Evans and Julius and Annetta Dresser, who unjustly read back into Quimby many of the concepts discovered by Mary Baker Eddy. For the Scientist, Quimby was a mesmeric mind curist who was entirely devoid of any religious framework for his theory and practice. His work was only subsequently spiritualized and "scientized" by disciples who concealed his fundamental reliance on the suggestion techniques of hypnotism. Again, the confusion of dating and authorship surrounding Phineas Quimby's manuscripts affords little help in clarifying the matter.

The best-selling book that provoked this welter of long and intense debate is Mrs. Eddy's *Science and Health* (1875). The work underwent numerous revisions—sixteen editions in all during her lifetime—each further clarifying and changing certain emphases. With regard to the book's real impact, sales figures of *Science and Health,* which are said to be in the millions, are deceptive because Christian Scientists were required to purchase each new edition, which averaged one every two years between the first edition in 1875 and Mrs. Eddy's death in 1910. From the beginning, however, despite these incidental alterations, the unique religious vision of *Science and Health* remained the same. Its most famous and controversial theological statement, on which its practice of healing rests, ventures a step beyond the idealism of transcendentalism and denies altogether the reality of matter. The physical world and the ills of mortality seen in sin, disease, and death are errors or illusions of humankind's mortal mind. Mrs. Eddy reasons to this conclusion from the premise that an all-good and wholly spiritual God could not create entities of matter and evil that contradict its essential nature.

Human consciousness, then, is only the manifestation of an entirely benign and spiritual Divine Mind. The more the individual apprehends the purely spiritual nature of his own being and his likeness to God, the more he is able to vitiate the effects of false belief in materiality and its woe-ridden by-products. Insofar as this goal is attained, the devotee becomes less susceptible to the sin and illness that result from belief in materiality. Healing occurs when the mind turns from its acceptance of the sway of material belief and is released to the pure contemplation of the love of God. Probably the largest intellectual problem with Christian Science—one often pointed out by its orthodox Christian critics—pertains to how the mortal mind, whose product is evil, however illusory, ever comes into existence if all reality is the spiritual manifestation of a good and completely spiritual deity. Defenders readily acknowledge the problem and let it rest as an enigma, suggesting that the truth of Christian Science can only be grasped from within its belief system, wherein exists a beautiful logic to its assertions.

The importance of Christian Science for an understanding of self-help and religion lies in its notion that adversity proceeds from wrong belief and attitudinal disorientation. Christian Scientists avow that their emphasis on spiritual struggle in discarding illusion and material trust distinguish it from the facile optimism of New Thought and positive thinking. There is a prominent strain, however, that regards first health and then economic success or "supply," as it is called by Scientists, to be reliable evidence of proper belief and God's favor. Indeed, Mrs. Eddy and her followers have stressed that the proof of their belief lies in the empirically observable effect of healing and improved health, which is but a step from economic reassurance. In any case, later disciples of both Quimby and Eddy were less cautious in ascribing wealth as well as health to new found trust in the power of mind and attitude to enhance spiritual, physical, and material well-being.

For a multitude of reasons involving cultural susceptability and readiness, Mrs. Eddy's Christian Science made a tremendous impact on late nineteenth-century American society. The woman, who at age fifty was penniless and working on a book no one would wish to publish, would retire three decades later as the spiritual and political head of a sizeable, well-established, and accepted, if not quite respected, church body. But there, in the transition from controversial sect to respectable denomination, Mrs. Eddy's influence in American culture ceases to grow, although it does not end altogether. The history of an energetic, radical, religious movement pioneered by a magnetic leader begins to assume the characteristics of institutional denominationalism. The authoritarian character of Mrs. Eddy's writing and self-understanding explicitly held that her particular interpretation of scripture and statement of doctrines were handed down by God and were therefore definitive and final. Any attempt by a Christian Scientist to rephrase or add to the substance of belief delineated in *Science and Health* was to be prohibited. This ultra-conservative theological rigidity led, during Eddy's life, to the expulsion of prominent Christian Scientists and, after the founder's death, to the absolute central control of the Church and the writings of all members by an executive board.

This same tenor is still evidenced today in the fact that while Christian Science worship services have largely copied mainline Protestant liturgy, they have supplanted the sermon with readings from *Science and Health*. Any further words of interpretation on matters of which Mrs. Eddy once spoke could only prove superfluous and risk inadvertent distortion. Christian Science initially produced a major ideological formulation on the dominance of spirit in man and provided strategies for self-cure. Given its prohibition against any re-expression by anyone of Mrs. Eddy's theology, and given orthodoxy's traditional suspicion of Christian Science's off-beat metaphysics, its persisting influence is open to question. This conclusion is supported by the failure of the denomination to sustain its dramatic early growth. Since the death of Mrs. Eddy, membership increases have paralleled population growth. The observer must look to the movement known as the New Thought—the other offspring of Phineas Quimby—to detect the route by which American culture became beguiled by the notion of self-help through religion.

To be sure, Mary Baker Eddy was not the only person healed by Phineas Quimby in his Portland housefront office. In 1863, the year after Quimby healed the founder of Christian Science, he successfully treated for nervous collapse Warren Felt Evans, who had just left the Methodist ministry for the Swedenborgian Church of the New Jerusalem. Six years later, and six years before Eddy's *Science and Health*, Evans published *The Mental Cure: Illustrating the Influence of the Mind on the Body, Both in Health and Disease, and the Psychological Method of Treatment* (1869). While it was not a best-seller, *The Mental Cure* enjoyed steady attention, going through seven editions in sixteen years. Evans's second book, *Mental Medicine* (1873), is known to have gone through fifteen editions in its first twelve years, indicating persistent interest in Evans's thought.

Evans was religious throughout his life, and when he met Quimby, he was enamored with the esoteric Swedish physicist-philosopher Emmanuel Swedenborg. Evans recognized in Quimby the use of the same principles by which Jesus healed and—still further—the logical and practical extension of philosophic idealism. Evans's fourth book, *The Divine Law of Cure*, is devoted to demonstrating the extent to which some of the best philosophic minds of Europe and America—for example, Hegel, Berkeley, Fichte, Coleridge, and Edwards—prepared a theoretical base for mental healing. By his fifth book, *The Primitive Mind Cure: The Nature and Power of Faith, or Elementary Lessons in Christian Philosophy and Transcendental Medicine* (1885), which went through five editions in one year, Evans had expanded his range of intellectual support to include Oriental thought, in which there was beginning to be considerable American curiosity. And in his last book, *Esoteric Christianity and Mental Therapeutics* (1886), Evans was even more characteristically like New Thought in his trust in a kind of philosophic universalism wherein ancient and modern creeds bear significant portions of fundamental truth. Like Evans, many subsequent and less prominent New Thought writers would seek intellectual support for their thinking. In America, they would most often find support in transcendentalism and Ralph Waldo Emerson, who chose to ignore both Christian Science and New Thought.

Throughout his six books, Evans reiterates basic conclusions from Quimby and shares many views with Mary Baker Eddy. There is always the insistence on the dominance of spirit or mind over matter. Unlike Eddy, Evans does not see matter as necessarily illusory, allowing rather that it does exist independently of human consciousness. Disease is the failure to recognize the ultimacy of spirit and the presence of Christ or God in every person, a potentiality made manifest through Jesus of Nazareth. The route to health is through dispelling the idea or conviction of the sway of disease, which results from partial recognition of a kindly and loving God that forms the true self, residing primarily in the subconscious portions of the mind. The sufferer is in need of affirmation and hopeful thinking, which is the medium of all cures and a method to be used by later New Thoughtists and Norman Vincent Peale. Wrong or pessimistic thinking brings bodily ills.

New Thought gradually gathered momentum from the enthusiasm of other Quimby followers and of dissidents and exiles from Christian Science. Among the other famous patients of Quimby was Julius Dresser, who first visited Quimby in 1860 and was healed. While there, he met fellow-patient Annetta Seabury, whom he married in 1863. Dresser decided to discard his ambition to become a Baptist minister; he entered journalism, moved west, and returned to Boston in 1883, where he and his wife set up mental practice according to Quimby. While they published little of their own, they did attract attention by accusing Mary Baker Eddy of pirating from the manuscripts of Phineas Quimby, a controversy that has yet to be successfully resolved. The son of Annetta and Julius Dresser, Horatio, became the chief and most respected chronicler of New Thought, having studied with William James at Harvard, where he won the Ph.D. in philosophy.

The middle-aged Ursula Gestefeld cured herself after reading *Science and Health.* A zealous supporter thereafter of Mrs. Eddy, she went so far as to write an adulatory book on Mrs. Eddy and Christian Science entitled *Ursula N. Gestefeld's Statement of Christian Science* (1888). For her efforts, she was driven out of the Church by Mrs. Eddy. She subsequently started her own periodical called *The Exodus*, which soon had a club of devoted followers.

Emma Curtis Hopkins similarly became a devoted follower of New Thought after being driven from Christian Science in a series of disputes with Mrs. Eddy. A powerful speaker, she soon attracted a large following, an organization bearing her name, and a theological seminary in Chicago. Such people as the Dressers, Ursula Gestefeld, Emma Hopkins, and numerous others, often with their own following, books, and periodicals, joined together in 1914 to form the International New Thought Alliance, which did much to spur the notions of New Thought. One such member of the New Thought movement was the prestigious Boston Metaphysical Club, which met for the first time in 1895. All these diverse people, whose exact number is impossible to gauge, shared in the general hopes and tenets of mental healing as spelled out by Quimby and Evans. The sole point of division was perhaps how much they individually wished to "theologize" notions of incarnation, sin, and the existence of matter. In any case, differences were not sufficiently acute to cause acrimony or schism.

New Thought received a new level of public attention and a controversial new theme in 1897, with its first authentic best-seller, *In Tune with the Infinite: Fullness of Peace, Power, and Plenty,* by Ralph Waldo Trine. The book contained straightforward explanations of the main precepts of New Thought. Its acceptance by a largely orthodox reading public resulted in part from the fact that Trine, a skilled stylist and expositor, tended to blur some of the key differences between conservative Christianity and New Thought, and when choices in phraseology came, Trine tended to use the language of tradition. As a whole, *In Tune with the Infinite* sought to emphasize the closeness of conventional Christian thinking and New Thought. Most readers saw in it the noble inspiration of established wisdom rather than the influence of esoteric philosophy or any particular healing cult. What readers encountered in Trine's book was an explicit presentation of a latent strain in New Thought and Christian Science—that is, the promise of prosperity and economic plenty as the inevitable result of being in tune with the Infinite.

Whether this new conspicuous element accounted for Trine's success is impossible to tell. Spiritual tranquility and physical well-being had been a part of Quimby's pioneering views and were expounded by his disciples. Here, the hope of wealth and personal power began to equal, if not surpass, the expectations of health and psychic repose. A little over a decade before, Warren Felt Evans had expounded on "the power of faith" to heal in *The Primitive Mind Cure*. But until Trine's book, the emphasis on "supply," as Mary Baker Eddy called it, had been largely subordinated to the individual's ability to influence his own person—the mind and the body. Trine's work extended control of the self outward to suggest a causal connection between spiritual attitude and financial reward and success.

If most readers were not aware of the New Thought they were getting in Trine's book, the same can be said for the wisdom and service offered by New Thought's only enduring and widely recognized organization, the Unity School of Christianity, founded in Kansas City by Emma Hopkins's disciples Charles and Myrtle Fillmore. In 1887, the Fillmores had been in ill health when they heard Dr. E. B. Weeks lecture on Hopkins's doctrines. For the first time, Myrtle Fillmore saw herself as a child of God over whom sickness had no power. So began a healing that took some two years, but healed she was. Impressed friends, as well as her initially skeptical husband Charles, began to inquire into the causes of Myrtle's healing. Eventually convinced, Charles began publication of a magazine called *Modern Thought* in 1889. In 1890, the Society of Silent Help was announced in its pages. This organization grew out of weekly prayer meetings by the Fillmores and their friends, wherein they would specifically pray for the suffering, troubled, and needy, using the New Thought healing concept known as "absent treatment" or thought transference. The group grew quickly, becoming known simply as Silent Unity, and requests for prayers flooded the magazine's offices. Today, this service is offered around the clock, and one hundred fifty people are employed to handle over half a million requests annually. So successful have been its methods that they are now imitated by evangelist Oral Roberts and possibility-thinking television preacher Robert Schuller.

Eschewing the opportunity to become a church, Silent Unity became the Unity School of Christianity, devoted to the soft-sell promulgation of its New Thought Christianity through books, pamphlets, and media advertising, and to the daily practice of healing and aid first initiated by Silent Unity. Today, Unity continues to publish *Wee Wisdom*, begun in 1893, the oldest children's magazine in America, with a circulation of around a quarter of a million readers. Begun in 1924, *Daily Word*, a monthly inspirational booklet for adults, has a circulation of one hundred eighty thousand. In addition, there are *Weekly Unity* (1909), a mixture of newsletter and magazine; *Progress* (1924), which is oriented toward adolescents; and *Good Business* (1924), advocating the proposition that Christian ethics is good business practice. The message of Unity finds its way into even more homes through television and radio advertising that features inspirational talks by prominent Hollywood celebrities.

While it is not a formal church, Unity has found it necessary to authorize leaders and ministers for the local Unity centers that have sprung up across the country. Unity's publishing enterprise and its extensive headquarters-campus in suburban Kansas City is supported mostly by small contributions from donors. The organization is run by the children and grandchildren of the founders. While its rhetoric sounds like orthodox Christianity, it remains very much a descendent of New Thought in its emphasis on the partial divinity or Christliness of each person, the possibility of healing through the recognition of that Christly potential, and the ready supply of material blessing.

One of the best known of all avowed New Thought figures in the twentieth century, amounting to national celebrity status, was Emmet Fox, a best-selling author and a noted preacher who regularly preached to thousands in New York's Hippodrome and in Carnegie Hall. In 1930, in order to carry on the work started in his native England, Fox came to America where he found an enthusiastic following. The titles of his popular books amply illustrate his connection to New Thought, of which he was an ordained minister in the Church of Divine Science. *Power Through Constructive Thinking* (1932), *Make Your Life Worthwhile* (1942), and *Find and Use Your Inner Power* (1940) announce the unlimited and divine potentiality of each individual, which is unleashed through affirmative prayer that eliminates pessimism and fear, the sources of psychic stress, illness, and failure. Realizing God and the reality of divine love and assuming a new mentality yielded tangible evidences of its truth and efficacy in increased health and prosperity.

Fox's prominence was soon upstaged from an unexpected and surprising source. From dour Dutch Calvinism and America's oldest denomination—the small Reformed Church in America—came the message of ex-Methodist Norman Vincent Peale, whose best-selling books and frequent radio and television appearances have made his name and his "positive-thinking" credo household words. Peale admits to having been influenced deeply by New Thought during a crisis of relevance early in his ministry. The insights learned then proved useful when Peale assumed his present pastorate in the 1940s at New York City's prestigious Marble Collegiate Church, where he encountered much psychic dis-ease among the well-to-do.

Along with psychiatrist Smiley Blanton, a future coauthor, Peale established an extensive psychological counseling service in his new parish. His main work, though, has been his books, whose titles once again show obvious connections with New Thought. *A Guide to Confident Living* (1948) was on the best-seller list for two years, selling over six hundred thousand copies, and *The Power of Positive Thinking* (1952) sold two and one-half million copies in four straight years near the very top of best-seller lists. Now in its thirty-third volume, the magazine *Guideposts: A Practical Guide to Successful Living*, edited and published by Peale, has a circulation of over one million readers. It is estimated that in 1957 Peale reached a weekly audience of thirty million people through an extensively syndicated newspaper column, a radio program reaching one million homes, a television show on more than one hundred stations, a column in *Look*, and the monthly *Guideposts*.

Peale, in effect, borrows many of his major ideas and methods from New Thought, although he is careful to de-emphasize theologically questionable matters, such as the presence of Christ in each person and the stature of Jesus. Nonetheless, Peale has retained emphasis on the impact of attitude or confidence on self-perception, social acceptance, and worldly success. Peale has further stressed the tangible evidences of fruits of changed thinking as witnesses to the efficacy of his theories. His literary method is largely comprised of strategies to accomplish these ideological ends. While previous New Thought writers have largely written straight and sometimes detailed exposition of their ideas, Peale's books are aphoristic and anecdotal, with patterns of statement and exemplum, ad infinitum.

The decades of Peale's success saw a popular ecumenical consensus about his goals of inner confidence and hope, if not his exact methods and inspiration. Boston Rabbi Joshua Loth Liebman's *Peace of Mind* (1964) stayed near the top of the best-seller list for three years, eventually selling well over one million copies. Liebman combined modern depth psychology with Judaism in a guide to overcoming self-hatred, disabling guilt, and social maladjustment. The liberal Protestant preacher of Riverside Church in New York City, Henry Emerson Fosdick, in *On Being a Real Person* (1943) and other books, again melded psychology with religion. A positive faith was necessary to overcome pessimism, lethargy, and loneliness. By cultivating one's inner resources, the person could engage in, as the title of another of Fosdick's popular books puts it, *Adventurous Religion* (1926).

In contrast to Liebman's and Fosdick's trust in the new psychology, Roman Catholic Fulton Sheen counseled a return to orthodox and mildly ascetic Christianity in his best-selling *Peace of Soul* (1949) and *Life Is Worth Living* (1953). Self-control and repose proceeded from bringing one's anxiety and self-seeking to God. Conservative evangelical Protestantism found a spokesman in revivalist preacher Billy Graham with his *Peace of God* (1953). Like Sheen, Graham's solutions to psychic distress ignored the new psychologies and partook of the well-established Protestant tradition of pietism. Graham repeated the same counsel more than two decades later in his best-selling manual *How to Be Born Again* (1977).

The fundamentalism in which Graham had his roots had long featured its own tradition of religion as a path to the solution of one's ethical, spiritual, and physical ills. Revivalist pleas have always manifested, at least implicitly, an appeal to self-interest insofar as the sinner was urged to accept God's grace and avoid the fires of hell. The more extreme healing sects have emphasized in addition faith as the route to emotional and physical well-being. A former revivalist and now a television personality and president of Oral Roberts University in Tulsa, Oklahoma, Oral Roberts began his ministry on such a platform. The best known of recent faith healers was revivalist-television personality Kathryn Kuhlman, who died in 1976. A similar strain appears in the faith-to-riches ministry of the Reverend Frederick J. Eicherenkoetter II—or "Rev. Ike," as he is better known—a black evangelist who promises prosperity in return for faith in God and economic generosity to the preacher's cause. These all follow in the tradition of the controversial faith healer Aimee Semple McPherson, a female Elmer Gantry in the eyes of many, whose public career was plagued by scandal.

Perhaps the most recent and well known of the active self-help preachers demonstrates the persistence of the New Thought-Peale tradition. Peale's mantle has seemingly passed to a younger disciple, Robert H. Schuller, a native of rural Iowa and also a son of the Dutch Reformed Church. Schuller began his controversial ministry atop a drive-in theater refreshment stand in Garden Grove, California, a suburban community near Disneyland. Schuller, too, has written many books on his own modification of Peale's famous credo, "possibility thinking." He is best known, however, for weekly telecasts from his impressive drive-in church. The services and sermons are, in effect, dramatizations of the literary method pioneered by Peale and the strain of thought alive in America for over one hundred years. Its persistence and vitality are amply indicated by Schuller's meteoric success; his weekly program, "The Hour of Power," is now broadcast nationwide. In addition, Schuller's congregation is now constructing on its already well-developed campus a fourteen-million-dollar all-glass "Crystal Cathedrale," designed by world famous architects Philip Johnson and John Burgee.

The tradition of New Thought, Christian Science, and the popularity of "positive thinking" presents, in effect, a second and influential self-help tradition in America that emphasizes the instrumental utility of religious belief. Faith or the acquisition of a new affirmative frame of mind becomes a means of mending one's psychic or physical ills. In the older Puritan-endorsed self-help philosophy, the individual sought justification of the success-getting strategies and goals by assessing the extent to which those methods and ends conformed to Christian principles of fairness, charity, and stewardship. The New Thought tradition inverted this older perspective by making the curative and endowing powers of God the vehicle to success and well-being. Right attitudes or affirmative prayer becomes the means by which the individual acquires the traits and attitudes necessary for becoming a success. Moral questions about the appropriateness of affluence or means of acquisition receive little or no attention. In a kind of mental behavioralism, the individual, through autosuggestion, produces an attitude and expectation of success that will yield the reality. The results validate faith and constitute an empirical test of the truth and efficacy of religion.

BIBLIOGRAPHY

Braden, Charles S. *These Also Believe: A Study of Modern American Cults and Minority Religious Movements.* New York: Macmillan, 1949.

______. *Spirits in Rebellion: The Rise and Development of New Thought.* Dallas: Southern Methodist University Press, 1958.

Burns, Rex. *Success in America: The Yeoman Dream and the Industrial Revolution.* Amherst: University of Massachusetts Press, 1976.

Burr, Nelson R., in collaboration with James Ward Smith and A. Leland Jamison. *A Critical Bibliography of Religions in America.* 2 vols. Princeton: Princeton University Press, 1971.

Carey, Ralph Allison. "Best-Selling Religion: A History of Popular Religious Thought in America as Reflected in Religious Best-Sellers, 1850-1960." Ph.D. dissertation, Michigan State University, 1971.

Cawelti, John G. *Apostles of the Self-Made Man.* Chicago: University of Chicago Press, 1965.

Dresser, Horatio W. *A History of the New Thought Movement.* New York: Thomas Y. Crowell, 1919.

Gottschalk, Stephen. *The Emergence of Christian Science in American Religious Life.* Berkeley: University of California Press, 1973.

Green, Robert W., ed. *Protestantism and Capitalism: The Weber Thesis and Its Critics.* Boston: D. C. Heath, 1959.

Griswold, A. Whitney. "The American Gospel of Success." Ph.D. dissertation, Yale University, 1934.

Harrell, David Edwin, Jr. *All Things Are Possible: The Healing and Charismatic Revivals in Modern America.* Bloomington: Indiana University Press, 1975.

Herberg, Will. *Protestant, Catholic, Jew: An Essay in American Religious Sociology.* Rev. ed. New York: Anchor Books, 1960.

Huber, Richard M. *The American Idea of Success.* New York: McGraw-Hill, 1971.

Judah, J. Stillson. *The History and Philosophy of the Metaphysical Movements in America.* Philadelphia: Westminster Press, 1967.

Lynn, Kenneth S. *The Dream of Success: A Study of the Modern American Imagination.* Boston: Little, Brown, 1955.

Meyer, Donald. *The Positive-Thinkers: A Study of the American Quest for Health,*

Wealth, and Personal Power from Mary Baker Eddy to Oral Roberts. New York: Pantheon Books, 1980.

Parker, Bail Thain. *Mind Cure in New England: From the Civil War to World War I.* Hanover, N.H.: University of New England Press, 1973.

Rodgers, Daniel T. *The Work Ethic in Industrial America 1850-1920.* Chicago: University of Chicago Press, 1978.

Schneider, Louis, and Sanford M. Dornbusch. *Popular Religion: Inspiration Books in America.* Chicago: University of Chicago Press, 1958.

Weiss, Richard. *The American Myth of Success: From Horatio Alger to Norman Vincent Peale.* New York: Basic Books, 1969.

Williams, Peter W. *Popular Religion in America: Symbolic Change and the Modernization Process in Historical Perspective.* Englewood Cliffs, N.J.: Prentice-Hall, 1980.

Wyllie, Irvin G. *The Self-Made Man in America: The Myth of Rags to Riches.* New York: Free Press, 1954.

Romantic Fiction

Kay J. Mussell

In the literary sense, all popular fiction is romantic. It embodies, in John Cawelti's phrase, a "moral fantasy" that allows its readers to transcend the bounds of real life and enter a world in which things occur as they are "supposed to," where certain kinds of desired experience can be lived vicariously. Popular fiction is not *realistic,* is not intended to be by its authors, and is not desired to be by its readers. All popular fiction could be called "romantic" novels, as defined by Richard Chase and other critics. However, within the publishing industry and among readers, a "romantic" novel refers to a specific type of story.

The romantic novel in popular fiction is a tale about a love relationship, a courtship, and a marriage. It may take the form that Robert Palfrey Utter and Gwendolyn Bridges Needham described in 1936 as "the typical plot of the English novel," which "has love for the starting-post and marriage for the finish line." Or, the plot can concern the problems of an already-achieved marriage, with difficulties between husband and wife being resolved at the end, when the wife is rewarded with a better marriage to her current husband or a new marriage with a new lover. In addition, some romantic novels, probably more accurately called "anti-romances," invert the love plot while still reinforcing the assumptions of the form. These are novels in which the value structure is unchanged, but in which the heroine behaves in such a way that she cannot be rewarded with marriage in the end. These, too, are romantic novels, although they serve as cautionary tales rather than as models to be emulated. Because the tensions and issues inherent in love stories are women's concerns, romantic fiction is almost entirely a female form of fantasy reading.

Many novels in literary history revolve around these questions of love, courtship, and marriage imagined from a woman's perspective. The tension for a woman in the process of achieving identity through a lasting marriage is a profound one that has been dramatized in fiction extensively from Samuel Richardson's *Pamela* (1741), to the most recent issue of *Redbook* or *Good Housekeeping,* or to this month's selection of full-length Harlequin

Romances, sent by subscription to women throughout the United States, Canada, and Great Britain. The satisfaction gained by many women through reading such fiction is unquestionable. What is perhaps most significant about the popular romantic novel, however, is how little the basic assumptions of the story have changed from some of its earliest manifestations in American fiction to its most recent.

The story of a romantic novel begins with an assumption—unquestioned and unexamined except in a few books—that the necessary, preordained, and basic goal of any woman is to achieve a satisfying, mature, and all-fulfilling marriage. The primacy of romantic love, in defining a woman's place in the world and her personal and moral worth, is rarely in doubt in these books. The plot is often diffuse, but it never loses sight of that goal. Although other kinds of events and actions by the protagonist may take up much of the novel, those events are always related eventually to the woman's marital status and condition of happiness at the end of the book. Thus, although much of the action of *Gone With the Wind* (1936) concerns Scarlett O'Hara's experiences during the Civil War and Reconstruction, the underlying value structure of the book is prescribed by Scarlett's relationships with men and, especially, by the contrast between Scarlett and Melanie Wilkes. Similarly, Maria Susanna Cummins's *The Lamplighter* (1854) traces the childhood and young adulthood of its main character, Gertie, showing how she learned to be a worthy and moral young woman through the influence of various other characters on her life. However, the novel confirms her identity at the end by allowing her to marry the young hero, who has seemed throughout most of the book to be merely a friend to Gertie while attracted to another, and wealthier, young woman.

Using John Cawelti's approach to popular fiction—that of formulaic analysis—it would be necessary to discuss romantic fiction as a group of formulas, rather than as a single one. Romantic formulas intersect with several other kinds of popular fiction: the gothic, the historical, the juvenile, the sentimental, the domestic, the seduction. But they cannot be entirely identified with any of these other formulas. In addition, the sustained critical work on romantic fiction is just beginning to emerge in scholarship, so there is no general agreement on the definitions of different types of romantic fiction. At the moment, perhaps the most useful approach is to cast a wide net, assuming that novels that tell the story of a romance and how it was all-important in the life of a woman, all other factors being in one way or another subordinate to an all-consuming love relationship, are romantic fiction. The fine formulaic definitions can develop out of the necessary bibliographical and critical work that remains to be done.

One of the difficulties in dealing with this sort of popular fiction is that it is such an ephemeral form. Some examples are so widely popular and so often reprinted that they come to mind immediately: Susanna Rowson's *Charlotte Temple* (1791) or Margaret Mitchell's *Gone With the Wind* (1936).

Others have certainly been lost forever as the last cracked and crumbling copy, published by a local printer as a favor to a neighboring author, has disappeared in the trash after an attic was cleaned. Romantic novels are almost never reviewed, unless they are highly publicized blockbusters. Authors who write them tend to be relatively private persons and are rarely interviewed or written about. Many authors of romantic novels are very prolific writers, publishing several books a year for a grateful and insatiable audience, making large amounts of money from their work, but reaping very little acclaim except from readers.

Romantic novels are the fare of public libraries, which have large circulations for these books but which do not rebind or reorder most of them when they wear out because the audience usually demands new ones. Such books are also commonplace in drug stores and grocery stores. Romantic fiction is a staple in women's magazines today, as it has been for almost two centuries. It has been common in subscription series of novels sold by "dime novel" publishers in the nineteenth century and as named series (Harlequin Romances, Silhouette Romances, Barbara Cartland's Library of Love) in the twentieth century. It is easy to find current examples of the form; it was probably as easy to find them in 1880 as it is today. But it is difficult today to find 1880 examples or even 1920 or 1930 versions because many of these novels leave very little trace, and many of them are impossible to identify as romantic novels from a mere title or author's name.

The first American example of a popular romantic novel was probably Susanna Rowson's *Charlotte Temple,* one of the great bestsellers of American literary history. First published in Britain by a woman who almost immediately thereafter moved to America to set up a school for young ladies, *Charlotte Temple* went through more than two hundred editions, forty of them before the author's death in the 1820s. The first American edition was published in Philadelphia in 1794. As recently as the early twentieth century, it was still in print; one 1905 edition contained a number of photographs, including one of Charlotte's reputed grave in New York City. *Charlotte Temple* was a classic seduction novel about a young girl who was so foolish as to allow herself to be carried off to America by an officer; when she became pregnant, he abandoned her, leaving her to die miserably after giving birth to a daughter, whose life was later chronicled by Rowson in *Lucy Temple or Charlotte's Daughter* (1828).

Many other seduction novels were written in the early nineteenth century. Mrs. Hannah W. Foster's *The Coquette* (1797), Eliza Vicery's *Emily Hamilton* (1803), and several anonymous novels, such as *Fidelity Rewarded* (1796) and *Amelia, or the Faithless Briton* (1798), told the familiar story. Most of these, incidentally, were presented to the public as true stories, thinly disguised by changing names and places. Since seduction stories served so consciously as cautionary tales, the claim for their truth is logical, although it might be just as reasonable to conclude that the novels claimed a factual basis to combat the contemporary prejudice against fiction as harmful because it was made up of lies. After the early nineteenth century, a full-blown seduction story was hard to find. The tensions of the precarious position in which a "loose woman" could find herself were still important in later romantic novels, but the explicit warning about men, the specific if somewhat euphemistic story about sexuality, was less significant in romantic fiction.

From the 1820s until after the Civil War, romantic fiction was dominated by a group of women novelists usually referred to as the "domestic sentimentalists." They included writers such as Catharine Maria Sedgwick, Lydia Maria Child, Fanny Fern (Ruth Payton Willis), Mary Jane Holmes, Ann Sophia Stephens, Maria Susanna Cummins, and others. The work of these women has been more thoroughly documented than that of any other romantic novelists, and new critical studies of their work emerge every year with the impetus of the women's studies movement in scholarship. Although critics disagree, sometimes diametrically, about the meaning of the work of these women, there seems little doubt that their stories are about relationships between men and women. Almost all the heroines are married, happily, at the end of the books. Between the beginning and the end, males may be less in evidence than females, as the heroines spend their time solving domestic difficulties and improving their characters, saving souls, and learning to be "true women." But despite the trials of domestic life, the reconciliation with woman's place in a good marriage is where the plots end.

These were the novels that prompted Nathaniel Hawthorne's heartfelt cry in a letter to his publisher in 1855, a few years after *The Scarlet Letter* (1850) had been less than enthusiastically received by the mass reading audience.

> America is now wholly given over to a d______d mob of scribbling women, and I should have no chance of success while the public taste is occupied with their trash—and should be ashamed of myself if I did succeed. What is the mystery of these innumerable editions of the "Lamplighter," and other books neither better nor worse?—worse they could not be, and better they need not be, when they sell by the 100,000....

It is ironic to note that the output of these women included a rather large number of historical novels about women in Puritan New England, some of whom ran afoul of the religious and civil authorities of the colony, although for offenses more acceptable to nineteenth-century taste than was adultery. Hawthorne might be forgiven if he found contemptible an audience that embraced Sedgwick's *Hope Leslie* (1827) and Eliza B. Lee's *Naomi* (1848) more willingly than his novel about Hester Prynne.

After the Civil War, much romantic fiction was found in dime-novel series and story papers, as well as in full-length novels, often serialized in newspapers and magazines prior to book publication. Augusta Jane Evans Wilson and Mrs. E.D.E.N. Southworth were especially popular, although the work of many of the domestic sentimentalists was still in print and widely read. Since there are few studies of romantic fiction in this period, it is more difficult to identify titles and authors, but the genre seems to have flourished. Romantic novels about working girls, written by Laura Jean Libbey, were one example; others were some of the historical novels of Mary Johnston and others. A particularly interesting writer of romantic fiction, who also wrote numerous advice books, popular history and Bible studies, and edited a magazine, was Isabella Alden (known as "Pansy"). Her niece, Grace Livingston Hill, was to become one of the bestselling romance writers of the twentieth century.

Lists of bestsellers are available from 1895 onward, so it becomes an easier task to identify romantic novels that did well in the marketplace. Those books that did not sell widely enough to appear in these compilations are still hard to retrieve, but enough information is available to indicate that the love story was in style and relatively unchanged. Kathleen Norris's novels of family and domestic drama were especially popular during the first thirty years of the twentieth century. Mary Roberts Rinehart, better known for detective and gothic novels, also wrote a few straight romances for her wide audience; her books were regularly on the bestseller lists throughout the period, regardless of their type.

Grace Livingston Hill's novels of romance and traditional religion were popular alongside the racier novels of Fannie Hurst and Faith Baldwin. Emilie Loring's books also sold widely. Only a very few romantic novels, however, were great best sellers until the 1930s. *Gone With the Wind* was a romantic novel that appealed to a much wider audience than most—to men as well as to women. It was, of course, an instant success immediately upon its publication; it was awarded the Pulitzer Prize and it was made into one of the classic films of Hollywood in 1939. The 1977 edition of the bestseller lists, Alice Payne Hackett's *Eighty Years of Bestsellers,* lists it as the number eleven book on the all-time hardbound bestseller list; it is the top fiction book on the list after several cookbooks, Kahlil Gibran's *The Prophet,* and five Dr. Seuss books. With the story of Scarlett O'Hara, romantic fiction made the big time in a way that it had not since Augusta Jane Evans Wilson's *St. Elmo* (1867). Incidentally, the number twelve book on the all-time list is also a work of romantic fiction—Anya Seton's *The Winthrop Woman* (1958), a novel of the Massachusetts Bay Colony, which seems to be an enduring setting in popular romantic fiction.

Following *Gone With the Wind,* the next big romantic book was Daphne duMaurier's *Rebecca* (1938), the work of a British author who has always been very popular in this country. Kathleen Winsor's *Forever Amber* (1944) was also important. Most recently, Rosemary Rogers's *Dark Fires* (1975) has reached the all-time list of books that have sold more than two million copies. It is significant to note that two of these books, *Gone With the*

Wind and *Forever Amber*, are inversions of the romantic story in that their heroines are women who do not deserve a happy marriage and who are left alone by the men they love. It may be that this inversion is more likely to appeal to an audience that is partly male than a book that is a more straightforward retelling of a love story.

The post-World War II period has been a very fruitful one for the popular romantic novel in America. Novels by British writers have been readily available in paperback and in libraries and have been widely read. There is little sense in trying to separate the works of British and American authors during this period, except for the record, since both sell widely in both countries and are almost routinely published on both sides of the Atlantic. Particularly popular in the last two decades have been British authors Georgette Heyer, Barbara Cartland, and Dorothy Eden, as well as the Americans Anya Seton, Frances Parkinson Keyes, Rosemary Rogers, and Janet Dailey. The Harlequin romances, cheap paperback originals published in Canada by arrangement with the British firm of Mills and Boon, have also been widely read and imitated. These books, like the dime novels of the nineteenth century, are sold on book racks as well as by subscription. Most of them are straightforward romances—love stories set in interesting or exotic places or about people with interesting or exotic lives.

In 1980, after a distribution agreement between Harlequin and Simon and Schuster broke down, the American firm challenged Harlequin directly by creating a new series of paperback romances titled Silhouette. Based on extensive reader research, Silhouette Romances employ an aggressive advertising campaign on television, reader panels to approve manuscripts, and blatant imitation of Harlequin design and plot types. So closely is the series modelled on Harlequin Presents that Silhouette was forced by a court decision to redesign its cover. Also, some of the most successful of the Mills and Boon/Harlequin authors—most notably, Anne Hampson and Janet Dailey—have been lured from Harlequin to Silhouette. Other publishing firms also have either begun new series of paperback romances or repackaged older ones to compete more effectively with Harlequin and Silhouette. The most innovative of these are the Candelight Ecstasy series (feature more "adult" characters and situations) and the Jove Second Chance at Love series (the title is descriptive of the content). In the summer of 1981, the Romantic Writers of America held its first annual convention in Houston, Texas.

Magazines have also flourished on love stories in their fiction pages, from the most serious and uplifting of the women's magazines such as *Godey's Lady's Book* in the nineteenth century to *Good Housekeeping* in the twentieth. Confession magazines, love comics, and pulps are twentieth-century versions of the nineteenth-century story papers.

The drama of courtship and marriage has had a strong hold on the imaginations of American women readers for two centuries. The specifics of the plot have changed over the years, but the value structure and shape of the books have changed relatively little. Amber, in *Forever Amber,* does not die for her adultery as does Charlotte Temple, but the lesson of the two novels is clearly related. Melanie is allowed a happy and fulfilling marriage that is denied to Scarlett, even though Scarlett may have had the greater love, since Rhett is so much more passionate than Ashley. In domestic sentimental novels, women spend their time in domestic trivia rather than in the social whirl of more recent romantic novels by Georgette Heyer and others, but their behavior and their reward for virtue have not changed.

In the absence of good critical studies and bibliographies, it is difficult to say just how widespread romantic fiction has been in American literary history, but the evidence is clear enough to indicate that it has been both pervasive and persistent. One suspects that there is more of it still submerged than seems possible even now.

BIBLIOGRAPHY

Baym, Nina. *Woman's Fiction: A Guide to Novels by and About Women in America 1820-1870.* Ithaca, N.Y.: Cornell University Press, 1978.

Beer, Gillian. *The Romance.* London: Methuen, 1970.

Bell, Michael Davitt. *Hawthorne and the Historical Romance of New England.* Princeton: Princeton University Press, 1971.

Brown, Herbert Ross. *The Sentimental Novel in America 1789-1860.* Durham, N.C.: Duke University Press, 1940; New York: Octagon Books, 1975.

Cawelti, John G. *Adventure, Mystery, and Romance: Formula Stories as Art and Popular Culture.* Chicago: University of Chicago Press, 1976.

Cornillon, Susan Koppelman, ed. *Images of Women in Fiction: Feminist Perspectives.* Bowling Green, Ohio: Bowling Green University Popular Press, 1972.

Douglas, Ann. *The Feminization of American Culture.* New York: Alfred A. Knopf, 1978. See also Ann D. Wood.

______. "Soft-Porn Culture." *New Republic,* 183 (August 30, 1980), 25-29. See also Ann D. Wood.

Hackett, Alice Payne, and James Henry Burke. *Eighty Years of Best Sellers.* New York: R. R. Bowker, 1977.

Hart, James D. *The Popular Book: A History of America's Literary Taste.* New York: Oxford University Press, 1950; Westport, Conn.: Greenwood Press, 1976.

Hofstadter, Beatrice. "Popular Culture and the Romantic Heroine." *American Scholar,* 30 (Winter 1960-61), 96-116.

Kelley, Mary. "The Sentimentalists: Promise and Betrayal in the Home." *Signs,* 4 (Spring 1979), 434-46.

Koch, Donald A. "Introduction." In *Tempest and Sunshine* by Mary Jane Holmes and *The Lamplighter* by Maria Susanna Cummins. New York: Odyssey, 1968.

Mann, Peter H. *The Romantic Novel: A Survey of Reading Habits.* London: Mills and Boon, 1969.

______. *A New Survey: The Facts About Romantic Fiction.* London: Mills and Boon, 1974.

Mussell, Kay J. *Women's Gothic and Romantic Fiction: A Reference Guide*. Westport, Conn.: Greenwood Press, 1981.

Nye, Russel B. *The Unembarrassed Muse.* New York: Dial Press, 1970.

Papashvily, Helen W. *All the Happy Endings.* New York: Harper, 1956; Port Washington, N.Y.: Kennikat, 1972.

Petter, Henri. *The Early American Novel.* Columbus: Ohio State University Press, 1971.

Robinson, Lillian S. "On Reading Trash." In *Sex, Class, and Culture.* Bloomington: Indiana University Press, 1978.

Smith, Henry Nash. "The Scribbling Women and the Cosmic Success Story." *Critical Inquiry,* 1 (September 1974), 47-70.

Utter, Robert Palfrey, and Gwendolyn Bridges Needham. *Pamela's Daughters.* New York: Macmillan, 1936; Russell and Russell, 1972.

Weibel, Kathryn. *Mirror, Mirror: Images of Women Reflected in Popular Culture.* Garden City, N.Y.: Doubleday (Anchor), 1977.

Welter, Barbara. "The Cult of True Womanhood." *American Quarterly,* 18 (Summer 1966), 151-74.

Wood, Ann D. "The 'Scribbling Women' and Fanny Fern: Why Women Wrote." *American Quarterly,* 23 (Srping 1971), 3-24. See also Ann Douglas.

Science

Annette M. Woodlief

Science has been too much honored and too little appreciated by the American public, according to Morris Cohen.[1] To that I would add that most Americans throughout history have seen science alternately as creator and destroyer of their more cherished ideals and material progress, but they have rarely tried seriously to understand the goals and methods of pure science, an ignorance fostered by the isolation imposed by increasing specialization.

Science has had an impact, though it has not always been great, on American intellectual and popular culture from our Colonial beginnings. The impetus to study science in the Colonies was threefold: to demonstrate the divine origin and workings of the universe; to keep up with British scientific societies; and especially to exploit the utilitarian benefits of science. Interest in such areas as astronomy, weather, agriculture, botany, and inventions was widespread but rarely organized and generally served the practical concerns involved in establishing a new country.

The Colonial period marked the heyday of the amateur gentleman scientist in America. European science was eagerly followed, especially Newton's ideas, and twenty-five Colonials were elected fellows of the Royal Society of London, including the three John Winthrops, Cotton Mather, and William Bryd. However, there was little effort to establish similar professional endeavors in this country. More typical was the recording of natural observations, written and read by educated Americans, such as the nature accounts of John and William Bartram, notes on Virginia's geology by Thomas Jefferson, Jonathan Edwards's childhood essays on flying spiders and rainbows, and Benjamin Franklin's descriptions of his experiments and inventions. Theoretical science was represented in almanacs, which sometimes added to weather and agricultural advice brief explanations of Newton's ideas and the new astronomy. Such discussions appeared as early as 1659 in Zechariah Brigden's almanac summary of Copernican astronomy and continued in Franklin's *Poor Richard* and in Nathaniel Ames's almanac. These popularized expositions, appearing also in pamphlet form, were read widely, especially by ministers who shared the ideas with their flocks for what they revealed of design in the universe.

The mid-eighteenth century saw the growth of science primarily in the Philadelphia area, encouraged by the efforts of men like Ebenezer Kinnersley, a Baptist preacher who lectured frequently on Franklin's electrical experiments. Louis Wright asserts that lectures such as these on popular science aroused as much interest as political controversies during the 1760s and 1770s.[2] More serious explorations in science were going on, with encouragement and library support from James Logan and Franklin, by John Bartram (botany), Thomas Godfrey (inventor of the mariner's quadrant), and David Rittenhouse (astronomer and mathematician). New Yorker Cadwallader Colden and Virginians John Banister, John Clayton, and Dr. John Mitchell were other active gentleman scientists, although they were more interested in communicating with the Royal society than with the general public.

A few societies devoted to natural history (minerology, botany, zoology, ornithology) were formed during the eighteenth century so that their amateur membership could share observations. The first society was the Junto, formed by Franklin in 1727 for discussion of intellectual and scientific subjects. In 1744 he founded the American Philosophical Society, which became more vigorous when it merged with the Junto in 1769 to become the American Philosophical Society Held at Philadelphia for Promoting Useful Knowledge.

By the end of the century, magazines took over from newspapers the publication of essays on scientific theories and discoveries. The most notable, although short-lived, magazines were *American Magazine* (1769), *Pennsylvania Magazine* (1775-76), *Universal Asylum and Columbian Magazine* (1786-89), *American Magazine* (1787-88), *Worcester Magazine* (1786-88), *Massachusetts Magazine* (1789-96), and *American Museum* (1787-92).

Science in the Colonial period, then, was open to any interested person who would observe, read, and perhaps tinker a bit. It was extolled, whether by ministers or popular magazines, primarily for its capability of providing useful knowledge and demonstrations of the sublime and divine order of nature. But most people were simply too busy to pay much attention to science for purely intellectual reasons.

Freedom from the most pressing political and physical concerns after Independence brought more time for intellectual study at the same time that it broadened the base of popular interest in scientific subjects. This popular support, though, focused on practical results with little appetite for abstract theory, an attitude which surely encouraged the emergence of professional scientific societies and university curricula. Many scientists in the universities worked hard to acquaint the public with the serious nature of their work, but this proved to be a time-consuming and generally losing battle.

The problem was first highlighted by Alexis de Tocqueville, who noted in 1831 that Americans displayed "a clear, free, original, and inventive power of Mind" for practical science, but few were devoted to "the essentially theoretical and abstract portion of human knowledge." He speculated that scientific genius in a democratic society, then, would have to pursue discoveries leading to physical rather than intellectual gratification.[3] Time has not proved him generally wrong here, although he failed to predict the movement of many serious scientists to their ivory towers and labs to protect their professional integrity against public demands for practical results.

The nineteenth-century public had many scientific enthusiasms not necessarily shared by the increasingly professional and specialized scientists. Applied science was linked with material and spiritual progress in the periodicals, a faith which continued even in religious magazines well after the evolution controversy erupted. For much of this period, science, at least the popular Baconianism, was seen as cooperating with religion, and few were disturbed by conflicts incipient in geology and evolutionary theory. Also, Herbert Spencer's social interpretation of Darwinism pointed the way for human behavior based on scientific models of progress.

Most public interest was in discoveries associated with comets, geology, microscopy, meteorology, physics, and especially curiosities of botany and zoology as reported in newspapers and general magazines. Wide support was given the many scientific expeditions, the developing science and natural history museums, and new technological advances, especially in transportation. Scientific nationalism was quite strong, and the popular press was filled with numerous unsubstantiated boasts about American scientific and technological prowess.

Scientific-appearing evidence began being cited to support many dubious theories, such as phrenology and the undesirability of education and birth control for women. As Charles Rosenberg says, almost every social problem of the time attracted scientific discussion, much of it quite ingenious.[4]

Along with the drift toward scientism and pseudo-science grew serious efforts to popularize science. Most notable and far-reaching was the Lyceum movement, founded in 1828 by Josiah Holbrook to spread his interest in natural science. Lectures on science, particularly biology, chemistry, and astronomy, were well attended in the almost three thousand lyceums. This popularity inspired similar lectures offered by the YMCA and the Chatauqua circuit and library exhibits of geological specimens and Holbrook's scientific apparatus. John Griscom, Louis Agassiz, and Benjamin Silliman were scientists who appeared almost as much before an eager public as before their university students. One of Silliman's chemistry lectures in Boston attracted crowds which filled the hall and the neighboring streets, and the New York *Tribune* immediately sold out the 1872 issues printing John Tyndall's lectures on physics.

A natural outgrowth of the lecture movement were publications that could reach more people and require less personal energy of the scientists. Early in the century, the only general scientific magazine was the *Medical Repository*, which reported on scientific and medical developments. Silliman's *American Journal of Science,* which began in 1818, was joined by *Scientific American* in 1845; Edward L. Youmans began *Popular Science Monthly* in 1872 to popularize evolutionary theory. General magazines such as the *Port Folio,* the *Friend,* and *Atlantic Monthly* also found good reception for their sections on science. The American Association for the Advancement of Science (AAAS) was organized in 1848 to promote the popular as well as the professional communication of science. Clearly, the more the pure sciences developed professionally, the greater the need to explain themselves to a public interested but not intellectually engaged, especially since these scientific endeavors did require considerable financial support.

The nineteenth century also saw the blooming of quasi-scientific nature essays and the conservation movement. Birdwatching and botanizing were favorite activities in the antebellum South and in the North. For writers like Henry David Thoreau, John Muir, and John Burroughs and their readers, nature provided curious wonders and avenues to spiritual truths.

The wonders were particularly evident in the many natural history and science museums, ranging from the small town hall exhibits to the Smithsonian Institution, founded in 1846. The original motivation for such institutions was primarily theological, to present the order of nature in terms of natural theology, but they continued because of increasing public interest in scientific discoveries. Early museums included the Peabody Museum of Natural History (Yale, 1802), Mineralogical Collection of the University Museum at Harvard (1784), Dartmouth College Museum (1783), and University of Ohio Museum (1823). Influential popular educators were the American Museum of Natural History in New York, the Field Museum of Natural History in Chicago, and the Academy of Natural Science at Philadelphia. Technological aspects of science were the focus of exhibits at the Franklin Institute of Philadelphia, the New York Museum of Science and Industry, and the Museum of Science and Industry in Chicago. Such museums flourish today, promoting natural science and techology through many media: periodicals (most notably the *Smithsonian Magazine* and *Natural History*) and books (such as the "Smithsonian Series"), lectures, films and television, and expeditions. Perhaps less legitimately scientific but decidedly popular are scientific and technological sections of numerous exhibits and World Fairs, beginning with the 1853-54 New York Exhibition. Even Disneyland and Disney World have recognized the entertainment value of such exhibits.

Several societies catering to this popular interest in nature arose in the nineteenth century and began publishing magazines. The National Geographic Society has published its magazine and supported expeditions since 1886; the Audubon Society has promoted popular ornithology in several magazines, beginnning with *Bird Lore.* Other magazines with popular appeal were the *American Naturalist* (now a more specialized biological journal) and *Popular Astronomy,* now *Sky and Telescope.* Although most scientists would question how scientific these museums, exhibitions, and publications were and are, there is no doubt that the general public has long found them educational as well as entertaining.

On the negative side, discoveries in biology and physics in the last part of the nineteenth century initiated a change in public attitude toward science. Science became a clear threat to the idea of divinely instituted progress and was no longer the handmaiden of theology. For educated people like Henry Adams, the thermodynamic concept of entropy suggested that civilization and life itself were running down, not progressing. But the issue affecting most people was that posed by Darwin's theory of evolution, and preachers like Henry Ward Beecher and Lyman Abbott hastened to the aid of scientists Louis Agassiz and John Fiske to demonstrate that evolution could be compatible with Biblical accounts of creation. The debate reached a peak with the John Thomas Scopes trial in 1925, but it continues in fundamentalist Christian circles, as the Smithsonian Museum of Natural History found when it received many letters of protest about its recent exhibit on the "Dynamics of Evolution."

Despite these questions, for much of the public from the Civil War well into the twentieth century, the scientist was the modern hero and science would provide. Surrounded by growing technology making life more comfortable and prosperous, Americans honored scientists as well as engineers and inventors such as Thomas A. Edison. Even the scientific method with its emphasis on objectivity and experiments was extolled, although its practical results were much more appreciated.

Popular fiction of the time reflected this positive image of science. Literary utopias from J. A. Etzler's to Edward Bellamy's were able to erase the problems of leadership (with responsible and rational scientists) and servants (with well-controlled technology) in their perfect worlds. Serious fiction became increasingly realistic, striving for more objective reporting and less sentimentality, led by writers like William Dean Howells, John De Forest, and Mark Twain. As Social Darwinism gained popularity, fiction became more naturalistic, revealing the so-called scientific determinism of social laws, especially for the lower classes. The science romance also reached its peak with the pre-World War I novels centered on scientists who use their vast knowledge to end all war (often by giving their powerful discoveries to the most responsible government, that is, the United States) and in Sinclair Lewis's *Arrowsmith* (1925).

The image of the mad scientist initiated by Mary Shelley's *Frankenstein*

(1818) did not develop in this country until progressive optimism began breaking down after World War I, although it had appeared in some of Nathaniel Hawthorne's stories. The film industry, science fiction magazines, and comics seized on this theme, particularly after the debut of the atomic bomb; the white lab coat is still menacing in mass culture media. Actually, the sterotyped scientist is rarely evil, insane, or avaricious, except in B-grade horror films. Like the original Dr. Frankenstein, he's more likely to be idealistic, eccentric, dedicated to his instruments and research, somewhat cold and unfeeling, and not especially interested in long-term practical effects of his discoveries, even if they prove disastrous. He may provide a villain with the means of creating evil or a detective with vital clues, but he is too absorbed in his work to notice. Generally, he is not interesting enough to be the protagonist of a work; the focus is on what he does, not who he is. His quest for order often leads to chaos because of his very human limitations and god-like powers. He may not be mad, but he cannot be trusted, says the popular myth.

The fact that science is complicated and isolated by vocabulary and activities and has access to powerful knowledge not shared by the general public has generated much fear in this century, as is reflected in the news as well as entertainment media. This is not necessarily an unjustified fear. As magazines, newspapers, and books keep reminding the public, there are real and persistent problems created by science and technology; atomic power, chemicals in the environment, and genetic research are among those arousing widespread debate in the past thirty-five years. The promised utopia now looks more like dystopia or even apocalypse for many people.

Science fiction provides a good example of the continuing mixed public response to science. This writing has, as a rule, taken science quite seriously, extrapolating from the known to the possible to create an orderly, logical world. Scientists have been presented as relatively benign, providing the means for plot and characters to operate. Even the pulp science fiction of the 1930s assumed that science, especially the theory of relativity, was useful and valuable, although the stories relied primarily on pseudo-scientific doubletalk. However, science fiction film quickly developed a strong anti-science bias as it exploited superstition, horror, and the fear of the unknown. Necromancy and special effects took precedence over science, even in films adapted from science fiction stories. The favorite line, first used in the 1936 *The Invisible Ray,* has been "There are some things Man is not meant to know," a statement guaranteed to infuriate many science fiction writers. One reason for this split in attitude toward science is not hard to find: the audience. Science fiction—at least that which draws on the physical sciences—has been addressed to readers interested in science and technology, whereas films entertain people who often know nothing about science, and fear can be an exciting common denominator. This deep division in American nonscientific culture between pro- and anti-science concerns can be seen throughout the century in every popular medium.

The vividness of popular anti-science expressions has led many scholars to ignore the fact that science has never been very popular or respected in America, though much of the hero worship has worn off. New discoveries, especially in astronomy, geology, space, and biology are widely heralded by the news media. Interest in scientific biography is indicated by the recent celebration in magazines, on television, and in special exhibits of the Einstein centennial and the good sales of *The Double Helix,* a rather irreverent account of the discovery of the molecular structure of DNA by James D. Watson. Television shows about science, beginning with the long-running Mr. Wizard series in the 1950s and continuing today with shows such as PBS's "NOVA," CBS's "Universe," specials from the National Geographic Society and Jacques Cousteau, and six PBS series on science, including the thirteen-part, $10 million "Cosmos" with Carl Sagan, have become more rather than less popular, although the accent is more on entertainment than education. Science journalism flourishes today in newspapers and magazines, and the many magazines devoted to science are read widely. A recent popular addition is *Omni,* a slick magazine with articles on science and science fiction and *Science 80;* several others are being planned with such titles as *Science Illustrated,* and *Radical Science.* The popularity of science today is further indicated by the fact that the Smithsonian and over four hundred other science-related museums attract millions of visitors each year.

Books on science were particularly big business in the 1970s. Hundreds of books explaining scientific ideas and discoveries, many in paperback or in series, sell substantially, although they might not make the ten best sellers list. Ironically, the books that sell best are often pseudo-science, presenting dubious ideas about UFOs, plants, the Bermuda Triangle, or astrology, wrapped in scientific-appearing evidence. Science fiction continues to be popular, but as the writing has improved the scientific content has decreased and the fantasy element increased. Most significantly, there is a growing yet unnamed genre of books with considerable scientific content and/or viewpoint plus philosophical and poetic musings which are read widely by educated audiences. Some of the most notable include Jacob Bronowski's *The Ascent of Man* (television series and book), Annie Dillard's Pulitzer Prize-winning *Pilgrim at Tinker Creek,* Robert Pirsig's *Zen and the Art of Motorcycle Maintenance,* Fritjov Capra's *The Tao of Physics,* and books by Loren Eiseley, Rachel Carson, Lewis Thomas, and Carl Sagan.

Scientists may decry the diluted and enthusiastic appropriations of their work, especially to support questionable theories, but they also benefit from the accompanying public support and prestige. Even anti-science expressions of fear and distrust indicate popular recognition of the power science holds. For better and for worse, in this century science has become part of the fabric of American popular as well as intellectual culture.

NOTES

1. Morris R. Cohen, *American Thought: A Critical Sketch* (Glencoe, Ill.: Free Press, 1954), p. 85.

2. Louis B. Wright, *The Cultural Life of the American Colonies: 1607-1763* (New York: Harper and Brothers, 1957), p. 236.

3. Alexis de Tocqueville, *Democracy in America,* ed. Henry Reeve, Francis Bowen, and Phillips Bradley, vol. 2 (New York: Knopf, 1966), p. 42.

4. Charles E. Rosenberg, *No Other Gods: On Science and American Social Thought* (Baltimore: Johns Hopkins University Press, 1976), p. 4

BIBLIOGRAPHY

Barron, Neil, ed. *Anatomy of Wonder: Science Fiction.* New York: Bowker, 1976.

Bozeman, Theodore D. *Protestants in an Age of Science: The Baconian Ideal and Antebellum American Religious Thought.* Chapel Hill: University of North Carolina Press, 1977.

Cohen, Morris R. *American Thought: A Critical Sketch.* Glencoe, Ill.: Free Press, 1954.

Curti, Merle. *The Growth of American Thought.* New York: Harper & Row, 1964.

Daniels, George H. *American Science in the Age of Jackson.* New York: Columbia University Press, 1968.

———. *Science in American Society: A Social History.* New York: Knopf, 1971.

Gardner, Martin. *Fads and Fallacies in the Name of Science.* New York: Dover, 1957.

Glick, Thomas F., ed. *The Comparative Reception of Darwinism.* Austin: University of Texas Press, 1972.

Hanley, Wayne. *Natural History in America: From Mark Catesby to Rachel Carson.* New York: Quadrangle/The New York Times Book Co., 1977.

Hindle, Brooke. *The Pursuit of Science in Revolutionary America, 1735-1789.* Chapel Hill: University of North Carolina Press, 1956.

Holton, George, and William A. Blanpied, eds. *Science and Its Public: The Changing Relationship.* Boston: Reidel, 1976.

Hovenkamp, Herbert. *Science and Religion in America, 1800-1860.* Philadelphia: University of Pennsylvania Press, 1978.

Huth, Hans. *Nature and the American: Three Centuries of Changing Attitudes.* Berkeley: University of California Press, 1957.

Isaacs, Leonard. *Darwin to Double Helix: The Biological Theme in Science Fiction.* London: Butterworths, 1977.

Johnson, Thomas C., Jr. *Scientific Interests in the Old South.* New York: Appleton-Century, 1936.

Kohlstedt, Sally G. *The Formation of the American Scientific Community: The American Association for the Advancement of Science, 1848-60.* Urbana: University of Illinois Press, 1976.

Marx, Leo. *The Machine in the Garden: Technology and the Pastoral Ideal in America.* New York: Oxford University Press, 1967.

Miller, Perry. *The Life of the Mind in America: From the Revolution to the Civil War.* New York: Harcourt Brace and World, 1965.

Reingold, Nathan, ed. *Science in America Since 1820.* New York: Science History, 1976.

Rosenberg, Charles E. *No Other Gods: On Science and American Social Thought.* Baltimore: Johns Hopkins University Press, 1976.

Silverberg, Robert. *Scientists and Scoundrels: A Book of Hoaxes.* New York: Crowell, 1965.

Stearns, Raymond P. *Science in the British Colonies of America.* Urbana: University of Illinois Press, 1970.

Struik, Dirk J. *Yankee Science in the Making.* Rev. ed. New York: Collier Books, 1962.

Tobey, Ronald C. *The American Ideology of National Science, 1919-1930.* Pittsburgh: University of Pittsburgh Press, 1971.

Wright, Louis B. *The Cultural Life of the American Colonies: 1607-1763.* New York: Harper and Brothers, 1957.

Science Fiction

Marshall B. Tymn

The roots of science fiction are elusive and difficult to debate. Science fiction is a phenomenon with a heritage reaching back into ancient times, to a pre-scientific world inhabited by peoples whose myths, legends, and superstitions became a way of thinking about and explaining the wonders of the universe. The seeds of science fiction were planted thousands of years ago, as the human species dreamed of the great unknown.

Author Isaac Asimov reminds us that science fiction, as we know it today, could not have existed before the creation of a new world by invention and technology. "Through almost all of man's history," he says, "there was never any visible change in the basic manner of life as far as the individual human being was concerned. There was, indeed, change. There was a time when fire was tamed, when agriculture was developed, when the wheel was invented, when the bow and arrow was devised. These inventions, however, came at such long intervals, established themselves so gradually, spread outward from the point of origin so slowly, that the individual human being, in his own lifetime, could see no change.

"There was, therefore, until modern times, no literature that dealt with the future, since there seemed nothing about the future that could not be dealt with in terms of the present. There were fantasies, to be sure, dealing with supernatural worlds of gods and demons; fantasies of faraway mythical lands such as Atlantis, or unattainable lands such as the Moon, but all was described as taking place in the present or the past.

"Those changes which did take place (however slowly) were invariably the result of technological advance.... By 1800...the rate of advance in technology...had increased to the point where an Industrial Revolution was spreading outward from its point of origin with unprecedented speed. And wherever the Industrial Revolution took hold, the rate of change increased to the point where it became noticeable in the single lifetime of an individual human being.

"As a result of the Industrial Revolution, people, *for the first time,* became aware that the future would be, would indeed have to be, different from the present, and that this difference would arise specifically through the application of technological advance.

"At last people became curious about the future that they would never see. For the first time in history they had occasion to wonder what life would be like in their grandchildren's time.

"Science fiction arose as the literary response to that curiosity."[1]

As the Industrial Revolution burst upon the Victorian world, people began to write fantastic tales based upon the possibilities of scientific discovery and invention, and the now-evident fact that the world was changing.

Some envisioned a future in which a Utopia might be achieved due to advances in science and technology; others foresaw a bleak, nightmarish future. From the beginning, science fiction has swung between these two poles of optimism and pessimism.

Brian W. Aldiss, the British author and critic, contends that science fiction as a literary genre "was born in the heart of the English Romantic movement with Mary Shelley's *Frankenstein*" (*Billion Year Spree,* 1973). When Shelley published her novel in 1818, she started a trend that left behind the supernatural elements of the Gothic horror tale and introduced "science" as an ingredient of fiction.

The nineteenth century was fascinated with ideas of science and progress, and its mood was generally one of optimism. The machine age had been inaugurated, and its impact on fiction was tremendous. Popular magazines, such as *Century, Cosmopolitan, Harper's, Atlantic Monthly,* and *Saturday Evening Post,* along with vehicles like the dime novel, kept the public interest keen with stories featuring new mechanical devices and scientific marvels. Nearly every major writer in America and many in Europe experimented with writing stories about the new science, but Jules Verne was the first to devote more than part-time effort to the task.

Jules Verne (1828-1905) championed the revolution in transportation with such works as *Five Weeks in a Balloon* (1863), *A Journey to the Center of the Earth* (1864), *Round the Moon* (1870), *Twenty Thousand Leagues Under the Sea* (1870), *A Floating City* (1871), and *Around the World in Eighty Days* (1873). Verne's success as a writer of fantastic adventure helped pioneer a genre and establish the voyage motif as one of the classic themes within the literature. His blend of science and invention in his "voyages extraordinaire" insured the survival of science fiction, and his fertile imagination made it exciting. Verne was not a great innovator of science fiction ideas, but he captured the optimistic spirit of the nineteenth century when he made technological achievements a subject for fiction. Thus science fiction gained its own identity and a measure of respectability as defined by Verne's prolific and highly profitable output. His worlds seem limited, though, when compared with the work of another nineteenth-century writer, H.G. Wells.

With his background as scientist, teacher and journalist, Herbert George Wells (1866-1946) published his first "scientific romance," *The Time Machine,* in 1895. This novel is historically significant for two reasons: For the first time in fiction, a mechanical device built by man, a machine which utilized "scientific" principles, became the vehicle for an extraordinary journey through time. More important, the novel contained social commentary. Wells criticized the exploitation of the working classes and asked far-reaching questions about the directions in which progress would take us. In *The War of the Worlds* (1898), the first sustained work dealing with interplanetary warfare, "Wells's picture of Martians landing in Great Britain and remorselessly taking over the land without any regard for the native Earthmen, whom the invaders clearly pictured as inferior beings with no rights that needed to be respected, was...inspired by the fact that the British themselves...had just completed the takeover of the African continent under precisely similar conditions" (Asimov, p. 29). With H. G. Wells science fiction became more a medium of ideas than a brand of adventure. His vision of the future was tempered by pessimism, unlike Jules Verne, who was invariably optimistic in his tales of the wonders of a new scientific age.

Although stories heralding the new technology popularized by Verne and others constitute the early core of science fiction, other motifs had emerged by the turn of the century. As a response to a movement in England calling for the reorganization of the armed forces to meet the threat of global war, the future war motif, characterized by George Chesney's "Battle of Dorking" (1871), established imaginary warfare as a viable theme for science fiction writers, with the warring nations depicted in Chesney's tale eventually replaced by alien conflicts. The interplanetary voyage motif, which had existed in various guises since the early eighteenth century, began to adopt the more technological orientation that remains a staple of modern science fiction. Catastrophe evolved from threats of world destruction by alien invaders to an Earth devastated by atomic war, overpopulation, or pollution, as revealed in post-World War II works.

By far the most popular of the early motifs on both sides of the Atlantic was the lost race, which developed out of the interest in geology, archeology, paleontology and exploration. Escape was the keynote of science fiction in the early years of the twentieth century, and tales of exotic lands and lost races provided readers with a temporary release from the cares of the mundane world.[2]

Edgar Rice Burroughs (1875-1950) was the most popular writer in this motif. He was a master storyteller whose works were packed with solid entertainment and whose Tarzan series made him the most widely read author in the English language.[3] Many of the Tarzan novels centered on lost cities and lost races. Burroughs also wrote a series of novels set on Mars, where the remnants of once mighty civilizations were depicted with great color and vigor and exotic splendor. Other series took the reader to Venus, the Moon, and to the center of the Earth. His adventures were light, his characterizations superficial, and his science almost nonexistent; his striking settings and spellbinding adventures offered readers an escape from the gloom of industrialized cities and the realities of World War I. A greedy audience, and the inclination of pulp magazine editors to publish escape fiction, not only enhanced Burroughs's reputation but also gave science fiction another popular outlet.

It was not until Hugo Gernsback (1884-1967), a Luxembourg immigrant, began publishing a succession of electrical magazines[4] which regularly featured science fiction that the contemporary label *science fiction* evolved.[5] Science fiction entered a new phase when, in 1926, Gernsback placed the first issue of *Amazing Stories* on the newsstands. It was the first magazine devoted exclusively to science fiction ("scientifiction," as Gernsback first termed it), and it was an instant success. With *Amazing Stories* the pulp era of science fiction begins, when this form of literature separates itself from the mainstream by submerging itself within a long line of specialist pulp titles that were to remain virtually the only outlet for science fiction writers until after World War II. By the 1930s, other science fiction magazines were appearing regularly, competing with *Amazing Stories* and other Gernsback titles for the growing number of science fiction readers.[6]

Gernsback steadfastly promoted science fiction as he filled his early issues with reprints of the classic tales of Verne, Wells, and Poe. Later, he featured the works of Edward E. Smith, David H. Keller, Ray Cummings, Jack Williamson, Edmond Hamilton, and Murray Leinster, among others. Most of the fiction appearing in *Amazing Stories* emphasized the wonders of science, and were filled with futuristic hardware and fantastic adventure—another brand of escape fiction. One of the most famous writers of the Gernsback era was Edward E. "Doc" Smith, whose Skylark series, with its indestructible heroes and super villains, interacting on a galactic scale, popularized the term *space opera.*

In 1952 Gernsback was guest of honor at the World Science Fiction Convention held in Chicago. The following year, at the Philadelphia convention, popular works of science fiction were awarded "Hugos," in honor of the man who first used the term *science fiction* and encouraged the development of new writers in the field.

Science fiction began to change shape and direction when, in late 1937, John W. Campbell assumed the editorship of *Astounding Stories.*[7] Campbell, a regular contributor to that magazine himself, recruited writers with science backgrounds and demanded from them greater sophistication of style and technique. Writers refined their plots and characters, while emphasizing human relationships, and were encouraged by Campbell to tap psychological, political, philosophical, and other areas of inquiry. Among the new writers to appear in the pages of *Astounding* during the early years of Campbell's editorship were Isaac Asimov, Robert A. Heinlein, A.E. van Vogt, Theodore Sturgeon, L. Sprague de Camp, Katherine Maclean, Lester del Rey, Clifford D. Simak, C.L. Moore, and Henry Kuttner. Many of these writers still dominate the field. Under Campbell's tutelage, science fiction altered, matured, and entered what fans refer to as its "golden age," roughly the period from 1938 to 1950. Campbell remained editor until his death in 1971; *Astounding* changed its name to *Analog* in 1960 as part of an alteration of its overall format, and is today one of the world's largest-selling science fiction magazines.

The science fiction field continued to broaden and improve as influential magazines such as *The Magazine of Fantasy and Science Fiction* (1949), under the editorship of Anthony Boucher and J. F. McComas, and *Galaxy* (1950), edited by Horace L. Gold, appeared, and as science fiction spilled over into the paperbacks. But even in the post-World War II period, science fiction experienced a new direction of growth while preserving its romantic-escape and technological orientations.

The social sciences became important subjects as writers in the 1950s and 1960s came to examine the human consequences of technology, over-population, ecology, governmental abuse of power, racial conflict, and a host of other social themes. Science fiction's response to this new set of problems came, largely, at first, from a group of young writers, such as Michael Moorcock, J.G. Ballard, Brian Aldiss, Norman Spinrad, Harlan Ellison, Samuel R. Delany, Joanna Russ, and Thomas M. Disch. The "New Wave," as they came to be called, warned of the chaos and despair threathened by the potential for war and internal corruption in a technological society.

The New Wave writers also lent a fresh approach to the writing of science fiction, which, by the end of the 1950s, had become set in its ways. Eventually the New Wave movement was absorbed into the system, but before the movement faded, it was responsible for several important and permanent changes in the quality of science fiction writing, and helped to establish science fiction as a literature of serious social comment.

Science fiction continued to grow and develop in the 1970s. Robert Silverberg hit his stride with the publication of eight novels during the period 1970-1972.[8] Ursula K. Le Guin, who began her career in 1968 with *A Wizard of Earthsea,* has become an accomplished craftsman and a symbol of the high standards of quality of which the field is capable. Philip K. Dick and Fritz Leiber have maintained their important reputations: Dick, with works such as *Flow My Tears, the Policeman Said* (1973) and *A Scanner Darkly* (1977); and Leiber, now the most honored writer in the field, with eight Hugo and four Nebula awards to his credit. Brian Aldiss continued in the 1970s to be one of the least predictable of SF writers, "restlessly exploring new territory in each novel, refusing to be shackled by the traditional reader's expectation that an author's next book should be much like his last."[9] Michael Moorcock has continued to enjoy enormous popular success with his numerous fantasy works. Among the established writers, it was Frederik Pohl who made the greatest impact in the seventies. Following a period of low productivity and indifferent success, he has powerfully re-established his reputation with his novels *Man Plus* (1976), *Gateway* (1977), and *Gem* (1979), each of which has won major awards in the field.

Among the prominent new writers whose careers began in the seventies are George R.R. Martin, James Tiptree, Jr., Vonda McIntyre, Joe Haldeman, John Varley, Christopher Priest, Joan Vinge, Michael Bishop, Gregory Benford, C.J. Cherryh, and Ian Watson. Many other writers, too numerous to mention here, entered the field during the seventies; it was a fruitful decade for science fiction. As Robert Holdstock has pointed out, "the field has diversified to the point where to describe it any longer as a genre, while a convenient shorthand, is hopelessly inadequate. SF, if the term means anything, is a form of contemporary metaphor, a literary device for examining our world and our lives from another perspective. It is a significant form of the contemporary novel: not a substitute for it, not a poor relation of it, but an integral part of it. Its species of imaginative metaphor is one which has been attracting more intelligent readers and more serious and dedicated writers in the 1970s."[10]

The decade of the 1980s hold high promise, with a new generation of talented writers entering the field. Indeed, science fiction now attracts more writers than ever before in its history and is now the most popular form of the specialized literary genres published in the United States today. It has come a long way since the pulp magazines of the 1930s and 1940s provided a training ground for new talent; and in many ways the literature is still growing, altering its forms, modifying its techniques and subject matter. This constant change in style and direction is typical of a fiction that, above all else, is concerned with evaluating the forces affecting the shape the future may take and providing a vision of the possibilities open to society and the human race.

NOTES

1. Isaac Asimov, "Science Fiction and Society," in *Teaching Science Fiction: Education for Tomorrow,* ed. Jack Williamson (Philadelphia: Owlswick Press, 1980), pp. 26-27.

2. For additional commentary on early motifs see Thomas D. Clareson, "Introduction: A Spectrum of Worlds," *A Spectrum of Worlds* (Garden City, N.Y.: Doubleday, 1972).

3. *Tarzan of the Apes,* Burroughs' second published novel, first appeared in the October 1912 issue of *All-Story.* His first novel, *Under the Moons of Mars,* appeared in the February 1912 issue of the same magazine and ran as a six-part series; for its book publication in 1917 the title was changed to *A Princess of Mars.*

4. Gernsback published science fiction as early as 1911, when his own story, "Ralph 124C 41+," appeared in *Modern Electrics.* He also published science fiction in *Electrical Experimenter* (1915-1920), *Science and Invention* (1920-1928), *Radio News* (1919-1928), and *The Experimenter* (1924-1926).

5. The term was first used in Gernsback's editorial, "Science Wonder Stories," in the premiere issue of *Science Wonder Stories,* dated June 1929.

6. Gernsback launched *Amazing Stories Annual* in 1927, *Amazing Stories Quarterly* in 1928, and *Science Wonder Stories* in 1929. These were followed by *Air Wonder Stories, Scientific Detective Monthly,* and *Science Wonder Quarterly;* in 1953 he published his last title, *Science Fiction Plus,* a large-format magazine.

7. *Astounding Stories of Super Science* began publication in January 1930 under the editorship of Harry Bates; the next editor was F. Orlin Tremaine (1933-1937), who was replaced by John W. Campbell. The magazine changed its name to *Astounding Science Fiction* in 1938, and to *Analog Science Fact-Science Fiction* in 1960, with a minor change to *Analog Science Fiction-Science Fact* in 1965.

8. *Downward to the Earth* (1970), *Tower of Glass* (1970), *A Time of Changes* (1971), *The World Inside* (1971), *Son of Man* (1971), *The Second Trip* (1972), *Dying Inside* (1972), and *The Book of Skulls* (1972).

9. Robert Holdstock, ed., *Encyclopedia of Science Fiction* (London: Octopus Books, 1978), p. 176. I am indebted to Holdstock for information on trends in the 1970s.

10. *Encyclopedia of Science Fiction,* p. 189.

BIBLIOGRAPHY

REFERENCE WORKS

Barron, Neil, ed. *Anatomy of Wonder: Science Fiction.* 2d ed. New York: R.R. Bowker, 1981.

Brown, Charles N., and Dena Brown. *Locus: The Newspaper of the Science Fiction Field, 1968-1977.* Boston: Gregg Press, 1978.

Contento, William. *Index to Science Fiction Anthologies and Collections.* Boston: G.K. Hall, 1978.

Currey, L.W. *Science Fiction and Fantasy Authors: A Bibliography of First Printings of Their Fiction and Selected Criticism.* Boston: G.K. Hall, 1979.

Day, Donald B. *Index to the Science-Fiction Magazines 1926-1950.* Portland, Oreg.: Perri Press, 1952.

Franson, Donald, and Howard DeVore. *A History of the Hugo, Nebula, and International Fantasy Awards.* Rev. ed. Dearborn, Mich.: Misfit Press, 1980.

Hall, H.W. *Science Fiction Book Review Index, 1923-1973.* Detroit: Gale Research, 1975.

———. *Science Fiction Book Review Index, 1974-1979.* Detroit: Gale Research, 1981.

New England Science Fiction Association. *Index to Science Fiction Magazines 1966-1970.* Cambridge, Mass.: New England Science Fiction Association, 1971; *The N.E.S.F.A. Index. Science Fiction Magazines: 1971-1972 and Original Anthologies: 1971-1972.* Cambridge, Mass.: NESFA, 1973; *The N.E.S.F.A. Index. Science Fiction Magazines* [*1973*] *and Original Anthologies* [*1973*]. Cambridge, Mass.: NESFA 1974; *The N.E.S.F.A. Index: Science Fiction Magazines and Original Anthologies 1975.* Cambridge, Mass.: NESFA, 1976; *The N.E.S.F.A. Index: Science Fiction Magazines and Original Anthologies 1976.* Cambridge, Mass.: NESFA, 1977.

Nicholls, Peter, ed. *The Encyclopedia of Science Fiction.* London: Granada; Garden City, N.Y.: Doubleday, 1979.

Reginald, R. *Science Fiction and Fantasy Literature: A Checklist, 1700-1974 with Contemporary Science Fiction Authors II.* 2 vols. Detroit: Gale Research, 1979.

Strauss, Erwin S. *The MIT Science Fiction Society's Index to the S-F Magazines, 1951-1975.* Cambridge, Mass.: The MIT Science Fiction Society, 1965.

Tuck, Donald H. *The Encyclopedia of Science Fiction and Fantasy Through 1968.* 2 vols. Chicago: Advent, 1974, 1978.

Tymn, Marshall B., ed. *The Science Fiction Reference Book.* Mercer Island, Wash.: Starmont House, 1981.

______, Roger C. Schlobin, and L.W. Currey. *A Research Guide to Science Fiction Studies: An Annotated Checklist of Primary and Secondary Sources for Fantasy and Science Fiction.* New York: Garland, 1977.

GENERAL STUDIES

Aldiss, Brian W. *Billion Year Spree: The History of Science Fiction.* London: Weidenfield & Nicolson; Garden City, N.Y.: Doubleday, 1973; rpt. New York: Schocken Books, 1974.

Carter, Paul A. *The Creation of Tomorrow: Fifty Years of Magazine Science Fiction.* New York: Columbia University Press, 1977.

Gunn, James. *Alternate Worlds: The Illustrated History of Science Fiction.* Englewood Cliffs, N.J.: Prentice-Hall, 1975; rpt. New York: A&W Visual Library, 1976.

Scholes, Robert, and Eric S. Rabkin. *Science Fiction: History, Science, Vision.* New York: Oxford University Press, 1977.

AUTHOR STUDIES

Olander, Joseph D., and Martin Harry Greenberg, eds. *Writers of the 21st Century.* New York: Taplinger, 1977-.

Schlobin, Roger C., ed. *The Starmont Reader's Guides to Contemporary Science Fiction and Fantasy Authors.* Mercer Island, Wash.: Starmont House, 1979-.

Scholes, Robert, ed. *Science-Fiction Writers.* New York: Oxford University Press, 1980-.

Currey, L.W., with Marshall B. Tymn. *Masters of Science Fiction and Fantasy.* Boston: G.K. Hall, 1980-.

Sports

Robert J. Higgs

What is sport? The truth is that no one knows, and the challenge to define it, or at least to describe its characteristics, has engaged the attention of some of the best scholars of our time, always with beneficial results but never with answers that satisfy completely. Says Johan Huizinga in *Homo Ludens*, a book that is *sine qua non* on any aspect of the subject of sport, "In our heart of hearts we know that none of our pronouncements is absolutely conclusive."[1] Like Tennyson's flower in the crannied wall, we know that sport *is*, but we do not know with certainty what it is. Nevertheless, we are compelled to seek understanding of anything that so engages the interest of mankind as sport or play. In fact, play has become so important that it can no longer be left exclusively to the players. The influence of games on societies, from "the bloody Roman spectacles" to the staged demonstrations of the modern Olympiad and the Super Bowl, is simply staggering. Sport, as one observer has claimed, is the new opiate of the masses, as it has probably always been, though never so freely administered as in the modern world.

Drawing upon earlier works, Paul Weiss in *Sport: A Philosophic Inquiry* has grappled admirably with the problem of definitions and provided worthwhile distinctions among sport, play, and game, but does not, and indeed cannot, remove the overlap that exists in the common understanding of the terms. Since time and space do not allow me to delve into the nuances that Weiss establishes, I must, out of necessity, proceed, not on differences of opinion between him and others, but upon some common ground of agreement, with an invitation to the interested scholar to go directly to the sources himself.

" 'Sport', 'athletics', 'games', and 'play'," says Weiss, "have in common the idea of being cut off from the workaday world."[2] Here he is in agreement with Huizinga as he is with Roger Caillois who claims that play is *free*, *separate*, *uncertain*, *unproductive*, and governed by both *rules* and *make-believe*.[3] "Sport," as Weiss reminds us, "means" to disport, "that is, to divert and amuse." Hence in this study I regard sport as that aspect of culture by which men divert themselves from labor as opposed to work. This important distinction between labor and work is well made by Hannah Arendt in *The Human Condition* in her discussion of the difference between *animal laborans*, laboring animal, and *homo faber*, man the maker or artist, which is so succinctly implied in the phrase "the work of our hands and the labor of our body."[4] Today it is essential to realize that in professional sports, especially in professional sports, the athlete is quite often player, laborer, and artist all, one who laboriously sculpts a life of meaning out of his physical nature. Though lines between different activities frequently become blurred, in this chapter I regard sport as a diversion from labor. I am considering sport as "unnecessary" action in the sense that it is not *required* for survival as are forms of labor, such as farming. I must also add that I regard sport as an activity that requires the expenditure of a substantial amount of physical energy, more than that needed to play a game of bridge or checkers, though these too are certainly forms of play and diversions from labor.

"What is play? What is serious?" Huizinga asks. The Puritans would have had far less difficulty in answering these questions than we would today. For them, any effort not devoted to the good of the colony was to be eschewed, and games did not seem to lend themselves to the general welfare. In 1621 Governor Bradford rebuked the young men he found "in ye streete at play, openly; some pitching ye barr and some at stooleball, and shuch like sports." There should not be, in the governor's view, any "gameing or revelling in ye streets" nor if we are to judge from the incident of the maypole of Merry Mount any reveling in the country either. "Had the leaders at Plymouth, Salem, and Boston been in Parliament in 1643 they would have voted with the majority that all copies of the *Book of Sports* be seized and burned."[5]

The Puritan hostility to games took the form of official prohibition and even punishment. In 1647 in Massachusetts Bay a court order was issued against shuffleboard, and in 1650 the same injunction was extended against "bowling or any other play or games in or about houses of common entertainment."[6] In 1693 in eastern Connecticut a man "was fined twelve shillings and sentenced to six hours in the stocks for playing ball on the Sabbath. . . . Apparently, either he was playing alone or his teammates were let go with a warning, since he was the only man convicted."[7] The Puritan attitude toward fun and games in the view of many is perhaps best illustrated in Macaulay's remark that bear-baiting was stopped not because it gave pain to the bear but because it provided pleasure to the spectators.

The "Detestation of Idleness" was not confined to New England. In Virginia in 1619 "the assembly decreed that any person found idle should be bound over to compulsory work; it prohibited gaming at dice or cards, strictly regulated drinking, provided penalties for excess in apparel and rigidly enforced Sabbath observance."[8] Interdictions against racing within the city limits of New Amsterdam were issued in 1657, and two years later Governor Peter Stuyvesant proclaimed a day of fast on which would be forbidden "all exercise and games of tennis, ball-playing, hunting, fishing, plowing, and sowing, and moreover all unlawful practices such as dice, drunkenness–."[9] Restrictions of activities in some form on Sunday could be found wherever the new American civilization was extended on the frontier.

As John A. Krout, Foster Rhea Dulles, and others have pointed out the theocracy did not represent all of New England, and the narrow sanctions of the ruling class had in the long run little chance of being obeyed. The human propensity to play could not be stilled. Sport grew not only in New England but all along the frontier. Hunting and fishing flourished frequently as a means for gaining food but also as a form of diversion. Forests and rivers seemed to contain an endless supply of game and fish, and many availed themselves of the abundance. "Even Cotton Mather fished. Samuel Sewall tells of the time when the stern old Puritan went out with line and tackle and fell into the water at Spy Pond, 'the boat being ticklish'."[10] For those who have read Mather's prose, this is a pleasing image indeed.

The growth of recreation, even during the latter part of the seventeenth century, can be inferred from the journal of Sarah Kembell Knight, who wrote of her travels through Connecticut in 1704: "Their diversions in this part of the country are on lecture days and training days mostly: on the former there is riding from town to town . . . and on training days the youth divert themselves by shooting at the targets, as they call it (but it very much resembles a pillory). When he that hits nearest the white has some yards of red ribbon presented to him, which being tied to his hattband, he is led away in triumph, with great applause, as the winners of the Olympiak Games."[11]

At the beginning of the nineteenth century there was a wide diversity of amusements in the North, at least as reported by President Timothy Dwight of Yale: "The principal amusements of the inhabitants are visiting, dancing, music, conversation, walking, riding, sailing, shooting at a mark, draughts, chess, and unhappily, in some of the larger towns, cards and dramatic exhibitions. . . . Our countrymen also fish and hunt. Journeys taken for pleasure are very numerous, and are a very favorite object. Boys and young men play at foot-ball, cricket, quoits, and at many other sports of an athletic cast, and in the winter are peculiarly fond of skating. Riding in a sleigh, or sledge, is also a favorite diversion in New England."[12] Ninepins, skittles, and bowls were common at inns in the North for the convenience of the guests,[13] while in the South shooting matches were preferred, with "beef shooting" being one of the favorite forms.[14]

The sports that seemed to attract the most attention in the South, however, were cockfighting and horse-racing. According to Hugh Jones in

1724, "the common planters don't much admire labour or any other manly exercise except Horse racing, nor diversion, except Cock-Fighting, in which some greatly delight." In tones suggestive of William Byrd, he adds, "This Way of Living and the Heat of the Summer make some very lazy, who are then said to be Climate-struck."[15]

While the foreign traveler, especially the English, as Henry Adams notes, "charged the Virginians with fondness for horse-racing and cock-fighting, betting and drinking, . . . the popular habit which most shocked them, and with which books of travel filled pages of description was the so-called rough and tumble fight. The practice was not one on which authors seemed likely to dwell; yet foreigners like Weld, and Americans like Judge Longstreet in 'Georgia Scenes' united to give it a sort of grotesque dignity like that of the bull-fight, and under their treatment it became interesting as a popular habit."[16]

The rough and tumble, Adams argues, did not originate in Virginia, but came to America from England, as did, according to Jennie Holliman, most American sports, excepting those practices learned from the Indians, such as methods of hunting and trapping deer and bear, the use of bows and arrows, fishing at night with lights on canoes, lacrosse, and even rolling the hoop. Still the predominant influence was from abroad. The gun itself is a good example. "Up to 1830," says Holliman, "a few fine guns had been made in America, but they did not sell to an advantage simply because they were not imported." The same was true for fishing equipment, twine, tackles, hooks, flies, and rods, which came from Holland as well as England. Sleighs also came from Holland while bridles, harness, and saddles came from England.[17]

Cockfighting eventually disappeared in the South except in a few isolated areas but horse-racing, as everyone knows, has grown into both a major sport and industry with interest in the Triple Crown equaling that of the World Series and the Super Bowl. Wagering for the 1977 Kentucky Derby exceeded $3,500,000, breaking all previous records.

The history of horse-racing has to a large extent been the history of selective breeding of which Diomed and Messenger provide excellent examples. Diomed was brought to Virginia in 1798 and came to be held in such esteem that his death in 1808 caused almost as much mourning as that for Washington in 1799.[18] Messenger, bred by the Earl of Grosvenor on his Yorkshire farm, was brought to America a few years after the Revolution by Thomas Berger of Pennsylvania. Prized as a stud, Messenger was the sire of a long line of racing immortals, including American Eclipse, who defeated Sir Henry of Virginia at the Union course on Long Island in 1823, the first intersectional race that illustrated once and for all the popular appeal of the sport. Another offspring of Messenger was Hambletonian, the horse that turned harness racing into a national mania. "In the 1850's, the nation worshipped Hambletonian. It bought commemorative plates on which his likeness was inscribed. Children talked about him as if he were human."[19] Spurred on by the creation of jockey clubs, the establishment of race courses, and support of the aristocracy, horse-racing became America's first organized sport and has remained unquestionably one of its most popular.

The wide interest in the turf helped to bring about the rise of sporting literature in the three decades before the Civil War. The first sporting magazine in America was the *American Turf Register*, published in Baltimore in 1829 by John Stuart Skinner. Ten years later Skinner sold the *Register* to William Trotter Porter who had already begun his own weekly sporting publication called *Spirit of the Times*, one of the most famous of all American publications and a reservoir of history of American popular culture from 1831 to 1861. Prominent among contributors to this magazine was Thomas B. Thorpe, who inaugurated "the Big Bear school of humor," and the Englishman Henry William Herbert who wrote under the pen name of "Frank Forester" and who introduced "something of the English point of view of sport for sport's sake."[20]

Baseball, like horse-racing, has its roots in the nineteenth century and also like horse-racing owes more perhaps to the English than we are inclined to admit. The myth that Abner Doubleday invented baseball is totally without foundation. "The rules of baseball attributed to Doubleday in 1839 were identical to those in a rule book for the English game of rounders published in London in 1827."[21] In America rounders became known as town ball and was played at Harvard as early as 1829. In *The Book of Sport* (1827) Robert Carver related that many Britons, like the Americans, were calling the game by a new name, "base ball," and that it was "becoming a distinct threat to cricket."[22] Both the game and the new name caught on quickly in America, and by the 1850s the *Spirit of the Times* was calling it "The National Game."[23] By the 1880s daily attendance at the games was some sixty thousand. It has become "far and away the leading spectator sport."[24]

As Foster Rhea Dulles has observed, the role of colleges in the rise of sports in the decades after the Civil War was not one of leadership. The only sport that undergraduates developed was football, and again the English influence is incontrovertible. Basketball, in fact, is the only popular American ball game whose origins are not English, being invented by James A. Naismith in Springfield, Massachusetts, in 1891. American football evolved from soccer to Rugby to "American" Rugby and finally to the game we know today. While the basic forms derived from England, the Americans had long demonstrated a fondness for games of mayhem. Harvard, for example, "had a festival in the early 1800's which qualified vaguely as football. It was called Bloody Monday, but the upperclassmen mostly kicked the freshmen and only occasionally the ball."[25] Though it was essentially soccer instead of Rugby, what is called the first intercollegiate football game took place in 1869 between Princeton and Rutgers at New Brunswick. Rutgers won, no thanks to the player who, becoming confused and endearing himself to all future generations, kicked the ball through Princeton's goal. The first contest was played before a small crowd but approximately twenty years later Princeton played Yale before a crowd of almost forty thousand.[26] Thus long before the turn of the century football was well established as a mass spectator sport.

The one overriding fact concerning sport in America is its phenomenal growth. From William Bradford's injunction against games on Christmas Day in 1621 to Super Sunday 1977 there has been a complete reversal of attitudes. A few facts on salaries of the super stars tell much of the story. Fran Tarkenton estimates his net worth at $7,000,000, Kareem Abdul-Jabar is earning $2,500,000 for five years with the Lakers, Jim "Catfish" Hunter $1,000,000 more than that for the same period of time with the Yankees, and Muhammad Ali grossed over $16,000,000 in 1976.[27]

How did such changes occur? No one seems to be able to offer any conclusive answers except the human love of sport and the need for heroes. One thing is undeniable, however, and that is the contention that the widespread acceptance of sport was brought about in part by the revolution in technology in the decades after the Civil War. Says John R. Betts, "Ante-bellum sport had capitalized on the development of the steamboat, the railroad, the telegraph, and the penny press, and in succeeding decades the role of technology in the rise of sport proved even more significant."[28]

Of major importance in the promotion of sports has been the press, a major product of technology. Following the lead of the *Spirit of the Times*, new periodicals drawing attention to sport began to appear after the war. Among these were *Baseball Magazine*, *Golfer's Magazine*, *Yachting*, and *Saturday Evening Post*. Newspapers from coast to coast began to devote more and more space to sports until finally they had a section of their own. "Frank Luther Mott designated the years 1892-1914 as a period in newspaper history when sporting news underwent remarkable development, being segregated on special pages, with special makeup pictures, and news writing style."[29] Books, too, continued to arouse interest, especially among the younger generation. Among the many writers bringing dreams of fair play and heroism to millions of American youth were Gilbert Patten (Burt L. Standish), Henry Barbour, Zane Grey, and Edward Stratemeyer.[30] The champion producer of all in this group of juvenile writers was Gilbert Patten who wrote a Frank Merriwell story once a week for nearly twenty years and had only one nervous breakdown. Estimates of the sales of Merriwell novels run as high as five hundred million copies.[31]

The press helped bring together heroes and hero worshippers, but other developments also played crucial roles in the expansion of sports. It would be hard, for example, to overestimate the importance of the railroad and the telegraph in the spread of games. Because of the growing rail network, the Cincinnati Red Stockings could travel from Maine to California, and John L. Sullivan could go on a grand tour of athletic clubs, opera houses, and theaters. Revolution in mass transit meant mass audiences, and for those who could not come to the games the telegraph provided instant news of results. The Atlantic cable, electrification, radio, and television all influenced sport in profound ways that are still only vaguely understood. Because of technology the city of New Orleans could build in 1974 a bronzed-topped stadium with a gigantic screen for instant replays at a total cost of over $285,000,000. As Wells Twombly asks, "Was this only the beginning . . . or was it the end?"

NOTES

1. Johan Huizinga, *Homo Ludens: A Study of the Play Element in Culture* (Boston: Beacon Press, 1960), p. 212.
2. Paul Weiss, *Sport: A Philosophic Inquiry* (Carbondale: Southern Illinois University Press, 1969), p. 134.
3. Roger Caillois, *Man, Play, and Games,* trans. Meyer Barash (New York: Free Press, 1961), pp. 9-10.
4. Hannah Arendt, *The Human Condition* (Chicago: University of Chicago Press, 1958), p. 85.
5. John A. Krout, *Annals of American Sport*, Vol. 15, *The Pageant of America* (New Haven: Yale University Press, 1929), p. 10.
6. Herbert Manchester, *Four Centuries of American Sport, 1490-1890* (1931; rpt. New York: Benjamin Blom, 1968), p. 16.
7. Wells Twombly, *200 Years of Sport in America* (New York: McGraw-Hill, 1976), p. 18.
8. Foster Rhea Dulles, *America Learns to Play: A History of Popular Recreation, 1607-1940* (New York: Peter Smith, 1952), p. 5.
9. Manchester, p. 17.
10. Dulles, p. 25.
11. *Private Journal* (Albany, 1865), pp. 52-53. Quoted in Dulles, p. 29.
12. Quoted in Henry Adams, "The United States in 1800," *Henry Adams: The Education of Henry Adams and Other Selected Writings,* ed. Edward N. Saveth (New York: Washington Square Press), pp. 72-3.
13. Jennie Holliman, *American Sports (1785-1835)* (1931; rpt. Philadelphia: Porcupine Press, 1975), p. 81.
14. Ibid., p. 23.
15. Quoted in Dulles, p. 35.
16. Adams, p. 74.
17. Holliman, pp. 6-7.
18. Ibid., p. 108.
19. Twombly, p. 30.

20. Manchester, p. 77.
21. Twombly, p. 43.
22. Twombly, p. 46.
23. Manchester, p. 127.
24. Dulles, pp. 223-224.
25. Ivan N. Kaye, *Good Clean Violence: A History of College Football* (Philadelphia: Lippincott, 1973), p. 17.
26. Dulles, p. 198.
27. Jay Rosenstein, "Sweating Gold," *Playboy*, April 1977, pp. 106, 112, 238-240.
28. John R. Betts, *America's Sporting Heritage, 1850-1950* (Reading, Mass.: Addison-Wesley, 1974), p. 69.
29. Ibid., p. 68.
30. Ibid., p. 237.
31. Gilbert Patten (Burt L. Standish), *Frank Merriwell's "Father": An Autobiography* (Norman: University of Oklahoma Press, 1964), p. 181.

BIBLIOGRAPHY

Betts, John R. *America's Sporting Heritage, 1850-1950.* Reading, Mass.: Addison-Wesley, 1974.

Caillois, Roger. *Man, Play, and Games.* Translated by Meyer Barash. New York: Free Press, 1961.

Dictionary Catalog of Applied Life Studies Library. Boston: G.K. Hall, 1977.

Dulles, Foster Rhea. *America Learns to Play: A History of Popular Recreation, 1607-1940.* New York: Appleton-Century, 1940.

Edwards, Harry. *The Revolt of the Black Athlete.* New York: Free Press, 1969.

Finley, M.I., and H.W. Pleket. *The Olympic Games: The First Thousand Years.* New York: Viking, 1976.

Gardiner, E. Norman. *Athletics of the Ancient World.* London: Oxford University Press, 1930.

Haley, Bruce. "Sports and the Victorian World." *Western Humanities Review,* 22 (1968), 115-25.

Henderson, Robert W. *Early American Sport.* New York: The Grolier Club, 1937. Reprint. Cranbury, N.J.: Associated University Presses, 1977.

Holliman, Jennie. *American Sports (1785-1835).* 1931. Reprint. Philadelphia: Porcupine Press, 1975.

Huizinga, Johan. *Homo Ludens: A Study of the Play Element in Culture.* Boston: Beacon, 1960.

Kaye, Ivan. *Good Clean Violence: A History of College Football.* Philadelphia: Lippincott, 1973.

Krout, John A. *Annals of American Sport,* Vol. 15, *Pageant of America Series.* New Haven, Conn.: Yale University Press, 1929.

Lardner, John. *White Hopes and Other Tigers.* Philadelphia: Lippincott, 1956.

Manchester, Herbert. *Four Centuries of American Sport, 1490-1890.* 1931. Reprint. New York: Benjamin Blom, 1968.

Menke, Frank G. *The Encyclopedia of Sport.* 5th ed. Cranbury, N.J.: A.S. Barnes, 1975.

Olsen, Jack. *The Black Athlete: A Shameful Story.* New York: Time-Life Books, 1968.

Robinson, Rachel S. *Sources for the History of Greek Athletics.* Cincinnati, Ohio: University of Cincinnati Press, 1955.

Scott, Jack. *The Athletic Revolution.* New York: Free Press, 1971.

Strutt, Joseph. *The Sports and Pastimes of the People of England.* 1833. Reprint. New York: A. M. Kelley, 1970.

Stage Entertainments

Don B. Wilmeth

Other than the occasional staged variety show, the lone stand-up comic attempting to eke out a living in the few surviving night clubs or cabarets, or the spectacular revues of Las Vegas, popular live stage entertainment appealing to a large mass of Americans is a phenomenon of the past, replaced today by spectator sports, mass media, and rock concerts. In 1932, when the movies took over the Palace Theatre in New York, vaudeville symbolically died, although its slow death began in the 1890s as the motion picture slowly assimilated vaudeville and then replaced it as a more efficient and inexpensive medium. When the Minsky brothers introduced full-fledged strippers into their burlesque empire in the 1930s, burlesque as a unique and significant form of stage entertainment began its slow death. As Charles West, manager of his wife/stripper Evelyn "$50,000 Treasure Chest" West, commented as he observed the death of St. Louis's last burlesque house, burlesque's American decline began when taped music replaced bands, elaborate settings were eliminated, and comedians were canned. The decline, of course, began earlier, but he was correct when he added, "All that was left were the strippers." Each major American form of stage entertainment underwent a similar demise or merged into newer forms and vanished.

In the nineteenth century, however, the climate was right for live entertainment to prosper. Prior to the late eighteenth century, it was not possible for popular stage entertainments to appeal to large audiences, for it was necessary that there be a more concentrated society and the incorporation of the majority of the population into that society in order to foster popular entertainment. In this country, with the rise of technology and the rapid expansion of the frontier during the nineteenth century, Americans found increased time for leisure activities and developed a hunger for entertainment to fill what was for many a dreary and difficult existence. As cities grew and Americans were concentrated into cohesive urban or near-urban units with common social, economic, and cultural characteristics, a huge market for entertainment was created.

Although often similar in structure and form to the more legitimate, mainstream theatrical forms, popular stage entertainment offered the ordinary man a vital and appealing alternative theater that satisfied his needs and desires. Professional showmen quickly perceived what would be accepted and consciously attempted to appeal to the majority, creating entertainment that was neither complex nor profound but readily comprehended, thus popular in the sense that the majority of people liked and approved it, with few deviations from its standards and conventions. Hundreds of professional troupes and individual performers emerged during the mid-nineteenth century to provide a variety of entertainment forms, some new, some adaptations of earlier forms, but all aimed at a new audience seeking amusement. Urban centers developed theaters and "palaces" of entertainment; rural America depended upon the traveling troupe, be it a circus, a Wild West show, a repertoire company playing town halls, an opera house, or even a tent, Lyceum and Chautauqua troupes performing under the guise of religion or culture, and variety companies of all sorts and descriptions.

DIME MUSEUMS AND MEDICINE SHOWS

Prior to the American Revolution, strolling exhibitors of curiosities operated in the colonies along with numerous other mountebanks and itinerant entertainers. They presented crude and disorganized entertainments —animals, freaks, mechanical and scientific oddities, wax figures, peep shows, and the like. By the beginning of the nineteenth century showmen had begun to organize such exhibits into "museums" or "cabinets of curiosities," with little competition from legitimate or serious museums. By mid-century the dime museum was established as a major form of American entertainment, and the first formidable American showman emerged, Phineas T. Barnum, entrepreneur of the American Museum in New York, beginning in 1841.

Barnum's museum established the ultimate pattern for the museum rage, with exhibits of every sort and a so-called lecture room where visitors witnessed extra "edifying" attractions running the gamut from jugglers and dioramas to comics, musicians, and popular theater fare, such as *The Drunkard*. The museums, operating under the thin veneer of culture and learning, soon spread to every medium-sized city in America and survived as a uniquely American institution until World War I. The dime museum filled an important void; unsophisticated Americans and recent immigrants could find here cheap and comprehensible entertainment that was acceptable on moral and religious grounds.

Like the itinerant pre-Revolutionary mountebank, the roving, performing quack selling his tonics and elixirs evolved into a major form of American entertainment, the medicine show, which, with the phenomenal growth of the American patent medicine industry in the nineteenth century, became a major business. Before the turn of the nineteenth century, the traveling medicine show, with its pitchman and frequent humbug Indian spectaculars, was a flourishing form of entertainment, borrowing everything that was taking place in the American theater and adapting it to its own needs.

THE MINSTREL SHOW

Of the major forms of stage entertainment, the first unique American show business form was the minstrel show, which, beginning in the 1840s, literally swept the nation, producing in time a tremendous impact on subsequent forms, in particular vaudeville and burlesque. Using what they claimed were credible black dialects, songs, dances, and jokes, white showmen in blackface created extremely popular and entertaining shows while at the same time perpetuating negative stereotypes of blacks that endured in American popular thought long after the show had vanished. The popularity of the black native character dates from about 1828 when Thomas D. Rice created his "Jim Crow" song and dance routine. Evolving out of the "Ethiopian delineators" of the 1820s, the name for blackfaced white entertainers, four performers calling themselves the Virginia Minstrels and organized by Dan Emmett developed the first full-length example of the new entertainment in 1843; soon a flood of competitors followed. In 1846 E. P. Christy gave the minstrel show its distinctive three-part structure: repartee between the master of ceremonies, or interlocutor, and the endmen (Bruder Tambo and Bruder Bones) sitting on either end of a semi-circular arrangement of the company, followed by the "olio" or the variety section, and culminating with a one-act skit.

Minstrelsy was the first major stage entertainment to avoid the elitist reputation of legitimate drama and commit itself to the new common-man audience. It was immediate, unpretentious, and devoted to fun, the emotional outlet that its urban patrons needed so desperately. Its use of music and comedy created its greatest appeal and most lasting influence. With its endmen and interlocutor the audience was engulfed with an endless string of puns, malapropisms, riddles, and jokes, delivered as rapid fire exchanges and carried over into the later urban humor of vaudeville, burlesque, and even radio, motion pictures, and television.

After the Civil War, the minstrel show expanded in diversity and scope, incorporating elements from newer forms of entertainment, reaching its peak in 1870. Although the changes prolonged its life for a short time, its uniqueness was destroyed. By 1896 only ten companies remained, and the minstrel show was no longer America's major stage entertainment; its new replacement was vaudeville.

VAUDEVILLE

Like the minstrel show, American vaudeville was largely indigenous, the product of American saloon owners' efforts to attract eager and free-spending drinkers by enticing them with free shows. Early variety shows included risqué girlie shows, and their reputation soon became blighted. By the 1890s the older variety had been renamed vaudeville, capitalizing on the more elegant sound of the French word for light pastoral plays with musical interludes but having nothing in common with its French namesake. Instead, vaudeville developed its own brand of a highly organized, nationwide big business. Vaudeville became, after the early efforts of Tony Pastor (1837-1908), a symbol of Americanism; its performer, according to Robert Toll, the constant symbol of individual liberty and pioneer endeavor.

Modern vaudeville's heyday lasted a scant fifty years or so, from the 1880s to the early 1930s, but during its time Americans of all classes were amused and found relief from the relatively new industrial complex. Huge circuits of vaudeville theaters, led by such magnates as E. F. Albee, B. F. Keith, Marcus Loew, Martin Beck, F. F. Proctor, and Alexander Pantages, were in constant competition and, as rivalries blossomed, vaudeville flourished. The Keith-Albee combine, the most prestigious of them all, developel a formula catering to family audiences with continuous shows in luxurious vaudeville palaces. To protect their interests, managements formed conglomerates; performers quickly retaliated by founding the White Rats, modeled on the British music hall performers' union, the Water Rats, but with little success.

Although vaudeville appeared to its audiences as an unstructured collection of dissimilar acts, it was actually a meticulously planned and executed balance of "turns" designed to control the audiences' responses and interest, while enhancing the appeal of each act and providing a smorgasbord of the best available entertainment—magicians, vocalists, jugglers, comics, animal acts, skits, and even recitations and guest appearances by celebrities of the day. In 1913, the international star Sarah Bernhardt opened at the Palace in New York City and collected $7,000 for her talents. Because of its tremendous popularity, vaudeville helped to dictate morals and attitudes, whether consciously or not. Ethnic humor, for example, was a powerful force and, although immigrants were aided in their assimilation into the American populace by ethnic comics, their jokes helped to sustain the stereotyped misunderstandings and mythologies that still permeate American culture.

BURLESQUE

By the turn of the century a new form of stage entertainment had begun to assert its own unique brand of amusement, burlesque. The origins of burlesque are complex and confusing. Its components can be traced to numerous forms: English and American literary burlesque and parody, the circus, the knockabout farces of the medicine show and dime museums, the farces of such popular theater writers as Edward Harrigan and Charles Hoyt, the sketches of the minstrel show, concert saloons and beer gardens, Western honky-tonks, and even the stage Yankee. It is, however, misleading to attach the American form of burlesque to the older and more reputable forms, for American burlesque was clearly rooted in native soil. Historians usually date its true beginnings to the 1860s when a troupe of stranded ballet dancers in 1866 were incorporated into a musical extravaganza called *The Black Crook* at Niblo's Gardens in New York, followed in 1869 by Lydia Thompson and her "British Blondes" appearing in burlesques that emphasized feminine charms more than parody, the previous thrust of burlesque. As significant as these events were, they were less important than the influence of the honky-tonk, half beer hall and half brothel, with its variety entertainments of the most vulgar sort. The audiences were unsophisticated, and the atmosphere was similar to that of the early English music hall, rough and convivial. The first burlesque impresario, M. J. Leavitt, who began his career in 1870, combined the atmosphere of the honky-tonk with the structure of the minstrel show, took it out of the saloon, and put it into theaters. Soon burlesque assumed its standard form: variety acts and "bits" mingled with musical numbers, featuring beautiful women and bawdy humor. By the turn of the century the comedian was the center of the performance, despite the slow but constant increase of interest in the sensuous presence of the female form, made more prominent beginning with Little Egypt's "cooch dancing" in 1904 at the Louisiana Purchase Exposition in St. Louis. The comic retained his central position, however, until the advent of the striptease in the early 1930s.

The "golden age" of burlesque began in 1905 with the organization of the Columbia circuit or wheel and began to change in the 1920s when the new Mutual Burlesque Association added greater permissiveness. With an increase in its sexual overtones burlesque came to appeal primarily to male audiences, reaching its height of popularity just prior to World War I. As erotic stimulation replaced bawdy humor, burlesque audiences became jaded and bored; burlesque fell on bad days. Without its basically cheerful humor, never bitter or moralistic, burlesque, like the minstrel show before it, lost its identity and its uniqueness.

POPULAR THEATER

From the earliest days of the American theater, a popular fare dominated much of the best of native production, beginning with the stage Yankee, Jonathan, in Royall Tyler's *The Contrast* (1787). As more common people found their way into theaters, the popularization of drama became a necessity. Native actors gained prominence in plays with native themes and types: James Hackett as the Yankee with his common sense and rustic manners; Joseph Jefferson III, as Rip Van Winkle, providing the audience a momentary escape into a world of fantasy and freedom; Frank Mayo as the idealized American hero Davy Crockett; Frank Chanfrau as the Irish volunteer fireman from the Bowery, "Mose the Fire Bhoy." By the late nineteenth century, some versions of all the most popular plays began to reach small-town America. The earlier stock resident company gave way to "combination" traveling companies. During the last thirty years of the century, with the increase of railroad mileage after the Civil War, previously inaccessible towns became important and profitable stops for touring companies. Nearly every village and hamlet began to construct a local "opera house" to accommodate traveling entertainments, creating a vast theatrical network known as "the road." If an "opera house" or "academy of music" was unavailable, traveling shows turned to existing courthouses, schools, town halls, churches, or other large halls.

The most enduring form of theater that appealed to the common people and reflected their desires, needs, and tastes was the melodrama, which dominated the popular stage during its heyday, 1850-1920. Although much of the popular fare, called *10-20-30 melodrama* after its admission prices, was poorly written, its formula was such that it could accommodate any setting, time, or character, and the simplistic dramatis personae were immediately identifiable to the audience. To a public that found its traditional values exalted, melodrama was more real than reality. Although melodrama rarely dealt with social issues or problems, several of the more prominent examples were significant exceptions: *Uncle Tom's Cabin*, ostensibly against slavery but popular because of its emotionally moving, melodramatic scenes and its spectacle, gave rise to dozens of touring companies called *Tommers* or *Tom shows* which toured the nation well into the twentieth century; *Ten Nights in a Barroom* and *The Drunkard*, temperance plays, created patronage for the theater from people who had condemned it as immoral.

The thirst for a nostalgic look at the American past and a reminder of simpler, nobler times, as well as the need for the reinforcement of stable values that were rapidly changing, gave melodrama writers fertile ground for creation, from Denman Thompson's 1876 study of rural America, *The Old Homestead*, to William F. Cody's mythic creations of genuine western heroes in both drama and wild west shows, to Civil War dramas that ignored the broad issues and the causes of the suffering and the divisiveness in the 1880s.

In time, small towns were invaded by too many touring companies, each doing much the same thing. During the season of 1900, 340 theatrical companies were touring; by 1920 the number had dwindled to less than fifty. As the new century began, a trend developed toward outdoor entertainment, and tent show repertoire became very much a part of the movement. As repertoire companies found themselves squeezed out of many opera houses, in part because of the control of established houses by theatrical trusts, they looked toward more remote areas where one-night stand companies never appeared, and where, as William Lawrence Slout points out, audiences could not compare entertainment values, and obscurity was a protection against tightened copyright enforcement. The solution for many was the canvas pavilion used by the circus, as well as medicine shows and other forms of variety entertainment. Ironically, the movement was encouraged by cultural and religious organizations, first the Millerites in 1842 and the most popular of the movements, the Chautauqua, during the first quarter of the twentieth century. Between 1900 and 1910 there were well over one hundred repertoire companies under canvas. By the summer of 1921, faced with a recession, the golden years of tent repertoire ended.

Emerging from the tent tradition was one of the last native stock characters, Toby, a redheaded, freckle-faced, rustic country boy who became a nightly fixture and feature attraction with many tent rep companies. As tent show dramas lost relevance for rural audiences and Toby became so exaggerated as to lose identity with them, a final chapter in American popular theater fell into decline. While it lasted, however, American drama truly belonged to the people. The combined yearly attendance at tent shows exceeded that of the New York theater, despite the makeshift, shabby quality of the performances.

Like virtually every form of stage entertainment, popular theater was ultimately taken over by films which could be brought into America's heartland inexpensively and with a minimum of effort. Americans would never again be able to shape and mold drama in their own image.

EARLY MUSICAL THEATER AND THE REVUE

The nineteenth century spawned one last major form of American stage entertainment, and, in many respects, the last strong effort to create a form of amusement that would appeal to a large popular audience, although cutting across class lines. The American musical theater and the revue grew out of a blend of elitist European culture and American popular entertainment. By the 1890s, after the success of *The Black Crook*, George L. Fox's pantomime extravaganza *Humpty Dumpty* (1868), the parody *Evangeline* in 1874, Kiralfy's production of *Around the World in 80 Days* (1875), and *The Brook*, a production with Nate Salisbury's Troubadors in 1879 incorporating vernacular music and dance, an American form of the book musical slowly began to evolve. Edward Harrigan and Tony Hart, known as the American Gilbert and Sullivan, introduced their city low life and immigrant characters in a series of Mulligan Guard plays beginning in 1879; Charles H. Hoyt and George M. Cohan continued the trend toward a musical theater centered around urban life and people; and Victor Herbert, Jerome Kern, and Irvin Berlin helped to shape a naturalized American form of musical comedy.

Despite the tremendous popularity of American musical comedy, twentieth-century musical theater merged as part of the mainstream. The last true vestige of popular stage entertainment, then, grew out of the same roots as vaudeville and burlesque. The revue's immense popularity dates from the opening in 1905 of the New York Hippodrome, the home of early lavish circusy revues with a $2 top. In 1907 Florenz Ziegfeld unfurled his first Follies, which continued annually until 1932. The 1920s and 1930s saw a wave of revue series cashing in on Ziegfeld's success: The Passing Shows (1912-24), Greenwich Village Follies (1919-28), George White's Scandals (1919-39), The Music Box Revues (1921-24), and Earl Carroll Vanities (1923-32). Despite later efforts to perpetuate the revue, the great days of Ziegfeld and Earl Carroll, mixing radiant showgirls, humor, and spectacle on a level of sophistication and wit but still retaining a popular appeal, could never again be repeated. Instead, the revue propelled artists, especially songwriters and individual stars, into new avenues of show business.

Popular stage entertainments were quickly assimilated into those new media of mass communication, radio, and the motion picture. Modern technology and its new techniques for duplicating and multiplying materials, along with more efficient methods of production and distribution, quickly spread popular culture in this century, while at the same time replacing the need for live, professional entertainment aimed at a large popular audience.

BIBLIOGRAPHY

Allen, Ralph G. "Our Native Theatre: Honky-Tonk, Minstrel Shows, Burlesque." In *The American Theatre: A Sum of Its Parts.* Edited by Henry B. Williams. New York: Samuel French, 1971.

Baral, Robert. *Revue: The Great Broadway Period.* New York: Fleet Press, 1962.

Bordman, Gerald. *American Musical Theatre: A Chronicle.* New York: Oxford University Press, 1980.

Christopher, Melbourne. *The Illustrated History of Magic.* New York: Thomas Y. Crowell, 1973.

Csida, Joseph, and June Bundy Csida. *American Entertainment. A Unique History of Popular Show Business.* New York: Billboard/Watson Guptill, 1978.

DiMeglio, John E. *Vaudeville U.S.A.* Bowling Green, Ohio: Bowling Green University Popular Press, 1973.

Gilbert, Douglas. *American Vaudeville: Its Life and Times.* 1940. Reprint. New York: Dover Publications, 1968.

Graham, Philip. *Showboats. The History of an American Institution.* Austin: University of Texas Press, 1951, 1969.

Green, Stanley. *The World of Musical Comedy.* 4th ed. San Diego: A.S. Barnes, 1980.

Hamm, Charles. *Yesterdays: Popular Song in America.* New York and London: W.W. Norton and Co., 1979.

Harris, Neil. *Humbug: The Art of P.T. Barnum.* Boston: Little, Brown, 1973.

Laurie, Joseph. *Vaudeville: From the Honky-Tonks to the Palace.* 1953. Reprint. Port Washington, N.Y.: Kennikat, 1972.

McCaghy, Charles H., and James K. Skipper, Jr. "The Stripteasers." *Sexual Behavior,* 1 (June 1971), 78-87.

McKechnie, Samuel. *Popular Entertainments Through the Ages.* 1931. Reprint. New York: Benjamin Blom, 1969.

McNamara, Brooks. "'A Congress of Wonders': The Rise and Fall of the Dime Museum." *Emerson Society Quarterly,* 20 (1974), 216-32.

______. *Step Right Up: An Illustrated History of the American Medicine Show.* Garden City, N.Y.: Doubleday, 1976.

Matlaw, Myron, ed. *American Popular Entertainment.* Westport, Conn. and London: Greenwood Press, 1979.

Mickel, Jere C. *Footlights on the Prairie.* St. Cloud, Minn.: North Star Press, 1974.

Morrison, Theodore. *Chautauqua.* Chicago: University of Chicago, 1974.

Nathan, Hans. *Dan Emmett and the Rise of Early Negro Mistrelsy.* Norman: University of Oklahoma Press, 1962.

Slout, William Lawrence. *Theatre in a Tent: The Development of a Provincial Entertainment.* Bowling Green, Ohio: Bowling Green University Popular Press, 1972.

Smith, Cecil, and Glenn Litton. *Musical Comedy in America.* Rev. ed. New York: Theatre Arts Books, 1980.

Toll, Robert C. *Blacking Up: The Minstrel Show in Nineteenth Century America.* New York: Oxford University Press, 1974.

______. *On with the Show.* New York: Oxford University Press, 1976.

Wilmeth, Don B. *The American Stage to World War I: A Guide to Information Sources.* Detroit: Gale Research Co., 1978.

______. *American and English Popular Entertainment: A Guide to Information Sources.* Detroit: Gale Research Co., 1980.

______. *The Language of American Popular Entertainment: A Glossary of Argot, Slang, and Terminology.* Westport, Conn. and London: Greenwood Press, 1981.

Wittke, Carl. *Tambo and Bones. A History of the Minstrel Stage.* 1930. Reprint. Westport, Conn.: Greenwood Press, 1968.

Zeidman, Irving. *The American Burlesque Show.* New York: Hawthorn Books, 1967.

Stamps and Coins

John Bryant

In recent decades Americans have turned to leisure activities with an intensity that nearly belies the function of "rest and relaxation." Like sports, hobbies are for millions an outlet or even substitute for passion, controlled forms of mania which allow the participant to escape from or create order in a restless world. The most popular type of hobby is collecting. Our compulsion to collect, notes W. D. Newgold in the *Encyclopaedia Britannica,* probably dates back to those happy, preliterate days when man foraged for nuts and berries.[1] But today's collector does not forage in order to consume; he catalogs and displays his nuts and berries. The modes of collecting are as numerous as the objects that can be collected, and today anything that is abundant enough to be accessible yet scarce enough to be a challenge can become a "collectible." Some collect natural specimens. (We are told that Howard Hughes collected bits of himself.) Some collect rare books or art. Others collect the detritus of our industrial civilization: tinfoil, beer cans, or barbed wire. More collect antiques or dolls. But most people who collect, collect stamps or coins.

The American Philatelic Society reports that its membership now numbers fifty thousand individuals. A likelier estimate of serious stamp collectors is more than double that figure, and the number of "nonprofessional" collectors—the child or adult who keeps a cigar box or tidy album of stamps—undoubtedly swells into the millions. The U.S. Postal Service claims that upward of 20 million Americans use its philatelic windows each year. The American Numismatic Association reports a smaller membership of 34,000, but the recent interest in coin investment is quickly transforming a once elite avocation into a popular hobby.

More impressive than these figures is the remarkable activity that philatelists and numismatists precipitate in both the business and leisure worlds. Many governments maintain philatelic agencies designed to promote collecting and coordinate the year's steady stream of colorful new issues. Coins, too, in recent decades have assumed eye-catching designs. Collectors in both fields belong to local, national, and international associations, nearly all of which hold exhibitions ranging from modest hotel gatherings to major expositions with juried exhibits, lectures, and dealers' tables. Over 130 stamp and 26 coin groups meet regularly to examine special aspects of the hobbies. Each week over one hundred syndicated stamp or coin columns address the general reading public. Also, America's presses generate a bewildering array of books, scholarship, catalogs, and at present well over two hundred specialized stamp or coin periodicals.

To touch the past, to gain mental control over a proliferating world by gathering specimens of it, or simply to research a project—these are human needs that are routinely satisfied by putting a stamp or coin in an album. Determining the social and psychological roots of the collecting phenomenon is challenging; equally fascinating are the cultural implications of the stamps and coins themselves. Overtly, both stamps and coins serve basic economic functions; covertly, they are modes of governmental propaganda. From an aesthetic perspective, they provide unique popular art forms combing miniature and medallic art, engraving, mass production, and, in some cases, the work of premiere American artists and artisans. (At various times, for instance, Americans have been able to purchase an engraved Gilbert Stuart reproduction on a stamp with a coin designed by Augustus St. Gaudens.) Finally, as social icons, stamps and coins reflect shifting American ideologies and may in guarded cases be used as evidence supplementing a scholar's historical or cultural observations.

Since postal and monetary history are academic fields in their own right and plump bibliographies exist for them elsewhere, I shall not detail the histories of the mails or money except when such details directly influence the development of the two hobbies. Generally speaking, three factors have shaped the growth of philately and numismatics: "democratization," or the spreading of an elite hobby among the masses; "commercialization," or the transformation of the hobby into a business; and "specialization," or the creation within the hobby of special, even scholarly, modes of collecting.

STAMPS

Unlike coins, which are as old as sin, postage stamps are an invention of the industrial age and imperial Britain's need for an efficient communication system. Sir Rowland Hill introduced postal reforms and adhesive postage stamps to the public in 1840. Previously, letters were ink-stamped, and the price of delivery was paid by the receiver to the courier on delivery. Numerous private delivery agencies competed in an open market. Hill instituted a government postal monopoly and essentially inverted the process of mail delivery. Now senders paid for delivery by purchasing one-cent "Penny Black" stamps, which they then affixed to their letters. The result was more revenues going directly into government coffers and broadened mail circulation. Although an American allegedly introduced the idea of prepaid postage stamps to Hill, Americans were slower to adopt the new system. The first official U.S. stamps were not printed until 1847, and the government did not gain a monopoly until 1863.

Serious stamp collecting began some twenty years after Hill's invention. In the 1840s stamps were a fad but not a hobby: a socialite in British Mauritia printed her own "Penny Blacks" to adorn party invitations, and in England something called a "stamp ball" was the rage. The less affluent fancied stamps, too, using them to decorate their walls and lapels. By the 1860s, however, the fad had clearly grown into a hobby. Used stamp transactions were a common sight in the open markets of Europe. London could boast sixty stamp dealers, and French officials, fearing that stamp markets encouraged forgeries and the corruption of youths, closed the Paris markets twice before letting hobbyists be. Philatelic literature ("how-to" books, catalogs, price lists, and even books on counterfeit detecting) appeared as early as 1862. In 1865, British dealer J. W. Scott set up business in New York, and his new company (still a major U.S. stamp firm) stimulated an already growing market in this country.

From the beginning philately shared in the democratic spirit of the age. Although more prominent philatelists have generally been wealthy men (John K. Tiffany, Count Ferarri, King Farouk, Franklin Delano Roosevelt), the hobby has been a relatively cheap, accessible, and convenient pastime shared (as handbook authors like to crow) by "kings and kids" alike. Even the earliest guides to the hobby proclaim philately's universal appeal. Stamps were easily packaged and mailed for trade or purchase; they were generally inexpensive and required no costly paraphernalia (such as the traditional coin cabinet). A working-class child with a few resources could acquire a modest collection through trade and discovery, if not purchase. Moreover, stamp collecting was seen then as now as a form of play providing moral instruction, knowledge, and good preparation for social advancement. The publisher of Henry J. Bellars's *The Standard Guide to Postage Stamp Collecting,* for instance, argues that young collectors "have a more perfect knowledge of their studies, and, above all, obtain a quicker experience of actual life, *and the value of money.*"[2] More than a pastime for the idle rich, philately adhered to the Protestant ethic and gave youngsters a boost up the ladder of success.

To be sure, the major advances and research in the nineteenth century were made by the wealthy. The London (now Royal) Philatelic Society, founded in 1869, was followed in 1886 by the American Philatelic Association (now Society) organized by John Tiffany, a collector since 1859 and a bibliographer of philatelic literature. J. W. Scott presided over the first years of the Collectors Club of New York, founded in 1896, which listed among its members some of the nation's elite. The backbone of American philately, however, was in the middle and working classes; from 1870 to 1890 interest in the hobby was strong enough to sustain some three hundred popular and scholastic periodicals in the United States.

By the turn of the century, major stamp exhibitions in Antwerp (1887) and New York (1889) established philately as an international hobby. In 1890 a third such fair in London celebrated the fiftieth anniversary of Hill's invention and introduced an important decade in the commercialization of the hobby. Until this time governmental postal issues had been predominately portrait stamps. England had Victoria; America had Washington and Franklin. The first major step in the transformation of the hobby into a big government business occurred when authorities reckoned that prettier stamps might attract the eye and pennies of collectors. In the long run they were right, but the idea did not catch on immediately. As early as 1876 the U.S. government had, in fact, issued a series of seven "pictorial" stamps with vignettes of the signing of the Declaration of Independence, the landing of Columbus, and various "icons" such as a locomotive, steamship, and mounted courier; but these stamps did not sell well. A more notorious "experiment" in stamp marketing occurred in 1893, when N. F. Seebeck of the Hamilton Note Company of New York designed and printed a set of colorful stamps for certain Central and South American nations. Called "Seebecks," these stamps were primarily meant to be sold to collectors. The scheme failed, but in 1894 the republic of San Marino set up its philatelic agency to do precisely what Seebeck had hoped to do—create stamps not as postage but as collectors' items.

At first collectors were scandalized by any government's attempt to capitalize on the hobby, but the trend toward special and commemorative stamps was irreversible, and today most government postal services actively promote stamp collecting. The frequency of special issues has grown slowly but distinctly in the United States since the printing in 1893 of our first special issues commemorating Columbus's discovery of America. By the 1920s the United States was printing only about three special issues a year. However, 1932 was a banner year for U.S. commemoratives; nineteen in all were issued. The average number of issues in the 1950s was eleven; but since the Bicentennial the figure has approached thirty a year. Government stamp sales are a significant source of income ranging in the millions of dollars. Some speculate, too, that nearly 40 percent of U.S. stamps each year (almost 1.5 billion stamps in 1974) never circulate; they are collected or bought by dealers to be sold to collectors.

The boom in philately during the 1930s and 1940s deeply penetrated various sectors of American culture. Government, entrepreneurs, educators, churches, radio, and universities promoted the hobby. During his administration Franklin Roosevelt assumed complete control over stamp issues, and his flamboyant Postmaster General James Farley was responsible one year for a $1 million clear profit on the sale of stamps. Also at this time, philately was introduced as a teaching device in public schools. Junior-level history books, for instance, used stamps to "tell the story of America." Church-affiliated stamp clubs sprang up. Bell Telephone encouraged employees to collect, and Ivory Soap sponsored a long-running radio program for collectors. Even the University of Michigan offered a course in philately. Since World War II national and local stamp organizations have strengthened their civic-mindedness. The three major associations, the American Philatelic Society (APS), the Society of Philatelic Americans (SPA), and the American Topical Association (ATA), maintain close ties with civic and educational groups through slide shows, displays, and lecture programs.

For the most part the 1950s and early 1960s brought a continued expansion of philately's democratization and commercialization. More people were adopting the hobby, and the hobby business, in both private and government sectors, was growing. The notion that stamps make good investments has always been an important part of philately's commercial side, but it was not until the early 1950s and the advent of swift inflation that the idea began to sink in. Stamp guides, such as Henry M. Ellis's *Stamps for Fun and Profit,* indicate the trend. Temple University's Business School went so far as to offer a two-year course in philately. Since the Vietnam War, investors have turned more to stamps and coins as hedges against inflation, and Ed Reiter, coin columnist for the *New York Times,* recently reported that in 1980 Adelphi College offered courses in philately and numismatics to educate dealers and investors in the ways of the market.[3] Thus, the history of the commercialization of the postage stamps has moved from fad to hobby to private and government business to speculative finance.

To a certain degree, a history of philately can be keyed to the emergence of new ways to collect or specialize. Just as Jaques discerns seven ages of man, there are roughly the same number of "ages" of specialization for the collector. The first age is the generalist who collects any and all stamps. The first step toward specialization is the focus on the stamps of one nation or a particular historical period. A slightly more refined third "age" is collecting types of stamps (airmail, revenue, postage due) or stamps with peculiar markings or arrangements such as "overprints" and "perfins" (stamps pre-cancelled with perforated initials).

A fourth form of specialization is considered by many to be the height of traditional collecting (and, of course, madness, by the lay person). Here, a philatelist will focus on one particular stamp (usually a regular issue) and collect all of its plate, color, and press variants. Such a mode requires scholastic aptitude since the focal stamp's printing history must be meticulously researched down to the hairline cracks that appear in certain plates. (The process is comparable to literary textual analysis, only more difficult.) Growing out of the need for the analysis of variants and counterfeits was the foundation in 1940 of the Philatelic Research Laboratory of New York, which introduced various technological innovations to the hobby.

Anathema (it seems) to traditional philately is the fifth, upstart age of "topical" collecting. Here philatelists collect internationally but only along the lines of a particular subject matter depicted on the stamp. The American

Topical Association, organized in 1940 and now ten thousand strong, recognizes at least seven hundred categories, including John F. Kennedy; space; Americana on American or non-American stamps; journalists, artists, and poets on stamps (JAPOS); women, and so on up to an amazingly self-reflexive topic, stamps with pictures of stamps on them. Topical collecting (or "thematics" as the British call it) has grown in popularity, and some traditional philatelists disparage the mode because it develops an interest in a stamp's message rather than the stamp itself or its history. Government post offices, however, have shaped their special issues to attract the topicalist. In the last two decades the U.S. postal authorities have introduced new printing methods which allow for more color and experimental groupings. (Two or four related stamps, for instance, may be printed together in a strip or block. These are called *"setens"* from the French *se tenant,* and, yes, one can collect only *"setens."*) At the moment, topical collecting is becoming the dominant mode of collecting.

A sixth "age" of philately involves those who collect postal material rather than just stamps. Of recent interest to investors and long-standing interest to postal historians are mailed (or even unused) envelopes or "covers" that bear the intricate markings of the mail service. Cover philatelists may, of course, collect material dating before the invention of the postage stamp, but such items are quite often found in museums. Slightly more accessible modern rarities include air mail covers delivered to Paris by Charles Lindbergh or to the United States via zeppelin. Covers also allow collectors to examine postmarks. Up until the turn of the century, letters were hand-cancelled, and early regional postmasters carved their own cancellation marks. Pumpkins, devils, eagles, and other elaborately designed or "fancy" cancellations can be collected, cataloged, and displayed.

The final age of the philatelist (not to be compared too closely to Jaques's "second childhood") is the most academic: postal history. Today even philatelists do not fully understand the difference between postal history and cover collecting. Since collection categories are interpreted by national and international exhibition judges, we might expect clear distinctions from these authorities, but, as a seminar at a recent southeast Pennsylvania stamp exposition revealed, not all judges agree. Generally speaking, a cover collection is merely a collection of covers, but a postal history collection demonstrates developments in postal history. Thus, as one seminar participant put it, the two types of collections may use precisely the same material but the difference is whether the collection is "written up" to demonstrate history or merely to describe the covers. The philatelist of the future, then, must sharpen his rhetoric.

COINS

Coin collecting presents a significantly different pattern of development. Unlike philately, which began in the industrial age as a fad, spread democratically, yet has become as much an academic pursuit as a hobby, numismatics has been from the beginning and until only recently the concern of the intellectual and social elite. Old coins have always been attractive to the antiquarian; Petrarch, for instance, was one of the first to have collected antique Roman coins. By the eighteenth century no Sun King or even his lesser luminaries could feel properly furnished without a coin cabinet. Men of substance acquired coins as they would art or rare books. Also at this time numismatics entered the university. As early as the Renaissance, gentlemen had written brief treatises on the history of coins, but by the early 1700s in Germany (still the central arena for numismatic research) scholars were beginning to use coins as historical evidence. The compulsion that drove Schliemann a century later to dig at the layered ruins of Troy was in part the same desire that brought early scholars closer to coins. Since then numismatics has been an important handmaiden to the archaeologist and historian as well as the aesthetician.

The nineteenth century brought a number of developments that shaped and redefined numismatics from the study of coins to that of money in general and medals. As Elvira E. Clain-Stefanelli remarks in her monograph (used liberally here), *Numismatics—An Ancient Science: A Survey of Its History,* the Napoleonic wars generated many medals which were in turn studied in weighty French tomes. In the New World, British and American governments struck medals to "honor" American Indian peace alliances. The quickly expanding and contracting economies of the world also generated more varieties of currency: paper money, bank notes, scrip, tokens, and even unofficial yet negotiable coins. The shortage of coins resulting from Andrew Jackson's refusal to recharter the Second Bank of the United States forced banks and merchants to issue fractional currency and "hard times coins" as late as 1844 in order to make change. With more of such items to collect, numismatists began to focus on material of more recent vintage and of the modern nations. By mid-century, museums as well as universities had become the principal lodgings for major collections. More people were able to see the rarities; more people could also afford modest collections of their own. Yet more scholarly research, publication, and cataloging developed during this period. Thus, numismatics was able to broaden its appeal but also rise in academic respectability.

Although American Colonial coinage can be dated back to 1616, we have records of only a few eighteenth-century American coin collectors. American numismatics dates primarily from the mid-nineteenth century. Philadelphia, home of the U.S. Mint, was logically the first center of numismatic interest. As Clain-Stefanelli records, the mint's chief coiner, Adam Eckfeldt, began a collection at the mint that would become one of the United States's and the world's finest. In 1858 several Philadelphians formed the Numismatic and Antiquarian Society. Also founded that year but destined to outlive the Philadelphia organization was the scholarly American Numismatic Society (ANS). This group and the larger, more hobby-oriented American Numismatic Association (ANA), founded in Chicago in 1891, have become the country's principal numismatic organizations. During the latter half of the century, periodicals such as the *American Journal of Numismatics* (no longer in print), *The Numismatist,* and other more ephemeral publications provided amateurs and newcomers with an opportunity to prepare themselves for the rigors of numismatic technique. Landmark works in U.S. numismatic scholarship appeared in these decades. Consonant with international scholarship of that age, American numismatists tended to use currency as clues to economic development rather than as archaeological evidence. It has been only recently that scholars have begun to appreciate the artistic merit of America's coinage.

Although by the turn of the century numismatics was growing, it was still a gentleman-scholar's hobby horse. The democratization of the hobby was impeded by certain obvious physical problems. At the time, cumbersome coins required boxes, drawers, and cabinets for storage. Also, modern collecting was inhibited by the fact that governments (which are still conservative when it comes to coinage) rarely minted commemorative, special, or even new issues. At least three developments served to rectify these problems. First, from 1892 to 1934, the U.S. government experimented with commemorative coins, some of which were issued alongside similar commemorative stamps. Also during this period the mint, in an attempt to generate interest in collecting, made available "proof sets"of each year's new or newly dated coins. Unfortunately, the Depression and World War II slowed down the collection of such items until the 1950s. A third development was the marketing in the late 1930s of "coin books" made of cardboard pages with holes cut to fit individual coins. The convenient device gave the hobby its biggest boost. At the time, traditional numismatists laughed, but hobbyists today continue to search loose change and coin rolls for that elusive 1919 D one-cent to stick in their books.

Although numismatics preceded philately as an intellectual discipline, coin collectors of the 1930s did well by following commercial techniques that had been in vogue among stamp collectors for decades. Chatty but reliable journals such as the *Numismatic Scrapbook Magazine* provided trade and sale information. In 1942 Richard S. Yeoman (who first marketed the coin book) began publishing the *Handbook of United States Coins,* "an objective pricing guide" for dealers, and in 1946 he put out the first edition of the *Guidebook of United States Coins,* now an annual mainstay for collectors.

Since World War II the growth of the hobby can be gauged somewhat by the fact that the mint sold nearly 4 million proof sets in 1964 over the fifty thousand sold in 1950. In recent years private mints have promoted the medallic arts, but the most important force in the hobby today is investment—the hope that coin collecting will somehow keep the wolf of inflation at bay. This, however, may destroy rather than promote the hobby, since the price of gold and silver has recently made even collector's items more valuable if melted down. Ed Reiter reports that more coins are heading toward the furnace. This will reduce the number of collector's items and raise their value but also reduce the number of those who can afford to collect.[4] Thus, this century has seen numismatics develop in ways contrary to philately. Beginning as a highly specialized field, coin collecting has enjoyed an age of democratization which may be cut short by overcommercialization and speculative finance.

NOTES

1. Wilbert D. Newgold, "Hobbies," *Encyclopaedia Britannica: Macropaedia,* 15th ed. (Chicago: Encyclopedia Britannica, 1978), p. 973.
2. Henry John Bellars, *The Standard Guide to Postage Stamp Collecting* (London: John Camden Hotter, 1864), n.p.
3. Ed Reiter, "Numismatics: College Level Training," *New York Times,* December 23, 1979, Sec. D., p. 36.
4. Ed Reiter, "Numismatics: Is the Hobby Suffering from Growing Pains?" *New York Times,* December 30, 1979, Sec. D., p. 36.

BIBLIOGRAPHY

STAMPS

Brazer, Clarence. *Essays for United States Adhesive Postage Stamps.* New York: American Philatelic Society, 1941.

Brookman, Lester G. *Nineteenth Century Postage Stamps of the United States.* New York: Lindquist, 1947.

Dietz, August. *The Postal Service of the Confederate States of America.* Richmond, Va.: Dietz Press, 1929.

Fischel, H. A. "Philatelic Portrait of the Modern Jew," *Jewish Social Studies,* 23 (July 1961), 187-208.

Fuller, Wayne E. *The American Mail: Enlarger of the Common Life.* Chicago: University of Chicago Press, 1972.

Johl, Max. *United States Commemoratives of the Twentieth Century.* New York: Lindquist, 1947.

Kelen, Emery. *Stamps Tell the Story of John F. Kennedy.* New York: Meredith, 1968.

Konwiser, Henry M. *The American Stamp Collector's Dictionary.* New York: Minkus, 1949.

Postage Stamps: A Selective Checklist of Books on Philately in the Library of Congress. Washington, D.C.: Library of Congress, 1940.

Postage Stamps of the United States. Washington, D.C.: U.S. Government Printing Office, 1973.

Rosichan, Richard H. *Stamps and Coins.* Littleton, Colo.: Libraries Unlimited, 1974.

Scheele, Carl H. *A Short History of the Mail Service.* Washington, D.C.: Smithsonian, 1970.

Scott's Specialized Catalogue of United States Stamps. New York: J. W. Scott, 1980.

Stiles, Kent B. *Postal Saints and Sinners: Who's Who on Stamps.* Brooklyn, N.Y.: T. Gaus' Sons, 1964.

Stoetzer, O. Carlos. *Postage Stamps and Propaganda.* Washington, D.C.: Public Affairs Press, 1953.

Zareski, Michel, and Herman Herst, Jr. *Fancy Cancellations of Nineteenth Century United States Postage Stamps.* Shrub Oak, N.Y.: Herst, 1963.

COINS

American Numismatic Society. *Dictionary Catalogue of the Library of the American Numismatic Society.* New York: G. K. Hall, 1972.

Belden, Bauman L. *Indian Peace Medals Issued in the United States, 1789-1889.* New Milford, Conn.: N. Flayderman, 1966.

Clain-Stefanelli, Elvira E. *Numismatics—An Ancient Science: A Survey of Its History.* Washington, D.C.: U.S. Government Printing Office, 1965.

______. *Select Numismatic Bibliography.* New York: Stacks, 1965.

Coin World Almanac. Sidney, Ohio: Amos Press, 1979.

Criswell, Grover and Clarence. *Confederate and Southern States Currency.* New York: House of Collectibles, 1961.

Frey, Albert. *Dictionary of Numismatic Names.* New York: Barnes and Noble, 1947.

Grierson, Philip. *Numismatics.* New York: Oxford, 1975.

Judd, J. Hewitt, and Walter Breen. *United States Patterns, Experimental, and Trial Pieces.* Racine, Wis.: Whitman, 1962.

Loubat, Joseph F. *The Medallic History of the United States of America, 1776-1876.* New Milford, Conn.: N. Flayderman, 1967.

Reed, Mort. *Cowles' Complete Encyclopedia of United States Coins.* New York: Cowles', 1969.

Ruby, Warren A. *Commemorative Coins of the United States.* Lake Mills, Iowa: Graphic, 1961.

Salton, Mark. *Glossary of Numismatic Terms.* New York: Barnes and Noble, 1947.

Taxay, Don. *Comprehensive Catalogue and Encyclopedia of United States Coins.* New York: J. W. Scott, 1971.

______. *An Illustrated History of United States Commemorative Coins.* New York: Arco, 1967.

Vermeule, Cornelius C. *Numismatic Art in America: Aesthetics of the United States Coinage.* Cambridge, Mass.: Harvard University Press, 1971.

Yeoman, Richard S. *Guidebook of United States Coins.* Racine, Wis.: Western, 1978.

______. *Handbook of United States Coins.* Racine, Wis.: Western, 1978.

Television

Robert S. Alley

Technically television is in its fifties, culturally it is in its twenties. In the year 1926 there were practical demonstrations of living scenes viewed the instant they took place by audiences removed from the events. In London, Paris, and New York, the technology was similar and impressive. In 1927 the *New York Times* noted that television "outruns the imagination of all the wizards of prophecy." In that year the movies conquered the sound barrier with *The Jazz Singer*. Radio emerged at the same time as a startling source of instant information and live entertainment. Depression, war, and technical difficulties combined to deter the development of television even as its two media partners flourished. The irony was that television, maturing in the 1950s, radically changed the face both of radio and cinema, thereby challenging the existence of each. Only as the two accommodated themselves to the young upstart did they find hope for survival.

By 1951 the commercial television networks had established their hegemony and were developing means of transmitting signals coast to coast. Beer sales rose as baseball invaded the medium, and at least one doctor dolefully predicted that children would have stunted feet from too little walking. By 1953, television had attracted the likes of Bob Hope, Groucho Marx, Lucille Ball, Fred Allen, Jack Benny, Edgar Bergen, and George Burns and Gracie Allen. Thus radio, which had been a way of life for two generations of children, evaporated by the mid-1950s as quickly as it had burst upon us in the 1930s. Gone were the comedians and the dramas of a rainy afternoon. We were to discover that words, which had carried considerable weight, became conditioned by the visual.

The early 1950s was the era of television hearings—Kefauver and McCarthy—and of the so-called "golden age" of television. That age lasted only a few brief years as it claimed the talents of writers, such as Paddy Chayefsky, Reginald Rose, and Rod Serling; directors, such as Delbert Mann, Arthur Penn, and Sidney Lumet; and a luxury of talent including Paul Newman, Sidney Poitier, Kim Stanley, Rod Steiger, and Joanne Woodward. The remarkable success of the live anthological drama series that emerged with these personalities was all too short-lived. In the first place, the social comment of a play like *Marty* was in sharp contrast with the shiny world of the burgeoning number of eager sponsors. Second, the very success of television prompted a new breath of fresh air for cinema which began to drain talent from New York and consequently eliminate live television drama. Finally, the growing fear of both network executives and advertisers concerning controversial drama tended to stifle talent. Erik Barnouw dates the decline of these anthologies in the year 1955. Delbert Mann concurs. In a 1975 interview he noted that the early television dramas, starting in the late 1940s, appealed "to a small and rather specialized audience." As sets increased in number, the nature of the audience changed. The need to appeal to the mass audience was stimulated by the growing interest of manufacturers in advertising in the new medium. This coincided with the McCarthy era and the black listing of performers and writers. Mann noted that there was a pressure "not to offend." Thus was developed an inevitable pattern, of "restriction on the kind of material that could be used." Mann, like many other persons in the profession, left television for film by the end of the 1950s.

A great deal more was involved for television in the 1950s than fiction. The accident of technological discovery gave control of the television networks to the radio people. Radio, while deeply involved in entertainment, was a news-oriented medium for much of the public. And it was centered in New York. Quite naturally, then, the use of television after 1950 included a considerable emphasis upon public events. Had the motion picture industry controlled the medium, it is not altogether certain that such emphasis would have been as strong. Located on the East Coast and in close proximity to political and social phenomena which were shaping the nation, network executives promoted the beginnings of a vast news network. (For CBS that meant Edward R. Murrow.) David Halberstam noted in an excellent two-part study of CBS in 1976 that

> . . . television arrived simultaneously with the height of McCarthyism probably helped to narrow the parameters of journalistic freedom, but it was bound to happen anyway. Politically, television was simply too powerful a force, too fast, too immediate, with too large an audience, for the kind of easy journalistic freedom that radio and print reporters had enjoyed.[1]

Even in its restricted form television brought living drama into American homes regularly in its first decade. The Estes Kefauver Senate hearings on crime catapulted the senator into the Democratic nomination for vice-president by 1956. ABC moved quickly to televise the activities of the Army-McCarthy hearings in 1953. Concurrently millions of citizens had become more aware of the political process through the televising of the two party conventions of the previous year.

The first pronouncements of Richard Nixon were televised, and his classic "Checkers" speech was delivered in 1952. Many Americans heard about "old soldiers" from General MacArthur in that same year. In the aftermath of the Supreme Court's decision in *Brown* vs. *Board of Education* in 1955 came Little Rock and Governor Faubus, and a changing domestic scene. From Sputnik to the 1959 "kitchen debate," television provided a window on the world beyond the United States.

The American public felt the influence of television entertainment through language, comic heroes and classic portrayals. The phenomenon of families gathered silently around a small box to watch Milton Berle or Sid Caesar exploded in the 1950s in a dozen different directions. The culture of postwar America was straining under the old melting pot philosophy, and much of the comedy of that decade sought to reestablish the mentality of a secure middle-class picket fence community of the 1930s.

The 1940s gave the American viewers its most enduring television figure, Ed Sullivan in 1948. A less remembered role was that played by E. G. Marshall in "Mary Poppins" in the year 1949. The next year the crucial decade began with Sid Caesar, Jack Benny, Burns and Allen and "Broadway Open House" (forerunner of "Tonight"). Live drama was highlighted by Helen Hayes in *Victoria Regina*. In the early years American cultural roots remained in the radio era, a phenomenon that would disappear by 1955. The classics, "I Love Lucy" and *Amahl and the Night Visitors*, were produced early in 1951. The next year there were more comedians—Ozzie and Harriet, "Mr. Peepers," "Our Miss Brooks," and "My Little Margie." Sunday became the preserve of that special niche of television history called "Omnibus" and the sweaty hand of the forge became as well-known as Snap, Crackle, and Pop with the arrival of the Mark VII production "Dragnet."

Along with the inauguration of President Eisenhower, Red Skelton, Steve Allen, and Danny Thomas took to television. *Marty*, deftly directed by Delbert Mann and consistently described as a high point in television drama, was also produced in 1953. That same year viewers might have caught James Dean in *A Long Time Till Dawn* and Richard Kiley in *P.O.W.*, a drama about brainwashing and the Korean War. The heart of the picket fence era was probably 1954. The new offerings included "Father Knows Best," "Lassie," "Walt Disney Presents," "Love That Bob" (Bob Cummings), and "Private Secretary" with Ann Sothern. Live drama prospered in such offerings as *Twelve Angry Men,* written by Reginald Rose.

Little in the year 1955 warned Americans that their world was changing. Alfred Hitchcock entertained as did "The Honeymooners" and "Sergeant Bilko." "Captain Kangaroo" entered and became a traditional CBS figure for generations of children with Mr. Green Jeans, Dancing Bear, and Bun Rabbit. Meanwhile, American viewers focused on the past in drama and series. "Wyatt Earp" was the first, but "Gunsmoke" made it official; 1955 was the year the Westerns began. Drama was outstanding—Sidney Potier in *A Man Is Ten Feet Tall*, Raymond Massey and Lillian Gish in *The Day Lincoln Was Shot*, with Jack Lemmon as Wilkes Booth, Barry Sullivan in *The Caine Mutiny*, Maurice Evans in *The Devil's Disciple*, Michael Redgrave in *She Stoops to Conquer*, Lee Grant in *Shadow of the Champ*, and Humphrey Bogart in Delbert Mann's production of *The Petrified Forest*. Rod Serling contributed *Patterns*. Perhaps "never again on this stage" was the television epitaph for 1955.

The election year of 1956 saw the movement to Hollywood gather momentum. Film was replacing live drama, not always directly to its detriment but other effects were more subtle. Dramatically 1956 belonged to Rod Serling and his *Requiem for a Heavyweight*.

In 1957 television offered "Maverick," "Perry Mason," "Wagon Train," "Leave It To Beaver," and "Have Gun, Will Travel." The Westerns were on their way as was Jack Paar, who replaced Steve Allen that year on the "Tonight" show. Avid viewers may recall the maudlin conversations which Paar had with Hollywood personalities about bomb shelters and whether having one was cowardly.

Drama, now mostly on film, continued with high quality in 1958 with *The Bridge of San Luis Rey*, *The Days of Wine and Roses*, and *Little Moon of Alban*. Most lasting in impact was the "Untouchables," a product of Desilu which was also continuing to provide "I Love Lucy." The era of anthological dramatic shows was coming to an end with the television-film phase of 1955 and the discovery of video tape in 1957. "Studio One" moved to Hollywood in 1958, most other similar ventures faded and died. Even so, the last year of the decade offered some reason for hope that drama was not dead. There was Jason Robards in *For Whom the Bell Tolls*, George C. Scott in *Winterset*, Ingrid Bergman in *The Turn of the Screw*, and Laurence Olivier and Judith Anderson in *The Moon and Sixpence*. However, perhaps a greater harbinger of the 1960s was the debut of "Bonanza" that same year.

In the 1960s the stunning social dramas of the earlier decade became the live newscasts and made television fiction pale in comparison. The 1960 television debates between Richard Nixon and John Kennedy heralded the beginning of the decade of the newsman. A barrage of news-making events assailed the television viewer. If the event was not presented "live," it reached us within minutes thereafter—the Berlin Wall, the missile crisis, the assassination of John Kennedy and the subsequent killing of Lee Harvey Oswald "before our eyes," the reality of the war in Vietnam which every night on the news became more unreal, again assassination, Martin Luther King, Jr. and Robert Kennedy, riots at home from Watts in Los Angeles to Washington, D.C., men landing on the moon, and always the war in Southeast Asia. The Vietnam years were more devastating to our culture than perhaps any other event in our history. Distrust of government was rampant, with arrogance of power, depression and discontent among the dispossessed, fear and loathing to our youth, and destruction of decent models for children. Narcotics became a way of life for men called upon to commit mayhem abroad. Rising expectations and white stupidity created civil disorder from Watts to Washington. Television was there and it recorded a rare second chance in New Hampshire in February 1968 but America, after losing Robert Kennedy and Martin Luther King, Jr. to assassins, chose Richard Nixon. After that came Cambodia, Kent State, Attica, Agnew, Mitchell, Watergate, and pardons. In June 1977 Johnny Carson gave voice to many pent-up feelings when he noted upon the sentencing of John Mitchell and H. R. Haldeman to minimum security prinsons in Alabama that had it been you or I, we would have been put in a cell with Charles Manson. Clearly dramatic and comedic television had considerable competition in those years.

In the history of commercial television there have been four distinct types of comedy. The earliest was the personality, Milton Berle or Jack Benny or George Burns. There followed quickly the situation comedies of the "Leave It to Beaver," "Father Knows Best," and "Ozzie and Harriet" variety. Mild doses of fun were sprinkled among basic Puritan moralisms. By the late 1950s a third type of comedy emerged in "The Real McCoys." The 1960s saw the flowering of this genre with "Car 54 Where Are You?," "Gilligan's Island," and "The Beverly Hillibillies." Each poked fun at an authority symbol—the law, the scientist and socialite, or the banking profession. Some, like "The Munsters" and "The Addams Family," seemed to take on all social conventions, but it would be foolish to make too much out of this because each show was also designed quite obviously to match the public mood which increasingly seemed to desire escape. Lucille Ball interestingly reversed the trend. Her early shows were slapstick. Her comedy of the 1960s was similar to the earlier Ann Sothern efforts. Only with the appearance, largely via CBS, of "The Mary Tyler Moore Show" and "All in the Family" did a fourth comedy type begin to dominate. In style these shows owed much to the earlier "Dick Van Dyke Show" (1961-66). Their substance was probably made possible by the pioneering on CBS of the Smothers Brothers with social and political humor and on NBC by the freedom of "Laugh-In" with its sexual allusions, the former appearing first in 1965, the latter in 1968.

Of course even as the third comedy type dominated during the decade, the networks continued the traditional format with "My Three Sons," "Hazel," "That Girl," and "The Andy Griffith Show." The decline of the stand-up comic was a signal that the insatiable appetite of television, a new sketch every week, was beyond the capacity of comedians and writers. Indeed, this is a primary difficulty which television experiences unlike the theater, night club, or film. People like Johnny Carson have survived by creating a liturgy into which viewers enter as surely as the Sunday communicant. Thus the burden on the writers is largely relieved, but Carson is the exception and in that way has become a symbol of one important segment of the population. Carson makes trends and creates language styles. He is a primal popular cultural force, possibly more powerful than any other figure in the history of entertainment.

The decade of the 1960s was notable for three types of drama—police, Western, and medical. Apart from these types there were only a few dramatic series that survived long enough to remember—"The Defenders" (1962), "Combat" (1962), "Outer Limits" (1963), "East Side, West Side" (1963), "Mr. Novak" (1963), "Slattery's People" (1964), "Twelve O'Clock High" (1964), "Star Trek" (1966), "The Bold Ones" (1969), "Room 222" (1969)—an average of one new series per year.

From their beginnings in 1955 the Westerns expanded to number fifteen by 1960. That number was reduced to five by 1965. By the end of the decade it had diminished to three including "Bonanza" and "Gunsmoke." The history of police-detective drama is less consistent. When Americans entered their second ten years with television, they were watching "Naked City," "Peter Gunn," "Hawaiian Eye," "The Untouchables," and "The Detectives." "Dragnet" appeared and reappeared on the schedule during the same period. By 1964 there was not a single drama of this genre represented in network scheduling. In 1965 Quinn Martin, most persistent purveyor of the police motif, introduced the long-running "FBI," and by 1969 the schedule included no less than seven police-private eye shows. The 1970s saw that proliferate into over twenty in the 1975-76 season. The police dramas have been dominated by three producing giants—Martin, Jack Webb, and Spelling and Goldberg.

Medical drama moved in and out of the television scene in this period with the two long-running series, "Ben Casey" and "Dr. Kildare" debuting in 1961 and departing in 1966. By 1969 a new set, "Marcus Welby," "Medical Center," and "The Bold Ones" gave viewers three opportunities to experience vicariously the treatment of obscure and not so obscure diseases.

Documentaries burgeoned in the 1960s. The networks, spurred on by an obvious interest in public events, focused on social events (national and international) for material from migrant workers to Vietnam. Simultaneously domestic unrest bubbled to the surface and cascaded across the land in 1967 and 1968.

When the history of the 1970s is written, the portion devoted to television will undoubtedly emphasize the enormous success of a new comedy art in the business. Norman Lear, Grant Tinker, and Larry Gelbart will carry the credits along with Carroll O'Connor, Jean Stapleton, Bea Arthur, Mary Tyler Moore, Cloris Leachman, and Alan Alda. The similarities between "M*A*S*H" and "Maude" are more felt than defined, but the commonality was expressed both by audiences and actors. The flowering of the television comic short story may well be a most important cultural phenomenon. Beginning in 1971 the American public became conscious of Archie and Mary and Hawkeye. Every week these and other characters filled the screen with social bite in comic form. We laughed, often with a tear, and experienced what many knew finally to be reality joining hands with fantasy. Whatever new forms emerge for the 1980s, the television comedy of the 1970s had style and class and a social consciousness. Humanism dominated these shows and their companions—"The Bob Newhart Show," "Good Times," "The Jeffersons," "One Day at a Time," "Phyllis," and "The Odd Couple."

We were also deluged in this decade by an ever increasing assortment of gun-toting law enforcers. Television always upholds the law. It may be violent and sometimes in poor taste, but right does prevail. Not so in the movies or on the stage or in novels and magazines—these all offer alternatives to the triumph of the system. Television sustains it. To be sure not without criticism, but support there is, nonetheless. Baretta may condone small-time crime, and Kojak may bend the rules, but from Starsky and Hutch to Barnaby Jones to Charlie's Angels, the message is the same. Television has obviated certain cultural differences and leveled our language and dress. History may also affirm that it was the glue that held the clue to societal survival in the present decade. Certainly we all had television in common, and it has been affirming traditional social values. As early as 1968 the National Advisory Commission on Civil Disorders, commenting upon television coverage in 1967, noted:

> Content analysis of television film footage shows that the tone of the coverage studied was more calm and "factual" than "emotional" and rumor-laden. . . . Television newscasts during the periods of actual disorder in 1967 tended to emphasize law enforcement activities, thereby overshadowing underlying grievances and tensions. . . .
>
> In contrast to what some of its critics have charged, television sometimes may have leaned over too far backward in seeking balance and restraint.[2]

Television is a massive power of promotion and persuasion and its immediacy to our every thought makes it a likely target when cultural leaders search for a culprit upon which to blame the general tone of our society. It is new, it is beyond our control, and it is electronic. Television is popular culture. Although many social critics condemn and deride what television offers, for the majority of American people television is a friend, warts and all. It has become, as well, a critic in comedy and, less often, drama, of the flaws in our society. James Brown has written:

> The fact that the medium [television] produces several outstanding multi-hour presentations a month deserves more praise than the meager annual productivity

of Broadway. Books have been with us since movable type for over 600 years. How many books of true significance and public acceptance are published annually? Daily newspapers have been around for more than a century. Movies have been on the scene three-quarters of a century. But radio was first heard clearly in the land in 1920. Television has elbowed its way through exuberant adolescence and is now just beyond its teens. As a mid-twenty-year-old, it continues to try to find itself, to achieve its proper identity in society.[3]

In the early days the term *educational television* was used to apply to those stations normally expected to be unaffiliated with a commercial network. It was not until February 1950 that the first non-commercial station, WOI-TV in Ames, Iowa, was licensed and began operation. It was the one-hundredth station to begin television broadcasting in America. Because of the slow beginning of educational television, most of the stations occupied UHF channels which the Federal Communications Commission (FCC) had begun to assign in 1952. As late as 1956 there were only twenty-four non-commercial, educational channels on the air, and most of those were struggling. Television set manufacturers completely ignored UHF on early sets, and it was not until a decree from Congress required it, that all sets began to be sold with UHF tuners incorporated. Even then, the technology that allowed snap-lock tuning of VHF channels was not installed with the UHF tuner, and this meant long years of invidious comparison with the ease of tuning Channels 2 through 13. This problem was coupled with the fact that the UHF signal was usually more difficult to receive and had a much more restricted range. As late as 1968 only 55 percent of American families could receive UHF. In 1977 most hotels and motels were still not equipped with sets capable of receiving UHF broadcasts.

The original National Educational Television (NET) network survived through grit and grants from a small number of major foundations. Finally, in 1967, Congress took direct action and established the Public Broadcast System with federal funding. It still required substantial fund-raising by the local stations in order to guarantee survival. Since 1967, commercial networks have been quite guarded in their reactions to their new colleagues. Publications, such as *TV Guide*, have generally ignored the PBS activities except in the most obvious instances. Trade papers have tended to focus more attention on public policy regarding the new network than on the contributions it was making to television offerings.

Nevertheless, by 1975, with greater ease of reception becoming a reality for more and more of the viewing public, PBS began to attract more attention. There were two clear reasons—the huge success of "Sesame Street" and the prestige garnered from British offerings, such as "Masterpiece Theatre" and "Upstairs, Downstairs." However, the financial difficulties of PBS affiliates did not abate. Inadequate staffing and generally poor pay characterized many of the less affluent PBS members in comparison with the more prosperous channels in New York, Los Angeles, Pittsburgh, San Francisco, and Boston. Most of the new programming sprang from these more fortunate affiliates. Auctions and scrambling for any size grants became a way of life for most stations. Threatened with economic collapse, the temptation has been real to emulate the commercial networks in their quest for ratings. Further, there is the constant danger of government interference in the affairs of PBS even though every effort is made to eliminate politics from the system. There has been considerable pressure from some lawmakers for PBS to serve broader publics since it uses tax dollars. PBS has continued to offer more and more excellent quality programming to a solid minority of citizens. Properly funded, it can provide a healthy stimulus to the three major commercial networks, as it serves a significant public of its own.

NOTES

1. David Halberstam, "CBS: The Network and the News and the Power and the Profits," *The Atlantic Monthly*, 237 (January 1976), 63.

2. *Report of the National Advisory Commission on Civil Disorders* (New York: New York Times, 1968), p. 373.

3. Ward Quaal and James Brown, *Broadcast Management* (New York: Hastings House, 1976), p. 440.

BIBLIOGRAPHY

Adler, Richard, ed. *Television as a Cultural Force.* New York: Praeger, 1976.

Alley, Robert S. *Television: Ethics for Hire?* Nashville, Tenn.: Abingdon, 1977.

Atkin, C. K., J. P. Murray, and O. B. Nayman. *Television and Social Behavior: An Annotated Bibliography of Research Focusing on Television's Impact on Children.* Washington, D.C.: U.S. Government Printing Office, 1972.

Barnouw, Erik. *The Image Empire: A History of Broadcasting in the United States from 1953.* New York: Oxford University Press, 1970.

Bluem, A. William. *Documentary in American Television.* New York: Hastings House, 1965.

———, and Roger Manvell, eds. *Television: The Creative Experience. A Survey of Anglo-American Progress.* New York: Hastings House, 1967.

Blumler, Jay G., and Denis McQuail. *Television in Politics, Its Uses and Influence.* Chicago: University of Chicago Press, 1969.

Bogart, L. *The Age of Television.* 3d ed. New York: Frederick Ungar, 1972.

Brauer, Ralph. *The Horse, The Gun and The Piece of Property: Changing Images of the TV Western.* Bowling Green, Ohio: Bowling Green University Popular Press, 1975.

Brown, Les. *Television: The Business Behind the Box.* New York: Harcourt, Brace Jovanovich, 1971.

Cater, Douglass, and Richard Adler, eds. *Television as a Social Force: Approaches to TV Criticism.* New York: Praeger, 1975.

Cole, Barry G., ed. *Television: A Selection of Readings from TV Guide Magazine.* New York: Free Press, 1970.

Gans, Herbert J. *Popular Culture and High Culture: An Analysis and Evaluation of Taste.* New York: Basic Books, 1974.

Hazard, Patrick D., ed. *TV as Art: Some Essays in Criticism.* Champaign, Ill.: National Council of Teachers of English, 1966.

Head, Sydney W. *Broadcasting in America: A Survey of Television and Radio.* 2d ed. Boston: Houghton Mifflin, 1972.

McLuhan, Marshall. *Understanding Media: The Extensions of Man.* New York: McGraw-Hill, 1964.

Newcomb, Horace. *TV: The Most Popular Art.* New York: Doubleday, 1974.

______, ed. *Television: The Critical View.* New York: Oxford University Press, 1976.

Sterling, Christopher, ed. *Broadcasting and Mass Media: A Survey Bibliography.* Philadelphia: Temple University Press, 1974.

Terrace, Vincent. *The Complete Encyclopedia of Television Programs, 1947-1976.* 2 vols. Cranbury, N.J.: A. S. Barnes, 1976.

Trains and Railroading

Arthur J. Miller, Jr.

"Historically," according to Archie Robertson, "the railfan is at least as old as railroads." In his *Slow Train to Yesterday* Robertson provides a charming look at the railfan phenomenon:

> The Charleston & Hamburg..., earliest American railroad, ran its first trains for enthusiasts who just couldn't wait for the public opening. Before the Civil War the B&O ran excursions for camera fans from Washington to Harper's Ferry.... Fan trips were commonplace throughout the nineteenth century although no one called them that.[1]

The history of American railroading cannot, indeed, be separated from the public enthusiasm for rail travel or for the advancement and progress of the railroad industry. In the 1820s the railroad had taken hold in England, and by Christmas 1830 the first scheduled steam-railroad train run in America took place on the Charleston & Hamburg, carrying 141 passengers. The engine, the "Best Friend of Charleston," was the first commercially built U.S. locomotive. The expansion westward from the coast in the early nineteenth century led to rapid deployment of the railroad, at first in what might seem like unusual locations. The new technology captured the imagination and backing first of Southerners, whose seaports were suffering as the water routes further north—particularly the Erie Canal—drew trade to New York and the Northeast. Laying track to the interior offered a new chance for ports such as Charleston and Baltimore to compete. Boston, too, coveted New York's success and in the early 1830s wisely decided to build not more canals but railroads. The nation's first Railway Exhibit was in Boston in 1827, to which enthusiastic crowds paid admission to view the display of English locomotives.

By the 1850s the rail system reached to the Mississippi, as the various coastal establishments tied themselves to western settlements. Already the call for Manifest Destiny was to be heard, to build a railroad to the Pacific. Sectional rivalry, at first, was a stimulus to discussion: should the transcontinental line go across from a more northerly or southerly route, building from slave states or free? In the end the struggle's intensity was so great that it served to delay the transcontinental route until after the Civil War. The North's by then superior rail system contributed significantly to the preservation of the Union, and railroading today forms a key subgrouping of Civil War buff interest as a result; in the 1950s the "Great Locomotive Chase" was a popular story and film topic. But before this climactic encounter western cities had hosted railroad conventions to crystallize interest in a line—west from Memphis, St. Louis, or Chicago. As with the earlier Boston exhibition, these special events reflected and served to stimulate popular interest and support. Throughout the century the opening of new lines, anniversaries, and the great fairs of 1876 and 1893 were occasions for celebrating the progress, both geographical and technical, of the railroads.

After the Civil War forces were mobilized quickly, thanks to government incentives, creative management and engineering, and no little corruption, to forge the link to the Pacific. In 1869 the Union Pacific and the Central Pacific met at Promontory Point, Utah, ending the "Great Race." This epic feat was followed in rapid order by the completion of other lines to the north and south. By the end of the century the West was covered by a complete (often redundant) rail network, the Indians had been subdued, and the frontier (according to Frederick Jackson Turner) was closed.

From the end of the war to the closing of the frontier popular interest in the railroads was at a peak. The mighty task of crossing the continent was great by every measure: the profits, the speed at which track could be laid, the iniquity of life on the work gangs ("Hell on Wheels" and boom towns), the tall tales, the personalities (General Dodge, Jack Casement, and Charles Crocker), and the celebrations. In the years that immediately followed, Easterners and travellers from abroad made the trip across the plains and the mountains to San Francisco from Council Bluffs, Iowa, through prairie dog villages, mountain gorges, Indian lands, and deserts. Their accounts and the pictures by the illustrators and photographers who went along were printed and widely distributed, testifying to the railroad's popular appeal.

By the end of this period the railroads had begun to reach beyond opening new possibilities for Americans and immigrants. By the close of the century railroad domination had become a major issue particularly in the trans-Mississippi West. Popular support waned as scandals such as the Credit Mobilier matter, which concerned Union Pacific corruption, reached the public. Land prices, freight rates, and the continuing stock manipulations of the "robber baron" period turned first the Western farmers and later a majority of the public against railroad excesses. The Granger movement reflected the farmers' attempt to organize against the power of the railroads. And train robbers appeared as Robin Hoods in the popular imagination, dime novels, and the mass press. The spectacular exploits of Christopher

Evans and John Sontag in the San Joaquin Valley of California are reflected in Frank Norris's more ambitious novel of 1901, *The Octopus.* In general, *The Octopus* best characterizes the popular perception of the Western railroads at the end of the nineteenth century: greed, corruption, impersonality, manipulation, and oppression.

The railfan disappeared after the first blush of transcontinental travel. Archie Robertson reports that his return is first noted some half-century later, by the *Railway Age* in 1927.[2] By the late 1920s automobiles were no longer a novelty, and trains had gained the dignity of age and tradition and, says Robertson, "the sympathy which belongs to the underdog." This respected position has prevailed through much of the last half-century. Cors observes that "in the thirties...the rail hobbyist came into his own," with 1938 being a watershed year: the "first real railfan book," *Along the Iron Trail* by Frederick Richardson and F. Nelson Blount, appeared, along with Lucius Beebe's first rail book, *High Iron. Railroad Magazine* now served the railroad enthusiast as much as the working railroaders. In 1940 Kambach Publishing Company introduced *Trains,* the first "unequivocally" hobbyist periodical.[3] The war brought new reliance on the rail system, but this was short-lived. In the late 1940s further growth in automobile and air travel gave rail travel for passengers permanent underdog status and provided challenges for freight service as well. A new wave of nostalgia boosted modeling and other railfan occupations to record levels in the mid-1950s. The 1960s—with the space program, war, and social change—once again eclipsed railroading in the popular mind. But by the end of the 1970s the railfan had been "born again," as one hobby dealer reported.[4] The reason echoed the heydey of the 1940s: gasoline shortages and a much-heralded return to the rails, nostalgia for a simpler and more personalized era of travel, and a sense of national tradition and destiny. As the 1980s begin, a century and a half of popular fascination with railroading continues.

NOTES

1. Archie Robertson, *Slow Train to Yesterday: A Last Glance at the Local* (Boston: Houghton Mifflin, 1945), pp. 151-52.

2. Robertson, p. 152.

3. Paul B. Cors, *Railroads,* Spare Time Guides: Information Sources for Hobbies and Recreation, no. 8 (Littleton, Colo.: Libraries Unlimited, 1975), pp. 11-12.

4. Charles R. Day, Jr., "All Aboard for a Lifelong Hobby," *Industry Week,* 203 (December 1, 1979), 98.

BIBLIOGRAPHY

Adams, Ramon F. *The Language of the Railroader.* Norman: University of Oklahoma Press, 1977.

Beebe, Lucius. *High Iron: A Book of Trains.* New York: Appleton-Century, 1938.

Botkin, B. A. and Alvin F. Harlow, eds. *A Treasury of Railroad Folklore: The Stories, Tall Tales, Traditions, Ballads and Songs of the American Railroad Man.* New York: Bonanza Books, 1953.

Bryant, E. T. *Railways: A Readers' Guide.* Hamden, Conn.: Archon Books, 1968.

Condit, Carl W. *The Railroad and the City: A Technological and Urbanistic History of Cincinnati.* Columbus: Ohio State University Press, 1977.

Cors, Paul B. *Railroads.* Spare Time Guides: Information Sources for Hobbies and Recreation, no. 8. Littleton, Colo.: Libraries Unlimited, 1975.

Donovan, Frank P., Jr. *The Railroad in Literature: Brief Survey of Railroad Fiction, Poetry, Songs, Biography, Essays, Travel and Drama in the English Language and Particularly Emphasizing Its Place in American Literature.* Boston: Railway and Locomotive Historical Society, 1940.

Douglas, George H. "Lucius Beebe: Popular Railroad History as a Social Nostalgia." *Journal of Popular Culture,* 4 (Spring 1971), 893-910.

Goldsborough, Robert. *Great Railroad Paintings.* New York: Peacock Press/Bantam, 1976.

Hertz, Louis H. *The Complete Book of Model Railroading.* New York: Simmons-Boardman, 1951.

Hofsommer, Donovan L. *Railroads of the Trans-Mississippi West: A Selected Bibliography.* Plainview, Tex.: Wayland College, 1974.

Hudson, F. K., comp. *Railroad Bibliography, 1948-1972: A Comprehensive Guide to the Most Important Railbooks, Publications and Reports.* Ocean, N.J.: Specialty Press, 1972.

Jane's World Railways. London: Macdonald & Jane's, 1966-. Annual.

Jenks, George M. "A Bibliography of Books and Articles by and about Lucius Beebe." *Bulletin of Bibliography,* 37 (July-September 1980), 132-41, 155.

McPherson, James Alan, and Miller Williams, eds. *Railroads: Trains and Train People in American Culture.* New York: Random House, 1976.

Norris, Frank. *The Octopus.* Cambridge, Mass.: Robert Bently, 1971.

Richardson, Frederick H., and F. Nelson Blount. *Along the Iron Trail.* 2d ed. Rutland, Vt.: Sharp Offset, 1966.

Robertson, Archie. *Slow Train to Yesterday: A Last Glance at the Local.* Boston: Houghton Mifflin, 1945.

Shaw, Frederic. *Casey Jones' Locker: Railroad Historiana.* San Francisco: Hesperian House, 1959.

Stover, John F. *American Railroads.* Chicago: University of Chicago Press, 1961.

Verse and Popular Poetry

Janice Radway

While virtually every field in popular culture studies is plagued by the problems inherent in defining and identifying a proper object for analysis, these difficulties become particularly acute, in fact almost prohibitive, when the subject under scrutiny is popular poetry and verse. Several individual poets have become extraordinarily "popular" figures during the course of American cultural development, in the sense that they were, or are now, personally familiar to a large portion of the population. However, very few single volumes of actual poetry have ever achieved best-seller status at the time of their publication.

Frank Luther Mott, who conservatively defines the best seller as a work purchased in the decade of publication by 1 percent of the total population of the continental United States, lists only seven individual volumes of poetry by American poets as best sellers in the years from 1662 to 1945. Included in this list, however, is Walt Whitman's *Leaves of Grass* (1855), of which only a few hundred copies were actually sold in the year of publication itself. Mott is able to retain the work on his list only because, through cheap reprints, the requisite number of copies was eventually sold in the course of the entire decade. But there is an obvious and significant difference between Whitman's status as a popular poet and that of Henry Wadsworth Longfellow, whose *Hiawatha* (1855) sold two thousand five hundred copies during the week of publication alone and nearly eighteen thousand more during the next three months.

Although Mott's figures are therefore of little help to the researcher interested in identifying America's popular poets, assistance is not easily found elsewhere. Even if one could decide on an appropriate measure for the popularity of this genre, which has never approached the novel in sales, such publication figures for volumes of poetry are not readily available. Many literary historians of the eighteenth and nineteenth centuries do include poets now unfamiliar to us in their dictionaries and encyclopedias, but there is almost no way of determining whether such figures were truly popular or only minor poets who produced elitist verse of secondary quality.

The problem is further compounded by the fact that nearly every newspaper and popular magazine published in the United States has, at one time or another, included poetry that cannot be termed "elite" or "artistic." On the other hand, many of these same versifiers have neither produced an entire volume of poetry nor reached a national audience transcending regional, economic, and social limits. As a result, one has to question whether such poetry should be included in a study of popular forms, or whether it ought to be excluded as a variant of American folk culture.

These problems are of more than incidental significance because the way this field of study is delineated necessarily affects the character and validity of the conclusions drawn. Any thesis, therefore, about the place, development, or significance of poetry in the popular culture of the United States is, in reality, little more than a highly speculative hypothesis that can only be tested through further research.

The poets mentioned in the following survey have, accordingly, been selected on the basis of a fairly rigorous procedure. All of those occasional versifiers whose extant work is now limited to individual poems found in magazines, newspapers, or anthologies have been excluded. Of the remaining professional poets, only those for whom substantial sales figures or other indications of general popularity are available will be found in this history. In the case of the eighteenth- and nineteenth-century poets, I found it necessary to rely heavily on Rufus Griswold's *The Poets and Poetry of America*, a best-selling literary encyclopedia, which itself went through more than sixteen editions. If Griswold includes a poet, refers to his or her popularity, and I could confirm that popularity in some other source, then that poet has been added as well. Although the resulting list is therefore quite limited, these few figures are the only American poets whose work can be readily identified as poetry read by more than a very small portion of the population.

In the years immediately following the settlement of the American colonies, two distinct forms of verse emerged as the basis of a popular poetic tradition. While religious and practical considerations tended to diminish interest in the high art of poesy as it was then practiced in England, the early colonist found definite merit in religious poetry of a didactic nature and in informational verse designed for the circulation of news. Accordingly, it is not surprising to discover that the first truly popular American poems were those of the *Bay Psalm Book* (1640) and the numerous "broadsides" hawked by street peddlers.

While the two kinds of verse appeared vastly different on the surface, they exhibited a common interest in content as well as a very obvious disinterest in matters of aesthetic form. Indeed, the editors of the *Bay Psalm*

Book apologized for the rustic quality of their verse with the observation that "if therefore the verses are not always so smooth and elegant as some may desire or expect; let them consider that God's Altar needs no polishing."

Like the broadside verse that told of specific crimes, births, deaths, and holidays, early American religious poetry was thus designed to refer explicitly to the world inhabited by its reader. Language was not something to be manipulated for its own sake, but rather a tool to be used for instruction and information. It is this exclusive emphasis on the referential aspect of language that has continued to differentiate America's popular verse from her more self-conscious, deliberately aesthetic poetry of the elite tradition.

Throughout the late seventeenth and early eighteenth centuries, most of the poetry read by the majority of the populace was amateur verse published outside the three major literary centers of Philadelphia, New York, and Boston. Such verse was highly topical and therefore largely ephemeral. It was published by a local printer in pamphlet form and financed by the author himself. Much of the verse, like the "Massachusetts Liberty Song," centered about the revolutionary war, although religious teaching continued to be the primary subject of American amateur verse for the next one hundred fifty years. A vast quantity of this sort of verse was included in the almanacs that began to appear as early as 1639 and that quickly became an indispensable guide for every colonial home.

Two professional poets, however, did reach a relatively large audience even before growing industrialization began to revolutionize the printing industry. As far as can be determined, Michael Wigglesworth's *Day of Doom* (1662) was the most popular poem in America for well over one hundred years. The first edition of eighteen hundred copies was exhausted in the year of publication, a remarkable achievement considering the sparse population of the colonies at the time. While Wigglesworth's verse was certainly more accomplished than that of his amateur contemporaries, the poem probably achieved popular status because its theological content was remarkably expressive of the people's beliefs.

That this was the case with John Trumbull's "McFingal" (1775) is obvious since none of the poetry he later produced ever excited the interest of readers as did this patently political, Hudribrastic attack on the manners and men of Tory America. The poem went through thirty editions during the next century and, according to one literary historian, furnished many popular proverbs that were quoted long after the war that had sparked it had ended. "McFingal's" patriotic sentiments were quoted by innumerable political orators, and the poem itself was a standard entry in both poetic anthologies and school textbooks for the next hundred years.

Until Lydia Huntley Sigourney's poetry began to dominate the scene, most eighteenth-century Americans read little more verse than that appearing in the almanacs. Occasionally, a poem by a professional poet would strike the popular imagination and it would then be widely circulated and much discussed. It is, however, difficult to determine exactly how well known such figures as William Treat Paine, John Pierpont, or James Gates Percival ever became. Paine's publication of *Adams and Liberty* earned him $750, a very large sum for any book in 1797. Pierpont's "The Airs of Palestine" (1816) seems to have attracted a great deal of attention, as did Percival's sentimental Byronic epic, "The Suicide," which occupied twelve, long, magazine pages. While it is fairly certain that these men were widely known and read outside the small literary community of the period, none ever achieved the general popularity enjoyed by Mrs. Sigourney, the "Sweet Singer of Hartford."

Lydia Huntley Sigourney began writing poetry in 1798, published forty-six volumes of poetry in her lifetime, and, until the appearance of Longfellow, was America's most popular poet. Her first verse collection, *Moral Pieces in Prose and Verse* (1816), made it abundantly clear that for her, poetry was not a mere ornament to life, but rather a direct vehicle for moral instruction. Although her poems dealt with nearly every subject imaginable, each was designed to instruct the reader in the inestimable value of the chaste and moral Christian life. Her *Letters to Young Ladies* (1833) was especially popular—it eventually went through twenty American editions—and was followed by the equally popular *Letters to Mothers* (1838).

Mrs. Sigourney was one of the first American poets to compose lines upon request for the commemoration of special events. Her "occasional" poems memorialized many of her dedicated readers, whose relatives sought solace for their loss in her highly "poetical" sentiments and "uplifting language." It is important to note that although Mrs. Sigourney's poetry always referred directly to the world, it did so in language that clearly set itself off from the mundane discourse of everyday life. She was extraordinarily adept at striking a balance between the events of this world and the meaning they were thought to have in the more important ethereal realm of the spirit. While it is not completely accurate to think of American popular poetry as a "formula," Mrs. Sigourney's combination of the sublime with the small seems to have set a pattern followed fruitfully thereafter by nearly every popular American bard.

Lydia Sigourney's extraordinary popularity was challenged for a time in the 1830s by that of another occasional poet, Charles Sprague. He first attracted attention in 1829 when he delivered the Phi Beta Kappa poem at Harvard University's commencement. Although the poem was a highly conventional treatment of the forms "Curiosity" could take, it seems to have struck a popular chord, for it was widely circulated during the next ten years. Sprague thereafter wrote many odes for public and private occasions, including one "written on the accidental meeting of all the surviving members of a family."

Although William Cullen Bryant never became as popular a figure as Longfellow, he was able to earn a substantial living on the basis of his poetry publication. By 1842, he could command a fifty-dollar fee for a single magazine poem, while his individual volumes sold at the respectable rate of one thousand seven hundred copies per year. His work seems not to have excited as much general interest as that of some of his contemporaries, for he is included less often in anthologies and textbooks than either Mrs. Sigourney, Sprague, or the remarkable Longfellow. Still, he appears to have been generally known and popularly appreciated.

It was, however, Henry Wadsworth Longfellow who established himself most successfully in the minds of his fellow Americans as the country's unofficial poet laureate. At a time when the poetic vocation was still scorned as a generally ornamental, effeminate occupation, he was able to command respect as a spokesman for the American spirit. His first volume of poetry, *Voices of the Night* (1839), sold nine hundred copies in thirty days, four thousand three hundred in a single year. This seems to have set a precedent, for Longfellow earned more than $7,000 in royalties on *Hiawatha* alone in the next ten years. In fact, every volume he produced after the first was subject to advance sale. *Evangeline* (1847) sold 6,050 copies in the first two years after publication; twenty thousand copies of *Hiawatha* (1855) were purchased in the first three months alone; and in London, ten thousand copies of *The Courtship of Miles Standish* (1858) were sold in a single day.

No doubt many factors contributed to Longfellow's unprecedented popularity, not the least of which was the skill with which he played the part demanded of him by his readers. However, it is also certain that his ability to combine European erudition and a sense of the past with a characteristically American enthusiasm and optimism was also widely appreciated. This variation of Mrs. Sigourney's method, characterized by the combination of the elevated with the ordinary, served Longfellow well. He produced innumerable very learned poems, complete with classical allusions on ordinary topics familiar to his mass of readers. He was generally extolled for his high moral sentiment, for the depth of his feeling, as well as for the breadth of his knowledge. It did not matter to most of his readers that his versification was conservative, or that his poetic treatment occasionally bordered on the sentimental or the melodramatic. What was of primary importance to them was his ability to comment on the higher meaning of their daily lives in an easily comprehensible style. As Russel Nye has suggested in *The Unembarrassed Muse*, it was Longfellow's clarity and ability to unravel apparent complexities that most endeared him to his huge audience.

Longfellow was aided in his task of satisfying the young country's need for poetic interpretation and edification by men such as James Russell Lowell, Oliver Wendell Holmes, Josiah Gilbert Holland, and John Greenleaf Whittier. Although none ever came close to Longfellow's popularity, each was called on again and again to comment publicly on the "meaning" of the American experience.

Holmes was a well-known occasional poet who produced lines on commencements, feasts, town meeting, births, deaths, and special holidays. Lowell also produced topical poetry, but he was best known for his satirical verse in "The Bigelow Papers" as well as for his extravagant historical epic, "The Vision of Sir Launfal" (1848), which sold nearly one hundred seventy-five thousand copies during the decade after publication. Holland began his career as a poet in the magazines but graduated soon thereafter to complete volumes of verse. His two-hundred-page epic, *Bittersweet* (1858), setting forth the thesis that evil is part of the Divine Plan, first made his reputation as a poet of the people. When he composed the *Life of Abraham Lincoln* in 1865, eighty thousand readers snatched up his eulogy. Like his poetic forefathers, Holland's goal was didactic, and his message emphasized the need for religion in American life.

But even though Holmes, Lowell, and Holland were thus well known, their poetry did not touch the hearts of their fellow Americans in the exact way that the verses of John Greenleaf Whittier did. Indeed, Whittier's preoccupation with the pastoral values of rural existence seems to have endeared him all the more to America because it appeared at that precise moment when industry and urbanization were becoming a serious threat to a disappearing way of life. Although his first volume, *Lays of My Home* (1843), was well received, it was "Snowbound" (1866) which solidified Whittier's reputation with the masses. The poem's homely but sincere language, its nostalgic sentimentality, and detailed evocation of the hardship of country life made it especially attractive to a swiftly urbanizing people who were anything but sure that they wished to put the past behind them. Twenty-eight thousand copies of "Snowbound" were sold during the first year, and Whittier eventually realized more than $100,000 in royalties from its sale alone. As Van Wyck Brooks has pointed out, "Snowbound" was the safeguard of America's memory and the touchstone of its past. Whittier, like Longfellow and Sigourney before him, was remarkably good at couching America's highest sentiments about God, country, and the family in language slightly but definitely removed from the vernacular of the people. As a result, he was quoted and deferred to unceasingly throughout the nineteenth century as one of America's most honored sages.

Although Alice and Phoebe Cary never achieved the status of American sages, they did produce more than fifteen volumes between them that reached a specific segment of the American population. Born in Cincinnati, Ohio, the sisters composed verses on motherhood, family, and farm-life that were especially well known among women and in the midwestern United States. While their verse was neither so refined nor so polished as that of their better-known contemporaries, the sentiments they expressed were almost identical to those of Holmes, Holland, or Whittier. In fact, these lines from Alice's poem "Dying Hymn" (1865), while a bit more effusive, are not very different from numerous poems composed by the other three:

> That faith to me a courage gives
>   Low as the grave, to go:
> I know that my Redeemer lives:
>   That I shall live, I know.
>
> The palace walls I almost see,
>   Where dwells my Lord and King:
> O grave, where is thy Victory!
>   O death, where is thy sting!

Although many other poets like the Carys achieved regional popularity during the middle decades of the nineteenth century, none seems to have developed a reputation comparable to that of Bryant, Longfellow, or Whittier. John Godfrey Saxe, "the witty poet," was read for his satirical comments on the follies of social life, but he actually made his reputation by traveling throughout the country giving oral presentations. Nathaniel Parker Willis published nine volumes of verse throughout his lifetime, but he was better known as an editor, literary fop, and travel writer. In addition, many versifiers developed a following during the Civil War, when poetic sentiments were in particular demand. But as the war ended, and the broadsides in which they were published disappeared, so too did the poets.

This situation did not alter drastically in the last half of the century either. Thomas Bailey Aldrich achieved a measure of popularity with his "Ballad of Babie Bell" (1858) and thereafter published numerous poems on love, God, and the ubiquitous family. Still, he was most widely celebrated for his fiction and criticism, produced while he was editor of the *Atlantic Monthly*. Bayard Taylor, also an editor, produced a great deal of poetry that sold fairly well. However, his reputation was not strong enough to guarantee the success of any of his verse, for several of his epic poems, including "Lars, a Pastoral of Norway" (1873) and "The Prophet" (1874), were definite failures.

Perhaps the one poet of the late nineteenth century who came closest to rivaling the popular reputations of Longfellow and Whittier was James Whitcomb Riley, whose rustic Hoosier dialect and homespun philosophy struck a responsive chord in the now almost-wholly urban America. His idealizations of farm and country life were enormously popular throughout the country, despite the fact that the peculiar language he employed was nearly incomprehensible to some. Riley produced fourteen volumes of cheerful poetic sentiment, all of which were characterized by regular rhythms and easily memorized rhymes. Like nearly all of America's popular poets, he was obsessed with the family, childhood, and days gone by. His poetry, like Whittier's and Longfellow's, embodied the vision of America in which his fellow Americans most wanted to believe. The fact that the vision existed only in the poetry troubled almost no one, least of all Riley.

During the final decades of the century, three poets developed national reputations similar to Riley's in that they were identified with a unique section of the country. Will Carleton, a Michigan newspaperman, began his poetic career with "Betsy and I Are Out," a ballad about lost love, first published in *The Toledo Blade* in 1871. When newspapers across the country reprinted the poem, it was an immediate success. Three years later, Carleton published *Farm Ballads* (1873), a collection full of lavish sentiment and careful descriptions of the farming Midwest. The combination was perfectly suitable for the popular demand, and, by his death in 1912, more than six hundred thousand copies of the book had been sold.

Madison Cawein of Louisville, Kentucky, was never as popular as either Carleton or Riley, but his thirty-six volumes of verse did make him the most prolific southern writer of the decade. Although most of his lyrics were as sentimental, patriotic, and religious as those of nearly every other poet of the period, his realistic description of the southern landscape tended to set his work apart as something quite unique.

Joaquim Miller was not, like Cawein, known for the precision of his imagery. Indeed, he was extravagantly praised as the one American poet capable of capturing the grandeur of the magnificent West. Something of a showman, Miller exploited his frontier roots, traveling about the country dressed in buckskins to give poetry readings. Except for his evocative portrayal of the desert and the life of the American Indian, Miller's poetry is indistinguishable from the "heartfelt lyrics" of Carleton or Cawein.

This characteristic emphasis on sentimentality continued throughout the first years of the twentieth century. Most of the American popular verse published in 1900 was as closely centered about the home and family as it had been a century earlier. Although the kind of subject matter that could be treated in a poem had been extended and realistic description tended to appear more often, rhyme was still a necessary component, as was a lightly lilting rhythm. No doubt this was, in part, due to the continuing use of poetry for recitations in the schools and for orations at official occasions.

This public and rhetorical function slowly began to disappear, however, in the early years of the new century, when American popular verse gradually turned inward and became more contemplative and personal. There is no easy way to tell whether the change was produced by the difficulties of life in an increasingly impersonal world, or by the ridicule heaped on popular verse by the newly avant-garde elite poets. In any event, the change was generally noticeable, especially in the verse produced by America's newspaper poets, including Eugene Field and Ella Wheeler Wilcox. Field, who was associated with the city of Chicago, was particularly good at producing poetry about the innocence and beauty of childhood and was perhaps best known for "Little Boy Blue" (1887) and "Dutch Lullaby: Wynken, Blyken, and Nod" (1895). Wilcox, like Field, was adept at describing the inner life in subdued but sentimental terms and once remarked that her purpose was "to raise the unhappy and guide those who need it."

Poetry enjoyed something of a renaissance during World War I, when large numbers of people were willing to purchase single volumes of verse in addition to the traditional anthologies that had continued in popularity throughout the early years of the century. This increase in the "demand" for verse that spoke to the people is also evident in both the local newspapers and national magazines of the period. While many of the poems were written by the "mothers," "fathers," and "sisters" of the American soldier, by far the largest segment of verse was produced by the young infantrymen who had gone to Europe to "make the world safe for democracy." Among the most well known were John McCrae ("In Flanders Field" 1919), Alan Seeger ("I Have a Rendezvous with Death" 1917), and Joyce Kilmer ("Trees" 1913), all of whom were killed in the battlefields of France.

None of the soldier-poets, however, could match the popularity of the Michigan newspaper poet, Edgar A. Guest, who extended his early regional reputation by publishing large quantities of verse about the war. Although Guest did not participate in the conflict, it was the implicit subject behind most of his poetry. Indeed, his primary concern during the years 1914-1917 was the war experience as it was lived by those on the "home front." Then, throughout the 1920s, he consolidated his national reputation by continuing to write about home, work, and God. He rightly conceived of his verse as a "mirror" of the values adhered to by his audience, and that audience ratified his conception by purchasing his volumes in increasingly large numbers.

The history of American popular poetry after Guest is largely the history of anthologies, which continued to be successful despite the fact that few people were willing to purchase single volumes of verse. Most of these collections, like Burton Stevenson's *The Home Book of Verse* and Hazel Felleman's *Best Loved Poems of the American People*, were organized by subject matter rather than by poet, testifying to the fact that American popular poetry continued to function referentially for its audience by portraying a familiar world. Longfellow, Whittier, Bryant, and Riley continued as the traditional favorites although the least ambiguous poems by

Carl Sandburg and Robert Frost were also given prominent display. It is hard to determine, however, whether Frost's popularity was the result of his posture as the quintessentially American "poetic figure," or of a genuine interest in and demand for his poetry. The former speculation does seem more plausible since he was nearly always represented in the popular anthologies by the same two poems, "Stopping by Woods on a Snowy Evening" (1923) and "The Road Not Taken" (1915).

The only two poets who have managed to sell large numbers of single volumes of poetry during the second half of the twentieth century are Kahlil Gibran and Rod McKuen. Gibran first developed a large audience during the 1920s, when his Oriental mysticism satisfied the American public's interest in the exotic and the bohemian. He wrote eleven volumes before he died in 1931, all of which included a curious mixture of parables, aphorisms, verses, and short narratives. His best-known book, however, was *The Prophet* (1923), which was resurrected in the mid-1960s as a kind of handbook for the counterculture. To date, *The Prophet* has sold more than three million copies.

Also a phenomenon of the mid-1960s, Rod McKuen's poetry was especially popular with the young. His first book of verse, *Stanyan Street and Other Sorrows*, appeared in 1954 to a decidedly indifferent reception. But when *Listen to the Warm* was published in 1963, it immediately made the best-seller list, and McKuen became an instant celebrity. His verse differs somewhat from traditional popular poetry in that it is explicitly erotic, written in a free-verse style, and lacks any kind of end-rhyme. However, the language is as referential and familiar as that of Longfellow, Riley, or Guest, in that it explicitly describes the inner emotional life of the modern adolescent. Although his major themes—loneliness, lost love, and the need for human communication—are slightly different from those of his poetic forebears, the generally hopeful note sounded by his sentimental conclusions is not. In that sense, it is possible to see a direct line of development in American popular poetry extending from Lydia Huntley Sigourney through Henry Wadsworth Longfellow, James Whitcomb Riley, and Edgar Guest, to Rod McKuen.

BIBLIOGRAPHY

Brooks, Van Wyck. *Makers and Finders: A History of the Writer in America, 1800-1915*. 4 vols. New York: E. P. Dutton, 1956.

Cheever, George B. *The American Commonplace Book of Poetry*. Boston: Carter, Hendee, 1831.

Coates, Henry M. *The Fireside Encyclopedia of Poetry*. Philadelphia: Porter and Coates, 1879.

Cook, Howard. *Our Poets of Today*. New York: Moffat, 1919.

Cook, Roy J. *One Hundred and One Famous Poems*. Rev. ed. Chicago: Cable, 1929.

Early American Poetry, 1610-1820, a List of Works in the New York Public Library. Compiled by J. G. Frank. New York: New York Public Library, 1917.

Felleman, Hazel. *The Best Loved Poems of the American People.* New York: Garden City Publishing, 1936.

Griswold, Rufus Wilmont. *The Poets and Poetry of America.* New York: James Miller Publisher, 1872.

Hackett, Alice Payne. *Fifty Years of Best Sellers, 1895-1945.* New York: R. R. Bowker, 1945.

Hart, James. *The Popular Book.* Berkeley: University of California Press, 1961.

———. *The Oxford Companion to American Literature.* 4th ed. New York: Oxford University Press, 1965.

Kreymborg, Alfred. *A History of American Poetry: Our Singing Strength.* New York: Tudor, 1943.

Matthews, Brander. *American Familiar Verse.* New York: Longmans, Green, 1904.

Mott, Frank Luther. *Golden Multitudes.* New York: Macmillan, 1947.

Nye, Russel B. *The Unembarrassed Muse: The Popular Arts in America.* New York: Dial Press, 1970.

Onderdonk, James Lawrence. *History of American Verse, 1610-1897.* Chicago: A. C. McClurg, 1901.

Pattee, Fred Lewis. *A History of American Literature Since 1870.* New York: Century, 1921.

Scheick, William J., and Jo Ella Doggett. *Seventeenth-Century American Poetry: A Reference Guide.* Boston: G. K. Hall, 1977.

Shaw, John Mackay. *Childhood in Poetry: A Catalogue of the Books of English and American Poets in the Library of the Florida State University.* Tallahassee: Robert M. Strozier Library, Florida State University, 1967.

Stevenson, Burton. *The Home Book of Verse, American and English, 1580-1920.* 6th ed. New York: Henry Holt, 1930.

Thompson, Slason. *The Humbler Poets: A Collection of Newspaper and Periodical Verse.* Chicago: Jansen, McClurg, 1886.

Westerns

Richard W. Etulain

Until the 1950s little had been written about the Western, for it, like most types of American popular culture, was not considered worthy of scholarly scrutiny. The rise of the American studies movement in the 1950s and the birth of the Popular Culture Association in the late 1960s have encouraged students and teachers to examine the form and content of popular literary genres, such as the Western. It is now acceptable in many English, history, and American studies departments for a student to undertake a study of the Western for a thesis or dissertation. As yet, however, not much of this new interest in the Western has found its way into published articles and books; systematic study of the popular genre is still in its infancy.

The following essay deals with the popular Western, the formula fiction of such authors as Owen Wister, Max Brand, Zane Grey, Ernest Haycox, Luke Short, and Louis L'Amour. These writers follow the patterns of action, romance, and the clash of heroes and villains familiar to the Western. Their plots are predictable; they confirm rather than challenge or satirize American culture. Writers of Westerns do not produce the less stylized western novels of Willa Cather, John Steinbeck, Wallace Stegner, and Larry McMurtry. To make these distinctions between the *Western* and the *western novel* is not to denigrate the former and praise the latter but to make clear the subject of the following pages.

In recent treatments of the Western, two points of view about its historical development have emerged. One group argues that the Western is strongly tied to several nineteenth-century sources: the *Leatherstocking Tales* of James Fenimore Cooper, dime novels, and western local color writing. Another group asserts that though these early roots are significant for a large understanding of popular literature about the West, the Western is primarily the product of the dynamic climate of opinion surrounding 1900. The present account leans toward the second point of view while trying not to overlook the earlier influences upon the Western.

Many Americans did not take a positive view of the frontier until the last decades of the eighteenth century. Before that time, the earliest settlers and their descendants saw the frontier as a region for expansion but also as a forbidding and evil wilderness. As Richard Slotkin has recently pointed out in his book *Regeneration Through Violence*, it was not until John Filson published his legend-making volume, *The Discovery, Settlement and Present State of Kentucke* (1784), that Americans were provided with a western hero in the author's account of Daniel Boone.

In the fifty years following the publication of Filson's work, other information necessary for the creation of a western literature became available. Even before Thomas Jefferson became president, he was encouraging exploration of the West, and after he was elected, he sent Lewis and Clark to traverse the West and to provide written records of what they saw and experienced. The publication of their journals and the accounts of such travelers as Josiah Gregg, Jedediah Smith, and Stephen H. Long convinced many Americans that the empty spaces beyond the frontier were indeed a "passage to India" and part of the nation's "untransacted destiny."

The stage was set for an imaginative writer who could synthesize the information available about the West and the emotions that these facts and rumors had inspired. James Fenimore Cooper was able to use these materials to create the earliest full-blown hero of western fiction in Natty Bumppo (or Leatherstocking, the Long Rifle, or the Deerslayer). Many interpreters argue that Cooper produced the first widely read novels about the West and hence deserves to be called the father of the western novel.

Cooper used many ingredients in his fiction that later became standard parts of the Western. In the first place, his hero, Leatherstocking, embodied several of the virtues of the Romantic hero. He was a man of nature who loved animals, forests, and good Indians (Cooper made sharp distinctions between what he considered good and bad Indians) and was at home himself in the wilderness. Although Natty was interested in the women his creator provided for him, when he had the opportunity to choose between these heroines and his forest home, he selected the frontier rather than hearth, home, and domesticity. On numerous occasions Leatherstocking conflicted with white men or Indians who challenged his sense of territory or what he thought to be his rights. These conflicts foreshadowed the famous walkdowns that appeared later in such novels as *The Virginian.* And anyone acquainted with the modern Western will recognize its indebtedness to the chase-and-pursuit plot that Cooper utilized in his *Leatherstocking Tales.*

Cooper's western novels attracted thousands of readers throughout the world, and thus it is not surprising that several American authors rushed in to imitate his work. Such writers as James Hall, Charles Webber, Mayne Reid, and Emerson Bennett turned out dozens of adventure novels set in the West. By the Civil War, American readers were widely acquainted with the frontier West through the fiction of Cooper and other novelists. Then, in the next three decades, two developments changed the content and direction of western fiction and helped pave the way for the rise of the modern Western.

The first of these innovations was the appearance of the earliest dime novels shortly before the Civil War. Sales of the dime novel rose spectacularly until the late 1880s. And, as one might expect, authors of this new popular fiction, in their search for salable materials, made wide use of themes and formats contained in earlier writing about the West. Some writers sensationalized the deeds of historical persons, such at Kit Carson and Buffalo Bill; others like Edward Wheeler and Edward S. Ellis created the fictional characters Deadwood Dick and Seth Jones. As demands for the dime novel increased, writers were less inclined to stick to the Leatherstocking figure inherited from Cooper and fashioned instead heroes more adventurous and less reflective. Gradually the actions of these heroes—and heroines—were melodramatized beyond belief, and the potential power of the western setting was lost in the drive to turn out hundreds of dime novels in which action and adventure were paramount. The dime novel popularized the West, but its lurid sensationalism revealed a lack of serious intent in dealing with the western materials introduced earlier in the nineteenth century.

The other development that influenced writing about the West was the rise of the "local color" movement after the Civil War. In the first decades following Appomattox many American writers began to emphasize local dialect, customs, and settings in their fiction. Bret Harte was a well-known participant in this movement; indeed, his stories about Californian mining camps and prostitutes and hard-bitten miners with hearts of gold were path-breaking developments in the local color movement. Other writers like Joaquin Miller, Mary Hallock Foote, and Alfred Henry Lewis wrote poems, stories, and novels about explorers, engineers, and cowpunchers. These authors, whose works never sold as widely as those of the dime novelists, were more serious of purpose and proved that literary treatment of the West need not fall victim to sensationalism.

In addition to the rise of the dime novel and the local color movement, several other developments in late nineteenth-century America prepared the way for Owen Wister and the Western. Not the least of these was the realization of many Americans that the frontier was gone or rapidly disappearing. As the wide-open spaces vanished, cities, industrialism, and numbers of immigrants seemed to increase; and writers, sensing the public's desire to hold onto the frontier, began to write about the cowboy and other symbols of an older West. The same nostalgic mood helped popularize Buffalo Bill's Wild West Show, which played to large audiences in the United States and abroad. The show included real Indians, cowboys, and sharpshooters, and it aided in keeping alive an era that was rapidly disappearing. Probably the most important of the cultural "happenings" leading to the birth of the western novel was the discovery of the cowboy. A few dime novelists, journalists, and travelers mentioned the cowboy before 1890, but during the 1890s the fiction of Wister and the illustrations of Frederic Remington helped to make the cowboy a new cultural hero worthy of a major literary treatment.

And Wister was the man worthy of the task. Philadelphia-born and Harvard-educated, Wister first saw the West in the 1880s during a series of trips designed to relieve his boredom and restore his health. At first, he was satisfied to wander throughout the West as a dilettantish sightseer, but at the suggestion of his friends he began to record in his journals what he saw and experienced. Wister was a keen observer and talented writer—he had already published on a variety of subjects—and his first western stories published in magazines in the early 1890s attracted a good deal of attention. By the turn of the century, Wister was known as a prominent writer about western subjects.

Wister's position in 1900 was similar to Cooper's in 1820: he had at his disposal the materials necessary for a significant work of fiction, and his previous writings proved he could produce work that attracted readers. His first western books *Red Men and White* (1896) and *Lin McLean* (1897) dealt with cowboys, although these heroes were most often picaresque protagonists who were not as adventurous and winsome as many Romantic heroes. But in *The Virginian*, published in 1902, Wister put his brand on the most popular Western ever written, and after its publication western writing was never the same.

The Virginian occupies the central position in the historical development of the Western. The novel not only contains the action, adventure, romance, and good-versus-bad characters that had become standard parts of nineteenth-century western fiction; the work also reveals how much its creator was a participant in several cultural currents at the turn of the century. Wister's novel is shot through with nostalgia. From the prefatory note to the closing pages of the book, the tone is elegiac. The Virginian and the other cowboys are dealt with as symbols of a vanishing frontier. Wister also treats the West as another (perhaps the final) arena in which Anglo-Saxons can prove their superiority through vigorous competition with other people and the environment. In *The Virginian*, the hero and setting are used to illustrate these ideas: the Virginian is the Anglo-Saxon protagonist who wins his competition with others and who proves his superiority through conflict.

And yet there is an ambivalent strain in the novel. Though Wister seems drawn to the openness, the challenge, and the romance of the West, he also implies that life in Wyoming may turn men brutal and careless in their treatment of land, horses, and people. And it is necessary for Molly Wood, the Eastern schoolmarm, to bring civilization (as Eastern women had often done in earlier western fiction) to the West in the form of literature and culture. Finally, the marriage of the East (Molly) and West (the Virginian) is a union of the best qualities of each region and a union that bodes well for the future of America.

If Wister provided in *The Virginian* a paradigm for the modern Western, B. M. Bower (Bertha Sinclair), Zane Grey, Max Brand (Frederick Faust), and Clarence Mulford followed his lead and produced hundreds of novels that hardened the ingredients of Wister's novel into a durable formula. Although each of these writers turned out numerous works—most of which were notable for their predictable plots, stereotyped characters, and conventional morality—they exhibited individual talents and tendencies.

B. M. Bower, the only woman to produce a string of notable Westerns, is best known for her characters in *Chip of the Flying U*. She dealt authentically with the details of cattle ranching, and reviewers noted her use of humor and her varied plots. Like Wister, she used East-versus-West conflicts and tried to capture the complexities of a closing frontier. Her heroines were more convincing than those of her contemporaries, but the organization of her novels was often choatic, and conflicts between characters were too easily resolved. Even more damaging to her reputation was the fact that she seemed unable to deal with serious cultural or social issues and during her long career was reluctant to make changes in her plots and ideas.

Zane Grey was a much more well-known writer than Mrs. Sinclair. In fact, between 1910 and 1930 he did more than any other writer to popularize the Western. Not only did several of his works top the bestseller lists, he also portrayed a West of picturesque and restorative power that appealed to Americans increasingly distraught with urban, industrial, and international problems. The public seemed convinced that Grey's West, which was pictured as able to redeem effete Easterners, was a marvelous and wonderful place. His descriptive and narrative abilities were particularly alive in novels such as *Riders of the Purple Sage* (1912), *The U. P. Trail* (1918), and *The Vanishing American* (1925). Grey's popularity has endured, and many readers when asked to define the Western point to Grey's works as epitomizing the elements of the formula Western.

Max Brand (the most popular of Frederick Faust's seventeen pen names) was much less interested than Grey in specific settings, natural or historical, and Brand never placed a high value on his Westerns. While Grey was convinced that his novels should place him among the leading writers of his time, Brand referred to his novels set in the West as "Westtern stuff" or "cowboy junk." He was interested, however, in showing human nature in conflict, and to enlarge the significance of these battles he frequently made his heroes titan-like. Between the early twentieth century and his death in 1944, Brand turned out more than five hundred books, more than one hundred of which were Westerns.

Another writer, Clarence Mulford, was more serious than Faust in his approach to writing Westerns. Mulford prided himself on his careful research into the historical backgrounds of his fiction. He gathered a large library and boasted of knowing intimately the West even though most of his writing was carried out in Maine. Early in his career he introduced Hopalong Cassidy, a wise, humorous, and appealing cowboy, who appeared later in many of Mulford's Westerns and became one of the well-known series characters in western fiction. Hopalong was a working cowboy and rancher—much different from the image of Cassidy that William Boyd depicted in western movies.

By the early 1930s these novelists, in addition to such writers as Stewart Edward White, Emerson Hough, W. C. Tuttle, and Eugene Manlove Rhodes, had helped to identify the Western as a separate fictional type. Reviewers and readers were now aware of what the term *Western* meant when it was applied to a novel. Unfortunately, for many critics *Western* denoted a subliterary type that they considered beneath their scholarly interests.

Part of this negative reaction arose because the Western was associated with the pulp magazines of the 1920s and 1930s. Publishers found that after the demise of the dime novel and the popular story weeklies in the years surrounding the turn of the century, there was still a large audience for adventure fiction about the West. Firms such as Munsey's, Doubleday, and Street and Smith capitalized on this huge market. *Love Story, Detective Story, Western Story,* and *Adventure* were four of the most widely read pulps, but western stories and magazines were the most popular. By 1930, more than thirty western magazines were on the market, and writers like Frank C. Robertson, Frank Richardson Pierce, W. C. Tuttle, and Max Brand, especially dominated the pulp western scene.

From the middle 1930s until his death in 1950, Ernest Haycox was the premier figure among another group of writers of Westerns. Haycox had served his apprenticeship in the pulps during the 1920s, and by the mid-1930s his stories and serials were appearing in *Collier's*, which, along with *Saturday Evening Post*, was considered the leading slick magazine. When Zane Grey lost his place in the major serial markets in slick magazines, Haycox quickly moved into his vacated slot and won the attention of editors and many readers. Several writers of Westerns who began their careers in the 1940s and 1950s were later to testify that they learned their craft by reading and studying the Haycox serials in *Collier's*.

Haycox was interested in producing more believeable Westerns. Not only did he try to create more persuasive characters, he also tinkered with the stereotyped characterizations of the Western by using two or more heroes and heroines and thereby added a measure of complexity to an uncomplex genre. In addition, Haycox began to people his Westerns with what one interpreter calls *Hamlet heroes.* These protagonists were reflective men who often wrestled with their consciences in deciding what was the right course of action. These heroes were far more serious and contemplative than the leading men in the Westerns of Grey and Brand.

Finally, Haycox added a historical dimension to several of his Westerns. He was convinced that by resting his fiction on historical events he could increase the realism of the Western. In such novels as *The Border Trumpet* (1939), *Alder Gulch* (1942), and particularly in his novel on General Custer, *Bugles in the Afternoon* (1944), he carefully gathered data on historical occurrences and based his plots on recorded events. Because of his tinkerings with and his additions to the format of the Western, Ernest Haycox occupies a large niche in the development of the popular genre.

No single writer can be said to have inherited Haycox's mantle, but three authors of the last three decades have attracted more attention than other writers of Westerns. Henry Wilson Allen, who writes under the pen names of Will Henry and Clay Fisher, has adhered closely to the historical Western that Haycox popularized in the 1940s. Particularly in his Will Henry Westerns, Allen demonstrates an experienced hand in joining history and fiction to produce high caliber Westerns. His Clay Fisher Westerns, on the other hand, emphasize action and adventure and rarely deal with specific historical events. Among the best of the Will Henry novels are *From Where the Sun Now Stands* (1959), *The Gates of the Mountains* (1963), and *Chiricahua* (1972).

Frederick Glidden, better known by his *nom de plume*, Luke Short, was probably the most popular writer of Westerns during the 1950s and 1960s. Short emphasizes action, and he packs his Westerns with suspense. His novels are tightly written with carefully structured adventure. In several of his works, Short draws upon his knowledge of frontier and western occupations to make his characters more believeable. Sometimes he sets a Western in a twentieth-century mining town, but most of his settings are frontier communities of no specific location. Short frequently deals with town life, although he seems little interested in using historical characters or events in his novels. He is skillful in handling women and knows how to picture some of his heroes as good men who have made a mistake in the past and are now bent on redeeming themselves. In the 1950s Short's Westerns began to appear as original paperbacks after markets for magazine serials had disappeared. Since that time most Westerns have been printed as original paperbacks.

The third of the triumvirate of contemporary writers of Westerns is Louis L'Amour. During the early 1970s L'Amour reportedly became the bestselling living author of Westerns. Readers of L'Amour's novels praise his abilities as a storyteller. His speedy narratives seem to contain fresh stories within the familiar format of the Western. One survey of nearly two dozen of L'Amour's Westerns (he has written about sixty novels, more than four hundred stories, and about one hundred television scripts) noted a pattern in L'Amour's fiction: his emphasis on families, their origins and characteristics, and their historic roles in settling the West. Another critic stressed L'Amour's use of violence; in ten randomly selected Westerns, 156 persons were killed, not counting those destroyed in massacres and other mass killings. The same commentator observed that most of the heroes of L'Amour's Westerns are self-made men who espouse traditional and popular causes. It seems clear that L'Amour has gained his audience primarily because he produces Westerns that contain predictable characters, plots, and endings. His narrative skills hold his readers while he relates stories strongly tied to the familiar structure of the Western.

If Allen, Short, and L'Amour have made, at the most, tinkering changes with the content and format of the Western, other writers and film producers have given the popular genre a total overhaul. These people appear certain that the Western—like much of popular culture of the 1960s and 1970s—has not been very relevant to an understanding of America. Yet they also seem convinced that because the nature of the Western is so well-known, parodies of its tone, structure, and focus could be used to reveal dangerous tendencies in the formula Western and the popular genre's inadequacies as a moral and ethical base for American ideology.

In the 1960s such books and films as *The Rounders* (Max Evans, 1960), *Little Big Man* (Thomas Berger, 1964), *Cat Ballou* (1965), *North to Yesterday* (Robert Flynn, 1967), and *Soldier Blue* (1970) satirized the Western. Some of the treatments were gentle: *The Rounders* dealt with a pair of cowpokes cavorting about as drunken and lusting failures; *Cat Ballou* pictured a renowned western gunslinger as a drunk (Lee Marvin) and utilized a pretty and naive schoolmarm (Jane Fonda) as protagonist; *North to Yesterday* described a cattle drive which arrived two decades late in a Mid-western cattle town. (The novels of Richard Brautigan also seem, in part, gentle satires of the ingredients of the popular Western.) Other accounts are more biting: *Little Big Man* portrays General Custer as a vicious killer of Indians and suggests, on the other hand, that the Indians were *the* western heroes (the film based on Berger's novel was even more harsh and pro-Indian than the book); *Soldier Blue* implied that the army on the frontier was little more than a pack of killers who slaughtered Indians.

In 1960, E. L. Doctorow prefigured this attack on the Western in his first novel *Welcome to Hard Times*. Through his narrator-historian, Blue, Doctorow hints that early western experiences were, at best, depressing and more often savage. Most of the residents of Hard Times are grotesques: ludicrous whores, grasping merchants, and violent killers—all of whom rip into one another and show little or no sense of community. Another author, John Seelye, is equally devastating in his attack on the Western in his brief novel *The Kid* (1972). Seelye, who dedicates his work to Leslie Fiedler and who is obviously indebted to the writing of Mark Twain and Herman Melville, pictures a frontier Wyoming town ripe with violence, racism, and perversion. In addition to parodying the usual makeup of the Western, Seelye hints at the detrimental impact that violence, racism, and sexual prejudices have had on America. Thus, *The Kid* undercuts the form and content of the Western while it also attacks what the author sees to be the major weaknesses of American culture.

Finally, there are other small signs the Western is changing. Writers are dealing more explicitly with sex. For example, Playboy Press is publishing its line of Jake Logan Westerns which emphasize the hero's abundant sexual prowess. Other recent Westerns treat homosexuality. Women are playing a more conspicuous role; the protagonists in some Westerns are women (see Jack Bickham's novels dealing with a female character named Charity Ross), and more and more writers are avoiding picturing their heroines as merely pawns of their men. Moreover, the treatment of Indians, blacks, and Mexican-Americans is more balanced than in earlier Weserns. Indians, for example, are often described in these recent novels as embodying a culture different from white society, and it is obvious that these differences will lead to conflict, but the Indians who fight their white enemies are not portrayed as inferior people or as savages.

These innovations suggest that the Western is reflecting the changing ideas and customs of the United States during the last decade or so. If this surmise is true, the Western remains a valuable source for attempting to understand the American popular mind.

BIBLIOGRAPHY

Calder, Jenni. *There Must Be a Lone Ranger: The American West in Film and in Reality.* New York: Taplinger, 1975.

Cawelti, John G. *Adventure, Mystery, and Romance: Formula Stories as Art and Popular Culture.* Chicago: University of Chicago Press, 1976.

———. *The Six-Gun Mystique.* Bowling Green, Ohio: Bowling Green University Popular Press, 1971.

Easton, Robert. *Max Brand: The Big "Westerner."* Norman: University of Oklahoma Press, 1970.

Etulain, Richard W. "The American Literary West and Its Interpreters: The Rise of a New Historiography." *Pacific Historical Review,* 45 (August 1976), 311-48.

———. *Owen Wister.* Western Writers Series, no. 7. Boise, Idaho: Boise State University, 1973.

———. *Western American Literature: A Bibliography of Interpretive Books and Articles.* Vermillion: University of South Dakota Press, 1972.

———, ed. *The American Literary West.* Manhattan, Kan.: Sunflower University

Press, 1980. Includes "The Rise of the Western" (pp. 29-35) by Gary Topping and "The Modern Western" (pp. 54-61) by Michael T. Marsden.

———, and Michael T. Marsden. *The Popular Western: Essays Toward a Definition.* Bowling Green, Ohio: Bowling Green University Popular Press, 1974.

Fenin, George N., and William K. Everson. *The Western: From Silents to the Seventies.* New York: Grossman, 1973.

Folsom, James K. *The American Western Novel.* New Haven, Conn.: College and University Press, 1966.

Jackson, Carlton. *Zane Grey.* New York: Twayne Publishers, 1973.

Jones, Daryl. *The Dime Novel Western.* The Popular Western Writers Series, Richard W. Etulain and Michael T. Marsden, eds. Bowling Green, Ohio: The Popular Press, 1978.

Milton, John R. *The Novel of the American West.* Lincoln: University of Nebraska Press, 1980.

Nachbar, John G., ed. *Western Films: An Annotated Critical Bibliography.* New York: Garland Publishing Co., 1975.

Nye, Russel B. "Sixshooter Country." In *The Unembarrassed Muse: The Popular Arts in America.* New York: Dial Press, 1970.

Ronald, Ann. *Zane Grey.* Western Writers Series, no. 17. Boise, Idaho: Boise State University, 1975.

Slotkin, Richard. *Regeneration Through Violence: The Mythology of the American Frontier, 1600-1860.* Middletown, Conn.: Wesleyan University Press, 1973.

Smith, Henry Nash. *Virgin Land: The American West as Symbol and Myth.* Cambridge, Mass.: Harvard University Press, 1950.

Sonnichsen, C. L. *From Hopalong to Hud: Thoughts on Western Fiction.* College Station: Texas A & M Press, 1978.

Steckmesser, Kent Ladd. *The Western Hero in History and Legend.* Norman: University of Oklahoma Press, 1965.

———. "Zane Grey's West: Essays in Intellectual History and Criticism." Ph.D dissertation, University of Utah, 1977.

White, G. Edward. *The Eastern Establishment and the Western Experience: The West of Frederic Remington, Theodore Roosevelt, and Owen Wister.* New Haven, Conn.: Yale University Press, 1968.

Wright, Will. *Sixguns and Society: A Structural Study of the Western.* Berkeley: University of California Press, 1975.

Women

Katherine Fishburn

From the beginning, women have appeared in American popular culture in one way or another. At times, as readers, they seemed to be, in fact, its prime movers. They certainly have been among the major producers and purchasers of some of its most famous and profitable products. Not only did women demand and devour the early sentimental romances, but they also wrote most of them—and appeared in the "starring roles" with discouraging consistency. While these "scribbling women," as Hawthorne bitterly labelled them, were engaged in popular fiction, others were filling private journals with copious observations about colonial and Jacksonian era home life. With the invention of speedier and more efficient printing presses in the late 1800s, the ladies' magazines came into their own as one of the most potent social forces of the nineteenth century. They, in turn, have been replaced by the equally seductive women's magazines of the twentieth century. Nor has the female role been a minor one in the history of the movies. From the silent film to the eighties the image of women in film—either by her presence or, more recently, by her absence—has been a clue to the American way of life.

Since her appearance on these shores as a "lady," the American woman has been intimately involved with popular culture: as its source, sustenance, and subject. She can be described, without exaggeration, therefore, as the true mother of American popular culture. This is not to say, however, that the only image of women in American popular culture is that of the mother. Nor is it contained in the virgin-whore dichotomy. Rather, the image of the American female is as complex as her culture, appearing in various guises at different times.

In our very earliest popular culture, for example, in the Indian captivity stories, the conflict of good versus evil took center stage, with the grace of God overshadowing any human heroes or heroines. Believing that the Indian was the devil's disciple, the American colonists interpreted capture by the savages from a religious perspective, seeing the captivity itself as an opportunity for God to test their faith. The most popular of these tales was one by Mrs. Mary Rowlandson, which appeared in no fewer than thirty-one editions. It carried the descriptive, but cumbersome, title *The Sovereignty and Goodness of God..., Being a Narrative of the Captivity and Restoration of Mrs. Mary Rowlandson* (2d edition, 1682). Although its protagonist is a woman, its subject is religion. In time this would change, as the Indian captivity tales, in conjunction with the British novel of sensibility and the American accounts of witchcraft, were to provide the basis for our heavily formulaic and indisputably female fiction of the next two hundred years.

Perhaps the most stunningly successful of these forms was the sentimental tearjerker, best exemplified in Susanna Haswell Rowson's *Charlotte Temple: A Tale of Truth* (1791). A Britisher by birth, Susanna Haswell visited the colonies with her parents before moving here permanently with her husband William Rowson in 1797. As so frequently occurs in the strange history of women in American popular culture, the very women whose writings encourage mindless passivity in females have themselves been highly businesslike professionals. Not only was Rowson a notable author, but she also founded a girls' school in Boston and participated in numerous business and intellectual ventures.

Her heroine, Charlotte Temple, seems to be Rowson's negative print. Taking her cue from and riding the crest of Samuel Richardson's international popularity, Mrs. Rowson constructed a sentimental tale of seduction that became an archetype in its own right. Calling her novel "A Tale of Truth," she sought to disarm those critics who still considered fiction immoral. (In fact, *Charlotte Temple* is apparently based on events in Rowson's own family.) Through her heavy-handed didacticism, she used her story to convince readers that the wages of sin is death. Charlotte's "sin" is that of losing her virginity—a fall that would provide the plots of many forms of American popular culture in the years to come. Her punishment for her moment of foolish weakness is to die while giving birth to a daughter. Like other writers who followed her, Rowson makes it clear that any marriage at all is to be preferred to this ignominious ending. With this stand, she clearly deviated from Richardson's conclusion to *Clarissa* (1748), in which the death of the unmarried heroine is a kind of existential victory. In *Charlotte Temple*, Rowson also planted the seeds of the feminine mystique, whose influence American women are still struggling to overcome. For Charlotte, unlike her creator, is fate's plaything, the perfect victim who is unable to distinguish between true and false love.

The descendants of Charlotte Temple are alive and well and appearing in the immensely popular gothic and Harlequin romances, which sell in such large numbers that they have their own sections in many bookstores. The image of women in these escape fantasies, as in other popular genres such as detective and science fiction, is less than positive. With the exception of works like Ursula LeGuin's *The Left Hand of Darkness,* which skirts the issue through androgyny, popular fiction continues the tradition of portraying women as helpless, mindless creatures. If they are major characters in the romances, they are but booty to be won, princesses to be rescued, or companions to be tolerated in science fiction. Other roles for women are as monster robots and black widow spiders. Even such "feminist" best sellers as Alix Kates Shulman's *The Memoirs of an Ex-Prom Queen* seem to be nothing more than "sexploitation" told from a woman's point of view rather than from a man's. The contents of today's women's magazines reflect a similar transformation from muted to frank sexuality in their portrayal of women.

As early as 1709, when Richard Steele founded *The Tatler* and included a column intended for women, magazines have been alert to the needs and buying power of their female readers. In 1787, when Noah Webster founded *The American Magazine* in New York, he too had the interest of the ladies at heart, promising in his first issue that his "*fair readers* may be assured that no inconsiderable pains will be taken to furnish them entertainment." Toward this end, he published gothic and sentimental fiction and began the "how-to" columns that would later provide the substance of the specialty magazines of the twentieth century. In 1821, *The Saturday Evening Post* tried to attract women through its department called "The Ladies' Friend," which featured poetry and articles appropriate for the gentle sex. The purpose of these early magazines, as ostensibly was that of early novels, was instruction. Because of their popularity and because there were no public libraries where hungry readers might turn for more substantial fare, the influence of these publications was immense. The opportunity for female "education" contained in these isolated departments of the general magazines was nothing, however, compared to the power generated by the "ladies' magazines" themselves. Their history is at the heart of the development of American advertising: at the core of the mass marketing of mores, tastes, fashion, food, and literature that has transformed the face of America and that of the American woman in the past one hundred fifty years.

The *Ladies' Magazine*, established in 1828 in Boston by Mrs. Sarah Josepha Hale, was to become the foundation for the multibillion-dollar business of selling American housewives a bill of goods. Although the genesis of these ladies' magazines initially gave housewives a certain stature and pride in their work, their ultimate effect has been to glorify what many consider to be second-class citizenship. (One of the most powerful of the early editors, Edward Bok, discouraged women from entering business because there they would "lose their gentleness and womanliness.") Like the motion pictures that were to follow eighty years later, the magazines both recognized and codified the status of women in the United States. One of the most popular of these proselytizers was the brainchild of Louis Antoine Godey. *Godey's Lady's Book* was the hybrid born of the merger between Godey's own *Lady's Book* (founded in Philadelphia in 1830) and Sarah Hale's *Ladies' Magazine* (which he bought out in 1837). Sarah Hale was the editor from 1837 to 1877, during which time she increased circulation, encouraged female contributors to sign their names (rather than using just their initials or the anonymous "A Lady"), and, in general, left her mark on the magazine and on magazine history. Her editorial policy was to promote women's education, but to ignore politics. She featured recipes, health and beauty aids, embroidery patterns, and "embellishments"—the latter were those ornate illustrations and hand-painted fashion plates for which *Godey's* was justifiably famous. In short, Sarah Josepha Hale designed the archetypal magazine for women.

When *Godey's* folded in 1898, it simply left more room for its imitators and competitors, such as Cyrus H. K. Curtis's *Ladies' Home Journal.* (It was founded in 1883 as *Ladies' Journal and Practical Housekeeper,* but it appeared, from its ambiguously laid out masthead, to be entitled the *Ladies' Home Journal.*) As Godey's most astute move had been to hire Sarah Hale, so Curtis's was to hire Edward Bok, who took over as editor in 1889. And, in his turn, Edward Bok was to leave his mark permanently on the ladies' magazines. Setting out, in his own words, to "uplift" and "inspire" his readers, he made it a point to establish an intimate relationship with them. To do this, he wrote one advice column as "Ruth Ashmore" called "Side Talk to Girls" and, in a bold new move, another under his own name called "At Home with the Editor." In his zeal to reform America, he supported several causes, some more successfully than others; among them were campaigns against patent medicines, Paris fashions, aigrettes, and venereal disease—this last was a daring stand that cost him thousands of subscribers. Historically, perhaps his most significant contribution to the magazine trade was his decision in 1897 to widen the domestic coverage of the *Journal* by including architectural plans in the magazine; this feature was followed by photographs of the interiors of homes, which were categorized according to whether or not they were in good taste.

Although *Godey's* and the *Journal* were the "big two" of the early ladies' magazines, several others were being published concurrently. The fashion magazines, which had begun primarily as pattern catalogs, were represented by *The Delineator* (1873-1937), *Harper's Bazar* (1867, becoming *Harper's Bazaar* in 1929), and *Vogue* (1892). Other magazines modeled on the *Journal* were *McCall's* (1870), *Woman's Home Companion* (1873) and *Good Housekeeping* (1885). Although each magazine tried to promote its individuality through various gimmicks (the *Journal's* resilient slogan "Never Underestimate the Power of a Woman"; *McCall's* abortive "togetherness" campaign; the influential *Good Housekeeping* seal of approval), all directed their material exclusively to women—in particular, the mother who stayed at home.

Their formulas were magical until World War II. With the increasing availability of other diversionary and "instructive" media (such as television, radio, newspapers with colored supplements, cheap paperbacks, and movies), with a market glutted by virtually indistinguishable journals, and with the need for women to work because their men were at war, women's magazines began to decline. Their recent resurgence, along with such specialized publications as *Seventeen* (1944), is no doubt a result of their willingness to revamp their appearance. By modernizing their formats and raising their level of sexual tolerance, they have managed to hold their own in a competitive market.

Ironically, these current "ladies' magazines" are sometimes nearly indistinguishable not so much from each other as from their male counterparts, such as Hugh Hefner's *Playboy* (1953). Although their photography, fiction, and cartoons are not yet as graphic sexually as that of the men's magazines, they are certainly fully as suggestive. This state inevitably leads one to the conclusion that today's liberated housewife and/or career woman is just as susceptible to sexuality as her ancestors were to sentimentality. Perhaps the most interesting feature of their metamorphosis is that, except for the maverick *Viva* (1973) and the occasional *Cosmopolitan* (1886) centerfold, the fascination in both men's and women's magazines is with the female figure. In this, the modern glossies and their venerable ancestors share a common conviction that it is the images of women that sell magazines.

With the advent of the movies in the twentieth century, a new medium took over the task of determining American femininity. From Mary Pickford to Raquel Welch, and all the transformations in between, the movie actress has both reflected and projected an image of American womanhood: showing women what they are and, more importantly, what they can become. One of the trade secrets of the moneymakers in Hollywood has been an uncanny ability to depict and define the American taste in women: its virgins and viragos, its fantasies and nightmares. If the movies are not responsible for the American male's obsession with the breast, they at least brought the fascination to light, not incidentally making profits in direct proportion to bra size. Even before the days of Marilyn Monroe, the movies made "it"—the original version of "sex appeal"—a household word by promoting Clara Bow's role in *It* (1927). On the other hand, when necessary, the movies could even help the American war effort by portraying women not as sex objects but as Rosie the riveter in such movies as *Swing Shift Maisie* (1943) and *Since You Went Away* (1944).

It is no coincidence that the first big star of the silent era was the child-like Mary Pickford, who, with her innocent curls, epitomized the ideal of virtuous Victorian womanhood. Known to her fans as "The Girl with the Curl," Pickford made this image her hallmark until she was incapable of escaping its obvious limitations. Incredibly, like some sort of female Dorian Grey, as she matured off screen, she seemed to be changeless on-screen: playing a young child in *A Poor Little Rich Girl* in 1917 when she was twenty-four, and a twelve-year-old in *Little Annie Rooney* when she was thirty-two. Ironically, as so often happens with female pop-culture figures, these cinematic images of her as a girlish ragamuffin belied her real-life power and womanliness. Although she clung to her successful formula well into her thirties, she had the grace and good sense to retire at forty, after alienating her fans by trying to change her image to keep up with the Roaring Twenties.

If Mary Pickford was a genius at ruling the hearts of the American people by her ingenuous on-screen antics, David Wark Griffith was the man behind the throne. Personally enamoured of the girl-children he promoted, he single-handedly brought more of them to the screen than anyone else in this period. Among his other stars were Lillian and Dorothy Gish (sixteen and fourteen) and Mae Marsh (seventeen). Typical of his productions and moral proclivities is the infamous *The Birth of a Nation* (1915), in which Elsie Stoneman (Lillian Gish), white and pure, is threatened with rape by a black man. Her little sister (Mae Marsh), similarly threatened, throws herself off a cliff to her death. Griffith's classic scene, however, is in *Way Down East* (1920), where a young woman (Lillian Gish), having been deceived and seduced, is sent out mercilessly by her unforgiving father into a winter storm.

Complementing Griffith's rather unbelievable vestal virgins was Theda Bara's equally unbelievable voracious vamp. Rather than expressing purity, Bara exuded a crude Victorian sex appeal that was so extreme as to be rendered harmless. With her exotic makeup and costumes, her arrival on the screen (*A Fool There Was*, 1915), signaled a period of sexual freedom in film not to be rivaled again until recently. The cinematic sex she created was symptomatic of the changing social mores and the increasing freedom of the American woman. Drawn out of the home by the war, middle-class women began to assume responsibilities unheard of in their ranks since colonial times. Accompanying their vocational rehabilitation and emancipation was a new interest in more sophisticated movies. At the top of the list were Cecil B. De Mille's creations, such as the splashily successful and shockingly open (for the times) film about marital infidelity, *Old Wives for New* (1918).

All this innocent easy sexuality was brought to a grinding halt in the early 1930s by the implementation of the Production Code—the film industry's self-imposed censorship that severely limited the roles allowed women. It certainly spelled the doom of one of the screen's greatest originals, the self-sufficient and outrageously funny Mae West, who was unable to survive a climate inimical to her brand of sexuality. After the complexities and mysteries of the almost-androgynous Greta Garbo and Marlene Dietrich and the tough sexuality of Jean Harlow—all of whom were sex stars of pre-Code days—audiences were forced to content themselves with the more wholesome images of Katharine Hepburn, Jean Arthur, and the young Shirley Temple. The women in the comedies of the 1930s were no longer sensual; they were clever and witty companions to their men or feisty competitors engaged in the battle of the sexes. During this period many of the most successful screenwriters were themselves women; two of the major ones were the recently rediscovered Anita Loos and Frances Marion.

After the war ended, and the need for women factory workers and escape fantasies waned, the movies returned once more to the tried and true formula of women's sexuality in the unmistakable form of Marilyn Monroe and her many mammary imitators, such as Jayne Mansfield and Kim Novak. The reign of these sex goddesses was stormy but brief, confined primarily to the 1950s and early 1960s. Although the Production Code has been gradually circumvented in the industry's double-edged attempt to keep afloat financially and encourage artistic freedom, the latest images of women are less than attractive. The new freedom has brought with it a new fear of women's sexuality, it would seem, as directors such as Sam Peckinpah continue to depict women's sex drives as rape fantasies.

If the movies that included women in their scripts in the 1960s and early 1970s were almost paranoid about female sexuality, they were matched film by film by stories in which women played minor roles at best. These "macho" films, such as *Easy Rider* (1969), *Butch Cassidy and the Sundance Kid* (1970), and *Midnight Cowboy* (1969), seem to suggest a disturbing lack of interest in women that is reflected in television programming of this period. Although several movies have appeared in the last year that would suggest a return of major roles for women (*The Turning Point*, *An Unmarried Woman*, *Julia*), it remains to be seen whether this will be a passing fancy or an important shift in cinematic values. The future of women directors is also uncertain as Claudia Weill, Joan Tewkesbury, and Jane Wagner begin to break into the male bastions of the feature film. Whether or not these women will be the Dorothy Arzners of the 1970s and 1980s should become apparent shortly as their works gain public attention.

BIBLIOGRAPHY

Baym, Nina. *Woman's Fiction: A Guide to Novels by and about Women in America, 1820-1870.* Ithaca and London: Cornell University Press, 1978.

Bell, Roseann P., Bettye J. Parker, and Beverly Guy Sheftall, eds. *Sturdy Black Bridges: Visions of Black Women in Literature.* Garden City, N.Y.: Doubleday Anchor Press, 1979.

Christian, Barbara. *Black Women Novelists: The Development of a Tradition, 1892-1976.* Westport, Conn.: Greenwood Press, Inc., 1980. Contributions in Afro-American and African Studies, no. 52.

Cornillon, Susan Koppelman, ed. *Images of Women in Fiction: Feminist Perspectives.* Bowling Green, Ohio: Bowling Green University Popular Press, 1972.

Douglas, Ann. *The Feminization of American Culture.* New York: Alfred A. Knopf, 1977.

Ehrenreich, Barbara, and Deirdre English. *For Her Own Good: 150 Years of the Experts' Advice to Women.* Garden City, N.Y.: Anchor Press, 1978.

Flexner, Eleanor. *Century of Struggle: The Woman's Rights Movement in the United States.* Cambridge, Mass.: The Belknap Press of Harvard University Press, 1975. Revised edition.

Goffman, Erving. *Gender Advertisements.* Cambridge, Mass.: Harvard University Press, 1979. Introduction by Vivian Gornick.

Harris, Barbara J. *Beyond Her Sphere: Women and the Professions in American History.* Westport, Conn.: Greenwood Press, Inc., 1978. Contributions in Women's Studies, no. 4.

Haskell, Molly. *From Reverence to Rape: The Treatment of Women in the Movies.* New York: Holt, Rinehart & Winston, 1973.

Higashi, Sumiko. *Virgins, Vamps, and Flappers: The American Silent Movie Heroine.* St. Albans, Vt.: Eden Press Women's Publications, 1978.

Jeffrey, Julie Roy. *Frontier Women: The Trans-Mississippi West, 1840-1880.* New York: Hill and Wang, 1979.

Ladner, Joyce A. *Tomorrow's Tomorrow: The Black Woman.* Garden City, N.Y.: Doubleday & Company, Inc., 1971.

Lerner, Gerda. *Black Women in White America: A Documentary History.* New York: Pantheon Books, 1972.

Oglesby, Carole A., ed. *Women and Sport: From Myth to Reality.* Philadelphia: Lea & Febiger, 1978.

Rosen, Marjorie. *Popcorn Venus: Women, Movies & the American Dream.* New York: Coward, McCann & Geoghegan, 1973.

Rothman, Sheila M. *Woman's Proper Place: A History of Changing Ideals and Practices, 1870 to the Present.* New York: Basic Books, 1978.

Ryan, Mary P. *Womanhood in America: From Colonial Times to the Present.* New York: Franklin Watts, 1975.

Scott, Anne Firor. *The Southern Lady: From Pedestal to Politics, 1830-1930.* Chicago: The University of Chicago Press, 1970.

Springer, Marlene, ed. *What Manner of Woman: Essays on English and American Life and Literature.* New York: New York University Press, 1977.

Terris, Virginia R. *Woman in America: A Guide to Information Sources.* Detroit: Gale Research Company, 1980. Vol. 7 in the American Studies Information Guide Series.

Tuchman, Gaye, Arlene Kaplan Daniels, and James Benet, eds. *Hearth and Home: Images of Women in the Mass Media.* New York: Oxford University Press, 1978.

Twin, Stephanie L., ed. *Out of the Bleachers: Writings on Women and Sport.* Old Westbury, N.Y.: The Feminist Press, 1979. Series: Women's Lives Women's Work.

Walsh, Mary Roth. *Doctors Wanted: No Women Need Apply: Sexual Barriers in the Medical Profession, 1835-1975.* New Haven: Yale University Press, 1977.

Weibel, Kathryn. *Mirror Mirror: Images of Women Reflected in Popular Culture.* Garden City, N.Y.: Anchor Books of Anchor Press/Doubleday, 1977.

The Study of Popular Culture

Michael J. Bell

At first glance, popular culture seems to be exclusively modern. If the idea brings anything to mind, it is probably images of television, movies, popular music, automobiles, comic books, or fast food, all of which, by their very nature, seem to depend upon an extremely diverse, technological world to explain their existence and to justify their impact upon human life. Such appearances, however, are deceiving. In truth, there has always been a popular culture. Something is popular, after all, if it succeeds in reaching and pleasing as many people as possible. And, popular culture attempts precisely that, no more, no less. At its simplest popular culture is the culture of mass appeal. A creation is popular when it is created to respond to the experiences and values of the majority, when it is produced in such a way that the majority of the people have easy access to it, and when it can be understood and interpreted by that majority without the aid of special knowledge or experience. Every human society at every stage of human history has had artists and craftsmen who have produced such materials. Artisans have always sought to fashion objects and ideas which appealed to a select few and to fashion others which delighted audiences as wide as could be imagined. Equally, human communities have long recognized that their productivity and vitality rested not only on their ability to create for small groups with distinctive interests but also upon their ability to satisfy the concerns and desires of broad majorities of people. Still, it is not unreasonable to see popular culture as somehow especially modern. For while that world did not produce the first popular culture, it was the first to define its nature, its worth, and its difference.

Popular, elite, and folk culture are different because they define different experiences. But, their differences are not ones of quality. The three are different because they describe different kinds of relationships between producers and consumers. Elite culture is exclusive. Its artists define their task as the creation of something different, something which has never existed before, and, yet something which can be evaluated in relation to the known great works of previous times. Elite creators seek to produce "classics" in which the mixture of the subjective part, the artist's personal self, and the objective part, the accepted rules for the production of aesthetic experiences, are combined to produce new ways of confronting and experiencing the human condition. Elite audiences, likewise, accept the idea of creation as a consciously aesthetic act and expect that they will be provided with products and entertainments which will be novel and daring. They know their creators; they expect them to seek out complexity and use it as an end in itself. Elite creations, therefore, even when they are intended for some useful purpose, tend to exist for their own sake. They are appreciated for what they are, for how they compare to the creations of the past, and not for what they might do.

Folk culture is personal. It is the culture of everyday life. Folk creators work with the facts of ordinary experience and with the most regular and routine relations of social life. They and their audiences are immediately present to each other, and they are bound together by the fund of traditional knowledge and practice through which communities hold themselves together from generation to generation. This tradition sets the boundaries by which social life proceeds from moment to moment and by which individuals in that life find and orient themselves with one another. Those who create folk culture, therefore, work with and within the tried and true patterns of experience, and those who are its audience expect that their experiences will reflect the conventions of what has gone before and served them well in the past. Folk culture, accordingly, is a culture of continuity, governed by traditions and the expectation that the experience of daily life, lived as most people do most of the time, will continue largely as it has gone before.

Popular culture is comprehensive. Unlike either folk or elite culture, its creators are seldom known by or know their audiences. They work for the large mass of people and they seek to satisfy as many and offend as few of those people as possible. Their concern, therefore, is not complexity or profundity, though both may result, but that they will reach, be understood, and, perhaps, even move their audiences. The audience for popular culture seeks most of all to be entertained or to have a product that will serve a purpose. They want their values, their expectations, and their experiences to be validated. In a sense, they want novelty but they do not want that novelty to be overwhelming. The audience for popular art or products wants to recognize themselves in what is being presented to them. They want it to conform to their personal set of critical standards, to be what they like. Popular culture, thus, tends to be responsive to the marketplace. It aims for a consensus among its public and for the possibility that in reaching out to the majority of the community it can affirm what is already valuable in their lives and offer direction toward what ought and might become important in their world.

One way of visualizing this relationship is to see it not as a jumble of elements randomly piled one on top of another but as an integrated whole in which each component is dependent upon all the others for its existence and meaning. In such a relationship, the whole is greater than the individual parts. The pieces which make up the system are subject to the same rules. They do not simply exist in the presence of each other but continually interact and exchange information. Thus, they are always mutually influencing each other, producing change. And, this change produced in any one part in turn produces change in all the other parts. In this way the elements in the relationship take on distinctive features which they could never have on their own. They become bearers of information about themselves and about how they have interacted, are interacting, and will interact with the other components in the system. In sum, they communicate.

A working model of this communication can be diagrammed, drawing on the work of Roman Jakobson, in the following manner:

context

text

creator(s)............audience(s)

media

Each element in this model represents one of the essential elements out of which a communication develops. For such an exchange to take place, someone must convey something to someone in a certain way under certain conditions. A creator, in this case, offers a text to an audience. That act happens at a specific time and place, a context, and is transmitted by specific means. For popular culture, such a communicative relationship might involve a movie director producing a movie which is literally turned into a film to be shown to an audience in a theater, or a cartoonist producing a comic book which will be printed and sold in stores. Specifics aside, however, what is important is that all of these individual components only become meaningful because they are involved with each other and because that involvement adds important, new information to the whole that no single part could acquire on its own.

Each element in this model also represents a vantage point from which contemporary critical analysis attempts to describe, define, and explain cultural phenomena. Since each component is dependent upon the others, each stands as a way into the whole cultural meaning and significance present in the relationship. They act as refined perspectives from which the others can be watched. By focusing on one feature, it is possible to use it as a window through which the other features can be observed. The text, held constant or privileged to use the modern term, can lead the analyst back to its creator or forward to its audience. Equally well, it can speak to its historical times, and depending on whether it is oral or written or filmed, to the available methods for transmission that exist for its presentation to the world. Critical methodology, the way one examines a cultural phenomenon, and critical theory, the justifications for such examinations, therefore, are simply ways of perceiving through one feature to the meaning of the whole event. Not by any means, however, does this mean that either theory or method are themselves simple ideas or simple procedures. What it means is that despite their complexity both remain ways of seeing and interpreting.

The best starting point in the model for describing the various ways of studying popular culture is the text. Texts are easily recognizable. They seem somehow to have substance, to be real, tangible objects that can be held and touched. People can hold a book, see a movie, drive a car, or listen to a song. Seldom, however, can they have as direct a contact with the people who produce such products or who create them. Moreover, texts are usually the first classroom objects that students are asked to criticize. They hold that book in their hands, or are shown that film, or, even, take that car apart, all in order to explain how it is put together and what makes it work. In terms of the model and popular culture studies, however, the idea of a text refers to more than just the most obvious associations. Text here defines any self-contained product presented by a creator to an audience. It can be the traditional book, but it could also be a car, or a television show, or an actor's performance, or a comic's routine. A text is anything that is presented as a manufactured whole. It can be as simple as the words on a page or as complex as the performance of a play.

Not surprisingly, texts are the component around which the most well-developed body of method and technique have developed. Like ordinary people, scholars, too, have recognized the high visibility of the self-contained object, and they have responded with a number of different means for discovering what such objects are attempting to communicate. The simplest of these approaches, known as the *rhetorical,* is concerned with analyzing the basic components of the surface of a text. It is based on two assumptions. The first states that the text is intended to do something. It does not just exist; it has a definite purpose. The second is that that purpose can be discovered through a careful analysis of the relationships out of which the immediate presence of the text is constructed. Whatever the text is designed to do, it asserts, can be found in the words, the characters, their relationships, the plot, the style, the very techniques out of which the work is made. Once these assumptions are accepted, however, rhetorical analysis divides into two very different forms, New Critical and dramaturgical.

New Critical approaches to the text argue that the self-contained quality of the text is so powerful that such objects can be said to exist apart from the world and from their creators. Texts, for the New Critics, stand alone. Arguing that the author's intentions are unknowable and the audience's perceptions untrustworthy, they treat the text as understandable on its own terms. The author's intentions are unknowable because they are not in the text. Regardless of what an author/creator thought he was doing, there is no final way of determining if that is in fact what he did. He might have thought he was doing one thing and, in the end, produced quite another. Moreover, an author/creator's own description of intention is unreliable because there is no guarantee that he is telling the truth. He might be telling the truth as he believed it, but whether it was the only truth or the whole truth can never be known. Similarly, audiences could not be trusted to respond in precisely the same ways or in reliable ways. Knowing what one liked was not a substitute in New Critical analysis for knowing the most correct meaning that could be drawn from the text. Hence, New Critics rely on what the text reveals about itself. Texts are seen as powerfully defined, very specific cultural events whose design contains some special meaning. There is a message in the surface construction of the text, in the immediately observable choices made to unify the text, in the ideas it portrays and the solutions it produces. How does the plot move its characters forward? What happens in these relationships? Do they represent human complexity or do they act out events and situations in simplified and conventional manner? All of these questions seek to draw from the text any and all of the potential messages that it can offer up. For the practice of New Critical analysis, the formal relations of these features of the text constitute a logically circumscribed artifact directed toward a goal which succeeds or fails solely in terms of its internal construction. The analyst's task becomes to trace that logic and to determine if it fulfills the intended meaning. What the text means, therefore, is in the end a function of the messages that can be read out of its surface. The more complexly and richly detailed that surface is, the more numerous will be its meanings.

Dramaturgical analysis differs from New Critical over the question of intentionality. Like the New Critics, those who approach a text dramaturgically begin with the text as a self-contained artifact containing a message to be deciphered. They see the text, however, as still within the world. For dramaturgical analysis the text is a performance. It is constructed by someone with a specific purpose in mind and it contains in its organization and use the evidence of that purpose. The object of inquiry, therefore, is to discover how this purpose is performed. What specific events and situations, symbols and activities, roles and words are used to create what kind of impression? What does that impression convey to those for whom it is presented? In dramaturgical analysis, the goal is to take apart the specific arrangement of information inside the text and measure how that particular information moves its audience from one point of view to another. Overall, then, it does not matter for dramaturgical analysis what the limits of the text are. Objects small enough to be held and whole cultural events can be treated in exactly the same fashion. The parts out of which they are made stand as strategies used by the creator to develop certain images.

Granted the impact of these strategic manipulations cannot be precisely predicted. As before, authorial intention can be frustrated. Despite careful construction, audiences can still see different things than they were intended to see. Nonetheless, the assumption of dramaturgical analysis is that the text is trying to do something to its audience and that that goal is discoverable and describable. A dramaturgical approach, therefore, is as interested in the effect of the text as it is in the message presented. Texts are evaluated not only on their order but on their success. The question is not only how is intention presented but also did it accomplish anything. Texts succeed when they motivate their audiences, and they succeed best when those motives bring the audience to new understandings. Another way of saying this is that texts promise and their value depends upon how and how well their promises are kept.

A second critical approach which takes the text as its subject is formalist analysis. Unlike the rhetorical approaches which evolved as almost natural responses to the visibility and availability of the text, formalism began as a particular methodological attempt to solve a specific textual problem. It resulted from the attempts by a group of Russian linguists and folklorists, particularly the latter, to discover if there were any precise limits to the objects they studied. Their problem was that the texts that interested them seemed to be extraordinarily diverse. Folktales, costumes, even spoken language can display a wide range of differences even when they are arguably the same text. One word can be spoken in a variety of ways; two tales can tell exactly the same story and yet have characters and locations that do not at all match. How then, they questioned, was it possible to form scientific opinions about the meaning and use of such objects when they appeared to show contradictory messages about themselves. Their answer was to search for some method of classification which was capable of accounting for the bewildering variety of individual examples which any one cultural form could create. The major initial success of this movement was the work of Vladimir Propp. Through an approach which he characterized as *morphological,* Propp was able to demonstrate that there existed a distinctive, specific, and regular set of features which underlay the construction of all folktales and which made stories as diverse as Snow White and Little Red Riding Hood fundamentally the same. In his *Morphology of the Folktale,* Propp argued that the analysis of the folktale could not proceed from the examination of their surface features. These were obviously too diverse for careful study. Instead he began by analyzing character, who did something, in terms of what that action did to advance the flow of the narrative. From this, he determined that these character-action relationships were of a limited number and, more importantly, followed a rigorous pattern of occurrence. Ultimately, he showed that folktales consisted of thirty-one functions, as he defined these relationships, following in only two distinct patterns.

Growing from Propp's work, modern formalist analysis takes as its task the discovery of the underlying fundamental pattern or patterns which give any particular text its particular form. For formalists, texts are understood as the surface reflections of a deeper set of rules for their production. These rules stand behind the actual texts and govern how they are to be manufactured. They act, therefore, as a formal scaffolding, holding the text together and allowing its audience to recognize that it is like other texts of the same type. Rules are discovered through the application of several fairly basic methodological steps. First, the formalist attempts to discover the component parts out of which the text is constructed. These abstract units of construction are then analyzed in order to determine if they follow any logical pattern and if that pattern is consistent for other texts sharing the same surface similarities. Finally, the formalist attempts to formulate a single consistent pattern of function and action which can account for all the real and potential text which might occur within a single form.

Accordingly, formalism can be said to be concerned primarily with the discovery and analysis of textual convention. Its central questions, therefore, are defined in terms of the essential organization of form and genre. What are the conventions, the component parts, of specific texts? What is it that makes detective stories alike, or westerns similar, or situation comedies the same? What are the relationships of these parts to each other? Does the appearance of a hard-boiled detective demand a specific kind of villain and make it impossible that any other kind should appear? Does one kind of hero push all other types off the page? Is there a logical and necessary order to the appearance of actions within an event and does that order determine the meaning any specific action can have? Can a threat to a hero's life be as real, with only twenty minutes left in an hour television drama, as one occurring in the first twenty minutes of the same show? In an even more obvious example, can the hero of a continuous series ever really be threatened? These questions, in turn, make it possible for the formalist to discover the true differences which make one cultural form or event different from any other. With this information, they argue, it is then possible to discover what is truly meaningful and what is simply the product of the formal rules for creation. In the end, therefore, the formalists assert that form determines both content and meaning. Component parts, the relationship of such parts, the wholistic ordering of those relationships, all these combine, argue the formalists, to produce single examples, the individual texts, that are spoken, or read, or worn. These in their turn open the door to meaning. Insofar as an individual creator follows the necessities of pattern, the text defines itself as within a known form. Insofar as that creator introduces special information and insight, the text acquires its specialness and its character.

The last form of textual analysis is *structuralism.* Like formalism, structural analysis is concerned with getting beyond the surface of the text to the basic organizing principles which make the text possible. Unlike formalism, however, these rules and patterns are not seen as abstractions from the text. For the structuralist, the formal meaning of the text grows from the actual surface of content. This difference in orientation is immediately evident in the manner in which structuralists approach the systematic nature of the text. Like the formalists, the structural analysts consider the text to be an organized whole whose meaning is greater than the sum of its parts. They, however, are more explicit in defining the nature of that wholeness. For the structuralists, texts are understood to function as languages. They are ordered in the way language is and they are best analyzed in the manner in which linguists analyze their languages. Thus, structuralists draw their assumptions and their procedures from linguistics.

In particular, they begin with the assumption that there is a fundamental difference between language and speech. The former, they argue, is what communities share in order to produce speech. It is the system of rules which permits individuals to speak and understand each other. Speech is what is produced from a knowledge of those rules. Speech, therefore, is an expression of personal freedom. It is what an individual speaker can produce, sometimes imperfectly, when the rules of language are brought into play. Language, however, extends beyond the acts of any individual. It is a social institution, a competence, shared by all the members of the community, which stands apart from individual action and intention. Moreover, this social competence means that language is not a random or free phenomenon. Language is coded. It makes its individual sense because the ideas communicated, if they are to be understood, have to be expressed in a form that the community recognizes and understands. Thus, if a speaker of English wishes to speak to a speaker of French, they either must both be able to speak the same language or they must be capable of developing between them a third language in which to speak their ideas. If they cannot discover such a means of encoding their ideas, then no matter how urgently they need to speak *to* each other they will only be able to talk *at* each other.

Within this linguistic model, meaning is produced through the interaction of two distinct relationships. The first is called syntagmatic. A syntagmatic relationship is one which exists between any linguistic element in a grammatical construction and those other elements immediately next to it. For example, "David" and "runs" can be placed next to each other in English and produce a conventional construction in a way that "David" and "tree" cannot. The first, thus, is a possible syntagmatic relationship while the second is not, and, obviously, the first means while the second does not. One element of meaning, therefore, is dependent upon the number and kinds of syntagmatic relationships which are possible and practical in a given language system. The second kind of relationship is called paradigmatic. A paradigmatic relationship is one which exists between those linguistic elements which can replace one another in syntagmatic relationships without destroying their sense. Thus, in the previous example, any noun could replace "David" and any verb could replace "runs" and the two elements would still be in a syntagmatic relationship. This would stay the case even if the two replacements made no ordinary sense. "Frog philosophizes" is not an ordinary English construction and, probably, would never occur in conversation, but it still conforms to the syntagmatic expectation of a noun-verb relationship. Accordingly, language is represented as a system of difference, of presence and absence, in which any single element, no matter how large or small, develops its identity in terms of what it is, of what it can replace or be replaced by, and by what it may or may not be placed next to.

For structural analysis, meaning in texts grows out of this system of association and replacement. Like language itself, the texts are built out of codes which are themselves the products of syntagmatic and paradigmatic relationships. These codes may be as simple as the rules and procedures by which sentences and paragraphs are produced or they may be as complex as the rules and procedures by which fashion, myth, or culture, itself, is produced and made meaningful. Within these codes, and, more importantly, from these codes, individual creators construct texts whose meaning is a function not only of what is present and given to the audience but also of what might be there and instead is absent. The text, therefore, speaks as a statement of social intentions. In its organization are the coded relationships, the interplay between the various parts that are present and those which might have served as appropriate substitutes: from these are constructed the basic, acceptable, cultural meanings of the text, the structures out of which the rules of social experience grow.

The undertaking of a structuralist analysis, therefore, follows certain predictable steps. Initially, structural study begins with the distinctive features out of which a text or a collection of similar texts are constructed. Once these patterns are established, then the analyst traces the syntagmatic relationships which exist between the distinctive features, and these in their turn make it possible to isolate the possible alternatives which might have been constructed. More specifically, the analyst begins by attempting to discover a pattern which explains how the text has its particular effect on its audience. What is the outline of relations between characters in a story or set of stories? How do 'A' and 'B' interact, and how does their relationship affect the flow of the narrative? With this pattern, the analyst then examines the process by which it is used to produce critical meanings. How, in the immediate contents of the text, is this pattern articulated and what does this articulation speak to social codes by which the community forms its ideas about itself and the world? Finally, the analyst attempts to discover the play of contrasts against which these codes and conventions can be read. What else might have occurred without making nonsense of the whole, and what does the presence of one choice and the absence of another say about the immediate text and the culture which produced it? Once this is completed, it is possible to describe the internal relationships which permit the text to say something significant to those communities that know and preserve them.

Another perspective from which the popular culture relationship can be studied is that of the author. In the same way that the idea of the text defined something more than the limited notion of single, constrained object, the idea of the author represents more than the commonsense perception of a single individual who creates a single event from whole cloth. In popular culture, author covers the possibility of a single individual working alone but it also describes a whole other range of different behaviors. In fact, in popular culture single authorship is not the norm. Most popular cultural forms are produced in several stages, and at each stage of the process several individuals may be directly affecting the creative structure. Movies are the perfect example. They begin with a script which may have been produced by a single author and then rewritten by several more; they then become the concern of a director and entire production crew any one of which might affect how the words are transformed into images and sounds, and they then still remain incomplete until they are realized in an actor's performances. Even then movies remain incomplete until they are cut and edited into the product that audiences see when they go to their local theater. Still, despite this potential complexity, examining the popular cultural relationship from the perspective of the author offers some interesting and productive information.

Methodologically, authorial analysis is *biographical.* Its main concern is to recover from the text or event at hand the intentions of the creator. These intentions are seen as the key to the text's meaning and as a reflection of the creator's internal state at the time of creation. Author-oriented criticism, therefore, assumes a direct relationship between what an author desires and what an author produces. The final text is what its creator intended it to be. It is a closed book that the audience can only receive and respond to. In this sense, there is the further assumption that the author is always more powerful than the reader. Not only do readers receive, they fail at their task if they are incapable of discovering and interpreting what the author wants them to know. Thus, authorial criticism is always a process of puzzle solving. The text has been given a right order and only that order "correctly" explains the content of the work.

Within these critical assumptions, there are two perspectives from which the intentions of the author can be considered. The first concentrates on the external features of the author's life and interests and questions the relationship of these experiences to the created work. What does an author know? What unique or particular events have formed his point of view? Are there social, political, cultural or philosophical problems that have interested a particular creator or have been central to the world in which a creator lived and worked? How have any or all of these entered into the creative process, and how have they molded or altered the final work? In essence, the questions grow from the belief that creativity cannot feed on anything but what an author knows, believes, or experiences. It is this reservoir that supplies the basic building blocks from which any and every creation must be formed. Hence, the contents of the work, no matter how they are finally transformed, begin as an outgrowth of the known world of the creator. The task of the analyst is thus one of interpretation and of the validation of interpretation. The critic is faced with the responsibility of discovering what it is that the creator wants to stand as the message of the work and then of discovering how that message is related to the life experiences of the individual who produced it.

The second biographical approach focuses on the internal, or *psychological,* features of authorial intention. Psychological criticism is concerned with the relationship between conscious intent and unconscious desire. The psychological critic argues that the text is more than just a composite of the biographical "facts" of its creator's life. These, of course, are fundamental. But they are only half of experience. Equally important, for psychological criticism, are the subjective feelings and attitudes which shape how a creative individual responds to the facts of the world. These mold the personality of the individual, they argue, and thus stand as a screen between the world and any individual's experience of the world. Moreover, the psychological critic argues that these patterns of subjective response and reaction between the self and the world are formed in the very first processes of human life. They begin in infancy as each human being learns to cope with reality through interacting with the members of their immediate family. Thus, psychological criticism asserts that these early life experiences, many of which occur before an individual is even aware of the social rules for defining what experience is, will act to determine how a creative individual will perceive the world. Accordingly, the text for the psychological critic is a projective device. In it, the creator has constructed from the traditional, public symbols of his society an object which is neither wholly objective nor wholly subjective. Instead, it is a creative sharing of his own private interpretation of the way the world is ordered and the public expectation of the way the world is and ought to be. Thus, the final product displays information which is simultaneously more personal than intended and more universal than expected. It is more personal because the creator is largely unaware, as is any individual, of the patterns of relationship which have produced his or her individual self, and hence unaware of the particular patterns which have gone into organizing the facts of life presented in their work. It is more universal because, at an abstract level, every individual in a community has had to undergo a similar process of socialization to the world if they are to be counted as appropriate members of the group. Thus, in finding an audience, the text will touch in some way the unconscious organization by which each individual accounts himself or herself as different from others.

The ability to say something about what a creator "really meant" is very appealing, but it is also what makes the psychological approach the most difficult form of critical analysis. Those who undertake such analyses must not only know the necessary biographical facts of a creator's life and the necessary historical facts of a creator's times which make sense of that biography, but they must also be working with a psychology of the human mind that provides some insight into how a functioning personality is formed and maintained in the world. The great danger, therefore, is that a failure in any one of these areas will make the critic's conclusions, at best, incorrect, and, at worst, ridiculous and dangerous. Psychological criticism should be approached with caution, therefore. It can be done. It does provide important insight. But it demands the highest concentration to make it work properly.

The third facet of the model which can be taken as a perspective for analyzing the popular cultural relationship is that of the audience. In one sense, audience-oriented criticism reverses the major assumptions of authorial analysis. Critical studies that concentrate on the audience begin with the assumption that the created expression is somehow incomplete until it is received and interpreted by someone. They argue that the audience completes the text by making it mean. Before an object or event has been received, they believe, it has nothing but the potential to reach and affect. After it has been received, it has only the effects that its audience creates for it. Hence, audience-based criticism starts by declaring the freedom of those who receive a text to make of it what they will. The audience is, thus, seen as the final arbitrator of taste. It decides what the contents of an object or experience explain, and it determines if these messages mean anything to the world at large. In their most extreme, audience approaches argue that there can be no wrong interpretation of any text since each individual experience is a valid one for the person who is having it. By and large, however, audience-oriented criticism is not naive or simplistic. Rather, it falls into two distinct categories depending on whether or not the concern is with the individual receiver of a text or with the overall effect of a text on its widest audience.

Critics concerned with how the individual responds to the text are interested basically in the discovery of the conditions under which readers create meaning. Texts, they argue, are multiple realities. They are full of information. One reading may introduce an individual to one particular theme or interest, and a second reading might call attention to a wholly different perspective within the work. One viewing may do even more, since, of course, as the number of senses brought into the process are increased, the amount of information which has to be processed increases rapidly and geometrically. Thus, such critics assert that the relationship between creator and audience is open-ended, and itself creative. Many different interpretations exist, accordingly, because no single act of interpretation can ever hope to exhaust all that the text has to say. Given this, individual-oriented critics ask what are the constraints which control the nature of the reception process. These they define in four different ways.

First, it may be that the text cannot say all it might because the author is not aware of all that has been included or of all the ways in which his or her intentions might misdirect the audience. Second, in creating the work, the creator might have intentionally or accidentally misinterpreted a source. Perhaps, a source is too painful or too obvious, and, thus, has to be disguised or distorted in order that the author's originality can shine through. Third, it may be that the text is so controlled by convention that it is incapable of allowing the audience any freedom in its interpretation. Perhaps it is so commonplace that it does not leave any room for thinking and reduces its audience to the role of passive observers. Finally, it may be that the audience is itself blind to the potentials of the text. They may through their culture be incapable of perceiving the differences in a text as anything but aberrations. Thus, the text that attempts to go beyond the ordinary boundaries of social expectation is seen as too radical, or too strange, or too repugnant to qualify as something of value. In the last analysis, therefore, the critic's task is to sort between these various possibilities until one or several succeed in opening the text to interpretation. This is aided, of course, by the recognition that the critical process is also subject to the same constraints as the "reading" process, and, hence open to the same forms of interplay.

The approach to the broadly defined audience operates within the same methodological universe as do those which are concerned with individual response. Here, however, the focus is shifted from the qualitative to the quantitative impact of the work. How widely is the work received? Are there any differences in the types and kinds of receptions? What constraints are involved in the reception? The assumption is, thus, that there is a direct relationship between the distribution of a creative work and the effect it has on a community. The methodological task becomes, therefore, to create effective techniques which can examine this problem of distribution. Surveys of audience awareness or of consumption, how many know of or have used the product, are the central procedures through which such information is gathered. Beyond this, those interested in the broad audience response are also concerned with the impact of the various ways of distributing information on the audience's ability to see and value products. What are the relationships between the appeal of a work or object and the various methods in which it can be presented to the public? Does the multidimensional presentation of an image or message increase or decrease the value of an event? Here, accordingly, the concern is broadened to include the problem of availability and its effects on the amount and kind of information an audience has when it acts to interpret a message. Can a message be experienced in more than one way and do these various experiences reinforce or contradict each other? The broadly focused audience perspective, then, seeks to locate the effects of a product within the network of its presentation. Those who know it constitute the body of people who can be affected by it. Thus, the meaning of the work can only be known and measured in terms of the patterned reception it did or did not receive from the public world into which it was launched and within which it has existed.

Though these last questions derive from a concern with the audience's perspective, they reflect equally well another of the perspectives from which the popular cultural relationship can be studied, that of *media.* Media studies focus on the relationship between the form of a message and its impact. They argue that there is a direct relationship between the formal method in which information is communicated and the response it brings forth from its audience. For media studies, print, television, radio, oral speech, dance, and the like constitute methods of encoding and transmitting information. They represent distinct and wholly individual ways in which the same message can be presented. Accordingly, media specialists are concerned with the problem of choice. Since the different media present and represent information in different ways, the choice of one way of transmitting an idea or image over another determines in the most basic manner how the message can be perceived. Knowing, therefore, what choices were made, why they were made, and what effects they had on the nature, quality, and distribution of the message allows media analysts to describe not only what was experienced by the audience but also how that particular experience was actually created.

Media analysis approaches these problems from the perspectives of capacity and constraint. Capacity, at its most technical level, refers to the absolute quantity of information a particular channel can carry. It is the analysis of what a communication relationship, for example a speaker and a hearer, can tolerate before the messages dissolve into nonsense. Thus, though the human voice can speak much faster than 150 words per minute, the human ear can only absorb sound at or near that rate. If a speaker wants to be understood, therefore, he or she should not exceed that rate. In popular culture studies, capacity is treated less technically. Analysts begin with the technical information on how much any sensory system of the human mind can deal with and, using that as a guide, question the particular cultural constraints which expand or limit a particular channel of mass communication. Cable television is a particularly good example of a form upon which such an analysis is conducted. The ability of television to transmit information is nearly limitless. It can use the full range of verbal and visual codes to entertain an audience, to persuade them to buy a product, to believe an idea, or to take a "fact" for granted. Moreover, though it is a public medium, television creates a private relationship between creator and audience. Millions may be watching at any one time but most do so in their own homes, alone or with family. Cable television expands even this enormous capacity. Through its use of satellite transmissions and its vast expansion of the number of individual channels, it offers the possibility of transmitting anything that can be created and for which an audience exists. Some cable systems, in fact, already transmit everything imaginable. Still, most communities are much less liberal in what they will allow their cable systems to transmit. They establish boards of review and constantly monitor what is being presented. Thus, an unlimited capacity to communicate is brought under the control of community standards, and these determine the kind and quality of events which can be viewed.

This focus on capacity can be even more refined. Instead of examining a medium in revolution, it can be used to draw attention to the cultural constraints which affect the transmission of single ideas or themes. Thus, media analysis can focus on the transmission of violence or sex through a single medium, examining the kinds which can be transmitted, the contexts in which it can appear, the results it produces in the audience. Using television, again, media analysts have examined the violence in children's programming or sex in soap operas, or the stereotypic characterizations of women and minorities in comedies. In these cases, the analyst begins by establishing the criteria which frame the form to be constructed. What kinds of characters or relations are used to create particular messages? How do the limits of time organize what can be presented? If a story has to be ready for the 6 o'clock news, it might have to be reduced to its bare essentials, while if it is for the next day's newspaper, it might contain all sorts of extra detail. Within these criteria, the analyst next attempts to determine how the particular ideas or images are formulated against the background of the method in which they are to be presented. How, they ask, for example, does the use of one ethnic type as villains affect the public's perception of that group, or conversely, how does the continued use of another type as heroic characters affect that group's image? The key in each case is a concentration on the conditions under which the idea or image is experienced. How is what is given made meaningful by the manner in which it is given?

The analysis of the cultural capacity of particular media can even be further refined through a focus not on what is intentionally given, but rather on what is unconsciously or unintentionally presented. Here what is questioned is the relationship between the ability of certain mass communication techniques to overwhelm the audience with information and the audience's selective acceptance of that information. Thus, what is examined is, for example, the organization of messages within an advertisement and the impact it has. Where is the announcement of the hazardous effects of smoking in relation to all the other "facts" in the advertisement? Alternatively, how does the display of information within a news broadcast affect the audience's perception of the quality of life within its community? Do people see the world as violent or safe because the order of stories emphasizes "bad" news over "good"? Overall, then, media analysis discusses the convergence between the pattern of input, what is put into the text, and the pattern of output, what is taken out by the audience. Its subject, accordingly, is human linkage. It seeks to explain the ties that bind people together, the conditions under which messages can be exchanged, in order to answer how those ties make people into what they are.

The final perspective from which the popular culture relationship can be examined is that of *context*. The goal of contextual analysis is to locate the text in some place. It assumes that objects, events, and even ideas cannot exist in isolation from the constraints of the real world. They happen in time and space, that is what makes them real, that is how people know they exist, that is the only way they can be reacted to by an audience. The environment, therefore, provides the boundaries in which experiences quite literally happen. Accordingly, the problem for contextual analysis is twofold. First, it is necessary to determine the limits of the event. What, to use Erving Goffman's term, are the *frames* of experience? Where do objects or events begin and end? For example, defining the limits of a football game would seem a simple proposition. Football is what happens on the field between the opposing teams. This behavior is monitored by the referees and controlled by the rules of the game. Finally, it is limited by the size of the field, 100 yards by 50 yards, and the length of time the game can be played, four quarters of 15 minutes each. This context of football, however, does not take into consideration what happens on the sidelines, the place of coaching, or any of the other immediate activities which can be a part of the "game." Neither does it consider the relationship between what happens on the field and what goes on in the stands among the fans whose cheering or booing might directly affect the play of the game.

Even when the frames are well-defined, contextual analysis is still faced with determining the relationships between the individual boundaries and with describing their effects on each other. To continue the same example, imagine that the context of the football game is drawn to include everything that happens inside the stadium from the moment the game begins until the moment it ends and that the boundaries between each individual frame, playing field, sidelines, grandstands, behind the stands, are precisely delineated. The question still remains as to how each individually bounded event connects to the others. Are the players responding to the activities of the fans in the stands when they accomplish something unexpected, or do they motivate their own behaviors? What are the lines of influence and responsibility? How is the power to control or command distributed? Each of these questions, then, seeks to expand on the nesting of context within context to inquire into the location of meaning.

In terms of its practice, contextual analysis operates at three distinct levels. The first is concerned with the immediate *frame* of an object or event. A story, as an example, does not just come out of the blue. Usually, someone wants to tell it, someone is there to listen, there is a reason for its telling, and it happens in some particular place at some particular time. The immediate level of contextual analysis is concerned with these last phenomena. Are the contexts of stories individualized? Can, for example, the same kind of joke be told at a party as could be told in a church? How do the different contexts of experience, classrooms, hallways, bars, barbershops, offices, expand or contract the abilities of individuals to think certain ways, to say certain things, or to feel different emotions? Can such places contain the same events and acts, and can those experiences be interpreted in the same way?

The second level of contextual analysis is *cultural.* At this level, the concern shifts from the experience as it is actually lived, from a participation in the event, to the social community which makes the event possible. Culture is concerned with group. It is generally defined as the knowledge an individual needs to be a functioning member of a specific enclave. It takes as its subject the conditions under which group membership is possible. What does being Irish, or Polish, or German mean? How does membership in such a community (or any other type of social community that might be defined) affect individual response to an idea, object, or event? How does one group's understanding of its own identity affect its ability to evaluate another group? In popular cultural studies, cultural analysis is particularly important because so much of the popular nature of the materials is constructed out of the conventional images and ideas that make up American society. Thus, often, the texts of popular culture deal in the stereotypes one community has of itself and of the other communities in its world. These, in turn, evoke expected responses such as the beliefs that the "others" are really like their presentations in popular culture, that the media misrepresents the real identities of the communities it draws its images from, but they also serve to raise questions about how culture itself molds and operates through the lives of individuals. Thus, cultural analysis of popular culture permits the examination of how the various structures of identification that individuals use to define themselves as alike and different from the others around them create meaning out of the artifacts of the social world.

The final level of contextual analysis is the *historical.* Historical analysis is concerned with the problems of origin and change. Its goal is to discover where something came from, how it got to be the way it is, and what it went through to get that way. Historical analysis seeks to understand the social, political, and intellectual constraints that permit one kind of object to arise and not another. What is it about the times of an event that make the choice of one cultural form appropriate? For example, what is the relationship between the rise of a particular genre of popular literature such as science fiction or western novels and the world in which they are created? Can they only exist in a world of a certain type and experience or can they transcend their context and exist under any conditions? Certainly, science fiction has survived for a hundred years as a popular form, but an enormous amount of such fiction is hopelessly outdated and unread. Did these works by limiting themselves to the science of their times, and thus doing what they needed to do in order to not be seen as nonsense, also make it impossible for them to be seen as sensible at any other time? As well, historical analysis seeks to map out the progress of such change through time. The western novel, for example, began at a time when the presence of the American Indian was not perceived as a threat to the white settling of the New World. It also arose at a time when those Native Americans were seen by some Romantic thinkers as Noble Savages somehow apart from the destructive influences of civilization. Indian characters were varied in their presentations, therefore, with a surprising number actually being shown as more honest and moral than their white counterparts. As the availability of land became a question and the Indian presence an impediment to its occupation, Indian characters were increasingly portrayed as vicious savages incapable of any human virtues, suitable only to be exterminated. This image continued well into the twentieth century, long after the settlement of America was complete, and only shifted in the last decades under pressure from Indian activists rightfully offended with their unfair, biased presentation in the media. Thus, a historical analysis of this process would seek to discover the relationship between these "facts" and the different times they represented.

Accordingly, contextual analysis, at whatever level it is practiced, argues that the social surroundings of an activity influences the perceptions of the people within its boundaries. Within the walls, literal, cultural and historical, of such social organizations, it attempts to explain how events are defined and how such definitions of situation create meaning for the moment, for the community, and for the times. And, in this, it asserts that the sense of identity and community shared by the members of a social group arises not only from what the members know and do but also from the social situation that holds such knowledge and action together.

Knowing the kinds of questions to ask and the reasons why they are important is only the first step in research. It is also necessary to know what else has been written on the same subject. Research, after all, is not just solving an interesting problem. That is a legitimate beginning, but it is of little use if the problem has been solved already, or if the new solution fails to say all that it could because it does not take into account the ideas and discoveries of previous scholars. Accordingly, the starting point of research, of studying popular culture in this case, is to examine the basic bibliography of the topic that has been chosen. This material can be found in the individual bibliographies at the end of each of the chapters in this volume. These contain the major articles and books on each particular topic and provide the necessary information about the kinds of studies that have been done. By examining them and using their perspective it is possible to see concrete examples of how individual scholars have approached a popular cultural form and attempted to say something significant about it.

The bibliographic essay which follows attempts to do much the same for the practice of critical analysis with some differences. It, too, is designed to provide the basic introductory texts, collections of essays, and articles for each approach that has been described, but it does not attempt or pretend to be comprehensive. There are an enormous number of works which use each of the methods described, and any number of these could be included in this survey. Long lists of theoretical and methodological discussions, however, can sometimes be overwhelming to the non-specialist, as they often are for the specialist. Accordingly, rather than overpower with lists of texts for each approach, this bibliographic survey contains only a selection of each critical practice. The individual choices, therefore, do not tell the whole story on any one method of analysis. They are intended to open the doors to each method in the simplest and easiest manner, but more reading will be required if any particular method is to be used. The choices, then, are mini-introductions. Each section is designed to point up what each critical practice hopes to accomplish, to point out where other relevant information can be found, and, finally, to serve as model of how a successful use of a particular method might look when it is finished.

Because it is the oldest method discussed, New Criticism has the broadest and most established bibliography. Still, for the beginning student, the best starting point is the essays and arguments which initiated the approach. Several of these can be found in William K. Wimsatt, Jr., and Monroe C. Beardsley, *The Verbal Icon: Studies in the Meaning of Poetry* (Lexington: University of Kentucky Press, 1953). As well, an insight into the workings out of the approach can be found in Cleanth Brooks, *A Shaping Joy: Studies in the Writer's Craft* (London: Methuen & Co. Ltd., 1971) and Elder Olson, *Tragedy and the Theory of Drama* (Detroit: Wayne State University Press, 1961). Finally, a non-literary approach that uses an approach similar to that of the above works can be found in E. H. Gombrich, *Art and Illusion* (Princeton, N.J.: Princeton University Press, 1961).

The most accessible examples of dramaturgical analysis can be found in the writings of its founder, Kenneth Burke, of Hugh D. Duncan, and of the sociologist Erving Goffman. Burke's output has been wide and varied, and nearly any of his works provide an interesting introduction to this approach. One of his best, however, is the collection of essays, *The Philosophy of Literary Form: Studies in Symbolic Action* (Baton Rouge: Louisiana State University Press, 1941). Duncan's use of the dramaturgical approach can be found in his *Communication and Social Order* (London and New York: Oxford University Press, 1968). Like Burke, Erving Goffman has produced an expansive body of work. Two of his works that exemplify his use of dramaturgical concepts are *The Presentation of Self in Everyday Life* (Garden City, N.Y.: Doubleday, 1959) and *Frame Analysis* (New York: Harper and Row, 1974).

Though it can, at times, be complex, the best starting point for understanding formalist analysis is Vladimir Propp's *Morphology of the Folktale* (Austin and London: University of Texas Press, 1968). This work began the rise of formalist technique and still demonstrates how best it can be applied. A more concise explanation of the method can be found in Alan Dundes, "From Etic to Emic Units in the Structural Study of Folktales," *Journal of*

American Folklore 75:95-105. As well, Dundes' "On Game Morphology: A Study of the Structure of Non-Verbal Folklore," *New York Folklore Quarterly* 20:165-74, offers an interesting use of the approach with non-narrative materials. Lastly, Tzvetan Todorov's *The Fantastic: A Structural Approach to a Literary Genre,* tr. Richard Howard (London and Cleveland: Case Western University Press, 1973), provides an informative example of the manner in which the method can be further developed and the kinds of new insights that such developments can provide.

Like formalist analysis, structuralism has an identifiable beginning in the work of a single individual, the French anthropologist Claude Levi-Strauss. His works, *Structural Anthropology* (New York: Basic Books, 1963), and *The Savage Mind* (Chicago: University of Chicago Press, 1966), are the best statements of his very complex approach. However, the beginning student is better off starting with less formidable introductions. Two collections of essays and interpretations which provide such entry are Michael Lane, ed., *Structuralism: A Reader* (London: Jonathan Cape, 1970), especially Lane's introduction, pp. 11-43; and Ino Rossi, ed., *The Unconscious in Culture: The Structuralism of Claude Levi-Strauss in Perspective* (New York: E. P. Dutton & Co., 1974). Finally, Roland Barthes, *Mythologies* (Paris: Editions du Seuil, 1957), stands as perhaps the most witty and literate introduction to the practice of structural analysis.

The practice of biographical criticism depends upon exactly what facts are or can be known about the individual under analysis. Its starting point, therefore, has to be a gathering of all the basic facts of the individual's life and work. Only then can the work of relating the two begin in earnest. This means, however, that each example of such analysis is as unique as the life it attempts to describe. Some readable and potentially useful examples are F. O. Matthiessen's *American Renaissance; Art and Expression in the Age of Emerson and Whitman* (London and New York: Oxford University Press, 1941), and Martha Saxton, *Louisa May: A Modern Biography of Louisa May Alcott* (Boston: Little Brown & Co., 1977). Another useful text which is not focused on a single biography, but which mixes history, biography and social analysis is Raymond Williams' *The Country and The City* (London and New York: Oxford University Press, 1973).

As stated earlier in this essay, psychological criticism is the most difficult of all the methods described and must be undertaken with the greatest restraint. For those interested in attempting this approach, the best starting point is a collection of essays edited by Hendrik M. Ruitenbeek titled *Psychoanalysis and Literature* (New York: E. P. Dutton & Co., 1964). These offer an intelligent introduction to the terminology of psychological criticism as well as a variety of well-documented, well-written analyses of the relationship between the individual mind of a creator and its creative products. Another excellent collection of psychoanalytically oriented essays is *The Practice of Psychoanalytic Criticism* (Detroit: Wayne State University

Press, 1976), edited by Leonard Tennenhouse. Two useful works which employ psychoanalytic methodology and which are also excellent as introductions to how extended analysis can be carried out are Norman N. Holland's *The Dynamics of Literary Response* (London and New York: Oxford University Press, 1968), and Martin Grotjahn's *Beyond Laughter* (New York: McGraw-Hill, 1958).

Audience-oriented critical approaches which focus on the individual's particular response to the text in question come in a wide variety and with extreme differences in difficulty. Students interested in this approach, therefore, should take their time and move slowly through this potentially complicated methodological terrain. A good starting point is Wolfgang Iser's essay, "The Reading Process: A Phenomenological Process," *New Literary History,* Vol. 3, No. 2, 278-99. Another potential beginning can be found in Maurice Merleau-Ponty's essay "Cezanne's Doubt," found in his collection of essays *Sense and Non-Sense,* tr. Hubert L. Dreyfus and Patricia Allen Dreyfus (Evanston, Ill.: Northwestern University Press, 1964), pp. 9-24. Other useful works which expand on these two are Iser's *The Art of Reading* (Baltimore: Johns Hopkins University Press, 1966) and *The Implied Reader* (Baltimore: Johns Hopkins University Press, 1972) and Jonathan Culler's *Structuralist Poetics* (London: Routledge & Kegan Paul, 1975). Sociological approaches to the audience's involvement in the creation of meaning, often grouped under the names of cognitive anthropology and ethnomethodology, can be found in Alfred Schutz, *The Phenomenology of the Social World* (London: Heinemann, 1974), and in Harold Garfinkel, *Studies in Ethnomethodology* (Englewood Cliffs, N.J.: Prentice-Hall, 1967). An excellent translation of their ideas into practical techniques can be found in John Lofland's *Analyzing Social Situations* (Belmont, Calif.: Wadsworth Publishing Company, 1971).

Approaches which utilize the broadly conceived audience model can be found in Russel B. Nye, *The Unembarrassed Muse* (New York: Dial Press, 1970). This work is a classic in popular culture studies and contains many useful surveys of how popular tastes have been transformed in different historical contexts. Other useful works which cover this same ground are James D. Hart's *The Popular Book: A History of America's Literary Taste* (Berkeley: University of California Press, 1950), and Luther Mott's *Golden Multitudes* (New York: Macmillan, 1947). Non-literary uses of the approach can be found in Gerald Mast, *A Short History of the Movies* (New York: Pegasus, 1971) and Arthur Knight, *The Liveliest Art* (New York: New American Library, 1959).

A good, if quirky, introduction to media studies can be found in Marshall McLuhan's *Understanding Media* (New York: McGraw-Hill, 1964). In a similar vein, Russell Lynes' *The Tastemakers* (New York: Harper & Row, 1971), offers insight into the relationship between the manner in which messages are communicated and their effects. Also extremely useful in understanding the area of media analysis are Alfred G. Smith, ed., *Communication and Culture* (New York: Holt, Rinehart & Winston, 1966); Joseph T. Klapper, *The Effects of Mass Communication* (New York: Free Press, 1960); and Frank E. X. Dance, ed., *Human Communication Theory* (New York: Holt, Rinehart & Winston, 1973). Though not directly concerned with the media themselves, two works by Raymond Williams, *Culture and Society: 1780-1950* (New York: Columbia University Press, 1958), and *The Long Revolution* (London: Chatto and Windus, 1960), provide marvelous insight into how changes in technology and the creations of new communicative media act to transform both popular taste and the structure of society itself.

There are a number of excellent works which offer an introduction to the practice of contextual analysis. A good place to acquire an overall picture of the approach is Peter L. Berger and Thomas Luckmann, *The Social Construction of Reality: A Treatise in the Sociology of Knowledge* (New York: Doubleday, 1967). Dell Hymes has written a series of articles which explore the whys and hows of the ethnography of context. Among the best are Dell Hymes, "Introduction Toward Ethnographies of Communication," in John J. Gumperz and Dell Hymes, eds., *The Ethnography of Communication* (*American Anthropologist,* 1964: 1-34); Dell Hymes, "The Ethnography of Speaking," in T. Gladwin and William C. Sturtevant, eds., *Anthropology and Human Behavior* (Washington, D.C., 1963); and Dell Hymes, "Models of the Interaction of Language and Social Setting," *Journal of Social Issues,* 33: 8-28. Examples of the method in action can be found in Dan Ben-Amos and Kenneth S. Goldstein, eds., *Folklore: Performance and Communication* (The Hague: Mouton, 1975), and Michael J. Bell "Social Control/Social Order/Social Art," *Sub-Stance,* 22:49-65.

Analyses which focus on the cultural context of a particular subject matter, since they constitute the domain of the discipline of anthropology, are almost so numerous as to be overwhelming. Two extremely helpful introductions which make this material manageable are Edmund Leach, *Culture and Communication: The Logic by Which Symbols Are Connected: An Introduction to the Use of Structural Analysis in Social Anthropology* (New York and Cambridge: Cambridge University Press, 1976); and James P. Spradley, ed., *Culture and Cognition: Rules, Maps and Plans* (San Francisco: Chandler Publishing Co., 1972). Also useful for understanding the reach of this type of analysis is the work of Roger D. Abrahams. His *Deep Down in the Jungle: Negro Narrative Folklore from the Streets of Philadelphia* (Chicago: Aldine Publishing Co., 1970) and *Positively Black* (Englewood Cliffs, N.J.: Prentice-Hall, 1970), are two superb examples of how specific cultural materials are used to construct the major social institutions of a community.

A good, solid example of historical analysis with a specific popular culture orientation is Norman Cantor and Michael Wertham, eds., *The History of Popular Culture* (New York: Macmillan, 1968). Equally useful is Russel

B. Nye's *The Unembarrassed Muse* (New York: Dial Press, 1970), especially for its annotated bibliography. Beyond these, examples of historical analysis are as varied as the histories that can be described. Accordingly, the best approach to historical analysis is to find topics that are interesting and to examine the different ways in which individual historians have handled the same material. Two works which offer excellent exemplifications of what can be accomplished through the use of the historical approach are Lawrence W. Levine, *Black Culture and Black Consciousness: Afro-American Folk Thought from Slavery to Freedom* (New York: Oxford University Press, 1977), and Anthony F. C. Wallace, *Rockdale: The Growth of an American Village in the Early Industrial Revolution* (New York: Alfred A. Knopf, Inc., 1978).

A final word. It may seem at this point that research in popular culture, or in anything for that matter, is overly concerned with the matter of method. That is not the case. Method is important. It determines the final quality of the work in question. It permits scholars to validate their work, to say to one another: this is the manner in which I gathered my data; these are the procedures I used to discover my facts; and these are the conclusions I have drawn. But it is not why scholars ask questions, nor is it why it is important to know how something can be studied. Knowing about methodology is important because that knowledge makes it possible for anyone, beginning student, interested amateur, or professional scholar, to make a genuine contribution to the advancement of knowledge. That may sound farfetched and even corny, but truly it is not. In fact, it is particularly true in the field of popular culture studies. The idea of a discipline of popular culture is relatively new and the number of active scholars, though growing, is not that large. Students, at all levels, therefore, have the opportunity of participating in making the discipline into what it can become. But this can only happen if these beginning contributions try to follow the rules of scholarship, try to say what they have to say in some coherent and intelligible way, and, above all else, try to operate within the consistent universe that a method provides. Scholarship works because it tries to inform its reader, and, in the process, to see aspects of the world that were hidden from view. Method helps because it insures that the writer and the audience understand the rules for seeing what is intended. In the end, however, both depend for their success upon the person doing the research. The choice, therefore, to do research cannot be only a choice of an interesting way to proceed. The researcher also has to want to think, to reflect, and to say something about something that has not been said or seen in the same way. Research, then, is not only the desire to discover. It is also an insistence on showing what has been found in order that others may know.

Index

The Contributors

ROBERT S. ALLEY is professor of humanities and director of American studies at the University of Richmond in Virginia.

ROY M. ANKER chairs the department of language and literature at Northwestern College, Orange City, Iowa.

ROBERT A. ARMOUR is professor of English and film at Virginia Commonwealth University in Richmond.

MICHAEL J. BELL is associate professor of folklore and English at Wayne State University in Detroit.

WILLIAM C. BENNETT is production coordinator for the Smithsonian Collection of Recordings at the Smithsonian Institution in Washington, D.C.

JAMES J. BEST is associate professor of political science at Kent State University in Ohio.

BILL BLACKBEARD is director of the San Francisco Academy of Comic Art in California.

MARK W. BOOTH is assistant professor of English at Virginia Commonwealth University in Richmond.

JOHN BRYANT is assistant professor of English at Pennsylvania State University, Shenango Valley Campus, Sharon, Pennsylvania.

CHARLES CAMP is Maryland state folklorist and adjunct professor of folklore at the University of Maryland and the American University.

LORETTA CARRILLO is assistant professor of English at Clemson University in South Carolina.

EARLE J. COLEMAN is associate professor of philosophy and religious studies at Virginia Commonwealth University in Richmond.

ROBERT K. DODGE is associate professor of English at the University of Nevada in Las Vegas.

MAURICE DUKE is professor of English and coordinator of creative writing at Virginia Commonwealth University in Richmond.

RICHARD W. ETULAIN is professor of history at the University of New Mexico in Albuquerque.

KATHERINE FISHBURN is assistant professor of English at Michigan State University in East Lansing.

ROBERT GALBREATH is coordinator of the honors program at the University of Wisconsin in Milwaukee.

SUZANNE ELLERY GREENE is professor of history at Morgan State University in Baltimore, Maryland.

CLAUDIUS W. GRIFFIN is professor of English and director of the composition and rhetoric program at Virginia Commonwealth University in Richmond.

ROBERT J. HIGGS is professor of English at East Tennessee State University in Johnson City.

THOMAS W. HOFFER is associate professor of communication and a filmmaker at Florida State University in Tallahassee.

M. THOMAS INGE is professor and head of the department of English at Clemson University in South Carolina.

ROBERT H. JANKE is associate professor of speech in the department of theatre at Virginia Commonwealth University in Richmond.

ANNE HUDSON JONES is assistant professor of literature and medicine at the institute for the medical humanities at the University of Texas Medical Branch in Galveston.

R. GORDON KELLY is associate professor of American studies at the University of Maryland.

LARRY N. LANDRUM is assistant professor of English at Michigan State University in East Lansing.

RICHARD N. MASTELLER is assistant professor of English at Whitman College in Walla Walla, Washington.

BERNARD MERGEN is associate professor of American civilization at George Washington University in Washington, D.C.

ARTHUR J. MILLER, JR., is college librarian at Lake Forest College in Illinois.

KAY J. MUSSELL is associate professor and director of the American studies program at the American University in Washington, D.C.

RICHARD A. NELSON is assistant professor of communication at the University of Houston Central Campus in Texas.

NANCY POGEL is associate professor of American thought and language at Michigan State University in East Lansing.

JANICE RADWAY is assistant professor of American civilization at the University of Pennsylvania in Philadelphia.

ANNE ROWE is associate professor of English at Florida State University in Tallahassee.

DOROTHY SCHMIDT is assistant professor of English at Pan American University in Edinburg, Texas.

RICHARD A. SCHWARZLOSE is associate professor of journalism at Northwestern University in Evanston, Illinois.

NICHOLAS A. SHARP is assistant professor of English and coordinator of non-traditional studies at Virginia Commonwealth University in Richmond.

PAUL P. SOMERS, JR., is associate professor of American thought and language at Michigan State University in East Lansing.

MARSHALL B. TYMN is associate professor of English at Eastern Michigan University in Ypsilanti.

JAMES VON SCHILLING is completing graduate studies in popular culture at Bowling Green State University in Ohio.

FAYE NELL VOWELL is assistant professor of English at Emporia State University in Kansas.

J. CAROL WILLIAMS is assistant professor of philosophy and religious studies at Virginia Commonwealth University in Richmond.

ELIZABETH WILLIAMSON is assistant director of admissions at Virginia Commonwealth University in Richmond.

DON. B. WILMETH is professor and chairman of the department of theatre arts at Brown University in Providence, Rhode Island.

RICHARD GUY WILSON is associate professor of architectural history at the University of Virginia in Charlottesville.

ANNETTE M. WOODLIEF is assistant professor of English at Virginia Commonwealth University in Richmond.